P9-CLG-667

Access® 2010

ALL-IN-ONE

FOR

DUMMIES®

Access® 2010

ALL-IN-ONE

FOR

DUMMIES®

by Margaret Levine Young,
Alison Barrows, and
Joseph C. Stockman

WILEY

Wiley Publishing, Inc.

Access® 2010 All-in-One For Dummies®

Published by
Wiley Publishing, Inc.
111 River Street
Hoboken, NJ 07030-5774

www.wiley.com

Copyright © 2010 by Wiley Publishing, Inc., Indianapolis, Indiana

Published by Wiley Publishing, Inc., Indianapolis, Indiana

Published simultaneously in Canada

No part of this publication may be reproduced, stored in a retrieval system or transmitted in any form or by any means, electronic, mechanical, photocopying, recording, scanning or otherwise, except as permitted under Sections 107 or 108 of the 1976 United States Copyright Act, without either the prior written permission of the Publisher, or authorization through payment of the appropriate per-copy fee to the Copyright Clearance Center, 222 Rosewood Drive, Danvers, MA 01923, (978) 750-8400, fax (978) 646-8600. Requests to the Publisher for permission should be addressed to the Permissions Department, John Wiley & Sons, Inc., 111 River Street, Hoboken, NJ 07030, (201) 748-6011, fax (201) 748-6008, or online at http://www.wiley.com/go/permissions.

Trademarks: Wiley, the Wiley Publishing logo, For Dummies, the Dummies Man logo, A Reference for the Rest of Us!, The Dummies Way, Dummies Daily, The Fun and Easy Way, Dummies.com, Making Everything Easier, and related trade dress are trademarks or registered trademarks of John Wiley & Sons, Inc. and/or its affiliates in the United States and other countries, and may not be used without written permission. Access is a registered trademark of Microsoft Corporation in the United States and/or other countries. All other trademarks are the property of their respective owners. Wiley Publishing, Inc., is not associated with any product or vendor mentioned in this book.

LIMIT OF LIABILITY/DISCLAIMER OF WARRANTY: THE PUBLISHER AND THE AUTHOR MAKE NO REPRESENTATIONS OR WARRANTIES WITH RESPECT TO THE ACCURACY OR COMPLETENESS OF THE CONTENTS OF THIS WORK AND SPECIFICALLY DISCLAIM ALL WARRANTIES, INCLUDING WITHOUT LIMITATION WARRANTIES OF FITNESS FOR A PARTICULAR PURPOSE. NO WARRANTY MAY BE CREATED OR EXTENDED BY SALES OR PROMOTIONAL MATERIALS. THE ADVICE AND STRATEGIES CONTAINED HEREIN MAY NOT BE SUITABLE FOR EVERY SITUATION. THIS WORK IS SOLD WITH THE UNDERSTANDING THAT THE PUBLISHER IS NOT ENGAGED IN RENDERING LEGAL, ACCOUNTING, OR OTHER PROFESSIONAL SERVICES. IF PROFESSIONAL ASSISTANCE IS REQUIRED, THE SERVICES OF A COMPETENT PROFESSIONAL PERSON SHOULD BE SOUGHT. NEITHER THE PUBLISHER NOR THE AUTHOR SHALL BE LIABLE FOR DAMAGES ARISING HEREFROM. THE FACT THAT AN ORGANIZATION OR WEBSITE IS REFERRED TO IN THIS WORK AS A CITATION AND/OR A POTENTIAL SOURCE OF FURTHER INFORMATION DOES NOT MEAN THAT THE AUTHOR OR THE PUBLISHER ENDORSES THE INFORMATION THE ORGANIZATION OR WEBSITE MAY PROVIDE OR RECOMMENDATIONS IT MAY MAKE. FURTHER, READERS SHOULD BE AWARE THAT INTERNET WEBSITES LISTED IN THIS WORK MAY HAVE CHANGED OR DISAPPEARED BETWEEN WHEN THIS WORK WAS WRITTEN AND WHEN IT IS READ.

For general information on our other products and services, please contact our Customer Care Department within the U.S. at 877-762-2974, outside the U.S. at 317-572-3993, or fax 317-572-4002.

For technical support, please visit www.wiley.com/techsupport.

Wiley also publishes its books in a variety of electronic formats. Some content that appears in print may not be available in electronic books.

Library of Congress Control Number: 2010923554

ISBN: 978-0-470-53218-8

Manufactured in the United States of America

10 9 8 7 6 5 4 3 2

WILEY

About the Authors

Margaret Levine Young has co-authored several dozen computer books about the Internet, UNIX, WordPerfect, Access, and (stab from the past) PC-File and Javelin, including *The Internet For Dummies (Wiley) and Windows XP Home Edition: The Complete Reference* (Osborne/McGraw-Hill). She met her future husband Jordan in the R.E.S.I.S.T.O.R.S., a high-school computer club before there were high-school computer clubs. Her other passions are her children, music, Unitarian Universalism (www.uua.org), reading, gardening, chickens, and anything to do with cooking or eating.

Alison Barrows has authored or co-authored books on Windows, the Internet, Microsoft Access, WordPerfect, Lotus 1-2-3, and other topics. In addition to writing books, Alison writes and edits technical documentation and training material. In real life she hangs out with her "guys" — Parker, 6, and Mason, 4, and Evan 2 — and tries to carve out some time to practice yoga. Alison lives with her family in central Massachusetts.

Joe Stockman has been using Microsoft Access since its initial release and has authored or co-authored several books on Access, including *Access 2007 Bible* and *Access 2007 Workbook For Dummies*. He's also developed courseware in Access and VBA and has been on the speaker circuit for Microsoft Access seminars. Joe works as a consultant and software designer for Facilities Survey Inc. in Pittsburgh, PA. He also enjoys music, cooking, and anything else that lets him express his creative side.

Dedication

To my husband Jordan, my kids Meg and Zac, and my supportive friends. (MLY)

To Matt, Parker, Mason, and Evan. (AB)

To Mom, as always. (JCS)

Authors' Acknowledgments

We would like to acknowledge the care of Kyle Looper and Chris Morris, and all the others who shepherded this book through the editing and production process, as well as all the folks listed on the Publisher's Acknowledgments page who worked on this book. (It takes ALL of these people, not just those of us on the cover.) We'd also like to thank the folks at Microsoft for making Access a wonderful tool to create robust database applications.

Margy thanks her co-workers for their support and for making work fun — the Information Technology team at the UUA: Sean, Matt, Nick, Michelle, Scott, James, Bob, and Mark.

Alison thanks Dotty, Christy, and Matt for taking great care of my guys so I can get work done. Matt (also known as Honey) gets special thanks as my hardware guru.

Joe thanks his mom and dad, for always encouraging but never pushing. Also thanks to my friends and family for their support and understanding of the time it takes to finish this project.

We're proud of this book; please send us your comments at http://dummies.custhelp.com. For other comments, please contact our Customer Care Department within the U.S. at 877-762-2974, outside the U.S. at 317-572-3993, or fax 317-572-4002.

Some of the people who helped bring this book to market include the following:

Acquisitions, Editorial

Sr. Project Editor: Christopher Morris

Acquisitions Editor: Kyle Looper

Copy Editor: Teresa Artman, Virginia Sanders, Heidi Unger, Brian Walls

Technical Editors: Dan DiNicolo

Editorial Manager: Kevin Kirschner

Editorial Assistant: Amanda Graham

Sr. Editorial Assistant: Cherie Case

Cartoons: Rich Tennant (www.the5thwave.com)

Composition Services

Project Coordinator: Patrick Redmond

Layout and Graphics: Carl Byers, Samantha K. Cherolis, Amy Hassos, Joyce Haughey

Proofreader: Toni Settle

Indexer: Christine Karpeles

Publishing and Editorial for Technology Dummies

    Richard Swadley, Vice President and Executive Group Publisher

    Andy Cummings, Vice President and Publisher

    Mary Bednarek, Executive Acquisitions Director

    Mary C. Corder, Editorial Director

Publishing for Consumer Dummies

    Diane Graves Steele, Vice President and Publisher

Composition Services

    Debbie Stailey, Director of Composition Services

Contents at a Glance

Table of Contents

Book IX: Going Beyond Access 663

Introduction

*W*hoa! What happened to menu bars, toolbars, and all that other stuff I used to have? Well, in case you haven't noticed yet, they're all gone. Of course, if you never used Access before in your life, you're starting fresh, so never mind. Whether you never used any version of Microsoft Access, and aren't even sure what a "version" is, you've come to the right book.

The basic idea behind Microsoft Access is to allow individuals and small businesses to manage large amounts of information the way the big corporations do — with relational databases. The difference is that while the big boys spend millions on computer hardware, software, and staffs of nerdy database-administrator types, Access allows you to do it all yourself with a run-of-the-mill PC and a realistic software budget.

Microsoft Access 2010 is the latest-and-greatest version of a long line of Access versions, starting (not surprisingly) with version 1. Not that this is the 2,010th version. Somewhere along the way, Microsoft switched from using sequential numbers for versions to using years — an idea first pioneered by the automotive industry, which sells things like "2010 Ford Mustangs" as opposed to "Mustang Version 9.3s."

Without going into boring detail about what's new in Access 2010, you find the usual kind of stuff you find in new versions these days — more power, more flexibility, and more things you can do with it. And of course — along the lines of the Holy Grail of Everything Computerish these days — more taking advantage of everything the Internet has to offer. But the most noticeable change for the Access-experienced is the new look and feel (introduced in the 2007 version) — along with some new ways of doing things.

About Access 2010 All-in-One Desk Reference For Dummies

If you ever have the misfortune of trying to read anything written by one of the aforementioned database-administrator types, you know all about being faced with a decision among the lesser of *three* evils:

(Option 1) Try to figure it out by guessing-and-poking until you break something.

(Option 2) Part with your hard-earned money to hire someone to do the work for you, only to have someone with poor taste in clothing look at you like you're an idiot every time you open your mouth.

(Option 3) Forget computers altogether and stick with index cards.

Option 1 is the one most people try first — until they get to the part where they start breaking things, and it starts costing money to get them fixed. Option 2 is too odious to warrant serious consideration. Option 3 just isn't very realistic nowadays, unless you're dealing with a tiny amount of personal information. Which leaves a new Option 4 — this book.

The nerds who wrote this book are aware of the fact that *nobody* on the planet was *ever* born knowing what *any* technical term means. In fact, if at all possible, we avoid technical terms like a root canal. But because you are probably faced with technical terms outside this book, we do explain what they mean along the way.

As a rule, big fat computer books aren't such a great option. For that reason, this isn't really a big fat computer book. It's several *smaller* computer books combined into one. Each small book represents a single topic that you can pursue — or ignore — as your personal tastes and immediate needs dictate.

The idea here is definitely *not* to try to read the book cover to cover, unless you're desperately seeking a cure for insomnia. Rather, use the Table of Contents up front, or the Index out back, to look up information when trying to figure it out by guessing just isn't cutting it.

To prevent this book from topping 3,000 pages, we don't explain every possible way to do every possible thing in Access. Instead, we chose what we think are the most important database-management tasks, and we show you the best way — at least in our opinions — to do each one.

Conventions

Speaking of insomnia, this book, like most books, follows certain conventions to alert you to different kinds of stuff, as follows:

Boldface: Stuff you actually *do* while sitting at your computer is shown in boldface, to distinguish it from boring information you probably don't care about anyway.

Italics: When reality rears its ugly head and we're forced to use a technical term, we always show that term in italics the first time it's used. Then we define that term, right there on the spot. Of course, that doesn't mean you won't forget the definition two minutes later. But you can easily flip back a few pages and locate the definition amidst all the other words on the page.

`Monospace`: Monospace text (text in that typeface right back there) represents *code*, instructions that are written for computers, rather than people, to follow. Computers are so stupid, the term "stupid" is a compliment. Unconscious, non-thinking, non-beings (a.k.a. *machines*) is more like it. Anyway, when writing instructions for a computer, you *really* have to spell it out for them, right down to the blank spaces between words. Monospace text makes seeing where you have to put the blank spaces to avoid making Access say "Huh?" easier. (Actually, it can't even say "Huh?" More likely, it says something really stupid like `"Syntax error in something or other."`)

Foolish Assumptions

Despite the fact that the word "Dummies" is clearly emblazoned on this book's cover and elsewhere, we don't presume that you're the junior partner in a ventriloquist act. (The machine you're working with, yes. You, no.) We do assume that you already know how to do some things, such as turn on your computer and click and double-click things with your mouse. Maybe type with at least one finger.

We also assume you know what those *key+key* symbols, such as "Ctrl+Esc," mean. But just in case you don't, they always mean "Hold down the first key, tap the second key, and then release the first key." Also, we always use the term "press" when referring to something you do with the keyboard. For example, the instruction "Press Ctrl+Esc" means "Hold down the Ctrl key on your keyboard, tap the Esc key, and then release the Ctrl key." *Click,* on the other hand, is something you do with the mouse pointer on your computer screen and the buttons on your mouse.

We also assume (perhaps foolishly) that you know how to work menus. Not that there are many menus in Access. But when there is a menu-like sequence, we use the word "Choose" followed by the commands to choose, separated by an ⇨ symbol. For example, when we say "Choose Start⇨All Programs⇨Microsoft Office⇨Microsoft Access Office 2010" that's short for "Click the Start button, click All Programs on the Start menu that appears, click Microsoft Office on the All Programs menu that appears, and then click Microsoft Office 2010 on the last menu that appears."

Click, of course, means "rest the mouse pointer on the item, and then tap the left mouse button." When we tell you to *drag* something, we mean for you to move your mouse pointer to the item, click, and then hold down the left mouse button while moving the mouse. To *drop* the item, just release the mouse button after dragging it.

We also show things like Web site URLs (addresses) — those `www.what ever.com` things you see all over the place. We may even throw in an occasional e-mail address (the `somebody@somewhere.com` things) without explaining how to use them. Hopefully these assumptions on our part aren't too foolish. But if we had to explain *all* that stuff here, there wouldn't be much space left for talking about Microsoft Access 2010.

What You Don't Have to Read

Because reading the instructions is something we all do only as a last resort — after guessing and trying to get help on the phone have failed — we try to point out things you really don't have to read. For example, *sidebars* (which have a gray background) are little chunks of text with their own titles. If the title looks boring, skip the whole thing.

We also put little *icons* (pictures) in the left margin to point out text that you can maybe skip over. Or in some cases, really shouldn't skip over. The icons are pretty self-explanatory. So if you want to skip the next section, that's fine by us.

Icons

As far as those presumably self-explanatory icons go, here are the explanations you can probably skip over or, at best, glance at:

This is stuff you probably don't want to ignore. Because if you do, you may regret it. Not that you're gonna blow up your computer or the Internet or anything if you do. But the consequences may be inconvenient or unpleasant enough to justify spending a few seconds to read what these little notes say.

May be worth reading if you're looking for a shortcut, or a better way to do things. Not as important as a warning. But probably worth a few seconds of your time.

This is either stuff we already told you and you probably forgot, or something that's at least worth trying to keep in the back of your mind. Even if it's way back there. Kinda like where you park your car when you go to the mall.

This *is* a reference book, and we certainly don't expect anyone to read it cover to cover. But sometimes, you just have to know "Subject *x*" before "Subject *y*" even comes close to making any sense. So when we're forced to talk about a "Subject *y*" kind of thing, we use this icon to point out where "Subject *x*" is covered.

Stuff that definitely falls into the "insomnia cure" category.

Organization

If you already looked up the Contents at a Glance up near the front of this book, or the Table of Contents right after it, you already know how stuff is organized here. In that case, you may now skip to the "Where to Go from

Here" section. But because showing the contents a third time is customary (albeit kinda dumb), without the benefit of page numbers, we follow suit here. This book is actually eight little books, organized as follows:

Book I: Essential Concepts: If this is your first time using Microsoft Access and you really don't know where else to go, starting here is a good idea. This is the stuff you really need to know to get anything done with Access.

Book II: Tables for Storing Your Data: Everything in Access centers around *data* (information) stored in tables (not the coffee kind, the columns-and-rows kind). You can't do much of anything with Access until you have some information stored in tables. This book is a good second stop for you *newbies* (beginners).

Book III: Queries (or Getting Information from Your Data): Data stored in tables tends to be pretty random and, eventually, pretty plentiful. This book shows you how to pick and choose the information you want to see, and how to organize it in a way that's more useful, such as alphabetically.

Book IV: Forms for Editing Data: You can definitely get away without making forms in your Access database. But if you get tired of looking at information stored in rows and columns, and you're up for being creative, forms are definitely worth getting into.

Book V: Reporting in Words and Pictures: Whereas forms are a way to get creative with stuff on your screen, reports are a way to get creative with stuff you print on your computer's printer. Here's where you can do things, for example, printing form letters, mailing labels, numbers with totals and subtotals, and stuff like that.

Book VI: Automation with Macros: There's a technical term for you — *macros.* Nothing to be intimidated by, though. They're just a way of writing simple instructions that tell Access how to do something you're sick of doing yourself. Optional, but more fun than the name implies.

Book VII: Database Administration: Sounds like a real yawn, we know. Sometimes you just gotta do things such as make backup copies of your information, or get other people to help you with boring stuff such as typing information into your tables. This is the place where we cover those kinds of things.

Book VIII: Programming in VBA: For the aspiring mega-nerd, we didn't let this topic slide. This is where the über-technogeeks make their money by automating Access using a language, rather than macros. Though you can skip it if you have no such aspirations.

Book IX: Going Beyond Access: Kind of like going beyond the final frontier, but with less excitement. This is where you use Access to interact with and move data to and from other programs on your computer — or computers all over the world.

After that comes an appendix on how to install Microsoft Access 2010, in case you haven't gotten that far. If Access is already on your computer, there's nothing noteworthy here. If you do need to install Access, and don't feel like looking there, here's the condensed version of the appendix: Insert your Microsoft Office or Microsoft Access disc into your computer's disc drive, wait a few seconds, and then follow the instructions that appear on-screen.

Where to Go from Here

If you patiently read the preceding "Organization" section, you probably know where you need to go next. If not, you beginners should head straight to Book I, Chapter 1 to get your bearings. For the rest of you who already know some of the basics of Access, just pick whatever book or chapter talks about what you're struggling with right now.

And by the way, thanks for buying (begging, borrowing, or stealing — just kidding with that last one) this book. We hope it serves you well. For those of you who bought an extra, thanks for helping us pay down our credit cards a little.

Book I

Essential Concepts

The 5th Wave   By Rich Tennant

"Hold your horses! It takes time to build a database for someone with as many parts as you have."

Contents at a Glance

Chapter 1: Introducing Access 2010

Access is the database-management program, part of the Microsoft Office suite, that enables you to maintain *databases* — collections of data arranged according to a fixed structure. Its structure makes the information easy to select, sort, display, and print in a variety of formats. With Access, you can create and maintain as many databases as you need. You can even share them with other people over a local area network or the Internet.

Access works with almost any kind of information. An Access database can be as simple as a list of addresses to replace your card file. Or you can create a wine-cellar database with information about each bottle in your cellar, or a bookstore-inventory database with information about books, publishers, customers, and special orders. Access can also handle complex databases that contain many types of information and lots of customized programming.

An Access database can contain lists of records about almost anything, from sales to sports scores. Unlike a spreadsheet program, Access makes information in lots of different formats easy to display — including alphabetical listings, formatted reports, mailing labels, and fill-in-the-blank forms.

Access 2010 comes as a part of the Microsoft Office 2010 Professional suite of programs, and it's also available as a separate, stand-alone product. Previous versions of Access have also been part of previous Office editions — Access 2007 in Office 2007, Access 2003 in Office 2003, Access 2002 in Office XP, and so forth. Because Access is part of Microsoft Office, sharing information with Word documents and Excel spreadsheets is easy.

In this chapter, we introduce you to the components of an Access database and explain some key concepts related to developing and using Access databases.

Why Use a Database?

Many people use Microsoft Excel, another Office program, to manage their databases. Excel works for storing lists of things — up to a point. Go ahead and start with Excel if you are already comfortable with it, but you'll know you are ready to move up to Access when:

✦ **You need to store the same pieces of information in several different places.** You can use Excel formulas to duplicate data around a spreadsheet, and you can use cut-and-paste to make copies, but both methods lead to errors.

✦ **You don't want to look at your data as columnar tables.** Excel's database features (such as they are) require your data to be laid out in rows and columns. But what if you need a report in some other format? Displaying data in lots of different formats is where Access shines.

✦ **Your information consists of more than one list of records.** If your database includes information about several types of things — like customers, orders, and products — then you are ready for Access. Excel doesn't have an easy way to connect and combine information from different columnar tables. Access is a *relational database* that enables you to create forms and reports that include information from related tables.

✦ **You want to check your data to ensure that it's correct.** Access allows you to validate data in far more rigorous ways than Excel does. Avoid "garbage in, garbage out"!

Plan, Plan, Plan

Databases are very different from spreadsheets and word processing documents. With spreadsheets and documents, you can just start typing, putting information where you want it to appear when you print the thing out.

Databases don't work like that. If you just start typing information into a database, you'll have a total mess. Not to lay a major downer on you, but a database requires planning so that you put the right information into the right place. It's not rocket science, but it's necessary.

The first step is to find out what makes up an Access database, which is what this chapter is about. Chapter 2 of this minibook gets you into the Access program, clicking around and seeing what's there. And Chapter 3 is where you make your plan — designing your own database.

The Six Types of Access Objects

Access databases are made up of *objects* — things you can create, edit, and delete, each with its own name and settings. *Object-oriented* systems allow you to create these things one piece at a time, using pieces that fit together.

These objects can store, display, and print your data, as well as contain programs you write. At first, you'll probably use only a few types of objects, but as you customize your database, you may end up using all six types. You start with *tables* for storing data, *forms* for editing data on-screen, *reports* for printing data, and *queries* for selecting and combining data. Later, you may create *macros* and *modules,* which contain programs that you write.

In this section, we describe each of the main types of Access objects: tables, queries, forms, reports, macros, and modules.

Tables for storing your data

Tables are where you put your data. A table is an Access object that is made up of a series of *records* — the electronic equivalent of the index cards that make up an address list. Each record contains information about one thing, with the same pieces of information. In an address list, each record contains information about one person: name, address, and other facts. Each individual piece of information — such as first name, last name, or street address — is called a *field*.

Your database can contain many tables. A bookstore database (for example) can contain a Books table (with title, publisher, price, and other information about each book), a Vendors table for companies from whom you buy books (with company name, address, discount terms, and other information about each vendor), and maybe a Customers table of your regular customers (with name, address, and other information). Figure 1-1 shows a table of names and addresses. Each row is a record, and the fields are shown in columns.

Figure 1-1:
A table contains records (rows) and fields (columns).

Contact	First Name	Last Name	Company	Address1	City	State	ZIPPostalC	Country
1	Tori	Pines	Arbor Classics	345 Pacific Coast Hwy	Del Mar	CA	98765	USA
2	Marilou	Midcalf		500, 999-6th Street SW	Edmonton	AB	T5J 2Z4	India
3	Wilma	Wannabe	Wannabe Whistles	1121 River Road	Cornball	IA	54321-1234	USA
4	Frankly	Unctuous		734 N. Rainbow Dr.	Staten Island	NY	19470	USA
5	Margaret	Angstrom		P.O. Box 1295	Daneville	AK	92067	USA
6	Simpson	Sarah		1370 Washington Lane	Buckingham	PA	19046	USA
7			ABC Productions	Haverston Square	Doylestown	PA	18901	USA
8	Hortense	Higglebotton		P.O. Box 1014	Escondido	AK	49384	USA
9	Penny	Lopez		P.O. Box 10	New Hope	PA	18938	USA
10	Matilda	Starbuck		323 Shire Lane	Skeedadle	OK	54321	USA
11	Scott and Nata	Schumack		228 Hollywood Drive	Hollywood	FL	18914	USA
12	Linda	Peterson		823 Paseo Cancun	Redmond	WA	91792	USA
13	Ino	Yasha		1788 Port Carlo Circle	Framington	NM	54321	USA
14			Wiley Widgets	97 Roberts Dr.	Nashua	NH	03063	USA
15	Dominic	Kryzwicki		45 Albany Road	Maritime	RI	08053	USA
16	Rosemary	Stickler		1205 Huntingdon Ct.	Willow Grove	PA	19090-3705	USA

Address Book

Record: 1 of 35   No Filter   Search

After you set up tables in your database and type in (or import) information, you can sort the records, select records that match a criterion, and then display and print the records. You can create new tables, or you can link (connect) to existing tables in other Access databases or in databases created using programs like SQL Server and MySQL.

Proper design of your tables — choosing how many tables to create and which fields are stored in which table — is key to creating a usable and flexible database. Chapter 3 of this minibook includes a step-by-step procedure for designing your database, and Book II explains how to create tables and fill them with data.

Queries for selecting your data

Queries are operations that slice and dice your data to answer specific data needs. The most commonly used type of query selects data from a table, perhaps the records you want to include in a report. You can create a query that shows you all the people in your address book who live in (say) Vermont, or all those for whom you don't have a phone number. To create this type of query, you enter *criteria* that specify what values you want to match in specific fields in the tables (for example, **VT** in the State field to find Vermonters, or nothing in the Phone Number field to find the phoneless, or both).

You can also use queries to combine information from several tables. A bookstore database may store book author names in the Books table and book ordering information in the Purchase Orders table. A query can pull information from both these tables — to show (for example) all the Terry Pratchett novels you ordered for the last month. Queries can also create calculated fields, including totals, counts, and averages.

Another type of query is the *action query,* which does something to the records you select — copy records from one table to another, make a change to all the records you select, delete records you select, that sort of thing. *Crosstab queries* help you analyze the information in your tables by summarizing how many records contain specific combinations of values.

Queries are the way you get useful information out of your tables — and you'll probably create zillions of them as you play with your database. Book III explains how to create and use queries of all kinds.

Forms for editing and displaying your data

An easy way to enter data, especially into more than one related table, is to use a *form* — an Access object that displays information from one or more tables on-screen. You can have all kinds of fun with forms; for example, you can

✦ Edit your data or type in new records.

✦ Choose the layout of the table's information on the form.

✦ Specify the order in which your items appear.

✦ Group items together with lines and boxes.

✦ Use pull-down lists, radio buttons, and other types of on-screen controls for entering and editing data.

Figure 1-2 shows a form for entering names and addresses for the Address Book table shown in Figure 1-1.

Figure 1-2:
A form shows information from one table record at a time.

But why stop there? You can build intelligence into forms, too — program some smart boxes that automatically capitalize what you type in, or check your entry against a table of valid values.

After your database goes into production — that is, you use it for its intended purpose — forms become the most-used Access object. As go the forms, so goes the database — so Book IV explains how to design, create, modify, and use forms.

Reports for printing your data

Forms are primarily designed to appear on-screen; *reports* (on the other hand) are designed to be printed, as shown in Figure 1-3. Like forms, reports display information from tables; you get to choose the layout of the information. Most reports are based on queries; you use a query to choose the information that appears in the report. The *report design* defines the order in which records appear, which fields appear where, and which fonts, font sizes, lines, and spacing to use. (Control freaks, rejoice!)

In addition to reports on normal paper, you can create reports for printing on envelopes, labels, or other media. Access comes with report wizards that make creating fancy reports easy. It can also print charts and cross-tabulations (*crosstabs*) based on the data in your database.

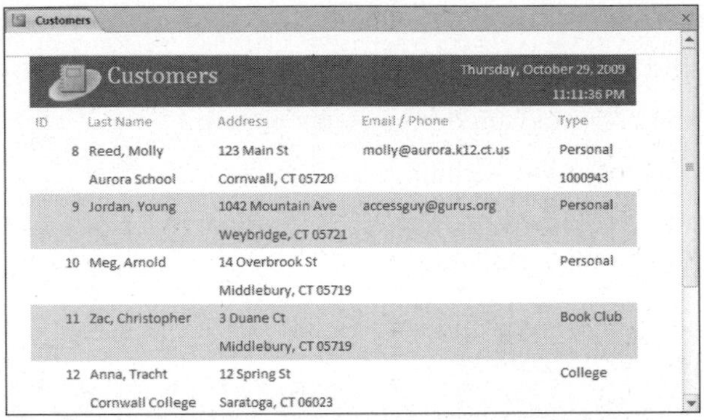

Figure 1-3:
A report
lets you put
Access data
on paper.

You're not limited to printing reports on paper; you can save reports as PDF (Portable Document Format) and XPS (Microsoft's equivalent of a PDF) files for e-mailing or posting on the Web.

Book V covers how to create and print reports, charts, and crosstabs.

Macros for saving keystrokes

Access includes two separate programming languages: one for macros and a separate one (VBA, or Visual Basic for Applications) for larger programs. *Macros* are programs that automate the commands you give when you use Access; every program in Microsoft Office enables you to write macros to work more efficiently. For example, you can write a macro that moves the cursor to the last record in the Orders table whenever you open the Order Entry form. (What are the chances that you'd want to edit your very first order? Most of us would be likelier to want to edit the *last* order or enter a new order.) Or you can write a macro that moves your cursor to the next applicable blank in a form, based on the entries you made so far.

After you get some practice at creating macros, you can create buttons on your forms that run the macros with a quick click. You can also tell your form to run a macro automatically whenever you move to a field on the form, or enter data into the field — handy! Access 2010 enables you to assign a *data macro* to a field in a table, too, so that you can trigger an action whenever your data changes. For example, you can automatically change other values to match, or validate other data against the values you just changed.

You don't have to be a programmer to create macros. Access helps you write them by providing menus of commands. Book VI explains how to create nifty and useful macros to clean up data entry — and a number of other items — automatically.

Modules for writing your own programs

Okay, now we come to the serious programming stuff: *modules* — another term for Visual Basic programs. *VBA* (Visual Basic for Applications) is a programming language based on the age-old BASIC language; it's specifically geared for working in Access and other Office programs. Macros are fine for saving a few keystrokes or cleaning up the data you enter in a field, but when the going gets complex, use VBA.

Programming isn't for the technologically faint of heart. Fortunately, it's rarely necessary. But when everything else is done in your database, take a look at Book VIII for an introduction to VBA programming. Writing small programs isn't all that hard — and if you acquire a taste for programming, who knows what you'll end up creating!

Essential Database Concepts

Here are the Five Commandments of databases. (Aren't you relieved there aren't 10?). You'll find lots more important rules and guidelines throughout this book as you discover how to work with various Access objects, but these five apply right from the start, no matter what kind of database you are using:

✦ **Store information where it belongs, not where it appears.** Where you store information has nothing to do with where it appears. In a spreadsheet, you type information where you want it to appear when you print the spreadsheet, but databases work differently. In a database, you store information in tables based on the *structure* of the information. (Don't worry — Chapter 3 of this minibook explains how to figure out the structure of your data.) Each piece of information likely appears in lots of different reports. For example, in a database for an online bookstore, book titles and authors' names appear on your invoices, purchase orders, and sales receipts. But the right place to *store* those book titles and author names is probably in the Books table, not in the Sales table or the Purchase Orders table.

✦ **Store information as it really exists, not as you want it to appear in a specific report.** This is a corollary to the first rule. If you want book titles to appear in all uppercase (capital) letters in your purchase orders, Access can capitalize the titles for you. Store the book titles with correct capitalization so you aren't stuck with them in all caps on every report. Access has built-in formatting options that control the way that text, numbers, and dates are formatted, as described in Book II, Chapter 1. Functions are also available for more advanced formatting, as you learn in Book III, Chapter 2.

✦ **Garbage in, garbage out (GIGO).** If you don't bother to create a good, sensible design for your database — and if you aren't careful to enter correct, clean data — your database will end up full of garbage. A well-designed database is easier to maintain than a badly designed one, because each piece of information is stored only once, in a clearly named field in a clearly named table, with the proper validation rules in place. Yes, it sounds like a lot of work, but cleaning up a database of 10,000 incorrect records is (pardon the understatement) even more work. See Book II, Chapter 5 for ways to avoid GIGO.

✦ **Separate your data from your programs.** If you create a database to be shared with (or distributed to) other people, store all the tables in one database (the *back end*) and all the other objects in another database (the *front end*). Then you can link these two databases together to make everything work. Separating the tables from everything else streamlines the whole rigmarole of updating queries, forms, reports, or other stuff later without disturbing the data in the tables. (See Book VII, Chapter 1 for how to separate a database into a front end and back end.)

✦ **Back up early and often.** Make a backup of your database every day. With luck, your office already has a system of regular (probably nightly) backups that includes your database. If not, make a backup copy of your database at regular intervals, and certainly before making any major changes. (See Book VII, Chapter 1 for how to make backups.)

Chapter 2: Getting Started, Getting Around

In This Chapter

✔ Starting Access and opening a database

✔ Understanding the Access window

✔ Choosing commands from the Ribbon and Quick Access toolbar

✔ Getting around via the Navigation pane

✔ Viewing and working with Access objects

✔ Managing your database in Backstage View

✔ Saving keystrokes with keyboard shortcuts

*B*efore you can do much with Access, you have to get it installed and running. If Access isn't already installed on your computer, see the appendix for what to do. Then come back to this chapter for pointers on how to run it and decipher the stuff you see in the Access window.

Running Access

Windows usually provides more than one way to perform a task; starting Access is no exception. To run it from the Start button, click Start and choose All Programs➪Microsoft Office➪Microsoft Access 2010 (unless you've rearranged your Start menu). After you've run it a few times, Access will probably appear on your Start Menu, so Start➪Microsoft Access 2010 will get it going.

Another way to get the program started is by double-clicking the name or icon of an Access database in any Windows Explorer window, or pretty much anywhere else you see files listed. (This method both starts Access and opens the database you double-click.) Or double-click the Access icon if it appears on your Windows desktop.

When you start Access without opening a database, the Access 2010 window looks like Figure 2-1, showing Backstage View. When no database is open, Backstage View shows your choices for opening an existing database or starting to build a new database. We describe opening and creating databases in the rest of this chapter. If you are running Access for the first time, see the sidebar, "Choosing whether to update Office automatically."

Choosing whether to update Office automatically

The first time you run any Office 2010 program, you see the Welcome to Microsoft Office 2010 dialog box:

Like Windows itself, Microsoft Office can download and install updates automatically. Both the Use Recommended Settings and Install Updates Only settings tell Office up to receive new updates whenever Microsoft makes them available. The first option also enables these features:

✔ Online help includes information from office.microsoft.com, where Microsoft posts updated support information

✔ Office may download and install small program files that help diagnose problems.

✔ You are signed up for Microsoft's Customer Experience Improvement Program, which enables them to collect anonymous information about how you and millions of other people use Microsoft software, so they can make new versions even better.

Choose the Use Recommended Settings or Install Updates Only setting, depending how you feel about these additional three features. Avoid that last setting: The Don't Make Changes setting prevents you from getting security updates that you might need for your computer to stay virus-free.

Figure 2-1:
Access's Backstage View displays lots of options for creating a new database.

When a database is already open, Backstage View displays information about the database as a whole — rather than about specific objects in the database — and the commands that affect the entire database. (See "Introducing Backstage View" near the end of this chapter.)

Opening a Database

Before you can work on a database, you open it in Access. If you have an Access database, you can open it by using the instructions in this section. For now, don't worry about which version of Access it was created in. For more details on that, see the next section.

Okay, but wait a minute: Before you can open a new database, you have to create it! If you want to try Access but you don't have a database to work with, skip ahead to the "Creating a sample database from a template" section to try Access with a sample database.

Only one database can be open at one time in Access. If a database is already open, Access closes it when you open a new database.

To open a database, follow these steps:

1. **Click the File tab on the Access Ribbon if you don't already see Backstage View (shown in Figure 2-1).**

   People missed having a File command in Office 2007, so Microsoft replaced 2007's Office button with the File tab — it's in the top-left corner of all Office 2010 applications.

2. **Click Open.**

   The Open dialog box appears, looking just like the Open dialog boxes used throughout Microsoft Office (and most other programs).

3. **Choose the filename and click the Open button.**

   You may need to browse to it. Use the icons on the left side of the Open dialog box to see different folders.

Access opens the database. If you see an alarming security message, check out the relevant nearby sidebar, "Security Warning: Certain content in this database has been disabled."

If you want to open a database that you used recently, the last four databases you opened appear just below Close Database in Backstage View, and you can click a filename to open it. To see a longer list of your recently-used databases, click Recent in Backstage View. In Windows 7, to start Access *and* open a recently used file, choose Start⇨Documents and choose the file from your Documents library.

Security Warning: Certain content in this database has been disabled

If you try to open a database containing any programming (in the form of macros, VBA procedures, or action queries, which we explain in later minibooks), Microsoft wants you to know that you are taking a chance, and displays the warning:

Or, you may see this warning:

Before you panic, consider that, unlike viruses in the real world, computer viruses don't just happen. A *virus* is a program that must be intentionally written by a human to do bad things and also make copies of itself.

So why the security warning? The warning appears whenever you open *any* document that contains any macros, VBA modules, or action queries. Access doesn't know whether the database contains viruses; it just tells you that programs of some sort — not necessarily viruses — are in the database. To protect you, Access opens the database, turns off the capability to execute code, and displays a warning.

What to do? It depends on where the database you are opening came from.

✔ **If the database is something you down-loaded from an unknown, dubious source,** leave the database content disabled, and look around it that way. To be even safer, close the database, create a blank database, and import the tables, queries, forms, and reports into it (but no macros or VBA code).

✔ **If the database comes from someone within your organization whom you trust,** click Open on the Open File Security Warning dialog box — or click the Enable Content button on the message bar — choose Enable This Content, and click OK. If the file is stored on a networked drive, you see a dialog box asking whether you trust the security for this drive — might bad guys be able to plant virus-infected databases there?

✔ **If you created the database and it's *sup-posed* to contain macros, VBA procedures, or action queries,** you can prevent Access from displaying the security message when you open the database. (See Book VI, Chapter 1 for how to set Access security settings for a database that contains macros or VBA modules.)

If you have antivirus software, you'd do well to scan any and all files you download from the Internet for viruses before you actually open such files. These days, most viruses spread through e-mail attachments or files down-loaded from the Web. Virtually all antivirus programs automatically scan all incoming e-mail attachments for viruses before allowing you to open them. *The Internet For Dummies* (by John R. Levine and Margaret Levine Young; Wiley Publishing) describes viruses, spyware, and how to avoid them.

When you work with a database, panes and tabs appear within the Access window. Exactly what you see depends on the database. A simple database displays the Navigation pane, described later in this chapter. Some databases display a form and hide the Navigation pane. You can also program the database to hide the standard Access components entirely (see Book VII, Chapter 3).

Opening oldies

Access 2007 introduced a new file format for Access, and Access 2010 uses the same format. (Phew! We're not faced with *another* new file format!) Access 2010 and 2007 create .accdb files, while Access 2003 and older versions saved databases as .mdb files.

Access 2010 can open databases created in Access 2003 and older versions — in addition, of course, to those created in Access 2007 and 2010. If you create new fields or objects that use new features in Access 2010, those objects will not work if you open the database later in an older version.

Saving in a different version

If you know someone with Access 2003 or older who needs to use your database, you can save it in the Access 2002-2003 format, or even in the Access 2000 format. Click the File tab on the Ribbon to display Backstage View, then click Share to see your Database File Types options, which include Access 2002-2003 Database and Access 2000 Database. You should not use the new-to-2010 features if you know you need to save the database in an older format.

I have that open already!

Access is a *multiuser database,* which means that more than one person can open an Access database at the same time. The usual way that this works is that several computers on a network (usually a local area network in an office) run Access — and all can open the same database at the same time. Access keeps track of who is doing what and prevents the users from (virtually) crashing into each other. Two people trying to edit the same thing at the same time can be tricky — Access locks out the second person until the first person is done with the edit.

For more information on multiple people using the same database at the same time, see Book VII, Chapter 2.

Creating a sample database from a template

If you want to look around in Access but haven't created your first database yet, you can create a ready-made database from one of the templates that come with the program. Many templates reconfigure the Navigation pane and make other changes to the way that Access looks, so you'll need to give a command or two to return Access to its usual appearance. Follow these steps:

1. **Run Access, using one of the many methods described earlier in this chapter.**

   For instance, click Start and choose All Programs⇨Microsoft Office⇨ Microsoft Access 2010. You see Backstage View, shown in Figure 2-1.

2. **Click New, if it's not already selected. In the Available Templates section, click Sample Templates and click one of the templates to select it.**

   If you aren't sure which template to choose, scroll down to the Task List template and click it. The Task List template includes a contacts list and a to-do list.

   When you click New, you can choose Blank Database to start from scratch. To make a database that links to SharePoint, Microsoft's Web-based, document-sharing system, choose Blank Web Database. Book IX, Chapter 3 describes sharing Access databases with SharePoint.

3. **Click Create.**

   Access creates a new database in your Documents (or My Documents if you're using Windows XP or earlier) folder, with a name that's based on the template. If you choose the Contacts template, the folder is named `Contacts.accdb`.

4. **Click Enable Content in the Security Warning message bar.**

   Even when creating a new database for you, Access just doesn't want to take any chances!

5. **If the Navigation pane doesn't appear, click the Shutter Bar Open/ Close button to display it.**

   The Navigation pane and the Shutter Bar Open/Close button are shown in Figure 2-2.

6. **Click the heading of the Navigation pane and choose Object Type from the menu that appears.**

   Now the Navigation pane should contain subheadings for tables, queries, and other types of Access objects.

There — now you have a database to explore.

Making Friends with the Access Window

After you have a database open, you're ready to have a look around. Figure 2-2 shows a typical Access window, with the major parts labeled. On the left is the Navigation pane, which lists objects in the database. (If all you see is a vertical stripe labeled "Navigation Pane," click it to see the Navigation pane; if you don't see a Navigation pane or a stripe, talk to the database developer to find out how the database is intended to be used.)

Across the top is the Ribbon, that super-menu that all Microsoft Office programs use. Below the Ribbon and to the right of the Navigation pane (if there's any space left on your screen) is space for you to see and work with the various objects that make up the database — the tables, queries, forms, reports, and the rest.

The Ribbon

If you are used to Microsoft Office 2010 or 2007, you're probably not alarmed that there's no menu — no "File, Edit, . . . " series of commands marching across the top of the window. Instead, you see tabs at the top of the window, and a bunch of buttons. If you're used to older Office versions, this is the Ribbon that replaced the menu and toolbars in Office 2007. And it's new and improved for 2010.

The Ribbon has five tabs that always appear, and additional tabs appear when particular objects are open — for instance, a Datasheet tab is available when a Datasheet is active. These additional tabs are known as *contextual tabs*.

Quick Access Toolbar

Shutter Bar
Open/Close button

File button

Ribbon

Minimize the Ribbon

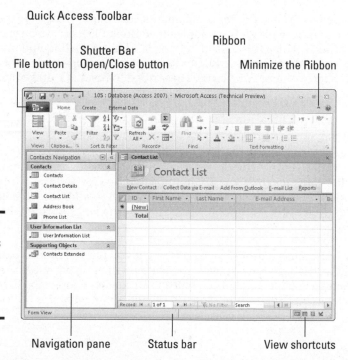

Figure 2-2:
The Access
window
with a
database
open.

Navigation pane   Status bar   View shortcuts

The tabs that always appear are

✦ **File:** This was the purple Office button in Access 2007, but so many people missed the old-fashioned File menu that the Microsoft team decided to bring it back. (Let's hear it for nostalgia as a motivator for software design!) Unlike the rest of the tabs, clicking the File tab displays Backstage View, described in the "Introducing Backstage View" section later in the chapter.

✦ **Home:** The first button on the Home tab (shown in Figure 2-2) is View, which allows you to change the view of the object displayed. You can view each object in Design view, to create and configure it, and use other views to actually use the object. The Home tab also contains buttons used for dealing with records: formatting, creating new records, creating totals, and spell checking, as well as sorting, filtering, and finding data. We describe many of the buttons on the Home tab in Book II, Chapters 3 and 4.

✦ **Create:** This is for — what else? — making new objects in your database. Books II through VI and Book VIII describe how to create each type of Access object.

✦ **External Data:** Contains commands for importing and exporting data and objects, collecting data via e-mail using Outlook (both are described in Book II, Chapter 4), and connecting and synchronizing with SharePoint (see Book IX, Chapter 3).

✦ **Database Tools:** Contains commands for running macros (described in Book VI), creating VBA modules (see Book VIII), creating relationships between tables (discussed in Book II, Chapter 1), documenting or analyzing your database (see Book VII, Chapter 1), connecting your database to SharePoint or SQL Server (described in Book IX), and other advanced tasks.

The Ribbon presents buttons in labeled groups, separated by vertical lines. The Home tab of the Ribbon in Figure 2-2 contains the Views, Clipboard, Sort & Filter, Records, Find, and Text Formatting groups. (The group names are at the bottom of the Ribbon.) In this book, we tell you (for example) to click the Filter button in the Sort & Filter group of the Home tab on the Ribbon. To find that button, first click the Home tab on the Ribbon, then find the Sort & Filter group on that Ribbon, and then find the Filter button within that group.

Every button has a descriptive *tooltip* — if you put the mouse pointer on the button, you will see the tip with the name of the button, a keyboard shortcut that can be used instead of the button (for instance, pressing Ctrl+F instead of clicking the Find button), and a sentence about what the button does.

Sometimes a group contains so many buttons that they don't fit on the Ribbon. In this case, the group has a little arrow in its lower-right corner. (Take a look at the Clipboard group in Figure 2-2.) Click that arrow to see the rest of the buttons, usually in a dialog box that pops up.

Minimizing the Ribbon

The Ribbon takes up lots of screen space. To minimize it, double-click the active tab, press Ctrl+F1, click the Minimize the Ribbon button (the upward-pointing caret above the right end of the Ribbon), or right-click a tab and choose Minimize the Ribbon.

Click any Ribbon tab to redisplay the Ribbon. However, the Ribbon will roll up again after you click a button. You can use keyboard shortcuts (covered near the end of this chapter) while the Ribbon is minimized. To redisplay the Ribbon for good, click the Minimize the Ribbon button again, or press Ctrl+F1 again, or double-click a Ribbon tab.

The Quick Access toolbar

Toolbars aren't completely gone! Access still displays a small toolbar (shown in Figure 2-2) immediately above the left end of the Ribbon.

The Quick Access toolbar includes three of the most commonly used buttons in Access:

✦ **Save:** Saves changes to the current object. (How long will they continue to use a floppy disk icon to mean save, even though most of us haven't touched a floppy disk in years?)

✦ **Undo:** Undoes the last undoable action.

✦ **Redo:** Redoes the last redoable action.

You can easily customize the Quick Access toolbar. Click the fourth button, the down arrow. A list of buttons that you can add to the Quick Access toolbar appears. Click any command (that is, Open, Quick Print, and so on) to add its button to the toolbar. If you don't see the command you want to add, see if you can find the button on the Ribbon, right-click it, and choose Add to Quick Access Toolbar.

If you can't find the button you want on the Quick Access toolbar anywhere on the Ribbon, add buttons to the toolbar by choosing More Commands from the Customize Quick Access Toolbar menu.

Mission Control: The Navigation Pane

The Navigation pane (shown in Figure 2-2) is the table of contents for your database. From it, you can open any table, query, form, report, macro, or VBA module in the database — all simply by double-clicking the object's name. By right-clicking objects in the Navigation pane, you can open the object in an alternate view, change the name of an object, copy an object, delete an object, import or export an object, hide or display an object, and view the object's properties.

F11 toggles the display of the Navigation pane — it can be rolled up into a narrow vertical ribbon. You can also toggle the display by clicking the Shutter Bar Open/Close button (such an egregiously long term for such a tiny little button!), which is the double arrow at the top-right corner of the pane.

You can make the Navigation pane narrower or wider by dragging its left edge.

Choosing how database objects are grouped

The Navigation pane displays the objects in the database in groups. Each group has a heading, and the group objects can be displayed and hidden by clicking the double arrow at the right of the group name.

By default, the Navigation pane shows database objects in Tables and Related Views. This option displays all tables, each with all objects that relate to that table.

The familiar way to group database objects is by object type, but there are other choices also. Click the drop-down list arrow on the Navigation pane title bar to see the grouping options (shown in Figure 2-3). The Navigation pane menu is really two menus displayed as one list — the blue highlighted words (Navigate To Category and Filter By Group) are the titles for each menu. The options on it vary, but you can select one option from the Navigate to Category options at the top of the list, and one from the Filter by Group at the bottom of the list.

Figure 2-3:
The Navigation pane menu for grouping options.

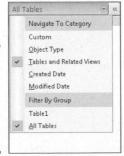

You can configure your Navigation pane in this way:

1. **Click the drop-down list arrow on the Navigation pane title bar.**

You see the Navigation pane menu. Table 2-1 shows what each option on the list does.

2. **From the Navigate To Category list, choose how you want objects grouped.**

The most popular options are Object Type (which lists tables, queries, forms, reports, macros, and VBA modules, each with its own heading) and Tables and Related Views (which lists all tables, each with the objects that relate to it).

3. **From the Filter By Group list, choose whether you want to show all objects, or only some of them.**

We usually like to see all objects, so we choose All Access Objects. When your database gets large, you can change your mind.

The Filter by Group options change when you choose a different Navigate to Category option to list the relevant choices. For instance, if you choose to navigate by Object Type, the filter options are different types of objects (tables, queries, forms, and so on). However, if you choose to navigate by Tables and Related Views, the filter options are the names of the tables in the database.

Table 2-1	Navigate to Category Options on the Navigation Pane Menu
Option	*How It Groups Database Objects*
Custom	Displays objects grouped in the way that you define. See the sidebar "Creating custom groups in the Navigation pane."
Object Type	Displays objects grouped by object type (Tables, Queries, Forms, Reports, Macros, and Modules), with a heading for each.
Tables and Related Views	Displays objects grouped by table — that is, group names are the same as table names, and the group consists of the table and objects that are related to it in the database. Objects may appear in more than one group.
Created Date	Displays objects grouped by create date. Groups are Today, Last Week, Two Weeks Ago, Last Month, and Older.
Modified Date	Displays objects grouped by the date they were last modified. Groups are Today, Last Week, Two Weeks Ago, Last Month, and Older.

Creating custom groups in the Navigation pane

Rather than using the default categories for Navigation pane groups, you can create your own custom groups using the Navigation Options dialog box, and then drag database objects into the new groups. For example, in a database for a small bookstore, you might want one group with objects that your purchase manager uses, and another group for your bookkeeper. Here's how it's done:

1. **Right-click the title bar of the Navigation pane or the empty space at the bottom of the Navigation pane, and then choose Navigation Options.**

   You see the Navigation Options dialog box. The Categories list on the left shows options that appear on the Navigate To Category list on the Navigation pane menu. The right-hand list shows the options for the selected category.

2. **In the Categories list, select Custom. Or create a new category by clicking the Add Item button and giving your new category a name.**

   Either way, the right-hand list shows the options for the selected category.

3. **Create new groups in the right-hand list by clicking the Add Group button, and select the check box of each group you want to appear in the Navigation pane. Change the order of the groups, if necessary, by using the up- and down-arrows that appear when the group is selected.**

Be sure to leave the Unassigned Objects category checked until you have assigned objects to their groups.

4. **Click OK to close the Navigation Options dialog box.**

5. **Click the drop-down list arrow on the Navigation pane title bar, and then choose Custom or the category you created from the menu.**

   You now see the groups you created in Step 3, and the database objects appear in the Unassigned Objects group.

6. **Assign objects to groups by following these steps:**

a. Select single objects, or select multiple objects by holding down Ctrl as you select.

b. Drag objects to their new groups — or right-click, select Add to Group, and choose the group name.

   When you add an object to a custom group, you create a shortcut to the object. (The shortcut arrow displays with the object type icon.) You can rename shortcuts by right-clicking them and choosing Rename Shortcut.

7. **When all objects are assigned to groups, you may choose to hide the Unassigned Objects group.**

Custom categories may be used to take the place of Switchboards that were used in earlier versions of Access.

Choosing size and details for Navigation pane objects

You can configure the Navigation pane to show object names, icons, or more information about each object. Right-click the title bar of the Navigation pane or the empty space at the bottom of the Navigation pane, and then choose from the View By menu. The options are

✦ **Details:** Displays the name of the object, the type of object, the date it was created, and the date it was last modified.

✦ **Icon:** Displays a larger icon for each object, leaving more space between listed objects.

✦ **List:** This is the default option — which you see in the figures throughout this book. Each object displays with an icon indicating the type of object it is, and its name.

Sorting objects in the Navigation pane

You can sort objects within a group in the Navigation pane by right-clicking the title bar of the Navigation pane or the empty space at the bottom of the Navigation pane, and then choosing from the Sort By menu. You can select both a sort order (ascending or descending) and an attribute to sort by (such as Name, Type, Created Date, or Modified Date). You can also Remove Automatic Sorts (the last choice on the menu).

Searching for an object

If your database contains dozens or even hundreds of objects, they can be hard to find. Luckily, the Navigation pane includes a Search bar, which appears just below the title of the Navigation pane. You can type words and press Enter to find objects that contain the words in their titles. If the Search bar doesn't appear, right-click the Navigation pane title and choose Search Bar. Choose the same command again to make the Search bar go away.

Viewing Objects in Your Database

Chapter 1 describes the six kinds of objects that make up an Access database — tables, queries, forms, reports, macros, and VBA modules. (No, you don't have to memorize this list!) When you open an object to work with it, you choose which *view,* or on-screen format, to display it in. For example, you can open a table in Design view to design the fields that make up the table, or you can open it in Datasheet view to enter and edit the data in the table. This entire book describes how to use views to create and configure objects and use them to manage your data.

When you double-click an object's name in the Navigation pane, Access opens the object in the default view for that type of object. (For tables, the default is Datasheet view, since once you have created a table, you are most likely to want to type records into the table.)

To close an open object, click the X on the same line as the object tab when the object is active, or right-click the tab and choose Close.

Viewing lots of objects at the same time

You can open more than one object at the same time. You can open a table in Datasheet view to look at your data while working on a form in Design view to create a form for editing the data. You've got these two options for viewing multiple objects in Access:

✦ **Overlapping windows:** Access 2003 and earlier versions used this system, where each object appears in its own windows within the Access window, as shown in Figure 2-4. You can resize them and move them around in whatever arrangement you like. However, half the time your windows cover each other, and you spend more time playing with your object windows than getting work done.

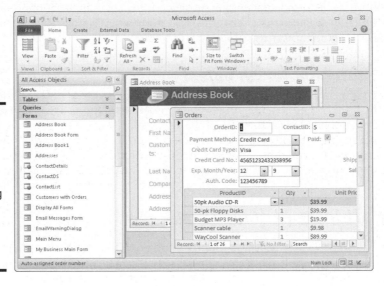

Figure 2-4: If you are used to the old, pre-2007 overlapping windows layout, you can still use it.

✦ **Tabbed documents:** Access 2007 instituted a new way of arranging the objects that you have open. Each appears with an object tab sticking up, with the name of the object on the tab. When you click the object tab, you see that object. Figure 2-2 — and all the rest of the figures in this entire book — show tabbed documents because we find them more convenient.

If you like tabbed documents, then you don't have to do a thing — that's the Access default. If you want to use overlapping windows for a specific Access database, you can. Click the File tab to display Backstage View, click Options, click Current Database, and set the Document Window Options to Overlapping Windows. To return to the default format, reset this option back to Tabbed Documents.

Switching views

After you have opened an object, you can look at it in a different view. Here are several methods:

✦ Click the icon on the View button at the left end of the Home tab on the Ribbon. (It's the only button in the Views group.) You switch between the current view and the most recently displayed view.

✦ To select from all the available views for the object, click the bottom half (the little arrow) of the View button and choose from the list that appears.

✦ Click one of the View shortcuts (shown in Figure 2-2) at the right end of the status bar, in the lower-right corner of the Access window. There's a button for each possible view; hover your mouse over a button to see the name of the view.

✦ Right-click the object tab and choose the view you want.

Creating, Deleting, Renaming, Copying, and Printing Objects

Throughout this book, we tell you how to create and modify tables, forms, reports, and other Access objects using the Navigation pane. A couple of tasks that work the same way for all Access objects crop up time and again, so you may as well find out about them right here.

✦ **Creating an object:** Click the Create tab on the Ribbon (shown in Figure 2-5) and then click the appropriate button. You usually see options to create the object by either running a wizard that steps you through the process or by using Design view — a window with settings for designing the object.

Figure 2-5:
The Create tab on the Ribbon.

See Book II, Chapter 1 for creating tables; Book III, Chapter 1 for queries; Book IV, Chapter 1 for forms; Book V, Chapter 1 for reports; Book VI, Chapter 1 for macros; Book VIII, Chapter 2 for VBA modules.

✦ **Deleting an object:** Select the object in the Navigation pane and press the Delete key. Simple enough! Clicking the Delete icon on the Home tab of the Ribbon works, too, as does right-clicking the object and then choosing Delete. Access asks whether you're really, truly *sure* before blowing the object away. Just remember that when you delete a table, you delete all its data, too.

✦ **Renaming an object:** Click the name of the object and press F2. Or right-click the name and choose Rename. Either way, a box appears around the object's name. Type a new name and press Enter. Press Esc if you change your mind.

✦ **Copying an object:** Select the object you want to copy, press Ctrl+C, move your cursor to where you want to create the copy, and press Ctrl+V. (The Copy and Paste buttons in the Clipboard group on the Home tab of the Ribbon work, too.) Access pops up a Paste As dialog box, asking what name to use for the copy. Type a name and click OK.

When you are creating a form or report, starting with a copy of an existing report (rather than starting a whole new one from scratch) is faster!

✦ **Printing an object:** Select or open the object you want to print and then press Ctrl+P. Or click the File tab on the Ribbon to display Backstage View, click Print, and choose one of the following: Quick Print (to use the existing printer settings), Print (to select printer settings), or Print Preview (to see what you're about to print before wasting paper on it).

You can find lots more about printing in Book V, Chapter 2, which talks about making and printing reports.

✦ **Creating a shortcut to an object:** If you frequently want to start Access, open your database, and immediately open a specific object, you can create a Windows shortcut that does all three tasks. The object shortcut can live on your Windows desktop or on your Start menu. Just drag the object from the Navigation pane to your Windows desktop — Windows creates the shortcut. You can then drag this shortcut to the Start menu if you want the shortcut on your Start menu.

Introducing Backstage View

Access 2007 had no File tab on the Ribbon; instead, there was a purple Microsoft Office icon. People the world over longed for their old friend, the File menu — didn't we all train ourselves to choose File⇨Save and File⇨Print in almost every program in existence?

Well, the File menu is back with a new name. In Access 2010, you click the File tab on the Ribbon to display Backstage View, a page of commands and settings that apply to the entire database or to your Access program. Figure 2-1 at the beginning of this chapter shows Backstage View when no database is open. Figure 2-6 shows Backstage View with a database open. The Info command is selected by default when you display Backstage View.

When the Info command is selected (as in Figure 2-6), you see buttons to view the log of any errors that have occurred, view the properties of the database, analyze the database, and other tasks that affect the entire database. And by using the commands directly below Info, you can also save the database, open a different database, or close the database.

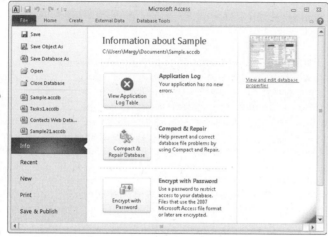

Figure 2-6:
The Info command in Backstage View shows information about your database.

✦ **Recent:** Shows a list of the databases you have opened recently.

✦ **New:** Shows ways you can create a new database.

✦ **Print:** This option is the only command in Backstage View that affects only the object that was selected when you clicked the File tab; it prints the selected object.

✦ **Save & Publish:** Enables you to save the database in another format, publish the database to the Web, or package your database to be installed on other computers.

✦ **Help:** Displays online help, activation information, and the version of Access you are running.

✦ **Options:** Displays the Access Options dialog box, which enables you to configure the Access program, including customizing the Ribbon and Quick Access toolbar.

✦ **Exit:** Closes the database and exits from Access.

Using Wizards

Years ago, in a land far, far away (Washington state, actually), Microsoft invented *wizards,* programs that step you through the process of executing a commonly used command. Instead of presenting you with a big, hairy-looking dialog box with zillions of options, a wizard asks you one or two questions at a time, and it uses the information you already provided before asking for more input. All programs in Microsoft Office, including Access, come with wizards.

Wizards appear in dialog boxes that pop up in response to a command. All Microsoft wizards follow the same pattern of asking a series of questions. Answer each question and click the Next button at the bottom of the dialog box to move to the next step. If you want to go back and change the answer you gave in a previous window, click the Back button. You can bag the whole thing by clicking Cancel. The Finish button is grayed out (and unclickable) until you provide enough information for the wizard to complete its task.

When using a wizard, you can select all items in a list by clicking the double arrow. Select one by clicking the single arrow. Deselect an item by using the analogous arrow buttons that point in the opposite direction. If you have questions, refer to the section of the book about that particular wizard.

Getting Help

Access offers online help, and it can be quite useful, so it's worth learning how to use it. To ask the Access Help system a question, here's the drill:

1. **Click the question mark in the upper-right corner of the Access window (or press F1).** Or, click the File tab on the Ribbon, click Help, and click Microsoft Access Help.

   The Access Help window appears.

2. **Type some search words in the Help box and then press Enter.**

   Access first searches its Help system for matches, and it then displays any search results in the window.

3. **Click a topic to see more information.**

When you're in Help, you can also click the book icon on the Access Help window to see the Table of Contents pane.

We find the following Web sites for getting answers to Access questions:

✦ **The Access Web:** www.mvps.org/access

✦ **Microsoft Support:** http://support.microsoft.com

✦ **The MSDN Library (Microsoft Developers' Network):** http://msdn.microsoft.com/access

✦ **TechNet Online:** www.microsoft.com/technet

Saving Time with Keyboard Shortcuts

Some people like to keep their hands on the keyboard as much as possible. For a fast typist, pressing keys is quicker and more efficient than pointing and clicking with the mouse. For those nimble-fingered folks, Access (like most other Windows programs) includes keyboard shortcuts — key combinations that issue the same commands you normally choose from the Ribbon.

To activate KeyTips, which help you navigate the Ribbon without the mouse, follow these steps:

1. **Press the Alt key.**

Letters pop up on the Ribbon — these letters correspond to tabs, sections of the Ribbon, buttons, or drop-down list items.

2. **Press the letter for the tab, section, or button you want and more letters will appear. Keep on typing until you've executed the command.**

• The letters don't change, so you can memorize common keystrokes so that you get your work done faster.

• Sometimes more than one character is used for a shortcut, for instance, FF for font face. Just type what you see to execute the command.

• If you press the wrong letter, press Esc to back up your command.

It's possible that the old menu commands whose keystrokes you memorized may still work. Give 'em a try before you give up and learn the new sequence. Table 2-2 shows a list of our favorite shortcuts.

Some of these keystrokes work only in specific situations — for example, when you edit something or work in a particular kind of window. Throughout this book, we tell you which keys do what and when.

Table 2-2	Shortcut Keys in Access
Key or Combination	*Action*
F1	Displays the Help window
Ctrl+F1	Hides or displays the Ribbon
F5	Goes to the record with the record number you type
F6	Moves the focus to another area of the window
F7	Checks the spelling in the selected object
F11	Hides or displays the Navigation pane
Delete	Deletes the selected object
Alt+Enter	In Design view, displays the properties of the selected object
Ctrl+C	Copies the selected text or objects to the Clipboard
Ctrl+F	Finds text (with the option to replace it) in the open table, query, or form
Ctrl+N	Starts a new database
Ctrl+O	Opens a database
Ctrl+P	Prints the selected object
Ctrl+S	Saves the selected object
Ctrl+V	Pastes the contents of the Clipboard to the active window
Ctrl+X	Deletes the selected text or object and saves it in the Clipboard
Ctrl+Z	Undoes the last action that can be undone (our all-time favorite!)
Ctrl+;	Types today's date
Ctrl+"	Duplicates the entry from the same field in the previous record
Esc	Cancels what you are typing

Chapter 3: Designing Your Database the Relational Way

*R*elational database design? Yikes! Sounds like a serious programming project. But what is it, exactly? Designing a database means figuring out how the information is structured — that is, which information should be stored in each table of the database, and how it all connects together. Unlike working with a spreadsheet or word processor, you have to design a database beforehand — you can't just start typing information in. (Well, sure, you can, but we don't recommend it — the result is usually a mess.) How easy it is later to enter and edit information and create useful queries, forms, and reports depends on how well your database is designed. A good database design can streamline your work in Access.

This chapter takes you through the process of designing the table(s) you need in your database, including the relationships between them. Book II, Chapter 1 contains instructions for creating the tables in Access.

What Are Tables, Fields, and Keys?

In Access, you store your data in *tables* — lists of records that work like the index cards that make up an address file. Each record contains information in the same format, in *fields* — specified places for individual pieces of information.

If you want to keep track of the customers of a small bookstore, you make a table of customers, with one record per customer. Each record is made up of the same set of fields, including fields that store the following types of data: customer's last name, first name, street address, city, state or province, ZIP or postal code, country, and phone number (as shown in Figure 3-1).

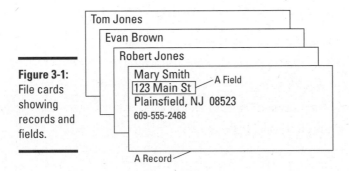

Figure 3-1:
File cards
showing
records and
fields.

After you use Access to create a table, you can *really* get busy — entering, editing, deleting, and sorting the records in various ways, and printing many types of reports (including columnar reports, forms, summaries, mailing labels, and form letters). Access allows you to create as many tables as you need in your database.

Designing a database means deciding (for openers) what tables your database will need to include, and what fields are in each table. At the most basic level, it means designing the needed forms and most likely required reports. This is the computer equivalent of designing the form or file card onto which you write the data, specifying which blanks need to be filled in and which are optional.

Data types

Fields can be different *data types,* depending on what kind of information you want them to store. Some fields contain textual alphanumeric information, such as a last name or street address. Other fields contain numbers, such as someone's age. Others contain logical information — a yes or no regarding some condition. Still others contain dates or times, such as the date that the record was added to the database. Table 3-1 lists the Access data types.

Table 3-1	Commonly Used Data Types for Fields
Data Type	What It Holds
Text	Short chunks of text up to 255 characters, or special codes that contain non-numeric characters, such as phone numbers ((xxx)xxx-xxxx) and ZIP codes (xxxxx-xxxx) that require parentheses and hyphens, which aren't allowed in numbers.
Memo	Like a Text field, but it allows more characters — up to 65,536 of them. A Memo field can contain rich (formatted) text, and you can set it to `Append Only` so that it can accumulate text notes without allowing the user to delete what's already there.
Number	Only numbers. You may use + or − before the number, and a decimal point. Number fields come in a bunch of different sizes, depending on how large the numbers are and how many decimal places you want to store. (See Book II, Chapter 1.)
Currency	Numbers with a currency sign in front of them ($, ¥, and so on). You can do numeric calculations with these fields.
AutoNumber	Numbers unique to each record and assigned by Access as you add records, starting at 1.
Date/Time	These fields calculate (what else?) dates and times.
OLE Object	Object Linking and Embedding. You can embed files containing other kinds of data in your database. However, when creating a new database, consider using the Attachment type instead because it stores data more efficiently than OLE Objects.
Hyperlink	This text string is formatted as a hyperlink. (If you click the link, it takes you to the page.) It's especially useful if there's information on the Web (or your organization's intranet) that relates to the data in your table.
Yes/No	Indicates whether a particular condition is in effect. Can be used for any two words, such as `True/False`, `On/Off`, or `Male/Female`.
Attachment	Using a system called complex data, you can store one or more entire files — pictures, sound, Word documents, even video — in one Attachment field. For example, you can store a picture of a person, or three Excel spreadsheets with data that relate to a transaction.
Calculated	You enter a formula that Access uses to calculate the value of this field based on other fields in the table. For example, a field named `Markup` could be calculated as `SellingPrice - OurCost`.

Primary key fields for your tables

A *primary key field* (or just *key*) is a field that uniquely identifies each record in a table. If (for example) each product in a Products table has a different product code, then the `ProductCode` field uniquely identifies a record in this table. If you search the Products table for a specific product code, you come up with — at most — one record.

However, not all tables have an obvious key field. You may have to combine two or three fields to come up with values that are different for *every* record in the table. In a Books table, for instance, you may have several books with the same title. If you assume that an author never writes more than one book with the same title, a combination of the `Title` and `Author` fields may work as a key field.

For an address list, you may think that the combination of first and last names would do the trick, but it doesn't take long before you realize that you know two Jim Smiths. You could use a combination of first name, last name, and phone number, but you have another, better alternative: Have Access issue each record a unique number, and use that number as the key field. If you can't figure out a good set of keys to use for a table, add an AutoNumber field, and Access automatically numbers the records as you add them.

Access doesn't absolutely require every table to have a primary key field (or fields), but if you plan to set up relationships between your tables, some tables definitely need them. Also, key fields speed up a search for records; Access creates an index for each primary key field and can zero in quickly on any record by using those primary key values. When Access offers to add a primary key for you, accept its offer!

What Are Relationships?

No trick question here — it's just that some projects (*most* projects) require more than one table. For example, a database for a store has to handle lists of customers, lists of products, and lists of vendors, for a start. All those bits of data have to be coordinated in some useful way.

That's where *relational databases* fill the bill. A relational database contains tables that are related — well, no, not as cousins or sisters-in-law. Two tables are *related* if they contain fields that match. If you have an online store, a relational database system probably includes related Products and Vendors tables like these:

+ **The Products table:** This is a list of the products you sell, containing one record for each product. Each record for a product includes a field that identifies the vendor from whom you buy your stock.

+ **The Vendors table:** This list includes name, address, and other information about each vendor.

The Products table and the Vendors table are related because the record for each product includes the name or ID code of a vendor, and the record for each vendor, of course, includes the name or ID code of the vendor.

Multiple products may come from one vendor. Figure 3-2 shows how such a *one-to-many* relationship (more about that in a minute) works in a database for a store that sells movies.

Figure 3-2:
A one-to-many relationship links the Products and Vendors tables — three products come from one vendor.

Products

Title	Vendor
Six Stories about Little Heroes	ART
Adventures in Asia-National Geographi	ROU
The Adventures of Curious George	ROU
I've Always Loved Airplanes	CHB
Aladdin and the Magic Lamp	EBA
Aladdin and the Magic Lamp	PV
The Alamo	COL
Amahl and the Night Visitors	MOV
The Amazing Bone and Other Stories	ROU

Vendors

VendorCode	Company	Address1
PV	Palace Video	
REE	Reel.com	1250 45th Street
ROB	Robert's Hard to Find	
ROU	Rounder Kids	1263 Lower Road
SCH	Schunick Productions	2 Winton Court

Well, sure, you *could* store product information and vendor information together, in one big table, but you'd soon be sorry. You may want to add fields to the Products table to contain the address of the vendor from which you bought the product. But here's the problem: Whenever a vendor's address changes, you have to make that change in the record for *every item* you buy from that vendor. What a pain!

A key principle of database design is this: *Store each piece of information once.* If you store information more than once, then you have to update it more than once. (In real life — trust us on this one — if you update it in some places but not in others, you end up with a mess.)

Here's a piece of geekspeak: *Normalizing* a database means figuring out the most efficient way to divide the information into tables so that each piece of information is stored only once, and related information is connected. This chapter steps you through the process.

How relationships work

Sorry, no advice for the lovelorn here — luckily, relationships between tables are much simpler than relationships between people. For two tables to be related, you specify one or more fields in one table that match the same number of fields in the other table. In Figure 3-2, the Products table relates to the Vendors table because the `Vendor` field in the Products table contains values that match the `VendorCode` field in the Vendors table. When you look at a record in the Products table, you can find out who you buy the product from by finding the record in the Vendors table that has the same value in the matching field.

Relationships, also called (less romantically) *joins,* come in several flavors:

✦ **One-to-many:** One record in one table matches no, one, or many records in the other table. The relationship in Figure 3-2 works this way because one vendor can provide many products.

✦ **One-to-one:** One record in one table matches one record (or no record) in the other table.

✦ **Many-to-many:** Zero, one, or many records in one table match zero, one, or many records in the other table.

The next three sections explain these three types of joins.

One-to-many relationships

This type of relationship is the most common among tables (by analogy, think of one person with a circle of friends). In a one-to-many relationship, many records in one table can match one record in another table. Here are some examples of one-to-many relationships:

✦ **Items in customer orders:** If you run a store, customers frequently buy several items at the same time. You may have an Orders table with one record for each sale you make, but a sale can include a number of products (say, someone buys two books and a pair of socks). One record in the Orders table could match several records in the OrderDetails table.

✦ **Vendors and invoices:** If your company buys many items from another company, you end up with a bunch of invoices from (and payments to) that company. The relationship between the Vendors table and the `Invoices` table in an accounting database is one-to-many.

✦ **People living in states or provinces:** The United States and Canada use standard two-letter state and province abbreviations, and if you have an address list, these codes should be correct. (Quick — is Quebec "QU" or "PQ"? No peeking.) To make sure you type in the valid state and province codes for the United States and Canada, you can create a StateProvinceCodes table against which you can validate entries in the `State` field of your Addresses table. One record in the StateProvinceCodes table can match many records in the Addresses table.

You use a one-to-many relationship to avoid storing information from the "one" table multiple times in the "many" table. For example, you don't want to store all the information about each student in the record for every course — unless you want to hear the groan of an overloaded disk drive. Storing each student's information in one place (the Students table), and storing only the student's name and/or student ID in the CourseRegistrations table is more efficient (and easier to maintain).

Many database designers call the "one" table the *master* table and the "many" table the *detail* table. In Access, *primary key* means the matching field(s) in the master table; *foreign key* means the corresponding field(s) in the detail table. In Figure 3-2, the Vendors table is the master table, and the Products table is the detail table. The primary key (in Vendors) is the `VendorCode` field; the foreign key (in Products) is the `Vendor` field.

One-to-one relationships

This type of relationship — where one record in one table matches exactly one record in another table — is much less common in database design. However, you may have reasons (perhaps *security* reasons) for separating information into two tables. Suppose, for example, you store information about the employees of your company. The Employees table contains the basic information about each employee (name, address, phone, and other personal information). The EmployeeHealth table contains information about each employee's health-insurance policy. (In your company, all employees have insurance.) Each record in the Employees table matches exactly one record in the EmployeeHealth table, and vice versa.

The question is: If you have exactly the same number of records in the two tables, and they match exactly, why not just combine them into one table? Most of the time, that's exactly what you should do. In the employee-database example, you can just add the health insurance information to the Employees table and do away with the EmployeeHealth table.

However, occasionally you have a good reason to separate information into two tables connected by a one-to-one relationship. We came up with three such scenarios:

✦ **Security:** One of the tables contains much more sensitive information than the other, and you want to restrict who can see the information in that table. Store the sensitive information in a separate table.

See Book VII, Chapter 3 for how to set up security for a database.

✦ **Subset of records:** Maybe only some of the employees in your company have health insurance. (This is the real world, after all.) Rather than leaving a lot of fields blank in the Employees table, storing insurance data in a separate, related table is more efficient. Not every record in your Employees table might have a record in the EmployeeHealth table.

✦ **Multiple databases:** Some information is stored in a separate database. When you use one database, you can *link* to a table in another database to work with the information in that table as if it were stored in your own database. If someone else's database has information you need and you link to it, you can't combine the two tables into one table, but you can set up a relationship. (See Book II, Chapter 4 for instructions.)

Don't be surprised if you almost never create one-to-one relationships between database tables; *we* hardly ever do.

For a one-to-one relationship, you need one or more fields that link the two tables. Make sure that both tables have the same primary key field(s).

Many-to-many relationships

Many-to-many relationships are more complicated than either one-to-one or one-to-many relationships. That's because a many-to-many is really two relationships in one. Here are some examples of tables in which zero, one, or many records in one table can match zero, one, or many records in the other:

✦ **Students in courses:** If you create a database to keep track of students in a school, many students are in each class, and each student takes many classes. You have many records in the Students table matching each record in the Courses table; that is, many students are in each course. You also have many records in the Courses table matching each record in the Students table; that is, each student can take many courses.

✦ **Committees:** If you set up a database for a club or religious group, you may want to keep track of who is on what committee. One person can be on lots of committees, and one committee can have lots of members. The relationship between the People table and the Committees table is many-to-many.

✦ **Books and authors:** One book can be written by a group of authors (such as this book). And one author can write many books. The relationship between the Books table and the Authors table in a bookstore inventory database can be many-to-many.

What should you do first?

Creating an Access database and setting up all the objects you will need can be a daunting task. Here's the order in which we usually set a new Access database.

1. Design the database, as described in this chapter.

2. Make the tables that you've designed, as described in Book II, Chapter 1.

3. If you are moving information from a spreadsheet, another database, or some other source, then import data into Access, as described in Book II, Chapter 4.

4. Set up the relationships between the tables, as described in Book II, Chapter 6.

5. Create the queries you know you'll need for displaying related data from multiple tables, as described in Book III, Chapter 1.

6. Make forms for adding and editing records, as described in Book IV, Chapter 1.

7. Set up the reports you want, as described in Book V, Chapter 1. You may need to make additional queries to use as the record source for some reports.

Figure 3-3 shows a many-to-many relationship between students and courses. Each student is in several classes; each course has its own bunch of students.

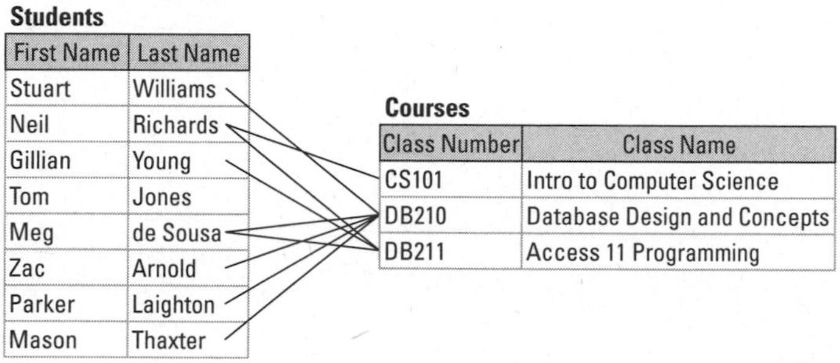

Figure 3-3:
Many
students
can be
in each
course,
and each
student can
take many
courses.

Students

First Name	Last Name
Stuart	Williams
Neil	Richards
Gillian	Young
Tom	Jones
Meg	de Sousa
Zac	Arnold
Parker	Laighton
Mason	Thaxter

Courses

Class Number	Class Name
CS101	Intro to Computer Science
DB210	Database Design and Concepts
DB211	Access 11 Programming

The problem is that Access (and most other relational-database programs) can't handle many-to-many relationships. Access refuses to accept that these relationships exist. (Don't we all know people like that?) But don't worry — you can work around this problem. You can create an additional table that saves the day: The new table records the *connections* between the two tables.

In the students and courses example, you can make a new table called CourseRegistrations. This new table is called a *junction table* and contains one field that matches the primary key for Courses and one field that matches the primary key for Students — each record in the CourseRegistration table connects one student to one course. The Students table and the CourseRelationship table have a one-to-many relationship: The Students table is the master table, and CourseRegistrations is the detail table. The Courses table and the CourseRegistrations table also have a one-to-many relationship: Again, the Courses table is the master table. In fact, you probably want this new table anyway because you need some place to record the student's grade in that course. (We frequently find that the new junction table is useful for storing more than just the relationship.)

Figure 3-4 shows the relationships among the three tables: Students, CourseRegistrations, and Courses. To provide a single primary key field that uniquely identifies each student, we added a StudentID field to the Students table. Each record in the CourseRegistrations table connects one student (by student ID) to one course (by class number). In real life, we'd add fields for the student's grade, registration date, payment date, and other information about the student's enrollment in the course.

Figure 3-4:
To store
a many-
to-many
relationship,
create a
junction
table that
connects
the two
tables.

Students

Student ID	First Name	Last Name
AR1002	Zac	Arnold
DE0014	Meg	de Sousa
JO4001	Tom	Jones
LA0056	Parker	Laighton
RI0014	Neil	Richards
TH2589	Mason	Thaxter
WI0143	Stuart	Williams
YO1567	Gillian	Young

CourseRegistrations

Student ID	Class Number
DE0014	CS101
TH2589	CS101
JO4001	DB210
RI0014	DB210

Courses

Class Number	Class Name
CS101	Intro to Computer Science
DB210	Database Design and Concepts
DB211	Access 11 Programming

Designing a Database

When you feel at ease with the concepts of tables, fields, and relationships,
you're ready to design your own relational database. The rest of this chapter
walks you through designing your database tables so your database is easy
to use, flexible, and efficient. We use the example of a bookstore as we go
through the steps to show you how the design process works.

Identifying your data

Find out what information is available, who maintains it, what it looks like,
and how it is used. Make a list of the possible fields. (Don't worry yet about
which fields end up in which tables.) For example, a bookstore needs to
track product descriptions, prices, purchase dates, customer names, who
bought what, shipment dates (for online orders), and other information.

If some of the information you need is already stored in another database —
whether it's in Access, SQL Server, MySQL, or another relational database —
find out whether the owner of the database will allow you to link to it. Also,
find out the name of the tables and the names and types of the fields in the
tables, so you can see how these tables and fields will connect with the rest
of your information.

Eliminating redundant fields

Look over the fields you identified — make sure they're all actually *needed*
for your application. Is each piece of information something that may appear
on a form or report later, or be needed to calculate something? If not, throw
it out.

In this case, it's worth repeating: *Don't store the same information in more than one place.* In a database, redundant information makes double the work when you're updating the information. Instead, figure out the right place to store the information, and store it there — once. If you can calculate one field from another field, then store only one. For example, storing both age *and* birth date is pointless; a person's age changes — the birth date doesn't. Store the birth date; you can always get Access to do the math for you.

The same is true for information that you can look up. For codes of all types (such as state and province codes, product codes, and the like), make a table for the code that includes a field for the code and a field for the code's meaning. Then all the other tables in your database store only the code — and Access looks up the code's meaning *when you need it to appear* in a form or report. For the online bookstore, you don't need to store the title and author of each item that a customer buys; instead, you can just store the book's ISBN (which is the unique number assigned to each book).

On the other hand, sometimes you can't avoid redundancy. For example, an item of information may change in one place but not in another, so you may have to store it in more than one place. In the bookstore system, when the price of a book changes, the amount that the previous customers paid for the book hasn't changed. In addition to storing the book's current selling price, you may want to store the book's price in the record for each sale.

Organizing fields into tables

Okay, you have a bunch of fields. Are they all in one table, or should you set up multiple tables?

One way to tell whether your system needs multiple tables is to check whether you have different numbers of values for different fields. Say the bookstore carries 2,000 different products (mainly books, we assume) and you have about 16,000 customers. You have 2,000 different product names, prices, and descriptions — while you have 16,000 different customer names, addresses, and sets of credit-card information. Guess what — you have two different tables: a Products table with 2,000 records and a Customers table with 16,000 records.

You could start out with a design like this, with two tables, Products and Customers:

Products

ISBN or Product Code

Title

Author

Publisher

Pub. Year

Price

Cover Photo

Taxable (Yes/No)

Shipping Weight

Vendor Name

Discontinued?

Product Type

Product Notes

Customers

First Name

Last Name

Street Address

City

State/Province

ZIP or Postcode

Payment Method

Credit Card Number

Credit Card Exp. Date

Check Number

Tax Exempt (Yes/No)

Book 1

Book 2

Book 3

Shipping Cost

Sales Tax

Total Price

Purchase Date

When you create the tables and fields in Access, you may not want to use spaces in your table and field names. During the design process, use readable English phrases for your table and field names, and consider removing the spaces, or replacing them with underscores later. Access works fine with spaces in table and field names, but most database programs are not. If you end up moving or linking your database with another database program, you'll have trouble. In your forms and reports, you can use more readable names for your tables and fields. In these examples, we're leaving the spaces in the names to make our example easier to follow.

As you look at these two tables, you'd soon realize that one customer can make more than one purchase. What happens when a customer buys something else, perhaps on a different date?

Combining customer information with purchase information won't work. Leave information about the customer in the Customers table — all the facts about the customer that don't change from one purchase to the next — and move information about a specific purchase into a separate Orders table, like this:

Customers

First Name

Last Name

Street Address

City

State/Province

ZIP or Postcode

Phone Number

Email Address

Tax Exempt (Yes/No)

Orders

Customer First Name

Customer Last Name

Purchase Date

Book 1

Book 2

Book 3

Shipping Cost

Sales Tax

Total Price

Payment Method

Credit Card Number

Credit Card Exp. Date

Check Number

But wait — what if the customer buys more than three books at a time? (We usually do.) If you own the bookstore, you don't want to put an arbitrary limit on how many items your customer can buy. (Limit your profit for the sake of your database? In a word, nope.) Any time your database design includes a bunch of fields that store essentially the same kind of information (for example, `Book 1`, `Book 2`, and `Book 3`), something is wrong. An order can consist of zero, one, or many books — does that sound familiar? Yes, a one-to-many relationship exists between an order and the items in that order, so you need to make a separate table for the individual items, like this:

Orders

Customer First Name

Customer Last Name

Purchase Date

Total Product Cost

Shipping Cost

Sales Tax

Total Price

Payment Method

Credit Card Number

Credit Card Exp. Date

Check Number

Order Details

ISBN

Quantity

Price Each

Now each time a customer places an order (or comes into your store to make a purchase), you create one record in the Customers table if this customer hasn't bought from you before, one record in the Orders table, and one record for each item purchased in the Order Details table. The Order Details table has room to store the quantity of that item, in case the customer wants more than one of something. You should also store the selling price of the book. Access can calculate the cost of that quantity of each book (price × quantity), so you don't need to store that information.

The following are really good reasons *not* to store multiple fields (such as `Book 1`, `Book 2`, and `Book 3`) in one table, and to create a separate table instead:

✦ **You can't anticipate the right number of fields.** If someone buys more than three things (as in this example), you have to create a separate order and enter everything twice.

✦ **You can't analyze the information later.** What if you want to see a list of everyone who bought the last *Twilight* book, so you can notify them that the next one is coming out? If you have multiple fields for this information, your query needs to look for orders that contain a *Twilight* book in `Book 1` or `Book 2` or `Book 3`. What a pain.

We don't want to drive this into the ground, but creating multiple, identical fields is a problem that many first-time database designers make for themselves. Be good to yourself and don't do it!

Add tables for codes and abbreviations

Look at your tables to see whether the fields contain any standard codes, such as two-letter state and province codes, ZIP codes, or other codes. For example, the bookstore's Customers table includes a `State/Province` field and a `ZIP/Postcode` field. The Products table contains a `Product Type` field so the bookstore can track sales of books (type `B`) versus other types of stuff (such as, `F` for food or `A` for audiotapes). Determine whether your system needs to do one of these tasks with the codes:

✦ **Validate the codes.** Wrong codes cause trouble later: Validating the codes when you type them in is always best. If someone types *VR* for Vermont, the post office may not deliver your package. And later, when you analyze your sales by state, you have some Vermonters with the right code (VT) and some with the wrong code. (See Book II, Chapter 5 for more information on how to set up validation in your database.)

✦ **Look up the meaning of the code.** Codes usually stand for something. Should your system print or display the meaning of the code? If you have a report showing total sales of products by type, printing `Books`, `Food`, and `Gifts` (rather than `B`, `F`, and `G`) is nice.

If you want to either validate or look up the codes you store, create a separate table to hold a list of your codes and their meanings. For example, you could add the following two tables to the bookstore database:

States/Provinces	*Product Types*
State or Province Code	Product Type Code
State or Province Name	Product Type Description
Country	

Although ZIP codes and postal codes *are* codes (well, yeah), most databases don't include tables that list them. The reason is simple: Pretty soon your system would be overstuffed with them (about 100,000 ZIP codes exist, for openers). Plus, you have to update the table constantly as the post offices issue — and change — ZIP and postal codes. If you *really* want to validate your ZIP codes, you can get a ZIP code database from the U.S. Postal Service at www.usps.com.

Choosing primary keys for each table

The next step in designing your database is to make sure each table has its own primary key field(s). Each table needs one or more fields that uniquely identify each record in the table. (We find that it's almost always better to use *one* field as your primary key.) Look for a field in the table that has a different value in each record. For example, in the Products table, each book has a unique ISBN (International Standard Book Number) — for a convenient example, look on the back of this book, and you can find its ISBN just above the bar code. If your bookstore sells stuff other than books — say, bookmarks, espresso, and expensive little pastries — then you can make up codes for them. If one field is different for every record in the table, you've found your primary key field. For lists of codes, the code field is the key.

Autonumbering your records

Well, okay, you may not find a unique field. It happens — tables that list people (such as the Customers table) can pose such a problem. Some people have the same name; family members or roommates can share an address and phone number. Most businesses end up creating and assigning unique numbers to people to avoid this problem. (For privacy reasons, don't even *think* of asking for anyone's Social Security number. Make up your own customer number!)

Fortunately, assigning each record in a table a unique number is easy in Access: Just add an AutoNumber field to the table, and Access numbers the records as you enter them. In your bookstore system, you can add a Customer Number field to the Customers table.

The advantage of using an AutoNumber key as the primary key field is that you can't change its values. After you relate two tables by using an AutoNumber field as the primary key, breaking the relationship between the tables if you have to edit the value of the AutoNumber field later is impossible.

For the Orders table, you can use `Customer Number` (instead of the customer's name) to identify who places the order. However, because one customer may make several purchases, you still don't have a unique key for the Orders table. One solution is to use a combination of fields as the primary key. How about using the `Customer Number` and `Purchase Date` fields together as the primary key? This solution works fine as long as a customer doesn't make two orders on the same day. (Hmm, that may not work — people sometimes forget to buy everything they need and come back later for one or two more items.) Instead, add an AutoNumber field to this table to provide a unique `Order Number`.

Two key fields are sometimes better than one

Sometimes using a combination of fields works fine. In the Order Details table, you'd better add a field for the `Order Number`, so you can get immediate access to whatever order contains these items. You don't need to add a `Customer Number` field in this case; after you identify the `Order Number`, Access can look up the `Customer Number` and other customer information.

The `Order Number` field doesn't uniquely identify records in the Order Details table because one order can (and a bookseller would really love it to) include lots and lots of books. Use a combination of the `Order Number` and the `Product Code` or `ISBN` as the primary key for the table — that way, one order includes one entry for each book purchased.

A sample order-entry database design

Figure 3-5 shows the new, improved table design for a bookstore system, with little key icons by the primary key fields. In this database, we've decided to use underscores in place of spaces in all our table and field names.

One other thing: We like to include a `Date_Last_Changed` or `Date_Updated` field in every table. This field almost always turns out to be useful, and it's required if you want to link to and update the table from another Access database. We omitted these fields from Figure 3-5 to save space, but we'd include them in the real database.

Linking your tables

If you end up with only one table, you can skip this step — but that situation is fairly rare. Almost every database ends up with a second table at the very least — to contain those pesky codes.

Figure 3-5:
Your
database
design
organizes
your data
into related
tables.

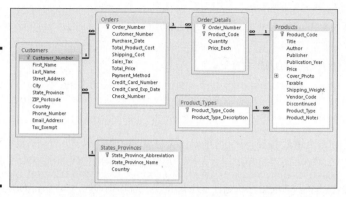

Look at the tables in your database and see which tables contain fields that match fields in other tables. Determine whether there's a one-to-one, one-to-many, or many-to-many relationship between the two tables (as described in the section "What Are Relationships?" earlier in this chapter). For each pair of related tables, you can determine which fields actually relate the tables by following these guidelines:

✦ **One-to-many relationships:** Figure out which is the "one" (master) and which is the "many" (detail) table in this relationship. Make sure that the detail table has a foreign key field (or fields) to match the primary key field(s) in the master table. The Customers and Orders tables have a one-to-many relationship in the bookstore example — because a customer may have no, one, or many orders. (Okay, someone who has no orders is technically not a customer but still counts as a one-to-many relationship; she's a potential customer.) The primary key field in the master table (Customers) is `Customer_Number`. To relate the tables, the Orders table has to have a `Customer_Number` field as the foreign key.

✦ **One-to-one relationships:** Make sure both tables have the same primary key field(s). (Our example doesn't include any one-to-one relationships.)

✦ **Many-to-many relationships:** Access can't store a many-to-many relationship directly. Set up a junction table to connect the two tables, containing the primary keys of the two tables. In the bookstore example, the Orders and Products tables have a many-to-many relationship: One order can have many products, and one product can occur in many orders. The Order_Details table is the junction table that contains the primary key of the Orders table (`Order_Number`) and the primary key of the Products table (`Product_Code`). This junction table can also include additional information. (The Order_Details table includes the quantity of the book that's ordered, as well as the price of each book.)

The related fields don't need to have the same name in the two related tables. But the types, lengths, and contents of the fields have to match. (We usually find giving the two fields the same names less confusing — preserving sanity is also good for business.) Figure 3-5 shows the relationships between your tables by lines between the related fields. For one-to-many relationships, there's a "1" on one end of the line and an infinity sign at the "many" end.

Refining your links

The relationships between your tables can be a bit more complex — what relationship isn't? — so you may need to make a few more decisions about how your table relationships work:

+ **Referential integrity:** This nifty feature means you can tell Access not to allow a record to exist in a detail table unless it has a matching record in the master record. For example, if you turn on referential-integrity checking for the relationship between the Customers and States_Provinces tables, Access won't allow you to enter a record with a `State_Province` code if the code doesn't exist in the `State_ Province_Abbreviation` field of the States table. It's a "No bogus codes!" rule, and doesn't require any programming (as you find out in Book II, Chapter 6).

+ **Cascading updates:** Another way-cool Access feature updates detail records automatically when you change the matching master record. For example, if you find out that you have the wrong ISBN for a book and you change it in the `Product Code` field in the Products table, you can configure Access to update the code automagically in the Order_Details table.

+ **Cascading deletes:** As with cascading updates, this feature deletes detail records when you delete the master record.

This feature is a bit more dangerous than cascading updates, and you may not want to use cascading deletes for most related tables. If a book goes out of print and you stop carrying it, deleting it from the Products table is a bad idea. Consider: What's supposed to happen to all those matching records in the Order_Details table (assuming that you sold *some* copies of the book)? Don't delete the Order_Details records — because then it looks like you never sold those books. Instead, mark the book as *unavailable* (in our example, set the `Discontinued` field in the Products table to `Yes`) and leave the records in the tables.

Now you have a fully relational database design. The last step is to clean up the loose ends.

What's in a name?

Table names should be plural (like `Products` and `Customers`). Field names should be singular (like `City` and `Quantity`). Access doesn't care, but it'll make things easier for you to read. Don't use all capital letters — you'll feel as though Access is yelling at you. We like to capitalize the first letter of each word.

Designing a Database **55**

Book I
Chapter 3

Designing Your
Database the
Relational Way

Naming things (for serious database designers)

If you really want to impress your programming friends, consider using prefixes on all your object names to show what kind of object you're naming. Here's a set of commonly used prefixes:

tbl   Table

qry   Query

frm   Form

rpt   Report

mcr   Macro

bas   Module

For example, you might rename the Products table as tblProducts.

Fewer programmers use prefixes for fields to show the data type of each field. If you want to, and if you want to read more about the Leszynski Naming Convention from which these prefixes come, go to MVPS.org and search for *Leszynski naming convention*.

In Figure 3-5, we used an underscore in place of a space in all the table and field names. Using spaces in names is a bad idea if you ever want to link the data from your Access database to a larger database, like a SQL Server or MySQL database. Also, it means that when typing formulas, you have to enclose the name in square brackets to tell Access where the name starts and ends. (And who wants to remember to do that?) Decide in advance whether you are going to use spaces, underscores in place of spaces (for example, `Product_Code`), or neither (`ProductCode`) in all your names. You can't use a hyphen because that means subtraction in Access.

Finally, don't use words that have specialized meanings to Access, including these words: *Name, Date, Word, Value, Table, Field,* and *Form.* You can actually confuse Access. It's not a pretty sight.

In general: Be consistent, to make it easier to remember table and field names. (Was that table name `Product_Codes`, `ProductCode`, or `ProductCODE`?)

Cleaning up the design

You have tables, you have fields, and you have relationships. What more could you want in a database design? You're almost done. Look at each field in each of your tables and decide on the following for each field:

✦ **Data types:** The section, "Data types," earlier in this chapter describes the types of information you can store in Access fields. Decide what kind of information each field contains, how large your Text fields need to be, and what kinds of numbers your Number fields hold. (Book II, Chapter 1 explains the sizes of Number fields.) Make sure to use the same data type and length for related fields. For example, if Product_Code is a Text field that is 16 characters long in the Products table, make it the same length in the Order_Details table.

If you use an AutoNumber field as the primary key in a master table, use a Long Integer Number field for the foreign key in related tables.

✦ **Required fields:** You can tell Access not to allow a field to be blank. For example, a record in the Products table should never have a blank Product_Code or Price field.

✦ **Validation:** You can set up validation (data-checking) rules for fields, as described in Book II, Chapter 5. Think about limits on the legal values for the field. For example, you may want to specify that the Price field in the Products table can't be over $1,000, or that the Publication Year field must be between 1500 and 2100. (This rule should work unless you run the bookstore for the Hogwarts School.)

✦ **Defaults:** Some fields have the same value for most records. For example, the Discontinued field in the Products table will be No for most records, especially when you first create the record. (How often would you type in an item that's already discontinued?) You can set the default value — the value that the field starts out with — to the most common value; you have to change it only for the records that have a different value.

✦ **Indexes:** If you plan to sort your table or search for records based on the values in a field, tell Access to maintain an index for the field. Like the index of a book, a database index helps you (or Access) find information; Access stores information about the field to speed up searches. Access automatically indexes primary key fields and foreign key fields, but you can designate additional fields to be indexed.

That's it! You're done designing your database!

Tips for Choosing Field Types

Now that you know the concepts and procedures for designing a relational database, here are a few suggestions for choosing field types for your information:

Choosing between Text and Yes/No fields

Fields that can have only two values (such as Yes and No, True and False, or On and Off) are also called *Boolean* or *logical* values. You can store Boolean information in a one-letter Text field, using Y and N. But if you use a Yes/No field, Access can display the information on forms as a check box, option button, or toggle button.

Another advantage of going the Yes/No field route is that you can easily switch between displaying the field as `Yes` and `No`, `True` and `False`, or `On` and `Off` by changing the Format property for the field. Using a custom format, you can choose any two text values to display instead of `Yes` and `No`. You can display the values `Discontinued` and `Available` for a `Yes/No` field.

Choosing between Text and Memo fields

Text fields are limited to 255 characters — if you need more than that, use a Memo field. An Access Memo field can contain more than 65,000 characters of textual information — but the extra elbow room costs you some versatility. You can't index Memo fields — and they can't serve as primary or foreign keys. If you plan to sort or search your records using the contents of this field — or use the information in it to relate one table to another — a Text field is usually your best bet. So is brevity. On the other hand, Memo fields can contain Rich Text — that is, formatted text. If you need bold, italics, and font changes in your text, you need to use a Memo field.

Some database designers avoid the Memo field altogether because they find that databases with Memo fields are more likely to get *corrupted* (become unreadable by Access). The same is true of OLE Object fields (used for storing pictures, spreadsheets, documents, and other large objects) — your database may get indigestion.

Choosing between Text and Number (or Currency) fields

Access displays and sorts Number and Currency fields differently from Text fields. Here are the differences:

✦ When displaying a Number or Currency field, Access drops any leading zeros. (For example, 08540 becomes 8540 or $8,540.)

✦ You can format Number and Currency fields in many ways, giving you control over the number of decimal places, specified currency symbols, and the use of commas. Access can vertically align these fields on the decimal points, which makes columns of numbers easier to read.

✦ Access can calculate totals, subtotals, and averages for Number and Currency fields, as well as do other numeric calculations.

✦ When sorting a Number or Currency field, values sort from smallest to largest. (At least they do when you're sorting in ascending order.) But when you sort a Text field, values are sorted alphabetically — starting at the left end of the field. This difference means that in a Text field, Access sorts 55 before 6, because the *5* character comes before the *6* character. The following table shows how Access sorts the same list of numbers in Number and Text fields.

Number Sort	Text Sort
1	1
2	11
5	2
11	21
21	44
44	5

Use Number fields for all numbers except numeric codes (such as ZIP codes or phone numbers), which are described in the next section. Store any number you may want to add to a total in a Number or Currency field. Choose a Currency field for money values.

Storing pictures and other files

Access provides two field types that allow you to store entire files of information, usually pictures. The old type, OLE Objects, provides a link to the file — but unless the files are small, doing so turns out to be a bad idea. The database reacts to a large OLE object like an anaconda trying to swallow a rhino — and its size balloons. Instead, you can use an Attachment field, which compresses the file before storing it in your database.

You have another option: Don't store the file in your database at all. If your pictures are large, if they change frequently, or if you use them for other purposes and need to store them as separate files anyway, store the pathname that leads to the files containing the pictures. In the bookstore example earlier in this chapter, the Products table includes a `Cover Photo` field. Instead of making that field into an Attachment field, you can store all the cover pictures in a separate folder on the hard drive — and store filenames for each picture in a Text field. If the pictures are in various folders, store the entire pathname in the field, as in the following example:

```
D:\Bookstore\Database\Products\Iliad.jpg
```

The disadvantage of this method is that if you move your database to another computer, you need to move all these files, too, so that the pathname is the same on the new computer as it was on the old one.

Storing names, money, codes, and other stuff

Here are a few other field-type suggestions:

✦ **People's names:** For lists of people, creating a `Name` field and putting full names into it is tempting. Don't do it: You'll want to sort records by last name, or create listings with last name first, or otherwise fool with the format of people's names. Create separate `First_Name` and `Last_Name` fields. You may even want `Middle_Name` and `Salutation` (like `Mr.` and `The Reverend`) fields.

✦ **Phone numbers and postcodes:** Use Text fields rather than Number fields, even if you plan to type only digits into the field. The test to use is this: Is there any chance that you'd ever want to do math with this information? If the answer is no, then use a Text field. (If you store a ZIP code in a number field, Access feels compelled to drop leading zeroes, so the ZIP code for Middlebury, VT turns from 05753 to 5753 — not good.)

✦ **Money:** Use a Currency field rather than a Number field. Calculations with Currency fields are faster than those with most Number fields.

✦ **Percentages:** To store percentages, such as a discount, create a Number field and enter decimal numbers between 0 and 1 (inclusive) for percentages between 0 and 100. When you create the table, you can format the Number field as a percent. Then, if you enter a value and habit makes you type **33%**, Access converts the value automatically to 0.33.

✦ **Calculations:** Access 2010 includes a Calculated field type, which stores the results of calculations that use other fields in the same table. Official relational database theory says that fields should contain only raw data — Access can always do the calculations later in your queries, forms, and reports. However, the space required to store a number is pretty small, and if there's a calculation that you'll need in lots of forms and reports, it's convenient to enter the formula just once as part of the table definition, so we say — go ahead! For example, we may want to enter a `Total_Price` field in the Order_Details table that multiplies `Quantity` with `Price_Each`, since this number is likely to show up on invoices, receipts, and sales reports.

Never create a field where you enter the result of a calculation yourself. If the numbers on which the calculation was based happen to change, the calculation is then wrong — which fouls up any calculations or reports based on it. An Access Calculated field will update the result automatically when other fields change.

✦ **Codes:** Decide on the formats to use for phone numbers, invoice numbers, credit-card numbers, purchase order numbers, and other codes. Decide whether to use all capital letters, and whether to include or omit dashes and spaces. If you ask Access to search for someone with a credit card number 9999–8888–7777–6666 and the card number is stored as 9999888877776666, the search won't find the record.

Secret keys

The primary key field for a table doesn't have to be information that the user sees. In fact, many programmers prefer to use a primary key field that has no other use than to uniquely identify records. If you create an AutoNumber field to act as a primary key field, the user of your database never has to see or type the values of this field.

For example, when you sign in to the Amazon.com Web site to order a book, you never have to type in your customer number. Instead, you sign in with your e-mail address, and Amazon looks up your customer number automatically. Similarly, when you order a book or other merchandise, you never have to type the item number. You just find the item you want and click the Add This Item to My Cart button.

Storing Single Facts

Some pieces of information exist all by themselves. They aren't part of a list — there's just one item. For example, the name of your organization is a single piece of information, and so is the pathname to the location of your database. If you want these pieces of information to appear on any reports, forms, or queries, or used in calculations or importing, typing them willy-nilly into said reports, queries, or other Access objects is tempting — but in practice, this turns out to be a lousy idea.

Here's the problem: What happens when one of these facts changes? Suppose that your organization's name or address changes, or you move your database's location to another folder on another computer. You sure don't want to have to root around your database looking for the places where such information appears.

Instead, create a table called Constants or Facts (or any name you like) *with just one record in it.* Create a field for each piece of information you need to store: Maybe your table contains `Our_Name`, `Our_Address`, `Our_City`, `Our_State`, `Our_ZIP`, and `Our_Phone_Number` fields. Be sure to include a `Our_State_Sales_Tax` field, too. Wherever you want this information to appear (reports, mainly), Access can look it up in your table. Then, if something changes (your telephone area code, most likely), you have to update it in only one place!

Creating a Database

Okay, if you faithfully read this book every night before bedtime — doesn't everybody? — you're 70 pages or so in by now. If you still haven't created your database, enough, already! You're armed with your database design and you're ready to start. (If you haven't been following along, then maybe you'd better review those 70 pages *before* you start.)

When you set out to create a new Access database, you have two options: Create it from scratch or use a template.

Creating a database from scratch

After you have a beautiful database design (allow us to recommend the — ahem — stellar example in this chapter), you can start with a blank database and create the tables, fields, and relationships. That means running Access without opening an existing database. Follow these steps:

1. Create a new database by clicking the File tab on the Ribbon and clicking New (as shown in Figure 3-6).

You see a number of choices for creating a new database.

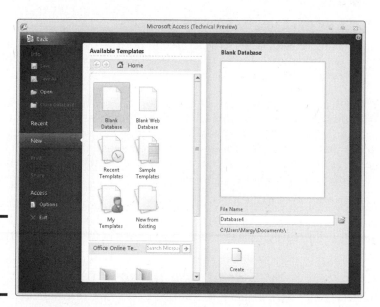

Figure 3-6: Creating a new database.

2. Click Blank Database.

The File Name task on the right side of the window appears, offering the option of naming the database file in the File Name box. If you don't choose to name the database on your own, Access will name it `Database1.accdb` (or another number, depending on how many databases you have created). (Wondering about that Blank Web Database button? See Book IX, Chapter 3 for details.)

3. **Navigate to the folder where you want to store the new database, and type the filename into the File Name box. Then click OK.**

   Access tells you where it plans to store the new database, but you can change this location by clicking the cute little folder icon on the far-right side of the File Name text box and choosing a different folder. If you are just trying this out, you can use the filename `Test`. Access automatically adds the extension `.accdb` to Access database files.

4. **Click the Create button.**

   Access creates a new, blank database. It assumes that the first thing that you will want to do is to create some tables, so it makes a new, blank table, too, and displays it in Design view.

5. **Create your tables.**

   Book II, Chapter 1 tells you how to do create tables. (You define each of the fields in the database, including the field name, data type, and field length.)

6. **Create relationships between the tables.**

   Making relationships is described in Book II, Chapter 6. Access displays a Relationships window that draws lines between related tables, like the diagram shown in Figure 3-5.

You can always rename the database later. Close the database, and run Windows Explorer by double-clicking My Computer on the desktop or choosing Start➪All Programs➪Accessories➪Windows Explorer. Navigate to the folder that contains the database and find its filename. Then click the filename, press F2, and type a new name for the database file. You can't rename an Access database within Access.

When you create a database, Access uses the newer `.accdb` format that was introduced with Access 2007. Note that Access 2003 and older versions can't open `.accdb` format databases — if you try, you'll just get an error message.

Creating a new database using a template

Access comes with a bunch of *templates* — databases that already include tables and relationships, but with no data. You get queries, forms, and reports, too — very handy! If you are creating a database for a purpose for which Microsoft has designed a template, you can use the template to provide the initial design, and then make changes to adapt the objects in the database for your own use. Looking at Microsoft's templates is a good way to get design ideas, too.

To create a database from a template, follow these steps:

1. **Click the File tab on the Ribbon, click New, and click Sample Templates.**

   You see buttons for lots of templates.

2. **Click a template, choose a folder location and a name, and click Create.**

   Choosing the folder and name works the same way as for creating a new, blank database, described in the previous section.

3. **Prowl around the database, looking at the tables to see whether the design will work for you.**

   Use the Navigation pane, described in Chapter 2 of this minibook, to see the tables. Open each one in Design view to see a list of the fields with their field types.

4. **Change the design as needed.**

   Book II, Chapter 1 describes how to change the design of an existing table. You can rename tables and fields, add fields that the template doesn't include, and delete fields you don't think you'll need.

If you make a new database from a template, and the template turns out not to be useful for you, you can always just delete the database and try another template, or start from scratch.

Analyzing and documenting your table design

Access comes with a wizard that can eyeball your database design, looking at the way that you divide your information into related tables. Specifically, it helps you fix a table that contains repeated values in some fields, splitting the table into two or more related tables. The Table Analyzer Wizard walks you through the process, creating the new tables and moving the fields and values. To run the wizard, click the File tab on the Ribbon, scroll down to the Analyze Database button, click it, and choose Analyze Table.

Another Access feature can provide documentation on almost any aspect of your new database, helps you to track the changes made to your database, and provides information to your users. The Documenter allows you to select the components of your database that you want to create documentation for and then creates that documentation automatically. It even allows you to select the format in which that documentation is stored. To run the Documenter, click the File tab on the Ribbon, scroll down to the Analyze Database button, click it, and choose Database Documenter.

Book II

Tables for Storing Your Data

The 5th Wave   By Rich Tennant

"My girlfriend ran a spreadsheet of my life, and generated this chart. My best hope is that she'll change her major from 'Computer Sciences' to 'Rehabilitative Services.'"

Contents at a Glance

Chapter 1: Creating and Modifying Tables

In This Chapter

✔ Making new tables with templates and wizards

✔ Making totally original tables using the Datasheet view

✔ Using datasheets to enter and view data

✔ Defining a primary key

✔ Navigating a datasheet

✔ Checking spelling in your datasheet

✔ Calculating totals for fields in the datasheet

✔ Printing your raw data

You've probably turned to this chapter because you have data — data already stored in Access that you want to look at, or data stored somewhere else, either on paper or in electronic form, and you (or someone you work for) have decided that Access is the right tool for storing and analyzing this data. You're probably right!

Tables are the basic building block of your database — they hold the data that you need to save and analyze. If you have data and are using Access, this chapter is a great place to start.

However, if you're getting ready to put data into Access, it's important that you first read the chapter before this one, Book I, Chapter 3. Even if you don't know what the title means, you need to read that chapter, which tells you how to gather all your data and look at it, how to decide how many tables to create to hold your data, and which fields will go in which tables. In that chapter, you also find out all about fields and records (that is, columns and rows in your table). After you've outlined the big picture of your database design, then this chapter is the next step — we tell you how to go about creating new tables and putting your data in them.

If you want to look at existing tables, skip to the section, "Working with a Datasheet Full of Data," later in this chapter. Then you may want to enter new data, change existing data, or refine field definitions. Look for those section headings in this minibook, in this chapter and the next.

Creating tables and entering data may not be the most glamorous things you do with your database, but having well-designed tables and correctly entered data makes your database as useful as possible. Once you've created a place to store your data in an organized way, you can put Access to work and analyze and view your data in any way that you want.

This chapter guides you through creating tables and defining fields in Datasheet view. Chapter 2 of this minibook goes into the details you need to know about creating and editing fields in Design view. The other chapters in this minibook cover all the other important details that keep your tables — and the data in them — in good shape for use in queries, forms, reports, and the other objects in your database, as well as other ways to analyze data using the tools available in a datasheet.

All the buttons on the Home tab in datasheet view are also available in a datasheet created by a query. The buttons on the Fields and Table tabs are only available in table Datasheet view.

Deciding How You'll View Your Tables

To display an existing table, find the Tables heading at the top of the list in the Navigation pane, followed by the name of all the tables in the database. Double-click the name of the table you want to display, and the table appears in Datasheet view.

The Navigation pane appears on the left side of the Access window, or as a grey bar along the left side of the window. (Click it to display the pane.) In the Navigation pane, if you don't see a Tables heading followed by all the tables in the database, here's how to get a look at them: Right-click the Navigation bar heading, choose Category, then Object Type. Now you should see the objects in the database, sorted by object type (that is, Tables, Queries, Forms, and Reports). (See Book I, Chapter 2 for more information on the Navigation pane and displaying database objects.)

You can view tables in these two views:

+ **Datasheet:** This view is similar to a spreadsheet — it displays your data in rows and columns. Rows are the records; columns are the fields. In Figure 1-1, you see a datasheet with all the parts labeled. Use a datasheet to view, enter, edit, and delete data. In Datasheet view, you can also create and delete fields, sort and filter data, check spelling, and find data. This chapter is all about table Datasheet view.

+ **Design:** In Design view, you don't see any data; instead, you define and edit field names and specify the type of data each field holds. You can also provide a field description. In addition, Design view contains *field properties* — more advanced ways to define fields and help make sure that data entry is accurate. In Figure 1-2, you see a table in Design view, with its various parts labeled. The next chapter in this minibook is all about Table Design view.

Don't stress about deciding whether you want to create a table by defining fields in Design view or by entering data in Datasheet view. It's easy to switch back and forth between Datasheet and Design views to define the tables and fields exactly the way you want them. If your data fits into a table template, use one. If you have data to enter, and you don't want to use a table template, start by entering data into Datasheet view. If you are defining an entire database and the data is coming later, define the table using Design view.

Record Selecter   Field

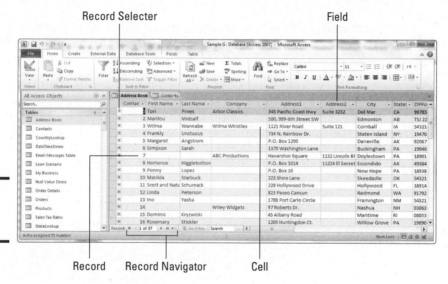

Figure 1-1:
Datasheet
view.

Record   Record Navigator   Cell

Field Selector   Fields

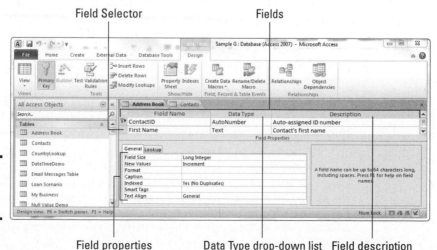

Figure 1-2:
Design
view.

Field properties   Data Type drop-down list   Field description

Once you've displayed a table, you can easily switch between Design and Datasheet view by clicking the View button, the first button on the Home tab of the Ribbon.

Making a Table for Your Data

Before you create a table to hold your data, take some time to consider the design of your database — that is, what fields and tables you need — so that your data is well-organized and easy to analyze. (Book I, Chapter 3 has all the information you need to know before you sit down and design your tables.)

After you figure out how to organize your data, you're ready to sit down with Access and create tables. If you are importing data, see Chapter 4 of this minibook for more information.

To create a table, first open the database that you want to hold the table. If you have just created a brand-new database, as soon as you name the database you'll see an empty table in Datasheet view ready for you to enter your data. If you are adding a table to an existing database, using the second group of buttons (the Tables group) on the Create tab of the Ribbon (see Figure 1-3) allows you to create new tables, as follows:

Figure 1-3:
Use a button in the Tables group to create a new table.

+ **Table:** Creates a new, blank table displayed in Datasheet view, allowing you to immediately enter data.

+ **Table Design:** Creates a new, blank table displayed in Design view, allowing you to define fields. See Chapter 2 of this minibook for more information on using Table Design view to refine your table and field definitions.

+ **SharePoint Lists:** Creates a list on a SharePoint site and a table in the database that links to the newly created SharePoint list. A SharePoint list stored on a SharePoint server allows you to securely share Access data with others who have access to the SharePoint server. See Book IX, Chapter 3 for more information on using SharePoint with Access.

Notice that the Tables group gives you two options for creating tables from scratch — Table and Table Design. If you want help creating your table, Access provides an additional two options — one is table templates, which allows you to choose from available tables with predefined fields. We discuss that in the next section. Another way to get help creating a table is to use field templates — predefined fields you can put in any table. (We talk about field templates in the upcoming "Entering data and creating fields" section.)

Starting with an application part

Microsoft is certainly aware that creating a database is not as simple as creating a Word document or an Excel spreadsheet. They also want you to be able to use the power of Access to work with data, so they've created all sorts of tools to make it easier for you. One of those tools is database templates, covered in Book I, Chapter 2. If your data fits or almost fits into a database template, you should use one.

**Book II
Chapter 1**

**Creating and
Modifying Tables**

A second option is to use an application part. To see the available Application Parts, click the Create tab and then the Application Parts button. Some of the Application Parts are available are Forms, and they are covered in Book IV, Chapter 1. However, the Quick Start options at the bottom of the Application Parts list insert part of a database into your database so that you can get your database built faster. These Quick Start application parts insert a table into your database, and also supporting queries, Forms, and Reports to help you enter and analyze the data in the table. They may even prompt you to build new relationships between existing tables and the new table to integrate the new data into your existing database.

There are currently only a few application parts to choose from, and none of them may be a good match for your data. However, you may want to consider using one of them — even if you have to change field names and definitions a bit — if it seems easier than starting from scratch. You may also want to check the Microsoft Web site for additional templates that may become available.

To add a table from Application parts, click the Application Parts button, the first button on the Create tab. The drop-down list shows Form templates at the top, and then Table templates under the Quick Start heading. Access may ask you to create a simple relationship to an already existing table in the database (and provides an option to create no relationship). For instance, you could create a relationship between people stored in a Contacts table and comments they make stored in a Comments table. If you do create a relationship when adding the Application Part to your database, you will see the related field in the new table in addition to the fields listed below. There are five template choices and what they contain:

✦ **Comments:** This table includes a Comments table with fields `CommentDate` and `Comment`.

✦ **Contacts:** This template includes a Contacts table with fields `Company`, `First Name`, `Last Name`, `E-mail Address`, `Job Title`, `Business Phone`, `Home Phone`, `Mobile Phone`, `Fax Number`, `Address`, `City`, `State/Province`, `Zip`, `Country`, `Web page`, `Notes`, `Attachments`, and calculated fields `ContactName`, and `FileAs`; ContactsExtended Query, ContactDetails Form, ContactDS Form, and ContactList Form; ContactAddressBook Report, ContactList Report, ContactPhoneBook Report and Label Report. This is a good template to use if you want to store an address book in Access.

✦ **Issues:** This template includes a Issues table with fields `ID`, `Summary`, `Status`, `Priority`, `Category`, `Project`, `OpenedDate`, `DueDate`, `Keywords`, `Resolution`, `ResolvedVersion`, and `Attachments`; `IssueDetail` form, and IssueNew form.

✦ **Tasks:** This template includes a Tasks table with fields `ID`, `TaskTitle`, `Priority`, `Status`, `Description`, `Start Date`, `DueDate`, and `Attachments`, and `Percent Complete`, TaskDetails form and TaskDS form This template can be part of a project management database.

✦ **Users:** This template includes a Users table with fields `ID`, `Email`, `FullName`, and `Login`; and `UserDetails` form.

When you've chosen the template you want to use, wait a second while Access creates the table and any other objects. After they are created, you can enter data or change the objects, just as you could if you'd created the objects from scratch.

Creating a new table using Datasheet view

The most straightforward way to create a new table is to create a datasheet and begin entering data. A datasheet looks like a spreadsheet; if you're familiar with Excel or another spreadsheet program, creating a table by entering data into a datasheet, and then changing field names and properties as needed are good places to start. In a datasheet, fields are columns, and records are rows. (If you're confused by this talk of fields and records, go to Book I, Chapter 3!)

Follow these steps to create a new table in Datasheet view:

1. **Open your database.**

If you're starting a brand-new database, Access immediately creates a new table in Datasheet view for you. Just skip to Step 4, and start entering your data!

2. **Click the Create tab on the Ribbon.**

3. **Click the Table button — the second button on the Create tab of the Ribbon.**

You see a blank datasheet in Datasheet view, as shown in Figure 1-4. Access names it Table1. (You can change that when you save the table.) Access automatically creates an ID field @md see the column labeled ID? The ID field automatically gives each record a unique ID number.

Notice that the Fields tab on the Ribbon appears automatically when you display a datasheet.

**Book II
Chapter 1**

**Creating and
Modifying Tables**

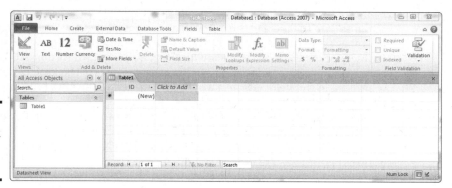

Figure 1-4:
A new blank
table, ready
for data.

4. **Save the table by pressing Ctrl+S or by clicking the Save button at the top-left corner of the Access window.**

Access displays the Save As dialog box.

5. **Type a name for the table in the** `Table Name` **field and press Enter.**

Use a descriptive name so you can find the table in the future. For more information on naming database objects, see Book I, Chapter 3.

Now that you have a table, you may want to do one of the following:

✦ **Enter data.** Press Tab to move from cell to cell. Access automatically saves the data when you move to the next cell. Hold Ctrl and type + to move to a new record, or use the New Record button at the bottom of the datasheet (or on the Ribbon's Home tab).

✦ **Create fields.** Enter data or use field templates.

✦ **Rename fields.** Double-click the field name, type a new name, and press Enter.

See Chapter 2 of this minibook for more information about defining fields and other tasks to define your table and fields in Table Design view.

Entering data and creating fields

When you have a new, blank database, start entering your data. Even if you want to create a form to enter data, it makes sense to enter one record's worth of data and then rename the fields. Then you'll have the basics of your table defined, and you can use the table to create a form, where you can continue to enter data.

As you enter data, Access determines the data type and defines the field accordingly. When one (or more) record has been entered, you can rename the fields and change any field properties as necessary.

Enter data by clicking the first cell and typing. It will save you some steps if you add the dollar sign for currency numbers percent sign when you're inputting a percentage, and type any dates in a recognized format (10-10/2010 or October 10, 2010, for instance). Then Access knows the type of data you are putting in the field, and you won't have to define the data type later.

After each entry, press Tab or Enter to move to a new field. For example, enter a first name, last name, street address, city, state, and ZIP code, pressing Tab to move from one entry to the next. Figure 1-5 shows a table with one record (row) of data entered.

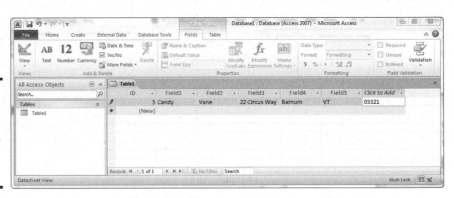

Figure 1-5:
Enter data, pressing Tab to move between fields.

Access uses the Pencil icon in the left border of the row (also called the *record selector*) to indicate that you are "writing" — that is, entering or editing — data. Access also italicizes the data in the active cell and shows the column outlined in yellow so that you can easily see where you are on the datasheet. Enter data in as many columns as you think you need in the table.

If you want to add more information than will fit, just go right ahead. Access can store way more information in a cell than it displays in the initial cell widths. You can easily increase the width of your column, or use a nifty little zoom box. (Use Shift+F2 to see the contents of the cell in the Zoom box.)

If you decide you need additional fields, you can add them using any of the three methods in the section that follows. For instance, if you create fields by entering data, you may create an additional field using a field template, or by defining it in Design view. Access is very versatile and doesn't lock you into one method.

Creating fields

After you've created a table, you're ready to create and define fields. Each field stores one category of data — for instance, first name or ZIP code. You may define fields by any of these methods:

✦ By entering data and letting Access figure out what kind of data is in each field, as detailed in the preceding section.

✦ By using buttons in the Add & Delete section of the Fields tab.

✦ By defining each field yourself in Table Design view. See the next chapter for all the details.

You may also choose to use a combination of all these methods. Using Design view to define fields and field properties is covered in the next chapter.

The Add & Delete section of the Fields tab provides an easy way to add fields to your table. Click the button for the type of data you will store in the new field, and Access creates a field of the correct type. The field will be called Field1, and before you do anything else, type a different name for the field. (The name of the newly selected field is selected so that you can rename it.) You can also click the field name and drag it to the location where you want it to appear in the datasheet.

Access 2010 has a number of predefined fields that you can insert into your table. To see the list, click the More Fields button in the Add and Delete group of the Fields tab of the Ribbon when you are viewing a datasheet. The More Fields list (shown in Figure 1-6) is displayed.

Fields are listed in categories. The first category is Basic Types, and the following categories contain options for the different types of data you may have: Number, Date and Time, and Yes/No (all of these field types are defined in the next chapter). The last category, Quick Start, is the most interesting: it contains data types that are common and relatively difficult to define manually: Address, Phone, Priority, Status, and Tags.

The field type defines the data type and format and may also include field properties. You can make the same changes to a field that you create using a field template that you can make to any field — you can change the data type, the field name, and any field properties.

Figure 1-6:
Click a field
template
to add a
field to your
table.

Quick-starting your table

If you are creating fields for your table, Access 2010 provides a way for you to Quick Start your table. The Quick Start fields found on the More Fields list in the Add & Delete group of the Fields tab are not single fields. They are groups of fields, and in some cases, selecting a Quick Start field might give you all the fields you need for your table. Each field is defined with the appropriate field properties. Here's a rundown of the Quick Start options:

✦ **Address:** Creates fields for Address, City, State Province, Zip Postal, and Country Region,

✦ **Category:** Creates a field with three choices on the drop-down menu: 1-Category, 2-Category, and 3-Category. Change these options by switching to Design view and editing the Row Source property on the lookup tab. (See the next chapter for more details on changing field properties.)

✦ **Name:** Creates fields for last Name, First Name, Contact Name, and File As. Contact Name and File As are calculated fields.

✦ **Payment Type:** Creates a field, Payment Type, with the options Cash, Credit Card, Check, and In Kind. Change these options by switching to Design view and editing the Row Source property on the lookup tab. (See the next chapter for more details on changing field properties.)

✦ **Phone:** Creates fields for Home Phone, Mobile Phone, and Fax Number.

+ **Priority:** Creates a field, Priority, with the options 1-Critical, 2-Major, 3-Minor, and 4-Trivial. Change these options by switching to Design view and editing the Row Source property on the lookup tab. (See the next chapter for more details on changing field properties.)

+ **Start and End Dates:** Creates fields for Start Date and End Date.

+ **Status:** Creates a field, Status, with the options 1-New, 2-Active, 3-Resolved, and 4-Closed. Change these options by switching to Design view and editing the Row Source property on the lookup tab. (See the next chapter for more details on changing field properties.)

+ **Tags:** Creates a field tag, with the options Tag 1, Tag 2, and Tag 3. Change these options by switching to Design view and editing the Row Source property on the lookup tab. (See the next chapter for more details on changing field properties.)

Choosing field names

When you create fields, give at least a couple of seconds of thought to the name you give them. Although you can change a field name, thinking of the name as permanent is safer. Pick a name that is descriptive, not too long, and easy to figure out. You often see the name without the description when you are building other objects, so naming fields well now saves you time later.

Some fields are used to connect tables — for instance, in your Holiday Gifts database you may have a person's name (or some unique identifier) in the table for listing addresses, as well as the table for listing the gift(s) you give them each year. Try to use the same name for fields that appear in multiple tables when the field is, in fact, the same. If the field is similar but *not* identical, give it a different name.

Starting every name with a number or a letter, and keeping names to 64 characters or fewer, is a good idea.

If you are even thinking of using your database in a SQL environment, don't use spaces in your field names. SQL does not like spaces!

Changing a field name

In the database-building process, changing field names is easier if you do it sooner rather than later — that is, before you use the field name a zillion times in tables, queries, forms, reports, and in code. Keep a table of old and new names in case any problems crop up.

You can rename a field in a single table, but if you use the field in other places in the database, be sure the Name AutoCorrect feature is on. To see the Name AutoCorrect options, click the File button near the top-left corner of the Access window, then click the Options button at the bottom of the menu. Click Current Database in the Navigation pane of the Access Options dialog box, and scroll down to see the Name AutoCorrect Options section. There are three Name AutoCorrect box check boxes — be sure the second (Perform Name AutoCorrect) is selected.

To change a field name in Datasheet view, right-click the current name, select Rename from the shortcut menu, type a new name, and press Enter. In Design view, simply edit the current name.

Saving your table

As soon as you enter data, Access saves it. So why do you need to save your tables? That's easy: In order to save both the structure of the table and its field definitions. What you save when you save a table is the table definition, which includes how the table looks in Datasheet view (such as the size and order of the columns) and the information in Design view (the field names, data types, descriptions, and field properties).

Save a table design by using one of these methods:

✦ Click the Save button (it looks like a disk, and is on the toolbar above the Ribbon).

✦ Press Ctrl+S.

✦ Close Design view and click the Yes button when Access asks whether you want to save the table.

✦ Click the File Button in the top-left corner of Access and choose Save from the menu.

Then, in the Save As dialog box, provide a name that describes the data stored in the datasheet. Chances are you'll use a table whenever you create other database objects; naming each table descriptively saves you time when you're looking for the data you need later.

Working with a Datasheet Full of Data

If you've inherited a database full of data, or if you've put lots of data into your database, or if you've created queries and displayed the results in datasheets, it is reasonable to expect that you may want to look at the data!

Double-click any table (or query) name in the Navigation pane to display the table (or query) in Datasheet view. (For more information about the Navigation pane and about opening database objects, see Book I, Chapter 2.)

Looking at a datasheet

A datasheet displays data in a table — it has rows (records), columns (fields), and cells that hold individual pieces of data.

If you're looking at a table in Design view, click the View button, the first button on the Home and Design tabs on the Ribbon, to see it in Datasheet view. The View button allows you to switch between Design and Datasheet views. There is a set of View buttons in the bottom-right corner of the Access window, just in case you find that more convenient. Let the cursor rest on a button to see the button name.

The important buttons in Datasheet view live on three tabs on the Ribbon: the Home tab, and the Table Tools tabs: Fields and Table:

✦ The Home tab contains tools to manage the data displayed in the datasheet — use them to cut and paste, change the appearance of data (font, color, justification, and so on), check spelling, filter the data displayed, and find the specific data you're looking for.

✦ The Table Tools tabs contains tools for manipulating the database through the datasheet. The Fields tab has buttons for adding and renaming fields, changing the data type and format of a field, and the Table tab has buttons for viewing relationships and object dependencies. If there is something you want to do to the datasheet that you might otherwise do in Design view, the tool for doing it is probably on one of the Table Tools tabs.

Navigating the data

Moving around in a datasheet is pretty straightforward. Use the vertical scrollbar (see Figure 1-7) or the Page Up and Page Down keys to move quickly up and down the datasheet (from record to record). Use the horizontal scrollbar to move from left to right, and press Enter or Tab to move the cursor from field to field.

If you know the number of the record you want (for example, the fourth record in the table), type the record number into the Record Number box at the bottom of the datasheet (refer to Figure 1-7) to jump straight to the fourth record. Record numbers are relative — records are not assigned a permanent record number. But when you want to go to the fourth record listed on the page, type **4** in the Record Number box and then press Enter. Sorting the datasheet so that records appear in a different order means that the record that is fourth changes.

You can move around in a datasheet three different ways:

✦ **Mouse:** Click a cell or use the scrollbars.

✦ **Keys:** Use Page Up and Page Down and the other keys in Table 1-1.

✦ **Buttons:** Click the record navigation buttons at the bottom-left corner of the datasheet (refer to Figure 1-7), or you can click the New Record button on the toolbar to jump to the end of your listings.

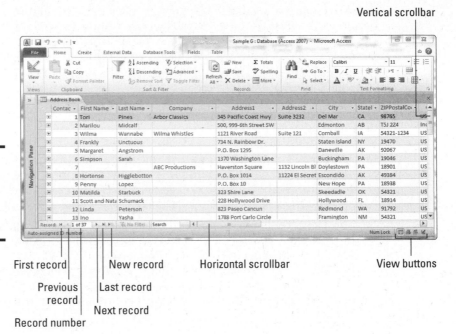

Vertical scrollbar

Figure 1-7:
Tools for
moving
around a
datasheet.

First record
Previous
record
Record number
New record
Last record
Next record
Horizontal scrollbar
View buttons

Table 1-1	Datasheet Navigation Keystrokes
Key	*Where It Takes You*
Page Down	Down a page
Page Up	Up a page
Tab	The next cell
Shift+Tab	The previous cell
Home	The first field of the current record
End	The last field of the current record
Ctrl+↑	First record of the current field
Ctrl+↓	Last record of the current field
Ctrl+Home	First record of the first field (top-left corner of the datasheet)
Alt+F5	Puts the cursor in the Record Number box — type a record number and press Enter to go to that record

Adding and Editing Records

To create a new record, start typing in a blank row. To move to a blank row, press Ctrl+ the plus sign (+) or click one of the two New Record buttons — you find one nestled with the record navigation buttons at the bottom-left corner of the datasheet and one in the Records group of the Home tab on the Ribbon. Type your data and press Enter or Tab to move to the next field. When you get to the last field of a record and press Tab or Enter, Access automatically moves you to the first field of a new record.

As you enter data, you may come across fields that are check boxes or drop-down lists. You can easily use the mouse to change a check-box setting or select from a list, but you can also use the keyboard — in these ways, for example:

> Press the spacebar to change a check box setting from selected to deselected
>
> or
>
> Press F4 to see a drop-down list, press the ↓ key to select your choice, and then press Enter.

If you change your mind about your entry, press the Esc key to cancel it. If you have already pressed Enter, you can undo the last entry by clicking the Undo button (a small button on the toolbar above the Ribbon) or by pressing Ctrl+Z. Another useful keystroke to know is Ctrl+' — it repeats the value in the record immediately above the cursor.

Table 1-2 lists all the keystrokes you ever want to use as you enter and edit data.

Book II
Chapter 1

**Creating and
Modifying Tables**

Table 1-2	Keystrokes in Datasheet View
Keystroke	*What It Does*
Ctrl+ plus sign (+)	Moves the cursor to a new record
Enter or Tab	Enters the data and moves to the next cell (to the right, or to the first field of the next record)
Esc	Cancels the current entry
Undo or Ctrl+Z	Undoes the last entry
F4	Displays a drop-down list (if present) in the current cell
Ctrl+C	Copies the selected data
Ctrl+X	Cuts the selected data
Ctrl+V	Pastes data from the Clipboard
Delete	Deletes the selected data
Ctrl+Enter	Enters a line break within an entry
Ctrl+−	Deletes the current record
Spacebar	Switches between the values in a check box or option button

Chapter 4 of this minibook covers cutting, copying, and pasting in detail.

Keystrokes that enter data

Access has a few extremely convenient keystrokes that enter data for you, and they're listed in Table 1-3. You can also use the Windows cut-and-paste shortcut keys. (Use Ctrl+C to copy the selected information to the Clipboard, Ctrl+X to cut the selected information and move it to the Clipboard, and Ctrl+V to paste the information from the Clipboard at the current cursor location.) (See Chapter 4 of this minibook for more information on using the Clipboard.)

Table 1-3	Entering Data with Keys
Keystroke	*Data It Enters*
Ctrl+ apostrophe (')	Repeats the entry for the field from the previous record
Ctrl+semicolon (;)	Inserts the current date
Ctrl+Shift+colon (:)	Inserts the current time
Ctrl+Alt+spacebar	Inserts the default value for a field

Editing the data you have

Editing is pretty straightforward. The only trick is to notice if you are in *overwrite mode* (where the entire contents is selected) or in *edit mode* (where a cursor is displayed). To get into edit mode, click with the mouse where you want to have a cursor, or press F2, and the cursor appears at the end of the data.

To edit data, simply place your cursor in the cell containing the data you want to change, use the Backspace or Delete keys to get rid of unwanted stuff, and then type in your replacement stuff.

Use these tricks when selecting text:

+ To replace the entire value, move the pointer to the left of the field until it changes into a big plus sign, and then click to select the whole cell.

+ Double-click to select a word or value.

+ Click at the beginning of what you want to select, press the Shift key, and then click at the end of what you want to select.

If you have lots of text in a cell and want to see it all at once, select the cell and press Shift+F2 to see the cell in a Zoom box (shown in Figure 1-8). You can make any changes, and then press Enter or click OK to return to the datasheet. Use the Font button in the Zoom box to change the font, and perhaps more importantly, the font size. Any changes you make are retained — the next time you display the Zoom box, you see the data with the new font settings. These font settings, however, do not affect how the data is displayed in the datasheet.

Figure 1-8:
Press
Shift+F2
to see the
Zoom dialog
box.

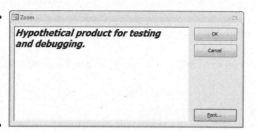

Table 1-4 lists keystrokes you can use while in editing mode.

Table 1-4	Keystrokes to Use While Editing
Keystroke	*What It Does*
Home	Moves to the beginning of the entry
End	Moves to the end of the entry
← or →	Moves one character to the left or right
Ctrl+← or Ctrl+→	Moves one word to the left or right
Shift+Home	Selects from the insertion point to the beginning of the entry
Shift+End	Selects from the insertion point to the end of the entry
Shift+←	Selects one character to the left
Shift+→	Selects one character to the right
Ctrl+Shift+←	Selects one word to the left
Ctrl+Shift+→	Selects one word to the right

Adding Calculated Fields to Tables

New in Access 2010 is the ability to add calculated fields to tables. In prior versions of Access, you were forced to create a query if you wanted to calculate a field. Now you can simply name the new field and add an expression to calculate a result.

To add a calculated field, display the table and click the Fields tab on the Ribbon. Click the More Fields button in the Add & Delete group and select the Calculated Field option at the bottom of the list. Then choose the type of data that you are calculating (choose from Text, Number, Currency, Yes/No and Date/Time).

Access displays the Expression builder, in which you can write your expression. For instance, in the Order Details table we can create a field to calculate Quantity times Unit Price.

The Expression Builder is covered in detain in Book III, Chapter 2.

Entering and Editing Hyperlinks

Working with fields with the Hyperlink data type can be a little tricky (but it doesn't have to be). Fields are defined as Hyperlink fields in one of two ways: If you create a table in Datasheet view and then type in hyperlink data, Access may define the field as a Hyperlink field (start Web links with **http://** to have Access recognize them as hyperlinks); alternatively, if you define the field in Design view with the Hyperlink data type, then the field you get is a Hyperlink field.

When you type something into a Hyperlink field in a datasheet, the text you type instantly turns to a hyperlink — blue, underlined text that you click to go to whatever site the link refers to. You can't click the hyperlinks to edit them — clicking a hyperlink always takes you to the linked file, which can prove tricky. The next section gives you the lowdown on editing hyperlinks.

A hyperlink entry can consist of four different parts:

+ The *underlined text* you see in a datasheet or form

+ The *address* that the hyperlink links to (the only required part)

+ The *sub-address* that the hyperlink links to

+ A *screen tip* — text that appears in a small box when the cursor hovers above the hyperlink

Because the full hyperlink entry consists of four parts, you may find the Insert Hyperlink and Edit Hyperlink dialog boxes an easier way to enter and edit hyperlinks (they are nearly identical).

The most common types of hyperlinks are links to Web pages or to files on your PC or LAN. You can enter those kinds of addresses by simply typing the address or path of the page or file you want to link to (or — an even easier method — paste it from your Web browser or Windows Explorer).

However, you may choose to enter or edit a hyperlink using the Insert Hyperlink or Edit Hyperlink dialog box (shown in Figure 1-9) in order to take advantage of the extra features found in this dialog box. To display the Insert Hyperlink or Edit Hyperlink dialog box (the two have the same options), do one of the following:

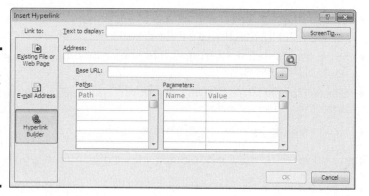

Figure 1-9: Press Ctrl+K to enter or edit a hyperlink in the Edit Hyperlink dialog box.

Book II
Chapter 1

Creating and Modifying Tables

✦ Right-click the Hyperlink field and choose Hyperlink➪Edit Hyperlink from the shortcut menu.

✦ Click in the field (if empty) or tab to the field and press Ctrl+K.

If a hyperlink is in the field, you can't click it without opening the hyperlink — instead, use the Tab key to move the cursor to that cell, hover the pointer over the upper-right corner of the cell until the pointer changes to a plus sign, and then click, or right-click, to see the shortcut menu.

Using the Edit Hyperlink dialog box, you can either change the text to display or change the address that the hyperlink points to (near the bottom of the dialog box).

You can also edit a hyperlink by tabbing to it and pressing F2, but what you get on-screen is the multipart hyperlink separated by # characters — a bit messy to deal with, to be honest — and you can't use the mouse to move the cursor. The dialog-box method is a more surefire method!

The Insert Hyperlink and Edit Hyperlink dialog boxes provides different options depending on the type of link you're creating. You can create a link to open any of the following:

✦ An existing file or Web page

✦ An e-mail address

Use the buttons on the left side of the dialog box — the ones under the Link To heading — to select the type of link before you enter any additional information about the hyperlink.

The following options always appear in the Insert Hyperlink dialog box, no matter what you end up linking to:

✦ **Text to Display:** The text that displays as a hyperlink. This can be but does not have to be the hyperlink address.

✦ **Some way to define the object that you're linking to:** The address or name of the object.

✦ **ScreenTip:** Click this button to enter text that appears when the cursor hovers over the hyperlink text.

✦ **Remove Link:** Deletes the hyperlink.

Other options in the dialog box change depending on the type of link you're creating.

If you link to an existing file or Web page, you see these browsing options for finding the file or Web page you want the hyperlink to point to:

✦ **Current Folder button:** Displays the current folder on your PC and allows you to enter a path or browse your PC or LAN.

✦ **Browsed Pages button:** Displays pages recently viewed with your browser.

✦ **Recent Files button:** Displays the contents of the Windows Recent Documents folder.

✦ **Browse the Web button:** Opens your browser.

✦ **Browse for File button:** Opens the Link to File dialog box, where you can browse to a file.

✦ **Address option:** Displays the URL of the file or page. Access fills this in automatically as you type, or you can type the address in manually. The drop-down list displays recently used files and URLs.

If you link to an e-mail address, specify the e-mail address and the subject of the e-mail message that is created when the user clicks the hyperlink.

You can remove a hyperlink by right-clicking and choosing Hyperlink➪ Remove Hyperlink from the shortcut menu. The text and the hyperlink are both removed.

Using the Hyperlink Builder

Using the Hyperlink Builder button in the Edit Hyperlink dialog box displays the settings shown in Figure 1-10. The Base, Path, and Parameters options allow you to define a relative hyperlink and also control how the link opens when the hyperlink is clicked.

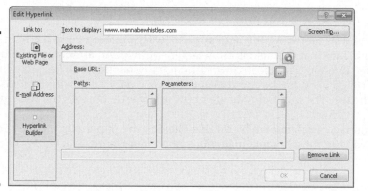

Figure 1-10: Advanced hyperlink settings are available when you choose Hyperlink Builder.

Using the Attachment Data Type

The Attachment data type is a relatively new data type, having been introduced with Access 2007. When a field is defined with the Attachment data type, you can store one or more files for each record in the field. For instance, you may store a picture of a person, or files containing correspondence about an order. Attachments can dramatically increase the size of the database, but since the attached file is stored as part of the database, you are not dependent on network drives being available as you would be if you included a hyperlink to the file. As a matter of fact, feel free to delete the original file after you attach it to the database so that you aren't storing it twice.

To use the Attachment data type, you must be using Access 2007 or 2010, and the database must be in the newer `.accdb` format. Individual files cannot be more that 256Mb, and all attached files cannot exceed 2GB (which is the size limit for an Access database). Once you've defined the data type of a field as Attachments, you cannot change it to any other data type.

Normally, a field holds only a single piece of information for each record. In an attachment field, however, you can store multiple attachments. (Access creates a hidden table to normalize your data.)

To create an Attachment field in your table, use one of these options:

✦ Insert a field based on the Attachment field template into your datasheet. (See the "Entering data and creating fields" section earlier in the chapter for details on using Field Templates.)

✦ Define the field data type as Attachment using the Data Type option in the Data Type and Formatting group of the Design tab on the Ribbon, or using the Data Type drop-down list in Table Design view.

In Datasheet view, the field appears with a paper clip in the field name box to indicate that the field is an Attachment field. An attachment field cannot be renamed in Datasheet view, although the name of the field can be changed in Design view. Each record also contains a paper clip with a number in parentheses. The number indicates how many attachments the record has.

Manage attachments by double-clicking the paper clip for the record to display the Attachments dialog box shown in Figure 1-11.

Figure 1-11: Manage attachment fields by using the Attachments dialog box.

Add an attachment by clicking the Add button in the Attachments dialog box. Then navigate to the file and click Open. Repeat to attach more files.

To view an attached file, open the Attachments dialog box and double-click the name of the attached file. It will open in its native application, if the application is available. (For instance, an .xls or .xlsx file opens in Excel.) You can make changes to the file and save it. To save files to the database, be sure to return to Access, click OK in the Attachments dialog box, and click Yes when asked if you want to save your updates to the database.

The Save and Save All buttons in the Attachments dialog box allow you to save attachments to your hard drive or another location so that they can be opened without opening the database.

Deleting records

It's inevitable that sometimes you want to delete data. Before you do that, however, here's a word to the wise. . . .

Deleted data cannot be recovered using the Undo button! And rather than deleting you may want to consider keeping old data in a new field. With that caveat firmly in mind, you can delete a record by following these steps:

1. **Select the record you want to delete by clicking the *record selector* to the left of it (or by putting the cursor anywhere in the record).**

   Remember that a record is a *whole row* of data.

2. **Press the Delete key or click the Delete Record button.**

   Access asks you if you are sure you want to delete the data.

3. **Click the Yes button to delete.**

   The row you select is deleted, and the data below the deleted row move up to fill the space.

Entering special characters

Occasionally, you may need to enter characters that aren't on your keyboard. Access doesn't provide an easy way to do that, but you can do it. If you know how to find your special character in another program, you may want to create it in that program first — and then cut and paste it into Access. Otherwise, follow these steps:

1. **Choose Start⇨All Programs⇨Accessories⇨System Tools⇨Character Map.**

   Alternatively, you can begin typing **Character Map** into the Start button search box, and click it when it appears in the list of possibilities.

   The Character Map appears. You see a grid of characters. The drop-down list at the top of the box lists the fonts. The box at the top is where the characters you select (in Step 3) appear.

2. **Browse to find the character you need.**

   Each font has a different set of characters, so you may need to browse through the fonts to find the character you want. Use the vertical scroll bar to see all the characters within a font.

3. **Double-click the character or select it and click the Select button to display it in the Characters to Copy box.**

   Repeat Step 3 until you have all the characters you need.

4. **Click the Copy button.**

   The contents of the Characters to Copy box copies to the Windows Clipboard.

5. **Return to Access and click the Paste button or press Ctrl+V.**

   If you don't see the character you copied, you may have to format it with the font you selected in Character Map.

Checking Your Spelling

 You can check your spelling in a datasheet or form by clicking the Spelling button in the Records group on the Home tab of the Ribbon. You can easily skip some fields that may have words that Access doesn't recognize, especially if they are full of codes or abbreviations. (See Table 1-5 for exactly how to do that.) You may also find that it makes sense to select a field or two to run a spell check on rather than check the whole datasheet. (You can select a field by clicking the field name; select several consecutive fields by selecting the first field and, while holding the Shift key, clicking the last field.)

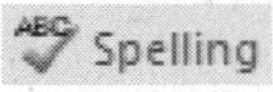

When you spell check, Access compares the words in the datasheet to the words in its own dictionary. Anything not found in the dictionary is considered misspelled. Of course, plenty of words that you use may not be in the Access dictionary, such as technical terms or unique product names. Don't assume that the Spelling dialog box is always right — your spelling may be just fine. Checking is a good habit.

A routine spell check goes like this:

1. **Click the Spelling button in the Records group on the Home tab of the Ribbon to open the Spelling dialog box (shown in Figure 1-12).**

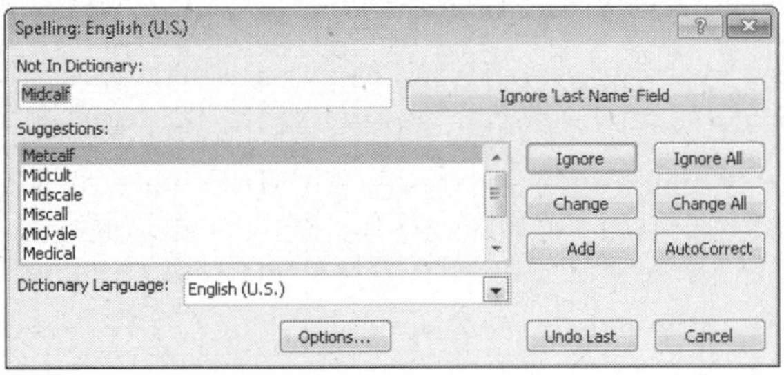

Figure 1-12: The Spelling dialog box helps you find and correct potentially embarrassing typos.

Access finds the first word that is not in its dictionary and displays it in the Not In Dictionary box. In the Suggestions box, Access lists possible correct spellings of the word.

2. **You decide how to deal with the word:**

   • Double-click a word from the Suggestions list to replace the misspelled word, or click the correctly spelled word once and then click the Change button.

   • Edit the word by clicking on it and making corrections and click Change or Change All.

- Click the Ignore button to ignore the word and find the next misspelled word.
- Click the Cancel button to exit the spell check and correct the word in the datasheet manually.

You may want to use the options in the Spelling dialog box listed in Table 1-5 as you check spelling.

Table 1-5	Buttons in the Spelling Dialog Box
Button	*What It Does*
Ignore "Field name" Field	Tells Access not to check spelling in the field where it has found the latest misspelled word.
Ignore	Skips the current word and finds the next misspelled word.
Ignore All	Skips all instances of the word.
Change	Changes the misspelled word to the word typed into the Not in Dictionary box or selected in the Suggestions box.
Change All	Changes all instances of the word typed into the Not in Dictionary box or to the word selected in the Suggestions box.
Add	Adds the word to the dictionary. Use this carefully as it's difficult to undo! Access uses main and custom dictionaries that are shared by all the Microsoft Office applications. You can use Microsoft Word to remove words from a custom dictionary — check Word's online help for details.
AutoCorrect	Adds the misspelled word *and* the correctly spelled word selected in the Suggestions box to the AutoCorrect list. AutoCorrect automatically replaces words when you enter them or press the spacebar.
Options	Displays the Access Options window; here you can tell Access whether to suggest words, whether to ignore certain words, and which dictionary to use. (You can specify a foreign language by using the Custom Dictionary option.)
Undo Last	Undoes the last change made by the Spelling dialog box.
Cancel	Closes the Spelling dialog box and retains any changes made.

You can change the way Access finds and corrects spelling errors by changing the settings in the Access Options⇨Proofing window. Click the Options button on the Spelling dialog box to see the Proofing options.

Using AutoCorrect for Faster Data Entry

AutoCorrect helps you in two distinct ways:

✦ It corrects misspelled words as you type.

✦ It replaces an abbreviation you type with more complete text, saving you time.

To change the way that AutoCorrect works, display the AutoCorrect dialog box, shown in Figure 1-13, by following these steps:

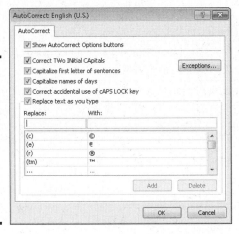

Figure 1-13:
The AutoCorrect dialog box helps you set up abbreviations for faster data entry.

1. **Click the File button (near the top-left corner of the Access window) to display the File menu.**

2. **Click Options at the bottom of the left panel of the File menu.**

The Access Options window appears.

3. **Click Proofing in the navigation portion of the Access Options window.**

Spelling and AutoCorrect options appear.

4. **Click the AutoCorrect Options button.**

The AutoCorrect dialog box appears. To turn on AutoCorrect, check to make sure that the Replace Text as You Type option is selected.

To add a common abbreviation to the AutoCorrect list, display the AutoCorrect dialog box and follow these steps:

1. **Enter the abbreviation in the Replace box.**

2. **Enter the full term in the With box.**

3. **Click the Add button.**

4. **Make sure that the Replace Text as You Type option is selected.**

You can delete an AutoCorrect entry by selecting it in the list and clicking the Delete button.

By default, all the options in the AutoCorrect dialog box are enabled (selected). You may want to disable (deselect) some or all of them if Access is making corrections that you don't want it to make.

The Exceptions button displays the AutoCorrect Exceptions dialog box (shown in Figure 1-14), where you can tell Access not to capitalize after a period that ends an abbreviation (on the First Letter tab) and when you want two or more initial caps to stay the way you enter them (on the INitial CAps tab).

Book II
Chapter 1

**Creating and
Modifying Tables**

Figure 1-14:
The
AutoCorrect
Exceptions
dialog box
makes
AutoCorrect
more
efficient.

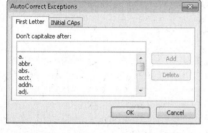

When AutoCorrect is turned on, it checks your typing after you press the space bar, Tab, or Enter after typing an error or abbreviation found in the AutoCorrect list. If you have chosen to display the AutoCorrect Options button (the first check box on the AutoCorrect dialog box), you see the button immediately after AutoCorrect makes a correction. Click the button to see the menu shown in Figure 1-15. The menu gives you the option of undoing the autocorrection in this one instance, in all instances, or displaying the AutoCorrect dialog box.

Figure 1-15:
The
AutoCorrect
Options
button lets
you control
each auto-
correction.

Formatting a Datasheet

Datasheets can't provide the good-looking output you get with a report or a form, but you can make some changes to make a datasheet more readable and attractive. The formatting options are available on the Home and Fields tabs on the Ribbon.

Format changes usually cannot be undone using the Undo button or Ctrl+Z. You can undo changes by closing the table without saving, but of course you lose all the formatting and design changes you made since the last time you saved the table.

Formatting a field

Field formats are covered in detail in the next chapter, but notice that you can format fields from the datasheet — you don't have to be in Design view. Select any value in a field to format the whole field, and then use the Data Type and Formatting options on the Fields tab of the Ribbon. If you can't make the change you want to make, check the field properties in Table Design view.

Be thoughtful about changing the data type — you may want to read the section in the next chapter about data types, as it is possible to lose data when changing the data type. (Access will warn you first, though.)

Use the buttons at the bottom of the Formatting section of the Fields tab to change the way the data is displayed. You can change numbers to display with a currency symbol, in percentages, or in the comma number format. You can also increase or decrease the number of decimal points displayed using the Increase Decimals and Decrease Decimals buttons.

Changing the font

In an Access datasheet, the font and font size of all the data are the same — you can't change the font for just some of the data (the exception: fields with the Memo data type support Rich Text).

Change the font by using the Text Formatting tools on the Home tab on the Ribbon. Changing the font, font style (bold, italic, or underlined), and font size will change that attribute for the whole datasheet. The Color option changes the color of the data in the datasheet.

Taking advantage of Rich Text

Access 2010 supports Rich Text. This means that you can store formatted text — words in a particular font, size, color, bold, underline, alignment, indents, numbering, bullets, and whether the field fills from left to right or from right to left. In other words, in the right kind of field you can have just about all the text-formatting capabilities you need to make pretty text. However, to take advantage of Rich Text, the field must be a Memo field. Otherwise, you will end up formatting the whole datasheet, rather than just part of one field.

To create a field to hold Rich Text, create a Memo field and set its `Text Format` property to `Rich Text`. You can change the data type in Design view, or select the field or any value in it, click the Data Type drop-down list in the Formatting section of the Fields tab of the Ribbon, and choose Memo. However, you have to flip to Design view to change the Text Format property to Rich Text. For more information on working in Design view to change the data type and field properties for a field, see Chapter 2 of this minibook.

Once you have created a Rich Text field, view your data in a datasheet or, even better, in a form, and format away. The formatting options on the Home tab on the Ribbon will all be available to you. To format text, first use the mouse to select the text you want to format, and then select the type of formatting you want to apply.

Rich Text can be displayed in a form or report in a Text Box control. The text box has a `Text Format` property that must be set to `Rich Text` for the text to appear on-screen with its formatting.

Changing gridlines and background color

Gridlines are the gray horizontal and vertical lines that separate cells in a datasheet. You can change the color of the gridlines or choose not to display them at all. You can even choose a special gridline effect other than plain lines.

Access 2010 has a secret button used to display the Datasheet Formatting dialog box (shown in Figure 1-16) — it's at the bottom-right corner of the Text Formatting group of the Home tab on the Ribbon. Click it to display the dialog box, make any changes (changes reflect in the Sample box), and click OK. You have the option of making the datasheet work from right to left instead of the usual left-to-right — not an option often used, but if you need it, you can find it here.

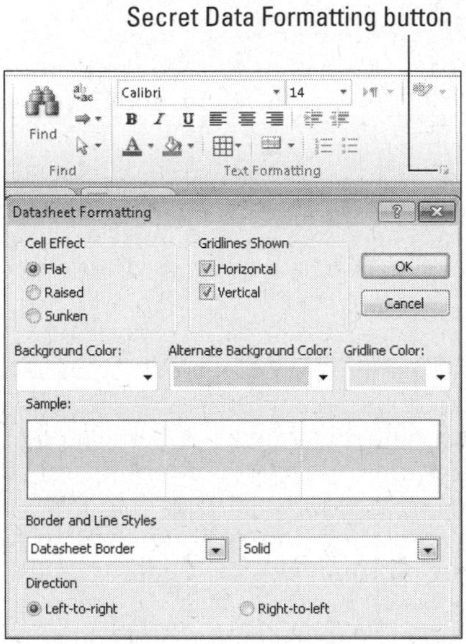

Secret Data Formatting button

Figure 1-16:
Use the
secret
button to
display the
Datasheet
Formatting
dialog box.

Rearranging columns in a datasheet

You can rearrange the order of fields in the datasheet in either Datasheet or Design view. Follow these steps to move columns in Datasheet view:

1. **Select the column you want to move by clicking the field name.**

You may want to select a block of columns by clicking and holding and moving to the last column you want to select, or by selecting the first column and then Shift+clicking the last field name in the block.

2. **Release the mouse button, and then click on any selected field name and drag the column(s) to its new position.**

As you move the mouse, a dark vertical line shows where the columns will be when you release the mouse button.

If you can't move a column, it's probably frozen. Right-click a field name and choose Unfreeze All Columns to unfreeze it. For more on freezing columns, see the aptly named section "Freezing columns" later in this chapter.

Changing column width

When you initially create a datasheet, all the columns have the same width. But column widths are easy to change, and when you save the table, the new column widths are saved too.

To change the width of a column, move the pointer to the bar separating the field names at the top of the column. The mouse pointer changes into a double-headed arrow (shown in the margin). Drag the bar to the appropriate width, or you can double-click to size the column to the widest data in the column.

You can change the width of several adjacent columns at the same time. Start by selecting them: Click the field name of the first column and then drag to the last field name, or click the first field name and then Shift+click the last. Then change the width of one column. All the selected columns have the same (new) width.

If you prefer, use the Column Width dialog box to change column width — right-click a field name and choose the Column Width option from the shortcut menu. Enter the width in number of characters. You can use the Standard Width check box to reset the column width to the standard, or use the Best Fit button to fit the column width to its contents. Click OK to close the dialog box.

Changing row height

You change the row height in one of two ways — with the mouse or with the Row Height dialog box. You have to change the height of only one row — all the rest change to match. All the rows change to the same height; you can't just change one.

 Changing row height with the mouse is very similar to changing column width: Move the mouse pointer to the record selectors until the pointer turns into a double-headed arrow (shown in the margin). Then drag up (to make the row shorter) or down (to make the row taller).

Alternatively, right-click a record selector and select the Row Height option from the shortcut menu to display the Row Height dialog box. Enter the row height in points. (There are 72 points in an inch.) The Standard Height check box formats the row height at the standard height for the font size that you have chosen (the point size of the font, plus a cushion for the top and the bottom of the row).

Inserting and deleting columns

Remember, columns are fields, so when you insert a column, you are adding a new field; and when you delete a column, you delete the field and all its data. You can add and remove fields in Design view — that's covered in Chapter 2 of this minibook.

To insert a generic field in Datasheet view, follow these steps:

1. **Right-click the field name of the column where you want the new, blank column.**

2. **Choose the Insert Column option from the shortcut menu.**

   A column with the name Field 1 (or some other number) is added. The selected columns and all the columns to the right move to make room.

3. **Rename the field name by right-clicking it and choosing the Rename Column option from the shortcut menu.**

4. **Type the new name and press Enter.**

   The new field also appears in Design view.

To delete a field and all its data (but think really hard about it first), right-click the field name and choose the Delete Column option from the shortcut menu. Click the Yes button to permanently delete the field and its data.

Buttons to insert fields with a defined data type, delete, and rename a field are also available in the Add & Delete group of the Fields tab on the Ribbon.

Hiding columns

If you want to hide a column in a datasheet (perhaps the data is sensitive), select the column or columns, right-click the selected field name(s), and choose Hide Columns. To display hidden columns, right-click any field name and choose Unhide Columns. A dialog box appears, where you can choose which columns to redisplay.

Freezing columns

When you're working with a wide datasheet, you may want to freeze one or more columns so they don't scroll off the left side of your screen. To freeze one column, first select it, and then right-click the field name and choose Freeze Columns from the shortcut menu. The selected column pops to the left side of the datasheet, and stays there. To freeze more than one column, select them, right-click a field name, and then choose Freeze Columns. To unfreeze columns, right-click the field name and choose the Unfreeze All Columns option from the shortcut menu.

Changing default formatting for new tables

Access allows you to change default formatting for tables using the Design tab of the Access Options window. Any changes you make affect only new datasheets, and not tables and queries already created.

Display the Options dialog box by clicking the File (near the top-left corner of the Access window) to display the File menu. Click Options in the left panel to display the Access Options window. Click Datasheet in the navigation portion of the Access Options window to display default formatting options for datasheets in the current database.

Use the options to change colors, font, gridline, and cell-effect options.

Most of the options in this dialog box (text colors, text font, gridlines, and cell effects) have already been discussed in this chapter.

Taking Advantage of Subdatasheets

Access has a nifty feature that allows you to display data from related tables in your datasheet. This feature makes related data easy to view and enter data from different tables — without using a form.

Access automatically creates subdatasheets in a datasheet if you create a one-to-one relationship with another table, or if the datasheet is on the one side of a one-to-many relationship with another table. (You need to define a relationship in the Relationship window, or use the Lookup Wizard that creates a relationship as the wizard creates a drop-down list.) Queries may have subdatasheets also. (See Book I, Chapter 3 and Chapter 6 of this mini-book for more information on relationships.)

When a subdatasheet is available, you see a + (plus) sign in the first column of the table. Click the + sign to see the subdatasheet. When the subdatasheet displays, the + sign changes to a – (minus) sign. Click the – sign to remove the subdatasheet. By default, subdatasheets display for one record in the parent table. To display all data from the related table, click the More button in the Records group of the Home tab on the Ribbon, choose Subdatasheets⇨Expand All. To hide all subdatasheets, click the More button and choose Subdatasheets⇨Collapse All.

Figure 1-17 shows a datasheet with two levels of subdatasheets. The main datasheet shows names and addresses of customers. The first-level subdatasheet lists order information; the second-level subdatasheet lists order details (items ordered).

When a subdatasheet is displayed, you can use it as you would use a table — to view, format, enter, edit, or delete data.

Access determines which table to display as a subdatasheet based on the relationships you define in the database. However, you can select a table or query to be used as a subdatasheet on the Table Property Sheet. (Display the table in Design view and click the Property Sheet button on the Design tab.)

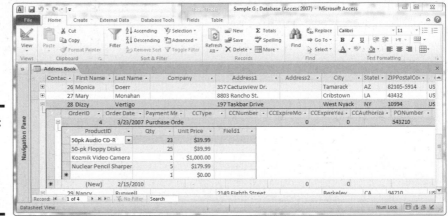

Figure 1-17:
This table displays two levels of subdatasheets.

You can use a query as a subdatasheet — doing so allows you to filter the data displayed in the subdatasheet using criteria defined in the query.

When you select a subdatasheet manually, you need to know the name of the table or query you use as the subdatasheet, as well as the names of the two related fields — one in the parent table and the other in the subdatasheet table. The two fields need to meet the requirements of related fields. (See Chapter 6 of this minibook.) Follow these steps to select a table or query to be used as a subdatasheet:

1. **Click the More button in the Records group of the Home tab on the Ribbon.**

2. **Choose Subdatasheets⇨Subdatasheets from the menu.**

The Insert Subdatasheet dialog box (shown in Figure 1-18) appears.

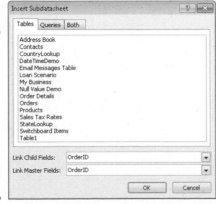

Figure 1-18:
Use the Insert Subdatasheet dialog box when you want to specify the subdatasheet.

3. **Select the table or query you want to use as a subdatasheet.**

   To view just your tables, click the Tables tab; to view just your queries, click the Queries tab; to view both tables and queries, click the Both tab.

4. **Use the Link Child Fields drop-down menu to select the field from the subdatasheet table that you want to use to link the two tables.**

5. **Use the Link Master Fields drop-down menu to choose the field from the parent table that you want to use to link the two tables.**

6. **Click OK.**

Adding a Totals Row to the Datasheet

Access 2010 has a handy feature that allows you to add a totals row to a datasheet. A *totals row* can be used to count the number of items in a column, calculate a sum or average, or find the minimum or maximum value. These are all examples of aggregate functions — you can use them in queries, but now you can also use them in a totals row of a datasheet.

Follow these steps to create a totals row:

1. **Display the datasheet and click the Totals button in the Records group of the Home tab on the Ribbon.**

   Access creates a row titled Total at the bottom of the datasheet.

2. **Click one of the blank cells in the Total row to display an arrow; click the arrow to display a drop-down list of aggregation options.**

3. **Choose the kind of total you want to display.**

   The choices are None, Sum, Average, Count, Maximum, Minimum, Standard Deviation, or Variance. For Text and Memo fields, you can choose Count to count the number of entries in the field. For Date fields, the choices are limited to Average, Count, Maximum, and Minimum.

   Access displays the aggregate as shown in Figure 1-19. To change the kind of aggregation, simply select the cell and choose another option from the drop-down list.

To clear the totals row, simply click the Totals button again. If you change your mind and want your aggregates back, Access will remember the type of aggregation you chose. You may also want to add a Totals row to queries displayed in Datasheet view. See the next minibook for more on queries.

The totals will adjust when a filter is applied to the datasheet. See the next chapter for more on filters. Totals rows do not appear in subdatasheets.

Totals

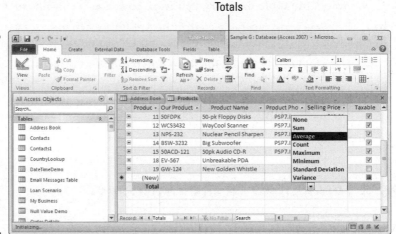

Figure 1-19:
Click the
Totals
button on
the Home
tab of the
Ribbon,
then choose
the type of
aggregation
you want for
the field.

Chapter 2: Refining Your Table in Design View

In This Chapter

✔ **Creating and fine-tuning fields using Design view**

✔ **Choosing the correct field type**

✔ **Formatting a field with field properties**

✔ **Defining a primary key**

The previous chapter covered how to create tables using Datasheet view. This chapter covers creating and refining tables using table Design view.

In Design view, you can access many settings for all the fields just a little more easily than in Datasheet view. If you are creating a table and won't immediately put data into it, then Design view is a good place to do that. And if you want to make changes to how your fields work and what data they will accept, Design view is a good place to work.

Getting to know how to work in Design view may be a little intimidating to begin with, but if you become comfortable in Design view you can make your database work better. In Design view you can work with field definitions without having to look at data. You can even define fields when for data to be input later. Datasheets are similar to a spreadsheet; design view takes you into the database realm and allows you to take control of your data by using, for instance, the data integrity tools in Chapter 5 of this minibook.

Creating Tables Using Design View

Design view is a good place to create a table if you know a lot about the type of data you put in the table — and you want the fields you create to be designed for the data you have to put into them. If you're creating the table but don't yet have any data, Design view is the perfect place to start. Of course, you can always switch to Datasheet view by clicking the View button on the Home or Design tab of the Ribbon to enter data at any time.

Follow these steps to create a table in Design view:

1. **Click the Table Design button in the Tables group on the Create tab of the Ribbon.**

   Access opens a blank table in Design view. Notice the flashing cursor in the first row of the Field Name column.

2. **Type the name of the first field. Press Tab to move to the Data Type column.**

   The field properties for the field fill in automatically (down at the bottom of the screen in Design view), and the data type is set to the Text option.

3. **Select a data type from the Data Type drop-down list.**

   Common choices are Text, Memo, Number, Date/Time, and Currency. Data types are covered in detail later in this chapter.

4. **Type a description of the field in the Description column. (This is optional, but we recommend it.)**

   The description can be especially useful if many people use the database, or if you may not use the database for a while. Use the Description column to explain exactly how you intend the field to be used.

5. **Define additional fields in the table by repeating Steps 2 through 4. You can press Tab to move to the next row, where you enter the next field name. Figure 2-1 shows six fields defined.**

6. **Click the Save button or press Ctrl+S to save the table. Type a descriptive name in the Name field and press Enter.**

7. **When Access asks whether you want to define a primary key, choose Yes or No.**

   Don't worry; whatever you choose, you can change later. If you feel the need to make an informed decision now, skip ahead to the section, "Defining the Primary Key," later in this chapter. If you choose to create a primary key now, Access creates a new, numbered field that gives each record a unique number. (The first field shown in Figure 2-1 is an AutoNumber field, defined as the primary key.) If you want to skip this step, be sure you define a primary key manually when you know which field(s) you want to use to uniquely identify each record.

After you have defined the fields in Design view, you have the option of displaying the table in Datasheet view and entering data. Use the Datasheet view button on the status bar in the lower-right corner of the Access window. However, you also have the option of entering data through a form.

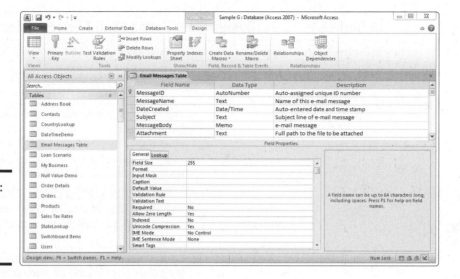

Figure 2-1:
Defining
fields in
Design
view.

Refining Your Table Using Design View

Design view is the place to go when you want to be really specific about
what you want a field to hold. Design view also provides some tools you
use to make sure that the data entered in a field is what you want it to be —
that's covered in more detail in Chapter 5 of this minibook.

The top part of the Design View window lists the fields in the table and their
data types. Descriptions also appear in that part of the window if they've
been added.

The bottom part of the Design View window displays *field properties* — configuration information about the current field. If you're a novice Access user,
don't worry about field properties. You don't have to do anything with them
at all; if you do need them at some point, however, we tell you exactly how
to use them.

Many (but not all!) tasks you do with Design view can also be done in
Datasheet view. Datasheet view is covered in more detail in Chapter 1 of
this minibook. The Data Type and Formatting groups of the Fields tab of the
Ribbon (which you can display when a Datasheet is active) contain options
for changing the data type, format, and some field properties (Unique and Is
Required) for a selected field.

Design view has its own Ribbon of tools — to display them, click the Design
tab that appears at the end of the Ribbon when Design view is displayed.

Table 2-1 lists Design view Ribbon tools.

Table 2-1   Design View Buttons and Their Functions

Button	*Name*	*What It Does*
Primary Key	Primary Key	Makes the selected field the primary key field for the table.
Builder	Builder	This button is grayed out in many contexts (when creating an expression is not an option). Displays the Expression Builder to help you build a field or expression. Available when the cursor is in Field Name, Default Value, Validation Rule, or Smart Tags.
Test Validation Rules	Test Validation Rules	Tests Validation Rules. See Chapter 5 of this minibook for more information.
Insert Rows	Insert Rows	Adds a row (field) to the table design where the cursor is, or inserts as many rows as are selected.
Delete Rows	Delete Rows	Deletes the current row, or selected rows of the table design view.
Modify Lookup	Modify Lookup	Creates a *lookup field* — that is, a field that lists values stored in another field. See Chapter 5 of this minibook for more information.
Property Sheet	Property Sheet	Displays the properties sheet for the selected field. A *properties sheet* allows you to set even more controls for the field. (Many of the field properties are covered in Chapter 5 of this minibook.)
Indexes	Indexes	Displays the Indexes window with the indexed fields in the table and their index properties.
Create Table Events	Create Table Events	Creates a macro.
Manage Table Events	Manage Table Events	Displays the Table Logic manager, where the macros attached to the Table are listed.
Relationships	Relationships	Displays the Relationship window, where the relationships in the database are displayed (and can be created and edited).
Object Dependencies	Object Dependencies	Displays the Object Dependencies window, where you can see which database objects depend upon the table you're viewing, and which objects the table depends upon.

Using the Caption property

Access gives you the option of giving a field a *caption.* A caption is text that is used on the datasheet, forms, and reports instead of the field name. The field name must still be used in expressions and in code.

To give a field a caption, use the `Caption` field property in Table Design view.

The Caption property can also be accessed using the Name & Caption button on the Fields tab in Datasheet view.

Adding a field

If you want to add a field in the middle of a table in Design view, place the cursor where you want the new field to appear (or select the row) and then click the Insert Rows button in the Tools group of the Design tab of the Ribbon. Rows at and below the cursor are pushed down to make room for the new field. Fill in the Field Name and Data type for the new field, and you've created a new field.

Copying a field

You can copy a field definition easily — be aware that by using this method you copy only the definition, not the data. You can even copy a field definition from one table to another — which is an easy way to be sure that related fields have the same definition. Remember, however, that usually only one field needs the primary key designation; be sure to remove the primary key designation from the other field.

To copy a field in Table Design view, follow these steps:

1. **Click the record selector (the gray box to the left of the field name) to select the field.**

2. **Press Ctrl+C or click the Copy button in the Clipboard group of the Home tab on the Ribbon.**

3. **Move the cursor to an empty row in the table into which you want to copy the field.**

4. **Press Ctrl+V or click the Paste button in the Clipboard group of the Home tab on the Ribbon.**

5. **Type a new name in the Field Name field, if necessary, and press Enter.**

   The field title is highlighted, so when you type a new name, you replace the old name.

Moving a field

To move a field, select the row by clicking the record selector — you can select multiple rows by dragging the row selectors. Then drag the record selector up or down to where you want to drop it. As you move the mouse, a dark horizontal line shows where the row moves when you release the mouse button.

Moving a field in Design view also changes its position in the table datasheet.

Deleting a field

You can delete a field in Design view. Deleting a field deletes the field definition and all the data stored in the field.

Follow these steps to delete a field:

1. **Select the field by clicking the record selector (the gray box to the left of the field name).**

2. **Press the Delete key or click the Delete Rows button in the Tools group of the Design tab on the Ribbon.**

   If the field has no data, Access deletes it. If the field has data, you see a dialog box that asks you to confirm that you do, indeed, want to permanently delete the field and its data.

Choosing a data type

Access provides eleven data types for you to choose from. Choose the data type that best describes the data you want to store in the field and that works with the type of analysis you need to use the field for. For instance, storing phone numbers in a text field works fine because you probably never need to add or subtract numbers. Prices, however, should be stored in a Number or Currency field so you can add, subtract, or even multiply them by the number of units ordered and create an invoice.

A few fields need data types that may not be obvious, mainly telephone numbers and ZIP codes and other such fields. Generally, even though these fields store numbers, you want to set these fields to Text data type. Doing so allows you to store leading zeros (so that 02138 doesn't appear as 2138) and add characters such as dashes and parentheses. The Input Mask Wizard (covered in Chapter 5 of this minibook) helps you define fields for phone numbers, ZIP codes, Social Security numbers, and dates. The Input Mask Wizard is also useful for any codes you may use in your database, or other types of fields that may sometimes appear with spaces or dashes (such as credit card numbers) or other punctuation, so that the data is always entered consistently, and you can find it when you need it.

Table 2-2 lists the data types and describes when to choose each.

Table 2-2	Data Types	
Data Type	*What It Holds*	*When to Use It*
Text	Numbers, letters, punctuation, spaces, and special characters (up to 255 characters).	All text fields except really long ones. Also good for ZIP codes and phone numbers. You can't do number-type calculations with a Text field.
Memo	Text, and lots of it — up to 65,536 characters.	When you have lots of text, such as comments. Can't be indexed, and can't be a key field.
Number	Numbers. When you select the Number type, you may want to change the Field Size property to the option that best fits the field. (Field sizes are explained in Table 2-3.)	For numbers that you may want to add, multiply, and do other calculations with. You can also use decimal points and + and – (to designate positive and negative numbers) in a Number field.
Date/Time	Dates and times.	For dates and times. You can do calculations such as finding the number of days between two dates, or adding hours to a time to calculate a new time.
Currency	Numbers with a currency sign in front of them.	When you store monetary values, such as prices. Like number fields, currency fields can do calculations. Calculations with Currency fields are faster than those with Single or Double Numbers field sizes (the kinds of numbers that can include fractions for cents). Single and Double field sizes for number fields are explained in Table 2-3.
AutoNumber	A unique number generated by Access for each record.	When you want each record to have a unique value that you don't have to type in. The value starts at one and is incremented for each record.

(continued)

Table 2-2 *(continued)*

Data Type	What It Holds	When to Use It
Yes/No	Binary data such as Yes/No, Male/Female, True/False, and so on.	When you have a field that can have only one of two entries. Appears as a check box on the datasheet; can appear as a check box, option button, or toggle button on forms; can be either on or off. Use the Format field property to define the values — for instance, true/false, male/female, or available/discontinued.
OLE Object	An electronic object such as a picture, a sound, or another object created with OLE-compatible software.	When you want to store something in Access or link to something created and opened with another application. The new Attachment data type is usually preferred over the OLE Object data type.
Hyperlink	URLs, e-mail addresses, and other types of links.	When you want to link to a Web page, e-mail address, or file. See more about hyperlinks in Chapter 2 of this minibook.
Attachment	Use to store one or more attachments (files).	Ultimately requires less database space than OLE. Also, more than one attachment can be entered in a record.
Lookup	Not really a data type — this option runs the Lookup Wizard.	When you want to select a table or a Wizard list to use as a drop-down list for the field.

Some database designers avoid the Memo field altogether because they find that databases with Memo fields are more likely to become corrupted (that is, become unreadable by Access). The same is true of OLE Object fields, which are used for storing pictures, spreadsheets, documents, and other large objects. The new Attachment data type is a good alternative to the OLE Object type. Sections on using Hyperlink and Attachment fields appear in the previous chapter.

AutoNumber fields have one and only one purpose: to act as the primary key field for tables that don't have an existing field that uniquely identifies each record. Don't use AutoNumber fields for anything else. In fact, most Access database designers use AutoNumber fields to create primary key fields — and then make sure those key fields never appear on forms and reports.

Here's why the key fields are often hidden: You have no control over the numbers that Access issues when numbering your records. If you start adding a record and then cancel it, Access may decide that particular number is already used — and skip it the next time you add a record. You can't change the AutoNumber field's value. If you need a series of numbers to not end up with holes (skipped numbers), then don't use an AutoNumber field.

Book II
Chapter 2

Refining Your Table in Design View

If you use an AutoNumber field to keep track of invoices, and it issues your invoice numbers, you end up with skipped invoice numbers. If this isn't a problem for you, fine — make the Invoice Number category an AutoNumber field and print it on your invoices. But if missing invoice numbers is a problem, use a regular Number field for your invoice numbers and don't use the unique AutoNumber field on forms and reports. You may want to use the Index field property setting set to Yes (No Duplicates) if you want to make sure that each value in the field is unique. Find out more about the Index field property later in this chapter.

If you want to start numbering invoices at 1001 rather than 1, create an Invoice Number field. If you want to get fancy, create a macro that automatically fills in the next invoice number in the sequence. But if an incorrect check number is entered by mistake, you can go back and make changes without changing the value of the primary key field.

Formatting Fields with Field Properties

Field properties are generally used for formatting fields. They can also be used to validate data, which we cover in Chapter 5 of this minibook.

Field properties are defined for each field (not surprisingly!). You can see the field properties for only one field at a time. To see the field properties for a field, select the field in the top half of the Design View window. You can select the field by clicking the field selector (the gray box to the left of the row) or by clicking anywhere in the row. The selected field has a triangle arrow to its left. Select a new field to see a whole different set of field properties. The field properties you see depend on the data type of the field — for instance, you won't see the Decimal Places property for a Text field.

Click a field property to see a short description to the right — that tells you if it's a formatting property and/or a data-validation property. (Some properties can be used in both ways.)

How do you use field properties to format a field? For number fields, you can define the number of decimal places you want to display. For text fields, you can tell Access to change the text to all capital letters or all lowercase. You can even use the Format property to add extra characters to a Text or Memo field. (Although for most applications, the Input Mask Wizard is easier to use than the Format property. — see more about input masks in Chapter 5 of this minibook.)

Formatting Number and Currency fields

You can use the Field Size and Format properties together to define how fields display. The common formats for Number and Currency fields are built right into Access — you can choose from those listed in Table 2-3.

Table 2-3	Number Formats
Number Format	*How It Works*
General Number	Displays numbers without commas — and with as many decimal places as the user enters.
Currency	Displays numbers with the local currency symbol (determined by the Regional settings found in the Windows Control Panel), commas as thousands separators, and two decimal places.
Euro	Displays numbers with the euro symbol, commas as thousands separators, and two decimal places.
Fixed	Displays numbers with the number of decimal places specified in the Decimal Places property (immediately after the Format property; the default is 2).
Standard	Displays numbers with commas as thousands separators and the number of decimal places specified in the Decimal Places property.
Percent	Displays numbers as percentages — that is, multiplied by 100 and followed by a percent sign.
Scientific	Displays numbers in scientific notation.

The Field Size property can affect the format.

You can define your own number format using the following symbols:

Symbol	What It Does
#	Displays a value if one is entered for that place.
0	Displays a 0 if no value appears in that place.
.	Displays a decimal point.
,	Displays a comma.
$ (or other currency symbol)	Displays the currency symbol.
%	Displays the number in percent format.
E+00	Displays the number in scientific notation.

Book II
Chapter 2

Refining Your Table
in Design View

To create a number format with comma separators and three decimal places, type the following: **###,##0.000**.

You can define a numeric format so that the format depends on the value. You can define formats for positive and negative numbers, for zero, and for null values (when no value is entered). To use this feature, enter a four-part format into the `Format` property, with the parts separated by commas. The first part is for positive numbers, the second for negatives, the third if the value is 0, and the fourth if the value is null (for example, `#,##0; (#,##0); "-"; or "none"`). Using this type of format, you can display positive and negative numbers in different colors, if you like, such as positive in green and negative in red. Put the desired color in square brackets in the correct section of the expression. The available colors are black, blue, green, cyan, red, magenta, yellow, and white. In Forms, conditional formatting is available, and you can specify an expression to determine format — for instance, displaying unshipped status in red.

To store percentages, such as a discount, create a Number field with a Single field size (to keep the size of the field small — see the next section) and enter numbers between 0 and 1 (inclusive) for percentages between 0 and 100. When you create the table, you can format the Number field as a percent. When you enter a value, you type **33%**, and Access converts the value to 0.33.

Setting the field size

Using the `Field Size` property correctly can keep your database efficient; doing so keeps the field size as small as is practical — making for a smaller, more compact database. For Text fields, the `Field Size` property can also help you screen out incorrect data — if you know that you need only (say) four characters in a certain field, then set the field size to 4. Anything longer produces an error message. (For more about screening out incorrect data, see Chapter 5 of this minibook.)

Using the `Field Size` property for any of your Number fields is a little more complicated, but again, using the shortest practical field size makes your database more efficient. Table 2-4 shows your choices for the field size of a Number field. (These are listed from the smallest amount of space required to store each value to the largest.)

Table 2-4	Field Sizes for Number Fields	
Setting	*What It Can Hold*	*When to Use It*
Byte	Integers from 0 to 255.	Use if values are small integers less than 256.
Integer	Integers from −32,768 to 32,767.	Use for most fields needing integers, unless you need to store values greater than 32,768.
Long Integer	Integers from −2,147,483,648 to 2,147,483,647.	Use when the Integer setting isn't enough.
Single	Numbers from about −3.4E38 to −1.4E−45 for negative numbers and from about 1.4E−45 to 3.4E38 for positive values. Decimal precision to 7 places.	Use for numbers with decimal values. Holds big numbers and lots of decimal places — Double holds even more. Generally speaking, Single is sufficient, but you can change the setting to Double without losing data.
Double	Numbers from about −1.7E308 to −4.9E324 for negative numbers and from about 4.9E−324 to 1.8E308 for positive values. Decimal precision to 15 places.	Any values that Single won't hold.
Decimal	Numbers from -10^28−1 through 10^28−1 in .mdb (Access database) files. Numbers from -10^38−1 through 10^38−1 in .adp (Access project) files. Decimal precision to 28 places.	Use for values with lots and lots of decimal places.
Replication ID	Globally unique identifier (GUID) used for replication.	Use for an AutoNumber field that is the primary key when you replicate the database and add more than 100 records between replications. (Not a common choice!)

The default field size for Text fields is 255; for Number fields, it's Long Integer. You can change the default size on the Access Options dialog box by clicking the File button in the top-left corner of the Access window and then clicking the Access Options button at the bottom of the menu. In the resulting Access Options window, click Object Designers in the Navigation pane. The default field sizes are the first three settings on the dialog box.

You can change a field size after you enter data, but if you shrink the size, any Text data longer than the new setting is truncated and any Number data that doesn't meet the requirements is rounded (if you choose an Integer setting) or converted to a Null setting if the value is too large or small for the new setting.

Formatting Date/Time fields

Access provides the most common formats for dates and times — click the down arrow in the `Format` field property to see the formats. You can also create your own Date/Time format (for online help, press F1 or use the Help button on the toolbar) that provides all the codes you need. Combine them in the same way you combine the text or number codes to define a format.

Formatting Text fields

Use the `Field Size` and `Format` properties together to format Text fields. The `Field Size` property limits each entry to the number of characters you specify. You can change the field size from a smaller size to a larger size with no problems. If you change a larger size (say, 20) to a smaller size (say, 10), you lose characters past the 10th character.

You enter symbols into the Format property in a kind of code:

For This Format	Type This Format Property
Display text all-uppercase	> (greater-than sign)
Display text all-lowercase	< (less-than sign)
Display text left-aligned	!
Specify a color	Enter one of the following colors between [ ] square brackets: **black**, **blue**, **green**, **cyan**, **magenta**, **yellow**, **white**.
Specify a certain number of characters	Enter @ for each required character. (See also Chapter 5 of this minibook.)
Specify that no character is required	**&**
Display predefined text	**/text** (The `Default Value` property may also be useful.) For instance, enter **/NA** to display the text NA. Appears in all records until another value is entered.

**Book II
Chapter 2**

Refining Your Table
in Design View

Defining the Primary Key

The *primary key* is a field in each table that uniquely identifies each record in the field. (Primary keys are described in Book I, Chapter 3, including how to choose which field or fields to use for your primary key.) The simplest primary key field is a counter with a value of one for the first record, two for the second record, and so on. You can create a counter field by using an AutoNumber field. If you allow Access to create a primary key for you, it creates an AutoNumber field.

Another example of a primary key is a Social Security number in a table where each record contains information about a single person and each person is listed only once in the table. Sometimes each record may be uniquely identified by the combination of two fields, such as an item number and the manufacturer. Note that first names and last names may not always be unique!

After you define a field as a primary key, Access prevents you from entering a new record with the same primary key value. When in doubt, an AutoNumber field is a good bet for a primary key, but the AutoNumber field doesn't allow Access to help you avoid repeating data as another field does.

Follow these steps to create a primary key:

1. **Display the table in Design view.**

2. **Click in the row containing the primary key field, or select the row by clicking the record selector.**

   To select multiple rows to create a multiple field primary key, click the first record selector, and then Ctrl+click the record selectors you want for any additional fields.

3. **Click the Primary Key button on the Design tab of the Ribbon or right-click the row selector and select Primary Key.**

   Access displays the key symbol in the record selector for the field.

   If you already have data in the field and two records have the same value, you cannot make the field the primary key for the table.

   The primary key field has to uniquely identify each record.

Indexing Fields

When you index a field, Access sorts and finds records faster using the Index field. An index can be based on a single field or on multiple fields. The primary key field in a table is indexed automatically, and you can choose other fields to index as well.

Although indexing speeds up many operations, it slows down some action queries because Access may need to update the indexes as the action is performed.

To index a field, choose one of the Yes values for the field's Indexed property. Three values for the Indexed property are available:

✦ **No:** Doesn't index the field.

✦ **Yes (Duplicates OK):** Indexes the field and allows you to input the same value for multiple records.

✦ **Yes (No Duplicates):** Indexes the field and doesn't allow you to input the same value for more than one record. The primary key automatically gets this value.

Indexes

You can see details on the indexed fields by clicking the Indexes button to see the Indexes window, shown in Figure 2-2.

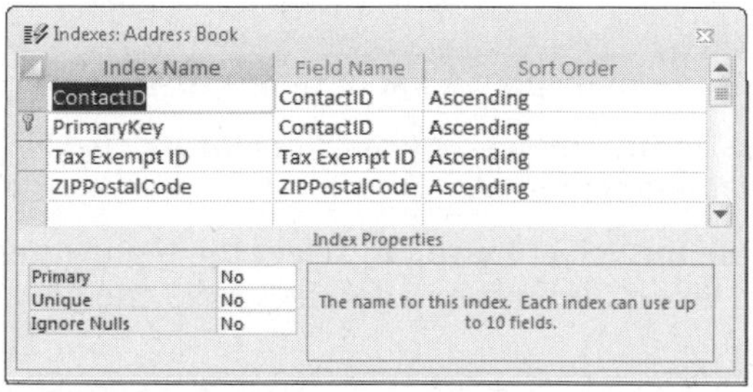

Index Name	Field Name	Sort Order
ContactID	ContactID	Ascending
PrimaryKey	ContactID	Ascending
Tax Exempt ID	Tax Exempt ID	Ascending
ZIPPostalCode	ZIPPostalCode	Ascending

Index Properties

Primary	No	
Unique	No	The name for this index. Each index can use up
Ignore Nulls	No	to 10 fields.

Figure 2-2:
The Indexes window.

The Indexes window displays all the fields in the table that are indexes, their default sort order (which you can change), and their index properties. The index properties are as follows:

✦ **Primary:** Yes when the field is the primary key for the table, No otherwise.

✦ **Unique:** Yes when the value of the field for each must be unique, No otherwise.

✦ **Ignore Nulls:** Yes when *nulls* (blanks) are excluded from the index, No when nulls are included in the index.

Printing Table Designs

Printing the Design view of your table is not as easy as clicking the Print button — as you may have noticed already, the Print button is not available when Design view is displayed. Luckily, Access includes a cool feature called the *Documenter dialog box* to help you document your database. To print your field definitions with field properties, follow these steps:

1. **Click the purple File tab near the top-left corner of the Access window. Click Info, and choose Analyze Database. Select Database Documenter from the menu of ways to analyze your database.**

   Access displays the Documenter dialog box, as shown in Figure 2-3. (Of course, your Documenter dialog box will show different objects.)

Figure 2-3:
The
Documenter
dialog box
displays
a tab for
each type of
object in the
database.

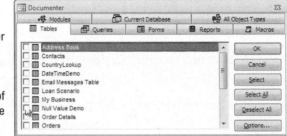

2. **Click the Tables tab to display a list of tables in your database.**

3. **Select the table definition(s) you want to print by clicking the check box in front of the table name.**

   Alternatively, use the Select button to select the highlighted table(s) or just click the Select All button to get the whole enchilada — all the tables.

4. **Click the Options button to display the Print Table Definition dialog box, as shown in Figure 2-4.**

   Use the Print Table Definition dialog box to choose those aspects of the table definition you want to print.

Figure 2-4:
The Print
Table
Definition
dialog box.

5. **When you're done, click OK to close the Print Table Definition dialog box.**

   The Documenter dialog box makes its return.

6. **Click OK in the Documenter dialog box to display the object-definition report in a form that can be printed.**

   The contents of the report depend on the settings you selected in the Print Table Definition dialog box, but the default display shows the following:

   - The properties of the table at the top
   - The name of each field with its properties
   - How the table is related to other tables in the database
   - The table index fields
   - The primary key

7. **Click the Print button on the toolbar, the Print button on the Print Preview menu, or click the File tab and choose Print from the menu to print the report.**

Book II
Chapter 2

Refining Your Table
in Design View

Chapter 3: Sorting, Finding, and Filtering Data in a Datasheet

In This Chapter

✔ **Sorting data in a datasheet**

✔ **Finding a specific record**

✔ **Using filters to find a subset of a datasheet**

A datasheet is a good place to start analyzing your data, especially if you only need to look at the data in one table. Within a datasheet, you can sort (alphabetize) — using any field and filter — to find records that are alike or that meet simple criteria. And if you're looking at a datasheet generated by a query, these datasheet tools may be just what you need to find the data you want without redefining the query.

Sorting the Rows of a Datasheet

You may enter data randomly (and that's not a bad thing), but it doesn't have to stay that way. Use the Sort buttons to sort the records (rows) into an order that makes sense.

Before you sort, decide which field you want to sort, and then place your cursor somewhere in that field. Then use one of the two Sort buttons on the Home tab of the Ribbon to sort the datasheet. Another way to sort the field is to click the down arrow next to the field name — the first two choices on the drop-down menu are Sort Smallest to Largest and Sort Largest to Smallest. (The exact text of the menu options varies depending on the type of data in the field.)

When you sort a Number field in ascending order, Access lists records from the smallest number to the largest. When you sort a Text field in ascending order, records are alphabetized from A to Z. When you sort a Date field in ascending order, records are listed from oldest date to most recent date. Descending order is the opposite in all three cases: largest-to-smallest number, Z to A, or most recent to oldest date.

Sort Button	Sort Order
↓ Ascending	Sorts from smaller to larger and A to Z.
↓ Descending	Sorts from larger to smaller and Z to A.
Remove Sort	Clears All Sorts button returns records to their previous order.

When you add a new record to a sorted datasheet, the datasheet does not automatically resort itself — you have to use the Sort button again to sort the new records in with the already existing records.

If you want to return records to their unsorted order, click the Clear All Sorts button on the Home tab on the Ribbon. However, if you have an order that you want to be able to return to (for instance, the order in which the records were entered), it's a good idea to have a field that you can sort on when you want to re-create that order.

Sort-order oddities

When sorting a Number or Currency field, values sort from smallest to largest. (At least, they do when you are sorting in ascending order.) But when you sort a Text field, values are sorted alphabetically, starting at the left end of the field. This difference between the two fields means that in a Text field, Access sorts 55 before 6, because the 5 character comes before the 6 character. For example, Access sorts the same list of numbers in Number and Text fields like this:

Number Sort	Text Sort
1	1
2	11
5	2
11	21
21	44
44	5

If you need to sort the numbers in a text field into numerical order, Access online Help has an excellent help page on the topic. You'll have

to create a new field, using an expression to convert the text into a numerical value — and then you can sort using that new field. You can find the information in the Filtering and Sorting section of the help system.

Sometimes you need to know exactly how Access sorts blanks and special characters. The sort, in ascending order, looks like this:

- **blanks** (null)

- **space**

- **special characters** such as !, ", #, %, &, (, comma, period, [, ^, `, ~ (in that order, incidentally)

- **letters** (Access does not distinguish between uppercase and lowercase letters when sorting.)

- **numbers**

If you need to know how Access sorts some characters that aren't listed here, make a test table with the characters you need to sort, and sort them!

An AutoNumber field often serves the purpose of resorting data into its original order, but if an AutoNumber field won't work for the order you want, consider adding a field that you can sort on to get your data in order. Don't let the order of records be a hidden clue to your data — include the data to sort on explicitly in a field.

Finding (and Replacing) Data

Do you like a quick-and-dirty approach, or are you more thoughtful and refined? Access accommodates both personalities. To search quickly for data in a datasheet, use the Search box at the bottom of the datasheet; it's located to the right of the Record Navigator and to the left of the scroll bar. Type your search text into the box, and with no further ado, Access takes you to the first instance of the text. You don't even have to press Enter. In fact, as you type, Access is moving the focus in the datasheet to the first instance of the text you're typing. To find the next instance, press Enter. Continue at will!

If you want to be more specific about what you're looking for, you may prefer the Find and Replace dialog box. Access even takes the text you typed in the Search box and puts it into the Find and Replace box automatically, so you have it as a starting point. Display the Find and Replace dialog box (shown in Figure 3-1) by pressing Ctrl+F or by clicking the Find button in the Find group of the Home tab on the Ribbon.

If you want to look within a single field, put the cursor anywhere in that field's column before you begin the search. To search the whole datasheet, change the Look In setting on the Find and Replace dialog box.

Book II
Chapter 3

Sorting, Finding, and Filtering Data in a Datasheet

Figure 3-1:
Press Ctrl+F
to see the
Find and
Replace
dialog box.

Using the Find and Replace dialog box for quick-and-dirty searches is as easy as 1-2-3:

1. **Press Ctrl+F to display the Find and Replace dialog box.**

2. **Type what you're looking for in the Find What box.**

3. **Press Enter or click the Find Next button.**

Access highlights the first instance of the Find What text.

Quick-and-dirty may work just fine for you, but you need to know about a few refinements to the Find and Replace dialog box — such as telling Access to limit its search to particular places. The default settings on the Find and Replace dialog box tell Access to search the field the cursor is in, and to match your search term word for word. You may find, however, that other options in the dialog box make it easier to find exactly what you're looking for. Keep reading to find out more!

Exploring the Find and Replace dialog box and its options

If you don't know how to use the options in the Find and Replace dialog box, it won't help you much with finding what you're looking for. So a guided tour is in order.

The Find and Replace dialog box has the following options:

✦ **Find What:** Here's where you type in the text or value that you're looking for.

✦ **Find Next:** Finds the next instance of the Find What text.

✦ **Look In:** Here's where you tell Access where to look — the field the cursor is in (Current Field), a series of fields, or the whole table (Current Document). If you select a bunch of fields or records *before* displaying the Find and Replace dialog box, Access searches the selected cells — and you can't change the Look In option. (Select contiguous fields by clicking the first field name and then Shift+clicking the last field name.) If you don't select a particular field, you can choose either the field where the cursor is, or the whole table. (The table name will be listed.)

✦ **Match:** Choose how the search results match the Find What text. You can choose from the following options: Any Part of Field, Whole Field, or Start of Field. The Any Part of Field option finds the most instances. If you search for Flamingo using the Any Part of Field option, Access finds Lawn Flamingo. The Whole Field option finds only cells that match the whole word, Flamingo — it does not find Lawn Flamingo. The Start of Field option finds cells that begin with Flamingo, such as Flamingos.

✦ **Search:** Choose the direction (from the cursor) to search: Up, Down, or All.

✦ **Match Case:** Match the case of the text — if you want to find THIS but not This, use the Match Case option.

✦ **Search Fields as Formatted:** Finds data according to how it looks, rather than how it was entered. If you use an input mask on a telephone-number field (for example), you may input ten digits one after another, but they appear with parentheses around the area code and a hyphen after the exchange. If you use the Search Fields as Formatted option, you can search for (508) to find phone numbers in the 508 area code.

The broadest search uses the following options: Look In *Tablename* (the whole table), Match Any Part of Field, Search All, and deselect Match Case. Other choices in the Look In, Match, and Search options narrow the search — and may miss particular instances of the Find What text. That's not necessarily a bad thing, by the way — especially if you have a very clear idea of where you want to find what you're looking for.

Replacing the data you find

To replace data with new data, first define what you're looking for using the Find tab, as described in the previous section, and then use the Replace With option on the Replace tab to define how you want to replace it.

You can replace instances one at a time by using the Replace (to replace) and Find Next (to skip that instance) buttons. Or you can replace all instances using the Replace All button.

The Undo button can undo only the last replacement made — it won't undo a whole slew of them, so use the Replace All button carefully.

If the Find and Replace dialog box isn't quite what you need, you may want to filter your datasheet and then make replacements, or you may want to try out action queries. For more on filters, see the next section; for more on action queries, check out Book III.

Filtering a Datasheet

Filtering a datasheet is a way to focus on specific records, rather than all the records in a table. You can filter out records that aren't relevant to what you're trying to do at the moment.

When you filter data, you use criteria to tell Access what you want to see. A *criterion* is a test that the data passes in order to display after the filter applies. For example, you may ask Access to show you the records with an order date of 5/1/10. A more advanced criterion is orders with a date *on or after* 5/1/10. Access will then show you only the data that meets your criteria. All other records are hidden until you remove the filter.

There are some cases when a filter is not the best tool for the job. If you are looking for the top or bottom values in a field, or unique or duplicate values, then you need to use a query. And if you want to use the same filter repeatedly (for instance, every day, week, or month), then creating and saving a query is likely to be a better solution for you.

Filtering the filtering basics

Filter

If you want to get a handle on the whole filtering concept, start out by taking a look at the parts of a datasheet that relate to filters. To start with, you can display the filter menu for any field by clicking the arrow next to the field name. To see what common filters are provided, choose the item above all the check boxes — in Figure 3-2, it reads Number Filters. To filter to a particular selection, use the check boxes (more about that in a sec).

Figure 3-2 shows a datasheet with the filter buttons and indicators marked. This datasheet has a filter applied — you can tell because of the Filtered datasheet indicators at the bottom of the datasheet. Also, the Toggle Filter button is highlighted — if it's clicked again, the filter is removed, and all the records in the datasheet display. If you hover the mouse pointer over the filter indicator next to the field name of the filtered field, a screen tip appears, showing the current filter definition.

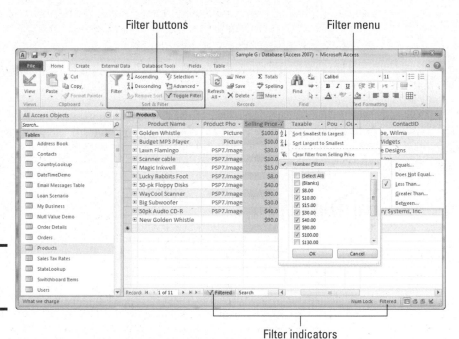

Filter buttons

Filter menu

Filter indicators

Figure 3-2:
A filtered
datasheet.

You can apply a filter to any datasheet — that includes a table, of course, but also subdatasheets and datasheets generated by queries. (When you apply a filter to a subdatasheet, all the data displayed from the subdatasheet table is filtered, not just the record where you apply the filter.) You can enter and edit data in a filtered datasheet as usual. Just be aware that the filter has no effect on any new records until you re-apply the filter.

To remove a filter, click the Toggle Filter button in the Sort & Filter group of the Home tab on the Ribbon. To re-apply the last filter you applied, click Toggle Filter again. The Filtered/Unfiltered indicator next to the Record Navigator at the bottom of the datasheet works the same way as the Toggle Filter button. To clear the filter so that it is not applied when you click Toggle Filter, choose Advanced➪Clear All Filters from the Sort and Filter group of the Home tab on the Ribbon.

If you apply a filter to one field, and then apply a filter to another field, Access will use both filters to choose the records to display. However, only one filter at a time can be used on each field — the second filter will override the first — so it's a good idea to know how to remove (that is, clear) your filters:

✦ Clear the filters from a single field by clicking the arrow next to the field name and choosing Clear Filter from *field name*.

✦ Clear all filters from the table by clicking Advanced and choosing Clear All Filters.

A filter runs a simple query on one table — a good way to start analyzing your data. Filtering can help you warm up to creating more complex queries. If you're confused about queries, creating a filter can help you figure out how to write criteria for a query (and so can Book III!). When you create the filter, click Advanced and choose Advanced Filter/Sort to see it in the design grid. Look at the Criteria row to see what the criteria look like. To close the design grid, click the Close button.

If you want to use the filter to create forms and reports, save it while in the Advanced Filter/Sort window by clicking Advanced and choosing Save as Query.

Filters appear in the `Filter` property of the Properties sheet. You can filter a table by entering an expression there — but almost no one does that because the filter stays applied, and some records may be filtered out the moment you open the table.

Using different types of datasheet filters

Since the 2007 version, Access has new filtering abilities, enabling you to easily apply common filters, for instance, to filter data from a particular month. These common filters are built in to every view that displays data, displayed on the menu that appears when you click the down arrow next to a field name. Here we discuss how to use them in Datasheet view. Table 3-1 tells you how to use each of the filter options.

Table 3-1	Types of Datasheet Filters
Type of Filter	*When You Should Use It*
Common Filters	When you want to find dates from a certain month or text with certain similar characteristics, or use a logical operator to filter a number field.
Filter by Selection	You have a record with a certain value in a field, and you want to find all the other records that have the same value in that particular field.
Filter by Form	You have more than one criterion; for instance, you want to find orders placed before 6/1/06 paid for by credit card.
Advanced Filter/Sort	You want to do more than the other filters allow, such as sorting and applying criteria to multiple fields. Advanced Filter/Sort creates a query using only one table.

Filtering by selection

Filtering by selection is the simplest kind of filter — it finds records with matching values in one field. To filter by selection, follow these steps:

1. **Find a record with the value or text you want to match and then place your cursor in that cell to match the whole value.**

   - To find all products with the price of $29.99, place the cursor in a Price cell with the value 29.99.

   - To match the beginning of the value, select the first character and as many thereafter as you want to match. To find all entries in the field that start with La, for example, highlight the La in Lawn Flamingo before filtering.

 Selection ▾

2. **Click the Selection button in the Sort & Filter group of the Home tab on the Ribbon.**

3. **Select the first choice, Equals X.**

   Access filters the datasheet to display only records that have the same value in that field.

To see the entire table, click the Toggle Filter button (which toggles the filter off and on).

By selecting a value in a datasheet, you can easily filter to find values equal to the value you're looking for (as you just did), or go after those *unequal* to that value (a process known as *filtering by exclusion*). Depending on the data type, other options are also available:

✦ **Number fields and Date/Time fields:** Filter to values greater than or less than the selected value. The Selection button also offers a Between option so that you can specify an upper and lower limit for the values you want to see in the filtered datasheet.

✦ **Text:** Filter to records that either contain the selected text or do not contain the selected text. These two options are useful if you have selected a portion of a text field.

Filtering with common filters

Common filters are now built in to Access. The filters available depend on the data type of the field that you are filtering. The most interesting choices are for Date/Time fields.

Follow these steps to use common filters to filter a field:

1. **To see the filters available for a particular field, click the arrow next to the field name, or click the Filter button when the cursor is in the field.**

At this point you may want to filter to a specific value. To first deselect all values, click the first check box, Select All. This check box toggles between two options: selecting all check boxes and deselecting all check boxes. You can then select the values you want to see when the datasheet is filtered. Click OK to see the filtered datasheet.

2. **To choose from more filtering options, highlight the menu option immediately above the check boxes.**

The name of this menu option changes with each data type. It is called Date Filters for Date/Time fields, Text Filters, Number Filters, and so on.

3. **For Date/Time fields, highlight All Dates in Period to display another level of choices.**

From this submenu, you can choose to see data in one quarter or one month of the year. Figure 3-3 shows all the filtering options available for a Date/Time field.

Filtering using criteria on multiple fields

When you have criteria for multiple fields, you can simply apply the filters to the various fields using the techniques you've already learned in this chapter, and Access will display only the records that meet all the criteria. Another choice, which is more flexible, is to use the Filter by Form feature to find the records you need.

To Filter by Form, click the Advanced button in the Sort & Filter group of the Home tab on the Ribbon, and then choose Filter by Form. Access displays a form that looks like a single row of the table you're filtering. Use the form, as shown in Figure 3-4, to specify the criteria you want to use to filter your data.

Figure 3-3: Date/Time fields have many, many filtering options.

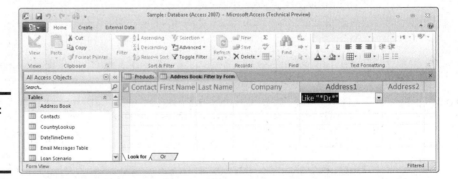

Figure 3-4: The Filter by Form window.

When you filter by form, you not only get to use multiple criteria, you also get to choose how the data filters through whatever multiple criteria you set up. Do you want a record to meet *all* the criteria before it shows up on-screen? Or is just meeting one criterion enough to display the record on the filtered datasheet? The following two operators are what you use to tell your criteria how they should act together:

✦ And: The criteria act together hand in glove — a record has to pass all criteria in order to display on the filtered datasheet.

✦ Or: A record has to pass only one criterion in order for it to display on the filtered datasheet.

You may use more than two criteria using both the Or and And operators. The way you put criteria in the form defines how multiple criteria act together. Use the Look For and Or tabs at the bottom of the form:

✦ Criteria on a single tab act as if they are joined by the And operator.

✦ Criteria on separate tabs act as if they are joined by the Or operator.

To take advantage of all this versatility, follow these steps to filter a datasheet by form:

1. Click the Advanced button in the Sort & Filter group of the Home tab on the Ribbon, and choose Filter by Form.

Access displays the Filter by Form window, which looks like an empty datasheet.

2. Move the cursor to a field you have a criterion for.

For instance, if you want to see addresses from only Pennsylvania, move the cursor to the State field. A drop-down list arrow appears in the field.

3. Click the arrow to see the list of entries in the field.

You may want to type the first letter or digit of your criteria to move to that point in the drop-down list.

4. Select the value in the drop-down list that you want the filtered records to match.

Access displays the text that the filter is looking for inside quotation marks.

If you aren't looking to match the entire field but are looking for a match in part of the field, type **LIKE** *"value that you're looking for"* (remember to include the quotation marks). For example, type **LIKE "new"** in the City field to find all records with new in the city name. You can use more complex criteria, too — for more information, see Book III, Chapter 3.

5. If you have a criterion for another field that needs to be applied at the same time as the criterion you set in Step 4, repeat Steps 2 through 4 for the additional field.

Setting up criteria to work together illustrates the usefulness of the And operator. If you want to find addresses in San Francisco, CA, set the State field to CA and the City field to San Francisco.

6. **If you have a completely different set of rules to filter records by, click the Or tab at the bottom-left portion of the Filter by Form window.**

   Access displays a blank Filter by Form tab. When you set criteria on more than one tab, a record has to meet all the criteria on only any one tab to appear on the filtered datasheet.

7. **Choose the criteria on the second tab in the same way you chose those on the first — click the field and choose the value that you want to match.**

   If, in addition to all the addresses in San Francisco, you want to see all the addresses from Boston, MA, set the State field on the Or tab to MA and the City field to Boston.

   When you use an Or tab, another Or tab appears, allowing you to continue adding as many sets of Or criteria as you need.

8. **Click the Toggle Filter button on the Ribbon to see the filtered table.**

Filtering Using Advanced Filter/Sort

The Advanced Filter/Sort feature in Access is really a query — the simplest kind of query. It allows you to find and sort information from one table in the database. This option is available from a datasheet by clicking Advanced and choosing Advanced Filter/Sort.

Use Advanced Filter/Sort when you want to use the more familiar Query by Example (QBE) grid to sort and filter a table. (In fact, you can load filter criteria from an existing query by choosing Advanced⇨Load from Query in the Sort and Filter group of the Datasheet tab on the Ribbon.)

Figure 3-5 shows the Advanced Filter/Sort window.

This section gives you the basics of performing an advanced filter-and-sort operation, but because the features of the Advanced Filter/Sort window are nearly identical to the features of queries, you may want to read Book III, Chapter 1 for more details.

Follow these steps to sort and filter a table using the Advanced Filter/Sort feature:

1. **Open the table you want to filter in Datasheet view.**

2. **Click the Advanced button in the Sort & Filter group of the Home tab on the Ribbon and choose Advanced Filter/Sort.**

Field names   Table name

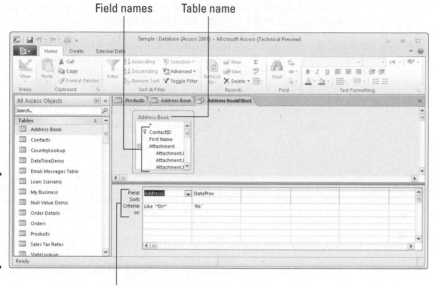

Figure 3-5:
The
Advanced
Filter/Sort
window.

Query by Example (QBE) grid

Access displays the Filter window, which has two parts, just like Design
view for queries. Notice that there is now a tab for the table and a tab
for the filter that you are defining.

3. **In the top half of the window, you see a box with the table name and
   all the fields in the table listed. Double-click the first field you want to
   use to filter the table.**

   The field appears in the Field row of the first column of the QBE grid in
   the bottom half of the window.

   Instead of double-clicking a field, you can choose a field from the Field
   drop-down list in the QBE grid. Click in the Field row of the grid to see
   the arrow for the drop-down list.

4. **Click the Criteria row in the first column and type the criteria to limit
   the records you see.**

   If you want to see only items that cost more than $10, select the
   Selling Price field as the field you want to use as your filter, and
   then type **>10** in the Criteria row of the same column of the QBE grid.

5. **Repeat Steps 3 and 4 to add other fields and criteria to the grid.**

6. **(Optional) Choose a field by which to sort the resulting table and then
   choose Ascending or Descending order.**

A drop-down list appears for the Sort row in the column, containing the field you want to sort. Access sorts the table that results from the advanced filter in ascending or descending order, using the field listed in the same column as the sort key.

7. **When you finish creating all the criteria you need, click the Toggle Filter button to see the resulting table.**

   Access displays all the fields in the original table, but it filters the records and displays only those that meet the criteria.

You can do several things with the resulting filtered table, including the following:

✦ **Filter it again.** Use the filter options to filter the table even more.

✦ **Print it.** Click the Print button.

✦ **Sort it.** The best way to sort is to use the Sort row in the design grid. (Click the tab for the Filter window to display the QBE grid again.) But you can use the Sort Ascending or Sort Descending buttons to sort the table by the field that the cursor is in.

✦ **Fix it.** Click the tab for the Filter window to display the Filter window again to fix the criteria or other information in the grid.

✦ **Add data to it.** Add data to the table by clicking the New Record button and typing in the data.

✦ **Edit data.** Edit data the same way that you do in the datasheet. When you look at the unfiltered table, you see any changes you made in the filtered table.

✦ **Delete records.** You can delete entire records if you want — click the record you want to delete and then click the Delete Record button.

✦ **Toggle between the filtered table and the full table.** Click the Toggle Filter button.

   • If you're looking at the full table, clicking the Toggle Filter button displays the filtered table (according to the last filter that you applied).

   • If you're looking at the filtered table, clicking the Toggle Filter button displays the full table.

If you want to save your advanced filter, you have to save it in Design view. After you apply the filter, return to Design view by clicking the tab for the filter. Right-click the Filter tab and choose Save to save the advanced filter. You can find the filter, after it's saved, listed with the Queries button in the Navigation pane.

Creating a report or form with a filter

After you get the hang of filtering a datasheet, you may realize that what you really want to do is create a form or report with the same filter you've just applied to your datasheet. You can — and quite easily — by using the buttons on the Create tab of the Ribbon. First, filter the datasheet, and then select the type of object you want to create. Access prompts you to save the table. Then you can either display the new object (if you select AutoForm or AutoReport) or display the New Form or New Report dialog box. You can find the filter you created in the `Filter` property of the Properties sheet for the new object. Pretty slick.

Chapter 4: Importing and Exporting Data

In This Chapter

✔ Copying and moving data with the Clipboard

✔ Importing data from other programs into Access

✔ Linking data from other programs into Access

✔ Cleaning up your imported data

✔ Exporting data from Access

✔ Collecting data though e-mails

*E*ven if you love Access, you may not end up using it for every single data-oriented task you need to do. Because of that, you may need to get data from another format (such as an Excel spreadsheet) into Access. Or you may want to take data from an Access database and use it elsewhere — say, a statistical report, spreadsheet, or word-processing document.

But never fear — you can get data from other applications into Access. Or, if you prefer, you can leave your data in other applications and have Access link to it there. (Although you should have a really good reason to do that, because it can get tricky.) Access provides a number of ways to import and export data.

The rest of this chapter covers different methods of getting data into and out of Access, starting with the easiest method — cutting and pasting.

If you are looking for more sophisticated methods of getting Access to share data, such as using SharePoint and using Access as a front end for other databases, check out Book IX.

Cutting, Copying, and Pasting

The most basic way to move information is cutting and pasting (or copying and pasting) using the Windows Clipboard or the Office Clipboard. Cutting and pasting is a straightforward (and relatively simple) way to move or copy information into or out of Access, or from one place to another within Access.

You can use the Cut, Copy, and Paste commands in at least two ways: by clicking buttons or by pressing shortcut keys. Figure 4-1 shows the buttons, and Table 4-1 lists keystrokes for cutting, copying, and pasting.

Figure 4-1:
The Cut,
Copy, and
Paste
buttons are
found in the
Clipboard
group on the
Home tab of
the Ribbon.

 ——Secret Clipboard button

Table 4-1	Cutting, Pasting, and Copying Options
Keystroke	*What It Does*
Ctrl+X	Cuts the selection and stores it on the Clipboard
Ctrl+C	Copies the selection to the Clipboard
Ctrl+V	Pastes the contents of the Clipboard

To copy or cut and paste data, follow these steps:

1. **Select the data or object that you want to cut or copy; for instance, double-click to select a word.**

2. **Choose your favorite method (Ribbon button or hot key) to cut or copy what you selected.**

You can also right-click the selection and choose Cut or Copy.

When you cut something, it disappears from the screen and is stored on the Windows Clipboard. When you copy something, it stays where it is, and Access also places a copy on the Windows Clipboard.

3. **Move the cursor to the place where you want the item to appear.**

4. **Choose your favorite method (shortcut menu, Ribbon button, or hot key) to paste the item.**

Using the Office Clipboard

Using the Windows Clipboard works the same as using the Office Clipboard, except that the Office Clipboard has more features — mainly, it stores up to 24 clips. The Windows Clipboard stores only one clip. You can use the Office Clipboard when cutting and pasting within Office applications. You can use the Windows Clipboard for copying and pasting in any Windows application that supports its use. When you cut or copy something to the Clipboard, it is saved on both the Windows and Office Clipboards. When you paste from the Clipboard using a keystroke or a button, you get the most recent thing you put on the Clipboard, which is also the top item on the Office Clipboard.

If you always get the most-recently-copied item, what's the point of the Office Clipboard storing up to 24 of your recent clips? The Office Clipboard stores items from all Office applications — Access, Excel, Word, Outlook, and PowerPoint. If you want to see your clips, click the secret Clipboard button (okay, technically it's the Clipboard Dialog Box Launcher, but seriously, what was Microsoft thinking making those little tiny grey shadows and calling them buttons?) on the Home tab of the Ribbon. (It's to the right of the word Clipboard, under the Paste button — see Figure 4-2.)

Book II
Chapter 4

Importing and
Exporting Data

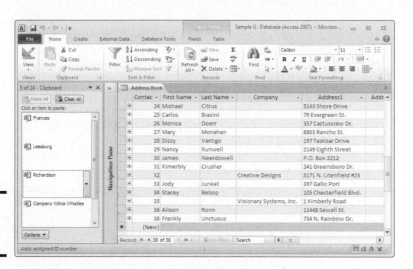

Figure 4-2:
The Office
Clipboard.

The Clipboard task pane displays the clips that you cut or copy, along with an icon to show you what type of clip it is (from Access, Excel, Word, and so on). Paste any clip — not just the most recent one — at the cursor's position by clicking the clip. Delete a clip from the Clipboard by right-clicking the icon and choosing the Delete option from the shortcut menu. The Paste All button pastes all the stored items at the cursor's position.

Close the Clipboard task pane by clicking the Close button in the pane's upper-right corner.

If you want to keep track of what's on the Clipboard, you can set it to appear automatically whenever you cut or copy more than one item without pasting. Just click the Options button at the bottom of the Clipboard task pane and choose Show Office Clipboard Automatically.

Cutting and pasting small to medium-ish amounts of data

Cutting and pasting is most useful for small pieces of data, but you may also use that capability for a number of fields- or even records-worth of data. If you move lots and lots of data, look at the import and linking options covered later in this chapter — but if you're copying small or medium amounts of data, copying and pasting may work just fine. Access gets picky when you paste more than one piece of data into a datasheet; to help make pasting work most effectively, follow these guidelines:

✦ Fields (columns) need to be in the same order in the source document as in Access. You may need to rearrange columns in either Access or the source document.

✦ The data type of the data you are copying needs to match the data type of the field you're pasting into. The exceptions are Text and Memo data types, which can accept any type of data.

✦ You can't paste a duplicate value into the primary key field (just like you can't type a duplicate value into a primary key field).

✦ You can't paste into a hidden field. Unhide all the fields you're pasting data into before you paste data into them. To unhide, right-click any field name and choose Unhide Columns. However, if you don't have data for one field, and you want to paste into the fields on either side of it, hiding the field before pasting is a good option.

✦ Data you paste must meet any validation rules and work with any input masks. (See the next chapter for details on those features.)

✦ You can't copy data into an AutoNumber field. Access generates AutoNumber values for copied records.

✦ A good option for pasting multiple cells of data from a spreadsheet program is the Paste Append command. To append entire records (with the exception of any AutoNumber fields) from Excel or another spreadsheet, paste by using Paste Append — copy the data to the Clipboard, display Access, and then click the arrow under the Paste button on the Home tab of the Ribbon and select Paste Append.

✦ If you are adding data into a datasheet that already has data, you may want to paste the new data into a temporary datasheet to make sure the data look right before you paste it into the permanent datasheet. Another option is to append the table with the new data to the existing table. Append Queries, which do that job, are covered in Book III, Chapter 3.

✦ If you choose not to use Paste Append or the Append Tables query, you have to select multiple cells (fields, records, or both) if you want to paste content into multiple cells. You don't have to select the exact number of cells that you're copying into — if you don't want to count the exact number of rows or columns that you want to copy data into, just select more than you think the data will fill. To make new records, click the New Record button. You may need to put a piece of data in each record. The dummy data will be overwritten when you copy data into the records.

✦ One easy way to select cells in a worksheet is to click the first cell (in the upper-left corner of the range), and then Shift+click the last cell (in the lower-right corner of the range).

✦ You can't copy into subdatasheets as you copy into the main datasheet. Copy into one table at a time.

Moving data from Excel to Access

Do you have a relatively small amount of data you want to copy and paste from Excel to Access? If so, follow these steps for a very convenient way to copy and paste into a new Access table. (However, if you have a large amount of data to move, see the "Importing or Linking to Data" section for a better method.)

1. **In Access, open the database to which you want to copy the data.**

2. **In Excel, open the workbook and display the worksheet that contains your data.**

Make sure that the first row of data makes adequate field names. (You can always change them later.)

3. **Select the data in Excel and press Ctrl+C to copy the data to the Clipboard.**

4. **Click any table in the Navigation pane and press Ctrl+V to paste the data into a new table.**

5. **When Access asks if the first row of your data contains column headings, click the Yes button.**

Access creates a new table from the Excel data with the same name of the Excel worksheet that contained the data. You may need to rename your table, but wasn't that easy?

Alternatively, you open a new or existing table, arrange your windows so you can see both the data in Excel and the table where you want to put the data. Then drag the data from Excel to Access.

If you have large amounts of data, try the Import Spreadsheet Wizard, explained later in this chapter.

Importing or Linking to Data

If you have large quantities of data that you want to use in your Access database, or if you want to take advantage of the features offered by the Link or Import Wizards, you can import or link to the data.

Understanding what applications are compatible with Access

Here's the scenario: You were lucky enough to find the data you need for your database, and it's even in electronic form. But it's stored in dBASE, Excel, Word, another Access database, or some other file format — what do you do?

In most cases, Access knows how to either import the data directly or create a link to the data. If you can't import the file type directly, chances are that you can use the program in which the data was entered to save it in a file format that Access can import. Currently, you can import or link to files in the following formats:

✦ Microsoft Access data can be imported, linked and exported.

✦ Microsoft Excel spreadsheets can be imported, linked and exported.

✦ ODBC data (SQL Server, for example) can be imported, linked to and exported.

✦ Text files (delimited or fixed-width) can be imported, linked to, and exported (use this option for Microsoft Word files).

✦ XML documents can be imported and exported, but not linked to.

✦ PDF and XPS files can be created by exporting from Access, but cannot be imported or linked to.

✦ SharePoint lists can be imported, linked to, and exported.

✦ HTML documents can be imported, linked to, and exported.

✦ dBASE can be importcd, linked to, and exported.

 If you have data in a format that your version of Access can't use, you may be able to download updated drivers from the Microsoft Web site at www. microsoft.com. Or you can see if the application allows you to export the data to one of the accepted formats. Then you can import it into Access.

Making data available: To link or to import, that is the question

You have a number of choices about how to make your data available in Access. You must choose whether you want to actually store the data in Access (import the data) or create a link to the data.

✦ **Import:** Make a copy of the data in Access. (Copying and pasting is the simplest form of importing.)

✦ **Link:** Keep the data in another file and tell Access to get the data each time it is needed.

Some factors to consider when deciding whether to import or link include the following:

✦ **Storage:** When you import data, you may be doubling the storage required because you are storing the data in Access as well as in its original format.

✦ **Customization:** If the data is stored in a format other than Access and you want to define a primary key, enforce referential integrity, change field names, and/or customize field and table properties, you should import the data.

✦ **Maintenance:** Does the data get updated, and if so, how? If a system is in place to update data in another format, leaving the data where it is and linking to it makes sense, unless you're prepared to create a system to update it in Access. However, if the data is not analyzed in its current format, moving the data to Access and creating a system for updating it there makes sense.

✦ **Accessibility:** If you're leaning toward linking to the data, will the data always be available when you need it? Is it likely to move, or will you need it when you are traveling or not on your usual LAN? If the data is not accessible, Access will not be able to use that data for queries, reports, and forms.

If you need the data to get started in Access, and will then be using Access exclusively to update and analyze the data, you should import it. If data is collected and updated in another format, and you will be using the database from a computer that can always access the data source, then linking is probably a good option. But in this case, scheduled imports may work, too. You'll need to evaluate your situation, considering the preceding points to decide whether linking or importing is the better choice.

Getting external data

After you decide whether to import or link to your data, you're ready for the next step. If you can, look at the external data you want to use. Look for the following factors:

✦ **Are fields stored in columns and records in rows?** This is relevant to text and spreadsheet files.

✦ **Does the data you need begin at the top of the file?** For text and spreadsheets, Access expects to see one row of names and then the data.

✦ **Is all data within a field of the same type?** If not, the field imports as a Text or Memo field, which can't be used in mathematical equations.

✦ **Is the number of fields in each row the same?** This is of particular concern in a text file. If necessary, add null values to make your data line up. (For instance, "", two quotation marks with nothing between them, is a null text value.)

✦ **Are the field names in the data you are importing identical to the field names in the Access table?** When you append data, the field names you're importing must be identical to the file you're appending to.

Are you importing the data into a new table, or do you want to append the data to an existing table? Appending can be tricky because the data in the external source and in the Access table has to match in data type and in its relative location — you may want to first import into a new table in Access and then use an Append Query. (You find more on appending in general later in this chapter; for more on the Append Query in particular, see Book III, Chapter 3.)

When your data source is ready, you're ready to either import or link. The following are general instructions — followed by some particulars for specific file formats:

1. **In Access, open the database that you want to add external data to.**

2. **Display the External Data tab on the Ribbon and click the button for the kind of data that you're importing.**

There are buttons for Excel, Access, ODBC Database, Text file, and XML file. The More button drop-down list contains buttons for SharePoint List, Data Service (for Web services), HTML Document, Outlook Folder, and dBASE file.

When you've made your choice, Access displays the Get External Data dialog box (shown in Figure 4-3), where you specify the name of the file that contains the data you're importing or linking to.

3. **Use the File Name box to specify the source of the data. Click the Browse button to navigate to your data file.**

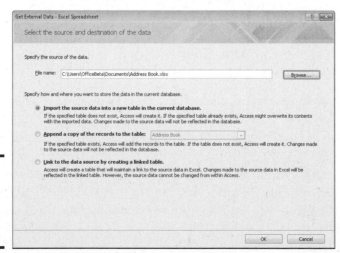

Figure 4-3:
The Get External Data dialog box.

Navigate through the folders (if necessary) to find the file that contains the data you want to use. Click the filename so that it appears in the File Name box.

If you are linking and the file that you are linking to is not on your computer (it is on a LAN or another remote computer), use the universal naming convention (UNC) path for the file rather than using a drive letter that is mapped. The UNC path is a more reliable way for Access to locate the data. A UNC path looks like the following:

`\\server\directory\file`

You have to know the server name in order to type the UNC.

4. **Choose how you want to store the data in the current database.**

   You can Import the data into a new table in the current database, Append the data to an existing table (all the fields must correspond exactly for this option to work), or Link to the data outside Access. The advantages and disadvantages to each of these options have been discussed in this chapter.

5. **Click OK.**

   Depending on the type of file you're working with, you may see a wizard that guides you through the process of choosing the data you want to import or link to.

   The windows you see depend on the type of file that contains the data you're importing or linking to. (The following sections guide you through the Text and Spreadsheet Wizards.)

   Other data types (including `.dbf`) immediately import, ready for use.

When the import or link is complete, you see a new table listed in the Database window. Imported tables appear just like other tables, and you use them like any other table — you can change field names and properties, create relationships, enter data, and edit data. Linked tables appear with an arrow and an icon, indicating the type of file that the link points to (such as dB for dBASE, X for Excel, and a fox for FoxPro).

You can use most linked tables like any table in the database — some types, however, are read-only, and you can't enter and edit data. You cannot change field properties or enforce referential integrity for linked tables.

The following sections provide details on using the Import and Link Wizards for text and spreadsheet files. You may see Import Wizards for other types of files, too, files that are similar to the text and spreadsheet files in the information they need — Access wants to know how to get to and use the file, and how to break the data into fields.

Importing text or spreadsheet data

If you import or link a text file, the Import Text Wizard or Link Text Wizard starts when you select the appropriate file using the Get External Data dialog box. The two wizards are very similar, but the Link Text Wizard has fewer steps.

Are you importing a whole worksheet? If not, you may want to create a named range in the spreadsheet to make importing exactly the data that you need easier. Access uses the first eight rows of data to determine the data type. If Access happens to select the wrong data type (based on the first eight rows), format the cells in your spreadsheet to the correct data type. For instance, if the first eight ZIP codes start with a digit other than zero, Access will format them as numbers. To keep the leading zero, format them in Excel as text.

Follow these steps to complete the Text Wizards:

1. **In the first wizard window (shown in Figure 4-4), select the Delimited option or the Fixed Width option to describe how your data is divided, and then click the Next button.**

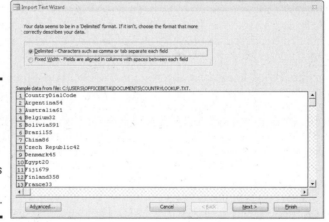

Figure 4-4:
The Import (or Link) Text Wizard can turn data like this into fields and records.

The Delimited option is for situations where commas, tabs, or other characters separate each field, whereas the Fixed Width option is for situations in which spaces make the columns line up.

2. **Further define where one field ends and the next begins in the second window. When done choosing your options, click the Next button.**

If you chose the Delimited option in Step 1, you see Figure 4-5, which asks you what character separates your fields. (Choose from the options or use the Other option to specify the character used.) Also specify whether the first row contains field names, and whether you're using a *text qualifier* (symbols that surround text, such as double or single quotation marks). Your data is shown with vertical lines to separate fields.

If you chose the Fixed Width option, you see a similar window, which shows you where Access guesses the field breaks go. If Access is wrong about the field breaks, fix them. Create a break by clicking, delete a break by double-clicking, or move a break by dragging.

3. **In the next window, click a column in the displayed data to change properties for that field, and then click the Next button.**

   For example, you can further define each field by typing a field name; choose the data type, whether to index the field, and specify whether to skip importing or linking to this particular field.

   You don't have to complete this information for each field — you can go with the choices Access makes.

4. **In the next window, select a primary key field, let Access create a new AutoNumber field as the primary key, or specify that the field doesn't have a primary key field. When you've finished your selections, click the Next button.**

5. **In the last window that appears, name the table by typing a name in the Table Name box, and then click the Finish button.**

   The last window of the Import Text Wizard contains a check box that runs the Table Analyzer Wizard. If you choose to have a wizard analyze the table, the Table Analyzer Wizard looks for duplicated data and recommends how to create multiple related tables that don't contain repeated data. You may also choose to display the Access Help system when the wizard is done.

   After you click Finish, Access creates the new table and lists it in the Database window.

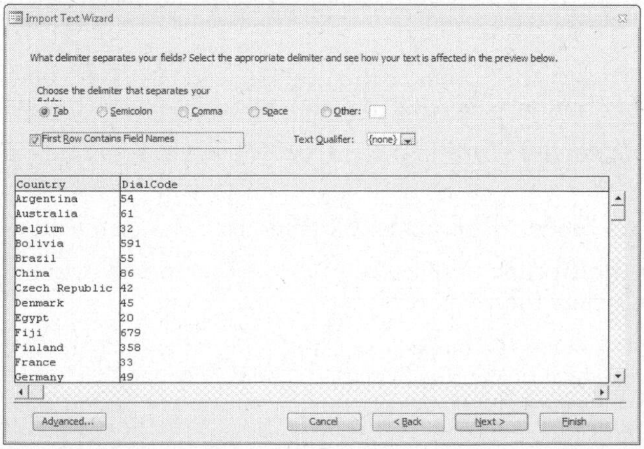

Figure 4-5:
Help Access figure out where each field in your delimited text file begins and ends.

Import Text Wizard

What delimiter separates your fields? Select the appropriate delimiter and see how your text is affected in the preview below.

Choose the delimiter that separates your fields:
◉ Tab ○ Semicolon ○ Comma ○ Space ○ Other:

☑ First Row Contains Field Names   Text Qualifier: {none}

Country	DialCode
Argentina	54
Australia	61
Belgium	32
Bolivia	591
Brazil	55
China	86
Czech Republic	42
Denmark	45
Egypt	20
Fiji	679
Finland	358
France	33
Germany	49

Advanced...   Cancel   < Back   Next >   Finish

Click the Advanced button in the last window of the wizard to display the Import Specification or Link Specification dialog box again. If this is an import or link that you may want to repeat, save the specs (using the Save As button).

The Import Specification dialog box, shown in Figure 4-6, displays all the specifications for the text-file import. You can edit these specs, save them, or import specs that you created and saved when you did another text-file import. This dialog box has options that you've seen before in the wizard (such as those for file format, field delimiter, and text qualifier), as well as the following options:

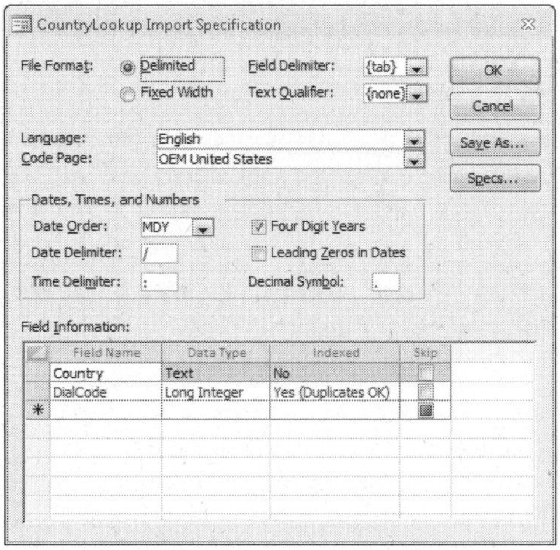

Figure 4-6:
The Import
Specification
dialog box
saves the
options so
you can
import your
file faster
next time.

- ✦ **Language:** Select the language for the text in your table.

- ✦ **Code Page:** Select a code page. Just keep the default selection unless you know for certain that the imported data is using one of the other available options.

- ✦ **Date Order:** MDY (month/day/year) is standard, but you can select another option as needed to match your date data.

- ✦ **Date Delimiter:** Type in the character used to separate month, day, and year.

- ✦ **Time Delimiter:** Type in the character used to separate hours and minutes.

- ✦ **Four Digit Years:** Deselect this option if your data uses only two digits to designate the year.

- ✦ **Leading Zeros in Dates:** Select this option if your data has zeros before single-digit months (for example, 02 for February).

✦ **Decimal Symbol:** Type in the character used as a decimal point. In the United States, the decimal symbol is a period, but in many European countries, the decimal is a comma.

✦ **Field Information:** Lists the field name in the file you are importing or linking (click to edit), the data type that Access has chosen (change by choosing from the drop-down list), whether the field is indexed (change by choosing from the drop-down list), and a check box if you want to skip the field.

✦ **Save As:** Saves the Import Specifications settings (or Link Specifications) for use with a later import or link.

✦ **Specs:** Lists saved specs that you can select from.

When you're done setting your options, click the OK button.

Importing with the Import Spreadsheet and Link Spreadsheet Wizards

If you import or link a spreadsheet file, the Import Spreadsheet Wizard or Link Spreadsheet Wizard starts when you select the appropriate file using the Get External Data dialog box. Follow these steps to complete the Spreadsheet Wizards:

1. **Select the sheet that contains your data in the first window that appears (as shown in Figure 4-7), and then click the Next button.**

You can import or link to data on only one sheet at a time. Use the Show Named Ranges option to see named ranges in the spreadsheet if you need to import part of a spreadsheet.

2. **In the second window of the wizard, tell Access whether the first row contains column headings, and then click the Next button.**

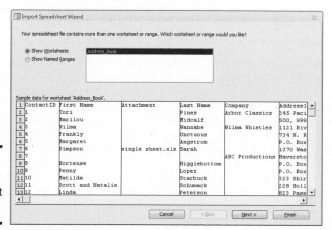

Figure 4-7:
The Import
Spreadsheet
Wizard.

3. **In the next window, change properties as necessary for each column: Click a column in the displayed data, change properties for that field at the top of the window, and then click Next when you're happy with the properties for all the fields.**

    This window allows you to further define each field by typing a field name, choosing data type, choosing whether to index the field, and choosing to skip importing or linking to this particular field. You don't have to complete this information for each field — you can go with the choices Access made.

4. **In the next window, select a primary key field, let Access create a new AutoNumber field as the primary key, or specify that the table doesn't have a primary key field. When you finish your selections, click the Next button.**

5. **In the last window, name the table and then click the Finish button.**

    The last window of the wizard contains a check box that runs the Table Analyzer Wizard. If you choose to have the wizard analyze the table, the Table Analyzer Wizard looks for duplicated data and recommends ways to create multiple related tables that don't contain repeated data. You may also choose to display the Access Help system when the wizard is done.

    When the wizard finishes, you see the database window with your new table listed.

Getting contacts from Outlook into Access

You can import contacts from Outlook into an Access table if you have Outlook, Outlook Express, or Microsoft Exchange Server installed on your computer and can log in to an e-mail account. If you want to import Outlook data but don't meet these requirements, open Outlook and export data in Access format or another format that Access can use.

Here's how to link or import Outlook data in its native form:

1. **Click the More button in the Import group of the External Data tab on the Ribbon and click the Outlook Folder button.**

    Access displays the Get External Data dialog box, where you can choose to Import the data into a new table, append the data to an existing table, or link to the data (that is, create a new, linked table). Access then asks you to choose a folder or address book to import from. It will look only at the Outlook files on your computer, and you must have a mail service set up on the computer you are working on. (There is to be no way to look at Outlook files available through network connections.)

The same rules apply for appending data to an existing table — the field names and data types must be the same in the imported data as in the existing table. The details on how to do this are in this chapter, at the beginning of the section on importing and linking data.

2. **Choose between importing from your Outlook Address Book and your Contacts folder.**

   If you're not sure which you need, it's easy enough to try one and then switch if you find you need the other. (Click Next to see the data, and then click Back to return to select a different folder.)

3. **After you have chosen a folder, click Next to see the data.**

   From this point, the import is identical to importing text or spreadsheet data. Access shows you the data and allows you to choose the fields you want. Outlook Contacts creates redundant fields — so check that you have what you need, and skip those that you don't. (Select the field and click the Do Not Import Field check box.) Empty fields (which are displayed as narrow columns) are created in a new Access table. If you don't want them, be sure to select the Do Not Import Field check box. Alternatively, you can delete the empty fields in Access.

Managing links

If you create links to external data sources, you may need to manage those links. For instance, when data changes in the source, you can tell Access to get the new data — and if the source file moves, you have to tell Access where to find it. Use the Linked Table Manager to manage your links:

1. **Right-click a linked table in the Navigation pane (linked tables have an arrow next to them) and choose Linked Table Manager from the shortcut menu.**

   Access displays the Linked Table Manager, as shown in Figure 4-8.

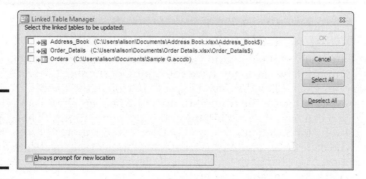

Figure 4-8:
The Linked
Table
Manager.

2. **Select the check box(es) for the table(s) whose links you want to refresh, and then click OK.**

   Access refreshes the data in the selected tables, using the external file listed in the table. If the external file isn't found, you see the Select New Location Of dialog box, where you can specify the new location. If more than one table was not found, Access searches the new location for all the missing tables.

   If you want Access always to ask you where the files are, select the Always Prompt for New Location check box before you click OK to update your data.

Cleaning up your imported data

If you import large amounts of data, you may need to clean it up a bit to make it efficient for use in Access. (If you have any doubt about what clean data looks like, review Book I, Chapter 3 on designing databases.)

One useful tool for cleaning up imported data is the Table Analyzer Wizard. This wizard looks for repeated data to determine whether to break a table into two or more tables. The various Import Wizards offer to run the Table Analyzer Wizard. You can also run it by clicking Analyze Table button in the Analyze group of the database Tools tab, or by clicking the File tab, choosing Info and clicking Analyze Database⇨Anaylze Table.

If you decide not to use the Table Analyzer Wizard, you may want to inspect your data for duplicate data. The primary key field cannot have duplicate data.

Your new table may need relationships defined with other tables in the database. (See Chapter 6 of this minibook for more on relationships.) You may also want to edit the table name or field names, and fields may need some fine-tuning — you can use Design view to edit data type and properties (as explained in Chapter 2 of this minibook).

Running and scheduling saved imports

If you have saved the definition of an import or export operation while using the appropriate wizard, you have the option of running the same import or export again. Click the Saved Exports button in the Export group of the External Data tab on the Ribbon to open the Manage Data Tasks dialog box. Here you can see all saved import and export definitions. (There are two tabs — one for Saved Imports and one for Saved Exports.) From this dialog box, you can run an operation, create an Outlook task, or delete a saved operation. You also have the option of changing the source or destination file — click the filename to change it.

If you create a task in Outlook, you can go to the Outlook task to add a date or define recurrence. You can run the task straight from Outlook by clicking the Run Export or Run Import button on the Ribbon when the Outlook task is open.

Getting Data from Another Access Database

If the data you need is already in an Access database, decide whether you want to import it or link to it. Read the section, "Importing or Linking to Data," earlier in this chapter if you need help deciding whether to link or import data.

You can also use the procedure below to import another database object (such as a query, form, report, and so on.)

If you want to import (or link to) a table and all its data from another Access database, the process is simple — follow these steps:

1. **Open the database where you want to use the data.**

2. **Click the Access button in the Import group of the External Data tab on the Ribbon.**

Access displays the Get External Data dialog box.

3. **Browse to the database that has the object you need.**

4. **Choose Import or Link. Either option results in a new database object — there is no option that appends data to an existing table.**

If necessary, you can use the Append Query to combine two tables after you have imported the data.

5. **Click OK.**

Access displays the Import Objects dialog box shown in Figure 4-9 (or the similar Link Tables dialog box).

6. **Select the table you want from the Tables tab.**

To select multiple objects, use Ctrl+click and/or Shift+click. Click the Select All button to select all objects displayed on the current tab (for instance, all tables). Click the Deselect All button to deselect all objects on the current tab.

Click the Options button and choose the Definition Only option if you don't want to import the data, just the table definition (table properties and field definitions).

7. **Click OK to import the objects (or create the link).**

The new objects appear in the Database window. You can view and edit them just as you would any other database object.

You can use this method to import any database object — not just tables.

Figure 4-9:
The Import Objects dialog box allows you to import database objects from another Access database.

Getting Data Out of Access

You can export any object from an Access database to another Access database — or to a file that isn't an Access file (a dBASE or Excel file, for example). You can also use this technique to create a static HTML file.

Exporting is a convenient way to go about moving data from one Access database to another. You can also export an object without any data — for instance, if you want to reuse a query definition. Exporting is similar to importing — the difference is which database you have open when you start.

You can even save your export definition if you export data to another application frequently. Notice the Save Exports button in the Export group of the External Data tab on the Ribbon.

To export an object, follow these steps:

1. **Open the database that contains the object you want to export.**

You can export a table with or without the data in it. You may also want to export a query with its data — which allows you to get specific information from your database.

2. **Select the object name in the Navigation pane.**

3. **Display the External Data tab on the Ribbon.**

Find the Export group of the tab.

4. **Click the button for the format you want to export to.**

   There are buttons for Excel, Text File, XML File, PDF or XPS file, E-Mail, Access, and Word Merge. The More button displays export options for Word, SharePoint List, ODBC Database, HTML Document, and dBase File.

5. **Select the file, or type a name for a new file to which you want to save the object by typing the name in the File Name box. Use the Browse button to choose a folder.**

   You may also need to select a file format, depending on the application you are exporting to. You can export to an existing Access database, but when you export to other file types, you create a new file (which you can then import into an existing file, if needed).

6. **Click OK.**

   What happens next depends on where the data is going:

   - If you're exporting to a file type other than an Access database, the object is exported.

   - If you're exporting to an existing Access file, you see the Export dialog box, where you can rename the object (if you want to) and tell Access whether you want to export all the data or just the object definition (field names, format, and any expressions).

   - When you save a report to HTML, Access asks you for the name of the HTML template file. You can find out about HTML template files from the Access Help system.

   Access quietly completes the export process and asks whether you want to save the export.

7. **If this is an export you will do again, select Save Export Steps to see additional options.**

   You'll have to name the export; we encourage you to make use of the Description field to describe the specifics of the export. (What does it do? When should it be used?) You also have the option of creating an Outlook task to remind you to repeat the export.

   You can make the Outlook task recur if you go into Outlook, choose the task, and click the Recurrence button.

8. **To see whether the operation worked, open the file to which you exported the object.**

Collecting Data with Outlook

Access 2010 allows you to collect data with an e-mail. You can send a form via Outlook, and then easily process the replies as you add the collected data to your database.

Before you begin the process of creating an e-mail message to collect data, you need a table or query in which to store the data. You may use an existing table or query, or create a new one. A query is a good way to collect data for more than one related table — create the query before starting the process of creating the e-mail. When you create the e-mail, you have the opportunity to select the fields you want to collect data for, so your table may contain more fields than you ask your recipients to fill in.

Another option with the data-collection feature is sending out existing data for users to verify. For instance, you can mail contact information using the e-mail address in each record and ask the recipients to edit or add to it. This option allows recipients to edit the information, and also to add new information. Note, however, that

✦ The recipients' e-mail addresses must be stored in the table beforehand if you're going to use this option.

✦ Data can be updated for only a single table.

✦ You cannot collect or edit fields that are Attachment type, AutoNumber, Multivalued, or OLE.

In order to collect data through Outlook, you must have Access 2010 *and* Outlook 2007 or 2010. You may also want to use InfoPath 2007, as the InfoPath form is easier to use. However, if you choose this option, all your recipients need InfoPath 2007 or 2010 as well — choosing the HTML form is safer. (It doesn't require recipients to have the extra software.) If you don't use InfoPath, recipients don't even need Outlook 2010, and they definitely don't need Access. They do, however, need an e-mail client that can read HTML e-mails. Here we cover how to collect data with — and without — using InfoPath.

Here's how to start and use the wizard to collect data through e-mail:

1. **To start the process, right-click a table name and choose Collect and Update Data via E-Mail, or click the Create E-Mail button in the Collect Data group of the External Data tab on the Ribbon.**

   The wizard starts and shows you a page that lists the six steps for gathering data through e-mail messages.

2. **Click Next to choose the type of form you want to send.**

3. **Choose HTML form. Click Next.**

   InfoPath provides many more features — including drop-down controls and in-form validation. Although HTML supports these types of controls, they are blocked by most firewalls and e-mail gateways and can't generally be used in e-mail. The HTML forms are simpler, and recipients without Access and Infopath can use them.

The next page of the wizard asks you whether you want to collect new information or update existing information.

Notice that to update existing information, the recipients' e-mail addresses must be part of the table. The update option is useful if you need people to review and update one record of information.

4. **Select the fields that you want to collect, using the wizard page shown in Figure 4-10. When you've selected all the fields you want to include in the e-mail, click Next.**

   Click the single arrow to move one field at a time, and the double arrow to move them all. The field names that appear in the box on the right are those that will be included in the e-mail. You can change the field name that the recipient sees by selecting the field name in the rightmost box and then changing the Label displayed in the Field Properties box.

   Required fields are those whose Required property is set to `Yes`. The Read-Only option allows you to send a field for the recipient to see, but not update.

5. **Specify how to process replies.**

   Generally, you'll want to select Automatically Process Replies and Add Data to *Tablename*. When data is automatically processed, it is added to your Access table when Outlook and Access are open and responses are received. Additionally, for responses to be processed automatically, the database

   • Must not be password protected.

   • Should be open in Exclusive mode, and the name and location of the database, requested fields, and relevant tables must not have changed. Also, you need to have the required permissions to add or update the tables or query.

Book II Chapter 4

Importing and Exporting Data

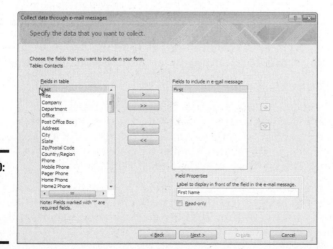

Figure 4-10: Select the fields you want to collect.

If you want to store responses in a folder with a name other than Access Data Collection Replies, click that folder link and then create a new folder, or rename the folder. (You can get to the folder by clicking the + next to Inbox in the Select Folder dialog box.)

You may want to change some collection options. Click the Set Properties to Control the Automatic Processing link to see the Collecting Data Using E-Mail Options dialog box shown in Figure 4-11.

If you choose to process replies manually, you must select each reply in Outlook, right-click, and choose Export data to Microsoft Access. You can manually process replies that fail to be automatically processed. If you allow multiple replies from each recipient, second and subsequent replies must be manually processed.

Figure 4-11:
Set properties for processing e-mails containing data.

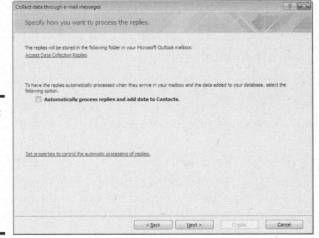

6. **Select e-mail addresses either by using addresses from Outlook (where you can type in addresses that aren't in your Outlook address book) or by using addresses stored in a field in the database. (If you are updating rather than adding data, this option doesn't appear.)**

   You guessed it — more options:

   • If you choose Outlook addresses, the next window you see allows you to customize the e-mail with a title and introductory text. Then the wizard creates the e-mail, and you can send it to your selected recipients using Outlook. (You type or select recipients in Outlook, too.) You can also alter the e-mail using Outlook.

   • If you choose addresses stored in the database, the next wizard window asks you to identify the field that contains the addresses. You can choose from the current table or query, or another table in the database.

• If you are choosing to use e-mail addresses from an associated table, first select the field in the current table that joins it to the table with the addresses. This is probably an ID field — the primary key in one of the two tables. The next step depends on whether there is more than one table associated with the original table. If not, simply select the name of the field with the e-mail addresses. If there is more than one table, first select the table, then select the field.

When you use addresses from the database, you cannot preview or customize the e-mail in Outlook.

7. **That's just about it! Depending on how addresses are being added to the e-mails, you either**

• Click Create to create the e-mail, if you are adding addresses in Outlook. The e-mail form will open in Outlook, and you can add addresses and send the e-mail as you usually do in Outlook.

• See a list of recipients with check boxes, if you are using e-mail addresses from the database. Deselect a check box to skip sending the e-mail to a recipient. Click Send to send the e-mails.

If you see any error messages on the final page of the wizard, you can use the Back button to go back and make corrections.

Click the Manage Replies button in the Collect Data group of the External Data tab on the Ribbon to see a summary of data-collection e-mails you have sent. This dialog box gives you the option of resending the message, and it allows you to change the collation options on the Collecting Data Using E-Mail Options dialog box.

If replies are being processed automatically, you will see new data in the table you specified as replies are processed. If you are manually managing replies, you can display the folder where replies are being stored, right-click each message, and choose Export Data to Microsoft Access. If you allow multiple replies from each recipient, second and subsequent replies must be manually processed.

The Access Help system has comprehensive help on sending e-mails to collect data.

Using Access Data in a Word Mail Merge

If you want to use data from Access in Word, chances are you need the Mail Merge feature. Mail merge is generally used when you want to write a letter and personalize it using an individual's name and address, inserted seamlessly into the letter. We're sure you can think of other uses for merging your Access data into Word.

Book II
Chapter 4

Importing and Exporting Data

The process of doing a mail merge consists of creating a Word document with special merge codes in it that, in the final document, display data from Access. You can create the document before you begin the merge process or after.

In order to use Access data in a Word document you should have some knowledge about using Microsoft Word. Creating the Word document is beyond the scope of this book. Word's help system is helpful if you have difficulties.

Follow these steps to export Access data to a Word document:

1. **To begin the merge from Access, select the query or table with the data you want to use in Word in the Navigation pane, display the External Data tab, and click Word Merge in the Export group.**

   The Microsoft Word Mail Merge Wizard starts and asks you whether you want to Link your data to an existing Microsoft Word document or Create a new document and then link the data to it. In this example we choose the second option. If you choose the first option, you will need to tell Access where the Word document is.

2. **Click OK. Microsoft Word opens with the Mail Merge options displayed. Proceed with creating your document in Word.**

   At step 3 of the Word Merge process you will see the name of your table (or query) and database as the recipients of the document. You can click the Edit Recipient List link to see your data.

3. **In step 4 of the Word merge process you insert the codes into your document that coincide with the fields in your database.**

   Word is pretty good at figuring out how to use your data. But if your field names do not match up well with Word's expectations, you can Match Fields manually (look for the Match Fields button as you are choosing the Address Block, and so on.).

That's it for the Access side of the merge. Mail merge can be difficult, but if you have a lot of data that you want in letters or a similar document, it's worth the effort.

Chapter 5: Avoiding "Garbage In, Garbage Out"

In This Chapter

✔ Using field properties to get the right data in the right fields

✔ Defining how data in a field looks with input masks

✔ Creating drop-down lists with lookup fields

✔ Filtering data with validation rules

*L*et's face it: If the data that goes into your database through tables and forms is garbage, then any output or analysis you do with queries and reports will give you garbage, too. Fortunately, Access offers lots of tools to help you make sure that the data that goes in each field is the data that's supposed to go in that field. Of course, we're talking about avoiding mistakes as data is entered — if someone is purposefully entering erroneous data, these tools may not help much! Some of these Access features we describe in this chapter are described in other chapters, but they deserve a mention here, too. The rest are exclusive to this chapter.

Finding the Right Tool to Keep Garbage Out

You can find many of the tools to keep garbage out in Table Design view. You can use the data type to keep inappropriate data out of a field, and many of the other field properties can work that way, too.

 Field properties appear in the bottom half of Table Design view — make sure you're viewing the field properties for the field you're working with by clicking the field name in the top half of Design view. Field properties are also covered in Chapter 2 of this minibook.

As you define a field in Design view, you can use the following field properties to make sure that the right data gets into the right field:

✦ `Data type`: Use the correct data type to eliminate data of the wrong type. Text and Memo data types accept just about any input, so use the Number, Date/Time, or Currency data types to screen out data of a different type whenever appropriate. (See Chapter 1 of this minibook for more about choosing data types.)

Although data type is technically not a field property, it appears in Design view and is your first line of defense against incorrect data.

✦ Field Size: Limits the number of characters. For instance, if you know that a field should never exceed four characters, set the field size to 4 characters. (See Chapter 2 of this minibook for more about field size.)

✦ Format: Makes the data look right. For instance, you can change text to all caps or all lowercase. Input masks, explained later in this chapter, work with the Format field property. (See Chapter 2 of this minibook for more about the Format field property.)

✦ Input Mask: An *input mask* limits the information allowed in a field by specifying what characters you can enter. Use an input mask when you know the form the data should take — for instance, if an order number has two letters followed by four digits. Phone numbers and ZIP codes are other examples of fields where input masks are useful. You find out lots more about input masks later in this chapter.

✦ Default Value: Defines a value that appears by default if no other value is entered. The default value appears in the field until another value is entered.

✦ Validation Rule: A rule that data must pass before it is entered. This property works with the Validation Text property rule. A Validation Rule property that applies to a whole record is in the Properties sheet. (You find more on validation rules later in this chapter.)

✦ Required: Specifies that the field must have a value in order for you to save the record. When no value is entered, Access doesn't create a new record when Tab or Enter is pressed, and the New Record button is grayed out. Required is also accessible from Datasheet view — it is a check box on the Datasheet tab of the Ribbon.

✦ Allow Zero Length: Specifies whether a zero-length entry such as " " (quotes without a space between them) is allowed (only for Text, Memo, and Hyperlink fields). A zero-length field allows you to differentiate between information that doesn't exist, and a null value (blank) that is unknown or hasn't been entered. When this option is set, it allows a zero-length string in a required field. You may want to use an input mask to make a zero-length field look different from a null value when both are allowed.

✦ Indexed: When you choose to index a field, you can specify that no duplicate values are allowed in the field. This property is also accessible from Datasheet view — it is a check box on the Datasheet tab of the Ribbon.

The rules that keep your data honest and help keep bad data out are sometimes called *data-integrity* rules. You can change a field property that controls data integrity (filters out garbage data) in a field that already has data — Access tells you (when you ask to view the datasheet) that the data-integrity rules have changed and gives you the option of checking existing data against the new rules.

Access only tells you whether existing data violates the new rules — it doesn't flag the offending records in any way.

The rest of this chapter covers input masks, validation rules, and the Lookup Wizard, which allows you to create drop-down lists and pick from existing data, eliminating the possibility of misspelling a new entry.

When you use both the Format field property and an input mask, the field property is used, and the input mask ignored.

Using Input Masks to Validate and Format Data

An *input mask* both formats the data and defines the type of characters and the order they can be entered. Input masks have two intertwined functions:

+ **They format data by adding punctuation or changing the look of certain values (for example, displaying asterisks instead of the text of passwords).**

+ **They block any data that doesn't fit the mold from being entered.** For instance, you can't enter twelve characters if the input mask specifies four, and you can't enter a digit followed by three letters if the input mask specifies two letters followed by two digits.

Use input masks when you know the form the data should take — for instance, a ten-digit phone number, a nine-digit ZIP code, or an item number that must be two letters followed by three or more digits.

In fact, a manually entered input mask is even more flexible than this because you can, say, require two digits and then allow a third, and the same with letters. See Table 5-1 for more details on defining a custom input mask.

Using the input mask, you can add formatting characters — for instance, you can add parentheses and a hyphen to phone numbers. And you can change the way a value appears — for instance, by choosing to display a date as 27-sep-06 or 9/27/06, or by displaying hyphens in a Social Security number. The input mask for the field is in effect when you enter data into the field from either a datasheet or a form.

If the data in a field varies or is not easily described, the field is probably not a good candidate for an input mask. For example, street addresses come in too many formats to describe easily, so making an input mask for an Address field is difficult. You can create input masks for Text, Number, Date/Time, and Currency field types; other data types don't have the Input Mask field property.

You can use an input mask with a validation rule to protect a field from data that is incorrect or that just doesn't belong there. Validation rules give you more flexibility in limiting the data you can enter — and there's more about them later in this chapter.

Input masks are commonly defined in Design view, where they become part of the field definition, and apply in forms also. However, you can also add input masks to queries and forms where data may be entered, and the input mask is defined only for that object. In all cases, you have to add an input mask from the Design view.

Using the Input Mask Wizard

The easiest way to create an input mask is to use the Input Mask Wizard. The wizard can help you create the input mask for your data — especially if the data in the field is a common type of data, such as a phone number or a ZIP code.

If your data is similar to one of the data types in the Input Mask Wizard, you may want to use the wizard and then edit the input mask in Design view.

To create an input mask with the Input Mask Wizard, follow these steps:

1. **Display the table in Design view.**

Right-click the table name in the Navigation and choose Design view.

2. **Select the field you want to apply an input mask to by clicking the record selector, or put the cursor somewhere in the row for that field so that you see its field properties.**

3. **Click the `Input Mask` field property on the General tab of the field properties.**

Access displays the Build button to the right of the Input Mask line.

4. **Click the Build button.**

Access displays the Input Mask Wizard, shown in Figure 5-1.

5. **Select the input mask that looks the most like the data that you want to allow in the field.**

You may see an exact match for your field, or you may see a pretty close approximation that you can edit to fit your data.

You can add an input mask to the list displayed in the wizard by clicking the Edit List button in the first window of the Input Mask Wizard and then filling in the details of the new input mask.

6. **Click in the Try It box and type some text to see how the field appears with data in it and the input mask applied.**

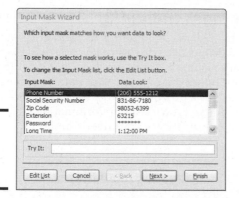

Figure 5-1:
The Input
Mask
Wizard.

Access displays a Try It box on each window so that you can see the effect of any changes you make — click in the Try It box to see what the input mask looks like when you enter data in the field.

7. **Click Next to see more questions about the input mask.**

   The questions you see depend on the type of data you chose in the first window; you may not see all the options in the next three steps.

8. **Edit the input mask, if you want to, using the characters listed in Table 5-1 (later in this chapter).**

   Access displays the input mask it has created, and you have the opportunity to edit it.

9. **Choose a placeholder character and then click Next to see the next window of the wizard.**

   A *placeholder* is a character that holds a place for every character that the user needs to enter so that the user can see that he needs to enter five characters or whatever the input mask defines. Choose a placeholder character from the drop-down list.

10. **Choose how to store the data and then click Next to display the final window of the wizard.**

    If you include punctuation or other additional characters in your input mask, you can choose how to save the data being entered — either save the characters entered plus the extra characters, or just the characters entered. Generally, you don't need to save the extra characters.

11. **Click Finish to tell the wizard to put the input mask it created into the `Input Mask` property for the field.**

    Access displays the Design view with the new input mask.

12. **Save the table design by clicking the Save button on the toolbar — otherwise you may lose your nifty new input mask!**

Creating an input mask manually

To create an input mask manually, enter a series of characters in the Input Mask property of the Field Properties pane to tell Access what kind of data to expect. Data that doesn't match the input mask cannot be entered. To block data from a field, first figure out exactly what data you want to allow in a field, and then use the characters in Table 5-1 to code the data in the Input Mask field property. If you have trouble formulating an input mask, you may find that a validation rule meets your needs better.

Table 5-1	Creating Input Masks
Input Mask Character	**What It Allows/Requires**
0	Requires a number
9	Allows a number
#	Allows a space, converts a blank to a space, allows + and -
L	Requires a letter
?	Allows a letter
A	Requires a letter or number
a	Allows a letter or number
&	Requires any character or a space
C	Allows any character or a space
<	Converts the following characters to lowercase
>	Converts the following characters to uppercase
!	Fills field from right to left, allowing characters on the left side to be optional
\	Displays the character following in the field (\Z appears as Z)
. ,	Displays the decimal placeholder or thousands separator
; : -/	Displays the date separator (The symbol used depends on the setting in the Regional Settings section of the Windows Control Panel.)
Password	Creates a password-entry text box; any character typed is stored as that character but displays as an asterisk (*)

Here's how to use characters to create some common input masks:

✦ **AA00999:** Requires two letters or numbers followed by two digits and then allows an additional three digits.

+ **00000-9999:** ZIP codes — this mask requires five digits, displays a hyphen, and provides space for an optional 4 digits.

+ **L0L 0L0:** Canadian postal codes — this mask requires a letter, a number, a letter, displays a space, requires a number, a letter, and a number.

+ **99:00:00 >LL:** Long time format — allows two digits, displays a colon, requires two digits, displays a colon, requires two digits, displays a space, requires two letters, which are displayed in uppercase.

Creating a Lookup Field

You want your database to be as easy to use as possible, right? But you also want data entered consistently. As orders are entered, for example, you want the name of each product entered so that Access can find it in the Products table. But what's the chance that the product name, entered as part of an order, actually matches the exact product name listed in the Products table? Pretty minimal . . . unless you create a lookup field.

A *lookup field* provides the user with a list of choices, rather than requiring users to type a value into the datasheet. You could think of it as adding a field from an existing table to your new table. Access uses the field from the other table to create a drop-down list of products that you carry for users to choose from as orders are entered. Lookup fields enable you to keep your database compact and the data entered accurate and consistent. Lookup fields are very useful — and not as complicated as they sound.

The items on the drop-down list can come from a list you type, or they can be from a field in another table. Storing values for your drop-down list in a table gives you much more flexibility if you want to modify the list or store additional information about the values. (For instance, if your list contains state abbreviations, you may also decide to include full state names and even state tax rates.) Storing the drop-down list data in a table enables you to display one field (for instance, the customer's full name) and store another (such as the customer number). Working with the logical relationship you set up between tables, you can store less data — thus keeping the database compact — and entering and manipulating your data is easy. So here's the hint — in almost all cases, it's better to keep the values for your lookup in a table; it gives you much more flexibility to work with your data.

When you have two tables with a one-to-many relationship, the values of the connecting field may be perfect for a lookup field. When you enter records in the detail table (the *many* table in the relationship), the foreign key (related field) needs to match the primary key of the master (*one*) table. Consider making the foreign key in the detail table a lookup field — with the primary field in the master table providing the list of possible values. For example, if you have a Products table (the master table) and an Order Detail table (the detail table), make the Product Code field (or whatever field identifies the product the customer is ordering) in the Order Detail table a lookup field, using the Product Code field from the Products table as the list of values. (You can find more information on relationships in Book I, Chapter 3 and in Chapter 6 of this minibook.)

Using the Lookup Wizard

An easy way to create a lookup field is with the Lookup Wizard. In this example, we show you how to use the Lookup Wizard to enter the Customer ID number (stored in the Address Book table) in the ContactID field in the Orders table. The Orders table lists information about each order, one record per order. Fields include the order date, the contact ID, payment, and shipping information. Items ordered are stored in the Order Details table.

Display the table you want set up to contain the lookup table in Design view and follow these steps:

1. **In the top half of Design view, find the field that you want to contain the drop-down list. Click the down arrow to display the Data Type drop-down list. Select the Lookup Wizard option. In our example, this means that you view the Orders table and select the ContactID field.**

   Access launches the Lookup Wizard.

   Alternatively, if you haven't yet created the field that will be the lookup field, display the table in Datasheet view, click any cell in the last column (the one labeled *Add New Field).* Click Modify Lookup in the Fields and Columns group of the Modify Fields tab on the Ribbon to launch the Lookup Wizard.

2. **Tell the wizard whether the values you want to appear on the field's drop-down list come from a field in another table or from a list that you type. Click Next.**

   Storing the values in a table is easier, even if you have to cancel the wizard and create a new table!

   If you don't want the drop-down list to display every value in the field in another table, you can base the drop-down list on a field in a query. Find out all about queries in Book III. For instance, if you want to retain discontinued products in the Products table, but not allow those products to be entered in new orders (that is, the lookup list), you could create a query that displays only products that are currently available.

3. **Choose the name of the table (or query) that contains the data that you want to appear in the drop-down list. Click Next.**

   If you want to see queries, click the Queries button. Click the Both button to show the names of both tables and queries.

If you tell Access that you want to type in the values, a table appears in which you can type the lookup list. Click in the table in the wizard window (which currently has only one cell), and type the first entry in the list. Press Tab — not Enter — to create new cells for additional entries. Skip to Step 7.

4. **Tell Access which field(s) you want to display in the drop-down list by moving field names from the Available Fields list box to the Selected Fields list box.**

   Double-click a field to move it from one column to the other. Select multiple fields to display multiple fields on the drop-down list. For instance, you may display the `Company`, `First Name`, and `Last Name` fields in the drop-down list.

   Access always adds the primary key of the table that contains the data for the drop-down list to the list of selected fields, and it always saves the value of the primary key field. While you may see and select from another field — for instance, the `First Name` and `Last Name` fields — the primary key of the Address Book table (which is called `ContactID` in this example) is the value that is stored. Generally, this is exactly what you want (even if you don't know it). If you're sure that you don't want the primary key stored, you can customize the lookup field after the wizard finishes its business.

5. **If you select more than one field (or only one field that isn't the primary key), select a field to sort by. Then click Next.**

   Using this window (shown in Figure 5-2) you can sort by up to four fields. Click the Ascending button to sort in descending order. (The button toggles between ascending and descending — click it to change from one to the other.) In this example, we sort first by last name.

6. **Format your drop-down list — change the width of columns to fit your data, change the order of columns, and choose whether to hide or display the primary key field. Then click Next.**

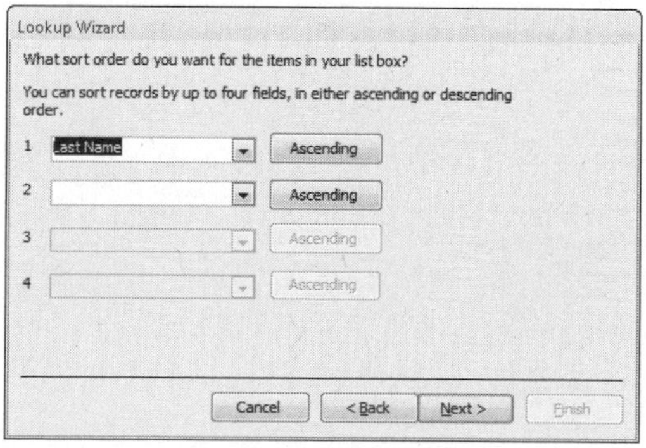

Figure 5-2:
Change the
way your
lookup list
looks.

Lookup Wizard

What sort order do you want for the items in your list box?

You can sort records by up to four fields, in either ascending or descending order.

1 Last Name ▼ Ascending

2 ▼ Ascending

3 ▼ Ascending

4 ▼ Ascending

Cancel   < Back   Next >   Finish

This window shows you a table with the values in the lookup list. You can change the width of the columns by clicking and dragging the border between field names; to automatically fit the widest entry, double-click the right edge of the field name that appears at the top of the column. You can change the order of columns by clicking the field name to select a column and then dragging the column to a new position.

The window also contains a check box, which, when selected, hides the key field. Depending on your application, you may want to display the key field by deselecting the Hide Key Column check box.

7. **In the final window, change the label (the field name) for the lookup column if you want to, and choose whether you want to Enable Data Integrity or Allow Multiple Values. (See Figure 5-3.)**

If you choose to Enable Data Integrity, you are telling Access to make sure that the two (or more) fields linked by the lookup option contain identical data. Data Integrity is covered in detail in Chapter 6 of this minibook.

A multiple value field allows the user to select more than one value for the field in each record when entering data. See the next section for more details.

When you have completed the options on the page, click Finish.

Access may tell you that you have to save the table before relationships are created — why argue? — go ahead and save the table. A relationship is created automatically between the table with the new field and the table with the field that appears in the drop-down list when you use the Lookup Wizard (more about that in a minute).

View your table in Datasheet view to see your new lookup field. When you click within the field, you see an arrow to display a drop-down list. Go ahead and display the list. (See an example in Figure 5-4.)

Figure 5-3:
Name the
new field
and decide
whether
you want
to Allow
Multiple
Values.

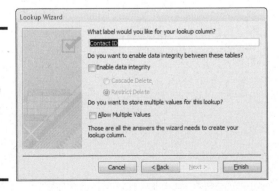

TIP

To make changes to the field by using the Lookup Wizard again, place the cursor in any value in the field (in the datasheet) and click the Modify Lookup button in the Fields & Columns section of the Modify Fields tab.

Figure 5-4: To input data, click the arrow to display the lookup list and click the option you want to use.

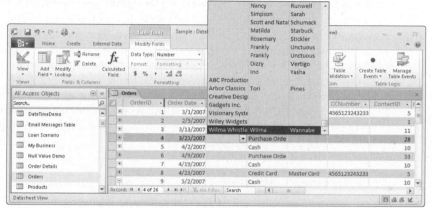

The default setting allows users to choose from the drop-down list or type in a value. To force users to choose from the drop-down list (or to enter a value that's on the drop-down list), display the table in Design view, click the Lookup tab in the field properties, and change the `Limit to List` property from the `No` setting to the `Yes` setting. Figure 5-5 shows Lookup properties. You may also want to enforce referential integrity, as covered in Chapter 6 of this minibook.

Figure 5-5: You can use the Lookup tab in the field properties to edit the lookup field.

Contact ID	Number

Field Properties

General | **Lookup**

Display Control	Combo Box
Row Source Type	Table/Query
Row Source	SELECT [Address Book].[ContactID], [Address Book].[Compar
Bound Column	1
Column Count	4
Column Heads	No
Column Widths	0";1";1";1"
List Rows	16
List Width	3"
Limit To List	Yes
Allow Multiple Values	No
Allow Value List Edits	Yes
List Items Edit Form	
Show Only Row Source V	No

The type of control to use to display this field on forms.

Using the Lookup Wizard creates a relationship between the table containing the lookup field and the table containing the data shown in the drop-down list for the lookup field — in our example, the relationship is between the `ContactID` field in the Orders table and the `ContactID` field in the Address Book table. If you display the Relationships window (click the Relationships button on the Database or Database Tools tab of the Ribbon), you see the relationship that the Lookup Wizard created. (You can find out more about relationships in Chapter 6 of this minibook.)

When to use the Allow Multiple Selections option

When you select the Allow Multiple Selections check box in the Lookup Wizard, your lookup list looks like Figure 5-6. Access creates a hidden join table to store the many-to-many relationship between the two tables — in this case, the Employee table and the Role table — involved in the lookup. In this case, the multiple value lookup is used to define multiple employee roles. For instance, if Matt is both a Manager and a Systems Administrator, a multiple value field lets you define him as both. You can run a query to find all managers and see Matt in the list, or to find all Systems Administrators and see Matt in that list also.

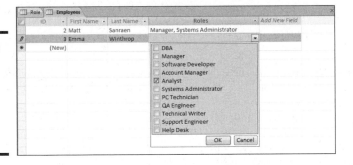

Figure 5-6:
The user can select multiple options in this drop-down list.

Allowing multiple selections in a lookup field can be a tremendously convenient feature if it is used correctly. It shouldn't be used when you need to add other information about the choice. For instance, in our Order Details table we don't want the item ordered to be a multiple value field even though a customer may, in fact, order multiple items. Instead we need each item ordered to have its own record so that we can record how many of the items the customer wants, and so we can do calculations with that data down the line (that is, to calculate the order total).

Access doesn't really store multiple values in one field — that would break the laws of good database design. Instead it creates a hidden join table. This intermediate table is the join table in the many-to-many relationship between the two tables. Although it's more work to set up the join table yourself, in many situations it is the right choice to make. You can then create a form to make data entry as quick as it would be with a multiple-selection lookup field.

Be aware that if you ever want to upsize your database to SQL server, the multi-value feature doesn't convert well, but if you're staying in Access or SharePoint, it's a great feature when used correctly.

Modifying the lookup list

Adding values to an existing lookup list is pretty easy. If the lookup list gets its values from a table, just add records to the table to see additional choices in the lookup list. If you typed values for the lookup list yourself, switch to Design view, click the field with the lookup, and click the Lookup tab in the field properties. (Refer to Figure 5-5.) You can add options to the Row Source property — just be sure to separate the values with semicolons.

Book II
Chapter 5

Avoiding "Garbage
In, Garbage Out"

Validating Data as It's Entered

Often, you are able to formulate a rule that data must pass before being entered in a certain field. For instance, you may know that the date is not before 1999, that the price is zero or greater, or that the entry must be five characters and begin with P. The Validation Rule field property (in field properties) enables you to specify a rule that data in a single field must pass in order to be entered in a particular field. Field validation rules are entered in the Validation Rule property for the field. Figure 5-7 shows a validation rule for the Order Date field.

Figure 5-7:
The Order Date field uses a validation rule to make sure the date is after December 31, 2005.

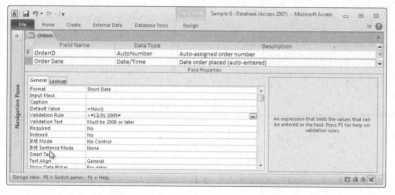

If you just want to require that a value be entered, set the Required field property to the Yes setting.

You can also specify a validation rule for a record (rather than a field). Record validation allows you to create a rule to prevent internal inconsistency in a record — for instance, you may want to check that the ship date is not before the order date. You can enter record-validation rules in the `Validation Rule` property, one of the table properties. Display Table Properties by clicking the Property Sheet button on the Design tab (when the Table Design view is displayed). Figure 5-8 shows a record validation rule.

Figure 5-8:
Use the `Valida-tion Rule` property on the Table property sheet to establish a rule for the record.

Table 5-2 shows a few examples of validation rules. If you have a complicated validation rule, read up on creating expressions in Book III. Use expressions the same way in validation rules as you do in query criteria. If the expression is true, then the data can be entered; if the expression is false, the validation text displays, and the data cannot be entered. Criteria are covered in Book III, Chapter 1. (Expressions are covered in detail in Book III, Chapter 2.) The Build button that appears next to the Validation Rule box when you are entering a rule displays the Expression Builder, which is also covered in Book III, Chapter 2.

Table 5-2	Validation Rule Examples
Rule for the Field	*Validation Rule*
Date not before 2006	`>#12/31/05#`
Price zero or greater	`>=0`
Five characters beginning with P	`Like P????`
Ship date equal to or later than order date	`[Ship Date]>=[Order Date]`

If a user attempts to enter data that does not pass a validation rule, the contents of the `Validation Text` field property pop up to guide the user, using the text you enter. Generally, the validation text guides the user to enter the right data. An exception may be if you don't want to give away too much information — maybe PO numbers are always two letters followed by three or more numbers, but you don't want users to guess at a PO number. Your validation text can simply say `Enter a valid PO number`.

The validation text cannot be longer than 255 characters.

Use operators to tell Access how to validate your data. *Operators* are symbols, (such as < and >) and words (such as `AND, OR,` and `NOT`) that tell Access how to limit your data. (Although +, –, *, and / are also operators, you aren't as likely to use them in validation rules.) You can also use expressions that include functions to create validation rules.

The validation rule cannot be longer than 2,048 characters.

To create a validation rule, follow these steps:

Book II
Chapter 5

Avoiding "Garbage
In, Garbage Out"

1. **Display the table in Design view.**

2. **Select the field to which you want to add a validation rule.**

    Place the cursor anywhere in the row that displays the field and data type, or click the record selector to select the field. When the field is selected, or when the cursor is anywhere in its row, you see the field properties for that field.

    If you want to create a record validation rule, click the Properties button on the Design tab of the Ribbon.

3. **Click in the `Validation Rule` property.**

4. **Type your validation rule.**

    Table 5-3 tells you how to create your validation rule.

5. **Enter an explanatory message in the `Validation Text` property.**

    Validation text appears when data entered into the field does not meet the validation rule. In most cases, you want this script to be helpful for the user to understand why the input was not accepted. (In some cases, you may not want someone to make up data that passes the validation rule, so your validation text may be more cryptic.)

You can test data entered prior to the validation rule by one of two methods:

✦ Clicking the Test Validation Rules button in the Tools group of the Design tab on the Ribbon

✦ Displaying the datasheet by clicking the View button and clicking the Yes button when Access asks whether you want to test existing data

Table 5-3	Creating Validation Rules
Validation Rule Example	*How It Works*
`"Boston" OR "New York"`	Limits input in the field to just those two cities
`Is Null`	Allows the user to leave the field blank
`<10`	Allows values less than 10
`>10`	Allows values greater than 10
`<=10`	Allows values less than or equal to 10
`>=10`	Allows values greater than or equal to 10
`=10`	Allows values equal to 10
`<>0`	Allows values not equal to 0
`In("Boston", "Concord")`	Allows text that is *Boston* or *Concord*
`Between 10 And 20`	Allows values between 10 and 20

The `Like` operator deserves its own explanation. Use the `Like` operator to test whether an input matches a certain pattern — use wildcard characters, such as the ones shown in Table 5-4, to help define the pattern.

Table 5-4	Using the Like Operator
Wildcard	*What It Signifies*
`?`	Any single character
`#`	Any single number
`*`	Zero or more characters

For example, you may define a ZIP code field to only allow five digits, as follows:

```
Like "#####"
```

You can also define a field to contain only names that start with the letter `S`, as follows:

```
Like "S*"
```

According to the preceding rule, a person can choose not to type any characters after the S, because the * wildcard allows zero or more characters. If you always want a certain number of characters to follow the S, use the ? wildcard instead. If you want users to type exactly three characters after the letter S, use this validation rule:

```
LIKE "S???"
```

You can use more than one expression in a validation rule by separating the expressions with AND, OR, or NOT. AND and NOT limit the entries that pass the rule. In the case of AND, an entry must pass both rules; in the case of NOT, an entry must pass one rule and fail the other. Using OR increases the likelihood that an entry passes the rule, because the entry only needs to pass one of the two rules separated by OR.

Chapter 6: Relating Your Tables and Protecting Your Data

In This Chapter

✔ Creating relationships between tables

✔ Protecting your relationships with referential integrity

✔ Using cascading updates and deletes to protect data integrity

✔ Printing the relationships between tables

Relational database-management systems such as Microsoft Access exist because the real world often requires that we store large amounts of data. And often, one-to-many or many-to-many relationships exist between pieces of data. For example, any one customer may place many orders (a one-to-many relationship). Any one order may be an order for many different products. In a school, any one student may enroll in many courses. Any one course has many students enrolled in it.

When information is spread across multiple tables, the data must always "link up" correctly. For example, if customer Hortense Higglebottom places an order on April 1st for five lawn flamingoes, the records from the various tables that record that information must jibe perfectly, so that she gets what she ordered, she pays the right amount for what she bought, and her five lawn flamingoes are sent to the correct address — and so she doesn't end up getting 37 Golden Whistles instead. The technical term for making absolutely sure that all the pieces line up correctly, at all times, is *referential integrity*. But before we get to the specifics of how you enforce referential integrity in your database, we provide you with a brief review of all the buzzwords and concepts surrounding the whole idea of storing chunks of data in separate tables.

Book I, Chapter 3 describes relationships among tables from a design perspective.

When two tables are related in a one-to-many relationship, the table on the "one" side of the relationship must have a primary key field that uniquely identifies each record. For this reason, the table on the "one" side is often referred to as the *master table*. For the customers-and-orders example, the Address Book table is on the "one" side of the relationship, and the primary key field, ContactID, has a unique value for each record — that is, each customer listed in the table has a value in the ContactID field that is unique to him. If we want to refer to a customer anywhere else in the database, we can use that unique ContactID value as a shortcut. (See Figure 6-1.)

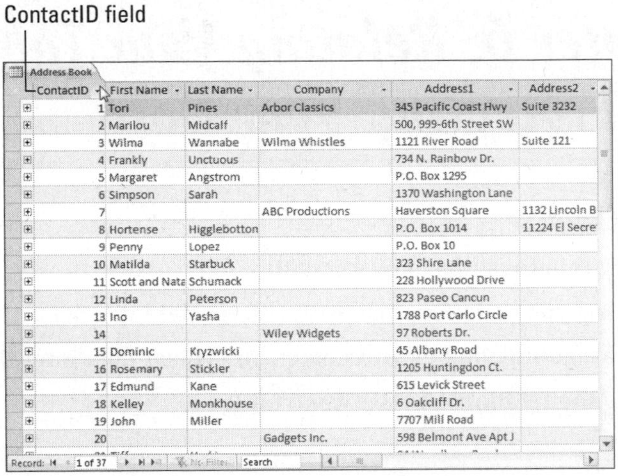

ContactID field

Figure 6-1:
The Address
Book table
has the
`Contact
ID` field as
its primary
key. The
field value
can be used
to identify
customers
in other
tables in the
database.

Address Book					
ContactID	First Name	Last Name	Company	Address1	Address2
1	Tori	Pines	Arbor Classics	345 Pacific Coast Hwy	Suite 3232
2	Marilou	Midcalf		500, 999-6th Street SW	
3	Wilma	Wannabe	Wilma Whistles	1121 River Road	Suite 121
4	Frankly	Unctuous		734 N. Rainbow Dr.	
5	Margaret	Angstrom		P.O. Box 1295	
6	Simpson	Sarah		1370 Washington Lane	
7			ABC Productions	Haverston Square	1132 Lincoln B
8	Hortense	Higglebottom		P.O. Box 1014	11224 El Secre
9	Penny	Lopez		P.O. Box 10	
10	Matilda	Starbuck		323 Shire Lane	
11	Scott and Nata	Schumack		228 Hollywood Drive	
12	Linda	Peterson		823 Paseo Cancun	
13	Ino	Yasha		1788 Port Carlo Circle	
14			Wiley Widgets	97 Roberts Dr.	
15	Dominic	Kryzwicki		45 Albany Road	
16	Rosemary	Stickler		1205 Huntingdon Ct.	
17	Edmund	Kane		615 Levick Street	
18	Kelley	Monkhouse		6 Oakcliff Dr.	
19	John	Miller		7707 Mill Road	
20			Gadgets Inc.	598 Belmont Ave Apt J	

Record: 1 of 37   No Filter   Search

The table on the "many' side of the relationship needs to contain a field that has (preferably) the same name, and (definitely) the same data type and field length as the primary key in the master table. In the table on the "many" side of the relationship, that field is referred to as the *foreign key*. Because that table contains the foreign key, it's often referred to as the *detail table*. In the customers-and-orders example, the Orders table is the detail table. Each order placed is listed in the Orders table, and the customer who placed the order is identified by his `ContactID` number. Taken together, the primary key and foreign key are often referred to as the *matching keys*. (There's a load of technical jargon for ya.)

You can see how the one-to-many relationship plays out when the two tables contain data. In Figure 6-2, looking up which orders are placed by Margaret Angstrom is easy; the `ContactID` happens to be 5.

In any given database, one-to-many relationships likely occur between several tables. A *many-to-many* relationship is just two one-to-many relationships among three tables, as we show in the Students-and-Courses example in Book I, Chapter 3. And in the orders example, there is a many-to-many relationship between products and customers. But you don't have to do anything special to define a many-to-many relationship. When you link two tables to a common third table, you create a many-to-many relationship.

Figure 6-3 shows relationships defined in an Access database. In the Relationships window, field names with a picture of a key to the left of the name are primary keys. The connecting lines show how the tables relate. In that example, the number 1 on a connection line represents the master table — the table on the "one" side of the relationship. The many symbol (an infinity sign, or sideways 8) represents the detail table — the table on the "many" side.

Figure 6-2: The Orders table uses the `Contact ID` field from the Address Book table to identify customers.

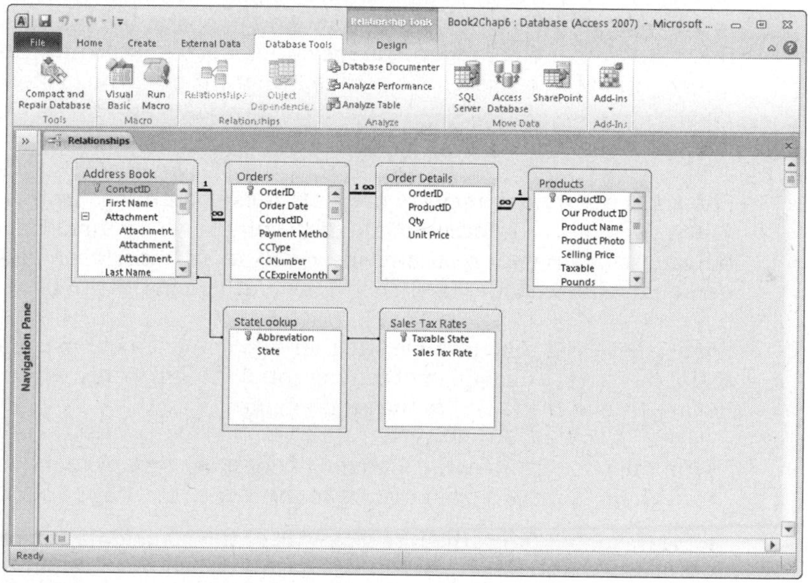

Figure 6-3: Multiple one-to-many relationships exist among the tables in this database.

Creating Relationships and Protecting Your Data with Referential Integrity

We're not referring to your personal relationships. (Well, maybe we are in an abstract sort of way.) Before you join two tables in the Relationships window, think about whether you want Access to enforce referential integrity between those tables. *Referential integrity,* as the name implies, is all about making sure that the relationship between two tables doesn't turn to total garbage.

To see how you convert a one-to-many relationship to garbage, consider the following scenario. Suppose a table named Products contains a primary key field named `ProductID` that uniquely identifies each record. Say a hammer in that Products table has a `ProductID` value of `232`.

The Order Details table in that same database *also* has a field named `ProductID`, which is the foreign key. Say 100 hammers are ordered to date, and 100 records in the Order Details table have the number `232` in their `ProductID` fields.

So now someone comes along and decides to change the hammer's `ProductID` code to `98765`. Or instead of changing the hammer's `ProductID`, that person just deletes that product from the Products table altogether. Either way, a record in the Products table no longer has a `ProductID` value of `232`.

So what becomes of the 100 records in the Order Details table that still have `232` in their `ProductID` fields? Do we leave them referring to the now non-existent record `232`? If we do that, we destroy the referential integrity of the relationship between the tables. How, you may ask, did we manage to do that? Well, a bunch of records in the Order Details table now point to absolutely nothing — there's no way to tell what product the customer bought. The referential relationship between the Products and Order Details tables has lost its integrity.

Enforcing referential integrity prevents these bad things from happening. When you enforce referential integrity, you prevent yourself from accidentally messing up your relationships. (Well, okay, that doesn't apply to your personal relationships, even abstractly, but you get the point.)

Some rules exist to determine whether you can even choose to enforce referential integrity. You can enforce referential integrity only when all the following are true of the tables in the relationship:

✦ In the master table, the matching field must be a primary key, or a field with its `Indexed` property set to the `Yes (No Duplicates)` setting.

✦ In the detail table, the foreign key is of the same data type as the primary key. Or, if the primary key is an AutoNumber field, the foreign key is a Number field with its `Field Size` property set to the `Long` width.

✦ Both tables are stored in the same Access database.

Deciding on the best path to take

Assuming all the rules for enforcing referential integrity are met — see the previous section for a refresher — you're ready to get started. Just keep in mind that you have a choice between these two distinct types of referential integrity you can enforce:

✦ **Cascade Update Related Fields:** This option ensures that if the value of the primary key field changes in the master table, the same change "cascades" to all records in the detail table. (This option doesn't apply if the primary key is an AutoNumber field. ***Remember:*** After an AutoNumber field receives a value, that value never changes.)

✦ **Cascade Delete Related Records:** This option ensures that if a record is deleted in the master table, all corresponding records in the detail table are also deleted.

You can choose to enable referential integrity as soon as you join two tables in the Relationships window — more about said window later. You can change or disable referential integrity options at any time, so you're not making a lifelong commitment or anything.

Opening the Relationships window

The place where you actually join tables and enforce referential integrity between them is called the Relationships window, the same window you see back in Figure 6-3. Clearly then, if you want to be able to set up referential integrity between two tables, you're going to need some hints on how to open the Relationships window. What the heck — how about some explicit instructions, such as the following . . . ?

1. **If any tables are open, close them.**

Access can't create a relationship if one of the tables involved is open.

Relationships

2. **Click the Relationships button in the Relationships group on the Database Tools tab of the Access Ribbon.**

Access opens the Relationships window.

The Relationships window may be empty when you first open it, but if we know you, it won't be that way for long; you can (and probably will) add tables to the window at any time, as the next section makes clear. It's possible that some relationships may have already been created, too, even if you don't remember creating them. There are ways to define relationships that don't use the Relationships window, such as using the Lookup Wizard.

Adding tables to the Relationships window

After the Relationships window is open, you can add tables to it by performing the following steps:

Show
Table

1. **Click the Show Table button on the (Relationship Tools) Design tab of the Ribbon.**

The Show Table dialog box appears.

2. **Click the name of any table you want to add to the Relationships window, and then click the Add button.**

Repeat Step 2 as many times as you wish to add multiple tables to the Relationships window. You can select multiple tables by holding down the Ctrl key as you select table names.

3. **Click the Close button in the Show Table dialog box.**

The Show Table dialog box closes and — voilà — the tables you chose are visible in the Relationships window. Not the entire table, of course. That would be too big. Only a *field list* that shows the names of all the fields in the table displays for each table you select. You can move those field lists around by dragging their title bars. You can size them by dragging any corner or edge.

Setting referential integrity between two tables

When you have two or more tables in the Relationships window, you can define their relationship and referential integrity. Here's how:

1. **Click the matching key in either table to select that field name.**

For example, if you're joining the Address Book and Orders tables shown in Figure 6-3, you click the ContactID field in either table.

2. **Drag that selected field name to the corresponding field name in the other table, and drop it there.**

The Edit Relationships dialog box, shown in Figure 6-4, opens.

3. **If you want to turn on referential integrity, select the Enforce Referential Integrity check box.**

The Cascading options (beneath the Enforce Referential Integrity check box) are now enabled.

4. **If you want matching records in the detail table to update automatically when the value of a primary key field changes, select the Cascade Update Related Fields check box.**

5. **If you want matching records from the detail table deleted automatically after you delete a record in the master table, select the Cascade Delete Related Records check box.**

Figure 6-4:
The Edit Relationships dialog box.

6. **Click the Create or OK button to save your changes and close the Edit Relationships dialog box.**

   (The OK button replaces the Create button when you edit an existing relationship, as opposed to creating a new one.)

If you join two tables without enforcing referential integrity, the connecting line (or the *join* line) in the Relationships window is just a thin black line, as shown in the top two tables in Figure 6-5. If you enforce referential integrity, the connecting line displays a 1 near the master table, and a "many" symbol (an infinity sign, or sideways 8) near the detail table, as shown in the bottom two tables in Figure 6-5.

The relationship you define is not etched in stone. You can change the relationship between two tables at any time.

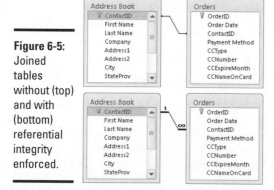

Figure 6-5:
Joined tables without (top) and with (bottom) referential integrity enforced.

Editing and deleting relationships

To change or delete the relationship between two tables in the Relationships window, you first need to select the relationship you want to change. Selecting a relationship is trickier than you think. Follow these steps to select the join line that represents the relationship you want to change:

1. **In the Relationships window, right-click the join line that you want to change or delete.**

   You see the options shown in Figure 6-6. If you see different options, you right-clicked too close to a table. Clicking directly on the line can be tricky: Try right-clicking nearer to the center of the join line you want to change.

2. **Choose from the following:**

   • If you want to delete the line (which deletes the relationship and turns off referential integrity), choose the Delete option.

- If you want to change something about the relationship, choose the Edit Relationship option.

If you choose the Edit Relationship option, the Edit Relationships dialog box opens, where you can change or disable referential integrity. Make your changes, and then click OK.

The Join Type button in the Edit Relationships window allows you to set a default join type to be used in queries. Join types have no bearing on referential integrity. See Book III, Chapter 1 for more on Join Types.

Figure 6-6:
Right-click a
connecting
line to
delete or
change it.

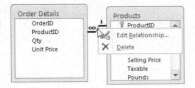

Referential Integrity with Many-to-Many Relationships

As we discuss in Book I, Chapter 3, a many-to-many relationship often exists among chunks of data. For example, a school has many students, enrolled in many different courses. To design a database that contains information about students, courses, and enrollment, you need three tables. One table, perhaps named Students, contains a record for each student with a primary key field named StudentID that uniquely identifies each student.

A second table, perhaps named Courses, contains one record for each course with a primary key named CourseID that uniquely identifies each course. To keep track of which students are enrolled in which courses, you need a third table (called a *junction table)* that contains a record that pairs a StudentID with a CourseID. For the sake of the example, say the junction table is named Enrollments, as in Figure 6-7. When looking at data in the tables, you see how each record in the Enrollments table links a student to his or her courses.

The same tables, and same relationships, link any given course to the students who are enrolled in it, as shown in Figure 6-8.

While a many-to-many relationship is conceptually its own beast, Access recognizes only one-to-many relationships. To set up referential integrity among the tables, you don't create a "special" many-to-many join. Rather, you just connect the fields and enforce referential integrity on each join line, as shown in Figure 6-9.

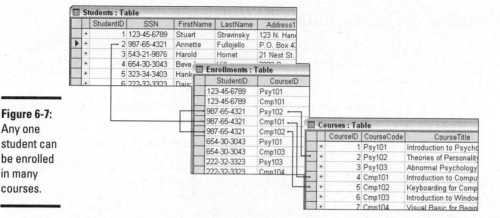

Figure 6-7:
Any one student can be enrolled in many courses.

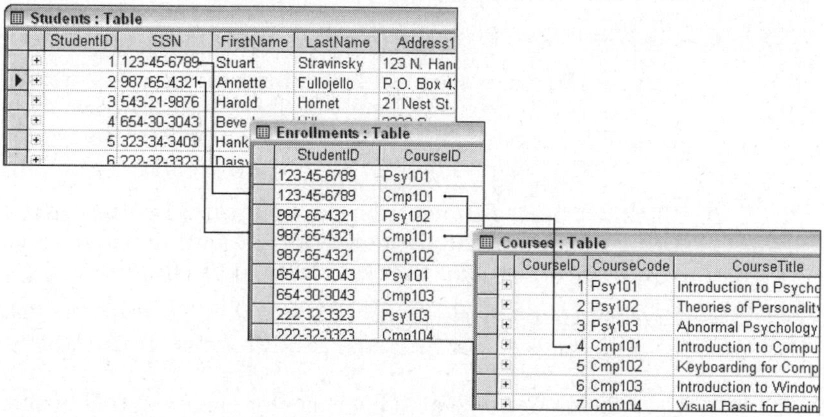

Figure 6-8:
Any one course contains many students.

Figure 6-9:
The relationships among the Students, Courses, and Enrollments tables are set to enforce referential integrity, as indicated by the 1 and infinity symbols.

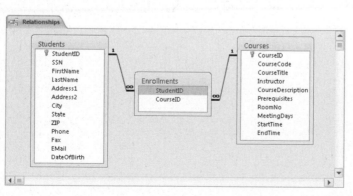

Printing the Relationships Window

You can print a copy of your Relationships window at any time. Doing so is not necessary. But if you'd like to have a printed copy to refer to in the future, you can just follow these steps:

1. **First make sure the Relationships window is open and looks just the way you want the printed copy to look.**

2. **Click Relationship Report on the (Relationship Tools) Design tab.**

   The printer won't start churning right away. Instead, a preview of what the printer will print appears in a new window.

3. **Click the Print button on the Ribbon.**

   Now the printer actually prints the relationships.

4. **Click the Close Print Preview button on the Print Preview tab.**

   A Report Design screen suddenly opens, but don't be alarmed. It appears in case you want to save a copy of the Relationships window as an Access Report. If you haven't gotten into reports yet, and don't know what that means, don't worry about it. You can just continue with the next step.

5. **Click the Close (X) button in the upper-right corner of the Report Design window, and then click the No button when asked whether you want to save the changes made to the Report.**

   You return to your Relationships window. To close the Relationships window, click the Close (red X) button in its upper-right corner.

As we said, you don't need to concern yourself with this business of reports right now, so don't worry about the weird stuff that happens when you print your Relationships window. But just so you know, Access reports are covered in Book V.

Book III

Queries (or Getting Information from Your Data)

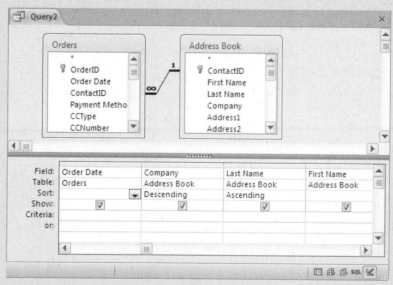

Selecting fields for a query

Contents at a Glance

Chapter 1: Creating Select Queries

In This Chapter

✔ Seeing what queries do — and what kind of queries you can make

✔ Creating a select query with a wizard

✔ Creating and editing a select query in Design view

✔ Using criteria and sorting to get the data you want from your queries

✔ Using query datasheets to enter and edit data

✔ Saving your queries

Queries are a way to ask questions of your data. Do you want to know who ordered a lawn flamingo? Which customers live in California? Which orders contain items that have been discontinued? What your top-ten bestselling items are? Queries can tell you all that and more.

Like tables, which we cover in Book II, queries have two views: Design view and Datasheet view. In Design view, you define your query — you tell Access which fields you want to see, which tables they come from, and the criteria that any record has to meet in order to appear on the resulting datasheet. In Datasheet view, you see the fields and records Access finds that meet your criteria.

You can use queries to do the following:

✦ Look at data from related tables.

✦ Look at *subsets* of your data — a selective slice that meets certain criteria that you specify.

✦ Sort and alphabetize data.

✦ Create new calculated fields.

You can make as many queries as you want to — usually some are made on the fly and not saved, and some are saved and used as the basis for forms and reports.

To create a query, you need to know what data — more specifically, which fields — you want to see and which tables those fields are in. As you define the query, you may have criteria that limit the data. After you define the query, you can view the data in a datasheet (or a form, a report, PivotTable, or PivotChart to see the data in a different format). The datasheet created by a query is dynamic — that is, you see the data that meets the query definition each time you view the datasheet. If data has been added, edited, or deleted, the query datasheet may display different data.

To create a query, you use either a wizard or Design view (or both) to tell Access which data you want to see. The easiest way for a beginner to create a query is to use the Simple Query Wizard, but after you understand queries, you may prefer to go right to Design view.

We start this chapter by telling you about the different types of queries that Access offers, and then introduce you to Design view. This chapter concentrates on select queries, which are the most common type of query, and the skills you use to create select queries. Then we guide you through creating a query, using the Simple Query Wizard. The Simple Query Wizard provides some features that are difficult for beginners to add in Design view, such as summary fields. Because the Simple Query Wizard doesn't allow you to define criteria (such as limiting records to those ordered this month, or only viewing products that cost more than $20), you probably want to move quickly to the next sections on using Design view and criteria. At the end of the chapter, you find all the details on working with your query data in a datasheet. Use the two tools together to get the data you want.

If you want to send a query through Access to an SQL database you need to create a pass-through query. See Book IX, Chapter 2 for more information.

Types of Queries

The many different types of queries that Access provides give you many different ways to select and view specific data in your database. You choose the type of query, choose fields you want to see, and define criteria to limit the data shown as necessary.

These types of queries are available in Access:

✦ **Advanced Filter/Sort:** The simplest kind of query, Advanced Filter/Sort allows you to find and sort information from a single table in the database. This option is available from any datasheet by clicking Advanced in the Sort & Filter group of the Home tab on the Ribbon and choosing Advanced Filter/Sort. Advanced Filter/Sort is covered Book II, Chapter 3.

✦ **Select Query:** A *select* query selects the data you want from one or more tables and displays the data in the order in which you want it displayed. A select query can include criteria that tell Access to filter records and display only some of them. Select queries that display individual records are detail queries; those that summarize records are Totals or Summary queries.

✦ **Totals or Summary Query:** These queries are a subset of select queries, but they allow you to calculate a sum or some other aggregate (such as an average) rather than displaying each individual record. (Totals queries are covered in Chapter 2 of this minibook.)

✦ **Parameter Query:** A parameter query asks you for one or more pieces of information before displaying the datasheet.

✦ **AutoLookup Query:** An autolookup query fills in information for you. (AutoLookup queries are covered later in this chapter.)

✦ **Action Query:** Action queries change your data based on some set of criteria. Action queries can delete records, update data, append data from one or more tables to another table, and make a new table. (We describe action queries in Chapter 3 of this minibook.)

✦ **Crosstab Query:** Most tables in Access, including ones generated by queries, have records down the side and field names across the top. Crosstab queries produce tables with the values from one field down the side and values from another field across the top of the table. A crosstab query performs a calculation — it sums, averages, or counts data that is categorized in two ways, as defined by the row and column labels. (Crosstab queries are covered in Chapter 4 of this minibook.)

Select queries are the most common type of queries used in Access. In fact, select queries are the most general type of query, and all the other query types add features to select queries. When you define a select query, you use the design grid to select which fields and records to display in the new datasheet. The skills you use to define select queries are also used to define the other types of queries.

Creating a Query in Design View

If you're completely new to queries, this section is for you. Here, we create a simple select query so you can see what, exactly, a query does.

Just follow these steps to create a simple query:

1. **Display the Create tab on the Ribbon.**

2. **Click the Query Design button in the Macros &Code group.**

Access displays Design view and the Show Table dialog box, as shown in Figure 1-1.

3. **In the Show Table dialog box, select the table that contains the fields you want to display in the query datasheet, and then click the Add button.**

Queries can show data from more than one table, but for this example, we're showing you a simple query that shows data from only one table.

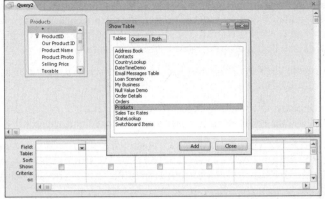

Figure 1-1:
Start your
query by
selecting
the table
that has the
data you
need.

4. **Click the Close button in the Show Table dialog box.**

   Design view displays the table you selected in its top pane and the empty design grid in its bottom pane.

   Notice the new tab that's available when you're working on a query design — the Design tab. It contains many options to help you refine your query.

   You can close the Query Property sheet if it's displayed — you don't need it right now. Redisplay it at any time by clicking Property Sheet in the Show/Hide group of the Design tab on the Ribbon.

5. **Double-click a field name in the top pane to display that field name in the bottom pane — the design grid. Repeat to include any additional fields.**

   You can drag a field name to the design grid or double-click a field name to move it to the grid. You can also use the drop-down Field and Table lists in the design grid to select the fields that you want to use. To select multiple field names in the Field list, use the standard Ctrl-click or Shift-click selection techniques, and then drag all selected field names to the design grid.

   Figure 1-2 shows the query we created, asking to view three fields from the Products table — the `ProductID`, `Product Name`, and `Selling Price` fields.

6. **Click the View button (the first button on the Design and Home tabs) to see the datasheet with the data selected by your query.**

   Our datasheet, shown in Figure 1-3, shows the three fields we put in the design grid.

Table used in query

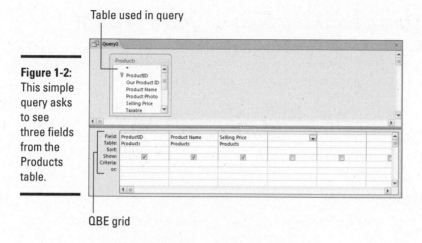

Figure 1-2:
This simple query asks to see three fields from the Products table.

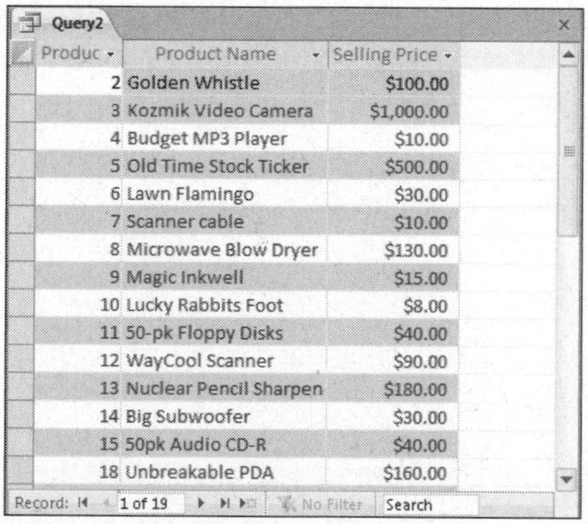

QBE grid

Figure 1-3:
The datasheet shows the data we asked for in the Query Design view.

**Book III
Chapter 1**

**Creating Select
Queries**

If you want to save the query, click the Save button on the toolbar. Give the query a name that indicates the data it selects. Remember that the next time you open the query in Datasheet view, you see updated data — if any records have been added, deleted, or modified, the query reflects that. You may choose not to save the query if you won't need it again. Just close it and then click the No button when Access asks whether you want to save it.

Now that you have the hang of what a query is, you're probably ready for more — getting summary data out of a query, sorting the results, limiting results with criteria, and so on. Read on!

Creating a Query with the Simple Query Wizard

The Simple Query Wizard does a great deal of the work of creating a query for you. It's most useful when you want to use fields from different tables and when you want a query that summarizes your data.

The Simple Query Wizard gives you the option of creating either a summary (totals) query or a detail query. A *detail query* lists every record that meets your criteria. A *summary query* (also called a *totals query*) performs calculations on your data to summarize it. You can create a summary query if the fields you choose for the query include both of the following:

✦ A field with values

✦ A field with repetitions or a field with dates, used to group the values

A summary query gives you the option of totaling (summing), averaging, counting the number of values in a field, or finding the minimum or maximum value in a field. A summary query creates new calculated fields that you can use in other queries or in reports.

Need an example? Here's one: If you have a field that lists the amount spent and a field that lists the dates on which the money was spent, the Simple Query Wizard creates a summary query for you that sums the amount spent by date. Pretty neat, huh?

Ready to give the Simple Query Wizard a spin? Just follow these steps to use the wizard to create a query:

1. **Display the Create tab on the Ribbon and then click the Query Wizard button.**

2. **Select Simple Query Wizard from the New Query dialog box and then click OK.**

    Access displays the first window of the Simple Query Wizard, as shown in Figure 1-4.

3. **Use the Tables/Queries drop-down list to choose the first table or query that you want to use fields from.**

    Many queries are based on tables, but you also have the option of basing a query on another query. For instance, maybe you already created a query to select sales data from only the year 2009. Now, without modifying the original query, you want to create a query that lists 2009 sales by state, or limits the analysis to just a few salespeople.

    When you select a table or query, fields from that object appear in the Available Fields list box.

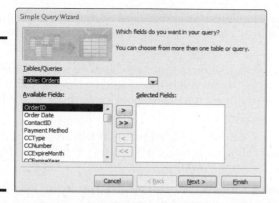

Figure 1-4:
Choose
fields
for the
query —
they can
come from
more than
one table.

4. **Move the fields you want to use in the query from the Available Fields list to the Selected Fields list by double-clicking a field name (or by selecting the field name and then clicking the > button).**

5. **If you're using fields from more than one table or query, repeat Steps 2 and 3 to add fields from the additional tables or queries to the Selected Fields list; then click Next.**

   From this point on, the windows you see depend upon the types of fields and the type of query (detail or summary) you choose.

6. **Choose the type of query you want: Detail or Summary. Depending on your selection, do one of the following:**

   - *If you choose a summary query,* click the Summary Options button.

   - *If you choose a detail query,* click Next and jump to Step 9.

   The Summary Options window displays, as shown in Figure 1-5, where you tell the wizard how to summarize each field. Use these summary calculations carefully. In some cases, you may need to write a calculation in the query to get the data that you need — the summary options may not be sufficient.

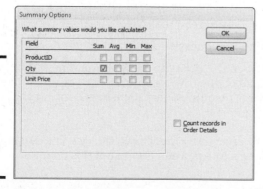

Figure 1-5:
Choose
how to
summarize
your data
using these
options.

7. Choose how to summarize your data and click OK to close the Summary Options dialog box. Then click Next to see the next window of the wizard.

Use the check boxes to indicate the new fields you want Access to create. For example, if you want to add all the values in the Qty field (to calculate how many items have been sold), select the Sum check box in the row for the Qty field.

Don't overlook the Count check box(es) that may appear in this window: Selecting a Count check box tells the wizard to create a field that counts the records within each grouping.

8. If the fields being summarized can be grouped by a Time/Date field, you will see a window where you can choose to group data by date. Choose the time interval the records should be grouped by and then click Next.

You won't see this window if your data doesn't contain a Time/Date field.

For example, if you choose to include the Order Date field in the query and to sum the Qty field, you can group by month to see how many of each item you sold in each month. You can choose to display totals by the following date grouping options: Day, Month, Quarter, or Year. The Unique Day/Time option groups records by each unique date and time; if your data includes times, each record with the same date and time is grouped together. If your data includes only a date without the time, each record from the same day is grouped together (the same as the Day option).

9. Type a name for the query in the box at the top of the window.

Choose from these options:

- *Open the Query to View Information:* This option shows you the query in Datasheet view.

- *Modify the Query Design:* This option shows you the query in Design view.

- *Display Help on Working with the Query:* Select this check box if you want to see the help screen that covers working with a query.

10. Click Finish to view the query.

If you chose the Open the Query to View Information option, you see the query in Datasheet view. If you chose the Modify the Query Design option, you see your resulting query datasheet, looking something like what you see in Figure 1-6.

You can edit the query created by the Simple Query Wizard using Design view, about which there's lots more in the rest of this chapter.

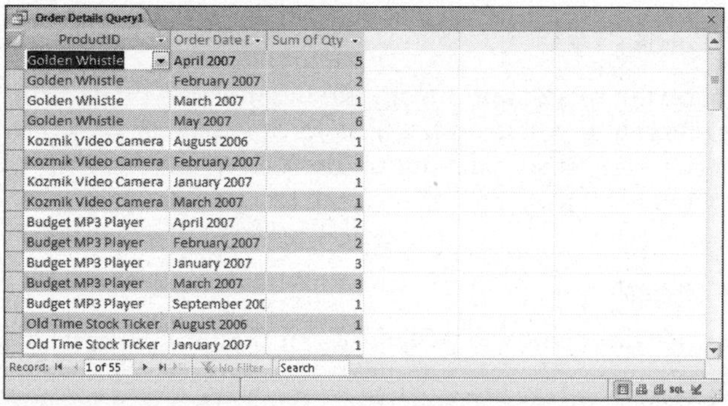

Figure 1-6:
The
datasheet
shows data
summarized
by product
and date.

ProductID	Order Date	Sum Of Qty
Golden Whistle	April 2007	5
Golden Whistle	February 2007	2
Golden Whistle	March 2007	1
Golden Whistle	May 2007	6
Kozmik Video Camera	August 2006	1
Kozmik Video Camera	February 2007	1
Kozmik Video Camera	January 2007	1
Kozmik Video Camera	March 2007	1
Budget MP3 Player	April 2007	2
Budget MP3 Player	February 2007	2
Budget MP3 Player	January 2007	3
Budget MP3 Player	March 2007	3
Budget MP3 Player	September 200	1
Old Time Stock Ticker	August 2006	1
Old Time Stock Ticker	January 2007	1

The Simple Query Wizard doesn't allow you to include criteria to choose which records you want to include in the query datasheet. If you want to include criteria in your query, open the query created by the wizard in Design view and add the criteria. (Details of Design view appear throughout this chapter.)

Viewing Your Query

After you create a query, you can look at it in any of these views:

✦ **Design view** displays the query definition where you can select tables, fields, create criteria, expressions, define sort order, and all the other things you need to do to define a query.

✦ **Datasheet view** displays the data from the query in a datasheet, just as if you were looking at a table datasheet.

✦ **SQL view** displays the query definition as a statement in SQL (Structured Query Language).

✦ **PivotTable** and **PivotChart views** summarize and chart the data from the query. (See Chapter 4 of this minibook for how to create PivotTables, and see Book V, Chapter 3 for how to create PivotCharts.)

The quickest way to view a query is to double-click the query name in the Navigation pane. When the query is open in Datasheet view, switch between Design and Datasheet views by clicking the View button (the left-most button on the Home tab of the Ribbon). To see the query in SQL view or one of the pivot views, use one of the five buttons in the bottom-right corner of the Access window; or, use the arrow on the View button to open the drop-down list of View options, and select the correct view.

Understanding Design View

If you're following this chapter from the beginning, you created a simple, one-table query, and you used the Simple Query Wizard to create another query. Queries can do so much more, though, so dive into Design view and figure out what's what.

Design view

Design view is where you tell Access about the data you're looking for. In Design view, you specify the tables (or other queries) where Access finds the data you want, the fields from those tables that you want to see, and any criteria that the data must pass in order to appear in the datasheet. You also use Design view to choose the type of query, specify calculations, and define the sort order of the resulting data.

The top half of Design view is the Table pane, where you view the tables (or queries) with fields that you will use in the query. The bottom half is the Query By Example (QBE) grid where you define the fields you want to see and any criteria to limit the data you want to see. Queries can do even more than that, as you'll see in the remainder of this minibook.

Here are our two favorite ways to display a query in Design view (shown in Figure 1-7):

Table names   Table pane

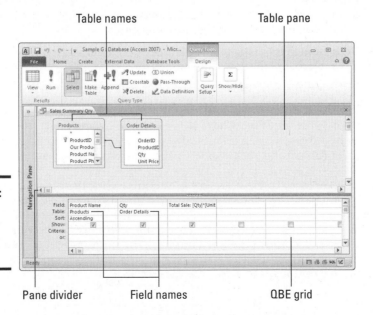

Figure 1-7:
A query
displayed
in Design
view.

Pane divider   Field names   QBE grid

✦ Click Queries in the Navigation pane, right-click the query name, and choose Design View.

✦ Click the View button on the Home tab of the Ribbon when the query is displayed in Datasheet view.

Table 1-1 explains what the most useful buttons on the Query Tool Design tab on the Ribbon do. (See Figure 1-8.)

Figure 1-8:
The buttons
of the
Query Tools
Design
Ribbon.

Table 1-1		Buttons in Design View
Button Name		*What It Does*
	View	Displays Datasheet view — the data set defined by the query.
	Run	Runs the query. (For a select query, clicking the Run button does the same thing as clicking the View button. When the query is an action query, the Run button performs the action. Use this button carefully.)
Query Type	Query Type group	Choose a query type: Select Query, Crosstab Query, Make-Table Query, Update Query, Append Query, or Delete Query. Union, Pass-Through, and Data Definition queries are covered in Book IX, Chapter 3.
Show Table	Show Table	Displays the Show Table dialog box so that you can add tables to the query.
Builder	Builder	Displays the Expression Builder dialog box. (This button can be clicked only when the cursor is in the Field or Criteria row.) See more about building expressions in Chapter 3 of this minibook.

(continued)

**Book III
Chapter 1**

**Creating Select
Queries**

Table 1-1 *(continued)*

Button Name	What It Does	
Insert Rows	Insert Rows	Insert a row in the QBE grid.
Delete Rows	Delete Rows	Delete a row in the QBE grid. The row deleted is the one containing the cursor.
Insert Columns	Insert Columns	Insert a column in the QBE grid to the left of the column containing the cursor.
Delete Columns	Delete Columns	Delete the column of the QBE grid (and its contents) that contains the cursor.
Return:	Top Values	Limits the result of the query displayed in the datasheet to the number of records or the percentage of records displayed in this option (for example, All, 5, 25%, and so on). You can choose from the drop-down list, or type values into this option.
Σ Totals	Totals	Displays the Totals row in the design grid. (Use the Totals row to create calculations that summarize your data.)
[?] Parameters	Parameters	Display the Query Parameters box.
Property Sheet	Property Sheet	Displays properties for the selected field or Field list.
XYZ Table Names	Table Names	Hides and displays the Table row in the QBE grid.

You can change the size of the panes in Design view by dragging the pane divider. Just move the mouse pointer to the divider, where it changes shape; then click, hold, and drag to move the divider.

Working with tables in Design view

The tables in the Table pane (the top pane of the Design View window) are really just little Field list windows that you can move and size the same way you move and size windows. Change the size of a table window by moving the mouse pointer to the border of the window; when the pointer turns into a double-headed arrow, drag the border to change the size of the window. To move a table in the Table pane, drag its title bar. This may come in handy when you work with related tables and want a clear look at the relationships between them.

If your query contains tables that have existing relationships that were defined with lookup fields (or created in the Relationships window), you see those relationships as lines between the related tables. (You can see more about relationships in Book II, Chapter 6.)

Introducing the query design grid

The bottom pane of Design view is technically called the Query by Example (QBE) grid, but is often simply called the "design grid." It's your handy visual aid for defining the data you want to select with your query. Each row in the design grid has a specific purpose. Table 1-2 lists how to use each of them.

Table 1-2	Rows in the Query Design Grid
Design Grid Row	*What It Does*
Field	Displays the name of a field that you want to include in a query.
Table	Displays the name of the table that the field comes from. (Hide/display this row via the Table Names button in the Show/Hide group of the Design tab of the Ribbon.)
Total	Performs calculations in your query. (This row isn't always visible — use the Totals button on the Design tab on the Ribbon to display or hide it.)
Sort	Determines the sort order of the datasheet produced by the query.
Show	Shows or hides a field. (If you want to use a field to determine which records to display on the datasheet, but not actually display the field, remove the check mark from the Show column for the field.)
Criteria	Tells Access the criteria — such as records with values less than 10, or records with dates after 12/3/2005 — for the field in the same column.
Or	Use for additional criteria.

Each of these query features gets more detailed coverage later in this chapter.

Navigating Design view

You can work in Design view by using the mouse (to click the pane that you want) as well as the scroll bars (to see parts of the view that don't fit on-screen). Or, if you prefer, you can use the keyboard to move around.

The keys in Table 1-3 move you around Design view.

Table 1-3	Shortcut Keys in Design View	
Key	*What It Does in the Table Pane*	*What It Does in the Design Grid*
Tab	Moves to the next table	Moves to the next row to the right
Shift+Tab	Moves to the previous table	Moves to the next row to the left
Alt+↓ or F4	Nothing	Displays the drop-down list (if the row has one)
Page Down	Displays more field names in the active table	Displays more OR criteria
Home	Moves to the top of field names	Moves to the first column in the grid

Displaying or hiding table names

You can view table names for each field in the query design in the Table row, or you can choose not to see the Table row.

To make the Table row appear or disappear, use one of these methods:

+ Right-click the design grid and choose Table Names from the shortcut menu.

+ Click the Table Names button in the Show/Hide group of the Design tab on the Ribbon.

Tips for Creating a Query

The "Creating a Query in Design View" section (earlier in this chapter) includes the basics for creating a query in Design view, but you can do so much more. This section delves in to a few more aspects of the Creating Queries story.

Adding tables to the query

To use a table's fields in a query, you have to display the table name in the top pane of the Design view. To do that, you need to view all table names by opening the Show Table dialog box:

+ Right-click the Table pane of Design view and then choose Show Table from the shortcut menu.

+ Click the Show Table button in the Query Setup group of the Design tab on the Ribbon.

After the Show Table dialog box opens, add a table to the query by using whichever of the following methods is most convenient:

✦ Double-click the table name in the Show Table dialog box.

✦ Select the table and then click the Add button.

After you add all the tables that you need, click the Close button in the Show Table dialog box to get back to work in Design view.

To remove a table from a query, just press Delete (on your keyboard) when the table in the Table pane is selected (that is, when any field in the table is highlighted). When a table is deleted from Design view, all the fields in the design grid from that table are deleted, too. Because deleting a table from a query is so absurdly easy — and can have damaging consequences for your query — take care when your fingers get close to the Delete key. And also save your query design often so that you can easily restore a saved version if you accidentally delete something important.

If you want to include a field generated by another query, you can add queries to a query by clicking either the Queries tab or the Both tab of the Show Table dialog box, and then double-clicking the query name.

Inserting fields in a design grid

You can move a single field from the Table pane to the design grid in three easy ways:

✦ **Double-click the field name.** Access moves the field to the first open column in the grid.

✦ **Drag the field name from the Table pane to the Field row of an unused column in the design grid.** This option is popular among dragging fans, or when you want to put a field in a specific location in the grid.

✦ **Use the drop-down list in the Field row of the design grid to choose the field you want.** If you use this method with a multiple-table query, you may find choosing the table name from the drop-down Table list before selecting the field name easier. If you don't have the Table row in your design grid, see the "Displaying or hiding table names" section, earlier in this chapter.

You can place all the field names from one table into the design grid in two ways:

✦ **Put one field name in each column of the grid.** If you have criteria for all the fields, you can put one field name in each column of the design grid in just two steps. Double-click the table name in the Table pane of Design view to select all the fields in the table. Then drag the selected

**Book III
Chapter 1**

**Creating Select
Queries**

names to the design grid. When you release the mouse button, Access puts one name in each column.

✦ **Put all the field names in one column.** This method is useful if you want to find something that can be in any field, you have one criterion for all the fields in the table, or you want to include all the fields in a table without criteria. To tell Access to include all field names in one column, drag the asterisk (above the first field name in each table window) to the grid. The asterisk is also available as the first choice in the drop-down Field list in the design grid — it appears as `TableName.*`.

Editing a Query

If you want, you can do some major reconstruction to your query in the design grid; for example, you can move columns, delete a column, or delete all the entries in the grid.

To do any of those things, though, you first have to select the column in the grid by clicking the *column selector* — the narrow block at the top of each column in the grid.

Table 1-4 lists some of the things you can do to make changes in the design grid.

Table 1-4	Editing Your Query
When You Want To . . .	*Here's What to Do*
Move a column	Click the column selector to select the column, click a second time, and then drag the column to its new position.
Delete a column	Click the column selector to select the column; then press Delete or click the Delete Rows button on the Design tab to delete the column.
Insert a column	Drag a field from the Table pane in Design view to the column in the design grid where you want to insert it. Access inserts an extra column for the new field, moving all other columns to the right to make space for the new column. Or use the Insert Columns button to insert a column to the left of the cursor. Select multiple columns before clicking to insert the same number of columns.
Change the displayed name	Use a colon between the display name and the actual name of the field in the Field row (display name: field name).

Sorting a query

You can sort or alphabetize the results of a query in several ways. The first way is to use the Sort row in the design grid. Use the Sort row to tell Access which field to use to sort the datasheet. The second way is to use the Sort Ascending and Sort Descending buttons on the Home tab of the Ribbon when a datasheet is displayed. (For more on sorting in a datasheet, see Book II, Chapter 3.)

If you sort a query by date, Access alphabetizes the months — which is usually not what you want. Reports, on the other hand, know how to put months in chronological order. If you have monthly data that you want to sort, a report is a better object to use than a query.

To sort by a field, display your query in Design view and follow these steps:

1. **Move the cursor to the Sort row in the column that contains the field by which you want to sort the records that the query selects.**

2. **Display the drop-down list for the Sort row.**

    Access displays the options for sorting: Ascending, Descending, and (not sorted).

3. **Choose to sort in ascending order or descending order.**

You can use the Sort row in the design grid to sort by more than one field. Say that you want to sort the records in the datasheet by last name, but more than one person may have the same last name. You can specify another field (perhaps `First Name`) as the second sort key.

When you sort by using more than one field, Access always works from left to right, first sorting the records by the first field (the *primary sort key*) that has Ascending order or Descending order in the Sort row, and then using the second sort key to sort any records that have the same primary sort-key value.

You can't sort by the following field types: Memo, OLE, Attachments, or multivalue Data Type.

Viewing top values

If all you care about are the top values produced by a query, you can tell Access to find and display only those records. Use the Top Values box on the Design View toolbar to see the top records produced by the query. A value in the Top Values box specifies exactly how many records in the datasheet you want shown; a percentage shows you that percentage of the records that the query finds.

Note that using a percentage does not show values that fall in the top *x* percent; it shows you the top *x* percent of the values. Say you're looking at test scores of 20 students. The test scores fall between 0 and 100 but are mostly in the 80s and 90s. If you ask to see the top 20 percent, Access shows you the top 4 scores (20 percent of 20 records) — *not* the scores that are 80 or higher. To see the scores that are 80 or higher, type the criterion **>=80** in the Test Score column in the design grid.

To display the top values found by a query, follow these steps:

1. **Create your query with all the fields and criteria that you need.**

2. **Choose the field you want to sort by, and then set the Sort row to either Ascending order or Descending order.**

   Access uses this to figure out which top values you're looking for. For instance, if we sort products using the `Selling Price` field, and sort in Ascending order, the cheapest products are at the top of the datasheet. When we ask for the top five prices, we get the five cheapest products. To get the most expensive products, we sort in Descending order so the most expensive products appear at the top of the datasheet.

3. **Change the Top Values option by typing in a value or a value followed by a percent sign.**

   You can also choose a value from the drop-down list. To see the top three values, type in **10**. To see the top three percent of the values, type in **3%**.

4. **Click the View button to see only the top values in the datasheet.**

Hiding fields

You can use fields to sort data — or use criteria for the fields to filter data — without having to display the field in the query datasheet. Deselect the Show check box (in the design grid) when you don't want to display the column in the datasheet. (The next time you open the query in Design view, you find that Access has moved the hidden field(s) to the right side of the grid. If the field is hidden and not used for sort order or criteria, Access removes it from the grid.)

Changing the format of a query field

The format of fields displayed in a query is determined by the field's properties in its native table. If the field is defined as having a currency format in its table, then that's what you see in the query. Note, however, that you can change the format of any field for the query.

To change the format of a field, follow these steps:

1. **In Design view, right-click anywhere in the column that contains the field you want to format, and then choose Properties from the short-cut menu.**

   If a Properties sheet is displayed already, just clicking the field displays the properties for that field.

2. **Click in the `Format` property, and then click the arrow to display the format options.**

   The list of available formats drops down.

3. **Choose a format option from the drop-down list.**

The format options in the Properties sheet are exactly the same as the options for the `Format` property in the field properties for a table, and you can use them exactly the same way. However, when you format a field in a query, you affect how that field appears only in the query datasheet. (Formatting fields is covered in detail in Book II, Chapter 2.)

Limiting Records with Criteria Expressions

In addition to using queries to select only a few fields to show, you may also (even often) use queries to display a limited selection of records. Criteria enable you to limit the records that the query displays. You use the Criteria and Or rows in the design grid to tell Access exactly which records you want to see.

Querying by example

Querying by example — QBE, for short — makes defining criteria easy: If you tell Access what you're looking for, Access goes out and finds it. For example, if you want to find values equal to 10, the criterion is simply `10`. Access then finds records that match — that are equal to 10.

The most common type of criterion is a logical expression. A logical expression gives a `Yes` or `No` answer. Access shows you the record if the answer is `Yes`, but does not show the record if the answer is `No`. The operators commonly used in logical expressions include <, >, `AND`, `OR`, and `NOT`.

Although we use uppercase to distinguish operators and functions, case doesn't matter in the design grid.

If you want to find all the addresses in California, the criterion for the `State` field is simply the following:

CA

You may want to add another criterion in the next line (OR) to take care of different spellings, as follows:

```
California
```

Access puts the text in quotes for you. The result of the query is all records that have either CA or California in the State field.

You can find records with null values by using the Is Null criterion. If you want all records except those with null values, use the Is Not Null criterion.

Using dates, times, text, and values in criteria

Access does its best to recognize the types of data you use in criteria; it relies on its best guess when providing characters to enclose the elements of the criteria expressions you come up with. You are, however, less likely to create criteria that Access doesn't understand if you use those characters yourself.

Table 1-5 lists the types of elements you may include in a criteria expression — as well as the character to use to make sure Access knows the element is text, a date, a time, a number, or a field name.

Table 1-5	Dates, Time, and Text in Criteria
Use This Type of Data . . .	*In an Expression Like This . . .*
Text	`"text"`
Date	`#1-Feb-97#`
Time	`#12:00am#`
Number	`10`
Field name	`[field name]`

You can refer to dates or times by using any allowed format. `December 25, 2009`, `12/25/09`, and `25-Dec-09` are all formats that Access recognizes. You can use AM/PM or 24-hour time.

Year numbers between 0 and 29 are prefixed with 20 (if you enter the year as 20, Access completes the year as 2020). Year numbers between 30 and 99 are prefixed with 19 (enter **45** as the year number, and Access completes the year as 1945). Of course, you have the option of entering all four digits of the year to make sure you enter the year that you want.

Using operators in criteria expressions

Don't be surprised if your criteria are frequently more complicated than "all records with California in the State field." You use operators in your criteria expressions to tell Access about more complex criteria.

Table 1-6 lists the operators that you're likely to use in an expression that specifies criteria.

Table 1-6	Using Operators in Criteria
Relational Operator	*What It Does*
=	Finds values equal to text, a number, or date/time. ("Equal to" is understood when you type a criterion without an operator — you don't need to type it.)
<>	Finds values not equal to text, a number, or date/time.
<	Finds values less than a given value.
<=	Finds values less than or equal to a given value.
>	Finds values greater than a given value.
>=	Finds values greater than or equal to a given value.
BETWEEN	Finds values between or equal to two values.
IN	Finds values or text included in a list.
LIKE	Finds matches to a pattern.

When you type your criterion, you don't have to tell Access the field name. Just put your criterion in the same column as the field, and Access applies the criterion to the field that appears in the same column.

Table 1-7 explains how different criteria affect the records that appear on-screen in the query datasheet.

Table 1-7	Examples of Criteria with Operators
When Field1 Has This Criteria	*These Are the Records You See*
<15	Displays records where Field1 is less than 15.
<#9/1/03#	Finds records where Field1 contains a date before September 1, 2003.
>15	Finds records where Field1 is greater than 15.

(continued)

Table 1-7 *(continued)*

When Field1 Has This Criteria	These Are the Records You See
`>#12:00am#`	Finds records where `Field1` is a time value after 12:00 a.m.
`>[Max Price]`	Finds records where `Field1` is more than the value in the field Max Price.
`<>15`	Finds records where `Field1` is not equal to 15.
`>10 AND <20`	Finds records where `Field1` is between 11 and 19.
`>=10 AND <=20`	Finds records where `Field1` is between 10 and 20, including 10 and 20.
`BETWEEN 10 AND 20`	The same as `>=10 AND <=20`.
`IN ("Virginia", "VA")`	Finds records where `Field1` contains either Virginia or VA.
`LIKE "A*"`	Finds records where `Field1` begins with the letter A. You can use `LIKE` with wildcards, such as `*`, to tell Access in general terms what you're looking for. For more information on the wildcards that Access recognizes, see Book II, Chapter 5.

Using multiple criteria

Often one criterion is not enough. You may want to prune down the records displayed by using multiple criteria for a single field or multiple criteria for different fields. To get the data you want, however, you do need to know how Access combines your criteria.

When you have criteria for only one field, decide whether you want to see records that meet all criteria (in which case, join the criteria with AND) or whether you want records that meet only one criterion (in which case, join the criteria with OR). Of course, you may have three or more criteria, and you can join them with both AND and OR.

To join criteria for a single field with AND, type them into the Criteria line of the grid with AND between them — like this:

```
<5 And >65
```

shows you records with values less than 5 as well as those greater than 65.

To join multiple criteria for one field with OR, use one of these methods:

✦ Type your expressions into the Criteria row, separating them with OR.

✦ Type the first expression into the Criteria row, and type subsequent expressions by using the Or rows in the design grid.

Whichever approach you take, the result is the same — Access displays records in the datasheet that satisfy one or more of the criteria expressions.

When you have criteria for different fields, you join them with either the OR or the AND operator. The operator is implied in the way you put the criteria into the design grid. Here's how that works:

✦ **Criteria on the same row are implicitly joined by AND.** Access assumes that you want to find records that meet all the criteria. If you type criteria on the same row for two fields, a record has to meet both criteria to be displayed in the datasheet.

✦ **Criteria on different rows are joined by OR.** Access assumes that you want to find records that meet at least one criterion. If you type criteria on different rows for two fields, a record has to meet only one criterion to be displayed in the datasheet.

✦ **When you use multiple rows for criteria, the expressions on each row are treated as though they are joined by AND, but each row's worth of criteria are treated as though they are joined by OR.** Access first looks at one row of criteria and finds all the records that meet all the criteria on that row. Then Access starts over with the next row of criteria, the Or row, and finds all the records that meet all the criteria on that row. The datasheet displays all the records that are found. A record has to meet all the criteria on only one row to display in the datasheet.

Using lookup fields in criteria

When you define a criterion for a query, you tell Access what you're looking for either by entering a value or by using a logical expression. However, if you use a criterion to limit the number of records displayed from a lookup field, you have to figure out exactly what value you want to find — and that may not be the value you see in the table. See Book II, Chapter 5 for how to create a lookup field.

How about an example? You want to find orders for the Budget MP3 Player. The Order Details table stores this data, shown in Figure 1-9. Notice that the `ProductID` field is a lookup field — it displays values from the `Product Name` field of the Products table, but stores the values from the Products table primary key field, which is `ProductID`. The Products table is shown in Figure 1-10.

Figure 1-9:
The
`Product`
`ID` field in
the Order
Details table
is a lookup
field.

Figure 1-10:
The
Products
table holds
the data
shown in
the Order
Details table
drop-down
list.

Because the `ProductID` field in the Order Detail table is a lookup field, the criteria need to refer to the value that is stored in the field, not the value that displays. The value stored is the primary key field from the Products table. The value that displays is the product name. If we enter `Budget MP3 Player` for the `ProductID` criterion and then try to view the datasheet, we see a `Data type Mismatch in Criteria Expression` error message. We need to go back to the Products table and find the `ProductID` number for the Budget MP3 Player. (**Remember:** A lookup field always stores the primary key field.)

The `ProductID` for the Budget MP3 Player is 4 (see the third line of Figure 1-10). With that information, we can create the query criteria — it is 4.

Queries with multivalue lookup fields
Multivalue lookup fields make queries a little more complicated. The question is whether you want to display the complete multivalue field with each

value separated by a comma, or to put each value on its own line in the query datasheet. If you want to do complicated analysis with multivalue fields, you may want to reconsider your database design, and add tables and fields to save the same data without the multivalue field.

Although a multivalue lookup field seems cumbersome, it can still give you the results that you want if you simply have your query display the multiple values separated by commas. If you want to deconstruct your data some — and ensure each value in a multivalue field has its own line — add the `Value` property to the field name. Here's how: Instead of just *multivalue field name* in the query grid, enter ***Multivalue Field name.Value***.

In addition to the special instructions about multivalue fields, remember the caveat about lookup fields: The value you see may not be the value that's actually stored. (Fortunately, the preceding section offers tips on using lookup fields in your criteria.)

Working with Multiple Related Tables

One powerful feature of queries is the ability to view related fields from different tables together in a query datasheet. For instance, using our database, we can create a query to list customer name and contact information with order dates and numbers, even though two different tables store the data. The relationship between the two tables is the `ContactID` field, which is the primary key of the Address Book table. The same field, `ContactID`, is in the Orders table — it identifies the customers who placed each order. (For more information about relating tables, see Book I, Chapter 3 and Book II, Chapter 6.)

For Access to display data from different tables, a relationship must be defined between the tables. A relationship between tables is created in one of these ways:

✦ A lookup field exists, creating a relationship between two tables. For more on lookup fields, see Book II, Chapter 5.

✦ A relationship was defined in the Relationships window, as described in Book II, Chapter 6. (Creating a lookup field automatically creates a corresponding relationship in the Relationships window.)

✦ Access automatically creates a relationship when it finds related fields in two tables: that is, if the two fields have the same name and data type, and one of the matching fields is the primary key of its table.

✦ You create a relationship in Query Design view.

When a relationship exists between two tables displayed in Design view, the tables appear joined by a line, as in Figure 1-11.

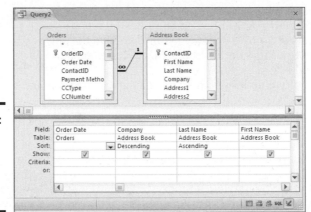

Figure 1-11:
A query
combining
data from
two related
tables.

If you use data from two tables that are not directly related, you have to make sure that any other tables that relate the fields you want to display in the query datasheet appear in the Query Design view.

If referential integrity is enforced, the 1 and ∞ symbols appear on the relationship line to denote the "one" and "many" sides of the relationship. If referential integrity is not enforced, those symbols don't appear on the line. (See Book II, Chapter 6 for more on referential integrity.)

Figure 1-12 shows the result of the query shown in Figure 1-11. Each order is listed once, with the name of the customer. Many customers have multiple orders, so they appear more than once in the datasheet.

Figure 1-12:
This
datasheet
shows the
results of
the query
shown in
Figure 1-11.

OrderID	Order Date	Company	Last Name	First Name
12	5/31/2007	Wiley Widgets		
11	5/25/2007	Visionary Systems, Inc.		
14	8/6/2006	Gadgets Inc.		
13	8/3/2006	Creative Designs		
2	2/5/2009	Arbor Classics	Pines	Tori
15	2/19/2007	ABC Productions		
1	3/1/2009		Angstrom	Margaret
16	2/27/2008		Angstrom	Margaret
8	4/23/2007		Angstrom	Margaret
10	5/24/2007		Escovedo	George
21	1/22/2009		Higglebotton	Hortense
6	4/9/2007		Junket	Jody
18	1/9/2007		Kane	Edmund
22	1/28/2008		Lopez	Penny

Record: 1 of 26   No Filter   Search

Joining tables in Design view

Although you can create or edit a relationship between two tables in Design view, remember that the relationship defined in Design view is used only for the query: It's not used in any other part of the database. You can use a type of join that you may not want to use in the database as a whole, but that you may find useful for a single query (which you may then use as the source data for a form or report). You can also delete a relationship in Design view without deleting the same relationship in the Relationships window. (To delete the join, click the line and then press Delete.)

To create a join, use the Table pane of Design view and follow the same procedure you use when creating a relationship in the Relationship window: You first identify the two related fields (each in a different table) you want to join, and then you drag the field from one table to the related field in the other table. *Voilà!* — a join!

Choosing the type of join and setting join properties

You can edit the join properties of a relationship for the query in Design view. To do so, double-click the relationship line to see the Join Properties dialog box, as shown in Figure 1-13. If you have trouble double-clicking the relationship line, keep trying! The tip of the pointer needs to be right on the line.

The new properties apply only in the current query and not in any other objects in the database except those based on this query.

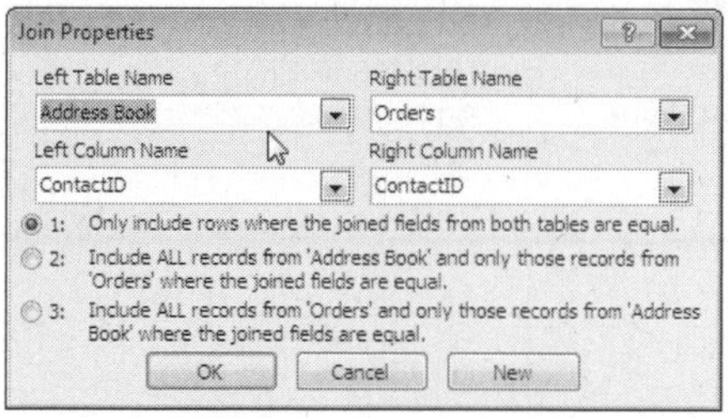

Figure 1-13: The Join Properties dialog box.

> **Join Properties**
>
> Left Table Name
> Address Book
> Right Table Name
> Orders
>
> Left Column Name
> ContactID
> Right Column Name
> ContactID
>
> ○ 1: Only include rows where the joined fields from both tables are equal.
> ○ 2: Include ALL records from 'Address Book' and only those records from 'Orders' where the joined fields are equal.
> ○ 3: Include ALL records from 'Orders' and only those records from 'Address Book' where the joined fields are equal.
>
> OK   Cancel   New

The Join Properties dialog box options are largely self-explanatory, but using the dialog box effectively requires knowledge of a few buzzwords that describe particular types of relationships — but don't appear in the dialog box. The buzzwords — *inner join, left outer join, right outer join* — are included in the descriptions of the following three options:

✦ **Option # 1 (inner join):** A query displaying records from both tables displays only those records that have counterparts in the related table. Records that don't have matching partners in the opposite table are hidden, as though they didn't even exist. This is the default, meaning that if you don't set a join type, this is what you get.

✦ **Option # 2 (left outer join):** A query displaying records from both tables displays all records from the table on the left. From the table on the right, only records that have matching partners from the table on the left appear.

✦ **Option # 3 (right outer join):** A query displaying records from both tables displays all records from the table on the right. From the table on the left, only records that have matching partners from the table on the right appear.

The line that connects two tables in the Relationships view (and in Design view as well) reflects information about how the tables are joined, as shown in Figure 1-14. The arrow points to the table that contributes matching records — all records from the other table display in the query datasheet.

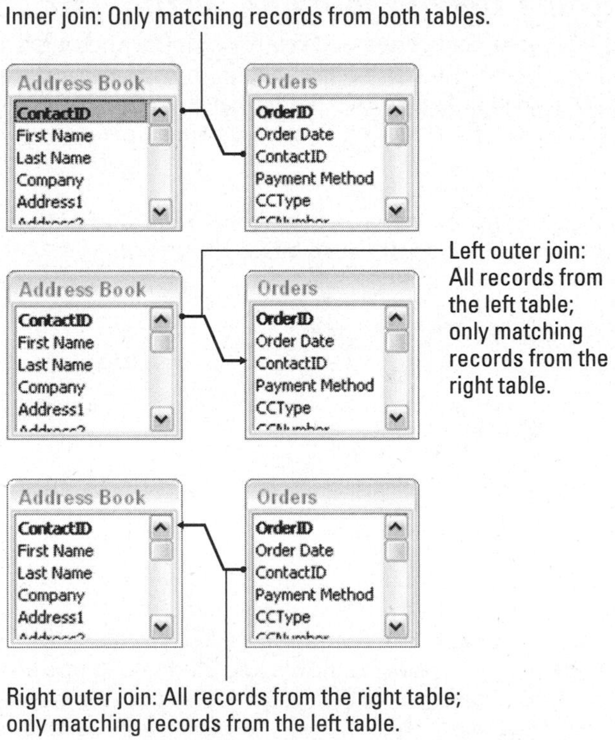

Inner join: Only matching records from both tables.

Left outer join: All records from the left table; only matching records from the right table.

Figure 1-14: Join lines and outer joins.

Right outer join: All records from the right table; only matching records from the left table.

When would you use an outer join? Say you create a sales report and want to see products that haven't sold at all: You want an outer join that shows all the products from the Products table, regardless of whether they appear in the Order Details table.

If you create a query with fields from two tables that don't have a relation-ship defined, Access doesn't know how to relate records, so *every* combina-tion of records between the two tables displays in the datasheet. Generally (as you might expect), these queries won't give you meaningful results.

Working with Query Datasheets

A query datasheet looks a great deal like a table datasheet — you can sort, filter, navigate, and in many circumstances, enter data in the query data-sheet. The data displayed in the query datasheet is sometimes referred to as a "dynaset" — a *dyna*mic sub*set* of your data.

The query result reflects changes in the data in your tables. The actual records displayed in a dynaset aren't stored in the database; only the design of the query is stored. Each time you open the query in Datasheet view, the query definition determines which records appear in the datasheet.

Because working with queries in Datasheet view is similar to working with tables in Datasheet view, turn to Book II for specific instructions on working in Datasheet view.

To toggle between Datasheet and Design view, click the View button, the first button on the Home and Design/Datasheet tabs on the Ribbon.

Using the query datasheet to edit data

In many cases, you can edit the data in the query datasheet and use the datasheet to add new records. Any changes you make are reflected in the table that holds the data you changed; edits are permanent and apply to the underlying tables and not just to the query.

When your query includes fields from multiple tables, you may see some funky things on-screen when you edit data. Not to worry — they're all features!

✦ You may see other data in the datasheet change when you make an edit. If your query includes related tables, you may see repeated data, such as the repeated names in Figure 1-12. If you make edits, you see all the repetitions of the name change when you change one instance. Because you're changing a single record repeated in the datasheet, the other instances change to reflect the change in the underlying table. When this happens, you have happened upon an AutoLookup query. The next sec-tion covers AutoLookup queries.

✦ If your query meets the qualifications of an AutoLookup query, Access may fill in fields after you enter a single value.

If you work with a query datasheet that shows data from multiple related tables, you may not be able to modify data. The rules get complicated, but generally all data on the "many" side of a one-to-many relationship can be updated. Data on the one side usually can be updated if you're not editing the primary key field.

AutoLookup queries to fill in data automagically

AutoLookup queries can be a terrific tool when you want to enter one value (such as a customer number) and see other data from the same table (such as the customer's name, address, and phone number). You may want to use this feature while you enter a new order: You can enter a customer number and see the contact information, and then enter the particulars of the order, such as the date and payment method. You can even create an AutoLookup query and use it as the basis of a form, where it may be more convenient to enter data. AutoLookup queries may sound complicated, but in fact, they're pretty simple.

The AutoLookup feature also works in forms.

The key to creating an AutoLookup query is that you must include the `Join` field from the "many" side of the one-to-many relationship (also known as the foreign key). Then when you enter a value for that field, Access fills in other fields from the "one" side of the relationship automatically.

For instance, the query in Figure 1-15 displays fields from the Orders and Address Book tables. The `ContactID` field comes from the Orders table (the key field on the "one" side, but displayed from the "many" table).

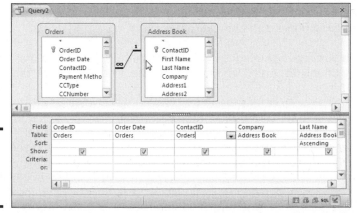

Figure 1-15: An AutoLookup query.

When new orders are entered into the query datasheet, only the customer number needs to be entered. Access automatically fills in the first name, the last name, and other contact information from the Address Book table. The rest of the Order information can then be added.

Saving Queries

A query doesn't store data; it just pulls data from tables and puts it in query datasheets for you to look at. A query is *dynamic* — as you add to or change your data, the result of the query also changes. When you save your query, you're not saving the table that the query produces; you're just saving the query *design* so you can ask the same question again.

You don't have to save a query. Often, you create queries on the fly to answer a question. No need to clutter your database with queries you're unlikely to need again.

That said, you can certainly save a query design when you need to. Use one of the following methods:

 ✦ **In Design or Datasheet view, click the Save button or press Ctrl+S.** If you haven't saved the query yet, Access asks you for a name for the query. Type the name in the Save As dialog box and then click OK.

 ✦ **Close the query (clicking the Close button is a popular method).** If you've never saved the query, or if you've changed the query design since you last saved it, Access asks whether you want to save the query. Click the Yes button to save the query. If you've never saved the query, give it a name in the Save As dialog box and then click OK.

Give your new query a name that tells you what the query does. That way, you won't have to open one query after another to find the one you're looking for.

If you want to create a query similar to one you already have in your database, select or open the query and choose Save As from the File tab of the menu to save the query with a new name. You keep the original query and make changes to the new copy.

If you want to save the query dynaset, create a snapshot query with the data (covered in Book V, Chapter 2) or export the data to its own file, using one or more buttons in the Export group of the External Data tab on the Ribbon. For more about exporting data, see Book II, Chapter 4.

**Book III
Chapter 1**

Creating Select Queries

Importing and exporting queries

If the query you need is in another Access database — or if you create a query that you want to use in another database — simply import or export it. Information on importing and exporting objects is in Book II, Chapter 4.

Chapter 2: Letting Queries Do the Math

In This Chapter

- Doing calculations in queries
- Writing expressions for math
- Going beyond basic arithmetic
- Calculating dates and times
- Manipulating text with expressions
- Writing decision-making expressions
- Creating flexible parameter queries
- Calculating totals, subtotals, averages, and such
- Finding duplicate records

*I*f you ever find yourself doing math to figure out what to put into a field, you made a mistake when designing your table. A table needs only the raw data — the factual information that cannot be calculated from known data. For example, a table may contain `Qty` and `Unit Price` fields to indicate how may items — and at what price — some product was ordered. Having an `Extended Price` or `Subtotal` field in the table is pointless, though, because Access is smart enough to determine that on its own by multiplying the `Qty` field by the `Unit Price` field for you.

Letting Access do the math for you has advantages beyond just saving you the time of doing the calculation yourself. For one thing, Access can do any mathematical calculation, no matter how complex, in less time than you take to blink your eye — and the calculations are always correct. No need to worry about typing a wrong value into an `Extended Price` field, or forgetting to change the field after you change the `Qty` or `Unit Price` fields. Just let Access do all the math.

Doing Math in Queries

Access can do the math for you in queries, forms, reports, and macros. In many cases, you should do the math in a query. That way, any forms, reports, or macros that use the query automatically have access to the calculated value. To do the math in a query, you create a *calculated field* within the query. Unlike a regular field in a query, a calculated field's name doesn't match any of the field names in the tables. In fact, its value doesn't come directly from any field in any table. The calculated field exists only in the query.

A calculated field starts out with a field name, followed by a colon, and then an expression that defines the field's contents, in this order:

```
fieldname: expression
```

where *fieldname* is any name you want (provided it doesn't match the name of a field in a table), and *expression* is a formula that tells the query how to do the math.

Take a look at Figure 2-1, which shows a query in Design view. The first four field names at the top of the Query by Example (QBE) grid — OrderID, Product Name, Qty, and Unit Price — are regular fields that get their values from either the Order Details or Products table in the top pane of the Design View window.

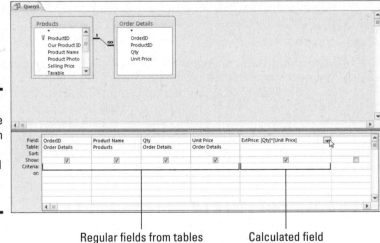

Figure 2-1:
The ExtPrice column is an example of a calculated field in a query.

Regular fields from tables   Calculated field

The last field:

```
ExtPrice: [Qty]*[Unit Price]
```

is a calculated field. The field name is ExtPrice (short for "extended price"). The expression is [Qty] * [Unit Price], which means "the Qty (quantity field) times the Unit Price field."

Figure 2-2 shows the same query as Figure 2-1, but in Datasheet view. Notice two things about this Datasheet view:

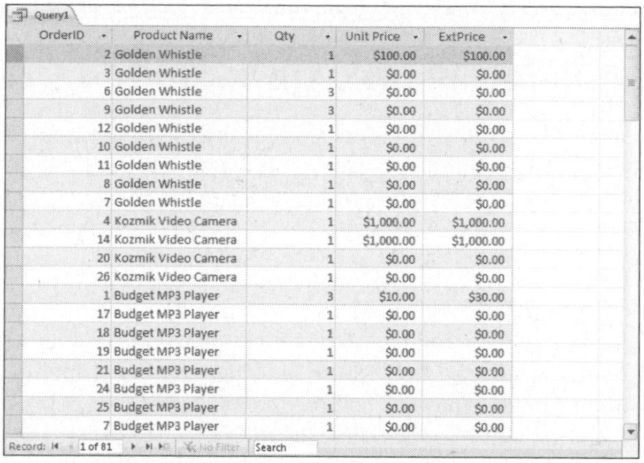

Query1

OrderID	Product Name	Qty	Unit Price	ExtPrice
2	Golden Whistle	1	$100.00	$100.00
3	Golden Whistle	1	$0.00	$0.00
6	Golden Whistle	3	$0.00	$0.00
9	Golden Whistle	3	$0.00	$0.00
12	Golden Whistle	1	$0.00	$0.00
10	Golden Whistle	1	$0.00	$0.00
11	Golden Whistle	1	$0.00	$0.00
8	Golden Whistle	1	$0.00	$0.00
7	Golden Whistle	1	$0.00	$0.00
4	Kozmik Video Camera	1	$1,000.00	$1,000.00
14	Kozmik Video Camera	1	$1,000.00	$1,000.00
20	Kozmik Video Camera	1	$0.00	$0.00
26	Kozmik Video Camera	1	$0.00	$0.00
1	Budget MP3 Player	3	$10.00	$30.00
17	Budget MP3 Player	1	$0.00	$0.00
18	Budget MP3 Player	1	$0.00	$0.00
19	Budget MP3 Player	1	$0.00	$0.00
21	Budget MP3 Player	1	$0.00	$0.00
24	Budget MP3 Player	1	$0.00	$0.00
25	Budget MP3 Player	1	$0.00	$0.00
7	Budget MP3 Player	1	$0.00	$0.00

Record: 1 of 81 No Filter Search

Figure 2-2: The query from Figure 2-1 in Datasheet view.

- The ExtPrice field looks just like any other field.
- The value shown in the ExtPrice column is equal to the value of the Qty field times the Unit Price field in each column.

Even though the ExtPrice column in Datasheet view looks like a regular field, it doesn't behave exactly like a regular field. If you try to change the contents of the ExtPrice field, Access won't let you. The contents of the ExtPrice field in this query *always* show the quantity × the unit price, and cannot possibly show anything else because it's a calculated field.

However, if you change the Qty or Unit Price field in any record, the ExtPrice field instantly — and automatically — changes to show the correct result based on the change you make. If (for example) you change the Qty field in the first record in Figure 2-2 from 1 to 2, the ExtPrice field for that record then shows $200.00.

Follow these steps to create calculated fields in queries:

1. **Create a normal select query, like any of those shown in Chapter 1 of this minibook.**
2. **Add any fields you want the query to display to the Field row of the QBE grid.**
3. **To add a calculated field, pick any empty column, type a unique, new field name into the Field row, followed by a colon (:) and an expression that performs the calculation.**

   What you get will look a lot like the ExtPrice calculated field shown in Figure 2-1.

Zooming in on expressions

The tiny space provided in the Field row of the QBE grid doesn't exactly make typing lengthy expressions easy. In fact, the text may be so small that you have difficulty seeing even when typing a short expression.

To see what you're typing, press Shift+F2 while the cursor is in the calculated field, or right-click in the calculated field and choose the Zoom option from the shortcut menu. The Zoom dialog box opens, showing what you already typed into the field (if anything). You can use all the standard Windows text-editing keys and techniques to type your expression. For example, press the End key to move the cursor quickly to the end of the expression.

To make the text easier to read, click the Font button. In the Font dialog box that opens, choose a larger font size and then click OK in the Font dialog box to accept the change. Type your expression, and then click OK in the Zoom dialog box to copy the expression into your calculated field in the QBE grid.

Your query can contain any number of calculated fields — you're not limited to having just one or two. The big trick, of course, is knowing how to write the expression. When writing expressions, the possibilities are almost endless although some basic tools and rules exist to help you create any expression, as we discuss next.

Writing Expressions in Access

An *expression* tells Access how to perform some calculation. An expression can contain operators, field names, literal text, or all of those — and can also use any of the Access built-in functions. Built-in functions can be mind-boggling, but if you take them one step at a time, you'll soon create them like a pro.

Literal text, in Access jargon, means text that isn't the name of some field or other object. Whereas `LastName` may be the name of a field in a table, `Smith`, `Jones`, and `123 Oak Tree Lane` are all examples of literal text. Always put your literal text in quotes (`"Smith"`). For a classic example of how to use literals, flip ahead in this chapter to the "Using literal dates and times in expressions" section.

Using operators in expressions

An *operator* is a character that operates on data. Some of the more commonly used operators are listed in Table 2-1. The operators are listed in *order of precedence,* meaning the order in which Access does the calculations when an expression contains two or more operators.

Table 2-1	Operators in Order of Precedence	
Operator	*Purpose*	*Example*
( )	Grouping	(2+2)*5 returns 20.
^	Exponentiation (raising a number to a specified power)	5^2 returns 25.
* /	Multiplication, division	5*6/3 returns 10.
+ –	Addition, subtraction	6+6–2 returns 10.
&	String concatenation (connecting chunks of text together)	"Hello" & "There" returns HelloThere.

The order or precedence that operators follow can be a real "gotcha" if you're not careful. Take a look at the following simple expression that includes an addition operator (+) and a multiplication operator (*):

5+3*2

When you do the math, do you get 16 — or do you get 11? If you do the addition first (5 + 3 = 8) and then the multiplication (2 * 8), you end up with 16. But if you do the multiplication first (3 * 2 = 6) and then the addition (6 + 5), you end up with 11. So which is the correct answer, 11 or 16?

Give up? 11 is the correct answer (and the one Access comes up with) because the order-of-precedence rules state that multiplication and division are always performed before addition or subtraction.

Multiplication and division are at the same order of precedence. If an expression involves both of those operations, they're executed in left-to-right order. In the following expression, the division takes place first because it's to the left of the multiplication:

10/5*3

The result of the preceding expression is 6 because 10 divided by 5 is 2, and 2 times 3 equals 6.

Addition and subtraction work the same way. If an expression includes both addition and subtraction, the calculations take place in left-to-right order.

You can control the order of precedence using the parentheses. Access always works from the innermost parentheses to the outermost. The following expression is an example:

5^2+((5–1)*3)

When faced with this expression, Access goes inside the innermost parentheses first (5-1) and does that calculation. So the expression (for a brief instant in time) becomes

```
5^2+(4*3)
```

Access next calculates the remaining pair of parentheses in the expression (4*3). For a brief moment the expression becomes

```
5^2+12
```

Because no more parentheses are left, Access uses the regular order of precedence to do the rest of the calculation. Exponentiation has a higher order of precedence than addition, so for a brief instant the expression becomes

```
25+12
```

Access then does the final math and returns the result, 37.

If you're a real math-head, you'll appreciate that two more operators have the same order of precedence as multiplication and division. One is the \ operator, which returns only the integer portion of a quotient, and the other is MOD (for *modulo*), which returns only the remainder after division. For example, while 16/3 (normal division) returns 5.3333, 16\3 returns 5, and 16 MOD 3 returns 1.

Field names in expressions

If you're thinking, "Big deal, I could have done those preceding calculations on my $2 calculator," that's certainly true. But Access expressions aren't limited to numbers and operators. You can use field names in expressions to perform math on data stored in fields. The sample query shown at the start of this chapter uses the field names [Qty]*[Unit Price] to multiply the value in the Unit Price field by the value in the Qty field.

Technically, you need to enclose field names in square brackets only when the field name contains a blank space, as in [Unit Price]. But you can put square brackets around any field name, just in case (so to speak). For the sake of consistency — and to make the field names in expressions stand out — we always put them in square brackets throughout this book.

The sample expression shown in the first query at the start of this chapter, [Qty]*[Unit Price], is a prime example of using field names in expressions. The expression, in English, simply means "the contents of the Qty field in this record × the contents of the Unit Price field in this same record."

Using functions in expressions

Wait, there's more. An Access expression can also contain any number of functions. A *function* is sort of like an operator in that it performs some calculation and then *returns* some value. How you use a function is different, though. Every function includes a name followed by a pair of parentheses. For example, the `Date()` function always returns the current date.

Many functions accept *arguments,* which are enclosed within the parentheses. To calculate the square root of a number, you use a `Sqr()` function. The `Sqr()` function accepts one parameter — a number, the name of a field, or an expression that contains a number. The `Sqr()` function returns the square root of whatever value passes to it as an argument.

As an example, the following expression returns 9 because the square root of 81 is 9 (because 9 × 9 is 81). In this example, we use a number as the argument to the `Sqr()` function:

```
Sqr(81)
```

Note that in the example, we use 81 as the argument to the `Sqr()` function. Another way to state that is to say we *pass* the number 81 to the argument. In other words, the term *pass* in this context means to use as an argument in a function.

The following `Sqr()` function uses an expression, `5*20`, as its argument:

```
Sqr(5*20)
```

Because the expression, `5*20`, is inside the parentheses, the multiplication happens first. For an instant, the function contains `Sqr(100)`. Then `Sqr(100)` returns 10 because 10 is the square root of 100.

You can use field names in functions as well. Suppose you have a table that contains a number field named `bigNumber`. The following `Sqr()` function returns the square root of whatever value is stored in the `bigNumber` field:

```
Sqr([bigNumber])
```

Dozens of functions are built in to Access. In fact, memorizing all the functions is nearly impossible. We recommend looking up functions as you need them, using Expression Builder as your guide. What's the Expression Builder? Read on and find out.

Using the Expression Builder

Expression Builder is a tool to help you write meaningful expressions using any combination of operators, field names, and functions. To use Expression Builder while creating a calculated field in a query, do the following:

1. **If you haven't saved the current query yet, do so now to name it. (Press Ctrl+S, type in a name for your query in the Save As dialog box, and then click OK.)**

2. **Type a new field name, followed by a colon (:) in the Field row of an empty column in the QBE grid.**

   The *Query by Example grid,* also known as the *QBE grid,* is in the bottom pane of the Design View window. For more on the QBE grid (and its lovely home, the Design View window), see Chapter 1 of this minibook.

3. **Right-click the empty space to the right of the colon you just typed and choose Build from the shortcut menu, or click the Builder button in the Query Setup group on the (Query Tools) Design tab on the Ribbon.**

   Expression Builder opens, looking like Figure 2-3. Any text you already typed into the QBE grid is already in Expression Builder.

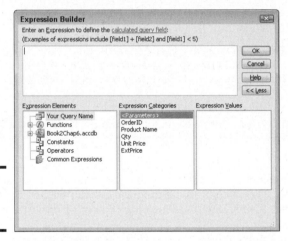

Figure 2-3:
Expression
Builder.

Within Expression Builder, the large white area at the top is where you compose your expression, as shown in Figure 2-4. You can type and edit in that large area using the keyboard and all the standard Windows editing techniques.

Not everything in Expression Builder is geared toward creating expressions for queries. Some features of Expression Builder are better suited to creating expressions in forms and reports. When you're working with a query, the main things you want to focus on are the following:

✦ **Expression:** This is where operators, fields, and functions appear when you choose them from the lower portion of the screen.

✦ **Query name:** Shows the name of the query that's open. When you click your query name, fields from that query appear in the center column. Clicking a field name in that center column adds the name to the expression.

Query name folder   Expression

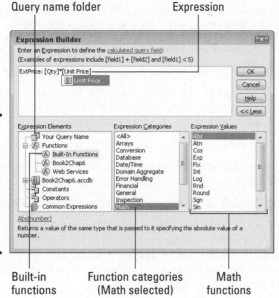

Figure 2-4:
Main
options for
creating
expressions
in a query's
calculated
fields.

Built-in   Function categories   Math
functions   (Math selected)   functions

If you don't save the query before opening Expression Builder, clicking
the Your Query Name folder in Expression Builder won't display
anything!

✦ **Built-In Functions folder:** If you double-click the + sign next to the
Functions folder, a couple of options appear. Click the Built-In Functions
folder to see categories and names of available functions in the center
column. Click a category name in the middle column to see in the right
column, names of functions within that category.

Whatever you insert into your expression is inserted at the blinking cursor's
position or at the end of whatever text is currently in the expression if no
blinking cursor is visible. If you need to move the cursor before inserting
something into an expression, just click at the spot where you want to position the cursor. You can also use the ←, →, Home, or End keys to position
the cursor. Use the Backspace and Delete (Del) keys to delete text in the
expression. To undo your most recent change to an expression, press Ctrl+Z.

Getting help with functions

Just seeing the name of a built-in function in the third column of Expression
Builder doesn't tell you much. You don't know what the function does or
how you use it, but you can get instant information by using the Help button.
Follow these steps to access a Help window:

1. **In the left column of Expression Builder, if the Functions folder has a + sign next to it, first click that + sign to expand the list.**

2. **Click the Built-In Functions folder in the first column.**

The category names appear in the center column.

3. **Click a category name in the middle column to see functions within that category listed in the third column (or click <All> in the middle column to see all functions in the third column).**

The functions for that category appear in the third column.

4. **In the third column, click the name of the function that you want to find out more about.**

5. **Click the Help button at the top right of Expression Builder.**

The Help window for that function opens. If you don't see specific help for the function, type the function name into the Access Help search box. Functions are listed by type in the Help system, so if you need to find a function in the Help system, you'll be able to find it quicker if you know if it's a Financial function, for example.

For instance, select the Financial category of functions in the center column, click the PV function in the third column, and then click the Help button. The Help page that opens not only describes what the PV function does, but it also describes the syntax required for using the function. The *syntax* of a function describes what information you need to pass (provide) to the function for the function to do its calculation and return a result.

The syntax for a function usually looks something like the following:

```
functionName(arg1,arg2,[arg3])
```

where *functionName* is the name of the function, and *arg1*, *arg2*, and *arg3* represent arguments the function accepts. The number of arguments that a function accepts varies. Some functions take no arguments; others take many. If a function accepts two or more arguments, they must be separated by a comma.

Any argument name in square brackets is optional, meaning that you can omit the entire argument.

Whether you use an optional argument or not, never type the square brackets into the function.

A function name is always followed by parentheses — even if the function accepts no arguments. `Now()`, `Sqr(81)`, and `PV(apr,TotPmts,Income)` are all examples of valid function syntax. Note as well that when typing an argument, you can use a literal value (like the name `"Smith"` or the number 10), a field name, or an expression as an argument. The following three expressions all pass literal values to their functions:

```
Sqr(100)
PV(.035,120,250)
UCase("howdy")
```

The next three expressions all pass data from fields to the function (provided that Hypot, Apr, Months, Amount, and Company are the names of fields in the current query):

```
Sqr([Hypot])
PV([Apr],[Months],[Amount])
UCase([Company])
```

In the next examples, we use expressions as arguments:

```
Sqr(227*[Hypot])
PV([Apr]/12,[Months]*12,-1*[Amount])
UCase([First Name] & " " & [Last Name])
```

We know these examples look weird, but we do have a reason for the madness. The ability to pass literal data, field names, and/or expressions to functions gives you a lot of flexibility.

About text in < and > brackets

When you use the buttons in the lower half of Expression Builder to insert text into your expression, that text often includes *placeholders* — text in angle brackets (< >). You may see placeholders, such as *<expr>*, *<interval>*, *<npers>*, or something equally bizarre in Expression Builder. Each of these brackety things is a placeholder for an argument that you need to type in.

If a placeholder represents an optional argument and you don't plan to use that argument, you can just delete the placeholder. If the placeholder represents a required argument, though, you need to replace the placeholder with valid data. Using the Help feature often when working with functions is very important. We doubt that anybody has ever managed to memorize all the functions because of the sheer number, all supporting so many different arguments.

Nesting functions

You can *nest* functions, meaning you can put a function inside another function. Because Access always works from the innermost parentheses outward, the inside function is always calculated first. For example, the Date() function always returns the current date. (It requires no arguments.) The WeekDay() function accepts any date as an argument, meaning its syntax looks like the following:

```
WeekDay(date)
```

Because the `Date()` function always returns a date, you can use it as the argument to the `WeekDay()` function. The expression turns out to be

```
WeekDay(Date())
```

A number between 1 and 7 returns, indicating which day of the week today is. If the current date is the 23rd, for example, and that day is a Tuesday, the `WeekDay()` function returns the number 3. (Day 1 is Sunday, 2 is Monday, and so forth.)

Going beyond Basic Arithmetic

Near the start of this chapter, we talk about how you can use the +, −, *, and / operators in expressions to perform simple arithmetic. As you know, not all math is quite that simple. Some calculations require more than addition, subtraction, multiplication, and division.

Access offers many mathematical and financial functions to help with more complex math. These functions all operate on numbers. For example, the math functions include `Cos()` (cosine), `Tan()` (tangent), and `Atn()` (arctangent) in case you need to do a little trigonometry in your queries. The financial functions include things such as `IRR()` (internal rate of return), `Fv()` (future value), and `Ddb()` (double-declining balance depreciation). You're unlikely to need financial functions unless your work specifically requires those sorts of calculations. Rather than list all the functions that allow you to do complex math, Table 2-2 lists a few examples to give you a sense of how they work.

Table 2-2   Examples of Built-In Math and Financial Functions

Function and Syntax	Returns	Example
`Abs(number)`	Absolute value (negative numbers convert to positive numbers)	`Abs(-1)` returns 1.
`Int(number)`	Integer portion of a number	`Int(99.9)` returns 99.
`Round(number [,decimals])`	The numerical value number rounded to a specified number of decimal places (decimals)	`Round(1.56789,2)` returns 1.57.
`Pmt(rate, nper, pv[, fv[, type]])`	Monthly payment on a loan or annuity	`Pmt(.058/12, 30*12, -50000)` returns 293.3765 (payment on a $50,000 30-year loan at 5.8%).

If you need help with any function in Expression Builder, you can find all the gory details that you need to make the function work for you in the Help system.

Formatting calculated numbers in queries

When you create a table and define a field as the Number data type, you can choose a format, such as Currency, for displaying that number. In a query, you don't predefine a field's data type. The number that appears as the result of a calculation is often just displayed as a *General number* — no dollar sign, no fixed number of decimal places.

Figure 2-5 shows a query based on a hypothetical table named Loan Scenarios. Within the Loan Scenarios table, the APR (annual percentage rate) is a Number field with its Format property set to Percent. The LoanAmount field is a Number field with its Format property set to Currency. Those formats carry over in the results of the query (the query's Datasheet view). But the calculated MonthlyPayment field's result displays as a General number with no currency sign, no commas, and a lot of numbers to the right of the decimal point, as you see in the lower half of Figure 2-5.

**Book III
Chapter 2**

**Letting Queries
Do the Math**

Percent format in table   Calculated field

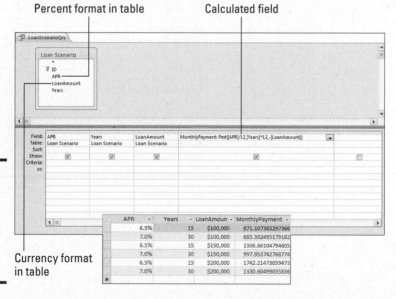

Figure 2-5:
Calculated
fields often
display in
General
number
format.

Currency format
in table

You can format a calculated field so the result appears in Currency format in a couple of ways. If you intend to build any forms or reports based on this query, you can just save the query and forget about formatting the field. Later, when designing a form or report based on the query, you just create a control for the calculated field like you do any other field in the query. Then set that control's Format property to the Currency format in the form or report. The data looks the way you want in the form or report, and you don't have to mess around with the query at all.

See Book IV, Chapter 1 for the goods on creating forms and reports. See the section on setting control properties in Book IV, Chapter 2 for the specifics on formatting controls.

Optionally, if you have no intention of creating any forms or reports based on the query, you can use one of the conversion functions to format the data. The conversion functions are listed in Table 2-3. They're all accessible via the Conversion category of the Built-In Functions folder in Expression Builder. As usual, you can click a conversion function name in the third column of Expression Builder, and then click the Help button for more information on the function.

Table 2-3	Main Built-In Conversion Functions	
Function	*Acceptable Expression Type*	*Return Type*
CBool(expression)	String or number	Boolean
CByte(expression)	Number from 0 to 255	Byte
CCur(expression)	Number	Currency
CDate(expression)	Date/Time	Date
CDbl(expression)	Number	Double
CDec(expression)	Number	Decimal
CInt(expression)	Whole number from −32,768 to 32,767	Integer
CLng(expression)	Whole Number	Long
CSng(expression)	Number	Single
CStr(expression)	Any	String
CVar(expression)	Any	Variant

Think of the starting letter *C* in each conversion function's name as standing for "Convert to." For example, CCur means "Convert to Currency."

Be careful when you use a conversion function because you're defining the data type, as well as the appearance, of the calculated field. Setting the format of a calculated field in a form or report, rather than directly in the query, is often easier.

The big trick is to enclose the entire expression (everything to the right of the field name and colon) within the conversion function's parentheses in the QBE grid. For example, to display the `MonthlyPayment` field from the sample Loan Scenarios query as Currency data, the entire expression must be contained within the `CCur()` parentheses as the following expression:

```
MonthlyPayment: CCur( Pmt([APR]/12,[Years]*12,-[LoanAmount]) )
```

Figure 2-6 shows the results of using `CCur()` in the `MonthlyPayment` calculated control to display the results of the expression in Currency format.

Calculated field

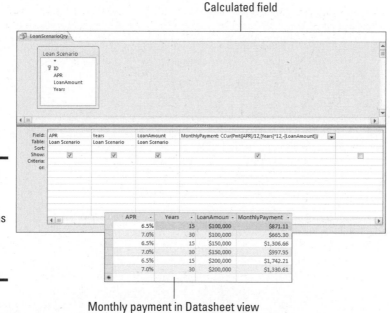

Figure 2-6:
Monthly payment calculations shown in Currency format.

Monthly payment in Datasheet view

What's with the 12s in the expression?

If you're wondering why the sample expression contains things like `/12`, `*12`, and such, it all has to do with how the `Pmt()` function works. The `APR` value is the annual percentage rate, and the term of the loan is expressed in years. When you want the `Pmt()` function to return a monthly payment, you need to divide the annual percentage rate by 12: `[APR]/12`. You also need to multiply the number of years by 12 to get the number of monthly payments: `[Years]*12`.

Typically, `Pmt()` returns a negative number as the result because each payment is a debit (expense). By placing a minus sign in front of the `LoanAmount` field name (that is, `-[LoanAmount]`), we convert that to a negative number (a debit), which in turn makes the calculated monthly payment into a credit (a positive number).

Avoiding problems with null values

Sometimes a field in a record may be empty because nobody ever typed any information into that field. The official name used to describe the value of an empty field is *null*. If a field contains nothing, we say that it contains a *null value.*

Mathematical calculations don't automatically treat a null value as being the same thing as 0 (zero). If any field that's used in a calculated field contains a null, the expression itself also returns null. In Figure 2-7, the SubTotal calculated field multiplies the contents of the HowMany field by the Price field. In the query results, shown at the bottom of Figure 2-7, any field that has a null in the HowMany or Price field ends up with a null value in the SubTotal field as well.

Calculated field

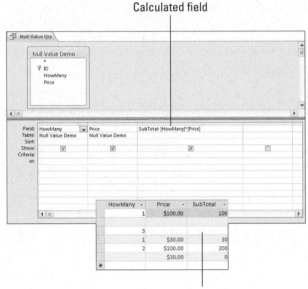

Figure 2-7:
Null fields
in a table
cause
calculations
on those
fields to be
null, too.

Null calculated result

Use the Nz() function to convert a null to a zero. What Nz() really means is, "If this field contains a null, then make that into a zero, and do the math using that zero." To use the Nz() function, put the entire field name within the function's parentheses. In Figure 2-8, the modified calculated field uses the following expression:

```
SubTotal: Nz( [HowMany], 0 ) * Nz( [Price], 0 )
```

In the Datasheet view of that same query, shown at the bottom of Figure 2-8, records that contain a null HowMany or Price field yield a zero result, rather than null, in the SubTotal field. That's because the modified calculated control tells Access to use a zero, rather than nothing (a null) to do the math when a field is null.

Modified calculated field

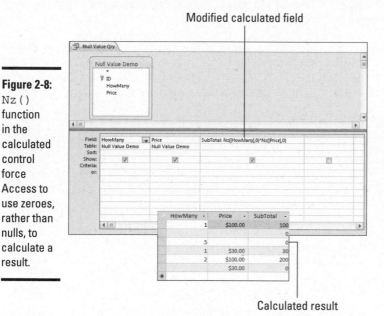

Figure 2-8:
`Nz()`
function
in the
calculated
control
force
Access to
use zeroes,
rather than
nulls, to
calculate a
result.

Calculated result

If you want the third column in Figure 2-8 to show results in Currency format ($100.00, $0.00, $0.00, and so forth), enclose the entire expression in a `CCur()` function, such as `SubTotal: CCur( Nz([HowMany], 0)*Nz([Price], 0) )`.

You can also use the `IsNull()` function to test for a null field. (See the section "Testing for Empty Fields," later in this chapter, for more information.)

Date and Time Calculations

The built-in Date and Time functions operate on data stored in Date/Time fields. You can perform some basic calculations — called "date arithmetic calculations" — on dates using simple + (addition) and – (subtraction) operators. Date arithmetic calculations follow a few simple rules:

+ **If you subtract one date from another, you get a number indicating the number of days between those dates.** For example, `1/15/2010– 1/1/2010` returns `14` because there are 14 days between January 15 and January 1.

+ **If you add a number to, or subtract a number from, a date, you get a new date, rather than a number.** That new date is the date that's *n* number of days away from the original date (where *n* stands for the number of days you add or subtract). For example, `1/1/2010+30` returns `1/31/2010` because January 31 is 30 days after January 1. The result of `12/31/2000-999` is `4/7/1998` because April 7, 1998 is 999 days before 12/31/2000.

Figure 2-9 shows a sample query that uses some basic arithmetic in query calculated fields. In the underlying table, the `StartDate` and `EndDate` fields are each defined as the `Date/Time` data type (with the Short Date format). The first calculated field is the following expression:

Design view

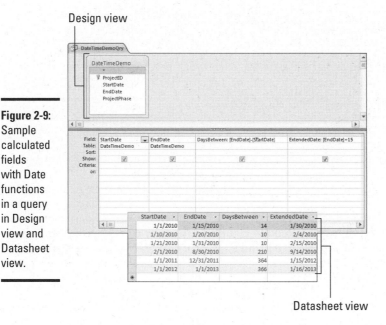

Figure 2-9:
Sample
calculated
fields
with Date
functions
in a query
in Design
view and
Datasheet
view.

Datasheet view

```
DaysBetween: [EndDate]-[StartDate]
```

and calculates and displays the number of days between the `StartDate` value and the `EndDate` value in each record. The `ExtendedDate` calculated field

```
ExtendedDate: [EndDate]+15
```

adds 15 days to whatever date is stored in the `EndDate` field. The lower half of Figure 2-9 shows the query results in Datasheet view. The `DaysBetween` column shows the number of days between the `StartDate` value and the `EndDate` value. The `ExtendedDate` column shows the date 15 days after the `EndDate` value, as specified by the expression in the calculated fields.

Using literal dates and times in expressions

When writing expressions that include dates, you can use a literal date, as opposed to the name of a field that contains a `Date/Time` value. A *literal date* is one that isn't stored in some field — it's just a specific date you want to use in the expression. However, you can't just type in the date using an everyday format like 12/31/2005 because Access interprets that as "12 divided by 31, divided by 2005." And you can't use quotation marks because those are used to define literal text. Instead, you have to use the awkward # character to *delimit* (surround) a literal date.

For example, `#01/01/2005#` is literally the date January 1, 2005. The expression `#01/01/2005# + 14` returns 1/15/2005, the date that's 14 days after January 1, 2005. The expression `#3/31/2005# - #1/1/2005#` returns 89 because March 31, 2005 is 89 days after January 1, 2005.

To express a literal time, use colons (`:`) to separate the hours, minutes, and seconds between the # delimiters. You can also tack on a blank space followed by AM or PM. For example, `#7:30:00#` is literally 7:30 AM, as is `#7:30:00 AM#`. The literal time `#7:30:00 PM#` refers to 7:30 at night. You can use military time as well: The literal time `#19:30:00#` is also 7:30 PM.

Using the Date/Time functions

You're not limited to basic date arithmetic in Access. Quite a few built-in Date/Time functions exist in Access that you can use to manipulate dates and times in other ways. Like with all built-in functions, you can find the Date/Time functions in Expression Builder. Again, if the Functions folder in the left column has a + sign next to it, click that + sign to expand the list. Then click the Built-In Functions subfolder in the left column, and the Date/Time category in the center column. Then click any function's name from the right column and click the Help button for details on the function.

We spare you the details of every available Date/Time function. Chances are that you may never need to use the more obscure functions. Table 2-4 lists some of the more commonly used Date/Time functions and provides examples of their use.

Book III Chapter 2

Letting Queries Do the Math

Table 2-4   **Examples of Access Date/Time Functions**

Function and Syntax	Returns	Example
`Date()`	The current date	Returns the current date, according to your computer's clock.
`Time()`	The current time	Returns the current time, according to your computer's clock.

(continued)

Table 2-4 *(continued)*

Function and Syntax	Returns	Example
Now()	The current date and time	Returns the current date and time, according to your computer's clock.
CDate (expression)	Converts *expression*, which can be any string that looks like a date, to an actual Date/Time value	CDate("Mar 31, 2010") returns 3/31/ 2010.
DateAdd (interval, number, date)	The date that is *number* of days, weeks, months (*interval*) from *date*	DateAdd("m",14, #1/1/2010#) returns 3/1/ 2011, the date that's 14 months after January 1, 2010.
DateDiff (interval, date1, date2 [, firstdayof week[, first weekof year]])	The number of hours, days, weeks, (*interval*) between two dates	DateDiff("w",#1/1/ 2010#,#1/1/2011#) returns 52 because there are 52 weeks between the two dates.
Day(date)	The day of the month expressed as a number between 1 and 31	Day(#1/15/2010#) returns 15 because 1/15/2010 falls on the 15th day of the month.
Hour(time)	The hour of a time	Hour(Now()) returns a number representing the current hour of the day.
MonthName (monthNumber [,abbreviate])	The month of a date, spelled out (if *abbreviate* is false) or abbreviated (if *abbreviate* is true)	MonthName(12,False) returns December; MonthName (12,True) returns Dec because December is the 12th month of the year.

As you can see in Table 2-4, the DateAdd() and DateDiff() functions allow you to specify an *interval* argument. That argument defines the time interval used for the calculation.

For example, if you just use plain date arithmetic to subtract two dates, the difference between the dates automatically displays as the number of *days* between those dates. By using the `DateAdd()` or `DateDiff()` function, you can change that so the difference between the dates is expressed in seconds, minutes, hours, weeks, months, or years — depending on which provides the accuracy you need.

To specify a time interval argument in a `DateAdd()` or `DateDiff()` function, you use one of the settings (enclosed in quotation marks) listed in the left column of Table 2-5.

Table 2-5   Settings for the *Interval* Argument in Date/Time Functions that Require an Interval

Setting	Description
`"d"`	Day
`"h"`	Hour
`"m"`	Month
`"n"`	Minute
`"q"`	Quarter
`"s"`	Second
`"w"`	Weekday
`"ww"`	Week
`"y"`	Day of year
`"yyyy"`	Year

Book III
Chapter 2

Letting Queries
Do the Math

Take a look at an example using an interval in a `DateDiff()` function. Without using the `DateDiff()` function at all, the expression `#12/25/2010#` − `#12/24/2010#` returns 1 because there is one day between those dates, and `"day"` is the default interval when subtracting dates. On the other hand, the expression `DateDiff("h",#12/24/2010#,#12/25/2010#)` returns 24 because the `"h"` interval specifies hours, and there are 24 hours between those two dates.

Manipulating Text with Expressions

You can use the contents of Text fields (also called *strings,* short for "a string of characters") in expressions as well. However, adding, subtracting, multiplying, or dividing with strings doesn't make sense. After all, `Smith times Jones` or `Smith divided by Jones` makes no sense at all. However, you can use the ampersand (`&`) operator to *concatenate* (join) strings.

For example, the expression [First Name] & [Last Name] joins the contents of the Last Name and First Name fields. If the Last Name field contains Pines and the First Name field contains Tori, then the expression [First Name] & [Last Name] returns ToriPines.

Adding spaces to text expressions

"But wait," you say, "shouldn't that be *Tori Pines* with a space in between?" To you and me, it should be — but that's not what the expression says. The expression says, "Stick the First Name value and Last Name value together." The expression doesn't say, "And put a space between them." Computers are literal minded; you can easily fix the problem by using literal text.

Literal text is any text that doesn't refer to a field name or function or anything else that has special meaning to Access. To use literal text in a calculated field expression, enclose the text in quotation marks. A blank space is a character — a chunk of literal text. So watch what happens if you rewrite the previous example expression like this:

```
[First Name] & " " & [Last Name]
```

The result is Tori Pines with a space in between. The expression says, "The contents of the First Name field, followed by a blank space, followed by the contents of the Last Name field."

Two quotation marks right next to each other, with no blank space in between, is a zero-length string, which is basically nothing at all. [First Name] & " " & [Last Name] returns something like Tori Pines, and the expression [First Name] & "" & [Last Name] also returns something like ToriPines (the first and last names with nothing in between).

Suppose that a table contains City, State, and ZIP fields. The following expression displays the city name followed by a comma and a blank space, followed by the state name, followed by two blank spaces, followed by the zip code:

```
[City] & ", " & [State] & "  " & [ZIP]
```

An example of the preceding expression may look something like this:

```
Los Angeles, CA  91234
```

Using the Access Text functions

Access provides several functions for working with text. You find them in the Text category in the middle column of Expression Builder. We focus on some of the more commonly used functions and show examples of their usage. For information on more Text functions and additional details, use the Help button in Expression Builder. Table 2-6 lists the more common Text functions.

Table 2-6	Examples of Built-in Text Functions	
Function and Syntax	*Returns*	*Example*
`LCase(string)`	*string* converted to lowercase	`LCase("AbCdEfG")` returns `abcdefg`.
`UCase(string)`	*string* converted to uppercase	`UCase("AbCdEfG")` returns `ABCDEFG`.
`Left(string,n)`	Leftmost *n* characters of *string*	`Left("abcdefg",3)` returns `abc`.
`Right(string,n)`	Rightmost *n* characters of *string*	`Right("abcdefg",2)` returns `fg`.
`Mid(string, start[, length])`	Middle *length* characters of string starting at *start*	`Mid("abcmnyz",4,2)` returns `mn`.
`Len(string)`	Length of *string*	`Len("Howdy")` returns 5.
`Trim(string)`	*string* with any leading and trailing spaces trimmed off	`Trim(" abc ")` returns `abc`.
`InStr([start,] string1, string2)`	Position of *string2* in *string1* starting at *start*	`InStr("abcxdef", "x")` returns 4 (because x is the fourth character in *string1*).

Writing Decision-Making Expressions

One of the most useful functions in Access is the `Immediate If` function, `IIf()`, which accepts three arguments, as the following shows:

`IIf(conditionalExpression, doThis, elseDoThis)`

where

+ *conditionalExpression* is an expression that results in a `True` or `False` value.

+ *doThis* is what the function returns if the *conditionalExpression* proves `True`.

+ *elseDoThis* is what the function returns if the *conditionalExpression* proves `False`.

The value of the `IIf()` function lies in its ability to make a decision about what to return based on the current situation. For example, suppose your business requires charging 7.25% sales tax to New York residents and no sales tax to everyone else. The `State` field in the underlying table contains the state to which the order is shipped. The following expression says, "If the `State` field contains `NY`, then return `0.7.25%`; otherwise, return 0 (zero)":

```
IIf([State]="NY",0.0725,0)
```

Note, in the preceding expression, that `0.0725` is just a way of expressing 7.25% as a regular decimal number (remove the `%` sign and shift the decimal point two places to the left).

Another example of an `IIf()` function is where a `Paid` field in a table is a `Yes/No` field. A `Yes/No` field can contain only either a `True` or `False` value. The field name alone is a sufficient conditional expression for an `IIf()` function, as in the following sample expression:

```
IIf([Paid],"Receipt","Invoice")
```

In English, the expression says, "If the `Paid` field contains `True` (or `Yes`), return the word `Receipt`. Otherwise, (if the `Paid` field contains `False`) return the word `Invoice`."

Making comparisons in IIf()

Access offers several *comparison operators* that you can use to define expressions that result in the `True` or `False` values. Buttons for these operators appear alongside the arithmetic operators in Expression Builder. Table 2-7 describes the Access comparison operators.

Table 2-7	Built-in Comparison Operators	
Comparison Operator	Name	Meaning
=	Equals	Is equal to
>	Greater than	Is greater than
>=	Greater than or equal to	Is greater than or equal to
<	Less than	Is less than
<=	Less than or equal to	Is less than or equal to
<>	Not equal to	Is not equal to
Between	Between	Is within the range of

An example of an IIf() function — using the >= comparison operator to make a decision based on the contents of a field named Qty — is the following:

```
IIf([Qty]>=10,"Discount","No Discount")
```

In English, the expression says, "If the Qty field contains a value greater than or equal to 10, then return Discount. Otherwise, return No Discount."

Combining comparisons

You can use the Access built-in *logical operators* to combine several comparisons into a single expression that results in a True or False value. The logical operators are listed in Table 2-8.

Table 2-8	Built-in Logical Operators
Logical Operator	*Meaning*
And	Both conditions are True.
Or	One, or both, conditions are True.
Xor	Exclusive "or" — one condition, but not both conditions, are True.
Not	Not True.

As an example, take a look at the following IIf() function, which uses the And operator:

```
IIf([Last Name]="Pines" And [First Name]="Tori","No Charge","Charge")
```

The conditional expression, [Last Name]="Pines" And [First Name]="Tori" says, "If the Last Name field contains Pines and the First Name field contains Tori." So one condition is that the Last Name field contains Pines. The other condition is that the First Name field contains Tori. If both those conditions are True, the expression returns No Charge. If either one, or both, of those conditions is False, then the expression returns Charge.

Another example using the Or operator is the following expression:

```
IIf([State]="NY" Or [State]="NJ","Tax","No Tax")
```

In the preceding example, the first condition is that the State field contains NY. The second condition is that the State field contains NJ. The Or operator says that either one (or both) of the conditions must be met for the whole conditional expression to return True. If the State field contains NY or `NJ`, the expression returns `Tax`. If the `State` field contains anything other than `NY` or `NJ`, then the expression returns `No Tax`.

To tax or not to tax?

A practical example of using an `IIf()` function in calculated field expressions is whether to tax. Suppose you have a query like the one in Figure 2-10. Your business requires that you charge 7.25% tax to all orders shipped within the state of New York. You charge no sales tax on orders shipped outside New York. The `StateProv` field in the query contains the state to which the order is shipped.

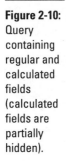

Figure 2-10: Query containing regular and calculated fields (calculated fields are partially hidden).

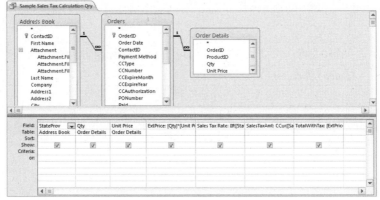

Obviously, you can't see all the expressions in the query — the QBE grid isn't wide enough to show all that. The following is a quick summary of what each field in the query represents:

✦ `StateProv`: A regular Text field from the underlying Address Book table, representing the state to which the order is being shipped.

✦ `Qty`: A regular Number field from the Order Details table, representing the quantity of items ordered.

✦ `Unit Price`: A regular Currency field from the Order Details table, representing the unit price of the item ordered.

✦ `ExtPrice`: A calculated field, `ExtPrice: [Qty]*[Unit Price]`, that multiplies the contents of the `Qty` field by the contents of the `Unit Price` field.

✦ `Sales Tax Rate`: A calculated field, `SalesTaxRate: IIf ([StateProv]="NY",0.0725,0)`, meaning "If the `StateProv` field contains `NY`, then put `0.0725` into this field. Otherwise, put `0` (zero) into this field."

✦ SalesTaxAmt: A calculated field, SalesTaxAmt: CCur([SalesTax Rate]*[ExtPrice]), that multiplies the extended price by the sales tax rate. The CCur() function makes the result appear in Currency format, rather than as a General number.

✦ TotalWithTax: A calculated field, TotalWithTax: [ExtPrice]+ [SalesTaxAmt], that adds the extended price to the sales tax amount.

Figure 2-11 shows the results of the query. Records that have NY in the StateProv field show a sales tax rate of 7.25% (0.0725). Records that don't have NY in the StateProv field show 0 (zero) as the sales tax rate. The SalesTaxAmt and TotalWithTax fields show the results of adding sales tax. (Because the SalesTaxRate value is zero outside of NY, those records end up getting no sales tax added to them.)

Figure 2-11:
Results
(Datasheet
view) of
the query
shown in
Figure 2-10.

Sample Sales Tax Calculation Qry

StateProv	Qty	Unit Price	ExtPrice	Sales Tax Rate	SalesTaxAmt	TotalWithTax
AK	1	$39.99	$39.99	0	$0.00	$39.99
AK	1	$39.99	$39.99	0	$0.00	$39.99
AK	3	$10.00	$30.00	0	$0.00	$30.00
AK	1	$9.98	$9.98	0	$0.00	$9.98
AK	1	$89.99	$89.99	0	$0.00	$89.99
CA	1	$100.00	$100.00	0	$0.00	$100.00
CA	1	$29.99	$29.99	0	$0.00	$29.99
CA	10	$7.99	$79.90	0	$0.00	$79.90
FL	1	$500.00	$500.00	0	$0.00	$500.00
FL	1	$0.00	$0.00	0	$0.00	$0.00
NY	23	$39.99	$919.77	0.0725	$66.68	$986.45
NY	25	$39.99	$999.75	0.0725	$72.48	$1,072.23
NY	1	$1,000.00	$1,000.00	0.0725	$72.50	$1,072.50
NY	5	$179.99	$899.95	0.0725	$65.25	$965.20
OK	1	$0.00	$0.00	0	$0.00	$0.00
OK	1	$0.00	$0.00	0	$0.00	$0.00
OK	1	$0.00	$0.00	0	$0.00	$0.00
NM	3	$0.00	$0.00	0	$0.00	$0.00
NM	1	$0.00	$0.00	0	$0.00	$0.00

Record: 1 of 81 ⏮ ⏭ No Filter Search

**Book III
Chapter 2**

Letting Queries
Do the Math

Testing for Empty Fields

Sometimes having an expression know whether a field is empty, or null, is useful. Access includes an IsNull() function that you can use to test whether a field is empty. The syntax of the function is pretty straightforward:

IsNull[*fieldname*])

where *fieldname* is the name of the field you want to test.

If the specified field is empty, IsNull() returns a True value. If the specified field isn't empty, IsNull() returns a False value. The next section provides an example of using IsNull() in an expression.

To treat a null field as a zero in mathematical expressions, use the Nz() function described in the section, "Avoiding problems with null values," earlier in this chapter.

Sort by name or company

A fairly common problem comes up in tables that store names and addresses. Some records in such a table may list a person's name, but no company name. Some records may contain a company name, but no person name. If you sort records in such a table by the Last Name, First Name, and Company fields, as in Figure 2-12, the records with empty Last Name and First Name fields are listed first.

Sort by Last Name, First Name, Company fields

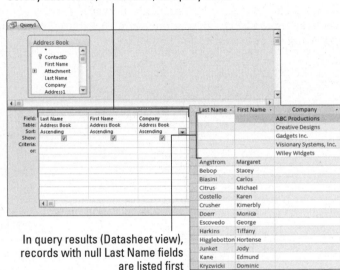

Figure 2-12: Sorting by name and company fields puts empty name fields at the top.

In query results (Datasheet view), records with null Last Name fields are listed first

Suppose you would prefer to see names listed in alphabetical order by person name — or by company name if there is no person name. In that case, create a calculated field in Design view. You can name this field anything you want, but in Figure 2-13, we named the field CustLookup. The expression for that field reads

```
CustLookup: IIf(IsNull([Last Name]),[Company],[Last Name] & ", " & [First Name])
```

The IIf() expression says, "If the Last Name field is null, put the company name in this field. Otherwise, put the person's last name followed by a comma, space, and the person's first name (for example, Pines, Tori) into this field." Setting the Sort row for that calculated field to Ascending order puts records into alphabetical order by last name or company (if there is no last name), as shown in Figure 2-13.

Calculated field

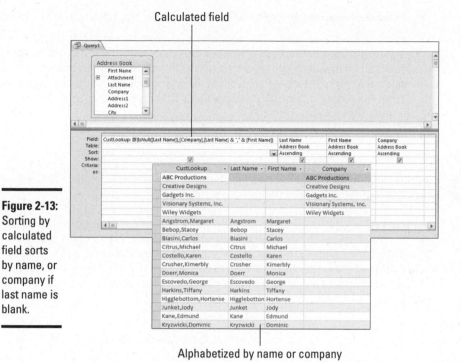

Figure 2-13:
Sorting by
calculated
field sorts
by name, or
company if
last name is
blank.

Alphabetized by name or company

Creating Flexible Parameter Queries

A *parameter query* is a query intentionally missing a piece of needed information so that you can enter the information on the fly when you open the query in Datasheet view. For example, suppose you create a query that shows orders from all records in a table (or tables) from all records in your database. You also like to have queries that show orders from each month.

Rather than create 12 different queries (one for each month), you can create a parameter query that asks for the month number. Then, as soon as you enter a month number, the query shows orders for just the month you specified. In other words, the month number that you're interested in becomes a parameter that you define and pass (provide) to the query just before the query opens.

To create a parameter query, start by creating a normal select query (as detailed in the previous chapter). You can add tables and field names just as you would any other query. Then follow these steps to make your query into a parameter query:

1. **In the Design View window, click Parameters in the Show/Hide group of the (Query Tools) Design tab on the Ribbon.**

The Query Parameters dialog box appears.

2. **Enter a parameter name and its Data Type in the appropriate columns.**

   The parameter name can be any name you like as long as it doesn't match the name of a regular field or calculated field already included in the table. The data type matches the type of data that the parameter will ask for, such as Text for text, Currency for a dollar value, or Date/ Time for a date or time. You can repeat this step to create as many parameters as you wish.

3. **Click OK to close the Query Parameters dialog box.**

In the QBE grid, you can then treat the parameter name like you do a value from a field. In fact, you enclose the parameter's name in square brackets, just like you would a field name.

In Figure 2-14, we created a Month Number parameter that contains an integer. In the Criteria row for the Order Date field in the QBE grid, we used the parameter name in the following expression, as shown in Figure 2-14. The criterion tells the query to show only those records where the month of the order date is equal to whatever we type in as the Month Number parameter.

Month Number parameter defined

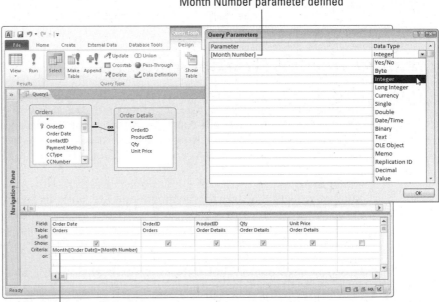

Figure 2-14: Defining and using a query parameter.

Month Number used in criteria

```
Month([Order Date]) = [Month Number]
```

After defining your parameter and using it in the QBE grid, you can save the query like you do any other query. The parameter doesn't really come into play until you open the query in Datasheet view. When you do, an Enter Parameter Value dialog box, like the one shown near the top of Figure 2-15, opens on-screen. You type in a value for the parameter and click OK. For the sake of our example, say you type **9** to view September orders only.

Then, when you click OK in the Enter Parameter Value dialog box, the query opens in Datasheet view, using the parameter value you specified. In this example, the query shows only records that have 9 as the month number in the Order Date field, as shown in the bottom half of Figure 2-15.

Before a query opens, you provide a parameter value

Figure 2-15:
The result
of opening
a parameter
query and
specifying
9 as the
Month
Number.

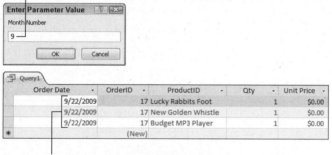

The opened query shows orders only for September (month 9)

You will also see the Enter Parameter Value dialog box if you have a typo or another error where Access doesn't recognize a field name in your query design.

Totals, Subtotals, Averages, and Such

So far, all the calculations in our queries operate on individual fields within records. Suppose you want a different sort of total — such as the total dollar amount of all sales, in all records. You can perform such calculations in two ways. The best — and perhaps easiest — way is to use a report rather than a query. Reports provide more flexibility, and allow you to display the information in more meaningful ways than queries do.

For the goods on creating reports with totals and subtotals, see Book V, Chapter 1.

The other approach is to use a *totals query*. A totals query doesn't give you the flexibility or pretty output that a report does, but a totals query is useful when you just want to perform some quick calculations on the fly without formatting a fancy report.

If you just want to do some quick subtotals, totals, or other multirecord calculations — and don't really care how the data looks on-screen or in print — you can use a query to do the math. As to the other multirecord calculations we just mentioned, Table 2-9 lists all the calculations you can do in a totals query.

Table 2-9	Operations Available in a Totals Query
Choice	*Returns*
Avg	Average of records in field
Count	How many records
First	Value stored in first record
Group by	Nothing — this is used only for grouping
Last	Value stored in last record
Max	Highest value in all records
Min	Lowest value in all records
StDev	Standard deviation
Sum	Sum of records in field
Var	Variance

To create a query that performs calculations on multiple records, start with a normal select query that contains the table (or tables) on which you want to perform calculations. Then do either one of the following:

✦ Click the Totals button in the Show/Hide group of the (Query Tools) Design tab on the Ribbon.

✦ Right-click the query grid and choose Totals from the shortcut menu.

The only change you see is a new row, titled Total, in the QBE grid. The next step is to drag any field name on which you want to perform math down to the Field row of the grid. Optionally, you can create a calculated field and then perform a calculation on that value.

After the field is in place, click the Total row, and then choose an option from the drop-down list, as shown in Figure 2-16. Repeat this process for each field on which you want to perform a calculation.

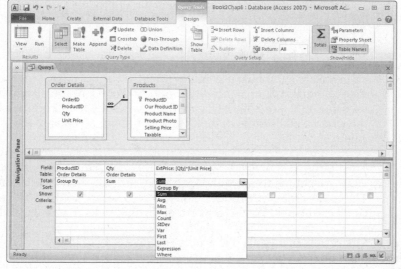

Figure 2-16: The Total row in a Totals query allows you to pick a calculation.

When you switch to Datasheet view to see the results of the query, don't be shocked if your large table, which consists of many records, is suddenly reduced to many fewer records. No, you didn't make an error — Totals queries work this way. The query shown in Figure 2-17 results in a datasheet that has one record for each product sold. The SumOfQty field is created automatically by the Totals query (using the Qty field that we included in the query.) The ExtPrice field lists the net income for each product.

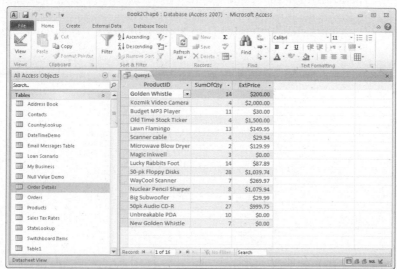

Figure 2-17: The query design in Figure 2-16 produces this datasheet, with one line for each ProductID (the Group By field).

To see a single value, the total income for all products, delete the `ProductID` field from the query design.

Calculating subtotals in a query

To calculate subtotals, use another field in the query that identifies the field the subtotals should be based on. Set the Total row for that field to a `Group By` value. In the top half of Figure 2-16, we added the `ProductID` field from the Order Details table to the QBE grid and set its Total row to a `Group By` value.

The bottom half of Figure 2-17 shows the results of that query in Datasheet view. We get the total extended price of orders for each individual product. The totals group by product. You can see that we sold $200.00 worth of Golden Whistles, $2,000.00 worth of Kozmik Video Cameras, and so forth.

The results of a totals query aren't always easy to interpret. Alas, the small amount of detail in the query results can make it difficult to see what the calculated values are based on. The lack of detail in queries is, in fact, the most important reason that reports are so much better than queries for totals and subtotals. In a report, you can include all the details you want — and arrange things in such a way that you can easily grasp the meaning of every calculated total just by looking at the report.

Filtering records based on calculated fields

You can filter records based on the results of a calculated field. Suppose you want to do a query like the one in Figure 2-16, but you want to see only those records where the total extended price is greater than or equal to $1,000. In that case, just set the Criteria row for the calculated field to `>=1000`. In Datasheet view, only those products with sales totals results greater than or equal to $1,000 show up.

Chapter 3: Doing Neat Things with Action Queries and Query Wizards

In This Chapter

✓ Using action queries safely

✓ Using update queries to change data into tables

✓ Creating new tables with make-table queries

✓ Adding data from one table to another table with append queries

✓ Gathering stray sheep with the Find Unmatched Wizard

✓ Getting the hang of the Find Duplicates Wizard

Chapter 1 of this minibook concentrates on creating select queries, which are the most common type of query created by Access users. You may not realize, though, that Access has other types of queries. Use action queries to make changes to your data; for example, you can set up a query to make a change to all the records that match a criterion. And two query wizards — the Find Duplicates Query Wizard and the Find Unmatched Query Wizard — can help you clean up the data in your database.

Creating Action Queries

Action queries are a way to make global corrections to your database. They are very powerful: They can be tremendously useful and save you a lot of time. However, they can also make an enormous mess of your database if used incorrectly.

Action queries differ significantly from select queries. A select query shows you data that meet your criteria; comparatively, an action query looks for the data that meets your criteria, and then does something with it, such as making changes to the data or moving records to a new table.

Four kinds of action queries, corresponding to four very specific tasks, exist. You may find that creating an action query saves you tons of time if you want to do any of the following things:

✦ Delete some records *(delete query)*

✦ Copy data from one table to another table *(append query)*

+ Update (change) information in some records *(update query)*

+ Create a new table from data stored in other tables *(make-table query)*

Make a backup *before* you run an action query. Action queries can make huge changes to your database — and even if you're careful, you may make a mistake. Making a backup doesn't take much time, especially compared with the time spent fixing what an action query did. You may want to back up the whole database or just make copies of the tables and the data in them that are affected by the query. (To find out about making copies of a database object, see Book I, Chapter 2; to find out about backing up a database, see Book VII, Chapter 1.)

The usual way to create a query is to click the Query Wizard or Query Design button on the Create tab of the Ribbon. When you create a query using either of these methods, Access automatically creates a select query. You can change the query type of any query, whether it's brand new or well used. To change the query type, choose the type of query you want from the Query Type group of the Design tab on the Ribbon (when the query is shown in Design view). (You can choose Make Table, Append, Update, or Delete Query to create an action query.)

The dangers of the Run button

As you may realize by now, action queries make changes; they don't just display data. You need to know how to safely create an action query without running it before you finish defining exactly how you want the query to work. The key is in when you use the View and Run buttons, and how you open the query:

+ When you work with a *select query,* the View and Run buttons do the same thing.

+ When you work with an *action query,* the View and Run buttons do completely different jobs:

• *View:* The View button displays Datasheet view with all the records that match your selection criteria, which is a good way to preview what records will change when you run the action query. The View button is a safe way to look at the datasheet of an action query to see whether the query will work the way you want.

• *Run:* The Run button executes the action — deletes or changes data in your database. You cannot undo the action after you click the Run button in an action query, so be very sure you set up the query correctly before you run it — and be sure to have backups of the affected tables just in case disaster strikes. (To find out about making copies of a table, see Book I, Chapter 2.)

You also need to be careful how you open an action query. Action queries are always rarin' to go. When you open an action query from the Navigation pane by double-clicking the query name, or by selecting it and clicking the Open button, you tell Access to *run* the query (not just to show it). Access does at least warn you that you are about to run an action query by telling you: `You are about to run a query that will modify data in your table`. If you don't want to run the action query, click No to cancel it. If all you want to do is work on the design, be sure to right-click the query name in the Navigation pane and choose Design view from the shortcut menu.

Recognizing action queries in the Navigation pane is easy because their icons are a little different from the icons that select queries have: All action query icons have an exclamation point.

It is possible that when you try to run an action query, you will see an error message. By default, Access disables all action queries unless your database resides in a trusted location, or unless the database itself is signed and trusted.

Settings for allowing Action Queries are in the Trust Center, which you access by clicking the File tab on the Ribbon and choosing Options from the menu. Then click Trust Center in the Options menu. Click the Trust Center Settings button to display the Trust Center options. Action queries are affected by the ActiveX options. The Trust Center is covered more extensively in Book VII, Chapter 3.

Try storing the database in a trusted location (such as your hard drive) to enable action queries.

Creating action queries safely

You need to perfect an action query before you run it so that you don't wreck your data. (Of course, if you make a mistake you have a backup — right?) You make the action query, look at it, maybe test it on a few records in a test table, and then finally run it.

The process for creating an action query is as follows:

1. **Back up your database, or make copies of the tables that the action query will change.**

   Because action queries can do so much work (good or bad), make a backup before you run the query.

2. **Create a select query to show the data needed for the action query.**

   On the Create tab, click the Query Design or the Query Wizard button. Add tables (or queries) and fields to the design grid. Define criteria and sort order as needed.

The point is to create a query that displays the records that the action query acts on.

View

3. View the records that the query will act on by clicking the View button.

You see the records that the query will act on. Make sure you see all the records you want to change, and none that you don't want to change.

4. Use the Query Type buttons to choose the type of action query you need — Make Table, Update, Append, or Delete.

You see the Query Type buttons when you are viewing a query — they are on the Query Tools Design tab.

5. Add the information about what you want the query to do — update data, append data, make a table, or delete data.

The details are covered in the following sections on each type of query.

You may want to use the View button again to see the records the query will act on.

Run

6. Click the Run button to run the query.

Access warns you that you are about to make changes that you can't undo.

If you see a message that the action has been blocked, refer to the steps at the end of the previous section.

7. Click the Yes button to run the query.

Access runs the query. Keep breathing!

8. Check your results.

Checking the results in the underlying tables is a good idea. If the action query acts on a field that you use in a criterion, you may not see the records that change after the query has run — you may have to look at the table, or create a new query to view the results.

The append and make-table queries create new tables. View those results in the affected tables, and not in the query datasheet.

9. If you won't be using the action query again, delete it.

They are dangerous things to have lying around!

Changing Data with Update Queries

You can use an *update query* to change a pile of data at the same time — to raise prices by 10 percent, for example, or to replace a product number with a new product number.

For instance, you may create a query to find orders that haven't yet been shipped that include a Golden Whistle, an item that is discontinued but has a substitute. You can then use the update query to change the item number in records that meet those criteria to `New Golden Whistle`, the replacement item.

Using the update query when you work on lots and lots of data or when you want to update multiple fields makes sense. But before you delve in to the complexities of an action query, consider whether you can use the much simpler Find and Replace dialog box to find and replace data instead. (See Book II, Chapter 2 for more information on the Find and Replace dialog box.) You can use the Find and Replace dialog box in a datasheet created by a query; if you change the data in the query, the table holding the underlying data reflects the change.

To create an update query, follow these steps:

1. **Back up the database and/or make copies of the tables and/or fields that will be affected by the update.**

Update queries can be hard to get right, so play it safe in case you need to get your data back the way it was before you ran the update query.

2. **Create a new select query in Design view.**

See Chapter 1 of this minibook for more information on creating a query.

Include tables that you plan to update or that you need fields from to establish the update criteria.

3. **Put fields in the design grid.**

Add the fields you want to see in the datasheet, the fields you want to use with criteria to tell Access exactly what to update, and the fields you want to change by using the update query.

See Chapter 1 of this minibook for more on using the design grid.

4. **Add the criteria to tell Access how to choose the records you want to update.**

Figure 3-1 shows the select query that finds all unshipped orders for the Golden Whistle. You see two fields included in the query — the `Shipped` field, because you are looking for orders that haven't been shipped (this is a `Yes/No` field, and you are looking for `No` values), and the `Product ID` field, because you are looking for orders that contain the Golden Whistle product.

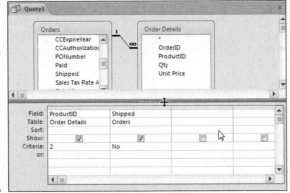

Figure 3-1:
This select query finds all orders for the Golden Whistle that haven't shipped.

View

5. **Click the View button to view the datasheet to check whether all the records you want to update, and none that you don't, are included.**

   Edit the query as needed until you see only the records you want to update in the datasheet. Figure 3-2 shows the datasheet for the query shown in Figure 3-1.

Figure 3-2:
The datasheet for the query in Figure 3-1, showing the Golden Whistle orders that haven't shipped.

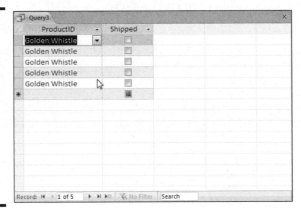

If you use an expression to define how a record is updated, you may want to create a test field now to write your expression and make sure it works in the way you want. For instance, if you want to increase prices by 10 percent, you can create a new field: `[New Price]: [Selling Price]*1.10`. The test field appears in the datasheet when you view it, and you can check it for accuracy. For more information about writing expressions, see Chapter 2 of this minibook.

6. **Return to Design view and click the Update Query button in the Query Type group of the Design tab on the Ribbon to change the query to an update query.**

   Access adds an Update To row in the design grid.

7. **Use the Update To row to tell Access how to update the field.**

   The easiest update is to change one value to another by simply typing the new value in the Update To box for the appropriate field. More complex updates include expressions that tell Access exactly how to update the field. For example, to increase the Selling Price field in a table by 10 percent, you use the expression [Selling Price]*1.10. You can use the Expression Builder to help you build an expression for the Update To row; just click in the box and then click the Build button. (See Chapter 2 of this minibook for more information on using the Expression Builder to create expressions.)

   If you created a test field in Step 5, move the expression to the Update To row for the field that will be updated, and delete the field you created to test the expression. Note that you move the expression that appears after the colon in the test field. You don't need to include a field name and a colon in the Update To row.

   Figure 3-3 shows the update query that finds all orders for the Golden Whistle and changes them to orders for the New Golden Whistle (the New Golden Whistle has a ProductID of 19).

**Book III
Chapter 3**

**Doing Neat Things
with Action Queries
and Query Wizards**

Figure 3-3:
This query finds all orders with a ProductID of 2 (Golden Whistles) that haven't shipped, and changes their ProductID to 19 (New Golden Whistle).

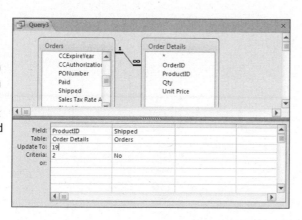

View

8. **Click the View button.**

Access displays the datasheet with the records the query changes when you run it. If the data isn't correct, return to Design view to correct the fields and criteria. This is the same data that you displayed in Step 5. You display it again to be sure you're making the changes you want to make. Check Design view carefully to be sure that the Update To row is correct.

You can display only those fields in the datasheet that the update query is updating. If you want to get a fuller picture of the records you're updating (see the data for all the fields, for example), you can change the query back to a select query, add additional fields, and view the datasheet that your criteria produce. When you change the query back to an update query, the Update To options you added are still there. Remove any additional fields from the query grid before you run the update.

Only fields that are updated or used for criteria are allowed in update queries.

Be aware that the datasheet shows the data that will be changed. You can't see what is changed until you run the query. If you use an expression in the Update To row, testing that your expression produces the desired result by using a calculated field in a select query is important (see Step 5).

Run

9. **Click the Run button to run the update.**

Access warns you that after the records update, you can't undo the changes, as shown in Figure 3-4.

Figure 3-4:
When you click the Run button to run an update query, you see a warning like this one.

10. **Click Yes to update the data.**

11. **Check the tables with affected fields to see whether the update query worked correctly.**

12. **Delete the query if you won't be using it again; press Ctrl+S to save it if you will need it again.**

Creating New Tables with Make-Table Queries

A *make-table query* is useful if you need to make a new table to export or to serve as a backup. You can use a make-table query to make a new table that contains a copy of the data in a table or query. The new table can contain some or all of the fields and records from an existing table, or combine the fields from two or more tables — similar to the results of a select query.

For instance, you can use a make-table query to create a table of customers who bought Golden Whistles. Say that you decided to share their addresses with a school that offers whistle lessons.

To create a table with a make-table query, follow these steps:

1. Create a select query that produces the records you want in a new table.

See Chapter 1 of this minibook for more information on creating a select query.

Figure 3-5 shows a select query that finds the contact info for all customers who ever ordered Golden Whistles. Notice that although you need only fields from the Address Book and Order Details tables, the Orders table is also included in the query to define the relationship between the Order Details and the Address Book tables.

**Book III
Chapter 3**

**Doing Neat Things
with Action Queries
and Query Wizards**

Figure 3-5:
The select query finds customers who ordered Golden Whistles (item number 2 and 19) and lists their names and addresses.

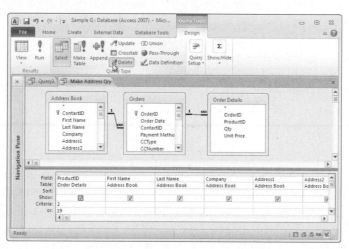

2. Click the View button on the toolbar to view the results.

Figure 3-6 shows the datasheet for the query.

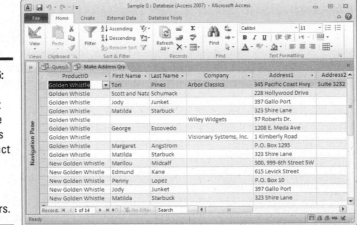

Figure 3-6:
The
datasheet
shows the
customers
and contact
info of
Golden
Whistle
purchasers.

3. **Click the View button on the toolbar to display Design view.**

   You don't want to include the `ProductID` field in the table that the
   make-table query creates, so return to Design view and deselect the
   check mark in the Show row for the `ProductID` field.

4. **Change the query type to a make-table query by clicking the Make
   Table button in the Query Type group of the Design tab on the Ribbon.**

   Access immediately displays the Make Table dialog box shown in
   Figure 3-7.

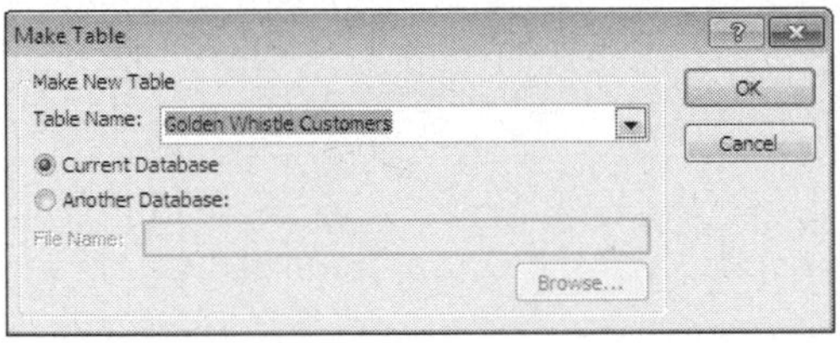

Figure 3-7:
The Make
Table dialog
box.

5. **In the Table Name field, type the name of the table you're creating.**

   Although you're offered a drop-down list, you'll probably want to create
   a new table with a new name, so type a name for the table that isn't the
   name of any table currently in your database.

6. **Choose whether to create the new table in the current database or in
   another database.**

If you choose the Another Database option, you can browse for an existing database, or create a new database with just the single table.

You cannot create a new database using a make-table query: only a new table in an existing database.

7. **Click OK to close the dialog box.**

   If you need to change the settings in the Make Table dialog box, click the Make Table button again to display the Make Table dialog box.

8. **Click the View button to see the records that will be in the new table.**

   You may need to return to Design view to edit the query until all the records you want in the new table appear in the datasheet when you click the View button.

9. **Click the Run button to create the new table.**

   Access asks whether you're sure — because you won't be able to undo your changes.

10. **Click Yes to create the new table.**

    Access quietly creates the new table.

11. **Check the new and old tables to make sure you get what you need in the new table.**

    You may want to edit the table design because the new table doesn't inherit the field properties or the primary key setting from the original table. (See Book II, Chapter 1 for more information on table design.)

Moving Data from One Table to Another with Append Queries

An *append query* copies data from one or more tables or queries in your database and adds the data selected by the query as new records to an existing table. Like with other queries, you can use criteria to tell Access exactly which data to append.

Append queries are used to archive information, to move data between databases, and other useful housecleaning chores.

Cutting and pasting may be an easier way to append records from one table to another if you are appending only a few records. (See Book II, Chapter 4 for more information.)

Access gets a little picky about data that you append with an append query, especially with primary key fields. You must follow these rules when appending records to another table:

✦ **Data that you want to append must have unique values in the primary key field.** Each value in the primary key field must be unique in the table to which the data is being added, because by definition, no value can repeat in a primary key field. If the field is blank, or if the same value already exists in the table, Access does not append the records.

✦ **If an AutoNumber field is in the table to which the data is being appended, do not append data in that field.** Access automatically generates new numbers in the AutoNumber field for the new records; old values cannot be appended.

✦ **The data type of each field you're appending must match the data type of fields in the table to which they're being added.**

To create an append query, follow these steps:

1. **Create a select query that produces the records that you want to add to another table. Display the query in Design view.**

   See Chapter 1 of this minibook for details on creating a select query.

   You can check the criteria by viewing the datasheet to see whether the query is selecting the data you want to append. Click the View button on the toolbar to display the datasheet, and click the View button again to return to Design view.

2. **Change the query type to an append query by clicking the Query Type button.**

   Click the Append button in the Query Type group of the Design tab on the Ribbon.

   Access immediately displays the Append dialog box shown in Figure 3-8.

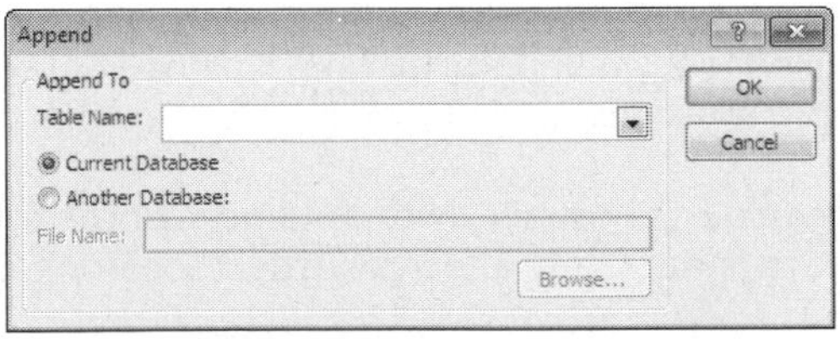

Figure 3-8:
The Append dialog box tells Access where you want to append data.

3. **From the Table Name drop-down list, choose the table to which you want to append the records.**

   You can add the records to a table in another database. Find the database by clicking the Browse button.

4. **Click OK.**

   Access adds an extra row to the design grid: the Append To row. If the field names match the names of the fields you're appending, Access automatically fills in the Append To row with the names of the fields in the table to which you're appending records.

5. **Carefully check the Append To row of the query grid and make any necessary changes.**

   The Field and Table rows show where the field comes from, and the Append To row shows where the data will be appended.

   If some of the fields don't have field names in the Append To row, display the drop-down list in the Append row and select the name of the field you want to append to. When you're finished, check each column to ensure that

   • The Field row contains the name of the field that contains data that you want to append to another table.

   • The Table row contains the name of the table that contains the data.

   • The Append To row contains the name of the field that the data will be appended to.

   • No field appears more than once in the Append To row.

6. **Click the Run button to run the append query.**

   Access tells you that you're about to append rows and that you won't be able to undo the changes.

   Be careful about running this query. If you run it twice, you append the records twice!

7. **Click the Yes button to run the query.**

   Access adds the records to the table you specified. You now have the same information in two tables.

8. **Save the query by pressing Ctrl+S if you think you'll use it again; otherwise, close it without saving.**

   Consider changing it back to a select query so that it doesn't get run accidentally.

9. **Check your results.**

   Check the table you appended to as well as the table you appended from to make sure that Access copied all the records you wanted copied.

**Book III
Chapter 3**

**Doing Neat Things
with Action Queries
and Query Wizards**

Deleting Lots of Records with Delete Queries

A *delete query* deletes whole records from tables, usually based on criteria you provide (although you can also use delete queries to delete all records in a table while keeping the field and table properties intact). Obviously, delete queries are a powerful feature, and should be treated with respect! Delete queries are dangerous — they permanently delete data from the tables in your database.

Always make sure that you have a backup before you run a delete query. You may want to back up the whole database or just the tables affected by the delete query.

Because delete queries can wreak such havoc with your database, you may want to consider whether manually deleting records meets your needs. You can delete a record by selecting it (click the record selector, the gray box to the left of the record) and pressing Delete or clicking the Delete Record button on the toolbar. You can select a group of records by double-clicking the first record selector and dragging to the last in the group, or by selecting the first record and then Shift+clicking the last in the group. You can use this procedure in a table or some queries.

Before you run a delete query, you need to be aware of how the table you're deleting data from is related to other tables in the database. In some cases, running a delete query can delete records in related tables. If the table you're deleting data from is on the one side of a one-to-many relationship and cascading deletes are enabled for the relationship, Access looks for related data to delete. For instance, the Products table (which holds information for all the sold products) is related to the Order Details table (where ordered items are listed). The relationship is one-to-many, with Products on the "one" side. When you created the relationship between the two tables using the Edit Relationships dialog box (displayed from the Relationships window), if you selected Enforce Referential Integrity and Cascade Delete Related Records, deleting records from the Products table results in Access deleting records from the Order Details table. Customers may not get the products they ordered, and no record of them ordering that item exists in the database. In this case, adding a `Discontinued` field to the Products table may be a better solution than deleting the records! (For more information on one-to-many relationships, see Book I, Chapter 4. For more information on referential integrity, see Book II, Chapter 6.)

When you tell Access to create a delete query, the Sort and Show rows in the QBE grid (the grid in the bottom pane of Design view) are removed, and the Delete row is added. The Delete row has a drop-down list with two options that you only see with delete queries: the Where option and the

From option. Use these two options to define the fields you want to see and the fields that you are using to define criteria to select the fields that will be deleted by the query:

✦ **Where:** Tells Access to use the criteria for the field to determine which records to delete.

✦ **From:** Displays the field when you view the datasheet for the query. You can choose the From option only when you use the * choice in the Field row to include all fields from a table. The asterisk appears as the first field for each table shown in the top half of Design view; when dragged to the design grid, Access displays all fields from the table. Viewing all fields from a table in the datasheet gives you a more complete picture of the data you're deleting; otherwise, all you see in the datasheet are the values from the fields included in the design grid with criteria — rather than the entire record that the delete query will actually delete when you run it.

Follow these steps to create a delete query:

1. **In Design view, create a select query that includes all the tables with records you want to delete.**

See Chapter 1 of this minibook for details on how to create a select query. Make sure you add to the query all tables containing records you want to delete.

2. **Drag the * option from each field list in the top half of Design view to the design grid to display all fields from the table or tables that contain records you want to delete.**

Using the * option allows you to view all fields in the table. When you change the query to a delete query, only the * allows you to display fields not being used for criteria.

3. **Add fields to the design grid that you have criteria for, and then define those criteria.**

4. **Click the View button on the toolbar to view the datasheet.**

The records you see should be the records that you want the delete query to delete. If you see records that should not be deleted, or you don't see records that you do want deleted, refine your query definition, and repeat until the query produces the correct records.

5. **Change the query type to a delete query by clicking the Delete button in the Query Type group of the Query Tools Design tab on the Ribbon.**

When you change the query type from select to delete, Access changes the rows in the design grid. The Sort and Show rows are removed, and the Delete row is added.

**Book III
Chapter 3**

Doing Neat Things with Action Queries and Query Wizards

6. **Choose a value for the Delete row (if it's not set automatically) from the drop-down list:**

   a. *Set the fields that you want to view to the From option.*

   b. *Set the fields that define criteria to the Where option.*

   Figure 3-9 shows an example of a delete query that will delete records with the `ProductID` value of `35` from the Order Details and Products tables. Note that when you view the datasheet, you're seeing data from two different tables. All that data will be deleted, so data will be deleted from both tables.

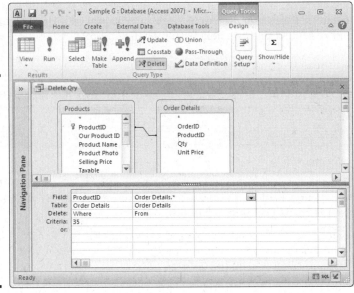

Figure 3-9: This delete query deletes records with the `Product-ID` value of `35` from the Order Details and Products tables.

7. **Click the View button to view the datasheet again. Check to make sure that you see only the records that the delete query should delete.**

   If you see data in the datasheet that shouldn't be deleted — or if data that you want to delete is missing — correct the design of the query before you run it.

   A delete query deletes entire records.

8. **Return to Design view by clicking the View button.**

9. **Click the Run button to run the query.**

   Access deletes the data that you saw in Datasheet view — it's gone for good!

Finding Unmatched Records with a Wizard

Access has two categories of Neat Things You Can Do with Queries — action queries and the two query wizards covered here. The Find Unmatched Query Wizard finds records in one table that have no matching records in another, related table. For example, you may store orders in one table and details about customers in another table. If the tables are linked by, say, a `Customer Number` field, the Unmatched Query Wizard can tell you whether you have any customers listed in the Orders table who aren't listed in the Customers table.

Use the Find Unmatched Query Wizard to find unmatched records in the following way:

1. **Display the Create tab on the Ribbon.**

2. **Click the Query Wizard button in the Macros & Code group on the Ribbon.**

   The New Query dialog box opens.

3. **Select the Find Unmatched Query Wizard option, and then click OK.**

   The first window of the wizard appears.

4. **Select the table (or query) that may have unmatched records in a second table, and then click Next.**

   For instance, if you're looking for customers with no orders, select the table that holds the names of customers in this window. If you're looking for orders for which you don't have the customer address, select the Orders table in this step. The final result of the query lists records from the table that you select in this step that don't have matching records in the table you select in the next step.

   If you want to choose a query, select the Queries or Both radio button.

5. **Select the table (or query) that should contain the matching records for the data in the table you selected in the previous step, and then click Next.**

   For instance, if you're looking for customers with no orders, select the table that holds the order information. If you're looking for orders that don't have the customer address, select the table that holds customer addresses when you do this step.

6. **Check to make sure that Access correctly guessed the related fields in the two tables you selected in the third window of the wizard (shown in Figure 3-10); if it did, click Next.**

**Book III
Chapter 3**

**Doing Neat Things
with Action Queries
and Query Wizards**

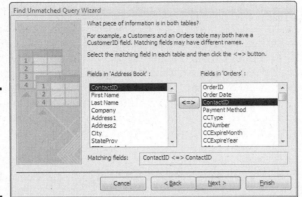

Figure 3-10:
Select
related
fields to find
unmatched
records.

The window shows field names in the two tables you selected. The names of the related fields are probably highlighted. Click the related field in each table if Access hasn't selected the correct related fields. The two fields that you select should contain the same information and be of the same data type.

7. **Select the fields you want to see in the query results in the next window of the wizard, and then click Next.**

   To select all fields, click the double arrow pointing to the right.

8. **Accept the name that Access gives the query or name the query yourself in the final window of the Find Unmatched Query Wizard.**

   Access is good at naming the results of this query descriptively. Notice whether the name reflects the query you thought you were creating. If not, use the Back button to redefine the query.

9. **Choose whether you want to view the results or modify the design; then click Finish.**

   Access displays the query in Design or Datasheet view as you requested.

Note that you don't have to use a wizard to create this kind of query. The query shown in Figure 3-11 finds unmatched records in the Address Book table by using an inner join between the tables and the `Is Null` criteria for the related field in the table where matching records are stored. (For more about inner joins, see Chapter 1 of this minibook.)

If you need to avoid unmatched records, define the relationship between the tables to enforce referential integrity. Define referential integrity to avoid creating orders for customers in the Orders table when you don't have contact information for them in the Address Book table. You may still find using the Find Unmatched Query Wizard useful, though. For instance, you may want to find customers who have not placed any orders, or products that have not been ordered. (For more information on referential integrity, see Book II, Chapter 6.)

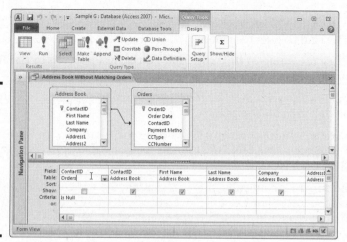

Figure 3-11:
Find
unmatched
records by
using an
inner join
and the
`Is Null`
criterion.

Finding Duplicate Records

When a table contains hundreds or thousands of records, spotting duplicates is not always easy, but the Find Duplicates Query Wizard can find them in an instant. Before you use the wizard, though, you need to really think about which combination of fields in a record constitutes a duplicate. For example, in a table of names and addresses, you wouldn't necessarily consider two records with the name `Jones` in the `Last Name` field duplicates because two different people in your table may have the name Jones.

Not even the `First Name` and `Last Name` fields combined necessarily pinpoint duplicate records because more than one Joe Jones or Sarah Jones can be in your table. On the other hand, if two or more records in your table contain the same information in the `Last Name`, `First Name`, `Address1`, and `ZIP Code` fields, there's a good chance that those records are duplicates. You can use loose criteria to find duplicates, though, because you can decide later whether to delete them. Perhaps looking at repeated addresses is a good start. If you do mass mailings, you may be sending two or more of every item to the customers whose records are duplicated.

Before you go looking for duplicate records, think about which combination of fields in your table will indicate records that are likely duplicates. Then use the Find Duplicates Query Wizard to locate those records. Because the Find Duplicate Query Wizard finds only duplicates, you can use your judgment to delete records that look like duplicates. Follow these steps to run the wizard:

1. **Display the Create tab on the Ribbon.**

2. **Click the Query Wizard button in the Macros & Code group of the Ribbon.**

   The New Query dialog box opens.

**Book III
Chapter 3**

**Doing Neat Things
with Action Queries
and Query Wizards**

 3. **Select the Find Duplicates Query Wizard option, and then click OK.**

    The Find Duplicates Query Wizard starts.

 4. **Click the name of the table that you want to search in the first window of the wizard, and then click Next.**

    Optionally, you can click the Queries option and choose a query to use as the basis for the search.

 5. **Use the > button to copy fields from the Available Fields list to the Duplicate-Value Fields list in the second window of the wizard, and then click Next.**

    Be sure to include all fields that contain the data needed to define duplicate records. For example, in Figure 3-12, we're about to find records that have identical information in First Name and Address 1 fields.

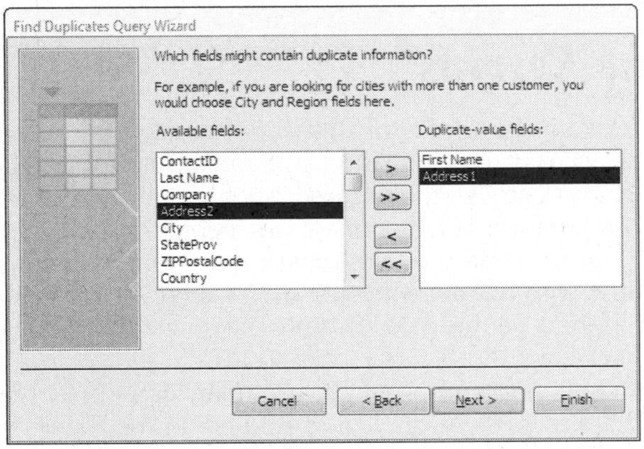

Figure 3-12:
Specify
fields to
compare in
the second
window
of the Find
Duplicates
Query
Wizard.

 6. **Choose the fields to be shown for additional information in the third window of the wizard, and then click Next.**

    The fields you specify aren't used for comparing records, but they will appear in the query results to help you better identify any duplicate records. If your table has a primary key and/or date entered field, both are good candidates for this third field.

 7. **Give the query a name.**

    Change the suggested name for the query, if you wish, or use the suggested name in the last window of the wizard.

 8. **Choose the View the Results option, and then click the Finish button.**

The results of the query appear in Datasheet view. If no records appear, no records have identical values in the fields you specified in the wizard. You have nothing to worry about.

The handy Unique Values and Unique Records properties

Sometimes, rather than finding duplicates and deleting them, you just want to hide them. For instance, you may only need to see a list of states that your customers come from — you don't need to see Massachusetts 56 times (if you have 56 customers in Massachusetts).

The Properties sheet has two properties that allow you to hide duplicate values:

✔ `Unique Values`: Set this property to the `Yes` value when you want to see only unique values for the fields displayed in the query. The `Unique Values` property omits duplicate data for the fields selected in the query. Every row displayed in the query datasheet is different.

✔ `Unique Records`: Set this property to the `Yes` value when you want to see only unique records based on all fields in the underlying tables. The `Unique Records` property affects fields only from more than one table. A record is considered unique if a value in at least one field is different from a value in the same field in another record. Note that the primary key fields are included when records are compared.

To display the Properties sheet, right-click an empty part of the Table pane in Query Design view (the top half of the design grid) and choose the Properties option from the shortcut menu; or, click the Properties button on the toolbar.

The `Unique Values` and `Unique Records` properties apply only to select, append, and make-table queries. Note that when both are set to the `No` value (which is the default), the query returns all records.

**Book III
Chapter 3**

**Doing Neat Things
with Action Queries
and Query Wizards**

On the other hand, if records do appear, you know you have duplicates. For example, in Figure 3-13, two records for Frankly Unctuous appear. Note the identical `First Name`, `Last Name`, and `Address1` fields. The `ContactID` field allows us to see that two records for this customer are, indeed, in the table.

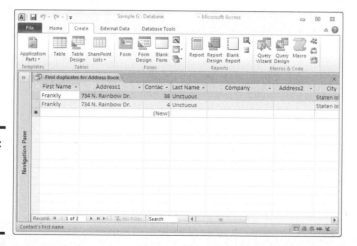

Figure 3-13: Frankly Unctuous has two records in the table.

Chapter 4: Viewing Your Data from All Angles Using Crosstabs and PivotTables

In This Chapter

✔ **Understanding Crosstab queries**

✔ **Running the Crosstab Query Wizard**

✔ **Creating Crosstab queries in Design view**

✔ **Understanding PivotTables**

✔ **Using PivotTable view**

✔ **Selecting filter, data, and category fields for your PivotTable**

Sometimes, instead of viewing your data in records, you want to see it organized and categorized (what a concept). You may want to see sales of each product by month, and you may want to see that information in a compact table, with months as the column titles, product names as the row titles, and the sum of sales in the body of the table. Access creates that kind of table in two ways — with a Crosstab query or a PivotTable. Both Crosstabs and PivotTables organize data and create totals using the aggregate function of your choice — sum, average, and count being the most popular. You create Crosstab queries in Design view. The PivotTable view is all mouse driven: You drag and drop fields where you want them, use check boxes to create filters, and do nearly everything else with buttons and menu commands.

If you want to look at your data in lots of different ways in a short period of time, you'll prefer PivotTables. You can look first at product sales by month and then quickly shift the view to see which salespeople are selling the most of which product, and then shift again to see which states your customers come from for each product. If you know exactly what you want and don't need to look at the data in another way (or if you want to use the results of the query as the record source for a report), you may prefer Crosstab queries. Take your pick — they're both covered in this chapter.

Aggregating Data in a Crosstab Query

A *Crosstab query* is a specialized query for summarizing data. Instead of creating a table with rows showing record data and columns showing fields, you can choose a field and group its data using two other fields as row and column labels. Access groups the data how you tell it and aggregates the grouped field in the body of the table; you can choose between the usual aggregate functions, such as sum, average, minimum, maximum, count, and all other available functions. For instance, if you chose the ProductName field for the column labels, the Order Date Month field for the row labels, and the field that contains the sales subtotal for the product (price × quantity) as the information to put in the body of the table, and you tell Access to sum the result, the Crosstab query appears, shown in Figure 4-1, where sales of each product are shown by quarter (you can choose the time period, too). The result is a compact, spreadsheet-like presentation of your data.

ProductID	Qtr 1	Qtr 2	Qtr 3
Golden Whistle	300	1100	
Kozmik Video Camera	3000		1000
Budget MP3 Player	80	20	10
Old Time Stock Ticker	1000	500	500
Lawn Flamingo	240	30	120
Scanner cable	40		
Microwave Blow Dryer	130	130	
Magic Inkwell	30	15	
Lucky Rabbits Foot	96	8	8
50-pk Floppy Disks	1080	40	
WayCool Scanner	450	90	90
Nuclear Pencil Sharper	1260		180
Big Subwoofer	60	30	
50pk Audio CD-R	1040	40	

Record: 1 of 16 — No Filter — Search

Figure 4-1: This Crosstab query shows sales by product and quarter.

If you want to aggregate data without using a Crosstab query, see Chapter 2 of this minibook, as well as the Forms and Reports chapters.

Using the Crosstab Query Wizard

The Crosstab Query Wizard provides an automated way to create a Crosstab query. The wizard works only with one table or query. If the fields you want to use in the Crosstab query are not in one table, you have to create a query that combines those fields before you use the Crosstab Query Wizard. However, because the wizard does give you the option of aggregating date data (taking a Date/Time field and combining the data into months), you don't have to write an expression to aggregate data yourself. For instance, the Orders table saves the time and day an order is submitted. The Crosstab Query Wizard takes that date field and converts it to just the month (or the year, quarter, or day). For the option to aggregate data, you must use the date field as a column heading.

Start the Crosstab Query Wizard by following these steps:

1. **Display the Create tab on the Ribbon.**

2. **Click the Query Wizard button in the Macros & Code group on the Ribbon.**

The New Query dialog box opens.

3. **Select the Crosstab Query Wizard option and then click OK.**

Access starts the Crosstab Query Wizard, shown in Figure 4-2.

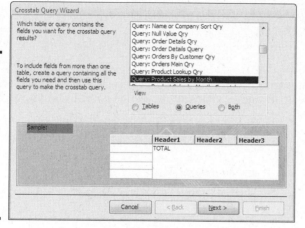

Figure 4-2: Choose the table or query that contains the fields you want to use in the Crosstab query.

Book III
Chapter 4

Viewing Data Using
Crosstabs and
PivotTables

4. **Select the table or query that contains all the fields you need for your Crosstab query, and then click Next.**

If you create a query to hold the fields you need, select the Queries or the Both radio button to see the query name.

5. **In the new window that appears, as shown in Figure 4-3, select the field(s) whose values you want to use as row headings and then click Next.**

You can select up to three fields to fine-tune the breakdown of your data. As you select fields, the sample at the bottom changes to reflect how your finished query will look.

Generally, the fields you select as row and column headings contain repeated data that is grouped in the Crosstab query. For instance, the `ProductID` field comes from the Order Details table and identifies products in each order. The Crosstab query can show you how many times a product is ordered, or how many units of each product is sold.

If you want the option of grouping date values, don't pick a Date/Time field here — use it for column headings instead.

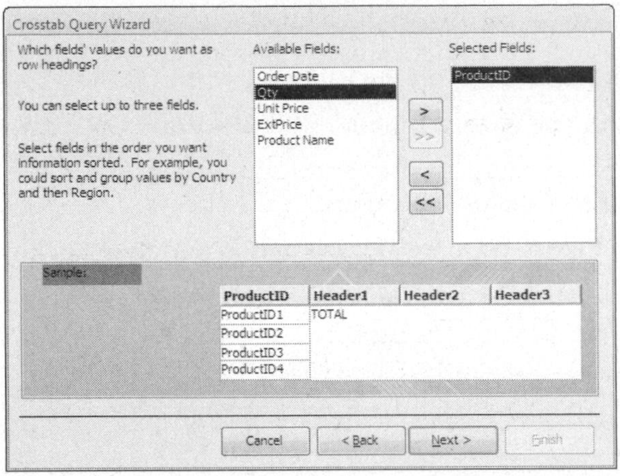

Figure 4-3:
Choose the field(s) that contains the data used as the row headings for the Crosstab query.

6. **In the new window that appears, as shown in Figure 4-4, select the field(s) whose values you want to use as column headings, and then click Next.**

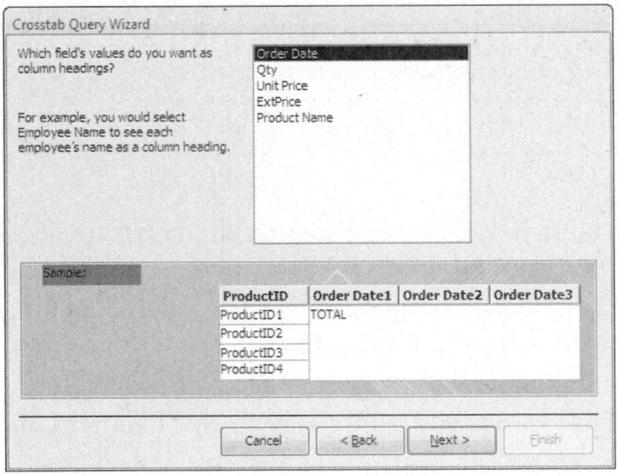

Figure 4-4:
Choose the field(s) you want to use as column headings.

You can select only one field to use as the column headings. You may want to use a field containing dates and tell Access to group date values.

7. **If you select a date field as the column headings, you see the window shown in Figure 4-5. Choose how to group dates from the list, and then click Next.**

Choose one of the options listed. The Date/Time option shows data by unique Date and Time. Data isn't grouped at all unless you have data with exactly the same time and date.

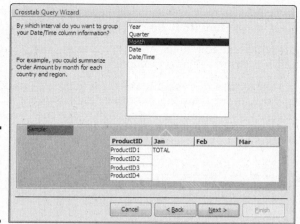

Figure 4-5:
Choose how
to group
date and
time data.

---

8. **In the new window that appears, shown in Figure 4-6, choose the field whose values you want to see grouped by the row and column headings that you selected.**

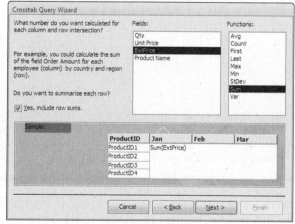

Figure 4-6:
Choose the
field that
contains
values for
the Crosstab
query, and
how you
want to
aggregate
them.

The field you select usually contains numerical data that can be aggregated in some way (added, averaged, and so on). The exception is if you want to count instances — then the field doesn't need to contain numbers.

Figure 4-6 uses the `Extended Price` field, which is price × quantity — the dollar amount of sales for each product.

9. **Select a grouping method from the Functions list.**

You can find out more about these functions in Chapter 2 of this minibook. You can easily change this function in Design view if you change your mind after you view the Crosstab query.

10. **Choose whether to include row sums by selecting the check box on the same page as the function choices, and then click Next.**

    If you choose to include row sums, Access creates an extra column that contains the sum of the row — in this example, the total sales for the product.

11. **Name the query (or use the name that Access suggests), choose how you want to view the query (viewing the query datasheet or viewing the query in Design view), and then click Finish to see the Crosstab query.**

    See Figure 4-7 to see how our sample Crosstab query turned out!

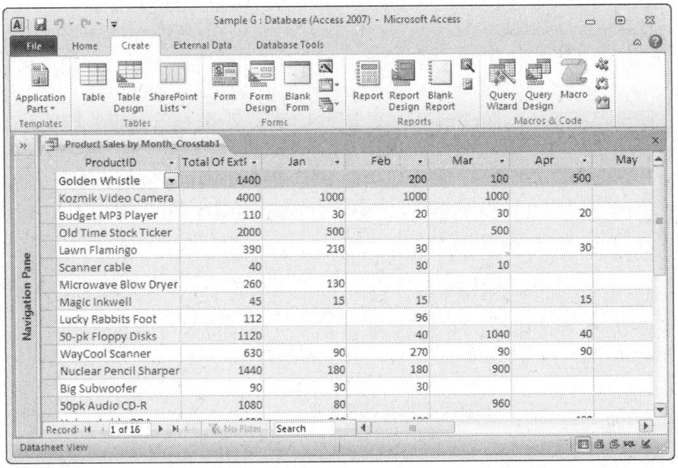

Figure 4-7: This Crosstab query shows sales of each product by month.

ProductID	Total Of Ext1	Jan	Feb	Mar	Apr	May
Golden Whistle	1400		200	100	500	
Kozmik Video Camera	4000	1000	1000	1000		
Budget MP3 Player	110	30	20	30	20	
Old Time Stock Ticker	2000	500		500		
Lawn Flamingo	390	210	30		30	
Scanner cable	40		30	10		
Microwave Blow Dryer	260	130				
Magic Inkwell	45	15	15		15	
Lucky Rabbits Foot	112		96			
50-pk Floppy Disks	1120		40	1040	40	
WayCool Scanner	630	90	270	90	90	
Nuclear Pencil Sharper	1440	180	180	900		
Big Subwoofer	90	30	30			
50pk Audio CD-R	1080	80		960		

Look at the results of the Crosstab Query Wizard in Design view to get ideas about how to create a Crosstab query from scratch. You can get your Crosstab query started with the Crosstab Query Wizard, and then put the finishing touches on the query in Design view, which is covered in the next section.

You can format your crosstab query data in Design view by selecting to column that defines the Value in the table, right-clicking, choosing Properties, and changing the Format on the Property sheet.

Creating a Crosstab query in Design view

A simple Crosstab query has three fields:

✦ One used for row headings (Date, for example)

✦ One used for column headings (Product, for example)

✦ The Value field, which contains the data that you want to appear in the cells of the table (such as an item subtotal). Tell Access how to summarize your data in the Crosstab query by choosing from these choices: Sum, Avg, Min, Max, Count, StDev, Var, First, or Last.

You also have the option of using an expression for any fields in the Crosstab query design (see Chapter 2 of this minibook for more information on creating a field with an expression).

Follow these steps to create a simple Crosstab query:

1. Create a new select query in Design view with the tables or queries that contain the fields you want to use in the Crosstab query.

Chapter 1 of this minibook covers creating select queries.

2. Change the query to a Crosstab query by using the Crosstab button in the Query Type group of the Design tab on the Ribbon.

Access displays a Crosstab row in the design grid (the grid in the bottom half of the Design window). You use the Crosstab row to tell Access how to build the Crosstab query. Access also displays the Total row in the design grid, which allows you to choose from the aggregate functions or choose the Group By option.

In the next steps, you double-click fields in the Table pane of Design view to move them to the design grid, and then choose from the Crosstab row drop-down list the way each field is used to create the Crosstab.

3. Double-click the field you want to use for row labels in the Table pane in the top half of Design view.

When you double-click the field name, Access moves it to the design grid.

4. Click in the Crosstab row and then click the down arrow. Choose the Row Heading option from the drop-down list.

Set the Total row to the Group By option for this column in the grid.

5. Double-click the field you want to use for column labels in the Table pane.

Access places the field in the design grid.

6. Click in the Crosstab row for the new field and then click the down arrow. Choose the Column Heading option from the drop-down list.

Set the Total row to the Group By option for this column in the grid. (Chances are you won't have to make this change. Click in the Total row to display the arrow for the drop-down list.)

7. Double-click the field containing the values that you want aggregated in your Crosstab query in the Table pane to put it in the grid.

This field — the `Value` field — provides the values that fill up the Crosstab query.

8. Click in the Crosstab row for the new field in the grid and then click the down arrow in the Crosstab row. Choose the Value option from the drop-down list.

**Book III
Chapter 4**

Viewing Data Using
Crosstabs and
PivotTables

9. Choose the option to summarize the data from the drop-down list in the Total row for the `Value` field column.

Sum and average are common, but one of the other options may be the one you need. See Chapter 2 of this minibook for more on these aggregate options.

Figure 4-8 shows Design view for a Crosstab query that creates a query similar to the one created by the Crosstab Query Wizard in the previous section.

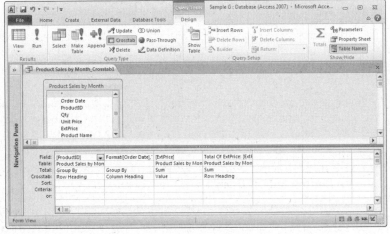

Figure 4-8:
This
Crosstab
query
shows sales
by product
and month.

10. Click the View button to view your new Crosstab query.

You may want to edit your query design, or make some of the modifications described in the next section.

Modifying your Crosstab query

After you figure out the basics of creating a Crosstab query — choosing fields for the row headings, column headings, and the value field; and then specifying how the data is aggregated — you may want to do any of the following to add more to the query design.

Using criteria

You can include criteria to narrow the data aggregated in a Crosstab query. You add criteria in the design grid to the fields used for row headings and column headings, but not to the field used for values. If you want to specify a criterion for the value field, you can put the field in the query a second time, set its Total row to the Group By option, leave the Crosstab row option blank, and define the criteria. Using the same method, you can add any field to the design grid and define criteria — just leave the Crosstab row blank.

Multiple fields for row headings

You can use more than one field for row headings. The resulting Crosstab query groups rows using both fields. Figure 4-9 shows hours grouped by company and project.

Figure 4-9:
This
Crosstab
query uses
two fields
as row
labels to
group hours
worked.

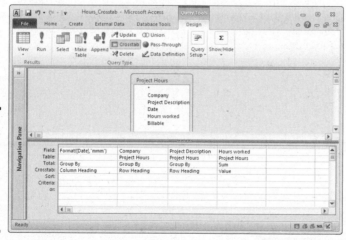

Company	Project Description	Jun	Jul	Aug	Sep	Oct	N
ABC Webworks	Short manual for WebWorks	6					
ABC Webworks	Trainers notes for WebWorks training man	32	27				
ABC Webworks	Training manual for WebWorks	10	6				
Dynamic Solutions, Inc.	General Marketing Brochure	28	9				
Dynamic Solutions, Inc.	Manual for WP software	9					
Lizard Web, Inc.	Edit text for Richards page		45				
Network Consultants, Inc	Compile specs for network hardware			23			
Network Consultants, Inc	General Marketing Brochure			8			
Network Consultants, Inc	Marketing description of consultants	13					
Network Consultants, Inc	User documentation for WebWorks netwo				3		
Network Consultants, Inc	Write article about top CIOs for newsletter					10	

To use multiple fields to group data by row, specify more than one field as a row heading in the design grid. Access figures out in which order to use the fields: The field on the "one" side of a one-to-many relationship displays first. Figure 4-10 shows the design grid for the same query.

Book III
Chapter 4

**Viewing Data Using
Crosstabs and
PivotTables**

Figure 4-10:
Specifying
two fields
as row
labels to
group hours
worked.

Adding aggregate columns

A *calculated* column is an additional column in the query that totals rows displayed in the query. For instance, you may add a column that calculated the total number of the product sold to a query that displays sales by month and product.

You can add calculated columns to a Crosstab query. They are added as row headings, and appear by default as the first column after the actual row headings. If you include row sums in a Crosstab query, a calculated column is automatically created as a row heading that uses the Sum option in the Total row. You may want to calculate other values using other aggregate functions.

Getting data in order

By default, Access sorts column and row headings in alphabetical or numerical order, but you can fix your Crosstab query to appear in any specified order in one of two ways:

✦ **Move columns manually in Datasheet view.**

    a. *Click the column heading to select the column.*

    b. *Drag the column heading to its new position.*

🗐 Property Sheet ✦ **Specify the sort order in the Property sheet for the query.**

    a. *Click anywhere in the column in Design View, which contains the Column Heading.*

    b. *Display the Property sheet by clicking the Property Sheet button on the Design tab on the Ribbon.*

    c. *Type the headings in order in the* Column Headings *property, using quotes around the headings and separating each heading with commas as shown in Figure 4-11.* Be sure to use the data as it appears on the datasheet.

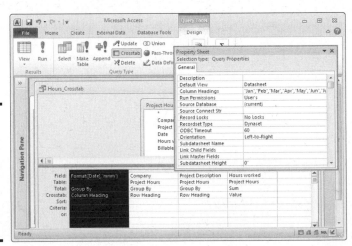

Figure 4-11:
Use the
Column
Headings
property to
list column
headings in
order.

Analyzing Data with PivotTables

A PivotTable is an interactive tool to help you analyze your data. When you work with a PivotTable, you can quickly drag fields and create new totals to present an entirely new view of your data, or drill down to see the individual pieces of data that make up a total. PivotTables are closely related to Crosstab queries in the way they present your data — they group data into rows and columns, with the row and column headings defined by fields. Using a PivotTable, you can select how to categorize data into rows and columns, choose fields to be summarized in the body of the table, and filter the data. And rather than using Design view to define the table, you create and make changes to a PivotTable just by clicking the table and dragging field names or choosing from automatically created drop-down menus that reflect your data.

Creating a blank PivotTable

To create a blank PivotTable, as shown in Figure 4-12, first create a query that contains all the fields you want in your PivotTable, and then use one of the following options:

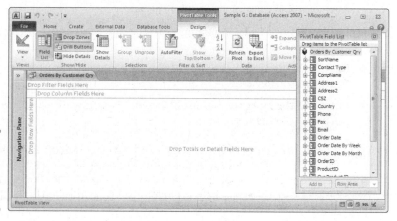

Figure 4-12:
At first, your
PivotTable
is blank.

**Book III
Chapter 4**

*Viewing Data Using
Crosstabs and
PivotTables*

✦ Open the query containing your data, and then click the PivotTable View button in the bottom-right corner of the Access window. (It's the second in the group of five tiny buttons.)

✦ Select the query containing your data in the Navigation pane. Then display the Create tab on the Ribbon and click the More Forms button in the Forms group. Select PivotTable from the drop-down list.

After you create a PivotTable using one of the methods, you see a blank PivotTable with a PivotTable Field List. If you don't see the Field list, click the Field List button on the PivotTable Tools Design tab on the Ribbon.

Displaying data in your PivotTable

To see data after you create a blank PivotTable, you need to drag and drop fields into the drop areas. Each field name in the PivotTable Field List has a plus sign *(expand indicator)* or a minus sign *(collapse indicator)* next to it. Click an expand indicator in the PivotTable Field List to see more options for fields to drag and drop. In particular, Access adds fields to categorize date data by week, month, quarter, and so on. In addition, you can create and display an unlimited number of calculated fields in a PivotTable. You can even sort by a calculated field.

The four drop areas are as follows:

✦ **Totals or Detail Fields:** Drag the name of the field that contains the values you want displayed in the body of the PivotTable to this drop area. The values in this field are organized by the values in the column and row fields. After you drag a field to the Totals or Detail Fields drop area, you see data in your PivotTable.

✦ **Column Field:** Drag the name(s) of the field(s) you want to show as column headings to this area.

✦ **Row Field:** Drag the name(s) of the field(s) you want to show as row headings to this area.

✦ **Filter Fields:** Drag the names of any fields you want to use for filtering purposes to this area.

You can start dragging fields in any order. After you drop a detail field onto the PivotTable, you see data in the table. Figure 4-13 shows a PivotTable with the `Product Name` field in the rows drop area, the `Order Date by Year` field in the columns drop area, and the `Qty` field in the body of the table. Fields used in the PivotTable appear in bold in the Field list.

Use these steps to see data in your PivotTable:

1. **Drag and drop a field from the PivotTable Field List into the main part of the PivotTable — the part labeled Drop Totals or Detail Fields Here.**

Choose the field that you want to see organized using other fields.

If the drop areas aren't visible in your PivotTable, click Drop Zones in the Show/Hide section of the Design tab.

A cell for each record of data appears. Now, by adding row and column labels, you can categorize that data. Later, you summarize it by using the AutoCalc button.

TIP

If you prefer not to drag and drop, select the field in the Field list, use the drop-down list at the bottom of the Field list to tell Access where you want to use the field, and then click the Add To button.

Fields used in the PivotTable appear in bold in the PivotTable Field List, as shown in Figure 4-14.

2. **Drag and drop a field into the Drop Row Fields Here section of the PivotTable — the section on the left — to create row labels.**

   You may want to click an expand indicator in the PivotTable Field List to see more options for fields to drag and drop. In particular, Access adds fields to categorize date data by week, month, quarter, and so on.

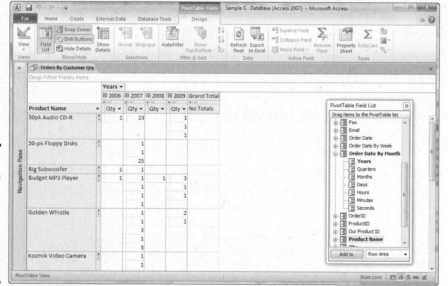

Figure 4-13:
A PivotTable showing ExtPrice organized by Product Name and Order Date.

**Book III
Chapter 4**

Viewing Data Using
Crosstabs and
PivotTables

Figure 4-14:
Bolded field names are used in the PivotTable.

3. **Drag and drop a field into the Drop Column Fields Here section of the PivotTable to create column labels.**

   Your table may look something like Figure 4-13.

   The resulting table may be confusing because you see each record rather than data totals. However, changing that isn't difficult.

4. **Click a column label that names the field displayed in the body of the table to see the totaled data. (In Figure 4-13, that's the Qty column.)**

   All like-named column headings are selected automatically.

Σ AutoCalc ▾

5. **Click the AutoCalc button on the Design tab on the Ribbon and choose the type of total you want to use.**

   See Chapter 2 of this minibook for more information about the aggregation choices. For Text fields, your only option is the Count total.

   You now see a Total column at the far right of the table (named according to the aggregation you picked) and a Grand Total row at the bottom of the table. Each cell in the table also gains an extra piece of information at the bottom of the cell: the sum, count, or other aggregation of the data in the cell. Also, the new field is added to the Pivot Table Field List.

🗐 Hide Details

6. **Click the Hide Details button on the Design tab on the Ribbon.**

   The table now displays aggregates, shown in Figure 4-15. You can show or hide the details for each row or column by clicking the expand (+) or collapse (–) indicator in the row or column heading.

   You can now add or remove categories to see your aggregated data in several different ways.

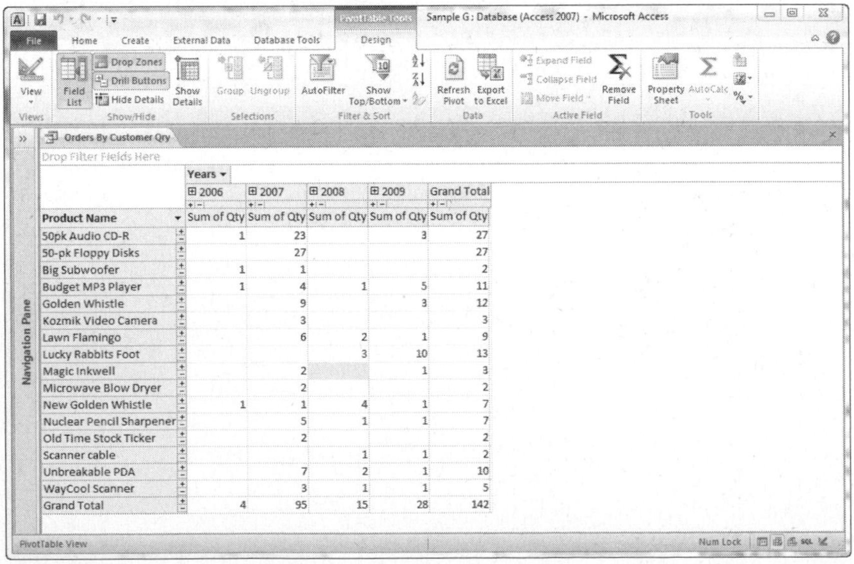

Figure 4-15:
This PivotTable shows aggregate data — total sales for each product for each month.

Working with dates

You may have noticed that the PivotTable Field List has a + next to each field name. Click the expand indicator (+) to see an indented list of fields, which is most useful when working with Date/Time fields.

Access does some neat things with `Date/Time` fields in the PivotTable Field List — it automatically creates fields to aggregate date data by year, quarter, month, week, day, hour, minute, and second. (Refer to Figure 4-14 to see date fields in the Field list.)

The two different date headings, Order Date by Week and Order Date by Month, allow you to use a date as a column field and a date as a row field, but you must select the dates from different indented lists. For instance, you may want to see years in columns and months in rows to compare monthly sales from year to year.

To view data by month, find the `Months` field in one of the date fields and drop it in the PivotTable.

After you have a date field in the columns or rows heading, you can expand the heading using the expand indicator (+) next to the field in the PivotTable (not in the Field list) to display date data in more detail.

When you use a lookup field in a PivotTable, you see the data that Access stores in the field, not the data usually displayed. (***Remember:*** A lookup field displays a drop-down list of data to choose from that is stored in a table or a list.) In general, you use the descriptive field in the PivotTable rather than the lookup field to see the appropriate data. We use the `Product Name` field rather than the `Product ID` field in this chapter even though (in most views) those two fields display the same data. (For more on lookup fields, see Book II, Chapter 5. For information on using lookup fields in queries, see Chapter 1 of this minibook.)

**Book III
Chapter 4**

Viewing Data Using
Crosstabs and
PivotTables

Modifying your PivotTable

After you have a basic PivotTable, you can modify it to look exactly how you want. You can add fields, move fields around to different drop areas, format your data, create new fields, expand and collapse details, and more.

For much of the work involved in modifying a PivotTable, your best friend is the PivotTable Tools Design tab on the Ribbon. Table 4-1 lists the buttons in the PivotTable tab and what they do.

If the data in your database changes while your PivotTable is open, be sure that the table reflects the most current data by clicking the Refresh Pivot button on the PivotTable toolbar.

Table 4-1	PivotTable Buttons
Name	*What It Does*
Save	Saves the format of the object, which includes the format of the PivotTable.
View	View the PivotTable in another view. PivotChart is always available. The other options depend on which kind of object you use to create the PivotTable — table or query.
Field List	Displays or hides the Field list available for this PivotTable.
Drop Zones	Displays or hides the labels for the areas where you can drop field names (that is, Drop Filters Here).
Drill Button	Displays or hides the + and – buttons that allow you to drill down into data.
Hide Details	Hides detail values (one value for each record of data) and displays only totals (if any are defined).
Show Details	Shows detail values (one value for each record of data).
Group	Allows you to create groups on the fly by selecting rows or columns and clicking the Group button. For instance, you could group state data into regions.
Ungroup	Ungroup a group by clicking the group name to select it, and then clicking this button.
AutoFilter	Applies (or removes) a filter already defined (such as a Show Top/Bottom Items filter).
Show Top/ Bottom Items	Choose to see top or bottom values. Choose either a percentage of values or a number of data points that you want to see. Click again to cancel the filter.
Sort Ascending	Sorts the selected part of the PivotTable in ascending order.
Sort Descending	Sorts the selected part of the PivotTable in descending order.
Clear Custom Ordering	Returns data to its unsorted order.
Refresh Pivot	Displays new and updated data.
Export to Microsoft Excel	Exports the PivotTable to Microsoft Excel (usually to make use of PivotTable functionality in Excel).
Expand Field	Expands the selected cell, column, or row to display additional data or options (equivalent to clicking +).
Collapse Field	Collapses the selected cell, column, or row to hide additional data or options (equivalent to clicking -).
Move Field	Displays a drop-down list allowing you to move the field to Field Area, Column Area, Filter Area, or Detail Area.

Name	What It Does
Remove Field	Removes the selected totals field.
Property Sheet	Displays PivotTable properties.
AutoCalc	Calculates an aggregate field by selecting the field to aggregate by clicking a field name in the table and then choosing from the AutoCalc drop-down list.
Subtotal	Calculates subtotals when the PivotTable has at least one total field and at least two fields as either row or column headings.
Formulas	Creates a new, calculated, total, or detail field.
Show As	Displays the values or percentage of a total.

Working with PivotTable data

Changing the way your PivotTable displays data is the fun part! Drag fields around, in, and out of the table to your heart's content — or until you have a table that shows the data you need in an easy-to-analyze format.

To change the data in your PivotTable, you have two basic options:

✦ **Add additional row and column categories.** Drag fields from the PivotTable Field List or from one part of the PivotTable to another. A blue line appears to show you where the field will drop. Watch the blue line — particularly the ends of the line — that tells you where you are dropping a field.

✦ **Remove categories.** Drag a field name off the table (until you see an *X* next to the pointer) to remove it from the table.

If you want to save the PivotTable data (that is, save it as is without seeing new data included in it), export it to Excel using the Export to Microsoft Excel button.

Showing/hiding details

By default, Access shows detail data, which means you see a heck of a lot of data. You may be interested only in summary data, though, such as totals.

You may have noticed that every row and column label on the PivotTable has expand (+) and collapse (–) indicators. When a category expands, you see details; when it collapses, you see only the total. Use these buttons to see more — or less — of the data. You can change an individual row or column, or you can expand or collapse an entire category by clicking a heading and then clicking the Collapse or Expand buttons on the toolbar.

Adding totals and grand totals

Σ AutoCalc ▾

Use the AutoCalc button to create totals. Select the field you want to total; then click the AutoCalc button and choose how to total the values. (See the section, "Displaying data in your PivotTable," earlier in this chapter.)

Here's how to add grand totals to the PivotTable:

1. **Scroll to the far-right column of the PivotTable until you get to the Grand Total column.**

2. **Drag the name of the field you want totaled to the Grand Total column, and drop it there.**

   You can drag the field name from the Field list or somewhere else in the PivotTable. The empty Grand Total column fills with totals.

Grouping data

You can easily group data on the fly in a PivotTable. For instance, if you want to create groups of products to see subtotals, just select the products in a group by clicking the first product and Ctrl-clicking subsequent products; then click the Group button. Figure 4-16 shows products sorted into two groups. The Other group can be further sorted as necessary: All you have to do is select the products you want to group and then click the Group button again.

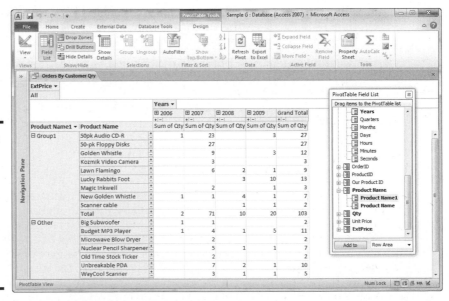

Figure 4-16: This PivotTable shows the products sorted into two groups using the Group button.

After groups have been created, you can use them to filter the PivotTable. Here's how:

1. **Click the drop-down arrow for Group parent (in Figure 4-16, that's the Product Name1 cell).**

   The filter options appear.

2. **Then click the group(s) that you want to display.**

3. **Click OK to see the resulting PivotTable.**

   The data is displayed with some groups hidden, and totals updated to match the new data. To unfilter, repeat these steps and choose All in the Filter options.

Adding a calculated field

You can also create a new, calculated field while in PivotTable view. *Calculated fields* are new fields that you create with an equation, known in Access-speak as an *expression*. When you create a calculated field in PivotTable view, you have the choice of creating a total or a detail field. A detail field has a value for every record, but a total field has only a value for every category shown on the PivotTable. For more about creating calculated fields, see Chapter 2 of this minibook.

Follow these steps:

1. **Click the Formulas button in the Tools group of the Design tab on the Ribbon.**

   Access displays a drop-down list.

2. **Choose the Create Calculated Total option or the Create Calculated Detail Field option.**

   Access displays the Calculation tab of the Properties sheet, as shown in Figure 4-17.

Book III
Chapter 4

**Viewing Data Using
Crosstabs and
PivotTables**

Figure 4-17:
Create a
new field
using the
Calculation
tab of the
Properties
sheet.

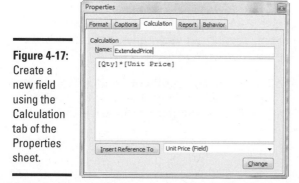

3. **Name the new field.**

   Type a descriptive name for the new field in the Name text box.

4. **Write the expression to calculate the new field.**

   You write the expression in the usual way (see Chapter 2 of this mini-book). In short, surround field names with square brackets and use operators such as +, -, *, and /. You can use the Insert Reference To button to put a field name into the expression.

   You can use functions, but you must know the exact syntax. (You may prefer to create the new field in Design view — see the tip after these steps.)

5. **Click the Change button to create the new field.**

6. **Use the other tabs on the Properties dialog box as needed to change the way the new calculated field looks and acts.**

   The Format, Report, and Behavior tabs are covered in the formatting section later in this chapter. The Captions tab allows you to specify a caption (text to appear instead of the field name) and formatting for the caption.

7. **Close the Properties sheet.**

   The new field appears in the PivotTable Field List. If the new field is a total field, it appears indented under the Totals category, at the top of the Field list.

After you create a new field, you can drag it into the table.

You can also create a new field in Design view. If you work in the PivotTable view of a query, switch to Design view (click the View button) and create a new detail field. When you switch back to PivotTable view, the new field is available in the PivotTable Field List. You can use Expression Builder when you create a new field using Design view, which is useful if you create an expression that uses functions.

Charting your PivotTable

You may find you want to view your PivotTable graphically. You can — with PivotChart view. Click the View button and choose the PivotChart option from the drop-down menu. PivotChart view reflects the layout of the PivotTable. (See Book V, Chapter 3 for more on how to use PivotCharts.)

If you change the layout of your PivotChart, your PivotTable reflects those changes — and vice versa. If you want both a PivotChart and a PivotTable to work with, create two identical objects (queries or forms) — one for the chart, and one for the table.

Formatting PivotTables

 Property Sheet PivotTables do have some formatting options. You find some of the normal text-formatting options through the Properties sheet: Click the Property Sheet button. When the Properties sheet appears (as shown in Figure 4-18), click the Format tab.

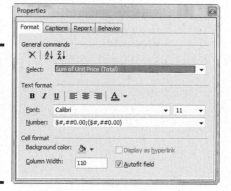

Figure 4-18: The Format tab of the Properties sheet changes text formatting.

Before you select format options, click the Select drop-down list to tell Access what part of the PivotTable you're formatting. To make changes to the whole table, follow these steps:

Book III
Chapter 4

Viewing Data Using
Crosstabs and
PivotTables

1. **Select the Microsoft Office PivotTable option.**

   If you prefer, rather than choosing a field from the drop-down list, click a part of the PivotTable while the Properties sheet is open.

   The Select option changes to reflect the part of the PivotTable that you clicked.

2. **Use the Delete button (which looks like an *x*) to remove the field that appears in the Select box from the PivotTable, and the Sort buttons to sort the field.**

   The other formatting options allow you to change the text format, alignment (where in the cell the data appears — left, center, or right), font, font color, font size, number format, background color, and column width.

3. **Select the Autofit check box to select the best size for the column.**

You can also change column width without the Properties sheet, by using the drag method that you use in a datasheet.

Another formatting option that you may want to use is the `Caption` property on the Captions tab of the Properties sheet. Using the `Caption` property, you can change the label used for the field. Here's the drill:

1. **Select the label you want to change, using the Select Caption drop-down list or by clicking the caption in the table.**

   The Properties sheet remains open.

2. **Type the new caption in the `Caption` property.**

   You can change the format of the caption, too, with the formatting options.

The Report tab, shown in Figure 4-19, has options that affect the way a field works — whether the headings are row or column headings, whether totals are calculated on the visible data or all data, and whether empty cells and rows/columns are displayed.

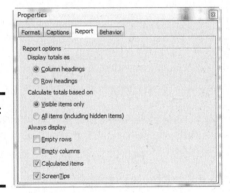

Figure 4-19: The Report tab of the Properties sheet.

The Behavior tab, shown in Figure 4-20, has options that affect the way the PivotTable as a whole works — whether expand indicators and drop areas are shown, defaults for the way fields expand, the default sizes for rows and columns, and whether the display works from left to right or the reverse.

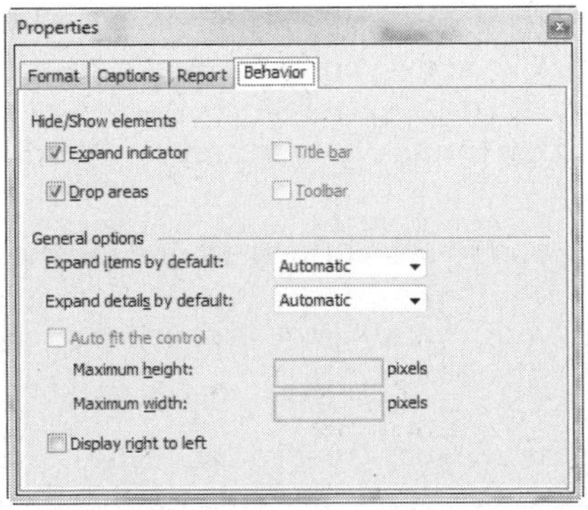

Figure 4-20: The Behavior tab of the Properties sheet.

Filtering the PivotTable data

You can filter data in a PivotTable in several ways. PivotTables can filter data, but they are set up for very simple criteria, such as excluding a single value at a time or displaying the top of bottom values. The Show Top/Bottom button in the Filter and Sort group of the Design tab of the ribbon allows you to choose to show the top (or bottom) values (you pick how many from the drop down list) or the top percent of values that you choose. For instance, choose to see the top 5% to see the highest values in your pivot table.

Another way to filter within a PivotTable is to select from a list of values. If you have a lot of data — as well as criteria that include a range of values — you may want to create criteria in a query, and then use the query data to create the PivotTable.

When you filter within the PivotTable, you can use a field in any drop area. If you don't want to use a field for the structure of the PivotTable (row, column, or data), simply drop it in the Filter drop area, and use it only to filter the data in the PivotTable.

Every field used in the PivotTable has an arrow to display a drop-down list. Use the drop-down arrow to display a check list of displayed data; click to remove check marks for data you don't want displayed.

Filter settings are retained when you remove a field. If you remove a field and later add the field back to the layout, the same items are again hidden.

Book IV

Forms for Editing Data

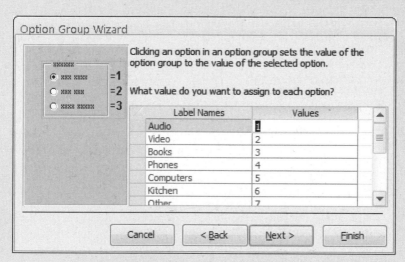

Specifying labels and values for buttons.

Contents at a Glance

Chapter 1: Designing and Using Forms (and Reports)

In This Chapter

✔ Understanding and using forms

✔ Creating a form using a wizard (the easy way)

✔ Using your new form to enter and edit records

✔ Creating or modifying a form using Layout view

✔ Changing the properties of a form

✔ Saving, copying, printing, importing, and renaming your forms

Although datasheets are convenient for looking at, entering, and editing the information in tables and queries, there's a lot to dislike about them as well. Datasheets show records one per row, and if your table or query has a lot of fields, you need to scroll left and right to see all the fields. Datasheets rarely look anything like the paper forms that your information may be coming from. And datasheets display information from only one table or query at a time, even though when you enter or edit data, you may need to make changes in related tables at the same time.

Forms to the rescue! When you design your own forms to display information on-screen, you choose where fields appear, what explanatory text appears, and what lines and boxes to add. Your forms can include calculations (such as the total number of items that a customer is ordering). You can also include *subforms,* which are small forms that display information (usually more than one record's worth) from a related table or query. You can also make forms that contain buttons that run programs (VBA modules), open other forms, print reports, or exit Access — your own Mission Control.

After you design a form (a first draft, anyway), you can save the form design as part of your database, and you can use it any time to view the table or query with which the form is associated. You can always change the design of a form later — no one makes a perfect form the first time. This chapter describes how to make simple forms (either by using a wizard or from scratch) and how to rearrange the fields on a form in Layout view. Chapter 2 of this minibook explains how to modify the design of a form after you create it using Design view. Chapters 3 and 4 of this minibook cover fancier forms, including forms with calculations, totals, and subforms.

Forms and Reports Are Secretly Related

This chapter describes how to make and edit forms, but it secretly also describes how to make and edit reports. Forms and reports are very similar. You *create* them with many of the same commands, tools, and properties to make stuff look good on-screen and on paper. But how you *use* forms and reports is different. Forms are for interacting with data on-screen, whereas reports are for printing data on paper.

This chapter describes how to create a form, but creating a report works the same way. To make a report, skim the instructions in this chapter, then skip to Book V, which is about the aspects of reports that differ from forms, like how they print.

Form Basics

A form doesn't store any data: It displays data from a table or query, called its *record source.* When you create a form, you tell Access what the record source will be for the form.

The things that appear on a form or report are called *controls,* and they include text boxes that display data from the database, text labels that explain how to use the form, buttons you can click to save, navigate, or other operations, check boxes, and more. Chapter 2 of this minibook explains how to use each of the available controls. You don't have to know much about controls when you get started making and using forms and reports, because Access can make entire forms and reports, including their controls, for you.

Many controls display the data from fields from the record source. Your form or report doesn't have to include all the fields in the record source. You can omit boring fields, for example, if the table has an Autonumber ID field that the user never needs to know about. And the fields don't need to appear in the same order in which they appear in the table or query.

Usually, a form displays the fields from a *single record* (either one record in a table or one record from a query result datasheet). However, you can also make a *continuous form,* which displays several records, one below another. You can even make a *split form,* which is a single record form with a datasheet below it: When you click a record from the datasheet, that record is displayed in the single-record form. We show you how to make all these types of forms. (Book V describes how to make various types of reports.)

What kind of form would you like?

Access provides several ways to create forms. The method you use depends on whether you want Access to do the work, whether you want complete control over what you see, or whether you want some combination of laziness and control.

Select the Create tab on the Ribbon and take a look at the Forms group to see the ways that you can create forms. Table 1-1 explains what each button does.

Table 1-1   **Creating Forms using the Forms Groups on the Create Tab of the Ribbon**

Button in the Forms Group	Name	What It Does	Where to Find More Info
Form	Form button	Creates a quick and easy form for the table, query, or report you have open or selected. You enter information into this kind of form one record at a time.	"Making the easiest possible form by using the Form button," later in this chapter.
Form Design	Form Design button	Allows you to design your own form from scratch, in Design view	Chapter 2 of this mini-book.
Blank Form	Blank Form button	Allows you to design your own form from scratch, in Layout view	"Making a new form from scratch in Layout view," later in this chapter.
	Form Wizard button	Walks you through the creation of a form, helping you to choose fields from multiple tables and queries and to add summary calculations. The results are bland and standard, but you can use Design or Layout view later to make changes.	"Wizard, make me a form!" later in this chapter.
	Navigation button	Creates switchboard-like forms with buttons that display any form or report you want.	"Creating a navigation form" in Chapter 3.
	More Forms button, then choose Multiple Items	Creates a datasheet-like columnar form.	"More super-speedy forms" later in this chapter.

Book IV Chapter 1

Designing and Using Forms (and Reports)

(continued)

Table 1-1 *(continued)*

Button in the Forms Group	Name	What It Does	Where to Find More Info
	More Forms button, then choose Datasheet	Creates a form designed to be viewed in Datasheet view rather than Form view.	"More super-speedy forms" later in this chapter.
	More Forms button, then choose Split Form	Creates a form that includes a regular form at the top and a datasheet below it.	"More super-speedy forms" later in this chapter.
	More Forms button, then choose Modal Dialog	Creates a form that keeps the focus and must be closed to return to where you came from. It is often confused with a dialog box.	"More super-speedy forms" later in this chapter.
	More Forms button, then choose PivotChart	Creates a PivotChart from a single table or query. A PivotChart graphically analyzes data as a bar or line chart.	Book V, Chapter 3 for more on PivotCharts.
	More Forms button, then choose PivotTable	Creates a PivotTable from a single table or query. A PivotTable is an interactive table that summarizes data by multiple fields.	Book III, Chapter 4 for more on PivotTables.

Making and Using a Form

The easiest way to create a form is to let Access create it for you. (Why work, when a program can do the work instead?) We show you how to make a form so you can see how it looks in Layout view, how to save it, and how to display a record in a form.

Making the easiest possible form by using the Form button

Follow these steps to make and save a form:

1. **In the Navigation pane, select the table or query that contains the records that you want to view or edit in the form.**

   For example, if you want to work with the records in your Address Book table, select it from the list of tables in the Navigation pane.

2. **Click the Form button in the Forms group on the Create tab of the Ribbon.**

   You don't have a lot of options — none, actually — but you get a usable form with no waiting. You see a form that displays all the fields in one record of your table or query, as shown in Figure 1-1. Access gives the form the same name as the table or query you selected in Step 1 (unless you already have a form by that name).

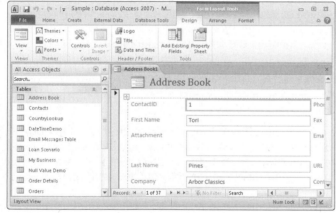

Figure 1-1:
Access whips up a form that displays one record at a time and shows the form in Layout view.

Access displays your new form in Layout view, a view that allows you to move the fields and labels around if you don't like where Access put them.

3. **Make whatever changes you see fit.**

   We describe how to use Layout view in the section "Getting Your Fields Lined Up in Layout View" later in this chapter.

4. **Save the form, so you can use it later, by right-clicking the object tab for the form and choosing Save.**

   In Figure 1-1, that's the AddressBook1 tab.

5. **When Access asks for a name for the form, accept its suggestion or type a different name; then click OK.**

That's it — you're done. You can close the form by clicking the X button at the right end of the object tab for the form. Or, right-click the object tab for the form and choose Close from the menu that appears.

Viewing a form

After you create a form, you can open it in any of these views:

✦ **Layout view** displays the form with some sample data, ready for you to move around the form elements into a more pleasing arrangement. You usually use this view right after you create a form, to fix layout problems. You can find out how to use Layout view in section "Getting Your Fields Lined Up in Layout View" later in this chapter.

✦ **Design view** displays the form elements with no data, so you can customize the form layout and behavior. You usually use this view after Layout view, when the form elements are in the right places, to tweak your design. See Chapter 2 for how to use Design view.

✦ **Form view** displays the form as you (or the Form Wizard or AutoForm) designed it, as described in the next section. When you've finished creating and customizing your form, this is the view you'll use on an ongoing basis to maintain the data in your database.

✦ **Datasheet view** displays the fields on the form as a datasheet. It ignores the layout of the form. Most forms have Datasheet view disabled. See the section "Some other cool form properties" for how to enable Datasheet view.

✦ **PivotTable and PivotChart views** are described in Book III, Chapter 4 and Book V, Chapter 3. These views are disabled for most forms. We don't cover them here because these two views are for summarizing and graphing your data, not for entering and editing data.

To open a form in Form view, just double-click it on the Navigation pane, where it appears in the Forms section. To open a form in any view, right-click the form name in Forms section of the Navigation pane and choose the view you want. (If there is no Forms section, then right-click the Navigation pane heading, choose Category, then Object Type. Now you see the objects in the database, sorted by object type, such as Tables, Queries, Forms, and Reports.) Datasheet, PivotTable, and PivotChart views don't appear for most forms, since they are usually disabled.

When the form is open, you can switch views by clicking the View button in the Views group on the Home tab of the Ribbon. The View button changes depending on which view you're in. When you're in Layout view, the default for the View button is Form view, and when you're in Form view, the default is Layout view. To get into Design view with the View button, click the bottom part of the button and choose Design View from the menu that appears.

You can also switch among the views by right-clicking the object tab or title of the form. Choose the view you want.

The View button provides different possible views depending on what type of object you're working on. The views available for tables and queries are different from those for forms.

Editing data in Form view

After you design and create your form, you can enter, edit, and display records. To open a form in Form view, double-click its name in the Forms section of the Navigation pane. The Address Book form in Form view looks very much like Figure 1-1, except now you can edit and add data.

The form itself doesn't store data: The data that a form displays comes from tables in the database (the record source), and any changes you make are stored in the tables. When you add a record via a form, Access stores the record in the table(s). If your form displays information from a query, the changes are stored in the tables that provide the records for the query. If your form has subforms, as described in Chapter 3 of this minibook, you can edit records from several tables at the same time.

In general, you use all the same keystrokes you use when editing records in Datasheet view, as described in Book II, Chapter 2. You can press Tab or Enter to move from one field to another. You can also use the navigation buttons at the bottom of the form to move to different records. There's a Search box at the bottom of the form that you can use to search for the text in whatever field your cursor is in.

If you prefer to use the keyboard to move around a form, check out Table 1-2 for a list of the keys to use and where they move the cursor.

Table 1-2	Using the Keyboard to Move in a Form
To Move Here in a Form . . .	*Press This Key*
Following field	Tab, Enter, or →
Previous field	Shift+Tab or ←
First field of current record	Home
Last field of current record	End
Subform	Ctrl+Tab
Main form	Ctrl+Shift+Tab
New record	Ctrl+(+) (Plus sign)

You can cut and paste, search, and filter your records just as if you were working in Datasheet view, as described in Book II, Chapter 3. To select an entire record, click the record selector (the gray box at the left edge of the window). You can cut and paste a record from another table into your form as long as the field names match: For all the fields with matching names, Access pastes the data into the correct field on the form.

Access saves the record when you move to another record. You can also save what you typed so far by pressing Ctrl+S or by clicking the File button on the Ribbon and choosing Save.

Creating Forms with Wizards

The Form button in the Forms group made you a form, but it may not be the kind of form you wanted. You have lots of ways to arrange fields on a form, and the form that Access made may not be what you had in mind. Before you give up and make a form from scratch in Design or Layout view, give the Form Wizard and More Forms a try.

Wizard, make me a form!

The Form Wizard lets you choose which fields to include and in what order to place the fields. This wizard is especially useful if you want to create a form that includes data from more than one table or query. The wizard can create subforms for you and even apply formatting to make the form look a little less vanilla. The Form Wizard can be a great way to get started with a complex form — you may not like the exact look of the finished form, but it works and has all the fields you want. After the wizard finishes, you can make all the changes you want in Layout or Design view.

Follow these steps to create a form with the Form Wizard:

1. **In the Navigation pane, click the Form Wizard button in the Forms group on the Create tab on the Ribbon.**

    You see the Form Wizard dialog box, which looks like Figure 1-2.

2. **Use the Tables/Queries drop-down list to choose the first table or query for which you want to include fields.**

    Choose the table or query from which the form gets the data to display or edit.

3. **In the Available Fields list, select the fields that you want to appear on the form. Move them to the Selected Fields list by double-clicking them or by selecting them and clicking the right-arrow (>) button.**

    The order doesn't matter. If you decide you don't want a field after all, double-click it in the Selected Fields list — or select the field and click the left-arrow button (<) button — to move it back to the Available Fields list.

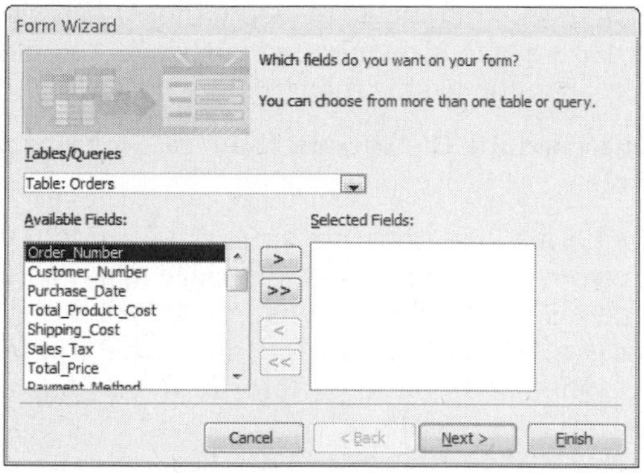

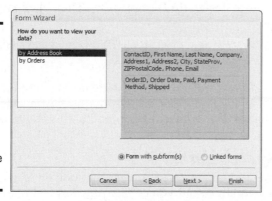

Figure 1-2:
The Form
Wizard
steps you
through the
process of
creating a
new form.

4. **Repeat Steps 2 and 3 to choose fields from other tables or queries.**

   The additional tables or queries have to be related to the first table or queries. Otherwise, Access asks you to use the Relationships window to create relationships, and you have to start the wizard over. See Book II, Chapter 6 for how to create relationships between tables.

5. **When all the fields that you want to display in the form appear in the Selected Fields list, click the Next button.**

   The Form Wizard displays the next screen of the dialog box. If you select fields from only one table or query, skip right to Step 10. Otherwise, the Form Wizard asks how you want to view your data, as shown in Figure 1-3.

Figure 1-3:
The Form
Wizard can
create a
form with a
subform for
information
from a
related table
or query.

**Book IV
Chapter 1**

**Designing and
Using Forms
(and Reports)**

6. **Choose the organization you want for your form by clicking the table or query by which you want to group records.**

   In Figure 1-3, the form includes fields from the Address Book table (which contains a record for each customer) and the Orders table (with one record for each order). Do you want the form to display one customer, with all the orders for that customer? Or do you want to display one order, with all its customers? (The second option makes no sense, because each order is placed by only one customer.) You decide, by clicking an option from the list on the left side of the wizard's window.

7. **Choose whether to include the second table or query as a subform or as a second form.**

   If you choose the Form with Subforms option, you end up with one form, with the records from the second table or query in a box (subform) on the form. If you choose the Linked Forms option, you get two separate forms, each in its own window, with a button on the first form to display the second form. When in doubt, try subforms. (See Chapter 3 of this minibook for how subforms work.)

8. **Click Next.**

   Access displays a window that asks you to choose the layout for the subform, if you're creating one. Otherwise, skip to Step 10.

9. **Choose the layout and click Next.**

   You can click a layout option to see what it looks like. If you're not sure which option to use, stick with the Tabular layout — using and editing the layout is easy.

10. **Give the form a name. If you created a subform or second form, give it a name, too.**

    This name is what Access uses when saving the form. The name doesn't have to appear on the form.

11. **Choose whether to open the form now (in Form view) or to make changes to the form design (in Design view). Then click Finish to create the form.**

    Why not open it first, to see how it looks? You can always edit the design later.

A form made by the Form Wizard is rarely totally usable right off the bat, but it's a good start. When you're done admiring your new form, close it with the Close button. To change its design, see Chapter 2 of this minibook.

More super-speedy forms

You have a few other predefined form choices that don't give you a lot of options — none, actually — but you get a usable form with no waiting. Try this:

1. **In the Forms section of the Navigation pane, select the table or query you want to use as the source of the records displayed on the form.**

2. **Click the More Forms button in the Forms section of the Create tab on the Ribbon.**

You see these options: Multiple Items, Datasheet, Split Form, Modal Dialog, PivotChart, and PivotTable. Later in this section, we list what kind of form each option creates.

3. **Click an option.**

Voilà — a form! Exactly what you see depends on which option you choose. The first four as described below. PivotCharts are discussed in Book V, Chapter 3 and PivotTables in Book III, Chapter 4.

If you like the form, save it when you close it. If you don't like it, just close it and decline to save it when Access asks. See the section "Storing Your Forms and Reports" at the end of this chapter.

Here's what you get when you choose one of the first four More Form options:

 ✦ **Multiple Items:** You get a form that displays more than one record. (It's called a *continuous form,* as described in the section "One record or many?" later in this chapter.) The fields are arranged in a column, like a datasheet, as shown in Figure 1-4. Unless your table or query includes only a few fields, the form is likely to be way too wide to be useful.

✦ **Datasheet:** Access creates a form to be viewed in Datasheet view. You can view it only in Design view (to choose which fields to include, as described in the next chapter) or Datasheet view (to add and edit records).

Figure 1-4:
Choosing Multiple Items from the More Forms button makes a form that looks like a dressed-up datasheet. You can customize the field sizes later.

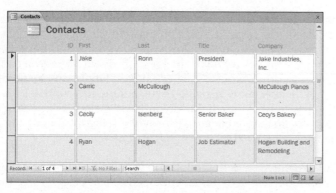

 ✦ **Split Form:** A *split form* displays some information in a regular form and some in Datasheet view, as shown in Figure 1-5.

Figure 1-5:
In a split
form, you
can select
a record
from the
datasheet at
the bottom,
and the data
is displayed
in the form
at the top.

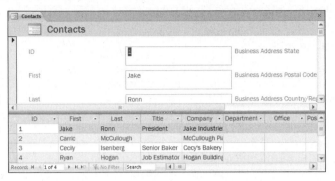

 ✦ **Modal Dialog:** Access creates a blank form for you, with an OK button
and not much else, configured to look like a dialog box. This type of
form is useful when you want a form that the user must deal with before
proceeding to other work.

Modifying Existing Forms (and Reports)

None of these wizards make forms that are perfect. These computer-generated
forms are a good place to start, but you usually want to make further refinements before the form is really usable. Two views are useful here: Layout
view and Design view. You can use these views to make new forms from
scratch, too.

Layout view, which was new in Access 2007, shows you your form with data
in it but allows you to make some changes to the form itself. The form looks
almost exactly as it will look in Form view, with the addition of some lines
and icons you can use to make changes. In Layout view, you can mess with
your controls (your text boxes, check boxes, labels, and so on), including moving them around, resizing them, adding the control for a field, and
removing the control for a field. Layout view makes it very easy to arrange
your controls tastefully because it provides a layout (hence the name) with
rows and columns, so that your controls line up nicely.

However, Layout view is limited. If you want to make other changes, like
adding validation rules to fields, you need to use *Design view.* Design view
doesn't look much like your form; no data appears, but you can see the controls on your form and configure the properties of each one.

In either Layout or Design view, you can display the *Property sheet,* which
shows the properties of the entire form, sections of the form, or individual
controls. Both views also work with the *Field list,* which lists the fields in the
record source.

Read on to try rearranging your fields in Layout view. Chapter 2 of this mini-book explains making all kinds of changes in Design view, setting the properties of controls and forms using the Property sheet, and adding controls by dragging fields from the Field list.

Getting Your Fields Lined Up in Layout View

Layout view enables you to impose a *control layout* on your form, which restricts where controls can appear on the form. When form controls are in a control layout, it's easy to get them to line up neatly, because Access does it for you. Access provides two control layouts:

✦ **Stacked:** The label for the control is to the left of the control, as shown in Figure 1-1 (earlier in this chapter). This control layout is useful for single-record forms.

✦ **Tabular:** The label for the control is at the top of a column of controls, as shown in Figure 1-4. This control layout is useful for continuous forms, which can display the data from multiple records in columns.

The Tabular control layout is useful only for continuous forms, which are described in the section "One record or many?" later in this chapter.

A form can have one or more control layouts, each occupying a rectangular part of the form, each with rows and columns containing controls displaying labels, fields, and other things. Each control layout appears in Layout view as a dotted rectangle; in Figure 1-1, a control layout encloses a column of controls and their labels. Your form may have a second control layout to the right of the first one if it has a second column of controls. Control layouts are invisible in Form view; you, the form designer, can see them in Layout and Design view.

If you can't see Layout view — if it just doesn't appear as an option in your menus and buttons — it may be disabled for this database. Click the File tab on the Ribbon, click Options to see the Access Options dialog box, and click Current Database to see the options for this database. Make sure that the Enable Layout View check box is selected.

Using a control layout to rearrange fields

Suppose you followed the steps in "Making the easiest possible form by using the Form button" to create the form shown in Figure 1-1. However, you don't like the arrangement of fields on the form. Well, we have good news for you: You can use Layout view to make some changes.

To open a form in Layout view, right-click the form name from the Navigation pane and choose Layout View from the menu that appears. The form appears, as shown in Figure 1-1, with the controls (text boxes and check boxes) and labels (the names to the left of each control) neatly lines up in a grid. The arrangement looks very much like a table in a word-processing document or spreadsheet. Faint dotted lines separate the rows and columns in the grid. When your form is in Layout view, three tabs on the Ribbon contain useful buttons: Design, Arrange, and Format.

You can move a field to another spot on the form by clicking and dragging its control. Access forces the field into a row and column in the control layout; if there isn't space for the field, Access inserts a row to make space. The control's label may not come along with it, so you may need to drag it to the spot to the left of the relocated field.

Adding and deleting fields

The easiest way to add fields to an existing form is to use the Field list. Display the Field list by clicking the Add Existing Fields button in the Tools group on the Design tab of the Ribbon. Click the plus sign to the left of table that contains the fields you want to display on the form, so you see the field names. Then drag the field name from the Field list to where you want it on the form. (Another way is to use the buttons in the Controls group on the Design tab of the Ribbon. We describe this method in Chapter 2 of this minibook.)

You can get rid of a field that you don't want to appear on the form. (Removing the field from the form doesn't delete it from the table where it's stored; Access just doesn't display the field on this form.) Right-click the field control and choose Delete from the menu that appears. You may need to delete the label or explanatory text about the field, too, in the same way.

Making a new form from scratch in Layout view

You can add a control for a field that doesn't appear on your form. In fact, you may want to create an entirely new form by starting with a blank form in Layout view, adding the fields you want. Here's how:

1. **Click the Blank Form button in the Forms group on the Create tab of the Ribbon.**

   Access creates a new form (tentatively named something like Form1) and displays it in Layout view. It also displays the Field list in a pane to the right of the form, as shown in Figure 1-6. (Click the Shutter Bar Open/Close button in the upper-right corner of the Navigation pane to shrink this list out of your way.)

2. **In the Field list, click the plus sign to the left of table that contains the fields you want to display on the form. If no tables appear, click the Show All Tables link.**

You see the list of fields in that table. (If you want the form to display fields from the results of a query, see "Where records come from" later in this chapter for how to change the record source for the form.)

Figure 1-6:
You can create a form from scratch in Layout view, dragging the fields from the Field List pane onto the form.

3. **For each field that you want to appear on the form, drag it from the Field list onto the form.**

   Access creates a control (usually a text box) and a label (text to the left of the text box) for the field.

4. **Keep adding fields, rearranging them as needed.**

5. **Close the form, clicking Yes when Access asks whether to save it, and typing a name for the form.**

Don't worry if you can't get your form to look right in Layout view. Design view, which we describe in the next chapter, gives you much finer control over your form. Layout view is great for getting the overall arrangement right, but you can't use it for everything.

Adding and deleting rows and columns in the control layout

You can open up some rows and columns in the control layout in Layout view, to make space for your new controls to go. Click the Arrange tab of the Ribbon to see the Rows & Columns group. Click a control on your form where you want to make a change and then click one of these buttons:

✦ **Insert Above** to add a row above the control

✦ **Insert Below** to add a row below the control

**Book IV
Chapter 1**

**Designing and
Using Forms
(and Reports)**

✦ **Insert Left** to add a column to the control's left

✦ **Insert Right** to add a column to the control's right

Then you can drag fields into these blank rows and columns in the control layout.

If you end up with an empty row or column in your control layout, you can get rid of it. Right-click in the empty row or column and choose Delete Row or Delete Column from the menu that appears.

Controlling your control layouts

What if you don't *want* your controls to line up neatly in rows and columns? For example, you may want the text boxes for `City`, `State`, and `Zip Code` fields to appear right next to each other, the way they look on an addressed envelope. You need to remove the control layout that forces these text box controls into line.

To see exactly what's in a control layout, click somewhere in the control layout and then choose Select Layout from the Rows & Columns group on the Arrange tab of the Ribbon. Orange lines appear around the control layout, separating its rows and columns. Here are some things to do with your control layout:

✦ **Change the spacing between the rows and columns.** You can adjust the padding (space) by selecting the control layout and choosing Control Padding in the Position group on the Arrange tab of the Ribbon.

✦ **Move it.** When you've selected a control layout, a little four-arrows icon appears in its upper-left corner. You can drag this icon around to move the entire control layout, including the controls that it contains.

✦ **Remove it.** To remove a control layout, so that the fields, labels, and other controls in that area of the form can roam free instead of being constrained into rows and columns, select the control layout, right-click in it, and choose Remove Layout from the menu that appears. The orange lines are still there, but when you click someone in the form to unselect that area of the form, the dotted lines that represented the control layout are gone.

If you have some controls that aren't in a control layout, but you wish they were so that they'd line up, you can put them into a control layout like this:

1. **Select all the controls that you want to enclose in the layout.**

Select the first control, and hold down the Shift key while clicking each of the other controls.

2. **Click either the Stacked or Tabular button in the Table group on the Arrange tab of the Ribbon.**

   Access moves all the controls into neat rows and columns, and you see the control layout dotted line around them all.

Trying out your new, improved form

After you make some changes to form, switch to Form view to see how it works. Right-click the object tab (the tab with the form's name at the top of the form) and choose Form View from the menu that appears, or click the View button in the Views group on the Design tab of the Ribbon. You can switch back and forth between Layout and Form view, making changes, until you like the result.

From time to time (maybe each time you sit back to admire your work), right-click the object tab and choose Save to save your form design. Or, press Ctrl+S to save the form.

Configuring the Whole Form or Report

Some properties apply to an entire form, such as what records appear in the form or report, how many records appear at the same time, and what scroll bars and buttons appear around the edges. You can view and edit the properties of any object in Access by using the Property sheet. This section explains how to set these form (and report) properties, and why you'd want to.

Reports have additional properties and sections, which are described in Book V, Chapter 1.

Follow these steps to display the properties that apply to the whole form or report:

1. **Open the form (or report) in Layout view or Design view.**

Property
Sheet

2. **If the Property Sheet pane isn't already open, click the Property Sheet button in the Tools group of the Design tab on the Ribbon to display it. Or, right-click anywhere in the form and choose Form Properties from the menu that appears.**

   Refer to Figure 1-7 to see the Property sheet when the entire form is selected. You see the properties of whatever object is selected — the entire form, a section of the form, or an individual control.

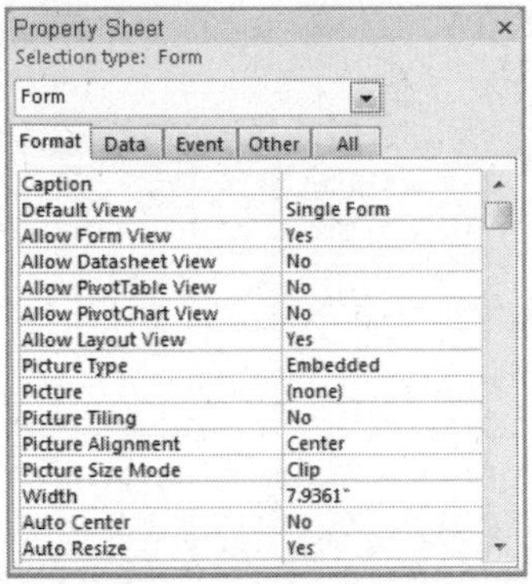

Figure 1-7:
The
properties
of a form
(or report),
a section
of a form,
or a single
control.

Property Sheet ✕
Selection type: Form

Form ▾

| Format | Data | Event | Other | All |

Caption	
Default View	Single Form
Allow Form View	Yes
Allow Datasheet View	No
Allow PivotTable View	No
Allow PivotChart View	No
Allow Layout View	Yes
Picture Type	Embedded
Picture	(none)
Picture Tiling	No
Picture Alignment	Center
Picture Size Mode	Clip
Width	7.9361"
Auto Center	No
Auto Resize	Yes

3. **To see the properties for the entire form (or report), make sure that the Selection Type at the top of the Property sheet is set to Form.**

   If you're looking at Design view, you can click the small box in the upper-left corner of the form, where the two rulers intersect.

   The Property sheet lists the properties in several categories (Format, Data, Event, and Other), each on its own tab, or you can click the All tab to see all the properties.

In addition to showing you the form properties, the Property sheet enables you to change their settings. The next few sections of this chapter describe properties you might want to change.

If the properties in the Property sheet look strange, you're probably looking at the properties for a part of the form, or maybe just one control on the form. The Property sheet displays the properties of whatever part of the form is selected. To see the properties of the entire form, set the Selection Type to Form. Chapter 2 describes setting properties for individual controls.

Naming the form

Every form has a name, and that name usually appears on the object tab for the form when the form is open. However, you can provide a different name to appear on the object tab. This feature is useful when your form name isn't very user-friendly. To change the caption — the name on the tab — change the Caption property, which is on the Format tab in the Property sheet. When the Caption property is blank, Access uses the form name, but you can type something else.

Where records come from

When you created your form or report, you (or an Access wizard) chose the *record source* — the table or query that provides the records to display. You rarely want to change the record source — if you want to use different data, you may as well start with a new form or report. To see or change the record source, open the form or report in Layout or Design view, display the Property sheet with the properties for the forms, and follow these steps:

1. **Click the Data or All tab in the Property sheet.**

Either way, the first property listed is the Record Source property. It shows the name of the table or query from which the form or report displays records.

2. **If you want to change the record source to a different table or query, click the down-pointing triangle button at the right end of the** Record Source **property and choose a different table or query from the list that appears.**

If the form or report is based on a query and you want to modify the query, click the Expression Builder button (the ... button to the right of the Record Source property). (See Book III for the details of how queries work.)

Application Parts forms

A new Access feature called Application Parts enables you to add preformatted (or even preprogrammed) objects to your database. To add a form from the library of Application Parts, click the Application Parts button in the Templates group on the Create tab of the Ribbon. You see a menu of precooked parts, starting with some blank forms:

When you click a blank form, Access adds a copy of the form to your database. Unfortunately, it doesn't ask what you want to call it, instead giving it a name like SingleOneColumnTopLabels, so you need to search the Forms section of the Navigation pane to find your new form.

When you open the new form in Layout or Design view, the first thing you need to do is to set its Record Source property, as described in the section "Where records come from." Then you can drag fields to the form in Layout view, and fine-tune the design in Design view.

If you're going to change the record source, do it *before* you spend a lot of time working on the design of the form. Having the correct record source makes creating and editing your form or report much easier, because Access already knows what fields may appear on it.

If you use the new Application Part feature to create a blank form, as described in the sidebar "Application Part forms," you need to set the Record Source property before you can add field controls to the form.

Deciding the order of the records

You can also control the order in which records appear. You may want to browse through your address book by last name or by city, or through orders by date. Normally, Access displays the records in the same order as the record source. If the record source is a table, records appear in primary-key order from that table. If the record source is a query, records are in the sort order specified in the query.

However, you can change the order of the records by changing the Order By property of the form or report, which appears on the Data tab of the Property sheet for the form. Type the field name into the Order By property. If you want the records to appear in reverse order, type a space and **DESC** after the field name (for descending order).

One record or many?

You usually want your form to show only one record at a time, like a paper form. Most forms display one record at a time. For example, the Address Book form in Figure 1-1 displays one record from an Address Book table. But sometimes you want to see more than one record at a time, as in the form in Figure 1-8. (Reports use a different system to determine whether one or many records appear on the report, as described in Book V, Chapter 1.)

To display more than one record at a time, change the form's Default View property. (It's on the Format tab on the Property sheet for the form.) To display one record at a time, set this property to Single Form; to display multiple records, change it to Continuous Forms.

Figure 1-8: A continuous form displays many records, one below the other.

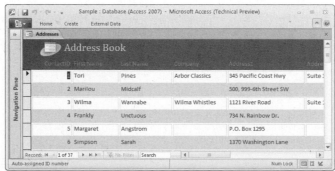

Continuous forms are useful when what you want is a glorified datasheet, with more than one row of fields for each record, more control over the layout of the fields, or other form features that aren't available for datasheets.

Some other cool form properties

A few other useful form properties appear on the Property sheet for the form. Here's what they do:

✦ **Datasheet view:** You can enable Datasheet view so that you can view the same set of fields that are on the form, but in a datasheet. Set the `Allow Datasheet View` property to `Yes` on the Format tab of the property sheet.

✦ **Read-only forms:** You can make the information in a form *read-only* — that is, not editable (look, but don't touch!) — by setting the `Allow Edits` property, which appears on the Data tab. This property is normally set to `Yes`, but you can change it to `No`. You can prevent adding new records by setting the `Allow Additions` property to `No`, and you can prevent deletions by setting the `Allow Deletions` property to `No`.

✦ **Record selectors:** A gray box — the record selector — appears to the left of the information for one record. When you're editing records using your form, you can delete or copy a record by clicking its record selector and pressing the Delete key or Ctrl+C. For a form that displays a single record (rather than a continuous form with lots of records), the record selector may not get much use, though, and you may not want to display it. You can control whether the record selectors appear on the form by setting the form's `Record Selectors` property, which appears on the Format tab.

✦ **Scroll bars and navigation buttons:** Normally forms include horizontal and vertical scroll bars if the form is too large to fit in the window. You also see navigation buttons to move to the first, previous, next, and last records. You can turn the scroll bars and navigation buttons on and off by using the `Scroll Bars` and `Navigation Buttons` properties, both of which appear on the Format tab.

Applying a theme to a form (or report)

Access comes with some predesigned themes, with a color scheme and font choices. When you apply a theme to a form (or report), Access sets the colors and fonts for the whole form (or most of the controls on the form). To apply a theme in Layout view, choose Themes from Themes group on the Design tab of the Ribbon, and choose a theme. As you hover your mouse over a choice, Access changes the open form to use that theme, even before you make your choice. (Try before you buy!) Or, you can apply just the color scheme to your form, by choosing Fonts from the same button group on the Ribbon.

Storing Your Forms and Reports

You spend oodles of time and energy getting your form or report looking just right. You don't want to lose all that hard work, do you? Save your form or report by pressing Ctrl+S or by right-clicking the form's object tab and choosing Save from the menu that appears. If Access displays the Save As dialog box (that is, if you haven't given this form or report a name yet), type a name. This name usually appears in the title bar of the form, although you can change this.

When you're done designing your form or report (or you're done for now, anyway), close it by clicking its Close button (the X in the upper-right corner). If you haven't saved it, Access asks whether you want to do so.

You can display the form or report any time from the Navigation pane — click its name from the Forms or Reports lists. If you want to change the design some more, right-click the name and choose Layout View.

Form and report management

You can rename, delete, and copy forms and reports from the Navigation pane, too. To rename one, click its name, press F2, edit the name in the little box that appears, and press Enter. To delete it, select the name and press the Delete key. To make a copy of the form or report design, click its name, press Ctrl+C, press Ctrl+V, and type a name for the new form or report.

Importing forms and reports from other databases

What if you create a terrific form or report in one database and you want to use the same one in another database? You can import a form or report from another Access database:

Access

1. **Click the Access button in the Import & Link group on the External Data tab of the Ribbon.**

   You see the Get External Data – Access Database dialog box, shown in Figure 1-9.

2. **Choose the filename of the Access database (either browse for it or type the path in); select the option labeled Import Tables, Queries, Forms, Reports, Macros, And Modules Into The Current Database; and click OK.**

   You see the Import Objects dialog box (shown in Figure 1-10).

3. **Click either the Forms tab or the Reports tab, depending on what you want to import.**

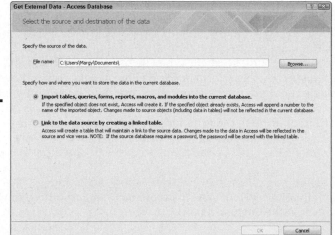

Figure 1-9:
You can
import a
form or
report from
another
Access
database.

4. **Choose the form(s) or report(s) you want to import.**

You can select a group of items by clicking the first one and
Shift+clicking the last. You can add a form or report to the ones you
already selected by Ctrl+clicking it.

5. **Click OK.**

Access copies the forms or reports from the other database into the current database. If you already have an object of the same type with the
same name, Access adds a 1 to the end of the name.

Figure 1-10:
The Import
Objects
dialog box.

**Book IV
Chapter 1**

Designing and
Using Forms
(and Reports)

Printing forms

Forms aren't designed to be printed — reports are the Access objects that give you the most printing and formatting options — but you can print them anyway. However, don't just click the File tab on the Ribbon and choose Print when you're using a form in Form view. Access prints the form for every single record in the table or query, not just the record you're viewing!

One method of printing the form for just the current record is to apply a filter to select only the current record, and then click the Print button. Be sure to remove the filter before trying to move to any other records.

Book II, Chapter 3 explains how to create, apply, and remove a filter. Chapter 3 of this minibook describes how to create a command button on your form that prints just the current record.

Chapter 2: Jazzing Up Your Forms (and Reports)

In This Chapter

✔ Creating new controls on your form (or report)

✔ Adding controls to display text, numbers, dates, and Yes/No fields

✔ Arranging and formatting the controls on your form

✔ Spiffing up your form with lines and boxes

✔ Controlling how the cursor moves from field to field when you use the form

Chapter 1 of this minibook explains how to make a form or report by using either a wizard or your bare hands. It also describes using Layout view to rearrange the fields on a form. In this chapter, you find out how to use Design view to create and configure *controls* — the objects on the form (or report) that actually display information. You use controls to add lines, boxes, and pictures to forms, too. You use Design view to fool around with your form (or report) and make it as clear and easy to use as possible.

The information in most of this chapter works for creating and editing reports, too. Just substitute the word *report* for *form* and give it a try!

An Efficient Way to Create New Forms

Here's how we usually make a new form:

1. **Create the form using a wizard, adding an Application Part, or making a blank form.**

   Decide among these options based on what you want your form to look like. You may want to run a few wizards and add a few Application Parts forms to see whether any of them look like good starting points for the form you want to create. You can always close them without saving if they aren't useful. These methods of creating a form are described in Chapter 1 of this minibook.

2. **Open the form in Layout view and drag the fields around where you want them.**

   See Chapter 1 for instructions.

3. **Open the form in Design view by right-clicking its name on the Navigation pane and choosing Design View from the resulting drop-down list.**

   See Chapter 1 of this minibook for how to open forms from the Navigation pane. If your form is already open in Layout view, click the bottom of the View button on the Design or Home tab of the Ribbon and choose Design View. You see your form in Design view, as described in the next section.

4. **Make a change — add a control, change an existing control, turn the background purple, or whatever.**

   Read on to find out how to make all kinds of specific changes.

5. **To see how your form looks with the change, switch to Form view by clicking the View button on the View group of the Design or Home tab of the Ribbon.**

   When either the Home tab or the Design tab is selected on the Ribbon, the View button shows a tiny form — it defaults to Form view. Clicking the View button when it's in tiny-form-mode tells Access to display your form in Form view — including a record from the table or query that the form is based on — so you can see whether you made the form better or worse. (See Chapter 1 of this minibook for the views available for forms.)

   For reports, you may often want to preview what the report will look like after it is printed. See Book V, Chapter 2 for how to preview and print reports.

6. **Switch back to Design view by clicking the bottom part of the View button and choosing Design view.**

   When you're in Form view, the View button defaults to Layout view, so you need to specifically choose Design view.

7. **Repeat Steps 4 through 6 until your form is gorgeous and works perfectly.**

   Be smart: Press Ctrl+S every few minutes to save your work, even before you're completely finished.

8. **Close the form's window. (It doesn't matter whether you're in Design view, Layout view, Form view, or Print preview.) If you haven't saved the form recently, Access asks whether you want to do so now — click the Yes button.**

Making All Kinds of Changes in Design View

If you are a glutton for punishment, you can create a form in Design view, by clicking the Form Design button in the Forms group on the Create tab of the Ribbon. However, we find it a lot easier to create a form as described in the preceding section, and we reserve Design view for improving the looks and behavior of an existing form.

Changing the layout of an existing form or report

To change the layout of an existing form or report, open it in Design view by right-clicking its name in the Navigation pane and choosing Design View from the menu that appears. Your form looks like Figure 2-1.

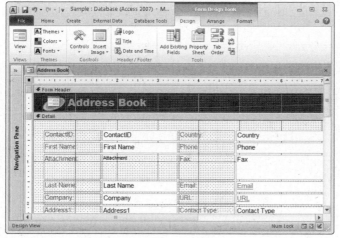

Figure 2-1: In Design view, you can configure each control individually, including text boxes and labels.

Design view shows the controls that make up your form or report, and enables you to create, move, and delete the controls. You can also set the properties of your controls to change how they look and act.

We can hear you asking, what's a control? A *control* is an object on a form or report that displays some information. Some controls display text, whereas others display check boxes, command buttons, drop-down menus, or pictures. You choose what information appears on your form by making controls to display that information. The all-time most popular controls are the following: a text box (to show text, usually from a field in your table), a label (to show explanatory text), a combo box (to show a drop-down menu), and a command button (to run a little program, either a macro or a VBA module). Table 2-1 (later in this chapter) lists other types of controls.

Other things you may see in Design view are the following:

✦ **Grid:** Access displays a grid of lines and dots in the background of the Design View window to help you align objects neatly, as well as rulers at the top and left sides of the window. Figure 2-1 shows the grid.

✦ **Design tab:** The Controls group on the Design tab of the Ribbon (viewable when a form is open in Design or Layout view) contains a button for each type of control you may want to create. There are also buttons for creating a header or footer for your form.

**Book IV
Chapter 2**

**Jazzing Up Your
Forms (and Reports)**

✦ **Format tab:** This Ribbon tab offers buttons for formatting text and numbers, setting a background image, and doing other kinds of formatting.

✦ **Field List pane:** This lists the fields in the table or query that this form is based on, as shown in Figure 2-2. You use it when creating a new control to display a field from your table or query. Display the Field list by clicking the Add Existing Fields button in the Tools group on the Design tab of the Ribbon.

Figure 2-2:
The Field list appears in a pane to the right of the Design view of a form.

✦ **Property sheet:** Shown in the previous chapter, this displays the properties of the selected object, which can be the whole form, a section of the form, or an individual control. Tabs display the different types of properties. The properties listed depend on the type of object that you select. Click the All tab to see all the properties of the selected item in one long list.

Display the Property sheet by clicking the Property Sheet button in the Tools group on the Design tab of the Ribbon. To change which control's properties display, you can choose another control name from the Selection Type list at the top of the Property sheet, or just click a control in Design view. To see the properties of the whole form, click the little black square in the upper-left corner of the form.

When you are in Layout or Design view, you can display the properties of a control on your form by double-clicking the control.

Changing the size of a form

If you use tabbed documents (described in Book I, Chapter 2), then when you open a form in Form view, it uses the entire space in the Access window (not counting the space that the Navigation pane takes up). With tabbed documents, the size of a form is defined as the size of the Access window: If the form is smaller, then the right and bottom parts of the form appear blank in Form view, and if the form is larger, then scroll bars appear so that you can scroll to see the rest of the form. Most people use tabbed documents because it's the default for Access databases.

In Design view, you can set the size of the form by dragging the lower edge of the grid upward or downward or the right-hand edge of the grid to the left or right. This may be a vestige of the time that most people used overlapping documents instead of tabbed documents, and it's still important if you view multiple objects in your database as overlapping documents. Although changing the size of the form in Design view doesn't change the way that the form appears in Form view with tabbed documents, you may still need to expand the grid in Design view if it's too small, preventing you from using the space available in Form view.

Taking Control of Your Form or Report

The heart of form design is the *controls* — the objects that appear on forms and reports. Controls on forms include boxes that display text and numeric data from fields, check boxes for Yes/No fields, drop-down menus for lookup fields, buttons you click to run a macro or VBA procedure, and other stuff you're used to seeing on computer screens. (On reports, all controls just sit there on the paper.)

To display or edit a field, you have to create a *bound control* — a control that is connected to a field in your table or query — so Access knows what information to display in the control. You can also display *unbound controls* that contain information that's not stored in your table or query, such as the form's title or explanatory text.

TIP

Form (and report) design tips

When designing your form, keep the following design tips in mind for perfect, or at least tasteful, forms:

✔ **Make sure that the Snap to Grid feature is turned on.** This feature tells Access to make all the edges of your controls line up with the grid that appears in Design view, which makes your form or report look neater. To turn this feature on, with the report open in Design view, click the Size/Space button in the Sizing & Ordering group on the Arrange tab of the Ribbon and see whether the Snap to Grid button appears to be selected in the Control Layout group. If its icon doesn't have an orange box around it, then it's not selected, and the feature is turned off: Click Snap to Grid to turn the feature on.

✔ **Before you make any big changes to your form or report, be sure to save it (by choosing Save from the File tab on the Ribbon or by pressing Ctrl+S).** If you want to be double-sure, choose Save As from the File tab to save it with a different name (like "Address Book Test") and fool around with the big change you're planning to make on the copy. Either way, if you don't like the results, close the modified version without saving it.

✔ **If you make a change and you're instantly sorry, press Ctrl+Z or choose Undo (the button with the backward curvy arrow) on the Quick Access toolbar to reverse your change.** Whew!

Designing a form or report (or changing the design of an existing one) consists mainly of adding controls where you want them to appear, getting rid of controls you don't like, and moving or configuring the controls that you've got.

Form control types

Table 2-1 lists the types of controls that can appear on forms and reports when the report is open in Design view, along with the buttons to create each type of control. The buttons are in the Controls group on the Design tab of the Ribbon. As with any button, hover the mouse pointer over a button to see the button's name. If your Access window isn't wide enough to display all the buttons, you see a single Controls button (as in Figure 2-1) that you click to see all the control buttons in a bunch, as shown in Figure 2-3. (If you used an earlier version of Access, this menu of buttons is what the Toolbox window turned into.)

Figure 2-3:
If your Ribbon isn't long enough (and whose is?), click the Controls button on the Design tab to see the buttons for creating controls.

Table 2-1		Types of Controls on Forms
Control Button	*Control Type*	*Description*
ab|	Text box	Contents of a field
Aa	Label	Text, not editable — hyperlinks are special types of labels. (See the section "Adding hyperlink controls.")
xxxx	Button	Button that performs an action when clicked

Control Button	Control Type	Description
	Tab	Tab for displaying different controls (like those at the top of many dialog boxes)
	Hyperlink	Clickable link to a Web page or other object
	Web browser	Web browser window displaying the Web page you specify in the properties of the control
	Navigation	Tab for displaying forms or reports from your database (See Chapter 3 of this minibook.)
	Option group	Group of option (radio) buttons, check boxes, or toggle buttons
	Page break	Division between one form page and the next
	Combo box	Drop-down menu from which you can choose an option or type in a new one
	Chart	Runs the Chart Wizard to define a bar, line, or pie chart
	Line	Straight line, for visual effect
	Toggle button	Button that is either on (pressed) or off (not pressed)
	List box	Drop-down menu from which you can choose an option, but you can't type new values
	Rectangle	Rectangle, for visual effect
	Check box	Box that contains or doesn't contain a check mark
	Unbound object frame	OLE or embedded object (graph, picture, sound file, or video) that is not stored in a field in a table
	Attachment	For Attachment type fields

Book IV Chapter 2

Jazzing Up Your Forms (and Reports)

(continued)

Table 2-1 *(continued)*

Control Button	Control Type	Description
⊙	Option button	Option (radio) button that is part of an option group
▦	Subform/ Subreport	Adds a subform or subreport to the form
XYZ	Bound object frame	OLE or embedded object (graph, picture, sound file, or video) that is stored in a field in a table
🖼	Image	Bitmap picture

Many of these are bound controls, displaying values from a field, like the text box (for text fields), check box (for Yes/No fields), and attachment (for attachment fields) controls. Others are unbound controls, like the image (for displaying an icon or picture not stored in a database table), line, or page break. This chapter shows you how to use many of these types of controls.

Making a new control by dragging a field

Making most forms (and reports) consists mainly of setting up the bound controls to display the fields from the record source. Access makes this easy, with a quick drag-and-drop procedure.

With your form open in Design view, display the Field list, if it isn't already displayed, by clicking the Add Existing Fields button in the Tools group of the Design tab on the Ribbon. Figure 2-2 (earlier in this chapter) shows you the Field list, with a list of the fields in your table or query. If your form doesn't have a record source, or the fields look like the wrong ones, see Chapter 1 of this minibook.

To make a control for a field, just drag the field from the Field list to the form, dropping it where you want a control for that field. Access creates a control (usually a text box) that is bound to the field you dragged. It also creates a label control containing the name of the field, followed by a colon. The text box (or other control) is where the contents of the field will appear.

Making a new control by choosing a control

The Field list helps you create a control for your field, but you don't get to decide what kind of control to make. If you don't like what the Field list provides, or if you want to create an unbound control (one that doesn't display a field at all), there is another way to create controls. To make any kind of control, open your form in Design view and follow these steps:

1. **Choose the appropriate Controls button for the type of control you want from the Controls group on the Design tab of the Ribbon.**

The selected Controls button turns a different color and has a box around it, so you know it's selected.

2. **Click the place on the form where you want the control to appear.**

Access creates a new control, and for some control types, runs a wizard to help you configure it.

Whether you use the Field list or the Controls buttons to create a control, you usually need to configure it by setting its properties on the Property sheet, as described in the next section. You can change the text of a label control, change the field that a text box control displays, make text bold, huge, or a different color, and other changes. The rest of this chapter describes how to configure your controls. You can change the properties of any of the components of the form, from text box properties to the background color of the form itself.

This chapter tells you everything you need to know about making and configuring text boxes, labels, and check boxes, along with drawing lines and boxes on your form. The next chapter of this book describes how to create and configure more advanced controls, including combo boxes, list boxes, toggle buttons, option groups (groups of radio buttons), and command buttons.

Setting control properties

After you create a control on a form or report, you can change what information the control displays, how the control looks, and how the control acts by changing its properties. To see or change a control's properties, open the form in Design view and follow these steps:

1. **If the Property sheet isn't already visible, display it by clicking the Property Sheet button in the Tools group on the Design tab of the Ribbon.**

You see the Property sheet, as shown in Figure 2-4.

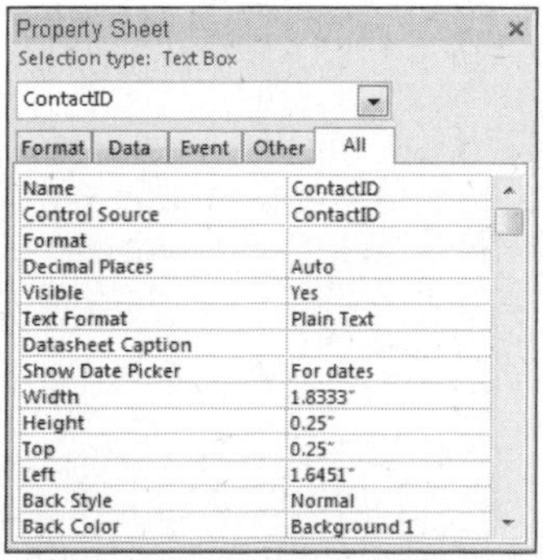

Figure 2-4:
The
properties
of a text box
control.

Property Sheet	×
Selection type: Text Box	
ContactID	▼

Format	Data	Event	Other	All

Name	ContactID
Control Source	ContactID
Format	
Decimal Places	Auto
Visible	Yes
Text Format	Plain Text
Datasheet Caption	
Show Date Picker	For dates
Width	1.8333"
Height	0.25"
Top	0.25"
Left	1.6451"
Back Style	Normal
Back Color	Background 1

2. **On the form in Design view, click the control whose properties you want to change.**

   Now the Property sheet shows the properties for that control.

3. **Find the property and change it.**

   Finding the property is the hardest part. You can guess which tab it's on, or click the All tab and scan the whole list. Wouldn't it be nice if you could see the properties in alphabetical order, to make them easier to find?

Advanced form designers can make macros or VBA modules run when users move the cursor in or out of the controls on the form. To connect a VBA module or macro to a form (or a control on the form, like a button), you set a property on the Events tab of the Property sheet — it's not that hard! See Book VI for how to create macros and connect them to form events, and Book VIII for creating VBA modules for forms.

Binding a control to data in the record source

The most important property of most controls is the `Control Source` property, which tells Access what information to display in the control. The `Control Source` property is usually a field in a table or query that is the record source for the form. For example, if a form's record source is the Address Book table in the database for a store, one text box may have the `ContactID` field as its control source — the text box displays the contents of the `ContactID` field in the current record of the Address Book table.

A control's name is usually the same as its control source, but not always. You can have a text box named `TextBox123` for which the control source is the `Selling Price` field in the Products table. Naming your controls with the same names as the fields that they display is good practice, though, and cuts down on the confusion. When you drag a field from the Field list to the form, Access usually names the new control after the field that it displays.

Making Controls That Display Text, Numbers, and Dates

Face it: The most important information on most forms and reports is text. Pictures are interesting, but text (including numbers and dates, which can be displayed as text) is usually where the heart of the matter is. Access has several types of controls that display text on forms and reports, including the following:

✦ **Label controls:** Display fixed text — text that isn't based on the record that you're displaying on the form.

✦ **Text box controls:** Display information from fields in the record source of the form, or calculated information.

✦ **List box and combo box controls:** Display drop-down menus of values, usually for a field in the record source.

This section describes how to create and format labels and text boxes. For combo boxes, list boxes, and option buttons (radio buttons), see Chapter 3 of this minibook.

Making and editing labels

Every form has a title on its object tab, which you can set by editing the `Caption` property of the form (as described in Chapter 1 of this minibook). But you may want some other titles on the form, including explanations of how to use the forms, headings for different sections of the form, or labels that apply to the controls for specific fields. Labels are unbound fields. (They don't take their information from a table.)

For reports, you use labels wherever you want to display text that doesn't come from the record source — such as the report title, the date, instructions, or any other text that's not stored in a table. (For more formatting options that are available on reports, see Book V, Chapter 1.)

To make a label, follow these steps:

1. **Click the Label button on the Controls group of the Design tab of the Ribbon.**

2. **Click on the form to create a tiny text box for your label.**

Don't worry — you can always move and resize it later.

3. **Type the text that you want to appear in the label and press Enter.**

As you type, Access makes the text box larger. (See Figure 2-5.) Pressing Enter tells Access that you are done typing, and it sets the text box to a size just large enough to display the text. If you want more than one line of text to appear in the label box, press Ctrl+Enter to start a new line.

To edit any text you entered, click the label control once to select it; then click it again or press F2 to edit the text. Press Enter when your edits are complete, or the Esc key to cancel editing. To change the font, size, or color of the label, see the section "Choosing Fonts, Colors, and Other Decorative Touches," later in this chapter.

Label control

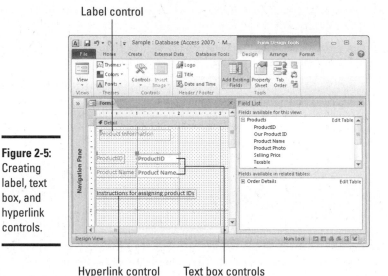

Figure 2-5:
Creating
label, text
box, and
hyperlink
controls.

Hyperlink control   Text box controls

Adding hyperlink controls

You can make a special kind of label that consists of a Web address (hyperlink) that you click to display a Web page. This kind of label may be nice if you want to provide helpful information about using the form on a Web site.

Caution: Is that an error?

When you create a label control, you may see a little error symbol — an exclamation mark in a yellow diamond. Access thinks that you may have made a mistake: Are you sure that you don't want this label to be associated with another control? Most labels are associated with text boxes or other controls, to provide a visible name or prompt for that control.

If you see the error warning icon, click it to see its diagnosis of the problem. In this case, it says "New Unassociated Label"

You also see your options. The most important two are

✔ **Associate Label with a Control,** which enables you to establish a connection between this label and another control, so that if you move the other control, this label moves along with it.

✔ **Ignore Error,** which tells Access to make the error box go away. This is the right choice if the label isn't associated with another control — for example, it's a title for the whole form, or part of the form.

Instead of clicking the Label button, choose the Hyperlink button in the Controls group on the Design tab of the Ribbon. In the Insert Hyperlink dialog box that appears (shown in Figure 2-6), type the text that you want to appear on your form in the Text to Display box, type the Web address into the Address box, and click OK. (You don't have to type the `http://` part; Access adds it for you.) You get a *hyperlink control* — a clickable label that displays the text you specified, as shown in Figure 2-5. In Form view, clicking the label switches to your browser (or runs it, if it's not already running) and displays the Web page you specified.

You can turn an existing label into a hyperlink label by changing its `Hyperlink Address` property. In the Property sheet for the label control, click the Format tab and type a Web address into the Hyperlink Address box.

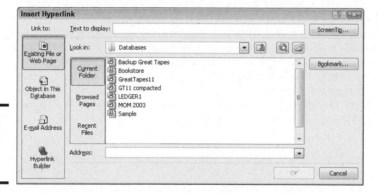

Figure 2-6:
Creating a hyperlink control.

Putting Text and Memo fields in text boxes

To make a text box for a Text or Memo field, drag the field name from the Field list onto the form or report where you want the text box to appear. Or click the Text Box button in the Controls group on the Design tab of the Ribbon and draw an outline where you want the text box to appear. Access makes a text box the size you indicated, along with a label control with the name of the field, as shown in Figure 2-5. Yes, you get two controls for the price of one!

You can format the contents of Text, Memo, and Hyperlink fields a bit, mainly controlling capitalization. Book II, Chapter 1 lets you in on how to display text in upper- or lowercase, limit what you type to a certain number of characters, and add preset characters to a field (such as dashes or parentheses in phone numbers) — you find out what magic characters to type in the `Format` property of your text box. For other types of formatting, such as fonts and colors, see the section "Choosing Fonts, Colors, and Other

Decorative Touches" later in this chapter. The next chapter explains ways to make your text boxes smarter, starting with preset default values and validating the information that people type in.

Displaying number, currency, and date fields

Number, Currency, and Date fields appear in text boxes, too, just like Text and Memo fields. You create text box controls to display Number, Currency, and Date fields the same way you create them for Text fields, using the Field list or button in the Controls group on the Design tab of the Ribbon.

Breaking Out of the Control Layout

In Chapter 1, we talk about using Layout view to arrange your controls. Layout view is where you can use a *control layout* to move your controls into neat rows and columns. However, control layouts insist that your controls appear in rows and columns, which isn't always where you want them. For example, for forms that include fields for an address, we like to use one label (something like "City, State ZIP") followed by three text boxes for the fields that contain the city, state/province, and ZIP code or postcode. You may want to tighten up the design in lots of little ways, as shown in Figure 2-7. That's not possible in a control layout.

Figure 2-7: What if you don't want your controls in rows and columns?

Removing the control layout

Even in Design view, control layouts restrict the positions of your controls. You can see the outline of a control layout in Design view as a dashed line, as shown in Figure 2-8. You can remove the control layout (without removing the controls *in* the control layout), by switching to Layout view, selecting the control layout, right-clicking in it, and choosing Remove Layout from the menu that appears. Now when you switch back to Design view, there's no dashed line indicating a control layout.

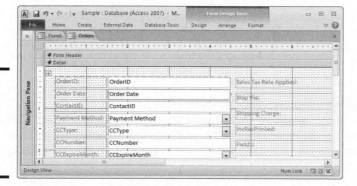

Figure 2-8: Control layouts work in Design view, too.

Remove the control layout only if you want to move your controls out of a strict row-and-column arrangement. You can leave the control layout in place when making other kinds of changes, like changing the color or numeric format of a text box control.

Moving or resizing a control

Now you are ready to move your controls anywhere on the form. First, select the control by clicking it. You can tell when the control is selected, because Access draws an orange box around the control. Little boxes, called *handles,* appear at the corners and the centers of the sides, as shown in Figure 2-5. You can click and drag the handles to resize the control. You can see a gray box at the upper-left corner of the control, which you can click and drag to move the control. If the control has a label associated with it, a gray box appears at its upper-left corner, too, so you can move the label independently of the control.

To move a control, click the control to select it. When your cursor is over the control, it appears as a four-pointed arrow icon; click and drag to move both the control and its associated label, if any. You can click the gray box in the upper-left corner to drag just the control. If the control has a label that moves along with it (an *associated label),* you can move the label separately by clicking the gray box in *its* upper-left corner and dragging it.

Now that you are free of the tyranny of the control layout, you can move the control anywhere you want. On the other hand, it can be very tricky to get the control in exactly the right place! (See the next section for help.)

You can select the label associated with a control separately from the control itself. To select only the control and not the label, click the gray box in the upper-left corner of the control. To select only the label, click the gray box in the label's upper-left corner. This method enables you to move the label closer or farther away from its control.

To change the size of a control, drag one of the handles to move that edge of the control. Exactly what happens depends on the control: Some controls can't be resized (such as a radio button). For labels, text boxes, and many other controls, the control stretches or shrinks as you drag its edge.

Neatening up your controls

You can spend hours fooling with the formatting of your forms and reports, moving controls around, getting all the labels to match, and choosing fonts and colors. (We certainly have!) One important aspect of design is neatness — forms are easier to use and reports are easier to read if they look neat and organized. People can find the information they are looking for — or the entries that they need to make — more easily if everything lines up nicely.

Luckily, Access has features that make it easy to line up your controls, so you don't have to squint at the screen and drag each control left or right by microscopic amounts. Instead, you can select a bunch of controls and deal with them all at the same time. To select more than one control, click one control and Shift-click the rest of the controls. Or drag your mouse around the group of controls: Access selects all the controls that are within that area (even if only part of the control is in the area).

After you select a bunch of controls, you can do the following things with them:

✦ **Move groups of controls.** If you want to move a bunch of controls together, select them all and then drag them to a new location. Access leaves the spacing among the controls unchanged.

✦ **Make controls the same size.** You can tell Access to make all the selected controls the same height or width. To make the widths of the selected controls all the same, click Size/Space in the Sizing & Ordering group on the Arrange tab of the Ribbon and choose To Widest to make all the controls as wide as the widest control you selected. Or choose To Narrowest to match the narrowest (left to right). To make the heights of the controls the same, choose To Tallest or To Shortest.

✦ **Line up your controls.** You can adjust the edges of your controls to line up with the grid lines that appear in Design view. With the controls selected, click the Align button in the Sizing & Ordering group on the Arrange tab of the Ribbon and choose To Grid. Access moves the edge of each control to the nearest gridline.

You can also get Access to move all the selected controls so they are left-aligned (that is, the left edges line up) or right-aligned. Click the Align button in the Sizing & Ordering group on the Arrange tab of the Ribbon and choose Left, or Right. We like to see labels right-aligned next to text boxes that are left-aligned, but it's a matter of taste!

You can turn on Snap to Grid for the whole form, so that when you move or resize controls, Access aligns their sides with the grid. Click Size/Space in the Sizing & Ordering group on the Arrange tab of the Ribbon to see whether Snap to Grid is selected (outlined in orange). If it isn't, click it!

✦ **Space controls evenly.** Controls look better if there is a consistent amount of vertical space between one control and the next — for example, one gridline or two gridlines. Rather than moving controls up and down by hand, Access can do this task for you. Select the controls you want to space and click Size/Space in the Sizing & Ordering group on the Arrange tab of the Ribbon and choose Equal Vertical. You can also move all the controls together or apart by choosing Decrease Vertical or Increase Vertical.

Renaming, Resizing, Deleting, and Copying Controls

Here are other things you can do after selecting a control:

✦ **Rename a control.** Change the Name property of the control, which appears on the Other tab of the control's Property sheet. The name doesn't affect what data appears in the control. (That's the Control Source property, on the Data tab.)

✦ **Delete controls.** Press the Del key. (Oops! If you didn't mean to delete it, then press Ctrl+Z or click the Undo arrow at the top-left corner of the page.)

✦ **Copy controls.** Press Ctrl+C to copy the control to the Windows Clipboard. Then press Ctrl+V to paste a copy from the Clipboard back into the Design View window. Then drag the copy where you want it to be. Cleverly, if you press Ctrl+V *again* to paste another copy of the control, Access tries to figure out where you want the new one based on where you dragged the last copy (a nice feature, we thought). After you copy and paste the control, you can modify it as you like.

You can also change the type of a control. For example, if you make a text box and wish later that it were a combo box (described in the next chapter), you don't have to delete the control and start over. Instead, right-click the control, choose Change To from the menu that appears, and choose the type of controls to which you want to change this control.

Book IV Chapter 2

Jazzing Up Your Forms (and Reports)

If you want to change a property for a bunch of controls, you can select them all and change the property for the whole group. First select the group of controls, by clicking the first one and Shift-clicking each of the rest. (Or sweep a rectangle with your mouse to select all the controls in that rectangle.) The Property sheet now says "Selection type: Multiple Selection" at the top. If you change the settings of any properties, Access makes the change to all the selected controls. Similarly, you can make changes on the Formatting toolbar to format all the controls at the same time.

Formatting Numbers and Dates

Numbers and dates appear in text boxes, but Access can display them in a lot of different formats. You can set the text box to display a currency sign (such as a dollar sign), to control the number of decimal places that appear, and to display thousands separators. (In the United States and Canada, we use commas for this.)

For dates in a text box, you can control the order of the month, day, and year; whether to omit the day or year; how many digits to show for the year; and whether to display the name or number of the month.

On the Format tab of the Property sheet for the text box, click in the `Format` property and then click the downward-pointing triangle at the right end of the setting (as shown in Figure 2-9). You see a list of numeric or date formats to choose from. To control the number of decimal places that appear, set the `Decimal Places` property. (The `Auto` setting means that Access decides how many places to display.)

Figure 2-9: Setting the format for a number in a text box.

For a date field, you can display a little calendar icon that the user can click to choose a date from a calendar. Set the `Show Date Picker` property to `For dates`.

If you want to make fancier numeric or date formats, see Book II, Chapter 1. Forms and reports can include calculated numbers and dates, too. For example, an order form can display the sales tax based on the total amount of the order. See Chapter 4 of this minibook for how to get Access to do your arithmetic for you.

Choosing Fonts, Colors, and Other Decorative Touches

You can format the label and text box controls in lots of ways, almost as if you were using a word processor. When you select a text box, label, or other control with text, numbers, or dates in it, you can use the tools in the Font group on the Format tab on the Ribbon, as shown in Figure 2-10. Or set properties on the Format tab of the Property sheet — your choice.

Figure 2-10:
Changing the font, background and foreground colors, and number formats on the Format tab of the Ribbon.

Here are some of the properties of labels, text boxes, and some other controls that you may want to set:

✦ **Font:** You can control the typeface by clicking the Font box in the Font group on the Format tab of the Ribbon, or by changing the `Font Name` property. Don't choose anything really fancy, or your text will be unreadable. (For most of the figures in this chapter, we used a font named Calibri.) Adjust the size of the text by clicking the Font Size box or setting the `Font Size` property. The Font group of the Format tab of the Ribbon also has buttons for boldface, italics, and underlining (or you can set the `Font Weight`, `Font Italics`, or `Font Underline` properties).

✦ **Color:** Text doesn't have to be boring black on ho-hum gray. With the control selected, click the downward-pointing triangle on the right side of the Font Color button in the Font group of the Format tab on the Ribbon and choose the color you want as the text color. (If you don't see the color you want, click More Colors.) To set another control to the same color, you can select the control and just click the button. (The

**Book IV
Chapter 2**

**Jazzing Up Your
Forms (and Reports)**

current color is the color of the bar below the "A" on the button.) You can set the background color the same way, using the Background Color button.

These buttons set the Fore Color and Back Color properties of the control, which are on the Format tab of the Property sheet. These properties appear as horrendous-looking seven-character codes — they use the same color-naming system used in the HTML formatting codes for Web pages. The first character is always #, followed by three pairs of two characters that represent the amount of red, green, and blue in the color.

✦ **Alignment:** To left-align, right-align, or center the text within the edges of the control, click the Align Text Left, Center, or Align Text Right buttons in the Font group of the Format tab of the Ribbon, or set the Text Align property on the Format tab of the Property sheet. If you really want to get weird, you can even display the text sideways within the box, by setting the Vertical setting on the Other tab of the Property sheet to Yes.

Copying your formatting

After you go to the effort of prettifying one control, why reinvent the wheel to make another control to match it? You can simply copy the formatting from one control to another by using the Format Painter. The Format Painter copies all formatting — colors, fonts, font sizes, border sizes, alignment, and anything else that you can think of. Select the beautifully formatted control and click the Format Painter button from the Font group on the Format tab of the Ribbon. Your mouse-pointer now has a paintbrush attached to it, so you know the tool is active. Click the control that you want formatted like the original control.

Make it red if it's bad news

Access has a cool feature called *conditional formatting* that lets you make a control look one way normally and a different way — maybe boldface and red — under special circumstances. For example, the total amount of an order for an online store ought to be a positive, unless the customer is due a refund. Wouldn't it be great if the form reached out and grabbed you when the total order amount is negative? Well, Access can't reach out of the screen, but it can make the control appear in bright red, boldface, or both.

To set up conditional formatting, you create rules based on two specifications:

✦ What **condition** must be true for the format to apply? For example, you can check whether a date is in the past (that is, it's < today), or whether a number is less than zero.

✦ What **formatting** applies? You can make the control a bright color (text or background), boldface, italics, or underlined.

You can create more than one rule — for example, if the order amount is more than $100, display it in green, while if it's less than zero, display it in red.

Follow these steps to set up conditional formatting:

Conditional
Formatting

1. **Select the control in Design view and click the Conditional Formatting button in the Control Formatting group on the Format tab of the Ribbon.**

   You see the Conditional Formatting Rules Manager dialog box, shown in Figure 2-11. You can use it to create rules that set the formatting based on the value of the field — or on values in other fields or records.

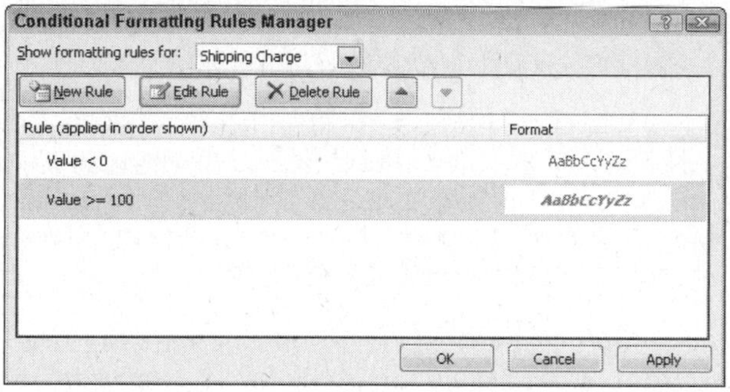

Figure 2-11:
The
Conditional
Formatting
Rules
Manager
dialog box.

2. **Click the New Rule button.**

   You see the New Formatting Rule dialog box shown in Figure 2-12.

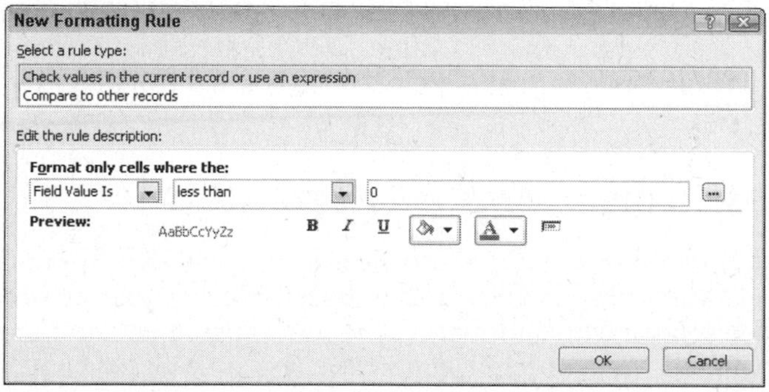

Figure 2-12:
Creating a
conditional
formatting
rule.

3. **Choose whether the condition is based on information in the current record or other records.**

4. **In the Edit the Rule Description section, set the boxes to display the condition. Click OK.**

   In Figure 2-12, the condition is that the value of the field is less than 0. After you click OK, you return to the Conditional Formatting Rules Manager, and the rule you just defined appears.

5. **Repeat Steps 2 through 4 to create other rules as needed.**

   In Figure 2-11, one rule turns negative amounts red, and another rule turns amounts $100 and over green and boldface. (You'll just have to imagine that these figures are in color!)

6. **Click OK.**

Creating Check Boxes for Yes/No Fields

When you drag a Yes/No field from the Field list to a form or report in Design view, Access assumes that you want to display the field as a check box — a `Yes` value appears as a checked box, and a `No` value appears as a blank box. You can't change the size of a check box — dragging its edges expands the box around it, but the check box just sits there.

 Another way to create a check box is by clicking the Check Box button on the Controls group of the Design tab of the Ribbon and then clicking where you want a check box to appear. If you use this method, you need to set the check box's `Control Source` property on the Data tab of the Property sheet to the name of the Yes/No field.

 Alternatively, you can display different information depending on whether the Yes/No field is `Yes` or `No`. For example, for tax-exempt companies, your order form can display a Tax Exempt ID box that appears only if the `Tax Exempt` field is set to the `Yes` value. See Chapter 3 of this minibook for how to display information that depends on other fields in this way.

Adding Lines, Boxes, and Backgrounds

Some forms and reports have several sections, and they are easier to use if you separate the sections by lines or boxes. For example, an order form may have one section with information about the customer, another section showing what items were ordered, and a third section with payment information.

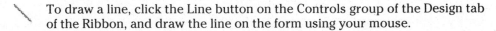 To draw a line, click the Line button on the Controls group of the Design tab of the Ribbon, and draw the line on the form using your mouse.

Drawing a box works the same way. Click the Rectangle button in the Controls group of the Design tab of the Ribbon and draw the box, starting at one corner and dragging the mouse to the opposite corner.

You can set the colors and thickness of a line or box by clicking the Shape Outline button in the Control Formatting group on the Format tab of the Ribbon. Click a color, Line Thickness, or Line Type.

You can specify a picture to display in the background of the form or report. Picture backgrounds seem like a demented idea to us — we hate forms and reports with clouds or sunsets in the background because they make forms look busier and more confusing. But if you want to jazz up your form or report, click the Background Image button in the Background group on the Format tab of the Ribbon and choose an image from their gallery or click Browse to choose a picture of your own. This button sets the `Picture` property on the Format tab of the Property sheet to the filename of a picture.

Controlling Cursor Movement in Your Form

You made a bunch of controls and formatted them nicely, and your form looks pretty spiffy. But here's a question you may not have thought about: When you (or other people) are using the form to enter or edit data, how does the cursor move from control to control? That is, when you press Enter or Tab to leave a text box or other control that allows you to edit information, which control does your cursor move to? Access calls this the *tab order* of the form.

Access stores the tab order for each form, which is a list of the editable controls on the form (that is, controls that allow data entry or editing in Form view). When you press Enter or Tab in Form view, your cursor moves from control to control in the same order as the Access list. Here's the problem: When you create a new control, Access adds it to the bottom of the list, even if the control is at the top of the form. As a result, your cursor skips around when you try to use the form.

The solution is to adjust the tab order of the form. To see the tab order list, follow these steps:

1. **With the form in Design view, click Tab Order in the Tools group on the Design tab of the Ribbon.**

   You see the aptly named Tab Order dialog box, shown in Figure 2-13.

**Book IV
Chapter 2**

**Jazzing Up Your
Forms (and Reports)**

Figure 2-13: Controlling the order in which your cursor moves from field to field on a form.

2. **Change the order of the controls by clicking the gray box to the left of a field name and dragging it up or down the list.**

   Alternatively, click the Auto Order button to tell Access to put the controls into order based on their positions — from top to bottom and left to right — on the form.

   Access reorders the controls, and you can look at the new order to see if Access got it right.

3. **Click OK when the controls are in the right order.**

   You probably already guessed this, but this whole tab-order discussion doesn't apply to reports.

Chapter 3: Creating Smarter Forms

In This Chapter

✔ Making drop-down menus and list boxes

✔ Displaying Yes/No fields as option or toggle buttons

✔ Grouping radio buttons

✔ Adding cool command buttons

✔ Making a Find box for searching records

✔ Adding headers and footers to your forms

✔ Displaying form data on multiple tabs

✔ Validating what people type

✔ Creating a main menu form for your database

✔ Setting a form to run automatically when you open the database

In Chapters 1 and 2 of this minibook, we explain how to make forms (and reports) and add labels, text boxes, check boxes, lines, and rectangles to them. You can go a long way with just those controls, but you'll miss a lot of the power of Access. Combo boxes and list boxes enable you (or your users) to choose values from lists instead of typing values in, and these lists can come from related tables in the database. If a field contains a small number of possible values, you may want to present them as radio buttons. And best of all, forms can display records from more than one table through subforms. This chapter explains all this — and more.

 This chapter doesn't apply to reports. Because you can't use reports for entering and editing data, the interactive features discussed in this chapter just don't work for reports (at least, not unless you have much fancier paper than we do!).

Creating and Configuring Combo and List Boxes

Combo boxes and *list boxes* are two controls that work like the drop-down lists that you see in Windows programs. Each box displays a list of values from which you can choose one value. The difference between the controls is how many values they display. A combo box shows only the currently selected value; you click the downward-pointing triangle on its right side to get the list to drop down so you can select a different value. A list box shows all the possible values (or as many as fit in the control, with a scroll bar to see the rest of the values), of which one is selected. Figure 3-1 shows a combo box and a list box.

Figure 3-1:
You can use a combo box or list box to choose from a list of values.

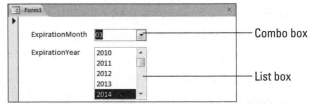

List boxes take up more room on forms than combo boxes, so they are used far less often. On the other hand, they allow you to see more values at the same time. We explain how to create both list and combo boxes (the process is almost the same), but our examples concentrate on combo boxes.

Before you create a combo or list box, consider the following questions:

✦ **Where will the values come from?** The combo or list box displays a list of values. Are the values stored in a table, or will you type them into the control's Property sheet? If you use this list of values in any other control on another form anywhere in your entire database, put the values in a table — just a plain old table, with one field for the value, and additional fields if you store other facts about each value. Make sure that the table has a primary key to uniquely identify each record. For example, if your bookstore has three types of products, these product codes need to be in a table, because you're sure to use them in lots of different forms and reports. Don't type them into the combo or list box's Property sheet.

✦ **If the values are stored in a table, which field (or fields) of the table do you want to appear in the control?** You can choose one or more fields; but don't choose too many, or the list gets enormous. For example, a combo or list box for a `StateAndProvince` field can display the two-letter state or province abbreviation, the full state or province name, or both.

✦ **When the user of the form makes a choice from this control, what happens to the selected information?** Most forms are used for editing the records in a table or query (the record source for the form). If the purpose of the combo box or list box is to help the user enter a value in a field, then make a note of the field name. On the other hand, you may want to use the combo or list box for another purpose, such as allowing the user to find a record (as described in the section, "Making a Find Box," later in this chapter).

For example, for an order-entry database, you may want a combo box that lists the states and provinces in the United States and Canada. You have a table called StateLookup with a field for the two-letter abbreviations, a field for the full names of the states and provinces, and a field for the sales tax rate you need to charge for orders from that state. You can have your combo box or list box display only the state or province name on the form, but have the control store only the abbreviation for the selected state or province in the order-entry table that you're editing.

Making combo boxes the really easy way

In the table that is the record source for the form, you can set up a field as a *lookup field* — a field that must match the primary key field in a table of codes. If you do this, Access creates a combo box when you drag it from the Field list to the Design View window of the form. Easy enough! By configuring the field as a lookup field, you've already told Access what table and field to use for the list of values. In the order-entry database example, when you set up the Customers table, you'd configure the StateOrProvince field as a lookup field that must match values in the StateLookup table.

To find out how to make a lookup field, see Book II, Chapter 5.

Running the Combo or List Box Wizard

To make a combo box or list box when you didn't designate the field as a lookup field, a wizard steps you through the process. Before you start, determine where the list of values comes from, as described earlier in this chapter. The Combo Box and List Box Wizards ask the same questions that we pose, so you'd better have the answers. We describe the Combo Box Wizard, because combo boxes outnumber list boxes 10 zillion to one in actual usage, but the List Box Wizard is similar.

To create a combo box with the Combo Box Wizard, follow these steps:

1. **Open the form in Layout or Design view.**

   If either Layout or Design view is new to you, jump back to Chapter 1 of this minibook for an overview.

2. **Click the Combo Box button in the Controls group on the Design tab of the Ribbon.**

   If you don't see the Combo Box button, click the Controls button and click the Combo Box button on the menu that appears.

3. **Click where you'd like the upper-left corner of the combo box to appear.**

   Don't worry if the combo box isn't in exactly the right spot — you can always move the edges later. Access displays the Combo Box Wizard shown in Figure 3-2.

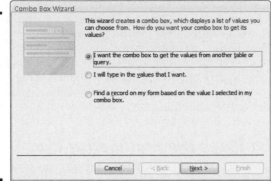

Figure 3-2:
The Combo
Box Wizard
steps you
through
creating a
combo box
(drop-down
list) on your
form.

4. **Choose where the list of values comes from, and click Next.**

   If the list comes from an existing table or query, choose the first option
   and go to Step 5. If the list of options doesn't exist in a table, choose
   the second option and go to Step 9. The third option is for creating a
   combo box that lets you jump to a specific record in your table. (See the
   "Making a Find Box" section later in this chapter.)

5. **If the list of values is already stored in your database, choose the table
   or query and click Next.**

   The wizard displays all the tables, all the queries, or both, so you can
   choose the table or query that you want. If the table doesn't have a primary key field, you can't choose it.

6. **When the wizard shows you a list of the fields in the table or query,
   choose the fields to display in the combo box, and click Next.**

   You can choose more than one field if you want more than one to
   appear in the combo box. Double-click a field in the Available Fields list
   to move it to the Selected Fields list (and vice versa). In Figure 3-3, both
   fields are selected.

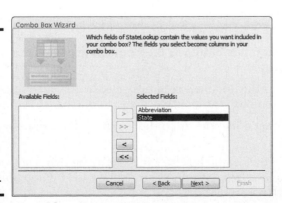

Figure 3-3:
Choose
which field
will appear
when the
user clicks
the combo
box and the
drop-down
list appears.

7. **Choose the order in which you want the records to appear in the combo box, and click Next.**

   The wizard allows you to choose Ascending or Descending order for up to four fields. Be sure that the field on which you're sorting also appears in the combo box, or the order can be confusing. For example, if you sort states and provinces by their two-letter codes, the names don't appear in order, which looks weird if the codes don't also appear.

8. **Adjust the widths of the columns by dragging the column divider left or right, and then click Next. Skip to Step 11 unless you're typing in values instead of using a table.**

   If you want the primary key field to appear in the combo box (for example, the two-letter code in a list of states), deselect the Hide Key Column check box.

9. **If you choose to type in the list of values, type them into the datasheet, one per row, and click Next.**

   The wizard displays a datasheet into which you can type the list. When typing in a list of values, you can create more than one column (for example, a code and its meaning), of which one will be stored in the record source of the form.

10. **Choose the field that identifies each row of the combo box, and click Next.**

    The wizard asks which field uniquely identifies each row in the combo box — the equivalent of the primary key field in a stored table. (Aren't you beginning to wish you'd just stored the list in the table? Hint, hint!) This value is what gets saved as the value of the combo box in the next step.

11. **Choose whether to remember the value for later use or store it in a field. Click Next.**

    The wizard asks what you want to do with the value of the field when the user chooses from the combo box: Remember the value for later use (for example, refer to it in a query parameter, macro, or VBA module); or store it in a field of the table or query that is the record source for the form. Most of the time, you want to store the value in a field; choose the field name from the list.

12. **Type a label for the combo box and click Finish.**

    The wizard creates your combo box.

13. **Adjust the edges of the control to resize the combo box. Drag its label to the right place.**

    We never get the size and position of a combo or list box right the first time, and Access never puts its label in the right place. Good thing Access gives us a chance to touch things up a bit! You can drag the control and its label around the form to the right positions.

When the wizard finishes, you end up with a combo or list box. The next section describes the properties you may want to change if you don't like the way your combo or list box turns out.

Changing the properties of a combo or list box

You can change the way a combo or list box works by editing its properties — you're never stuck with what a wizard creates. Click the Property Sheet button in the Tools group on the Design tab of the Ribbon to display the Property sheet. The properties you're most likely to change are shown in Table 3-1.

Table 3-1   Properties of Combo Boxes and List Boxes

Property	Description
Control Source	Field in the record source in which Access stores the value that you choose from the combo or list box.
Row Source Type	Where the items on the list come from: Table/Query, Value List, or Field List (That last option displays a list of the fields in a table or query.)
Row Source	If you choose the Table/Query or Field List options for the Row Source Type property, enter the name of a table or query (or a SQL statement). If you choose the Value List setting, type a list of values separated by semicolons (;).
Column Count	Number of columns to display in the combo or list box.
Column Heads	Whether or not to display headings for the columns of values.
Column Widths	Widths of the column(s) for the list. If you've got more than one column, separate the widths with semicolons.
Bound Column	Column number in the combo or list box of the column that gets stored in the control source.
List Rows	Number of rows that appear in the drop-down list of a combo box. If the list has more values than this number, a scroll bar appears so the user can display more values. (Not used for list boxes, because the size of the list box control on the form determines how many rows appear.)
Limit to List	Whether entries in the combo box are limited to values on the drop-down menu. Choose the No setting if you want to be able to type other values into the control. (Not used for list boxes, which are always limited to the values listed.)

Cool Looks for Yes/No Fields

Chapter 2 of this minibook describes how to create a check box for a Yes/ No field, which looks pretty spiffy. But you have other options for Yes/No fields: *option buttons* (little round radio buttons) and *toggle buttons* (rectangular buttons that appear pressed in when selected). You can display a Yes/ No field in a text box, too, but the Yes value appears as −1, and the No value appears as 0, which may not be what you want. Figure 3-4 shows a check box, option button, and toggle button.

Figure 3-4: Ways to display a Yes/No field.

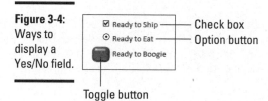

One of the easiest ways to make a toggle or option button for a Yes/No field is to create a check box for it, and then change it into a toggle or option button. Drag the field from the Field list to the desired location on your form, and Access makes a check box for the field. Right-click the field and choose Change To⇨Option Button, or Change To⇨Toggle Button, from the shortcut menu that appears. Adjust the size and position of the control and its label, and you're done!

Creating Option Groups

If a field is set to one of a small number of numeric, integer values — such as 1 to 10 — you can display the values in a box, with an option button by each value. When editing records using the form, you click the option for the value to which you want to set the field. Only one option can be selected at a time; clicking one option deselects the other options.

Making a group of option buttons for a field requires creating an *option group* — a rectangle within which you put an option button for each possible value of the field. Figure 3-5 shows option buttons in an option group. Luckily, Access comes with the Option Group Wizard that creates the option group and all the option buttons.

Before you run the Option Group Wizard, make a note of the values that the field takes. After the wizard is running, you can't open another table to see the values to which the field is limited. You may want to keep the table that lists the possible values open and visible in the corner of the Access window while you run the wizard.

Figure 3-5:
An option
group
contains
an option
button for
each value
that the field
can take.

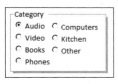

Note that option groups work only with integer, numeric values. You can show any label you want next to each option button, but the value that Access stores for the option group has to be a whole number. In the option group shown in Figure 3-5, the actual category codes may be the numbers from 1 to 7.

An option group can contain option (radio) buttons, check boxes, or toggle buttons. However, most people expect check boxes and toggle buttons to stand by themselves, not to be in a group of mutually exclusive options. We recommend sticking with option buttons in option groups.

To make an option group and option buttons for a field, display your form in Design view and follow these steps:

1. **Click the Option Group button in the Controls group on the Design tab on the Ribbon, and then click where you want the option group to appear on the form.**

   Access draws a box for the option group and then runs the Option Group Wizard. Don't worry if the rectangle for the option group is the wrong size; you can resize it later.

2. **The wizard prompts you for a list of the labels for the individual option buttons. Type them in, one per line, and click Next.**

   Don't press Enter after typing in a value; the wizard thinks you're clicking Next. Instead, press Tab or the down arrow to move to the next row in the datasheet. (If you accidentally press Enter, click the Back button to get back to this screen.)

3. **In the next window, choose the default value for the field, or choose the No I Don't Want a Default option. Click Next.**

   This answer determines whether one of the choices that you just typed starts out as selected when you create a new record in the table.

4. **You see a list of the labels that you typed in Step 2. In the right-hand column, type the number to store for each value, as shown in Figure 3-6. Click Next.**

   Each label must have a different value, and all the values have to be whole numbers.

Figure 3-6: When you create an option group, you specify a label and a value for each option button in the group.

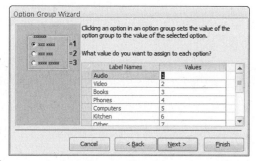

5. **Choose to save the value for later use or to store it in a field (and specify the field). Click Next.**

   If you're creating a form for editing a table, choose the Store the Value in This Field option. If the form is *unbound* (not connected to a record source) and the options are for use as an input to a query, macro, or VBA module, choose the Save the Value for Later Use option. (See Book VI, Chapter 1 for how to run macros from a form, possibly using inputs from the form.)

6. **Choose whether the options appear as option buttons, check boxes, or toggle buttons, and choose the style for the option group box. Click Next.**

   We strongly recommend choosing option buttons (the default), because most people expect option buttons to be in groups of mutually exclusive options and check boxes and toggle buttons to work independently of each other.

   The style for the option group controls the box that Access draws around the group of option buttons; it's an esthetic decision.

7. **Type a caption (label) for the option group and click Finish.**

   The caption appears at the top of the option group. When you click Finish, the wizard creates your option group and an option button (or check box or toggle button, if you callously disregarded our advice) for each value you specified.

**Book IV
Chapter 3**

Creating Smarter Forms

After the wizard finishes, you can resize the option group box and move the option buttons around inside it.

If you change the list of possible values later, the option buttons on your form don't change automatically. For example, if a set of option buttons shows all the categories of products that your store sells and you add a new product category, you need to remember to edit the form and add a new option button to the option group. For this reason, combo boxes are used more frequently to provide lists of possible values, because when you update a table from which the combo box gets its list of values, the combo box updates automatically the next time you open the form.

You can create a new option button to add to an option group by clicking the Option Button button in the Controls group on the Design tab of the Ribbon.

Creating Command Buttons

Dialog boxes contain command buttons, such as Save and Cancel, and your forms can, too. When you create a command button, you tell Access what program the button should run. Programs can take two forms: macros (described in Book VI) and VBA modules (described in Book VIII). Luckily, wizards can do a lot of the work for you. You don't need to know how to create either macros or VBA modules to make nifty command buttons on your forms.

This section covers how to run the Command Button Wizard to make command buttons that do useful stuff. The wizard creates a macro for the form to contain the programs for the buttons on the form. The wizard makes buttons with actions that it divides into these categories:

✦ **Record Navigation:** These commands are for moving from record to record. Most of them duplicate the navigation controls that appear at the bottom of most forms (Go to First Record, Go to Previous Record, Go to Next Record, and Go to Last Record), but you can also make a Find Record button that displays the Find and Replace dialog box or a Find Next button to repeat the previous search. If you want to make a box right on the form into which you can type a value, and a Find button that searches for that value, see the section, "Making a Find Box," later in this chapter.

✦ **Record Operations:** This category includes buttons for adding, deleting, duplicating, printing, saving, and undoing the edits to a record (the current record, in most cases). The Duplicate Record button adds a new record that is a duplicate of the current record. The Print Record button prints the form with the data for the current record.

✦ **Form Operations:** These commands apply or edit filters (which are described in Book II, Chapter 3), close this form, open another form, or print another form.

If you print another form, you get *all* the records in that form, so you may want to come up with another method.

You can also make a button that reloads the data on the form, in case it has changed since you loaded the form.

✦ **Report Operations:** You can make command buttons to preview, print, mail, or save a report to a file. However, there's no way to restrict the report to a specific record without editing the code behind the form.

✦ **Application:** These commands run other Microsoft Office programs (like Word or Excel) or other applications.

✦ **Miscellaneous:** This last group of commands includes commands to dial a phone number (assuming that your computer is connected to a dial-up modem and a phone), print a table in Datasheet view, run a macro, or run a query and display the resulting datasheet.

Making a Close button

Who needs a Close button when forms already have a big X button in the upper-right corner? Some people like to have a Close button anyway, and it's easy enough to make. Here's how:

1. **With your form open in Design view, click the Command Button button in the Controls group on the Design tab of the Ribbon.**

2. **Click in the form where you want the button to appear.**

   Don't worry about the exact location; you can always move it later. Access starts the Command Button Wizard shown in Figure 3-7.

Figure 3-7:
The
Command
Button
Wizard
includes
lots of pre-
programmed
commands
for your
button
to run.

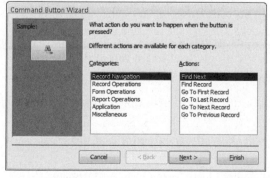

**Book IV
Chapter 3**

Creating Smarter
Forms

3. **Choose the Form Operations category and the Close Form action. Click Next.**

4. **Choose whether you'd like to have text or a picture on the button, specify what text or which picture, and click Next.**

    If you choose the Text option, you can edit the text in the box. (Access suggests "Close Form" for the text, which sounds pretty good to us.) If you choose the Picture option, you can choose from the list of suggested icons, or click the Browse button to look at the full set of icons Access provides; as you choose an icon, it appears on the left side of the dialog box. You can use any bitmap (.bmp) file as an icon.

5. **Type a name for your new control and click Finish.**

    The suggested name is something like Command7, so change it to something meaningful, like CloseButton. The wizard creates a command button control where you originally clicked the form. Now you can drag the edges of the button to resize it, or drag the whole button to another location.

After creating a command button using the wizard, you edit its properties, as described in the "Customizing your command button" section, later in this chapter.

Making a button to display a related form

You can make a command button to display another form. You can display any old form in the database, but this kind of command button is most powerful when you use it to display a form that shows the records of a table that relates to the records in your original form. For example, you may be working on an Order form that displays information about each order of your online store. You can add a command button that opens the Address Book form showing the record for the customer that placed the current order, including the customer's address, phone number, and other information.

Here's how to add a button to display another form:

1. **With the form open in Design view, click the Command Button button in the Controls group on the Design tab of the Ribbon.**

2. **Click in the form where you want the button to appear.**

    The Command Button Wizard fires up to create your button. (Refer to Figure 3-7.)

3. **Choose the Form Operations category and the Open Form action. Click Next.**

    Access displays a list of the forms in your database.

4. **Choose the form name you want the button to open, and click Next.**

    The wizard asks whether to display the form with all records available, or to display a specific record. In our example, it would be nice to display the Address Book record for the customer whose order you are editing.

5. **Choose the Open the Form and Find Specific Data to Display option, and click Next.**

    You see two lists of fields, as shown in Figure 3-8. The left-hand list shows the fields in the record source of the current form. The right-hand list shows the fields in the record source of the form you want the button to open.

6. **Choose the fields from the two forms that match. Click a field in the left-hand list, a field in the right-hand list, and then the <-> button. Click Next.**

    For example, if you are adding a button to display the Address Book form with record of the customer who placed the order displayed on the Orders form, the ContactID field on the Orders form should match the ContactID field on the Address Book form.

7. **Choose the text or picture to appear on the form, click Next, type a name for the control, and click Finish.**

    (How about `OpenAddressBookForm` for the control name? We don't mind using long names when they provide clarity.) The wizard makes the command button. Switch to Form view (by clicking the View button on the toolbar) to try out your new button!

When you click the button, Access opens the new form in a separate tab (or a separate window, if you have configured Access to use multiple windows).

Making a button to print the current record

The Command Button Wizard offers a number of print actions, but most of them don't work the way you might wish. The Print a Form action prints a form once for every single record in the form's record source, so you need to come up with a way to restrict the records to the one(s) you want. If you want to print the current record in the current form, run the Command Button Wizard, choose the Record Operations category, and choose the Print Record action.

If you want to print a report — rather than the current form — for just the current record, you need to do some extra work. Specifically, you need to make a macro or VBA module that the button runs, and you need to set up the macro or VBA to print the report with the records limited to those records that match the record currently displayed on the form.

Luckily, this macro is short and easy to make — see Book VI, Chapter 1 for specific directions.

Making other cool buttons

You can run the Command Button Wizard to make lots of other useful buttons. Command buttons do some of our favorite things. The following list shows how the wizard creates them:

**Book IV
Chapter 3**

**Creating Smarter
Forms**

✦ **Add a new record that's a duplicate of the current record.** Choose the Record Operations category and the Duplicate Record action.

✦ **Save the current record.** Choose the Record Operations category and the Save Record action.

✦ **Display the results of a query in Datasheet view.** Choose the Miscellaneous category and the Run Query action. For example, you could display all the other orders by the same customer, or all the recent orders for the same product.

✦ **Run a macro.** Choose the Miscellaneous category and the Run Macro action. (Book VI describes how to make macros that do all kinds of things.)

Hey, where's the "Run VBA Module" action? Microsoft is phasing out macros in favor of VBA, so why offer only macros here? Luckily, you can set the Event properties of a command button to run VBA modules, as described in the next section.

Customizing your command button

You can change the properties of a command button after you create it. To do so, display the button's Property sheet by double-clicking the command button in Design view.

Some of the most useful properties and what they do are in the following table.

Property	*Description*
Caption (on Format tab)	Text that appears on the button unless it displays a picture. (If the Picture property specifies a picture, the button shows the picture, not the caption.)
Picture (on Format tab)	Picture (icon) that appears on the button. The term (image) indicates that you selected a picture. Click the Build button to the right of the property to select a different picture. If the picture is blank, Access displays the Caption text.
On Click (on Events tab)	What program (macro or VBA module) Access runs when you click the button.

You can tell Access to run programs when you click, double-click, move into, or move away from the button (and at other times, too) by setting the Events properties of the command button — or almost any other kind of control, for that matter. See Book VI, Chapter 1 for how events on a form work.

Making a Find Box

When you're using a form, you can select a control, press Ctrl+F to display the Find and Replace dialog box, and jump directly to a record that matches the value you entered for the selected control. But wouldn't it be nice to have a combo box right on the form with the Find button next to it, so you can locate a record without bringing up a separate dialog box? Access makes this surprisingly easy.

For example, on an Address Book form, you could create a combo box that would list all the customers in your Address Book. When you choose a customer, the macro takes you right to that customer's record.

Follow these steps to create a Find box:

1. **With your form open in Design view, click the Combo Box button in the Controls group on the Design tab of the Ribbon.**

2. **Click in your form where you want the Find box to appear.**

   The Combo Box Wizard runs, as described in the "Running the Combo or List Box Wizard" section earlier in this chapter.

3. **Choose the Find a Record on My Form Based on the Value I Selected in My Combo Box option, and click Next.**

   Access displays a list of the fields in the record source of the form.

4. **Choose the field(s) containing the values from which the user can choose when finding a record. Click Next.**

   If you choose a field that is unique for each record (for example, the `OrderID` field for a form that displays orders), the combo box provides you with a list of the values for the field, and choosing a value takes you right to the order. If you choose a field that's not unique, the combo box displays a list with duplicate values and finds records unpredictably. You can choose more than one field — for example, `Last Name` and `First Name`.

5. **Adjust the width of the column(s) that will appear in the drop-down list by dragging the column divider(s). Then click Next.**

6. **Type a name for the combo box control and click Finish.**

   The wizard creates the combo box. Switch to Form view by clicking the View button on the toolbar, and then test it out. It looks something like Figure 3-8.

You can change the text of the label that Access creates for the combo box to something like "Find" or "Find by Name" — whatever you think will be clear to the user.

Figure 3-8:
You can
display a
form with
the record
that matches
the current
record of
the current
form.

Displaying Attachments

Attachments are files that can be imported into an Attachment-type field in a table. You can display attachments on a form by dragging the field from the Field list to the form in Design view. On the Field list, an attachment appears as a group of fields: the field itself followed by `FileData`, `FileName`, and `FileType`. In Figure 3-9, `CustomerDocuments` is an attachment field.

Figure 3-9:
Creating an
attachment
control
for an
attachment
field.

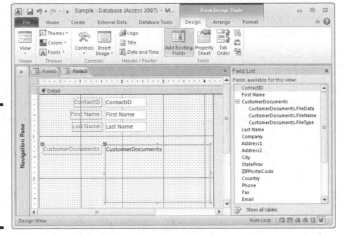

To create a control to display an attachment field, click the field name in the Field list to select the entire attachment field. When you drag it to the form, Access creates an Attachment control.

In Form view, the attachment control looks like an empty rectangle for records with no attachments stored in the field. If one or more pictures are stored in the attachment field for a record, the first picture appears in the rectangle, as shown in Figure 3-10. If you click the attachment field, three buttons appear: Back (to see the previous attachment for this record, if any), Next (to see the next attachment for this record, if any), and Manage Attachments, which displays the Attachments dialog box, shown in Figure 3-11. (Double-clicking the attachment control displays it, too.)

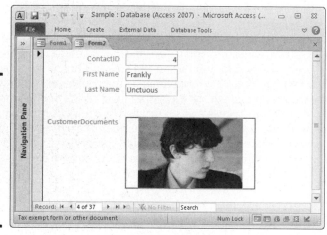

Figure 3-10: In Form view, you can see the attached files for the current record, one at a time.

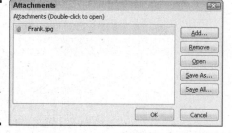

Figure 3-11: Managing the files stored for one record in an attachment field.

You can use the Next and Previous buttons to flip through the files stored in the attachment field for the current record. The files that aren't pictures appear as the icon for the program that can open them (Word for word-processing documents, Excel for spreadsheets, and so forth). The Attachments dialog box is where you can

✦ **Add** new files to the record.

✦ **Remove** a file from the record.

✦ **Open** the file using the default program for the type of file.

✦ **Save** the file **As** the name you specify.

✦ **Save All** the files attached to the current record.

Adding Form Headers and Footers

The part of the form that we've been working with so far is the Detail section — in Design view, a Detail divider bar runs along the top of the form (as shown in Figure 3-9).

However, you may want to display information at the top and bottom of your form. Yes, you can just put controls at the top and bottom of the Detail section of your form, and most people do just that. However, if the window displaying the form is too small for the whole form to fit, the information may not always be visible. Access's various wizards create forms that include a Header and Footer section, too — Figure 3-12 shows the Header section that one wizard creates. When you switch to Form view by clicking the View button, the controls in the header and footer sections are always visible, no matter what the size of your Form window.

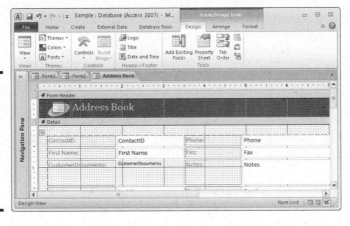

Figure 3-12: Forms can have headers and footers that always appear on the screen.

You can add a Form Header and Form Footer section to your form by opening the form in Design view, right-clicking anywhere in the form, and choosing Form Header/Footer from the menu that appears. (You can get rid of the sections by giving the same command again.) Access creates a new, blank Form Header section at the top of the form and a matching new, blank Form Footer at the bottom.

You can add controls to these sections by using the buttons in the Controls group on the Design tab on the Ribbon. And you'll find that the buttons in the Header/Footer group on the Design tab are useful, too.

✦ **Logo:** Adds a picture (which doesn't have to be a logo) in the Header section.

✦ **Title:** Adds a label in the Header section.

✦ **Date and Time:** Adds a text box with the current date, time, or both to the Header section.

To control the vertical size of the Header section, drag the top of the Detail divider bar up or down to make the Header section larger or smaller. Similarly, at the bottom of the form, you can drag the bottom edge of the Footer section up or down.

Creating Tabbed Forms

Sometimes you need to fit tons of information on a form, and you can see that the form is getting to be the size of Nebraska. In addition to not fitting on the screen, large forms are confusing: Where is the right box in which to type this information?

One way to fit lots of information on a form while keeping the window size down and making the form less confusing is to divide the form into tabs. We're talking about the kind of tabs that stick up from the tops of folders, like those on the Property sheet. Your forms can have tabs, too, with different controls on each one. The entire form can be on the tabs, or the tabs can occupy part of the form, with controls that remain visible regardless of which tab you're looking at. (We recommend the latter approach.)

To create tabs, you create a *tab control* on the form, and then you create controls on the tab. Before you start, decide how many tabs you want, and what controls go on each tab. Then follow these steps:

1. **With your form open in Design view, make some space on your form where you want the tabs to go.**

   If your form is already crowded, just expand the form outrageously by dragging its bottom edge downward or right edge rightward, and drag groups of controls out of the way of your new tabs.

2. **Click the Tab Control button in the Controls group on the Design tab of the Ribbon.**

3. Click in the form where you want the upper-left corner of the tabs to appear.

Access creates a tab control and two tabs (also called *pages*), usually named Page1 and Page2, as shown in Figure 3-13.

4. Drag the edges of the tab control to fix the size of the control.

If you want to move the whole tab control, click the first page (usually Page1) so that it's selected, and drag the black handle that appears in its upper-left corner. You can also drag the handles on the top, bottom, and sides of the control to resize it.

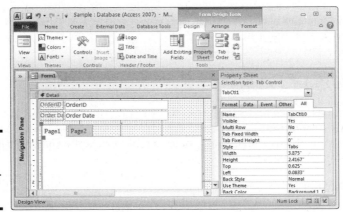

Figure 3-13:
Creating
tabs on your
form.

You can fix up your new tab control as follows:

✦ **Rename the pages.** Page1 and Page2 are probably not what you want to call your tabs. Click the tab to select the page, display the Property sheet by clicking the Properties button on the toolbar, and change the Name property on the Property sheet.

✦ **Add, delete, or reorder the pages.** If you want more than two pages, right-click the tab control (or any of its pages) and choose the Insert Page option from the shortcut menu that appears. To delete a page, select it, right-click it, and choose the Delete Page option from the shortcut menu. To switch the order of the pages, right-click any of the pages and choose the Page Order option; in the Page Order dialog box that appears, use the Move Up and Move Down buttons to reorganize the list of pages.

✦ **Put controls on the pages.** This is the good part — you can drag existing controls from the rest of the form, or you can create new controls on the form in the same way you create controls for the rest of the form. Click the page on which you want to put the controls so that the page appears "on top." Then move or create the controls you want.

Figure 3-14 shows a form with three tabs in Design view.

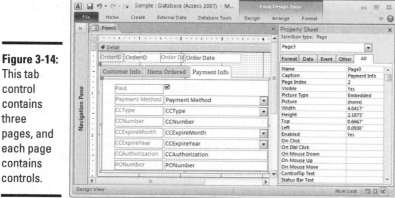

Figure 3-14:
This tab control contains three pages, and each page contains controls.

You Can't Type That Here!

The main purpose of forms is to provide easy-to-use on-screen display and editing for your records. Most people use forms rather than datasheets for entering and editing data. Book II, Chapter 5 describes how to create defaults and validation rules for your tables, to prevent the dreaded "garbage in, garbage out" syndrome that so many databases suffer from. You can add validation to your form controls, too.

Use validation in your tables when you want data to follow rules all the time, no matter how it is entered. Use validation in form controls when you want to validate one field against another, or do validation that applies only at certain times (like, when someone is using this form). For example, you may want to make sure the Ship Date can't be earlier than the Order Date, which you can't enforce using field validation in the table design.

Form controls that display data have properties with which you can validate and format that data. In fact, they are the very same properties that you can set as part of your table design.

+ **Default Value:** The starting value for this field when you add a new record

+ **Input Mask:** A pattern for field data to follow, including where letters, numbers, and punctuation appear, and how letters are capitalized

+ **Validation Rule:** A rule Access applies to values entered in this field

+ **Validation Text:** An error message you see if you try to enter data that breaks the validation rule

These settings appear on the Data tab of the Property sheet for controls. For help with creating input masks and validation rules (which can be a little complicated, frankly), click in the setting on the Property sheet and then click the Build button (to the right of the setting). For input masks, you see the Input Mask Wizard, and for validation rules, you see the Expression Builder. (For details about using these settings, see Book II, Chapter 5.)

Making a Main Menu for Your Database

As you set up your database, you end up with various forms and reports that you (or the users for whom you are creating the database) will use regularly. The database would be easier to use with a main menu from which these frequently-used objects can be chosen. Previous versions of Access used *switchboards* to create menus from which you could open forms and reports. Navigation forms replace switchboards, although switchboards in databases created in earlier versions of Access continue to work.

Creating a navigation form

A *navigation form* is a form that includes a *navigation control* that can display one or more forms and reports. The navigation control has tabs — which can appear down the left-hand side of the form, along the top, or other places — that you can click to choose the form or report to display. Very nice!

You can create a navigation form by running a wizard or by making it with your bare hands. Here are some suggestions for using both:

✦ **By wizard:** Click the Navigation button in the Forms group on the Create tab of the Ribbon. Choose from the options that the button displays to create a form with one or two levels of horizontal or vertical tabs (that is, form name tabs that run horizontally along the top of the form, or vertically down the left side of the form).

✦ **By hand:** Create it in Layout view, by clicking the Blank Form button in the Forms group on the Create tab of the Ribbon. You can create a navigation form in Design view, but Layout view makes it easier by positioning the forms nicely. Click the Navigation Control button in the Controls group on the Design tab of the Ribbon. Then click in the form to create the control.

Either way, you see a form with a navigation control: a box with an Add New tab near the top-left corner of the form. For each form for which you want a tab, drag the form from the Navigation pane onto the navigation control. Access creates a tab with the name of the form, and it displays the form in the main part of the navigation control, as shown in Figure 3-15.

Figure 3-15:
A navigation form can serve as Mission Control for your database.

A navigation form doesn't have to be the main menu for your whole database. You can make one for a specific function, like end-of-the-month reporting, or for things that the bookkeeper does. You can even include one navigation form on another: You might make a Main Menu navigation form that has a tab that opens a Bookkeeping Menu navigation form.

The alternative to navigation forms

You don't have to use a navigation control to make a main menu form for your database. You can use a regular old form with command buttons on it instead.

To make a main menu form, create an unbound form, that is, a form for which the `Record Source` property for the form is blank. (See Chapter 1 of this minibook for how to set the record source of a form, and Book VI, Chapter 2, for more on making a main menu.) Use labels to give the form a title (such as "Main Menu") and create a command button for each command you want available on the form. When the Command Button Wizard runs for each button, choose Form Operations and Open Form to open a form, or Report Operations and Preview Report to display a report that can be printed.

Many people use a one-record table to contain constants about their businesses or projects (see Book I, Chapter 3). If you use this trick, you may want to set this table as the record source of your main menu form. The form shown in Figure 3-16 contains two controls at the bottom of the form, showing data from a Constants table. These controls make seeing and editing these values easy for a database user.

Figure 3-16:
You can use a regular form with lots of command buttons as a main menu, too.

Opening a form automatically when the database opens

Now that you have a main menu, wouldn't it be nice to have it open automagically when the database opens? It's easy:

1. **Click the File tab on the Ribbon to see Backstage view.**

2. **Click Options to see the Access Options dialog box.**

3. **Click the Current Database button on the left side of the window.**

4. **Set the Display Form option to the name of the form you want to open.**

5. **Click OK.**

   Access warns you that you need to close and open the database for this change to take effect. Good enough!

Chapter 4: Doing Calculations in Forms and Subforms (and Reports)

In This Chapter

✔ Including calculated results on your forms (and reports)

✔ Using numbers in calculations

✔ Using dates in calculations

✔ Using strings — that is, text — in calculations

✔ Adding subforms to a form

✔ Using split forms to display a datasheet on a form

✔ Totaling and counting information from subforms (and subreports)

The first three chapters in Book IV explain how to make forms with all kinds of controls, showing information in all kinds of ways. In the process, you find out how to create reports, because creating and editing reports is so similar to working with forms. However, up to this point all the information we deal with is sitting there waiting for us, nicely contained in tables and queries. How about calculating data that isn't stored anywhere? Your forms and reports can calculate and display information, which you can also store in the record source for the form (that is, store the results so you can use them in other objects). For example, you may want the Order form for an online store to calculate the total price of all items ordered, the sales tax, and the grand total for the order.

In addition to calculating numbers, you can also do text, date, and logical calculations. For example, you can give Access instructions such as, "If `Tax Exempt` is `True`, then `Sales Tax` is 0; otherwise it's `Tax Rate` times `Product Total`." Text calculations include things such as keeping only the first five digits of a ZIP code, or capitalizing a text entry.

Doing Elementary Calculations

Sounds like algebra class, doesn't it? Don't worry; creating calculated values for your forms won't cause you to scream in terror like your high school algebra teacher did. You'll recognize some arithmetic signs (especially the equal sign), but the calculations are all easy.

A *calculated value* is a value that Access creates by doing a calculation based on other information, usually using fields from your tables. For example, Access can add the product total to the shipping cost for an order, to come up with the total cost.

To include a calculated value on a form or report, and the calculation isn't already stored in a calculated column in a table, create a text box and then enter an expression in the `Control Source` property of the text box. An *expression* is a formula that tells Access how to calculate an answer from field values and other values. Expressions start with an equal sign (=). If field names include spaces, enclose them in square brackets. (Actually, we enclose *all* field names in square brackets, just so we don't forget.) For example, this is an expression:

```
= [Product Total] + [Shipping Cost]
```

And here's another one:

```
= "Your total will be " & [GrandTotal] & "."
```

The expressions you use on forms and reports are the same as the expressions you use to create calculated columns in tables and calculated fields in queries. Turn to Book II, Chapter 1 for calculated columns in tables, and Book III, Chapter 2 for how expressions work in queries, including the operators and functions they can include.

Making a calculated control

A *calculated control* is a control that uses an expression, rather than a field name, as its `Control Source` property (as explained in Chapter 2 of this minibook). Usually, it's a text box control. To create a calculated control, follow these steps:

1. **With the form or report open in Design view or Layout view, choose the Text Box button from the Controls group on the Design tab of the Ribbon.**

   For an introduction to the tools in the Controls group, see Chapter 2 of this minibook. You have to use buttons in the Controls group, rather than the Field list, to create a control with a blank control source. (A control with no control source is called an *unbound control.*)

2. **Click the form where you want the text box to appear.**

   A text box appears. In Design view, it shows Unbound, while in Layout view, it's blank. The control has no control source — Access doesn't know what to display in the text box.

3. **Display the Property sheet for the control by double-clicking the new text box. Click the Data tab on the Property sheet.**

   The Control Source property is the first property on the Data tab — and lo! It's blank.

4. **Type an expression, starting with an equal sign, in the Control Source property of the text box.**

   Or, in Design view, you can click in the text box on the form and type the expression, and it appears in the text box as shown in Figure 4-1. Your choice.

Figure 4-1:
When you type an expression as the value of a text box, be sure to start it with an equal sign.

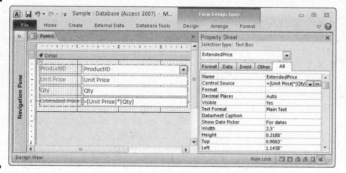

5. **Click the Other or All tab in the Property sheet and change the Name property to something descriptive.**

   Don't leave it named something like Text17, which won't give you much of a hint as to what you had in mind, when you look at this control later.

   If you want to edit the expression later, you can change the Control Source entry on the Property sheet.

Expressions can get long, and it can be hard to see them. When editing a long expression, press Shift+F2 to display it in a Zoom box, as shown in Figure 4-2.

**Book IV
Chapter 4**

**Doing Calculations in
Forms and Subforms
(and Reports)**

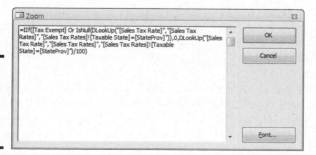

Figure 4-2:
A Zoom box displays a long, scary expression.

Should you put your calculations in tables, in queries, or on forms and reports?

When you want to include a calculated value in a form or report, you can do it in one of three ways:

✔ **In a calculated column in a table** that contains the fields that the calculation is based on. This new feature of Access 2010 is described in Book II, Chapter 1. Use this method if the calculation uses fields from only one table and will be used in more than one query, form, or report. If you need to change the way the calculation works, it's more efficient if you have to update it in only one place.

✔ **In a query** that you use as the record source for the form or report. Use this method if you plan to use the calculated value to select which records to include in the form or report so that you can set the Sort row of the query to ascending or descending for the calculated field. Also, use it if you use the calculation in more than one form or report that has this query as its record source, or if the calculation is based on fields from more than one table. See Book III, Chapter 2 for how to create calculated fields in queries.

✔ **In a text box control on the form or report.** Use this method otherwise.

Another way to enter or edit an expression is to click the Build button — the "…" button to the right of the Control Source box — or press Ctrl+F2 to run the Expression Builder, which steps you through writing an expression. See Book III, Chapter 3 for how the Expression Builder works.

Don't name the text box control with the same name as a field in the record source for the form or report! For example, if the table or query that provides the records has a field called Full Name, don't create a calculated text box with that name. Two objects with the same name confuse Access if you refer to that name — Access doesn't know whether you want the field or the control.

Checking your expression

After you type an expression into the Control Source property of a text box (or use the Expression Builder to create it), you see the expression itself in the text box. What about the answer?

To check whether the expression works, switch to Form view by clicking the View button on the Design or Home tab on the Ribbon. (For reports, switch to Print Preview.) Check the answer in several records to see whether the expression works as you expect.

Troubleshooting expressions

If you make a mistake in your expression, you may see one of three things in Form view or Print Preview: a wrong answer, #Name?, or another error message that starts with a #. If you find an error, check out these ideas for fixing your calculated text box and its expression:

✦ #Name? indicates that Access can't understand a field name in your expression. The most likely reason is that you forgot the equal sign (=) at the beginning of the expression. Or you may have misspelled a field name, or you may have forgotten to enclose it in square brackets. If your text box control has the same name as a field, Access can't tell which one you're referring to, so check the name of the text box, too. (It's the Name property on the All tab of the Property sheet.)

✦ #Div/0! means you're dividing something by zero, which is impossible in standard arithmetic. Check the fields in your expression to see if one might be zero for some records.

✦ #Error indicates some other problem — check the expression carefully.

Calculating and Formatting Numbers

To display a numeric calculation on a form or report, you can use the arithmetic operators that we describe in Book III, Chapter 3. Access also has numeric functions, described in the same section.

Some sample numeric expressions (you can guess what the fields contain from their names) are included in the following table.

Numeric Expression	Purpose
=[TaxableTotal]*[SalesTaxRate]	Sales tax on an order
=3.50 + ([ItemCount] * 2)	Shipping is $3.50 plus $2 per item
=[OrderSubtotal] + [SalesTax] + [Shipping]	Grand total for an order

After you type an expression in the Control Source property of a text box and switch to Form view or Print Preview to check that it works, you usually want to format the number — you may not like the number of decimal places, use of commas, or lack of a currency symbol in your calculated text box.

To format a number, display the properties of the text box and click the All or Format tab in the Property sheet, as shown in Figure 4-1. For a text box with numeric values, you can click in the Format property and click the down arrow at the right end of the property to see a list of numeric formats.

**Book IV
Chapter 4**

Doing Calculations in
Forms and Subforms
(and Reports)

Details about numeric formats are in Book II, Chapter 1 — they are the same formats that you can use to format the fields in your tables.

Calculating and Formatting Dates

Access includes operators and functions that work on dates, including finding the number of days between two dates, separating a date into its component parts (day, month, year, hour, minute, and second), and adding days to a date. Book III, Chapter 3 describes the operators and functions you can use. A few examples are in the following table.

Date Expression	Purpose
=DateDiff("w", [OrderDate], [ShipDate])	Number of weeks between ordering and shipping
=[InvoiceDate] + 30	30 days after the invoice date
=Date() + 10	10 days after today
=DatePart("q", [OrderDate])	Quarter in which order was placed

Access gives you lots of date formats to choose from, as listed in Book II, Chapter 1. You set them in the Format property on the Format (or All) tab of the Property sheet.

Calculating and Formatting Text

For forms and reports, you want things to look just right, and text expressions allow you to do all kinds of things to slice and dice the text that appears in your text boxes. Book III, Chapter 3 describes the operators and functions you can use with text values. A few examples are in the following table.

Text Expression	Purpose
=[FirstName] & " " & [LastName]	First and last names, with a space in between
=[LastName] & ", " & [FirstName]	Last name first, with a comma in between
=UCase([LastName])	Last name, in all capital letters
=Left([ProductCode], 2)	First two characters of the product code

You can create a so-called *input mask* that determines the formatting of a calculated text box, as we describe in Book II, Chapter 5. For example, an input mask can add parentheses and dashes to a phone number, or dashes to a Social Security number.

Displaying Values That Depend on Conditions

Some calculations have an *if-then* component — basically, *if* this is true, *then* we do this. For example, if the order is from your home state, then charge sales tax; otherwise, don't. Or if the order is above $100, then shipping is free. Access handles these types of if-then calculations using its `iif()` (immediate-if) function, which we describe in Book III, Chapter 3.

For example, if you charge sales tax for only Vermont orders, then you use this expression:

```
= iif([State]="VT", [TaxableTotal]*.06, 0)
```

The condition (`[State]="VT"`) is either true or false; if it's true, the expression is `[TaxableTotal]*.06` (6 percent of the taxable total); if it's false, the expression is `0`.

The condition can be a Yes/No field: if the field is `Yes` (true), the function returns the first value, and if it's `No` (false), you get the second value. For example, the following expression looks at the Yes/No field, `TaxExempt`, to determine whether this customer is exempt from sales taxes. For taxable customers, the function returns the value of the `TaxableTotal` field. For tax-exempt customers, it returns zero:

```
= iif([TaxExempt], 0, [TaxableTotal])
```

Here's the mind-boggling part: You can *nest* functions, including the `iif()` function — that is, you can use a function inside another function. The following expression (for example) combines the last two examples to calculate sales tax based on both the customer's tax-exempt status and the customer's state:

```
= iif([State]="VT", iif([TaxExempt], 0, [TaxableTotal]*.06), 0)
```

Formatting Calculated Controls

When you display calculated values on a form, the value isn't editable in Form view — that is, you can't type a different value in its place, or delete it. The expression controls what appears in the text box.

To make it clear which text boxes are editable, we like to make calculated text boxes look different from text boxes we type in. We recommend that you display the Format tab on the Property sheet for each calculated control and make the following changes:

✦ Set the `Back Style` property to the `Transparent` setting so that the background of the calculated value matches the background of the form itself.

✦ Set the `Special Effect` property to the `Flat` setting so that the value doesn't appear in a box at all.

Using a Split Form to Display a Datasheet

A *split form* is a form that displays a datasheet of the records from the record source, usually in the lower part of the form. A split form enables you to browse the records in datasheet format, and then view the current record in a form, which can arrange the fields so that they are all visible at the same time. It can include calculated fields.

The easiest way to create a split form is by following these steps:

1. **Select the table or query to be the record source of the main form, by clicking it in the Navigation pane.**

   In our example, you'd click the Orders table. (The Order Details table will be the record source of the datasheet, but that comes later.)

2. **Click the More Forms button on the Create tab of the Ribbon, and then choose Split Form.**

   Access creates a new split form in Layout view. A regular-looking form appears in the top part, with a control for each field in the record source. A datasheet appears in the lower part of the form, as shown in Figure 4-3.

Figure 4-3:
A split form shows a datasheet of the record source, plus a form showing one record.

3. **To adjust the properties of the form, display the Property sheet if it's not already visible, by clicking the Property sheet button in the Tools group on the Design tab of the Ribbon.**

   Make sure that the Selection Type is set to Form, so you see the properties of the whole form.

4. **Click the Format tab of the Property sheet and scroll down to the Script Form properties.**

   The properties that control split forms are listed in Table 4-1.

Table 4-1	Properties of Split Forms
Property	*Description*
Split Form Size	Specifies the height (usually in inches) of the part of the form that is *not* occupied by the datasheet. Defaults to Auto, so Access uses a height that displays the whole form.
Split Form Orientation	Specifies where the datasheet appears: Datasheet on Top or Datasheet on Bottom. The default is on the bottom.
Split Form Splitter Bar	Specifies whether a splitter bar appears in Form view. The user can drag the splitter bar up and down to change how much of the form appears.
Split Form Datasheet	Specifies what the user can do in the datasheet: Allow Edits or Read Only.
Split Form Printing	Specifies what to print if you print the form: Form Only or Datasheet Only.

Using a Subform to Display Detail Records

Sometimes you need to display information from two different tables or queries on the same form. For example, for an online store, if you have a form that shows information about one order from your Orders table, it would be nice if you could also see a list of the items that were included in the order, which may be stored in the related Order Details table.

Figure 4-4 shows an example. The main part of the form displays records from the "one" side of a one-to-many relationship — the Orders table — and the subform displays records from the "many" side — the Order Details table. As a result, the subform displays many records that relate to the "one" record on the main form.

Before you create a subform, make sure that the tables displayed by the form and proposed subform have a one-to-many relationship. Book II, Chapter 6 shows you how to tell Access about the relationships between tables by using the Relationships window.

A subform can have its own form layout and navigation buttons for moving around the records within the subform. One form can have more than one subform, if there's more than one table with a one-to-many relationship to the table shown in the main form.

Figure 4-4:
A subform
shows
the list of
products for
one order.

Each subform is stored as a separate form in Access — you see the subform's name in the Navigation pane. You create a subform just like a regular form because it *is* a regular form. To display it as a subform, you create a *subform control* on the main form, showing Access how and where you want the subform to appear on the main form.

Creating a subform

The easiest way to create a form is by using a wizard (surprise, surprise!). You can always edit and improve the subform later. (If you're creating a report, see the section on subreports in Book V, Chapter 1.)

To add a subform to a form, follow these steps:

1. **Display the main form in Design view.**

2. **If there isn't enough empty space on your form for the subform, make some space by dragging the bottom edge of the form downward.**

   Of course, you don't know yet exactly how much space your subform will occupy, but make a space a few inches high.

3. **Click the Subform/Subreport button in the Controls group on the Design tab of the Ribbon.**

4. **On the form, click where you want the upper-left corner of the subform to appear.**

   Access creates a subform control and runs the SubForm Wizard to lead you through the process of configuring the control. (If the wizard isn't installed on your system, Access offers to install it.)

5. **If you already have a form that you'd like to display as a subform, choose the Use an Existing Form option and choose the form from the**

list. Otherwise, choose the Use Existing Tables and Queries option. Click Next.

If you choose the Use an Existing Form option, skip to Step 8.

The wizard asks which fields you want to include in the subform, and what table or query the fields come from (that is, the record source of the subform), as shown in Figure 4-5.

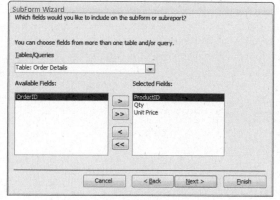

Figure 4-5:
You specify the record source and the fields to display on the subform.

6. **In the Tables/Queries field, choose the table or query to use as the record source of the subform.**

   The table or query that you select must contain a unique field that can act as the primary field in a one-to-many relationship with the records on the main form. For example, if you are adding a subform with order details (that is, the specific items that were purchased) to an order form, the Order Details and Orders tables may be related by an `OrderID` field.

7. **Choose the fields you want to display on the subform, by selecting fields and clicking the > button. Click Next.**

   Alternatively, you can double-click a field name to move it from one list to the other. If you want to display all the fields, click the >> button. As you select fields, they move from the Available Fields list to the Selected Fields list. Don't choose too many fields — you have to fit them all into the subform!

   Don't choose to include the primary key, which relates to the record in the main form. For example, if you're adding an order detail subform to an orders form, the main form displays one order at a time, including its order number. The subform displays all the order detail records that have the same order number. If you include the order number on the subform, you just see the same order number over and over, once for each record in the subform. What a waste of screen space!

8. **Choose a relationship from the list, or select the Define My Own option and choose the matching fields on the form and subform. Click Next.**

    The wizard needs to know how the records in the subform relate to the records in the main form. It displays a list of the relationships you have already defined, and this list usually contains the right relationship. For example, in Figure 4-6, the wizard suggests `Show Order Details for each record in Orders using OrderID` — it uses the `OrderID` field in the Order Details table to match the `OrderID` field in the Orders table (the record source of the main form).

    If you choose the Define My Own option, the wizard's window changes to allow you to choose the matching fields on the form (the "one" side of the relationship) and the subform (the "many" side).

Figure 4-6:
Tell the
SubForm
Wizard
how the
records in
the subform
relate to
the records
in the main
form.

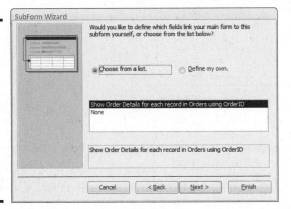

9. **Type a name for the subform or accept the wizard's suggestion. Click Finish.**

    The wizard creates the subform as a separate form in your database. It also creates a subform control on the main form, as shown in Figure 4-7. You can adjust the edges of the subform control by dragging them. You can delete the label for the subform if its function is obvious.

The subform may look totally wrong in Design view but fine in Form view. The subform appears in Datasheet view when the main form is in Form view, so the exact placement of the controls, background color, and other features doesn't matter.

To adjust the column widths of the subform, which is usually in Datasheet view, just drag the column dividers left or right in Form view. After you have nice-looking columns, switch the main form back to Design view and adjust the width of the subform control until it's the right size to fit your columns.

Figure 4-7:
In Design view, the subform looks terrible, but it looks better in Form view as a datasheet.

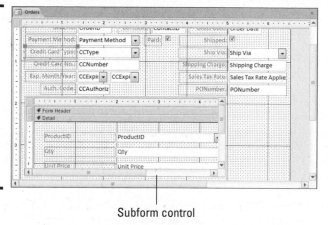

Subform control

The properties of subform controls

After you create the subform, you edit it in either of two ways:

✦ You can open the subform by right-clicking its name in the Navigation pane and choosing Design View from the menu that appears.

✦ When the main form is open in Design view, you can double-click the subform control to start editing the subform that appears in the control.

Either way, Access saves the changes to the subform separately from the changes to the main form. When you save your main form, Access saves changes to your subform, too.

While you're fooling with the fields on the subform, you may want to change the properties of the subform control that displays the subform on the main form. To see the properties of the subform control, display the main form in Design view, display the Property sheet, and then click in the subform.

Don't click in the gray box in the upper-left corner of the subform, or you end up seeing the properties of the form you're using as a subform, rather than the properties of the subform control.

When you're viewing the properties of the subform control, Selection Type at the top of the Property sheet shows the name of the subform control; if it doesn't, click the drop-down list and choose the subform control name.

Some useful entries you can change on the Data tab of the Property sheet for the subform control are the following:

✦ **Source Object:** The name of the form to display in this subform control.

✦ **Link Child Fields:** The field name in the record source of the subform. This field must match the `Link Master Fields` field.

✦ **Link Master Fields:** The field name in the record source of the main form. This field must match the `Link Child Fields` field.

Other properties have to be changed in the subform itself. Open the subform in Design view and display the Property sheet for the form. Or, with the main form open in Design view, click the subform control to select it, and then click the gray box in the upper-left corner of the subform to select the form properties. You may want to change these two properties, which are on the Format tab:

✦ **Default View:** The default setting is Datasheet view, in which the subform appears as a small datasheet of records. You can change the `Default View` property to `Continuous Forms` if you prefer; adjust the layout of the subform to make it look right.

✦ **Navigation Buttons:** If a subform doesn't show many records, you may not want to waste space on navigation buttons. Having two sets of navigation buttons — one for the subform and one for the main form — can be confusing, too. However, without navigation buttons, you have to click or use the keyboard to move from record to record in the subform.

If you're editing the properties of a subform in Design view of the main form, click elsewhere on the main form to tell Access to update the subform properties. Otherwise, your changes don't appear to have taken effect when you switch to Form view.

Adding Subtotals and Totals from Subforms

If your form includes a subform (or your report includes a subreport), and the information shown in the subform includes quantities, you may want to display a total on the main form. For example, on an Orders form that contains an Order Details subform, the main form can include the total cost of all the items in the subform, and maybe a count of the records in the subform. Figure 4-7 shows an Orders form with a subform listing the items that the customer is buying.

Unfortunately, you can't make a control on the main form that calculates a total for the records on the subform. You can, however, make a control on the subform that calculates the total, and then make a control on the main form that displays the value of this control. Seems like an extra step to us, but it works. The following sections cover what you need to know to create totals and counts of subform records.

Using aggregate functions

An *aggregate function* is a function that combines a bunch of values together. For example, the Sum() function adds a bunch of numbers together. (Simple enough!) When doing calculations based on a bunch of records, you can use the aggregate functions outlined in the following table.

Function	Description
Sum()	Totals the values.
Count()	Counts the values.
Avg()	Averages the values (sum divided by count).
Min()	Calculates the smallest value (for numeric values), the earliest date (for date values), or the first value in alphabetical order (for text values).
Max()	Calculates the largest value (for numeric values), the latest date (for date values), or the last value in alphabetical order (for text values).
First()	Uses the value from the first record.
Last()	Uses the value from the last record.

Aggregate functions work only where Access knows what set of records you want to work with. On forms, they work in the form footer of a subform. (See Chapter 3 of this minibook for a description of a form footer, unless you already guessed that a *form footer* is a section that appears at the bottom of a form.)

For example, you may have an Orders form, with an Orders Detail form that lists the items included in the order. The total of the Qty field in the Order Details subform would be useful to tell the shipping clerk how many items need to be shipped for this order. The expression is

= Sum([Qty])

If a field name contains spaces, you have to enclose it in square brackets. We enclose all field names in square brackets, just to be safe.

You can also total a calculation. To come up with the total cost of the items ordered, you use this expression:

```
= Sum([Qty] * [Unit Price])
```

If you want to total, average, or count all the records in an entire table or query, or selected records in a table or query, use the functions described in the sidebar, "Summarizing lots of records."

Summarizing lots of records

In addition to the functions that work with the field values in the current record, Access has *domain aggregate functions* — functions that work with field values in some or all the records in a table or query. (A *domain* is a fancy name for a table or query.) For example, you may want a form to display the grand total of all the orders so far this year, or the amount of the largest order placed. To total the value of a field for a bunch of records, you use the DSum function, which has this syntax:

```
DSum(expression, domain,
    criterion)
```

Replace *expression* with the field name that you want to total (or an expression such as [Price] * [Qty]), in quotes. Replace *domain* with the table or query name, in quotes. Optionally, you can include a *criterion* that limits which records to include.

For example, the following expression totals the extended price (price times quantity) for all the records in the Order Details table:

```
DSum("[Price] * [Qty]", "Order
    Details")
```

Some of the other domain aggregate functions you can use (they have the same syntax as DSum) are

✔ DAvg: Averages the values.

✔ DCount: Counts the values.

✔ DFirst: Value for the first record.

✔ DLast: Value for the last record.

✔ DMin: Minimum value. (For numbers it's the smallest; for text it's the first in alphabetical order; and for dates it's the earliest.)

✔ DMax: Maximum value. (For numbers it's the largest; for text it's the last in alphabetical order; and for dates it's the latest.)

One other useful domain aggregate function is DLookup, which returns the value of a specific field for a specific record in a table or query. For example, the following expression returns the date of OrderID 5000 from the Orders table:

```
DLookup("[Order Date]",
    "Orders", "[OrderID] =
    5000")
```

In this DLookup function, the expression is "[Order Date]", the date of the order. The domain is the Orders table. The criterion is "[OrderID] = 5000" — which limits the records to include only the record with that specific ID.

Referring to a control on a subform

To create a control on the main form that shows information from the subform, you need to know how to refer to a control on the subform. The format of an expression that displays a value from a subform is the following:

```
= [subform control name].Form![control name]
```

(This looks hideous, but hold on!) Replace `subform control name` with the name of the subform control on the main form that displays the subform. Replace `control name` with the name of the text box on the subform that displays the value you want to see.

For example, if your main form is the Orders form shown in Figure 4-7, its subform control is called `Order Details subform`. If you want to display the information from that subform's Order Subtotal text box, the expression would look like this:

```
= [Order Details subform].Form![Order Subtotal]
```

Creating the controls to total a subform

To calculate a total (or a count) of the values of a control on the subform and to display it on the main form, you create two controls: one in the form footer of the subform and one on the main form, wherever you want the total to appear.

Be careful when entering the expressions for calculating and displaying the total: In some cases, you type the name of the field while in other cases you type the name of the control that displays the field. It can get confusing!

Follow these steps to display the subform total on the main form:

1. **Open the subform in Design view and display its Property sheet by clicking the Property Sheet button in the Tools group on the Design tab of the Ribbon.**

    If you already have the main form open in Design view, you can right-click in the subform control and choose Subform in New Window.

2. **Add a Form Footer section (assuming that it doesn't already have one) by right-clicking on the location on the form you want to add a header or footer to and click Form Header or Form Footer.**

    If you see a Form Footer divider bar but space below it, click the bottom edge of the bar and drag downward to expand the footer so there's

**Book IV
Chapter 4**

Doing Calculations in
Forms and Subforms
(and Reports)

space for a text box or two. (See Chapter 3 of this minibook for more about form headers and footers.)

3. **Note the name of the field in the record source (not the control on the form) that contains the values you want to count or total. Or note the expression you want to total.**

Frequently, the control that displays a field has the same name as the field itself, but not always. Be sure to use the field name, not the name of any control on the form that displays the field. In our example, we want to total the expression [Unit Price] * [Qty].

4. **Make a text box by clicking the Text Box button in the Controls group on the Design tab of the Ribbon and clicking in the Form Footer section.**

Access creates an unbound text box.

5. **On the Data tab of the Property sheet for the text box, type the expression that you want to calculate into the Control Source property.**

For example, type = **Sum([Qty] * [Unit Price])** into the Control Source property, as shown in Figure 4-8. Access displays hints just below where you are typing, such as the names of fields and functions.

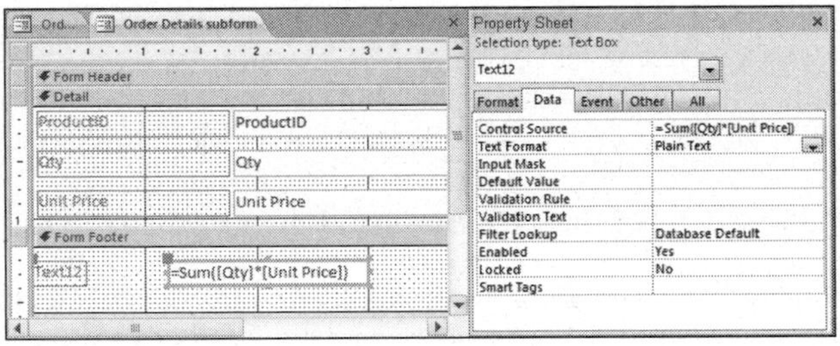

Figure 4-8:
Create a calculated control in the form footer to calculate totals of records on the form.

6. **Enter a descriptive name for the control in the Name property on the Other tab of the Property sheet.**

Make a note of the control name, because you need it to display the value on the main form. For example, you may name the control OrderSubtotal.

7. **Switch to Form view by clicking the View button, to make sure that the new text box works.**

   Because you're looking at the subform as an independent form, the subform shows all the records in its record source, and the calculation totals all the records, not just those for one order; so don't be surprised if you see a very large number. When this form is used as a subform, the linkage between the subform and the main form restricts the records in the subform to one order at a time, and the control totals the records for only the current order.

8. **If you plan to display the subform in Form view, not just in Datasheet view, hide the Form Footer section by setting its `Visible` property to a `No` setting.**

   Otherwise, you display the subtotal once on the subform and once on the main form, which looks odd. Most subforms appear in Datasheet view, which don't display form headers and footers. If you do need to hide the footer, click the Form Footer divider bar and find the `Visible` property on the Format tab of the Property sheet.

9. **Save and close the subform.**

   Press Ctrl+S to save your changes, and go ahead and close its Design View window — you're done with it.

10. **Open the main form in Design view and display the Property sheet, too.**

11. **Create a text box to control the total, by clicking the Text Box button and clicking on the form where you want the calculated control.**

    You get a new unbound control, ready to display your calculated total.

12. **Set the text box's `Control Source` property to an expression that refers to the calculated control on the subform.**

    For example, the expression referring to the calculated control shown in Figure 4-8 is this:

    ```
    = [Order Details subform].Form![Order Subtotal]
    ```

    `Order Details subform` is the name of the subform control.

13. **Format the new control with the numeric format you want, edit its label to a sensible name (like `Total Products` or `Order Subtotal`) and switch to Form view to test it out.**

    If you don't format the text box, Access usually displays way too many decimal places for calculated values. On the Format tab of the Property sheet, set the `Format` property to the `Currency` setting, or whatever format you prefer. Set `Decimal Places` to 2. If all goes well, you see a text box as shown in Figure 4-9.

If you see `#Name` or `#Error` instead of the subtotal, check the expression for the control on the main form carefully, and make sure that you entered the expression, the name of the control on the subform, and the name of the subform control — the control you put on the main form — correctly. (What a zoo!)

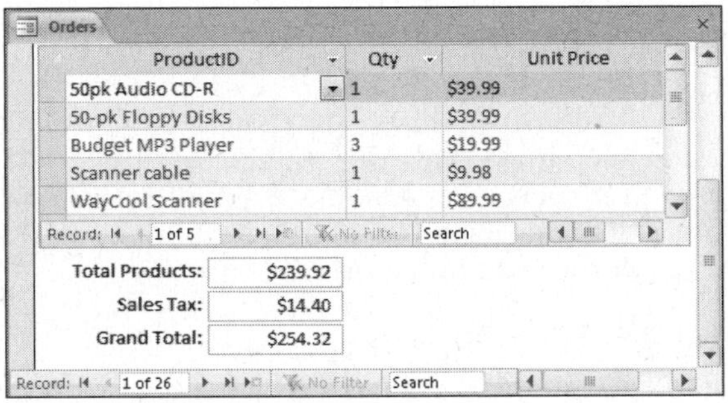

Figure 4-9:
You can display the total from the subform in the main form, and other calculations based on it.

	Orders			×
	ProductID ▾	Qty ▾	Unit Price	▲
	50pk Audio CD-R ▾	1	$39.99	
	50-pk Floppy Disks	1	$39.99	
	Budget MP3 Player	3	$19.99	
	Scanner cable	1	$9.98	
	WayCool Scanner	1	$89.99	▼

Record: ◄ ◄ 1 of 5 ► ►I ►⊠ 💱 No Filter | Search | ◄ ▥ ►

Total Products:	$239.92
Sales Tax:	$14.40
Grand Total:	$254.32

Record: ◄ ◄ 1 of 26 ► ►I ►⊠ 💱 No Filter | Search | ◄ ▥ ►

Book V

Reporting in Words and Pictures

The 5th Wave   By Rich Tennant

FIRED
YOU

"Nifty chart, Frank, but not entirely necessary."

Contents at a Glance

Chapter 1: Creating and Spiffing Up Reports

In This Chapter

✔ **Getting a handle on how reports are like forms**

✔ **Creating reports by running wizards and AutoReports**

✔ **Editing reports in Design view**

✔ **Adding page headers and footers**

✔ **Creating groupings and subtotals**

✔ **Printing information from related tables**

✔ **Viewing reports on-screen**

Reports are the best way to put information from your database onto paper, PDF files, and other formats. In a report, you can choose how to display your data, including which information to include (which tables and fields); where to print each field on the page; text fonts, font sizes, and spacing; and printing lines, boxes, and pictures.

Reports can include information from different tables — for instance, you can display the customer information, followed by all the items that the customer has bought from all orders. The Report Wizard simplifies creating reports that list, summarize, and total your data. You can also use calculations in reports to create totals, subtotals, and other results. You can create invoices, packing slips, student rosters, and all kinds of other reports. Thanks to the trusty Label Wizard, reports are also the best way to create mailing labels from addresses in your database.

This chapter explains how to create and modify reports so that they're ready to print. The next chapter talks about previewing and printing them. Chapter 3 of this minibook describes graphical reports — graphs and charts.

If You Know Forms, You Already Know Reports

Reports and forms are used very differently, but you create them in similar ways. You can create both forms and reports by running wizards. You can create or modify both forms and reports in Layout view, where you can create and rearrange controls, and Design view, where you can customize controls and sections of a report, along with their properties.

To see a list of the reports in your database — and, eventually, to open or modify a report — scroll down in the Navigation pane until you get to the Reports section. If you don't see the Reports section in the Navigation pane, click the title bar of the Navigation pane and select All Access Objects.

You can look at a report in four views:

✦ **Layout view:** Allows you to rearrange the controls on your report and create new ones. It works like Layout view for forms, which is described in Book IV, Chapter 1.

✦ **Design view:** This is where you can look behind the scenes at what fields the report displays where. It works like Design view for forms, which is described in Book IV, Chapter 2.

✦ **Report view:** Displays the report formatted with real data, as described in the section "Viewing Your Reports On-Screen" at the end of this chapter.

✦ **Print Preview:** Shows how the report will look when you print it, including page breaks, headers, and footers. See Chapter 2 in this minibook for how to check how your report will look before wasting paper printing it.

To open a report, right-click its name in the Navigation pane and choose a view from the menu that appears. You can switch between views by clicking the View button on the Home tab of the Ribbon. You can switch to any view by clicking the down arrow on the View button on the Home tab and selecting the view you want.

What view will open?

Now that Access has four (count 'em) views in which to open a report, it can be hard to guess which view you'll see when you double-click a report in the Navigation pane to open it — Report view or Print Preview. To clear up this confusion, you can set the `Default View` property of the report. With a report open in Design or Layout view, display the Property sheet for the form. (Double-click in the upper-left corner of the form in Design view, or click the Property Sheet button in the Tools group on the Design tab of the Ribbon in either Design or Layout view and set the Selection type to Report.)

On the Format tab of the Property sheet, set the `Default View` property to `Report View` or `Print Preview`. While you are at it, set the `Allow Report View` and `Allow Layout View` properties to `No` if you don't want to enable these views.

This chapter describes how to make reports by running wizards, as well as how to customize reports in ways that don't work for forms. For information about how to create and customize reports in Layout view and Design view, including adding controls and setting properties, applying themes and other formatting (including conditional formatting), and creating calculated fields, see Book IV, Chapters 1, 2, and 4.

Reports can include features that don't appear on forms, including these:

✦ **Grouping and sections:** When you design a report, you frequently want to have information grouped together. For example, a monthly sales report may list sales by product, with subtotals for each product. A mailing-label report may start a new page for each new ZIP code, and print the total number of labels that are in each ZIP code. You can have up to four grouping levels. You can add grouping levels by adding section headers to your report in Design view. (See the section, "Grouping your records," later in this chapter.)

✦ **Page headers, footers, and numbers:** Most reports have page numbers, and many need other information printed at the top or bottom of every page. See the section "Adding page headers, footers, and numbers" later in this chapter.

✦ **Margins, paper size, and paper orientation:** Reports usually end up on paper, and you can configure your report to fit. See Chapter 2 of this minibook.

But first, we cover how to create some reports the easy way — by using the wizard.

Creating Reports Automagically

You create a report the same way that you create other objects in your database. Take a look at the Reports group on the Create tab on the Ribbon to see some ways to make a report: The buttons are listed in Table 1-1.

Table 1-1		Creating Reports by Using the Reports Group of the Create Tab on the Ribbon	
Button on the Reports Group	*Name*	*What It Does*	*Where to Find More Info*
Report	Report	Creates a quick and easy report for the table, query, or form you have open or selected. You can customize the report later.	Book IV, Chapter 1

(continued)

Table 1-1 *(continued)*

Button on the Reports Group	Name	What It Does	Where to Find More Info
Report Design	Design View	Allows you to design your own report from scratch, in Design view.	Book IV, Chapter 2, for how to use Design view
Blank Report	Blank Report	Allows you to design your own report from scratch, in Layout view.	Book IV, Chapter 1, for how to use Layout view
	Report Wizard	Walks you through the creation of a report, helping you choose fields from multiple tables and queries. You can use Design or Layout view later to make changes.	"Running the Report Wizard" later in this chapter
	Labels	Creates a report to print data from one table or query on labels.	Book V, Chapter 2

Making the easiest possible report

You can use the Report button to create a report using the data from a single table or query. This button doesn't give you any options, but it makes a report in just a second or two.

To create a report based on a table or query, follow these steps:

1. **In the Navigation pane, choose the table, query, or form from which you want the data to come.**

   The report will include all the fields in this table, query, or form. (After you create the report, you can delete the controls for the fields that you don't want to appear on the report.)

2. **Click the Report button in the Reports group on the Create tab on the Ribbon.**

   Access creates a report in tabular format and displays it in Layout view, as shown in Figure 1-1.

3. **Customize it as you would any other report — use Layout view or Design view to get rid of the unwanted fields, widen the controls for the fields and field names you want to keep, or switch to landscape printing (or all three).**

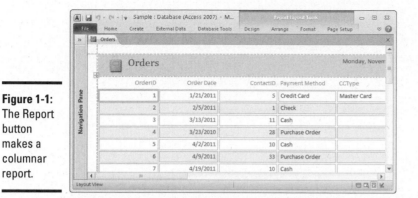

Figure 1-1:
The Report
button
makes a
columnar
report.

Running the Report Wizard

The Report Wizard is usually a better way to start making a report, especially
if you want to create a report that groups data using one or more fields, with
headings or subtotals for each group. When the wizard finishes, you can use
Layout view or Design view and add your own formatting touches.

One big advantage of using the Report Wizard is that you can choose fields for
the report from more than one table or query — you don't have to gather all the
data you want into one query. For example, if you have an online store, you may
want to create a report that lists all the orders for each customer. The information for this report comes from several tables: Address Book (which stores one
record for each customer, including name and address), Orders (with one record
for each order, including the order date), and Order Details (with one record for
each item in an order, including the quantity ordered and the price per item).

The Report Wizard asks different questions depending on the data in the
record source and on options you select, so don't be surprised if you don't
see every window each time you run it. Follow these steps to create a report:

1. **Click the Create tab of the Ribbon. Then click the Report Wizard
    button in the Reports group.**

    Access displays the first Report Wizard window, as shown in Figure 1-2.

2. **Use the Tables/Queries drop-down list to select the table or query that
    stores the records you want to include in the report.**

    If you plan to use information from several tables or queries, choose one of
    them. The Available Fields box lists the fields in the selected table or query.

3. **Select the fields you want to display in the report in the Available Fields
    box and add them to the Selected Fields list by clicking the > button.**

    Double-clicking a field name also adds it to the Selected Fields list. Click
    the >> button to add all the fields.

Figure 1-2:
The Report
Wizard
can build a
report from
one or more
tables and
queries.

4. **Repeat Steps 2 and 3 for fields in other tables or queries until all the fields you want to include in the report appear in the Selected Fields list.**

You can use some fields from tables and other fields from queries. For our customer-order listing, we select fields from the Address Book table, the Orders table, and the `Order Details Qry` query (which includes the `Ext Price` field, a calculated field that equals `Price × Qty`).

5. **Click Next to see the wizard's next question: Do you want to add any grouping levels?**

Access gives you a chance to choose how you want to group the data. For example, for a customer order report, grouping by customer is a good idea in order for all the information about one customer to be together. Within the section for each customer, the secondary grouping is by order, so that all the items in each order are listed together, as shown in Figure 1-3.

As you decide how to group your data, if you realize that you forgot to include any fields you need, click Back to return to Step 2 to add them.

Figure 1-3:
The Report
Wizard
enables you
to group the
information
in the
report.

To add an additional level of grouping, select a field from the list and click the > button. You can remove it by selecting it and clicking the < button. After you add a field, you can change the importance (grouping level) of a field by selecting the field and clicking the up-arrow and down-arrow Priority buttons.

6. **Use the Grouping Options button to customize how records are grouped.**

   Clicking the Grouping Options button (which is not always available, depending on your groupings) displays the Grouping Intervals dialog box. There you can specify exactly how to group records using the fields you choose.

   • For data fields, you can group by day, month, or year. For number fields, you can group by 10s, 50s, 100s, 500s, 1,000s, 5,000s, and 10,000s so that you can categorize values by magnitude.

   • For text fields, you can group on the first 1, 2, 3, 4, or 5 characters. Click OK to exit the Grouping Intervals dialog box and return to the main wizard window.

7. **Click Next to see the wizard's next question, about sorting your records.**

   Access automatically sorts by the fields on which you are grouping records. For example, if you are grouping records by customer and then by order, the customers appear in alphabetical order by name or in order of customer number. Within the lowest level of grouping, you can choose what order the records appear in — and specify up to four fields on which to sort. If you aren't grouping your records at all, you can also sort them here. In the customer orders report example, we've already grouped by customer and order, but we can sort the products in the order by product ID in each order.

8. **Choose how you want to sort the records within the lowest-level grouping.**

   Click in the 1 box (shown in Figure 1-4), choose a field, and click the Ascending button if you want to switch to a descending sort. Additional sort fields are used only when the 1 sort field is identical in two or more records — in which case, the 2 field is used. If the 1 and 2 fields are identical in two records, Access sorts by the 3 and then the 4 fields.

9. **Click the Summary Options button if you want to print counts, averages, or totals; specify which numeric fields to summarize; choose between the Detail and Summary and the Summary Only options; then click OK and click Next.**

   Access displays a list of the numeric fields in your report, with a check box for Sum (total), Avg (average), Min (minimum or smallest value), and Max (maximum or largest value), as shown in Figure 1-5. If you want only the summary values, without information for individual records, click Summary Only. If you want Access to calculate the percent of the total that each grouping represents (for example, the percentage of orders that each customer represents), click the Calculate Percent of Total for Sums check box.

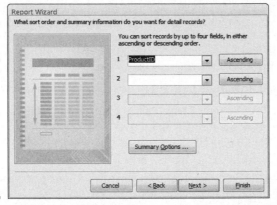

Figure 1-4:
You can
sort the
records in
your report
within the
lowest-level
grouping.

In the customer-order report we're cooking up here, you'd click the Sum
check box for the `Ext Price` field to get a total of the items in each
order and for each customer.

Figure 1-5:
The Report
Wizard can
add totals,
subtotals,
averages,
percentages,
and other
summary
statistics to
your report.

10. **Choose the layout for your report from among the Access canned lay-
    outs, and click Next.**

    You can preview the layout options by clicking one of the Layout radio
    buttons. The sample box on the left changes to show what your chosen
    layout looks like. If you want to print your report sideways on the paper,
    click the Landscape radio button. We can more or less guarantee that
    none of these layouts will be exactly what you want, and you'll end up
    adjusting them in Layout or Design view.

11. **Type a title for the report. Choose whether to display the report in Print Preview or in Design view, and click Finish.**

The title appears at the top of the report. The Report Wizard takes a moment to create the report, and then displays it in the view you chose.

The report may look close to perfect, or it may look like a complete wreck. For example, the customer-order report as created by the Report Wizard contains some of the right information, but it looks lousy. (Take a look at Figure 1-6.) Luckily, you can switch to Layout or Design view to fix it up.

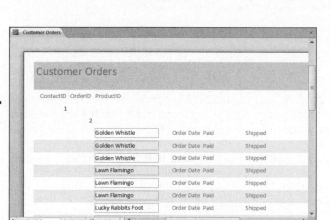

Figure 1-6: The Report Wizard's creation rarely looks right on the first try.

Editing Reports in Layout and Design View

Access has these two views for creating and modifying the design of a report (just like for forms):

✦ **Layout view** was new in Access 2007, and it shows your report with data in it. You can use it to move information around and add or remove information. See Book IV, Chapter 1 for how to edit reports in Layout view, including how control layouts keep information neatly in rows and columns.

✦ **Design view** is the traditional Access tool, and it enables you to make all kinds of changes to your report. Book IV, Chapter 2 describes how to use Design view. Figure 1-7 shows a report in Design view.

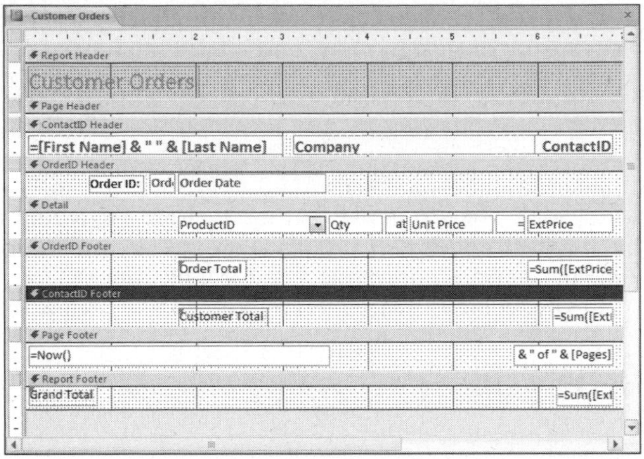

Figure 1-7:
A report
in Design
view.

You can modify your report in many ways, some of which work just as they do when modifying a form. Check out the following list for some of the ways — and for the chapter in Book IV that describes each one:

✦ **Creating, editing, moving, and deleting controls:** Controls are the boxes on the Design grid that display labels, data from fields, and other information. The easiest way to move them around is in Layout view, which is described in Book IV, Chapter 1.

✦ **Editing controls:** If you need to set the properties for a control, set fonts and columns, use conditional formatting, or make other fine adjustments, use Design view, as described in Book IV, Chapter 2.

✦ **Creating calculated controls:** To make a control that displays a calculated value, see Book IV, Chapter 4.

✦ **Drawing lines and boxes:** Book IV, Chapter 2 has a section devoted to this.

✦ **Setting report properties:** See Book IV, Chapter 1 for details.

✦ **Saving, importing, copying, and renaming reports:** See Book IV, Chapter 1 for details.

However, some things work differently for forms and reports. Reports don't have command buttons and drop-down lists. (They wouldn't work on paper!) Reports also have to fit correctly on the printed page, and they need page headers, footers, and headings for subsections. The rest of this chapter describes report-specific features, and the next chapter describes controlling how reports print.

Report Sections and How They Work

In Design view, your report is broken into parts called *sections*, as shown in Figure 1-7. The main part of the report is the *Detail section* — which shows information from fields in the table or query that is the record source for the report. The other sections come in pairs around the Detail section.

Sections provide headers and footers for your pages and allow you to group data using a particular field. If you have a number of reports with the same value in a field, you can display those records together in the report. For example, if your record source has a Date/Time field, you can create a section for that field and group records that have the same date, with subtotals by date. Table 1-2 lists the different sections that a report can include, with tips for how to use the section.

Table 1-2	Sections of Reports
Report Section	*Where It Appears and How to Use It*
Report Header and Footer	Appears at the beginning and end of the report. These sections are for summary information about the entire report. The report header can include a title page. The report footer can include totals for all the records in the report.
Page Header and Footer	Appears at the top and bottom of each page, and usually includes the report name, the date, and the page number.
Grouping Header and Footer	Appears at the top and bottom of each grouping (before the first record and after the last record) in a group that has the same value for a specific field. Your report may have more than one grouping header and footer (one pair for each grouping). The footer may include subtotals. Format your grouping headers and footers to make the hierarchy of the report obvious (for instance, larger fonts for first-level groups and smaller fonts for second-level groups).
Detail	Displays values for each record.

In Design view, the gray bar names the section, and the controls appearing underneath the bar appear every time that section of the report prints. In the report shown in Figure 1-7, the report header prints only once, at the very beginning of the report. The Page Header section is blank, so nothing prints at the top of each page. Records are grouped by customer, with customer information printing at the beginning of the section for each company (in the ContactID header). For each customer, the records are further grouped by order, using the OrderID header, which displays the order number and date. The Detail section prints information about each product in the order. The Order ID Footer section contains the total of the extended price (price times quantity) for all the items in the order (we seem to have omitted shipping from this report), and the ContactID footer totals the extended price for all orders by the customer. The Page Footer section includes the current date and time, the page number, and the total number of pages in the report. The Report Footer section has a grand total of the extended price for all records in the report. Figure 1-8 shows the report when printed.

Most sections are repeated many times in the report when you print it. For example, the ContactID header in Figure 1-7 prints once for each customer. The Detail section prints once for each product ordered in each order. The Page Header and Page Footer sections print once (each) per page.

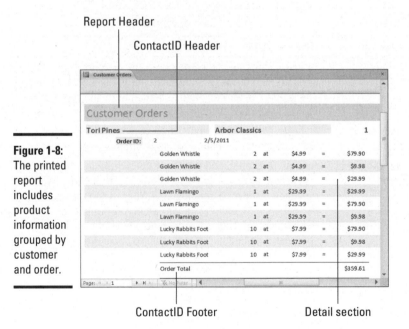

Report Header

ContactID Header

Figure 1-8:
The printed report includes product information grouped by customer and order.

ContactID Footer

Detail section

When you create a report using a Report Wizard, you get sections for each field on which you grouped the records. When you create a report from scratch in Design view, Access gives you just the Page Header, Detail, and Page Footer sections. You can add or delete sections in Design view, as described in the next two sections of this chapter. You can also adjust the size of each section by dragging the section dividers upward and downward.

You can't delete the Detail section. You can leave it blank, though, if you want a summary report with subtotals and totals but no data for individual records. Drag its lower edge (the top of the next section divider) upward to shrink the section to nothing. (In Figure 1-7, the Page Header section is shrunk to almost nothing.)

Setting report and section properties

As with most Access objects, each section and control in your report — as well as the entire report itself — has properties. You can display and change the properties on the Property sheet. (See Figure 1-9.) There are at least these three ways to display the Property sheet for the whole report:

✦ Double-click the report selector (the gray box in the top-left corner of the Design View window).

✦ Double-click the ruler at the top of the Design View window.

✦ Click the Property Sheet button in the Tools group on the Design tab of the Ribbon to display the Property sheet, and set the Selection type to Report.

Click the tabs to see the different categories of properties (or click the All tab to see all of them). Click in a property to change it.

Figure 1-9:
You can
set the
properties
of the entire
report or of
individual
sections or
controls.

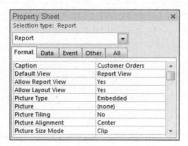

To see or change the properties of a particular section, double-click the section header or select the section header and click the Property Sheet button in the Tools chunk on the Design tab of the Ribbon. After the Property sheet is visible, you can click a section header or control to see its properties.

You can quickly display or hide the Property sheet by pressing Alt+Enter.

Adding page headers, footers, and numbers

To add Report or Page Header or Footer sections, right-click anywhere in the report in Design view and select Report Header/Footer or Page Header/Footer from the context menu. Access adds these in pairs: If you have a page header, you have a page footer. You can leave one or the other blank, though. To delete the Page or Report Header or Footer sections, choose the same command again: Access deletes the Header/Footer pair and all the controls in the sections (after warning you that it is about to do so).

If you want just a header or just a footer, change the height of the section that you don't want to appear by dragging the bottom border of the section up to the top border; the header or footer is still there, but you've shrunk it to nothing, so nothing prints.

Adding page numbers

Page
Numbers

After you have a Page Header or Footer section to put controls in, you can create controls in those sections, or drag them there from other sections. The easiest way to add page numbers — probably one of the most common controls you find in a report — is to click the Page Numbers button in the Header/Footer group on the Design tab of the Ribbon. When you see the Page Numbers dialog box (shown in Figure 1-10), choose the format of the numbering, the position, and the alignment (Left, Center, Right, Inside, or Outside). Inside and Outside page numbering refers to alternating left and right positions on odd and even pages. You can also omit the page number on the first page by deselecting the Show Number on First Page check box.

Figure 1-10:
Adding page numbers to your report.

If you'd rather make your own page-numbering controls, you can create your own text box control by following these steps:

1. **Open the report in Design view.**

2. **Create a text box control in the Page Header or Footer section by clicking the Text Box button in the Controls group on the Design tab on the Ribbon, and clicking in the Header or Footer section.**

Don't worry if the text box doesn't appear in exactly the right place — you can drag it there later.

3. **If Access created a label to go with the text box, delete the label by clicking in the label and then pressing the Delete key.**

    Your page number doesn't need a label!

4. **Display the Property sheet if it's not already on-screen.**

    You see the Property sheet with the properties of the text box you just created.

5. **Click the Data tab on the Property sheet, click in the `Control Source` property, and type the following expression:**

    ```
    = Page
    ```

    To display the word `Page` as well as the number, type

    ```
    = "Page " & Page
    ```

Adding the date and time

If you want to include the current date or time on your report, follow the same steps as in the preceding section, but type the following expression into the `Control Source` property of another text box:

```
= Now()
```

The `Now()` function returns both the date and time (for example, `6/25/04 1:55:48 PM`). If you want to print only the current date, format the box as a date using the `Format` property. (In the Property sheet for the text box, click the Format tab and set the `Format` property to one of the date formats, which omit the time.)

Controlling which pages get page headers and footers

You can also choose whether the Page Header and Footer sections print on all pages, all but the Report Header page (so your cover page isn't numbered), all but the Report Footer page, or all but the Report Header and Footer pages.

The following steps explain how to change the Page Header and Footer sections properties:

1. **With the report open in Design view, display the Property sheet for the report.**

2. **Click the Format tab in the Property sheet.**

3. **Set the `Page Header` and `Page Footer` properties.**

    Your options are `All Pages`, `Not With Rpt Hdr`, `Not With Rpt Ftr`, and `Not With Rpt Hdr/Ftr`.

TIP

Displaying the first value of a field in the Page Header section to make a telephone-book–style header is easy. Just create a text box in the Page Header section that displays the field. When you print the report, the text box shows the value for the first record on the page. You can also print the value of the last record on the page in the Page Footer section.

Grouping your records

To create *grouping sections,* you tell Access to group the records in your report by the value of one or more fields. For each field, you get a Grouping Header and Footer section for that field (as listed in Table 1-2 earlier in this chapter). For example, the report in Figures 1-7 and 1-8 lists customer orders, with records grouped by customer (identified by ContactID), and within customer by order (OrderID). If you choose to add both a header and footer section for each group, you end up with ContactID Header, OrderID Header, OrderID Footer, and ContactID Footer sections (in that order).

Group & Sort

To see and change your grouping sections, open the report in Design or Layout view and click the Group & Sort button in the Grouping and Totals group of the Design tab on the Ribbon. Access displays the Group, Sort, and Total pane, as shown in Figure 1-11. You see any fields that are currently used for sorting or grouping the records on your report. If more than one field appears, the topmost field is the major grouping, and other fields are subgroups.

Figure 1-11:
The Group, Sort, and Total pane defines how the records in your report are grouped for subtotals.

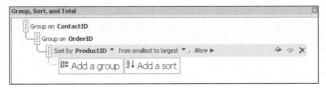

Adding a grouping

To add a group, follow these steps:

1. **Display the Group, Sort, and Total pane as described in the preceding text.**

2. **Click the Add a Group button and select a field from the Field/ Expression drop-down list to add a section (grouping).**

   You see a list of the fields in the record source for your report. After you select a field, Access automatically uses an ascending sort (with A at the top) for the new field. You can choose `expression` if you want to group on a calculated value.

   When you choose a field, Access adds a `Group` `on` line to the Group, Sort, and Total pane for this grouping. It also adds a Grouping Header to the report design. The `Group` `on` line includes drop-down lists for settings you can use to customize the grouping. The exact settings depend on the type of data in the field — there are different settings for text, numeric, and date fields.

3. **Customize the group as described later in this section.**

   You can sort in ascending or descending order, group by ranges of values rather than individual values, and make other changes.

4. **Close the Group, Sort, and Total pane by clicking the X button in its upper-right corner.**

Customizing your groupings

You can customize how each grouping works in various ways, using the Group, Sort, and Total pane. (See Figure 1-12.) Click the More button to the right of the field name to see your additional options, which vary depending on the data type of the field. (When the additional options are shown, you can click the Less button to hide them again.) Here are changes you can make to each grouping:

Figure 1-12:
In the Group, Sort, and Total pane, you can customize your groupings.

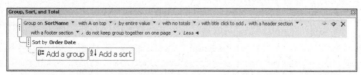

✦ **Sort the field in descending order.** Click the down arrow next to "from smallest to largest" (which appears for numeric fields), "from oldest to newest" (which appears for date fields), or "with A on top" (which appears for text fields) and select "from largest to smallest," "from newest to oldest," or "with Z on top."

✦ **Group on each individual value of the field, or ranges of values.** Click the down arrow next to "by entire value" and change it to the range you want. You see different options for text, numeric, and date fields.

✦ **Display subtotals and totals.** Click the down arrow next to "with no totals" and choose whether you want summary statistics, which can include totals, averages, minimum, maximum, or counts for each group or for the whole report. See "Calculating group subtotals and report totals" later in this chapter for more information.

✦ **Add a title.** Click the "with title click to add" link.

✦ **Hide or display headers and footers for the group.** Click the down arrow next to "with(out) a header section" and "with(out) a footer section" and make your choice.

✦ **Control page breaks.** Click the down arrow to the right of "do not keep group together on one page" and make your choice.

As soon as you choose to hide or display a group footer or header or add or remove a subtotal or total field, Access reflects your changes in the Design or Layout view.

To change what's displayed in a Grouping Header or Footer section, just create or remove controls in that section of the report in Design or Layout view.

Changes in the Group, Sort, and Total pane cause changes to the sections and controls in the report or to the properties of the grouping section. You can look at the properties of a section by double-clicking the gray bar at the top of the section in Design view.

Removing a grouping

To remove a grouping, click the X button at the right end of its line in the Group, Sort, and Total pane. If you want to remove the header or footer for a grouping, you can also delete all the controls in that section of the report and drag the divider below the section upward to shrink the section to nothing.

Sorting the records in your report

You can sort a report by sorting the record source — the table or query that provides the records for the report — before you print. But a more foolproof method is to use the Group, Sort, and Total pane to make a sort or a group for the field(s) by which you want to sort. When you tell Access to group by a field, you get sorting thrown in for free, so click either Add a Group or Add a Sort from the Group, Sort, and Total pane. If you make a group, selecting without a header section and without a footer section in the Group, Sort, and Total pane tells Access to sort by the field — but not to print any grouping sections.

To sort the records in a report by two fields, decide which field is the primary sort field and which is the secondary one. The secondary sort field works like a tiebreaker, used only when two or more records have the same value for the primary sort field. For example, to sort order records by customer name, you usually sort by last name (primary sort field) and first name (secondary sort field). If you have a large number of records, you may want additional sort fields. (For example, you could sort a mailing list by ZIP code, then last name, and then first name.)

When you add a group to your report, Access automatically sorts the group in ascending order based on the field on which you grouped the report. In the Group, Sort, and Total pane, click the down arrow next to "from smallest to largest," "from oldest to newest," or "with A on top" and select "from largest to smallest," "from newest to oldest," or "with Z on top."

You can sort by a calculated value that is not one of the fields in the record source of the report. Choose `expression` in the Sort By setting in the Group, Sort, and Total pane and enter an expression. See Book III, Chapter 2 for an introduction to expressions. For example, if you print a listing of products, you may want to sort them by profit margin — by `[Selling Price] - [Purchase Price]`.

Calculating group subtotals and report totals

If you use the Report Wizard to create a report, and you use the Summary Options button to request sums, averages, minimum values, or maximum values for each group, you already have subtotals and totals on your report. But you can make them yourself in Design view, too.

In the Group, Sort, and Total pane, you can display subtotals and totals in your report for the group. On the line for the grouping, click the down arrow next to "with no totals" and choose whether you want summary statistics, which can include totals, averages, minimum, maximum, or counts for each group or for the whole report. Set these options:

✦ **Total On:** This is the field that you want to summarize (total count, and so on), usually not the same field that you are grouping on. For example, if you are grouping on Contact ID (customer), you may want to total the `ExtPrice` field (price times quantity of each item ordered).

✦ **Type:** Choose what calculation you want Access to do. Your options are Sum, Average, Count Records (all records), Count Values (different values of this field), Maximum, Minimum, Standard Deviation, and Variance. (The last two are statistical analyses.)

✦ **Show Grand Total:** Select this to include a total at the bottom (or top) of the entire report.

✦ **Show Group Subtotal as % of Grand Total:** Select this to include a calculated field for each group, showing the percentage that the group is of all the records in the report.

✦ **Show Subtotal in Group Header:** Select this to include a calculated field in the header for each group, with the total, average or whatever Type calculation you chose.

✦ **Show Subtotal in Group Footer:** Ditto, but in the footer for each group (where totals usually appear).

In the group footer section, Access creates a text box control for each sum, count, or other summary information that you want to print. Or you can make these controls yourself. To print totals and counts for the entire report, make a text box in the Report Header or Report Footer section. Then type an expression in the `Control Source` property for the text box, using aggregate functions such as `Sum()`, `Avg()`, and `Count()`. (See Book IV, Chapter 4 for the scoop.)

When you use aggregate functions in a group header or footer section, Access automatically restricts the records to those in the current group. For example, the `Sum()` function totals the values of a field for all the records in the group. To subtotal the amount paid for each product in the current group, you use the following expression in a text-box control:

```
= Sum([Price])
```

To print the number of records in the report, type the following expression in the `Control Source` property (located on the Data tab of the Property sheet) for a text box in the Report Header or Report Footer section:

```
= Count(*)
```

Don't use aggregate functions in the Page Header or Page Footer sections of a report; you get an `#Error` message.

Figure 1-7 (earlier in this chapter) shows a report in Design view with `Sum()` functions in both the OrderID and ContactID Footers (for groupings) and in the Report Footer section (for the entire report). The `Sum()` function in the OrderID Footer section prints a subtotal of the cost for each order, the `Sum()` function in the ContactID Footer section prints a subtotal of the cost for all the orders for each customer, and the `Sum()` function in the Report Footer section prints the total cost for all the records in the whole report.

Formatting Tips and Tricks

The following list details a few tricks for making nicely formatted controls for your reports. Most of them involve setting report, section, or control properties on the Property sheet:

✦ **Printing calculations:** Print a *calculated field* — a field decided by an expression — the same way you display one on a form: Create a text box and enter an expression in the `Control Source` property. Be sure to set the control's `Format` property, too. (Book IV, Chapter 4 has the excruciating details of displaying calculations on forms; the same methods work for reports.)

✦ **Prompting for information to print:** Just as Access can prompt for information when running a query (as described in Book III, Chapter 2), you can use parameters when printing a report. Parameters allow you to specify information — usually in the Report or Page Header or Footer sections — that you want to print. Create a text box control where you want the information to print. For the `Control Source` property of the text box, enter the parameter prompt in square brackets so that it looks something like the following:

```
[Enter title line]
```

✦ **Avoiding space between fields:** When you display several fields in a row, you may not want to leave gaps between them. For example, in a mailing label or form letter, you may want to print fields containing first names and last names with only one space between them. To eliminate extra space between fields, regardless of the length of the values in the fields, *concatenate* them (glue them together) using the & operator. (We describe calculated fields and the & operator in Book III, Chapter 2.) Create a text box control and type an expression in its `Control Source` property, such as the following expression:

```
= [First Name] & " " & [Last Name]
```

This expression glues the first name, a space, and the last name together. If the first name were `Elvis` and the last name were `Presley`, you end up with `Elvis Presley` (the name, anyway).

✦ **Using conditional calculations:** You can print one thing in some circumstances and another thing in others by using the `iif()` function. (For more on the `iif()` function, see Book IV, Chapter 4.) For example, you may make a report that can print either an invoice or a receipt, depending on whether the customer has paid. At the top, you include a text box with an expression in the `Control Source` property that spells out that Access should print either an invoice or a receipt, depending on the value of the `Paid` field. That expression looks something like the following:

```
= iif([Paid], "Receipt", "Invoice")
```

✦ **Calculating a running sum:** You can tell Access to sum the values of a numeric field, showing the total of the current record (a *running sum*). Set the `Running Sum` property of the text box control displaying that field to `Yes`. You may want to include two text box controls for the numeric field: one to show the value for the current record (with the

`Running Sum` property set to `No`), and one to show the running sum (with the `Running Sum` property set to `Yes`).

✦ **Hiding duplicate values:** If a group of records have the same value for a control, and you want the value to print only the first time it appears, you can set the `Hide Duplicates` property of the field to the `Yes` setting. This setting is especially useful in tabular reports, in which each field appears in a separate column.

Don't use a field name as the control name for a calculated control. When you create controls, Access names them automatically, although you can change the names later. If you rename a calculated control, make sure that the name you assign isn't the same as any field mentioned in the expression (or any field in the record source of the report). Access gets confused about whether references to that name are to the field or to the control, and the report displays the `#Error` message.

Copying Forms to Reports

If you have a form that you want to print, you can certainly print it as is, but you have a lot more control over the format if you turn the form into a report first. You can then change the design for the report to print nicely without changing the format of the original form.

To save a form as a report, select the form in the Navigation pane, click the File tab on the Ribbon, and choose Save Object As from the menu. When you see the Save As dialog box, type a name for the new report and set the Save As drop-down list to the Report option. Access creates a new report based on the design of the form.

Most forms have colored backgrounds. After saving a form as a report, be sure to change the background of your new report to white before printing the report. Otherwise, you waste a lot of ink (or toner). Just right-click the background of each section, choose the Fill/Back Color option from the shortcut menu that appears, and choose the white box in the palette of colors.

Adding and Formatting Subreports

A *subreport* provides detail information from other tables. You can create a *subreport control* to print another report as part of your report. For example, if you have a report about customers, a subreport can list the orders for each customer. Figure 1-13 shows a report with two subreports in Design view, and Figure 1-14 shows the same report in Report view.

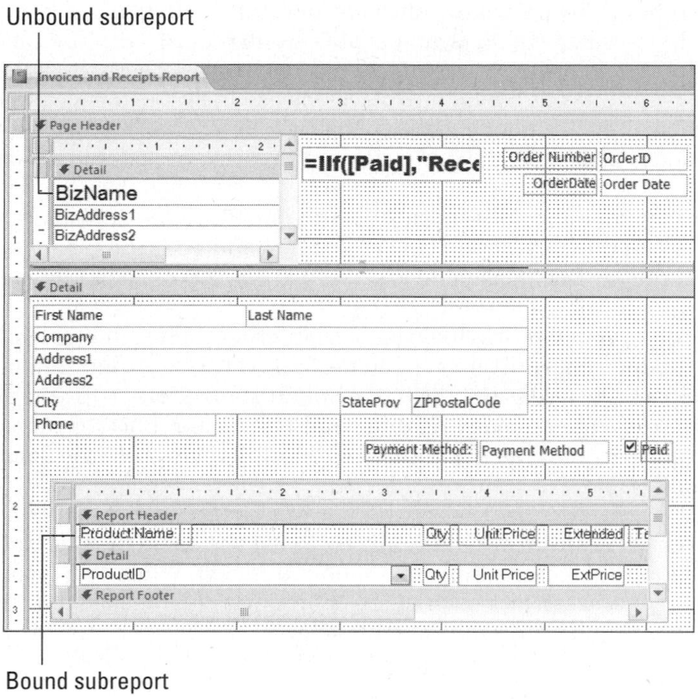

Unbound subreport

Figure 1-13:
A subreport
can be
bound or
unbound
to the main
report.

Bound subreport

Figure 1-14:
A report
with
subreports,
in Report
view.

An *unbound subreport* is not connected to the records in the main report: No
relationship exists between the record source of the main report and the

subreport. The unbound subreport in Figure 1-13 displays information from the My Business table, which contains one record, with the business's name, address, and other information. (We like to create a My Business table to store this information in one place, for use in all the forms and reports in the database. If your phone number changes, for example, you change it in the My Business table, and all your forms and reports are updated automatically.)

With an unbound subreport, Access prints the same information for each record in the main report. In Figures 1-13 and 1-14, the business information from the My Business table is printed at the top of each invoice or receipt.

A *bound subreport* provides detail from other tables. In Figures 1-13 and 1-14, the bound subreport lists the items in the current order, pulling the information from the Order Details table. Bound subreports help you print information from a one-to-many relationship: The main report displays records from the master (*one*) table and the subreport displays records from the detail (*many*) table.

If you always print two or more reports at the same time, include them as unbound subreports in a new, unbound report. When you print the new report, Access prints each of the subreports. Just make sure that all the reports require the same kind of paper!

Making a subreport

Subreports work just like subforms. (See Book IV, Chapter 4.) To create a subreport, whether bound or unbound, follow these steps:

1. **Create the report you plan to use as a subreport and save it.**

   For example, to make the report in Figures 1-13 and 1-14, you make one report appear as the unbound subreport, with the My Business table as its record source. You create another report as the bound subreport, with the Order Details table as its record source. When you preview the report by itself, Access displays all the records in the record source — but when a report serves as a subreport, Access restricts the records whenever the subreport prints, printing out only the records that match the current record in the main report.

   When you create this report, nothing about it says "subreport" — any report can be used as a subreport. We like to use the word "subreport" in the names of reports that never print on their own; they exist only as subreports of other reports.

2. **Open the main report in Design view.**

3. **Make space for the subreport control (also called a *Subreport/ Subform control*) in the Detail section of the report.**

   Drag your other controls out of the way.

4. **In the Navigation pane, scroll down to the Reports section.**

   This gets you ready to drag the subreport to the Design View window.

5. **Select the subreport-to-be from the Reports list in the Navigation pane and drag it onto the report where you want the subreport to appear.**

   Access creates a subreport control on the main report, containing the report you selected. The `Source Object` property for the subreport control contains the name of the report that you dragged.

6. **Delete the label that Access created for the subreport if you don't like it.**

   Access creates a label for the subreport with the name of the report, but you can select it and delete it if you want.

7. **Move and size the subreport control.**

   Drag the control to the location you want and drag its edges to adjust its size.

8. **Click in the subreport control and then click the Property Sheet button in the Tools group on the Design tab on the Ribbon to display the Property sheet for the subreport control.**

   Figure 1-15 shows the Property sheet for a subreport control with the Data tab selected. (While you've got the Property sheet displayed, you can adjust the format properties, too.) The `Source Object` property contains the name of the subreport that the control displays.

Figure 1-15:
The prop-
erties of a
subreport
control link
the records
in the sub-
report and
those in the
main report.

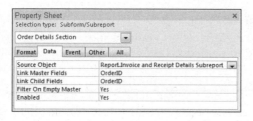

9. **Check the `Link Child Fields` and `Link Master Fields` properties on the Data tab of the Property sheet.**

   These properties contain the names of the fields that relate the main and subreports. The `Link Master Fields` property should contain the name of the field in the record source of the main report that relates to a field in the subreport. The `Link Child Fields` property contains the name of the matching field in the record source of the subreport.

Printing information from a subreport on the main report

Just as you can display totals from a subform on a main form, you can print totals from a subreport on the main report. (See Book IV, Chapter 4 for how to create a control on the main report to display a total from a subreport.)

When entering the expression in the text box control on the main report, use this format:

```
= [subreport control name].Report![total control]
```

Replace *subreport control name* with the name of the subreport control. Replace *total control* with the name of the text box control in the subreport that displays the total. For example, the following expression may display the total extended price (price times quantity) for the records in the report that display in the `Order Detail Subreport` subreport control:

```
= [Order Detail Subreport].Report![Total Ext Price]
```

Displaying Empty or Long Fields

Text and Memo fields can pose problems on reports because they can contain one or hundreds of characters. Anticipating how much space to leave for them is hard. Luckily, Access has some features to help deal with long fields.

Displaying long text

If a Text or Memo field in your report contains more than a few words, you may want the field to wrap onto additional lines. For example, the `Description` field in a Products table may contain a whole paragraph about the product. You could display the field in a very large text box control that can fit the largest description in the table, but Access would leave a large empty space in the report after short descriptions. Instead, each text box can expand or shrink vertically to fit the amount of text in the field for each record.

To make a text box grow, start off by making it big enough to fit just one line of text. (See Book IV, Chapter 2 for how to make a text box control.) Display its Property sheet by clicking the Property Sheet button in the Tools group on the Design tab on the Ribbon. Then set its `Can Grow` property (which is on the Format tab, a long way down the list of properties) to `Yes`. When

Access prints each record, the text box control expands until the entire value of the field fits. The remaining controls move down the page.

When you set a control's `Can Grow` property to `Yes`, Access sets the `Can Grow` property for the section that contains the property, too. When Access prints the report, the section expands as well as the control, so nothing gets cut off. If you don't want the section to expand, you can change its `Can Grow` property back to `No` to omit information that doesn't fit in the section. Set the `Can Grow` property to `No` when printing on forms of a predetermined size, such as mailing labels. (In Chapter 2, we show you how to set up a report that prints mailing labels.)

Displaying fields that may be empty

To avoid leaving blank lines when a field is blank, set the `Can Shrink` property for the text box to `Yes`. (This setting is on the Format tab of the Property sheet, just below the `Can Grow` property.) For example, many address lists are stored in tables that have two lines for the street address. If the second line is empty, the mailing label looks better if the City/State/ZIP line prints right below the first address line with no gap.

To make a text box control that shrinks when the value is blank, make the text box big enough to fit the longest value in the table. Then set its `Can Shrink` property to `Yes`. When printing the report, Access omits the control if the field value is blank.

When you set the `Can Shrink` property of a control to the `Yes` setting, Access does not automatically change the `Can Shrink` property of the section that contains the control. Leave the `Can Shrink` properties of the Detail section set to the `No` setting if the Detail section must always be the same size — as with mailing labels or other pre-printed forms. Otherwise, set these properties to `Yes`.

Viewing Your Reports On-Screen

Report view displays your report on the screen as it will appear on paper, except without page breaks, headers, and footers, as shown in Figure 1-16. You can't edit the data in the report (that's what forms are for), but you can use the report to find information that you are looking for. The Home tab on the Ribbon includes most of the same Sort & Filter, Records, and Find groups of buttons that you can use when viewing records in Datasheet view. Refer to Book II, Chapter 3 for how to use them.

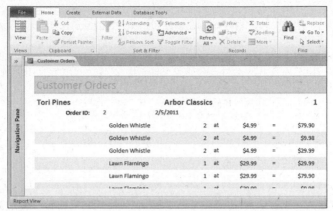

Figure 1-16: In Report view, the Home tab on the Ribbon enables you to find and filter the records.

Chapter 2: Printing Beautiful Reports

In This Chapter

✔ **Previewing your report on-screen**

✔ **Controlling report margins and page orientation**

✔ **Choosing which printer to print on**

✔ **Making reports that print mailing labels**

✔ **Saving Access reports in other Office formats**

✔ **E-mailing reports using Outlook**

After you create a good-looking report on-screen, the next step is to see whether it looks good on paper, or in a PDF file that simulates paper. To make it perfect (okay, close to perfect), you have to be able to control how the printer prints the report. This chapter describes page formats, margins, and other printer settings, as well as how to print mailing labels and export your reports to other Office programs.

Viewing Your Report

You can see how the printed report will look *before* you spend the time, paper, and ink or toner to print it. You can use Report view to see your report (as described in the previous chapter), but it doesn't include page breaks, page headers, or page footers, so you don't get a true idea of how the report will look on paper. Using Print Preview, you can see on-screen whether your controls are positioned as you want them, whether the right information appears in each control, and whether your headers and footers appear correctly.

To see how your report looks in Print Preview, try the following:

✦ Double-click the report name in the Navigation pane to open it. If its default view is Print Preview, there you are!

✦ With the report open in any other view, right-click the report's tab and choose Print Preview from the menu that appears.

✦ With the report open in any other view, click the bottom of the View button in the Views group on the Home tab of the Ribbon and choose Print Preview. (If the View button shows the Print Preview icon, you can just click the button.)

✦ Click the File tab on the Ribbon to see Backstage view, and then choose Print➪Print Preview.

The report appears in Print Preview, showing you the top of the first page of your report, or the entire report shrunk to a size too small to read, as in Figure 2-1.

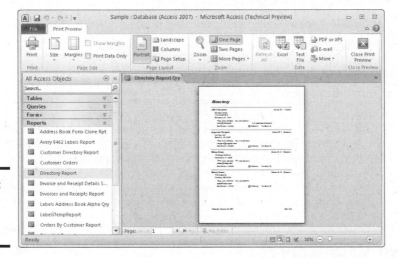

Figure 2-1:
A report
in Print
Preview.

You can display almost any Access object in Print Preview and then print it. When you're looking at a table in Datasheet view or a form in Form view, Print Preview is available by clicking the File tab on the Ribbon and choosing Print➪Print Preview. Reports have more formatting options than any other type of object in Access, but sometimes datasheets and forms are worth printing, too.

You can set page and print options in Design view, too. Use the Page Setup tab on the Ribbon, as shown in Figure 2-2.

Figure 2-2:
The Page
Setup tab
in Design
view.

Print Preview is different from most other views, in that it takes over Access. Only the File and Print Preview tabs are visible on the Ribbon. When you are done previewing (and possibly printing) the report, you can click the Close Print Preview button at the right end of the Print tab on the Ribbon to close the report.

Adjusting the view

When you're in Print Preview mode, your cursor changes to a magnifying glass, and your report is shrunk to display an entire page on the screen. Click anywhere on the report to zoom in. Click the report a second time to shrink it back to fit on the screen. Alternatively, you can use the Zoom control located in the bottom-right portion of the Access window — a slider between a minus (–) button and a plus (+) button. Click the minus (–) button to reduce the size by 10 percent. Click the plus (+) button to increase the size by 10 percent. Drag the slide control to change the size in other increments.

Use the vertical scroll bar or press the down arrow, up arrow, Page Down, and Page Up keys on your keyboard to scroll the report up and down within the Print Preview window. Use the horizontal scroll bar or press the left arrow and right arrow keys on your keyboard to pan sideways. To see other pages of the report, use the navigation buttons in the lower-left corner of the Print Preview window.

Looking at lots of pages

You can zoom *way* out by displaying two or more pages at the same time. Click the Two Pages button on the Print Preview tab on the Ribbon to display two pages at a time, side by side. Though useless for close proofreading, with this view you can tell where section breaks come and how full the pages are. To see more than two pages, click the More Pages button on the Print Preview tab on the Ribbon and choose an arrangement of pages: Your options are Four (as shown in Figure 2-3), Eight, and Twelve pages. Use the Zoom button to zoom in and out on Two Pages view and More Pages views.

Right-click the report and select a Zoom value of 5% to 1000% or type your own value in the Zoom menu option.

Right-click the report and point to Multiple Pages. You can select from 1×1, 1×2, 1×3, 2×1, 2×2, or 2×3.

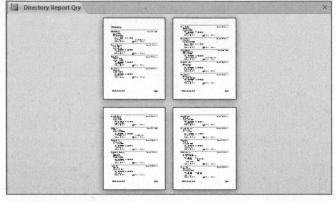

Figure 2-3:
You can see
two or more
pages at
a time, but
you can't
necessarily
read them.

Previewing reports with parameters

Some reports use parameters — the record source for the report or one or more report controls that contain prompts for information. (See Chapter 1 of this minibook for how to make a control that prompts for a parameter; see Book III, Chapter 2 for how to make a parameter query.) If your report has parameters, Access prompts you to type values for the parameters each time you preview the report. After you look at the report, you may want to try different values for the parameter(s). To enter new parameters, close the report and reopen it or switch to Design view and back to Print Preview.

Formatting the Page

Access stores print setup information with each report, so you can design different reports to be used with different printers or with different paper.

Selecting a printer

When formatting your report in Print Preview, Access takes into account the size and shape of the paper you plan to use. (Okay, most paper is rectangular, but you know what we mean.) Before you're ready to print, specifying what printer you plan to use is important.

If you plan to use the Windows default printer, you don't have to do anything. If you want to print to a different printer, choose the printer when you're ready to print. Click the Print button in the Print group (it's the only button in the Print group) to display the usual Windows Print dialog box, shown in Figure 2-4. Select your printer from the Name drop-down list.

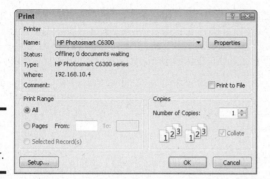

Figure 2-4:
Selecting
your printer.

 To see what printers your computer is configured to use — including the default — use Windows rather than Access 2010. In Windows, choose Start⇨ Devices and Printers (or Start⇨Control panel⇨Printers and Other Hardware⇨ Printers and Faxes, depending on how Windows is configured). A window appears, listing all the printers that your computer is configured for. The printer with an icon that includes a little check mark is the default printer. Right-click a printer and choose the Properties option on the shortcut menu to see how the printer is configured. To make a particular printer the default printer, right-click its name and choose the Set as Default Printer option from the shortcut menu that appears.

Setting margins, paper size, and paper orientation

Other print settings you can configure from the Print Preview tab on the Ribbon are the following:

+ **Margins:** Click the Margins button in the Page Size group to select Normal, Wide, or Narrow from the drop-down list. If you've set the margins in the Page Setup dialog box, then Custom Setting will be selected.

+ **Paper orientation:** Click the Portrait button in the Page Layout group to print normally on the page, or click the Landscape button to print sideways.

+ **Paper size:** Click the Size button in the Page Size group on the Print Preview tab on the Ribbon and select your paper size from the drop-down list.

+ **Columns:** Most people use columns only for printing mailing labels, but you can set any report to print in two or more columns. Click the Columns button to see the Page Setup dialog box with the Columns tab selected. Then choose the number of columns, the spacing, and whether records print across the columns then down to a next row, or down the page and then up to the next column.

If you end up changing the margins for almost every report you create, you can change the default margins for all new reports. Click the File tab on the Ribbon, then choose Options➪Client Settings, scroll down to the Printing section, and change the default margin settings, as shown in Figure 2-5.

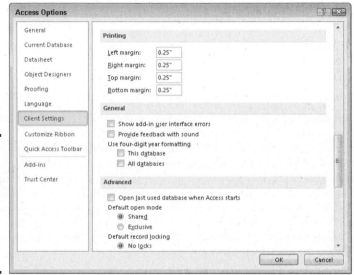

Figure 2-5:
Checking (and setting) the default margins for all reports in your database.

Controlling page breaks

Normally, Access fills each page from top to bottom, starting a new page only when the previous one is full. However, you can insert a page break (start a new page) at other times. You can add page breaks to a report in several ways:

✦ **After each record (print one page per record):** Set the `Force New Page` property of the Detail section to either the `Before Section` or `After Section` setting. If you choose the `Before & After` setting for this property, Access prints a blank page both before and after the page(s) for each record. With the report in Design view, double-click the gray bar at the top of the Detail section to display the Property sheet for the section, and then click the Format tab to see the `Force New Page` property.

✦ **After each group of records:** See Chapter 1 of this minibook for how to group records. Set the `Force New Page` property for the Group Footer to the `After Section` setting. Access prints the Group Header section, the Detail section for each record in the group, the Group Footer section, and then starts a new page for the next group of records.

 ✦ **Within a section of your report:** Use a page-break control. For example, the Detail section of the report may print a packing slip and an invoice for each order on separate pages. To add a page-break control to the

Detail section of the report, click the Page Break button in the Controls group on the Design tab on the Ribbon, and then click where you want the page break to occur. Access puts the page-break control at the left margin of the report.

Don't place page-break controls in the Page Header or Page Footer sections. Doing so starts a new page at the top or bottom of every page, which just creates confusion (and an error). You can put a page break in the Report Header or Report Footer, though, if you have multipage cover sheets.

Avoiding blank pages

Almost every Access user winds up with blank pages between each printed page of a report. The blank pages appear in Print Preview, but what causes them?

Access knows the width of your paper and how much space to leave for the left and right margins because these sizes are specified in the report's Property sheet. Access adds the width of your report to the left and right margins to come up with the total width of the printed report. If the total is wider than your paper, Access splits the report into vertical bands and prints the left and right halves of the report on separate pieces of paper, so you can tape them together to create a very wide report.

If the report is just a *little* bit too wide to fit across one piece of paper, the text of the report is all in the left half, leaving the right half blank. These blank right halves are the blank pages that Access prints. If the right part of the report has no controls in it, Access alerts you to this fact with the message, "The section width is greater than the page width, and there are no items in the additional space, so some pages may be blank."

To get rid of the blank pages, follow these steps:

1. **Click the File tab on the Ribbon, and then choose Options⇨Client Settings to display the Access Options dialog box. Scroll down to the Printing section.**

   You see something that looks like Figure 2-5.

2. **Subtract the left and right margin settings from the width of your paper to get the maximum width of the report.**

   Standard U.S. paper is 8½ inches wide. If the left and right margins are too wide, make them smaller in this dialog box, and then use the new values in your calculation. For example, if your paper is 8½ inches wide and you have half-inch left and right margins, your report can't be more than 7½ inches wide.

   You can change the margins if you want to use different defaults.

3. **Click OK to exit the Access Options dialog box.**

4. **In Design view of the report, note the report's width — the location along the ruler of the right edge of the grid area.**

   Alternatively, look at the Width property of the report in the Property sheet. (Double-click the gray box in the upper-left corner of the report in Design view where the rulers meet to display the Property sheet for the form.) This property is on the Format tab of the Property sheet.

5. **If the report is too wide to fit on the page, drag the right edge of the report leftward.**

   If the edge won't move, a control extends to the right of where you want the page to end. Move or shrink any control that extends too far to the right and move the right edge of the report to the left. Alternatively, change the Width property of the report. If you can't find the control that is in the way, use your mouse to select the apparently empty area of the report grid to see what appears when selected — frequently (in our experience) a horizontal line.

Another possible reason for blank pages is an incorrect setting for the Force New Page property of one of the sections of the report. See the preceding section for how to control page breaks before or after groups.

Printing only the data

If you're printing on a form, rather than on blank sheets of paper, you can design a report that looks like the form, including labels and lines that match the form. When you print the report, you can skip printing the labels and lines and print only the data. In Print Preview, select the Print Data Only check box in the Page Layout group on the Print Preview tab of the Ribbon. Access updates the Print Preview to show only your report data.

Printing the Report

After you have your page and margin options set, you're ready to risk wasting paper to print your report. You can print your report when it's open in Print Preview, in Design view, or not open at all.

Printing on an actual printer

Print

Open the report in Print Preview and click the Print button on the Print Preview tab on the Ribbon, click the File tab on the Ribbon, and choose Print⇨Print. Or you can simply press Ctrl+P. Access displays the Print dialog box shown in Figure 2-4 (the same Print dialog box that most Microsoft programs display). Click the Setup button if you want to take a look at the Page Setup dialog box. Click the printer name if you want to choose a different printer. Otherwise, click OK to send your report to the printer.

To send your report directly to the printer without displaying the Print dialog box, click the File tab on the Ribbon and select Print⇨Quick Print. Make sure you're really ready to print before you click!

You may want to print only part of a report — say, just the first page to see how the margins look — or reprint a specific page. In the Print dialog box (shown in Figure 2-4), in the Print Range section, click the Pages radio button and enter the starting and ending page numbers in the From and To boxes.

Creating a PDF, XPS, HTML, or other file of your report

PDF (Portable Document Format) files have become a standard way to distribute print-ready documents. Heck, even the IRS uses them for tax forms (at www.irs.gov). PDF enables you to distribute reports on the Web or by e-mail in a format that most people can open, read, and print — people don't have to have Access to see your reports.

You can download a free program (Adobe Reader) to display and print PDF files, from http://get.adobe.com/reader.

In the past, you've needed a separate program to create PDF files, usually a program that pretends to be a printer, so any program can "print" to it to create a PDF file. Office 2010 comes with PDF-creation software, along with the ability to export reports in several other formats. When you export a report (or other Access object), Access asks whether you want to save the steps that you followed to do the export, as shown in Figure 2-6. See the section "Automating your exports" at the end of this chapter for how this works.

Figure 2-6:
Saving export steps.

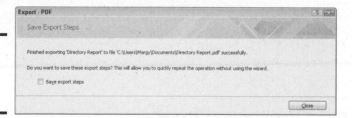

Here's how to create a file containing your report in one of these formats, once you have the report open in Print Preview:

✦ **PDF file:** Click the PDF or XPS button in the Data group on the Print Preview tab of the Ribbon. You see the Publish as PDF or XPS dialog box, shown in Figure 2-7. Make sure that the Save as Type setting is PDF and choose where you'd like to save the PDF file. Access automatically adds .pdf to the end of the filename. When you click the Publish button, Access exports the report in PDF format and then opens it in the default PDF reader program on your computer (if any).

✦ **XPS file:** The XML Paper Specification (XPS, or OpenXPS) format is Microsoft's version of PDF. You can create XPS files the same way you create PDF files — with the PDF or XPS button. Just change the Save as Type setting to XPS Document.

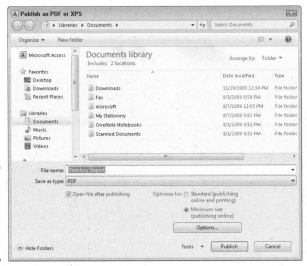

Figure 2-7:
Access now comes with a built-in PDF creator.

Creating Mailing Labels

A perennial database task is printing mailing labels from lists of names and addresses. The easiest way to create a report that prints on labels is to use the Label Wizard, which contains a long list of preset formats for all standard Avery brand and compatible labels. (Most boxes of label sheets include an Avery number that specifies the size of your labels.) After you create a report with the wizard, you can make further changes in Design view.

Running the Label Wizard

To run the Label Wizard, follow these steps:

1. **In the Navigation pane, select the table or query that contains the information you want to print on your labels.**

 2. **Click the Labels button in the Reports group on the Create tab of the Ribbon.**

   You see the Label Wizard, as shown in Figure 2-8.

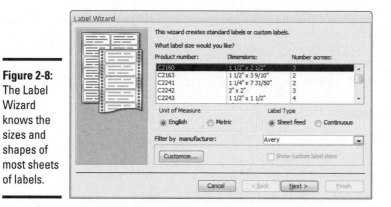

Figure 2-8:
The Label
Wizard
knows the
sizes and
shapes of
most sheets
of labels.

3. Choose the type of label from the Product Number list. Click Next.

Access normally shows the labels according to the numbers assigned
by Avery, a major manufacturer of labels. But you can see other types of
labels by changing the Filter by Manufacturer box:

- If you plan to print continuous-feed labels (where the sheets are
connected together) rather than sheets of labels, change the Label
Type setting.

- If you are printing on custom-printed labels, click the Customize
button, click the New button in the New Label Size dialog box that
appears, and tell Access about your labels.

**4. Choose the font, font size, weight (light, normal, or bold, among
others), and color. Click Next.**

Access uses these settings for the text boxes in the report. For mailing
labels, do your letter carrier a favor and choose a readable size, like 12
points.

**5. Choose the fields that you want to include on the label, as shown in
Figure 2-9. Click Next.**

The Prototype Label box shows the layout of fields on the label, including spaces, punctuation, and text that prints on every label (for example,
`"First Class"` or your return address). You arrange the fields and
other information in the Prototype Label box. Dotted lines show where
the lines of text can go. One line in the Prototype Label box is selected
(it's gray), showing that new fields are added to this line. You can press
the ↑ and ↓ keys to move to a different line.

To print a field on your mailing labels, click the field in the Available
Fields box and then click the > button to add it to the current line of
the Prototype Label box. (Double-clicking a field does the same thing.)
To add text, such as a space, comma, other punctuation, or words, just
move your cursor to the location in the Prototype Label box where you
want the text to appear, and type it.

Figure 2-9:
You tell
the Label
Wizard
what fields
you want
on your
label, and
the wizard
creates the
text box
controls.

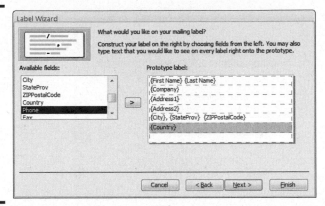

For example, the first line of a mailing label usually consists of the first name, a space, and the last name. With the first line of the Prototype Label box selected, you double-click the First Name field (whatever it's called in your table), type a space, and double-click the Last Name field. To move to the next line, press Enter or ↓.

If you put a field in the wrong place, click it in the Prototype Label box and press the Delete key to remove it.

Be sure to type a comma and a space between City and StateProv fields in the Prototype Label box, and a space between StateProv and ZipPostalCode fields, too.

6. **Choose the field(s) by which to sort the records. Click Next.**

   For example, to sort by last name within ZIP code, choose the ZIPPostalCode field and then the Last Name field.

7. **Type a name for the report and click Finish.**

   The wizard creates the report for you. Figure 2-10 shows a report created in the Wizard — it's just a regular report, but the layout will fit on the type of labels you specified.

Figure 2-10:
The Label
Wizard
creates a
report that
will print on
the labels
you chose.

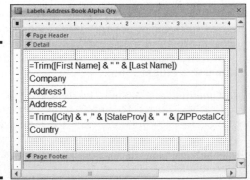

If the label report looks good in Report view, print it on a blank piece of paper before you start printing sheets of labels. Hold the printed sheet up to a blank sheet of labels and see whether the names and addresses line up with the labels. This method avoids wasting sheets of expensive labels while you refine your label report. See the next chapter for how to print reports.

Behind the scenes in a mailing-label report

The Label Wizard makes a report that looks like Figure 2-10 in Design view. You see the fields and text that you told the wizard to include, followed by enough blank space to reach down to where the text should start on the next label. Where more than one field (or text) appears on a line, the Label Wizard has cleverly written expressions (starting with =) that use the & operator to *concatenate* (glue together) the information. In expressions, the wizard encloses each field name in square brackets [ ] because, for field names that contain spaces, these brackets prevent the spaces from confusing Access. The wizard also uses the Trim() function to eliminate any extra spaces at the ends of fields.

For example, the first line of the label in Figure 2-10 contains a text box with this expression as its Control Source property:

```
=Trim([First Name] & " " & [Last Name])
```

This scary-looking expression glues the first name, a space, and the last name together — and then discards any spaces at the right end.

If you don't like the way information appears on your mailing labels, you can delete the text boxes, add new ones, alter the expressions in the existing text boxes, and change the formatting of the text boxes — the same kinds of changes you can make to the controls in any report.

Changing the page setup for labels

Unexpectedly, the report is only the size of a single label. You don't see a whole page full of labels. How does Access know how many labels to print across a row? The Page Setup tab on the Ribbon contains this information. If you specified the wrong Avery number in the Label Wizard (or if you have labels that don't have Avery numbers), you can change these settings.

With the report open in Design view, click the Columns button in the Page Layout group on the Page Setup tab on the Ribbon to display the Page Setup dialog box with its Columns tab selected (as shown in Figure 2-11). You see the following settings:

✦ **Number of Columns:** How many columns of labels per page.

✦ **Row Spacing:** How much blank space to leave between one row of labels and the next (usually zero, because Access includes this space in the report design).

✦ **Column Spacing:** How much blank space to leave between one column and the next (that is, between one label and the next across each row).

✦ **Column Size, Width and Height:** The size of the labels. If you leave the Same as Detail check box selected, Access adjusts these settings to be the same size as the Detail section of the report.

✦ **Column Layout:** The order in which the labels print on each page.

Figure 2-11:
The Columns tab of the Page Setup dialog box defines how your report prints on sheets of labels.

 You can use the settings on the Columns tab of the Page Setup dialog box to create newspaper-style "snaking" columns for any report, not just mailing labels. Make the Detail section of the report narrower than half the width of the paper, specify two columns, and set the `Column Layout` property to the `Down Then Across` setting.

Sending a Report to Another Application

The nice thing about Microsoft Office is that all the programs are designed to work together. Sometimes they even *do* work together.

For example, what if you want to include a report from your Access database in a Word document? You can export reports, tables, and queries in file formats that other Office programs can understand. If you export the same report regularly, saving it in the save folder with the same name, you can create a *data task* that you can run again and again.

Exporting your report to Excel

To export a report in Excel format, follow these steps:

1. **In the Navigation pane, click the report you want to export to Microsoft Word.**

2. **Click the Excel button in the Export group on the External Data tab on the Ribbon.**

   The Export – Excel Spreadsheet dialog box shown in Figure 2-12 opens.

   Another way to open this dialog box is to open the report in Print Preview, and then click the Excel button in the Data group on the Print Preview tab of the Ribbon.

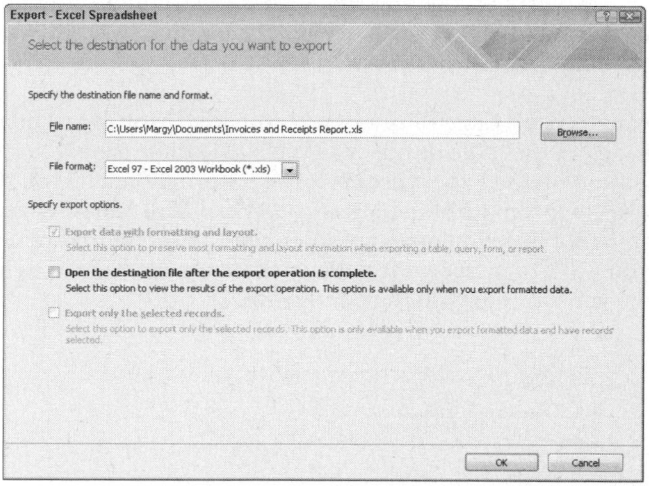

Figure 2-12:
The Export –
Excel
Spreadsheet
dialog box.

> **Export - Excel Spreadsheet**
>
> Select the destination for the data you want to export
>
> Specify the destination file name and format.
>
> File name: C:\Users\Margy\Documents\Invoices and Receipts Report.xls   Browse...
>
> File format: Excel 97 - Excel 2003 Workbook (*.xls)
>
> Specify export options.
>
> ☑ Export data with formatting and layout.
>   Select this option to preserve most formatting and layout information when exporting a table, query, form, or report.
>
> ☐ Open the destination file after the export operation is complete.
>   Select this option to view the results of the export operation. This option is available only when you export formatted data.
>
> ☐ Export only the selected records.
>   Select this option to export only the selected records. This option is only available when you export formatted data and have records selected.
>
> OK   Cancel

3. **Click the Browse button to choose the folder where you want to store the exported file, and type a name for the file in the File Name text box.**

   If you want to open the exported report automatically in Microsoft Word, check the Open the Destination File after the Export Operation is Complete check box.

4. **Click OK.**

   Access creates an Excel spreadsheet that has a column for each field and a row for each record on the report. It makes no attempt to preserve the formatting of the report; you get just the data.

5. **Click the Close button.**

   Access asks whether you'd like to save the steps you followed to create this export file (as shown in Figure 2-6, earlier in this chapter). If you want to try this, see the section "Automating your exports" later in this chapter before you click Close.

If your report contains subreports, Access creates a set of rows for the subreport under the row for the record in the main report, with the columns for the subreport fields off to the right. This format makes sense, because it keeps the data organized, with a column for each field, but it's hard to read.

Exporting your report to Word

More

You can export an Access report as a Word document in a similar way. Actually, the exported file is an RTF (Rich Text Format) file that can be opened in Microsoft Word or any other program that supports RTF.

To export to RTF, follow the same steps as for exporting an Excel spreadsheet, but click the More button in the Export group on the External Data tab of the Ribbon, or in the Data group on the Print Preview tab. Either way, you see a list of export formats that the Access folks couldn't shoehorn onto the Ribbon; click Word. Access creates an RTF file that looks in Word just about identical to the report in Access.

TIP

If you want to use a table or query with the Microsoft Word merge feature, you can. Select the table or query in the Navigation pane. Click the Word Merge button on the Export group of the External Data tab on the Ribbon and follow the prompts of the Microsoft Word Mail Merge Wizard, as shown in Figure 2-13. When you open the document in the Word document into which you want to merge your data, click Insert Word Field to include a field from your table or query in the document.

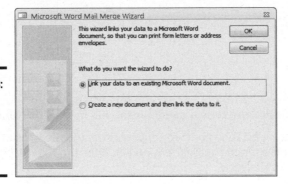

Figure 2-13:
The
Microsoft
Word Mail
Merge
Wizard.

E-Mailing your report

E-mail

If you use Microsoft Outlook, the e-mail program that comes with Microsoft Office, you can e-mail a report directly from Access. With the report selected in the Navigation pane, click the E-Mail button in the Export group on the External Data tab of the Ribbon. Or right-click a report that's open in Report view, and choose Send To➪Mail Recipient (As Attachment) from the menu that appears. Either way, you see the Send Object As dialog box shown in Figure 2-14. Choose a format, click OK, and Access fires up Outlook and creates a message with your report as an attachment.

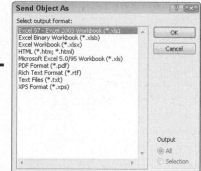

Figure 2-14:
How do you want to export your report for e-mailing?

If you don't use Outlook, you see an error message telling you to set up Outlook in order to use this feature.

Exporting your report in other formats

Access can export to a few other formats, using buttons in the Export group on the External Data tab of the Ribbon. Here are some of them:

✦ **Text File, by clicking the Text File button:** You can choose to preserve formatting, which tells Access to stick in spaces to approximate the layout of the report. Then it runs the Export Text Wizard, which helps you create a text file containing one line per record.

✦ **XML file, by clicking the XML File button:** XML (eXtensible Markup Language) is a standard data transfer format. It doesn't include any formatting, only data.

✦ **HTML file, by clicking the More button and choosing HTML Document:** You can save your report as a Web page. Not all formatting is preserved, but the results are usually pretty good. See Book IX, Chapter 3 for how to put your whole database on the Web, using SharePoint.

Automating your exports

If you plan to export this report regularly and you want Access to remember the directory and filename you specified, you can create a *data task* for the export. Select the Save Export Steps check box when you see the Export – *Whatever* dialog box. The dialog box expands to ask some additional questions, as shown in Figure 2-15.

Type a name for the export in the Save As box and, if you feel like it, a description in the Description box. If you use Outlook as your e-mail program and want to make a task in Outlook, you can select the Create Outlook Task check box. When you click Save Export, Access creates a data task with the name you specified.

To run the export again, click the Saved Exports button in the Exports group on the External Data tab of the Ribbon. Click the data task and click the Run button. (See Figure 2-16.)

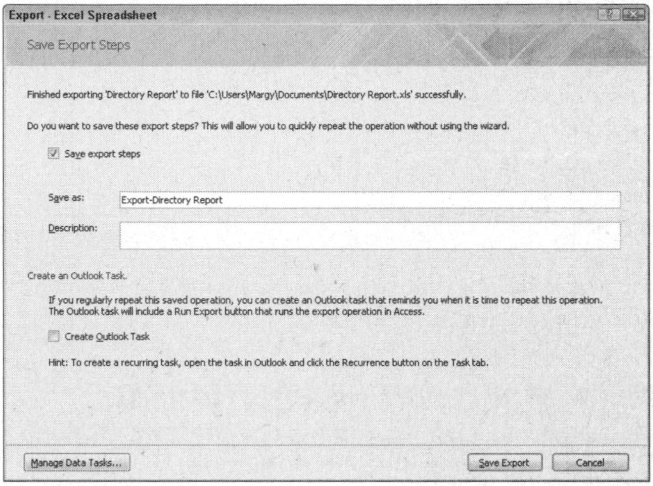

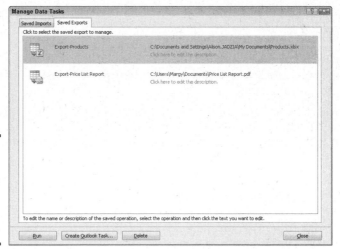

Figure 2-15:
Creating a data task that remembers how you created this export.

Figure 2-16:
Re-export an export by running the data task you created.

Chapter 3: Creating Charts and Graphs from Your Data

In This Chapter

✔ Adding data bars to your reports

✔ Making charts and graphs using the Chart Wizard

✔ Drawing bar charts

✔ Crafting line and area charts

✔ Displaying pie and doughnut charts

✔ Doing XY scatter and bubble charts

✔ Changing the format of your chart

✔ Making PivotCharts from PivotTables, tables, and queries

✔ Tweaking your PivotChart

Charts and graphs often communicate the meaning of your data better than columns of names and numbers. (What's the difference between a chart and a graph? Actually, they are two words for the same thing, so we'll call them "charts" from now on, to save ink.) You can add a chart to any report using the chart control. Access 2010 has a new feature called *data bars,* which are little bar charts that can appear as a part of any report.

PivotCharts are another Microsoft Office component that you can use with Access. A PivotChart is dynamic, which means that you can easily adjust it while you're looking at it. As you drag field names around the PivotChart, or make choices from drop-down lists, the chart changes immediately on-screen.

Which should you use — charts or PivotCharts? Depends on what you want to do with what you get. Here are some guidelines:

✦ PivotCharts are designed for the screen, where you can fool around with their settings and explore your data graphically.

✦ Regular charts are designed to print out, and include many more formatting options.

PivotTables are like PivotCharts — they also let you analyze your data on-screen. PivotTables display your data as text, whereas PivotCharts graph your data. For more information about PivotTables, see Book III, Chapter 4.

Pull Up a Seat at the Data Bar

You've probably heard of a bar chart, but who ever heard of a *data bar?* Microsoft coined this term to describe little horizontal bars that you can display on a report. If you display a bunch of data bars one below another, it makes a bar chart. Figure 3-1 shows a report with data bars showing the number of each product sold. The data bar displays both a horizontal bar and the quantity as a number.

Figure 3-1:
Data bars
are text
boxes that
contain
numbers
and are
formatted as
horizontal
bars.

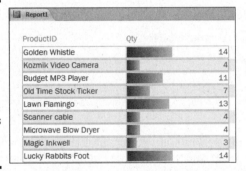

The data bar is actually a text box that contains a numeric value. To make the text box look like a horizontal bar, Access strangely uses conditional formatting to apply the format. Here's how:

1. **Create a new report, or open an existing report in Design or Layout view.**

   To make a new report, click the Report Design button in the Reports group on the Create tab on the Ribbon. To open an existing report in Design view, right-click the report and select Design View. (See Book V, Chapter 1 for how to edit reports in Design view and Layout view.)

2. **Display the Field list, if it's not already on-screen, by clicking the Add Existing Fields button in the Tools group on the Design tab of the Ribbon.**

   The Field list is described in Book IV, Chapter 1.

3. **Drag a numeric field from the Field list onto the report.**

   Access creates a text box with the field as its control source. Or you can use the Text Box button in the Controls group on the Design tab of the Ribbon, and set the Control Source property on the Property sheet.

Conditional
Formatting

4. **Click the text box to select it, and click the Conditional Formatting button in the Control Formatting group on the Format tab of the Ribbon.**

   You see the Conditional Formatting Rules Manager dialog box. This dialog box is described in Book IV, Chapter 2 because you can use it to format controls on both forms and reports.

5. **Click the New Rule button to display the New Formatting Rule dialog box, shown in Figure 3-2.**

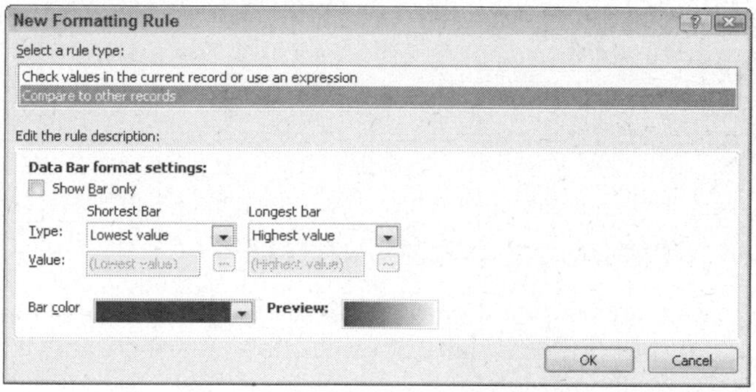

Figure 3-2:
To format a text box to appear as data bars, set the control's conditional formatting.

New Formatting Rule

Select a rule type:

| Check values in the current record or use an expression |
| Compare to other records |

Edit the rule description:

Data Bar format settings:

☐ Show Bar only

	Shortest Bar	Longest bar
Type:	Lowest value ▾	Highest value ▾
Value:	(Lowest value) ⋯	(Highest value) ⋯

Bar color ▾   **Preview:**

OK   Cancel

6. **Set the Select a Rule Type setting to Compare to Other Records.**

   Now the dialog box shows settings for data bars, and it looks a lot more like Figure 3-2.

7. **Configure your data bars.**

   Your options are as follows:

   • If you don't want a numeral to appear at the right end of the control, click the Show Bar Only check box.

   • Set the number that will be represented by the shortest bar. The default is for it to represent the lowest value in the field to be graphed. You can set Shortest Bar to Number and enter a specific number for the shortest bar to represent. (Zero may be a good choice for many charts.) Or you can set Shortest Bar to Percent and enter a percent (for example, .5 for 50%).

   • Ditto for the Longest Bar. The default value is for it to represent the highest value.

8. **Click OK to save your new formatting rule and OK again to dismiss the Conditional Formatting Rules Manager.**

In Layout view, you see your data bars right away. If you are using Design view, switch to Layout view or Print Preview to see them. (Right-click the tab for the report and choose Layout View or Print Preview.)

Access passes your charting requests to Microsoft Graph

Access itself doesn't include any graph-drawing features at all. Instead, chart controls are *object frame* controls that can contain a wide variety of things, including pictures, Word documents, Excel spreadsheets, sound files, video clips — you name it. What we call a *chart control* is actually an object frame control that contains a Microsoft Graph chart object. Luckily, you don't need to worry about object frames — you can just create your new chart control using a wizard. If you insist on making a chart control manually, see the sidebar, "Making charts the old-fashioned way," later in this chapter, but don't say we didn't warn you.

Displaying Information with Charts

Access databases contain different types of objects: tables, queries, forms, reports, and the rest. But what about charts? Where are they stored?

Access stores charts as controls on forms or reports because they are meant to be viewed (like forms) or printed (like reports). Before you make a chart, you create a new form or report — or open an existing one — and then add a chart control. In this chapter, we describe storing your chart controls in reports, but you can include them in forms if you prefer.

We recommend running the Chart Wizard and *then* customizing the chart afterward. Heck, why not make the wizard do most of the work? If you insist on making a chart control manually, see the sidebar, "Making charts the old-fashioned way," later in this chapter, but don't say we didn't warn you.

The Access Chart Wizard is very limited — Microsoft Graph can draw more types of charts. If you want to create a stacked bar chart, radar chart, or multi-ring doughnut chart, the wizard can't help you. You can make a similar chart with the wizard, and then modify the chart afterwards using Design view. Another method of making better charts is to export your data to Excel 2010 — yet another component of Microsoft Office 2010 — and use its more powerful Chart Wizard. See Book II, Chapter 4 for how to export records from Access to Excel.

Creating charts with the Chart Wizard

If you want to create charts in Access, the Chart Wizard is the only good way to start. You may want to add a chart to an existing report, or create a chart that stands alone (meaning that no other controls are on the report). The Chart Wizard allows you to do either.

Whether you create a new report for your chart or add a chart to an existing report, you start at the Reports list in the Navigation pane. If the Navigation pane isn't visible, press the Shutter Bar Open/Close button (>>). Then scroll to see the list of your existing reports.

You can add a chart to a report that you already created by adding a chart control to your report. Follow these steps:

1. **Determine which table or query contains the data you want to chart (a.k.a. the *record source*).**

To make a chart, you need at least one numeric field. Find a table or query (or make a query) that contains the fields you want on your chart. You don't have to use all the fields; the Chart Wizard enables you to select just those that you want.

 If you are charting values by date, make sure that your record source includes the date field. For example, if you want to chart sales per week for each week of the year, the record source needs to include both the sales number field and the sale date field. The fields don't have to be weekly totals: The Chart Wizard can total your fields for you.

2. **Create a new report, or open an existing report in Design or Layout view.**

3. **Click the Chart button in the Controls group on the Design tab on the Ribbon.**

Now, when you move your mouse pointer back to the Design View window, it appears as a teeny little graph.

4. **Click the section of the report where you want the chart to appear.**

A box appears on your report, and the Chart Wizard starts. It starts out just like the Report Wizard, asking what table or query contains the data that you'd like to graph.

5. **Click the Tables, Queries, or Both radio button to display the list from which to make your choice. Make your selection and click Next.**

The wizard asks what fields you want on your chart. This still looks just like the Report Wizard!

6. **Choose the fields you want to chart by moving them from the Available Fields list to the Fields for Chart list, and then click Next.**

To move a field from one list to the other, select the field and click the arrow button between the two lists. Or double-click a field to move it to the other list.

Later, you tell the wizard how to represent each field, and you don't have to represent all the fields you choose here. Go ahead and include any field that you *may* want to include on the chart.

7. Select the type of chart that you want to create from the screen shown in Figure 3-3, and then click Next.

When you select a chart type, the wizard displays the name of that type of chart as well as some information about that type of chart and the kind of data that it displays best. Click around to see what looks good and what will display your data clearly.

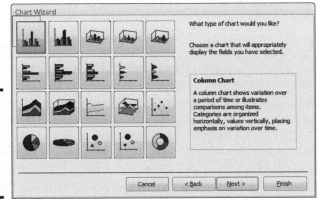

Figure 3-3: You're not limited to boring old bar and line charts!

After you click Next, the wizard displays a small version of the chart, as shown in Figure 3-4. The chart shows three labels: the Axis (the horizontal x-axis on most types of graphs), the Data (usually the vertical y-axis), and the Series (usually fields displayed in the chart as bars, lines, or other shapes).

The wizard guesses which field is on the x-axis, which is on the y-axis, and which are the Series. Sometimes its guess makes sense, and sometimes it produces a chart that is nonsensical, or just doesn't show what you had in mind.

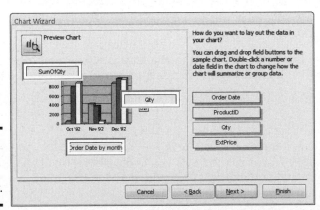

Figure 3-4: Laying out your fields on the chart.

8. **Drag fields onto the chart on the left side of the wizard window and tell the wizard how to use the fields you've selected, as shown in Figure 3-4.**

The fields that you choose appear as buttons on the right side of the window. Unused fields are parked over there. Fields that appear on the chart have only a shadowy box in that parking area, and their buttons appear on the chart as follows:

- The field that defines the x-axis appears below the x-axis.
- The field that defines the y-axis appears above the y-axis.
- The field(s) that appears in the graph appears to the right of the chart.

You specify how to use each field by dragging its field name to the parking area or to one of these three locations on the sample chart. If Access guessed wrong about how to use the fields, drag the field names around to more sensible locations. Don't worry about how the field names appear; you can fix the legends on the chart later.

How the Axis, Data, and Series settings work depends on the type of chart you are creating. The next four sections describe how to specify fields for bar, line, pie, and other types of charts. Remember: You don't have to use all the fields; you can leave some languishing in the parking area.

9. **Double-click a field's box and use the Group or Summarize dialog box that appears to control how the data is grouped or totaled.**

For date fields, the Group dialog box (on the left side of Figure 3-5) shows your options, while the Summarize dialog box (shown on the right side of the figure) shows how you can combine values for a numeric field.

Figure 3-5:
Choosing how a date field is grouped or a numeric field is summarized.

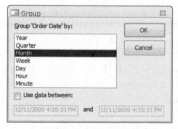

10. **Click the Preview Chart button in the top-left corner of the window to see how your chart looks so far. Check out the results and click the Close button to return to the Chart Wizard window.**

The Sample Preview window helps you figure out whether you chose the right fields for the X-Axis, Y-Axis, and Series settings.

11. **Repeat Steps 8, 9, and 10 until the chart looks right. When it does, click Next.**

If you omitted fields that you need, you can click the Back button to return to earlier questions that the wizard asked.

12. **Specify a title and whether to display legends, and click Finish.**

The title for your report appears at the top of the report. The wizard suggests the name of the table or query you chose as the record source. Legends (which are usually a good idea) show what the colors of the bars, lines, or pie sections mean.

The wizard creates a new chart control in your new or existing report.

In Design view, Access shows a sample chart, not the actual chart. The chart is of the type that you select, but with sample data. Don't worry; your real chart is on the report — switch to Print Preview to see the actual chart, as shown in Figure 3-6.

Figure 3-6:
Your actual chart doesn't appear in Design view, but you can see it in Print Preview.

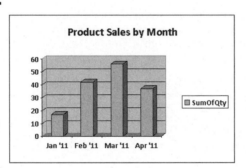

Product Sales by Month

13. **Drag and resize the chart control as needed.**

After the Chart Wizard creates your chart control, you can move the control around your report by dragging it. You can also resize the chart by selecting the control and then dragging the black handles on the edges of the control. (If you double-click the chart control, you find yourself in a strange new editing mode described in the "Formatting charts with colors, legends, and titles" section, later in this chapter.)

A report can contain more than one chart control. You may want to make a report that contains three chart controls that display three different charts. Just make the additional controls in Design view by clicking the Chart button in the Controls group on the Design tab of the Ribbon and clicking where you want the new control to appear.

Now you know how to use the Chart Wizard to create a chart. The next few sections describe popular types of charts — bar, line, and pie charts.

Making bar charts

The Chart Wizard can make a bunch of different kinds of bar charts. The types of bar charts in which the bars run vertically appear in the first row of buttons (as shown in Figure 3-3 earlier in the chapter). Here's some information on what you can create with those buttons:

✦ **Column Chart:** Flat, vertical bars.

✦ **3-D Column Chart:** Three-dimensional–looking vertical bars.

✦ **Cylinder Column Chart:** Same thing as a column chart, but the bars are cylindrical.

✦ **Cone Column Chart:** Another column chart, but with cones instead of bars.

✦ **Pyramid Column Chart:** Ditto, but with pyramids.

You can also make the same charts run horizontally. The following buttons appear in the second row of buttons in Figure 3-3:

✦ **Bar Chart:** Flat, horizontal bars.

✦ **3-D Bar Chart:** Three-dimensional–looking horizontal bars.

✦ **3-D Cylinder Bar Chart:** Same thing as a bar chart, but the bars are cylindrical.

✦ **3-D Cone Bar Chart:** Ditto, with horizontal cones. (They look rather odd, we think.)

✦ **3-D Pyramid Bar Chart:** Ditto, with horizontal pyramids (which look even odder).

Unfortunately, the Chart Wizard can't draw stacked bar charts — to make them, you have to choose another type of bar chart in the Chart Wizard, and then change the chart type to a stacked bar chart later. (See the section, "Changing your chart," later in this chapter.)

The key to creating bar charts with the Chart Wizard is to specify the right fields for the Axis, Data, and Series settings — the field selections you made in the previous section. Keep reading to find out how the Axis, Data, and Series settings work.

The X-Axis setting

For graphs with vertical bars (or other vertical shapes), set the X-Axis to the field that determines the labels that run along the bottom of the graph. For horizontal bar graphs, the x-axis runs up the left side of the graph. This setting also determines what bars sprout up from the x-axis. A bar graph has one bar (or group of bars) for each value (or range of values) of the X-Axis setting. Figure 3-7 shows two bar charts, one vertical (select Column Chart to get this particular chart type) and one horizontal (select Bar Chart for this one). The X-Axis setting in Figure 3-7 is the Order Date field, and the Y-Axis setting is the Qty field.

Figure 3-7:
Vertical and horizontal bar charts, with `Order Date` as the Axis setting.

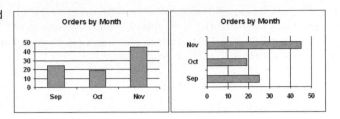

If you use a Date/Time field for the X-Axis setting, you can choose to group the dates into time periods such as a month or year. The X-Axis setting in the Chart Wizard window tells you how Access plans to group the information by date: An `Order Date` field may appear as `"Order Date by month"` — refer to Figure 3-4. To change the grouping, double-click the X-Axis field to display the Group dialog box, as shown in the dialog box on the left side in Figure 3-5. You can choose to group your data by year, quarter, month, and so on. The Group dialog box also allows you to choose to limit the values plotted on your graph to values within a specified date range. Just select the Use Data Between check box and enter the beginning and end dates you want for your chart. Access ignores records with dates outside that range.

You can't control how numeric or text values are grouped, or limit their ranges on the graph.

The Y-Axis setting

For vertical bar charts, drag the fields that determine the heights of the bars — along with the values that appear up the left side of the chart — to the Y-Axis setting. On horizontal bar charts, the Y-Axis fields control the lengths of the bars and the values that run along the bottom of the chart. In Figure 3-7, the Y-Axis field contains the number of items sold; it runs up the left side of the chart on the vertical bar chart and across the bottom of the chart on the horizontal bar chart.

If you group dates together along the x-axis, you can specify how the values are combined into the bars. If you want to graph sales by month and your record source has one record for each order, you may set the Y-Axis field to be the `Grand Total` field of each order. You can then specify how to combine the values of the orders into months — you may want the total value of all the orders for the month, or you may want the average value. The Y-Axis setting in the Chart Wizard window indicates how the values are combined: In Figure 3-4, the Y-Axis setting contains the variable `SumOfQty`, so Access sums up the `Qty` field for the orders in each month.

To change how Access combines the values of a Y-Axis field, double-click the Y-Axis field to display the Summarize dialog box, as shown in the dialog box on the right in Figure 3-5. Then choose how you want the values for each time period combined: Sum, Avg (average), Min (minimum value), Max (maximum value), or Count (number of records).

Unlike the X-Axis setting in the Chart Wizard, the Y-Axis setting can be more than one field. If you drag more than one field to the Y-Axis setting, you see a listing of the Y-Axis fields, as shown in Figure 3-8. For each Y-Axis setting, you get a separate bar.

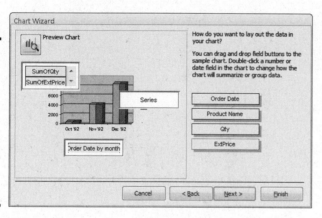

Figure 3-8: This chart has two bars for each month: one for Quantity and one for Extended Price.

You can drag the same field to the Y-Axis setting twice — for example, you may want to see the count and the total of the same field.

The Series setting

Unlike the X-Axis and Y-Axis settings, the Series setting in the Chart Wizard is optional — most charts leave this setting blank. The field used for the Series setting tells Access how to break down the bars (or columns, cones, or pyramids) into a group of smaller bars.

If you graph sales by month, each bar normally shows the total of the sales records for that month. If you drag a field to the Series setting, Access divides the bar for each month up into several bars according to the value of the Series field. If you set the Series setting to a field that represents which vendor sold you the product, you get a group of bars for each month, with one bar for each vendor. Figure 3-9 shows the Chart Wizard settings for a graph that separates sales by `Vendor Code`, and Figure 3-10 shows the resulting chart. (There are five categories.)

Figure 3-9:
The Vendor Code field is used as the Series setting, which splits each month's sales into separate bars for each vendor.

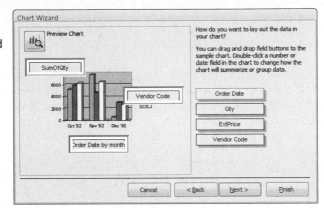

Figure 3-10:
The Axis field contains sales dates grouped by month, the Data field contains the values of the products sold, and the Series field contains the Vendor Code.

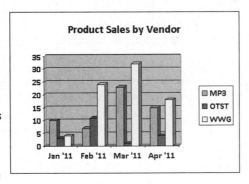

If you choose three or more fields to use in your chart, the Chart Wizard usually guesses that you want to use one of the fields as the Series setting. But for most charts, you use only the X-Axis and Y-Axis settings — just leave the Series setting blank. If the wizard puts a field there, drag it back over to the "parking area" list of fields on the right side of the wizard's window.

Making line and area charts

Line and area charts work similarly to bar charts. A *bar chart* draws a bar (or other shape) for each value of the X-Axis series, with its height determined by the Y-Axis series. A *line chart* works the same way, but instead of drawing a bar, Access draws a dot where the top of the bar would be, and then connects the dots. An *area chart* is basically the same thing, but Access colors in the area under the line, as shown in Figure 3-11. Line and area charts appear on the third row of buttons in Figure 3-3 earlier in the chapter. (They are all but the last button in that row.)

Figure 3-11:
Line and area charts work the same way bar charts do.

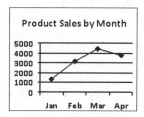

In a line or area chart, the X-Axis series defines the labels that run along the bottom of the graph, and the Y-Axis series defines the distance from the bottom of the chart up to each dot that the lines connect. If you have two or more Y-Axis series, a line chart shows a line for each one, as shown in the chart on the left in Figure 3-12. An area chart colors the area between one line and the next. A 3-D area chart shows each line with the area under the line as a colors slab, as shown in the chart on the right in Figure 3-12.

Figure 3-12:
An area chart with two series fields shows one area in front of the other (left). The Series field splits the quantity of the series field into several lines or areas (right).

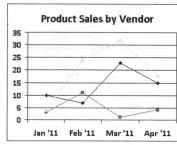
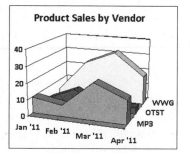

As with bar charts, Access uses the Series field to split the amounts for each line into several, lower lines. The charts in Figure 3-12 use `Vendor ID` as the Series field.

Making pie and doughnut charts

A *pie chart* shows how a total amount is split up by percentages. Access needs to know what field contains the numbers you want summed to make the total amount, as well as what field contains the information by which to split this total into pie slices. A *doughnut chart* is a line pie chart with a hole in the middle, except that you can specify more than one field, and you get a concentric ring for each field. Pie and doughnut charts appear on the fourth row of buttons in Figure 3-3 earlier in the chapter.

When you run the Chart Wizard, choose just two fields to include in the chart, as shown in Figure 3-13:

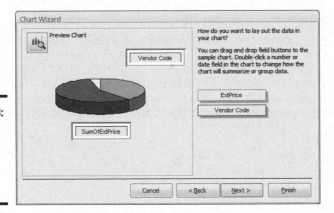

Figure 3-13:
Creating a pie chart using the Chart Wizard.

✦ The field below the sample pie chart is the one that contains numbers for Access to sum up to create the total pie. For a doughnut chart, you should be able to specify more than one field, and get a concentric ring for each field. If you can't specify all the fields in the Chart Wizard, you can add them later; see "Changing which data is charted," later in this chapter.

✦ The field to the upper-right of the sample pie chart can be numeric, text, Yes/No fields, or Date/Time fields. Access makes a separate pie slice for each value of this field.

Figure 3-14 charts total sales by vendor as a pie chart and a doughnut chart.

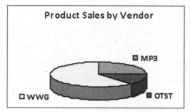

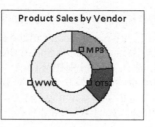

Figure 3-14:
A pie chart
(left) and a
doughnut
chart (right).

Making bubble and XY scatter plots

An *XY scatter plot* needs two numeric fields, and it plots one field against the other. For each record, you see a point with the horizontal and vertical position determined by the numbers in the fields. A *bubble chart* works the same way, except that Access draws a circle instead of a point, and the numeric value of a third field determines the size of the circle.

You can try making these graphs in the Chart Wizard, but we haven't had much luck. (Consider exporting the data to Microsoft Excel and charting it there.) If you want to try the Chart Wizard, drag the numeric field you want to graph along the horizontal (X) axis to the Series setting, and drag the field you want to graph along the vertical (Y) axis to the Data setting. If the wizard decides to aggregate either of the fields (you see `"Sum Of"` — the field name), double-click the field name and change the aggregation to the `None` setting.

Making charts the old-fashioned way

By far, the best way to create a chart is by using the Chart Wizard. However, if you want to create one without a wizard, be our guest — just don't say we didn't warn you. Follow these steps:

1. **With a report or form open in Design view, display the Design tab on the Ribbon.**

2. **Click the Unbound Object Frame button on the Controls group on the Ribbon, and then click in the Design View window where you want your chart to appear.**

   You see the Microsoft Access dialog box (which really ought to be called something like the Insert Object dialog box).

3. **If you've created a graph in some other program (perhaps in Excel or Word),** choose the **Create from File option, click the Browse button, and choose the file. If you are making a new chart, choose the Create New option and choose Microsoft Graph Chart from the Object Type list. Then click OK.**

Yes, that's "Microsoft Graph Chart," which sounds redundant, but the point is that you are creating a chart by using the Microsoft Graph program. Makes sense!

Access creates a sample bar chart based on sample data that appears in a Datasheet window. To replace the data with your own data, type your own headings and numbers in the Datasheet window. To change the type of chart, see the section, "Changing your chart."

Changing your chart

The Chart Wizard can't make all the types of charts that Microsoft Graph can draw. It can't even make all the charts that the Excel Chart Wizard can make — wouldn't you think that these two wizards would get together sometime and compare notes? Luckily, you can change the settings of a chart after the wizard creates it. You can fix charts that don't look quite right, as well as create charts that the Chart Wizard doesn't know about.

To modify a chart, you change the properties of the chart control on the report that contains the chart. This section gives you the general idea of how to modify a chart after you make it, while the next two sections provide more details.

To modify an existing chart, follow these steps:

1. **Open the report that contains the chart in Design view. (Right-click the report in the Navigation pane and select Design View.)**

   If the report is already open in Print Preview, then click the down arrow on the View button to switch to Design view. You see the report in Design view, including the chart control that defines the chart.

   In Design view, the chart control displays sample data, not the actual data. Don't worry — Access hasn't forgotten the actual data you want to plot. Just switch to Print Preview to see the real chart.

2. **Click once in the chart control to select it.**

   Now you can drag it to a different location on the report, or resize it.

   You can tell when the chart control is selected because a selected control sprouts handles — little squares at the corners and the middle of the sides — as shown in Figure 3-15. Drag anywhere in the middle of the chart control to move the chart. Drag a handle to resize the chart control.

   When the chart control is selected, click the Property Sheet button on the toolbar to display the Property sheet, which is also shown in Figure 3-15. In the Property sheet, you can change configuration settings for the graph, as described in the next two sections.

   The chart control appears as an Unbound Object Frame because the chart frame contains information that comes from another program, Microsoft Graph. The chart control is unbound because it's not connected to the records in a table or query.

3. **Double-click the chart control to start the Microsoft Graph program.**

   When Microsoft Graph is running, the chart control appears with a hashed line around it, as shown in Figure 3-16. Your Microsoft Access Ribbon goes away and is replaced by the Microsoft Graph menus and toolbars. The next two sections describe what some of the buttons on these toolbars do.

Microsoft Graph also displays a datasheet containing the sample data that it uses to make the graph that appears in Design view. Editing this sample data changes the chart in Design view; however — and this is important — editing the sample data has absolutely no effect on the real chart that appears in Print Preview (or on the data in the database).

Handle

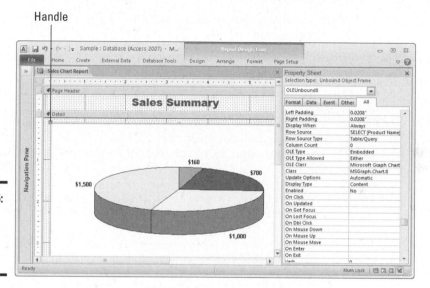

Figure 3-15:
A chart control in Design view.

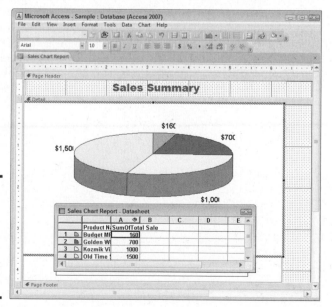

Figure 3-16:
Microsoft Graph is running, although you may not know it.

Click the View Datasheet button to get rid of the datasheet, or drag it out of the way.

4. **Make changes to your chart, as described in the next three sections.**

   The next three sections explain how to change colors, legends, titles, fields, and chart type.

5. **Exit Microsoft Graph by clicking on the report in Design view, outside the chart control.**

   The extra toolbars disappear, the funny border around the control disappears, and you are back in Access.

6. **Click the View button to see how your graph looks now in Print Preview.**

Repeat these steps until you have the chart the way you want it. When you save the report that contains the chart control, you save the changes to the control, too.

The next three sections describe changes you can make to your chart. You make some of these changes in the Property sheet for the chart control, some using buttons on the various Microsoft Graph toolbars, and some by giving commands while Microsoft Graph is running. (Don't worry — we let you know when to do what.)

Formatting charts with colors, legends, and titles

The Chart Options dialog box, shown in Figure 3-17, enables you to change the titles, axis labels, gridlines, legends, data labels (which appear on the graph itself), and data table placement. To display it, first double-click the chart control in the Design View window to get Microsoft Graph up and running, and then choose Chart⇨Chart Options from the main menu.

Figure 3-17:
The Chart Options dialog box contains lots of formatting settings for your graph.

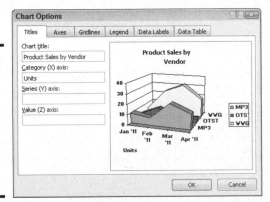

Some other ways that you can format your graph when Microsoft Graph is running (that is, when the chart control has a hatched border) are the following:

✦ **Background color:** Click a part of the graph and then click the down arrow to the right of the Fill Color button on the Standard toolbar and choose a color. You can also right-click the plot area (the graph itself) or a blank part of the chart and choose the Format Chart/Plot Area option from the shortcut menu that appears.

✦ **Gridlines:** To add or remove gridlines within the chart, click the Category Axis Gridlines and Value Axis Gridlines buttons on the Standard toolbar.

✦ **Title:** To change the title that appears on the graph, click the title to select it and then click again to edit the text. Move the title by selecting it (with one click) and dragging. You can also change the font by double-clicking it or right-clicking it and choosing the Format Chart Title option from the shortcut menu that appears.

✦ **Legends:** To display or remove the legend — the table that explains the meanings of the colors or symbols in the graph — click the Legend button on the Standard toolbar. Move the legend by dragging it to a new location within the chart control. Change the fonts by double-clicking the legend to display the Format Legend Entry dialog box.

✦ **Data table:** Click the Data Table button on the Standard toolbar to add a table to the chart showing the data used in the table. You'll need to make the control that contains your chart on your report bigger to make room for the data table.

You can change other formatting options using the Chart Objects drop-down list, which is the left-most item on the Standard toolbar. Choose Chart Area, Chart Title, Legend, or any of the other parts of the chart, and then click the Properties button on the same toolbar. (Actually, this button looks just like the Properties button in Access, but its name changes based on what object is selected. Anyway, just click it.) You see the dialog box with the settings for that object.

Changing how the data is graphed

When Microsoft Graph is up and running, you can also change the chart itself.

Just double-click the chart control in Design view to call up Microsoft Graph and follow these guidelines to make changes to the chart:

✦ **Type of chart:** If you want to switch from a bar chart to a line chart, from one kind of bar chart to another kind of bar chart, or if you want to make one of the types of charts that the Chart Wizard doesn't even know about, click the down arrow to the right of the Chart Type button and choose a different type of chart. For more options, choose Chart➪Chart

Type from the main menu, or right-click the chart control and choose the Chart Type option from the shortcut menu that appears.

✦ **Axes:** Because Microsoft Graph treats your data as if it were stored in a spreadsheet — graphing the data row by row or column by column — switching which field is represented along which axis of the chart is pretty easy. To see other ways of representing your data on the same type of graph, just click the By Row and By Column buttons on the Standard toolbar.

Save your chart first, in case you don't like the results. Switching your chart back to its original format is not always easy.

✦ **Trendline:** If your graph shows information over time (a Date/Time field is shown along one axis), you can add a *trendline* that shows the general direction of growth or decline in the numbers. Choose Chart⇨Add Trendline.

Changing which data is charted

Property
Sheet

If you want to change the fields included in the chart, you can change the Row Source setting of the chart control. Display the Property sheet for the chart control by single-clicking (not double-clicking) the chart control in Design view and clicking the Property Sheet button. (Microsoft Graph can't be running when you do this; to exit Microsoft Graph, click in the report outside the chart control.)

The Row Source setting (on the Property sheet Data tab) may contain an SQL statement that describes the fields to be graphed. (See Book VIII, Chapter 5 for information about SQL.) You can change the statement by clicking in the Row Source setting and then clicking the Build button to its right. Set the Row Source Type setting to Table/Query, and then click in the Row Source setting to see the Build button (the "..." button). You see a Query Builder tab, which looks just like Design view for queries. Each column in the Query by Example (QBE) grid corresponds to a field in the graph, although the exact number and use of the columns depends on the type of chart. Book III describes how to create queries using QBE.

If you make changes to the query, Access asks whether you want to save your changes when you close the window. (Or press Ctrl+S or click the Save button on the Quick Access toolbar before closing the window.) When you switch the report containing the chart control to Print Preview, you see the results of your changes.

Analyzing Your Data Graphically with PivotCharts

A *PivotChart* is an interactive tool that helps you analyze your data, selecting and summarizing your data by the fields that you designate. Both PivotTables and PivotCharts cross-tabulate records in a table or query, but a PivotTable presents the results as text, whereas a PivotChart graphs the results. Unlike a regular chart, you can instantly make changes to a PivotChart by dragging field names to the chart or choosing from drop-down lists that reflect your data. Figure 3-18 shows a PivotChart with information about sales by month and by vendor. The beauty of PivotCharts is that you don't have to create a whole bunch of different charts to show different types of data. Instead, create one flexible PivotChart that can be tweaked to show whatever you're interested in seeing at the moment.

You can read all about PivotTables in Book III, Chapter 4.

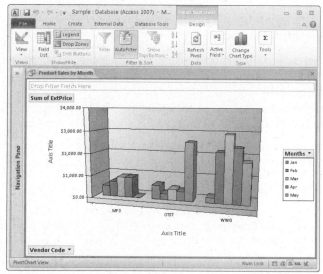

Figure 3-18:
You can change which fields are graphed on a PivotChart by dragging field names.

Creating PivotCharts

You can display the information from any table, query, or PivotTable as a PivotChart. When you create a PivotChart, you modify the layout of a table or query.

To create a PivotChart from any table or query, follow these steps:

1. **In the Navigation pane, double-click the table or query on which you want to base the PivotChart.**

   The table or query opens in Datasheet view.

2. **Right-click the table's (or query's) title tab and choose PivotChart View.**

   Access creates a view of the table or query showing the PivotChart. The Chart Field List also appears, showing the fields from the table or query on which the PivotChart is based, as shown in Figure 3-19. The Design tab on the Ribbon also changes to include buttons for customizing PivotCharts.

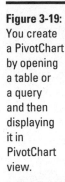

Figure 3-19:
You create
a PivotChart
by opening
a table or
a query
and then
displaying
it in
PivotChart
view.

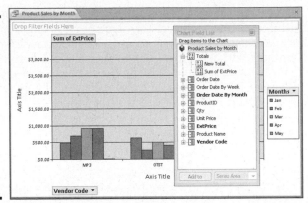

Access makes its best guess as to how you want to graph this data, but you can correct its guesses.

3. **Specify what's on your chart by dragging fields from the Chart Field list to the PivotChart drop areas.**

If the Chart Field list doesn't appear, click the Field List button in the Show/Hide group on the Design tab on the Ribbon. The Chart Field list is like the Field list that appears when you edit a form: It lists the fields available to drag to the PivotChart.

PivotChart *drop areas* are spots around the edges of the PivotChart where you can drag field names to control what data is included in your chart. They are

- *Filter fields:* Fields you want to use to filter the data shown in the chart. To filter the data, click the drop-down list and click to remove check marks — only check-marked data is included in the chart. This drop area works like the Criteria row in an Access query. This drop area is at the top of the chart, labeled "Drop Filter Fields Here."

- *Data fields:* Fields containing the data you want to chart (for example, the numbers that are represented by the heights of the bars of a bar chart). The values of these fields are measured by the numbers on the y-axis. This drop area is at the top of the y-axis, in the upper-left corner of the chart. (In Figure 3-19, the Sum of ExtPrice field is in this drop area.)

- *Category fields:* Fields that contain values that you want to run along the bottom edge (x-axis) of the chart. This drop area is below the chart (where Vendor Code appears in Figure 3-19).

- *Series fields:* Different values in these fields are represented by different lines in a line chart, different bars in a bar chart, or different-colored graph elements. If you want a stacked or clustered bar chart, a line graph with more than one line, or a multi-ring doughnut chart, drag more than one field to the Series drop area. (In Figure 3-19, it contains the Months field.) This drop area is to the right of the chart.

4. **Make changes to the type of chart, which fields are graphed, and which values of each field are included.**

   See the section, "Sprucing up your PivotCharts," at the end of this chapter, for details.

5. **To see the chart better, close the Chart Field list by clicking its X button.**

   You can always open it again if you want to add more fields: Click the Field List button again.

Saving and viewing your PivotChart

Like PivotTables, a PivotChart is a special view of a table or query. When you close a PivotChart, Access asks if you want to save the changes to the table or query on which the PivotChart is based. You can save your changes while editing a PivotChart by clicking the Save button on the Quick Access toolbar or pressing Ctrl+S.

To open a PivotChart again, open its table or query by double-clicking it in the Navigation pane. Then right-click the Title tab of the open table or query and choose PivotChart View. Access displays the PivotChart view of your table or query. The tab for the PivotChart view shows the name of the table or query that provides the record source for the chart.

You can switch to other views by right-clicking the tab of the table or query and choosing the view you want. Switching to PivotTable view shows the same information as rows and columns of text. Switching to Datasheet or Design views is usually pointless, though — you see only the datasheet or design of the underlying table or query.

Sprucing up your PivotCharts

After you create a PivotChart, you can change the type of chart, which fields appear where, and which values are included. As you make your changes, Access redraws the PivotChart immediately — unlike the charts made by Microsoft Graph, a PivotChart doesn't make you switch views to see your results.

Another dynamic aspect of PivotCharts is that you can see what each part of the chart means by simply hovering the mouse pointer over it. When you point to a section of the chart, Access displays a pop-up box with the values that make up that line or bar, along with its numeric value.

Here are some changes you can make to your PivotChart:

Change
Chart Type

✦ **Changing chart type:** If you don't want a bar chart (the default chart type), change the chart type by clicking the Change Chart Type button in the Type group on the Design tab on the Ribbon. Or right-click a blank place on the chart and choose Change Chart Type from the shortcut menu that appears. Either way, you see the Properties dialog box for the PivotChart with the Type tab selected, as shown in Figure 3-20. Click a type from the list at the left, and then a format from the examples shown.

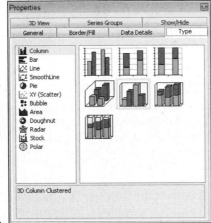

Figure 3-20:
Change the
type of chart
from the
Properties
dialog
box for a
PivotChart.

Field List

✦ **Changing which fields are graphed:** For each field on the PivotChart, you see a gray button with a downward-pointing triangle — a *field button*. Figure 3-19 shows buttons for the Sum of ExtPrice, Vendor Code, and Months fields. You can change or add the fields to the graph. Display the Chart Field list by clicking the Field List button in the Show/Hide group on the Design tab on the Ribbon. Then drag a field from the Chart Field list to one of the drop areas. (Turn to the "Creating PivotCharts" section, earlier in this chapter, if you need a refresher on drop areas.) You can have more than one field in each of the drop areas. To remove a field from a drop area, drag it anywhere outside the PivotChart window.

Switch Row/Column ✦ **Switching data and series fields:** You can switch the Data and Series fields (the fields shown along the x-axis and the fields shown by colors or symbols) by clicking the Switch Row/Column button in the Active Field group on the Design tab on the Ribbon. Click the button again to switch back.

✦ **Changing which values are included:** When you click a field button on the PivotChart (for example, the Vendor Code or Months buttons in Figure 3-19), the button expands into a list of the values for that field (as shown in Figure 3-21). The field button(s) in the filter fields drop area at the top-left corner of the chart are for fields that don't appear on the chart, but which are used to filter the records included. In the list of values, you can clear the check box for any value that you don't want included in the chart.

Figure 3-21:
You can
limit the
values
included in
the chart.

✦ **Displaying or hiding legends:** Click the Legend button in the Show/Hide group on the Design tab of the Ribbon to display or hide the legend that shows the meanings of the colors and symbols on the chart.

✦ **Changing other properties:** Click an item in the PivotChart and click the Property Sheet button in the Tools group on the Design tab of the Ribbon to see the Property sheet for that item. You can set the colors and borders of the bars, the background color, gridlines, fonts, and other settings.

Another way to change which fields are on the PivotChart, which values are included, and how they are arranged is to switch to PivotTable view (right-click the Title tab and choose PivotTable View) and make your changes there. When you switch back to PivotChart view, the same data is included in the chart.

Book VI

Automation with Macros

Main Menu		
	My Business	E-mail
	Address Book	Print Reports
	Products	
	Orders	Exit

A custom main menu

Contents at a Glance

Chapter 1: Making Macros Do the Work

In This Chapter

✔ What macros do

✔ Creating a macro

✔ Macro actions and arguments

✔ Running macros

✔ Telling Access to trust the macros in your databases

✔ Making macros run conditionally

A
ccess is a pretty smart program. Throughout the program are thousands of nice little features that make Access so intelligent, such as validation rules and formats that allow Access to help you keep your data neat and tidy. However, sometimes you want Access to be even smarter. You may want to format a field in a way that Access doesn't allow. Or you may want your form to include a command button that the Command Button Wizard doesn't make. No problem — you can make Access even smarter by writing your own programs within Access.

Strangely, Access includes two (count 'em) ways of putting a program together: macros and VBA. The differences between the two are

✦ **Macros** are the original Access do-it-yourself program makers, dating back to the Dawn of Access (1991). However, the macro language is limited, and Microsoft suggests that you not use them for any major programming tasks.

✦ **Visual Basic for Applications (VBA)** is the standard programming language for Microsoft Office and other applications. VBA is a version of Visual Basic that is similar to VB Script, which works on the Web. Microsoft recommends VBA for all significant programs. We describe VBA in detail in Book VIII.

So why use macros at all? Here's why: If you want to do something small and simple, making a little macro is a piece of cake (as you find out in this chapter). And you can always convert the macro to VBA later with the Access conversion command. This chapter explains how to make standalone, general-purpose macros, whereas Chapter 2 covers *data macros* (macros that are stored as part of a table) and macros embedded in forms and reports.

What Is a Macro?

A *macro* is a list of actions that happen when you run the macro. (That's a general definition that works for almost any programming language, actually.) For example, you may have a macro that performs these actions when you click a button on a form:

1. Saves the current record.

2. Prompts you to put a blank mailing label in the printer.

3. Prints a report, filtering the records to include only those that match the record currently displayed on the form.

Most macros are short and sweet, like this example. For more complex programs, you need VBA.

Macros can live as independent, standalone objects or embedded in tables, forms, or reports, as follows:

✦ **Standalone macros** are one of the types of objects that Access displays in the Navigation pane. (If the Navigation pane doesn't appear in your Access window, press F11 to expand it.) If you don't have any standalone macros, the Navigation pane doesn't display a section for Macros, even when you display objects by type. (Right-click the Navigation pane and choose Category➪Object Type.) When you have at least one macro, the section appears.

✦ **Data macros** are stored as part of a table. You can configure your table to run macros before or after a record is added, edited, or deleted. They are great for validating data or automatically setting values. See Chapter 2 of this minibook for how to set them up.

✦ **Embedded macros** are stored as part of a form or report. The macros are run only when the form or report, or objects on the form or report, trigger events. Chapter 2 of this mini-book describes how to create embedded macros that run when you use a form or report.

Creating and Editing Standalone Macros

Creating a standalone macro (a macro that's not embedded in a table, form, or report) is easy:

Macro

1. **Click the Macro button in the Macros & Code group on the Create tab on the Ribbon.**

   Access displays a tab with a new, blank macro, where you enter the actions that make up the macro. Figure 1-1 shows a macro with one action already entered. Macros in Access 2010 look quite different from the way they looked in Access 2007 and previous versions, but they contain the same information — a list of actions along with arguments (additional information) for each action.

You see the list of actions in the macro. The Action Catalog on the right side of the window shows a list of the actions that you can add to the macro, grouped by type of action. The Design tab on the Ribbon displays macro-related buttons.

Book VI
Chapter 1

Making Macros Do
the Work

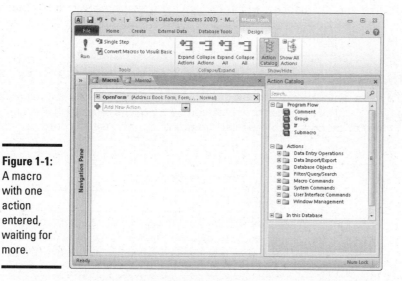

Figure 1-1:
A macro with one action entered, waiting for more.

2. **Enter the action that you want the macro to take, as described in the section "Taking action!" later in this chapter.**

3. **For each action, specify the arguments (additional information) for that action in the form that appears.**

   Click in each box in turn and set the value of the argument. For some arguments, you type a value, and for others, you can choose from a list. If a downward-pointing triangle button appears at the right end of the box, click it to see a drop-down menu of your options.

4. **Repeat Steps 2 and 3 for each action you want the macro to take.**

   When you run the macro, Access executes the actions you specified, starting on the first row of the macro and proceeding until Access reaches a blank row.

When you edit a macro, you open it in Design view. This view is also referred to as the Macro Builder.

Naming, saving, and editing macros

Before you run a macro, you need to save it with a name. Press Ctrl+S, click the Save button on the Quick Access toolbar, or click the Close button and click the Yes button to save the macro. The Save As dialog box appears the first time you save a macro. Name the macro and click OK.

You can edit your macro by right-clicking the macro name in the Navigation pane and choosing the Design View option from the shortcut menu that appears. You see the macro again in its own tab or window. When the macro is open in Design view, you can change actions and arguments as described in the following sections.

Taking action!

To tell Access what to do when running the macro, you specify actions and arguments to actions. Access provides you with dozens of actions that you can use in your macros. Table 1-1 lists some commonly used actions.

Table 1-1	Macro Actions
Action	*Comments*
Apply Filter	Applies a filter to the records in a datasheet, form, or report. Set the Filter Name argument to the name of an existing query or type an SQL WHERE statement as the Where Condition argument.
Beep	Beeps. (You were perhaps expecting it to do something else?)
CloseWindow	Closes an Access object.
FindNextRecord	Repeats the last search you performed. (Perfect for a Find Next button on a form!)
FindRecord	Searches the current datasheet or form for the record you specify.
GoToControl	Moves the focus (cursor) to the control you specify. Useful on forms.
MessageBox	Displays a message box with the text you specify.
OpenForm	Opens a form in Form or Design view or in Print Preview.
OpenQuery	Opens a query in Datasheet or Design view or Print Preview.
OpenReport	Opens a report in Design or Print Preview, or just prints the report, depending on what you specify for the View argument.

Action	Comments
OpenTable	Opens a table in Datasheet or Design view or in Print Preview.
PrintPreview	Displays the object that you specify in Print Preview. From there, the user can choose whether and what to print.
Requery	Recalculates the value of the current control, or reruns the record source query.
RunCode	Runs a VBA function. (See Book VIII.)
RunMacro	Runs another macro. When the other macro finishes running, the first macro continues with the next action.
RunMenuCommand	Runs an Access menu command.
SaveRecord	Saves the current record.
SelectObject	Selects the object that you specify.
SetProperty	Sets the property of a control, field, or other object to the value you specify (which can be an expression).
ShowAllRecords	Removes any filter from the current table, query, or form.

There are (at least) these three ways to add an action to a macro in Design view:

✦ Click the Add New Action box at the bottom of the macro and choose from the alphabetical list of actions.

✦ Double-click an action in the Action Catalog.

✦ Click an action in the Action Catalog and drag it where you want to add it in the list of actions in your macro.

Either way, Access adds this new action to your macro and displays a form with space for information about the action. (See Figure 1-2.)

The Action Catalog lists a *lot* of actions. We can never find the one we want. The solution? Type part of the action name into the search box at the top of the Action Catalog to display only actions that contain what you type in the action. To return to seeing all actions, click the Stop Filtering icon to the right of the search box.

Specifying arguments to actions

After you select an action, Access displays its arguments — additional information that Access needs to perform the action — of the currently selected action. (Refer to Figure 1-2.) Click in an argument's box to set it.

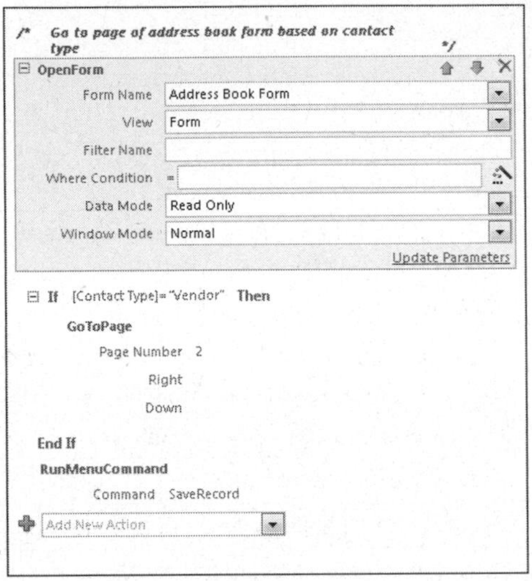

/* Go to page of address book form based on contact
   type   */
□ OpenForm   ⬆ ⬇ ✕

Form Name	Address Book Form	▾
View	Form	▾
Filter Name		
Where Condition	=	🔨
Data Mode	Read Only	▾
Window Mode	Normal	▾

                                    Update Parameters

□ If [Contact Type]="Vendor" Then

        GoToPage
                    Page Number   2
                        Right
                        Down

    End If
    RunMenuCommand
            Command   SaveRecord
⊕ [Add New Action   ▾]

Figure 1-2:
Macros can
have lots
of actions.
Click one
to enter its
arguments.

Some arguments start out blank, whereas others start with a default value. For example, the OpenForm action has a View argument that specifies which view you want the form to appear in. The default value for the View argument is Form view. (You usually want forms to open in Form view.)

These arguments appear in many macro actions:

✦ View: The view that Access opens the object in. For example, the OpenForm action includes the View argument, and you can choose the Form, Design, Print Preview, Datasheet, PivotTable, PivotChart, or Layout arguments from a drop-down menu — all the possible views for a form.

✦ *Object* Name: Name of the object (table, query, form, report, macro, modules, or data access page) the action affects. Access provides a drop-down menu of the objects of that type in your database.

✦ Filter Name: Name of a query (or filter saved as a query) that specifies which records to include in the action.

✦ Where Condition: Expression that specifies which records to include, written in SQL (Structured Query Language). Click the Build button to the right of the argument to display the Expression Builder. Book VIII, Chapter 5 explains how to use SQL.

When you have specified the arguments for an action, you may not want the action to occupy so much screen space. You can collapse the action by clicking the minus button to the left of the action so that the arguments are listed on the same line as the action. You can expand the action again any time by clicking its plus sign.

Moving your actions around

You can change the order of the actions in a macro by selecting an action (click it) and clicking the up or down arrow near the right end of the action (see Figure 1-2), or dragging the action up or down. You can delete the selected action by clicking the X at the right end of the action.

You can copy an action, too, which can be useful once you've created an action and entered all the appropriate arguments for the action. To copy an action, hold down the Ctrl key while you drag it to a new location; Access leaves the action where it is and creates a copy where you tried to drag it.

Adding comments

Previous versions of Access had a Comment column in the Macro window where you could type descriptions and explanations to make the macro more readable. In Access 2010, you add comments between actions, which is the way most programming languages work. To add a comment, drag the Comment action from the Action Catalog to anywhere in your macro. Or choose Comment from the Add New Action drop-down menu and then move the comment up to the spot where you want it. The first line of the macro in Figure 1-2 is a comment, shown as text enclosed in /* and */ characters. (These characters may seem like an odd choice, but several programming languages use them to mark where comments start and end.)

Adding comments to your macros is a great idea. Add a comment at the beginning of the macro that says what the macro is supposed to do. If the Access database is used by people other than you, also add your name and the date.

Creating subroutines in macros — submacros

Programs, even macros, can get long and confusing. Programs can also get repetitive; you may find yourself using the same series of actions in different macros. Programmers the world over use *subroutines* to store a set of actions (or commands) with a name. Instead of duplicating this set of actions in all the places they want them to run, they *call the subroutine* using its name. Later, if you think of a better way to perform that series of actions, you can change the subroutine, and all the programs that call it get the new, improved version. Very efficient.

Starting in Access 2010, macros now have subroutines, called *submacros*. You can put any actions you want into a submacro (even another submacro!), and you give the submacro a name. When you run a macro, it does *not* run the actions inside a submacro unless you specifically call the submacro by name.

**Book VI
Chapter 1**

**Making Macros Do
the Work**

To create a submacro in a macro, follow these steps:

Action
Catalog

1. **Display the Action Catalog if it's not already displayed, by clicking the Action Catalog button in the Show/Hide group on the Design tab of the Ribbon.**

2. **If the Program Flow group of actions isn't expanded (that is, doesn't have a list of actions below it), click the plus box to its left.**

   The Program Flow group is already expanded in Figure 1-2.

3. **Drag the Submacro action to your macro.**

   Access puts all submacros at the bottom of your macro and creates a group, with a name and actions, as shown in Figure 1-3. Another way to make a submacro is to right-click anywhere in your macro and choose Make Submacro Block from the menu that appears.

Figure 1-3:
A macro
can contain
as many
submacros
as you want.

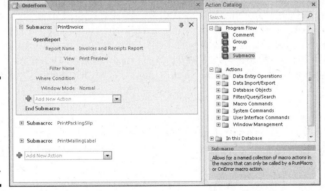

4. **Type a name for the submacro in the Submacro box.**

5. **Enter the macro's actions and arguments inside the submacro area, using the Add New Action drop-down menu, or dragging actions into the submacro box from the Action Catalog.**

When you run a submacro, you specify the name of the macro followed by a dot and the submacro name. For example, if you're working on a set of macros for use on your Orders form, you could call the macro `OrderForm`. One submacro might be the actions required to print an invoice; if you name that submacro `PrintInvoice`, then the submacro's full name is `[OrderForm].[PrintInvoice]`. (The square brackets are required for names that include spaces, and not a bad idea anyway.) Figure 1-3 shows a macro with three submacros. The first one is expanded so that you can see its actions, whereas the other two are collapsed so that only the name appears. To expand a collapsed submacro (sounds like a medical condition, doesn't it?) click the plus box to the left of the submacro name.

You can also create *groups* in macros, which allows you to enclose a set of actions in a box with a name. However, we're not sure what the point is. Stick with submacros, which are very useful!

Running Standalone Macros and Submacros

You can run a standalone macro directly by double-clicking the macro in the Navigation pane, or you can right-click it and choose Run from the menu that appears. If the macro contains only groups, Access runs just the first macro in the group.

The most common way to run a macro or submacro, however, is to assign it to an event on a form — for example, the `On Click` event of a command button. You specify the name of the macro, or the full name of the submacro (macro name, a dot, and submacro name) in one of the properties of a command button. But before we cover macros with forms (in Chapter 2 of this minibook), you can run macros in two other cool ways: auto-execution when the database opens and execution when certain keystrokes are used.

Running a macro when the database opens

We like our databases to automatically display a main menu form, or some other commonly used form, as soon as the database opens. If the first thing you usually do after opening the database is to open the Order Entry form, why not tell Access to open it for you? You may have other actions you'd like Access to take when your database opens — you may want to prompt the user for his or her name, or display a list of reports.

In order to tell Access to do something automatically when the database opens, you can write a macro with the actions you want Access to take, and then tell Access to run the macro on startup.

Running a macro when the database opens is a snap: Just name the macro `AutoExec`. That's the whole thing. When you open a database, Access looks in the database for a macro named `AutoExec`, and if there is one, Access runs the macro. Enter the actions and arguments for the `AutoExec` macro in the usual way.

If you *don't* want the `AutoExec` macro to run when you open the database, hold down the Shift key while the database is loading.

Another way to make something happen when your database opens is to tell Access to open a form. Click the File tab on the Ribbon, click Options to display the Access Options dialog box, click Current Database, and set the Display Form option to the name of the form you want to open.

Assigning macros to keys

Your database can contain a *key-assignment macro* — a macro that assigns keys on the keyboard to run macros. If you create a macro group named `AutoKeys`, and it contains submacros with the names of keys (or key combinations) on the keyboard, then Access runs the appropriate submacro when you press the key. Figure 1-4 shows an `AutoKeys` macro with a submacro assigned to function key F3.

Figure 1-4: An `AutoKeys` macro assigns submacros to keystrokes.

To name a key-assignment macro, use ^ to indicate the Ctrl key, + for the Shift key, and { } around key names that are more than one letter long. Table 1-2 shows the names of the keys you can use: You're restricted to letters, numbers, Insert, Delete, and the function keys, used in conjunction with the Shift and Ctrl keys. A few examples of key-assignment macros are the following:

✦ `^G`: Means Ctrl+G

✦ `+{F2}`: Means Shift+F2

✦ `{INS}`: Means the Insert key

All the submacros in the `AutoKeys` macro must be key-assignments with names of key combinations, or Access will complain when you save your macro.

Table 1-2	Key Names in AutoKeys
Key Name	*Key*
A	A letter key (ditto for the rest of the letter and number keys)
{F1}	F1 function key (ditto for the rest of the function keys)
{INS}	Insert or Ins key
{DEL}	Delete or Del key

If you assign a submacro to a key that normally does something else (such as Ctrl+F, which usually summons the Find and Replace dialog box), your submacro overrides the Access command.

Opening Databases That Contain Macros

Access 2007 added a new feature to guard against databases that contain viruses in the form of macros, and Access 2010 enhanced this feature. Unfortunately, this feature also guards against normal databases that contain macros, action queries, and VBA procedures. When you open a database that contains one of these types of objects, you may see a message asking whether you really want to take a chance on running the macros in the database, as shown in Figure 1-5. You can choose whether to open the database with the macros enabled. (See Book I, Chapter 2 for details.) If you or someone you trust created the database, click the Enable Content button in the message; otherwise, click the Close icon to dismiss the message, leaving some macros disabled.

**Book VI
Chapter 1**

**Making Macros Do
the Work**

Figure 1-5:
Access has
detected
that your
database
contains
macros.

When Access has disabled macros, you can read about it by clicking the File tab on the Ribbon, clicking Info, clicking Trust Center Settings, and clicking Macro Settings. If you don't see the security warning shown in Figure 1-6 doesn't appear, then macros are enabled.

Figure 1-6:
If macros
are
disabled,
you can
enable them
later.

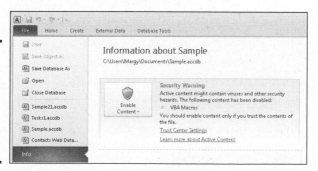

Can a macro be a virus?

Writing a virus is no small feat, and it requires pretty advanced programming skills. In order to qualify as a virus, the macro has to be intentionally written to do bad things to your computer, and to replicate itself. Writing code that makes copies of itself in other files on other computers is not easy. If you're concerned that you may accidentally create a virus, you can stop worrying about that. Creating a virus by accident is about as likely as writing an entire book, or driving across country, by accident.

If the database is something you created yourself, then it's absolutely, positively, 100-percent safe to enable the macros. You have several options:

✦ **Put up with the annoying security warning message every time you open the database, and choose the Enable Content button each time.** Actually, Access may not show you this message when you reopen the database if nothing significant has changed in the database. This method works, but it's annoying.

✦ **Store the database in a folder that you have indicated to Access can be trusted — a *trusted location*.** (We envision this folder looking like a CIA safe house in a spy movie.) We describe this in the next section, "Putting your database in a safe place."

✦ ***Digitally sign* your database by adding the security code that tells Access, "It's okay, this is my own database, and I can vouch for its safety."** This digital signature works only when you open the database on your own computer. The section "Signing your database" later in this chapter describes how to sign your database.

✦ **Enable all macros in all databases and just wait for a virus to come along.** We don't recommend this option. Access's security features may be annoying, but they were prompted by computers getting infected by viruses. We'll bet you don't want your computer to be one of them. If you do decide to change the security settings for Access, click the File tab on the Ribbon, click Options, click Trust Center, click Trust Center Settings, and click Macro Settings to see your options.

We recommend either storing your databases in a trusted location or digitally signing them. You don't have to put up with annoying messages, and you don't open up your Access program to viruses from other people.

Putting your database in a safe place

You can tell Access that a folder is a trusted location, that is, a place where only you and your trusted associates can store databases. To tell Access that the databases in a specific folder are safe, follow these steps:

1. **Click the File tab on the Ribbon.**

The Info option is already selected.

2. Click Trust Center Settings in the Enable Content section (as shown in Figure 1-5).

The Trust Center dialog box appears.

3. Click Trusted Locations in the left-hand column.

The Trust Center dialog box looks like Figure 1-7. Microsoft recommends that trusted locations be on your own hard disk, not on network drives, so the Allow Trusted Locations on My Network check box is normally not selected. However, if you share files with other people at your office (or your home, for that matter), you may need to store your database on a network drive.

**Book VI
Chapter 1**

Making Macros Do
the Work

Figure 1-7:
You can tell
Access that
a specific
folder is
safe — a
trusted
location.

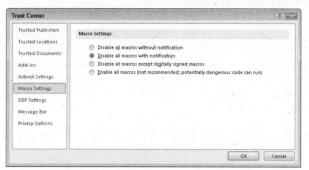

4. If you plan to store your database on a network drive, select the Allow Trusted Locations on My Network check box.

5. Click the Add New Location button.

You see the Microsoft Office Trusted Location dialog box, shown in Figure 1-8.

6. Browse to the folder where you (plan to) store your Access databases, and then click OK.

If you might store databases in subfolders, too, click the Subfolders of This Location Are Also Trusted check box. You return to the Trust Center dialog box, whether you can also modify and remove folders from the list of trusted locations.

7. Click OK to return to the Access Options dialog box, and OK again to return to your database.

Now when you open databases in the specified folder, Access won't display any alarming messages, or disable macros or VBA code in the databases.

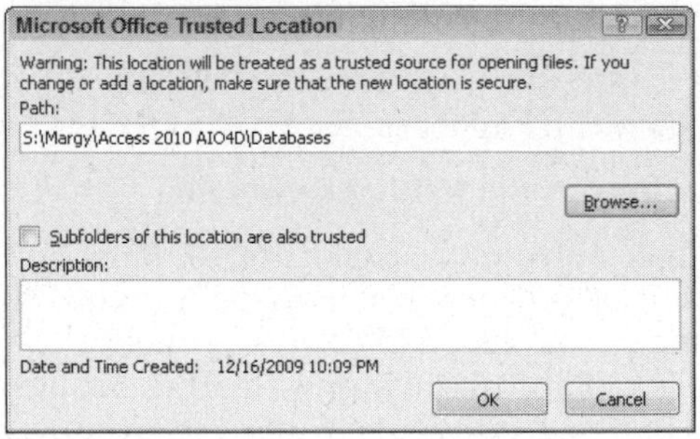

Figure 1-8:
Do you want
subfolders
to be
trusted, too?

Signing your database

Another way to turn off Access's security measures is by signing your databases. Signing a database for your own use is easy to do. First you create your own digital signature, and then you use it to sign your databases. This signature works only on your own computer: When other people open your database, they still see the security warning message. If you want to create a digital signature that works everywhere, then you need to contact a certification authority and buy one.

Follow these steps to create a digital signature for use on your own computer:

1. **Choose Start⇨All Programs⇨Microsoft Office⇨Microsoft Office 2010 Tools⇨Digital Certificate For VBA Projects.**

   Windows may prompt you to install this program, unless you've used it before. If so, follow its prompts. You see the dialog box shown in Figure 1-9.

2. **Type a name for your certificate (such as your own name) and click OK.**

   The program reports that it created a certificate, or digital signature.

3. **Click OK.**

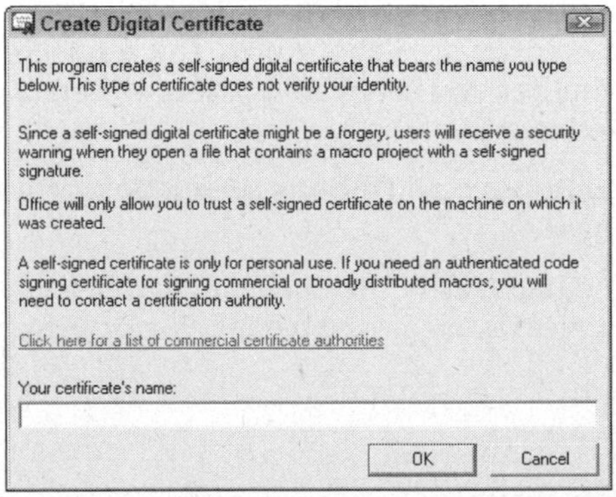

Figure 1-9:
Creating
a digital
signature
for use with
your own
databases.

If you plan to distribute your database to other people and you need a certificate that works on computers other than yours, you need to buy a digital certificate. See the VeriSign Web site at www.verisign.com/code-signing for information.

After you have a digital certificate, sign your database with the following steps:

1. **With your database open, click the File tab on the Ribbon and click Save & Publish.**

You see many options for saving your database in various formats, backing up your database, and uploading your database to a SharePoint site (described in Book IX, Chapter 3).

2. **Double-click Package and Sign in the Advanced section, under Save Database As.**

You see the Windows Security dialog box shown in Figure 1-10.

3. **Choose the digital signature and click OK.**

4. **Specify a filename for the signed database and click Create to save a signed version of your database.**

Access displays the Create Microsoft Access Signed Package dialog box, which looks just like a Save As dialog box.

5. **Choose where to store the signed copy of the database, and what filename to use. Click Create.**

Now, when you open this database, Access doesn't complain. Whew!

Book VI
Chapter 1

Making Macros Do
the Work

Figure 1-10:
You can
add your
own digital
signature
to your
database.

Which actions can you take?

Normally, when you edit a macro in Design view, Access shows you only the actions that it considers to be safe — for example, actions that don't allow you to change data outside the database. If you want to see all possible macro actions, click the Show All Actions button in the Show/Hide group on the Design tab of the Ribbon. More actions appear on the Add New Action drop-down menu and in the Action Catalog.

Run This Only If I Say So

Every programming language worth its salt has an if-then feature, which ensures that a command is carried out only under specific circumstances. For instance, you may want Access to print a report for the current order only if the order number isn't blank: If the order number *is* blank, don't print the report, and if the order number *isn't* blank, then do print the report. The technical term for such an if-then situation is *conditional execution*. The *condition* is a value or expression that can be either true or false (or, in geek speak, a *Boolean*).

If-then macros

The way you add condition execution to a macro action is by adding an If-Then block to the macro window and then typing in a condition. For example, you may want to print an invoice for the current order (using the `OpenReport` action), but you don't want to print it if the total amount of the order is zero. You use the `[Orders]![Total Product Cost] > 0` condition to specify that Access performs the action only if the order contains products that cost money. Follow these steps:

1. **Open your macro in Design view by right-clicking it in the Navigation pane and choosing Design View from the menu that appears.**

You see your macro, ready to edit.

2. **Click the Action Catalog button on the Show/Hide group of the Design tab on the Ribbon, if the Action Catalog isn't already visible.**

The Action Catalog appears to the right of the macro.

3. **Drag the If item from the Program Flow group on the Action Catalog to your macro.**

Or double-click the If item. Either way, you end up with an If block in your macro, which looks like Figure 1-11.

Figure 1-11:
The If block
is where
you type in
a condition
that controls
whether
Access
performs
a set of
actions.

CROSS-REFERENCE
...FOR DUMMIES

4. **Enter a condition in the Conditional Expression box. Or click the Expression Builder to its right to help you write the condition.**

   For the condition, you can use any expression that comes out to be either `True` (`Yes`) or `False` (`No`). Conditions work just like the criteria that you use when creating queries, as described in Book III, Chapter 1. You can compare values using comparison operators such as =, <, and >, and you can use `Is Null` and `Is Not Null` to spot (respectively) blank and non-blank values.

5. **Enter actions and arguments in the If-Then block, using the Add New Action box.**

   Or add actions from the Action Catalog. If the If command is selected in the Action Catalog, double-clicking another action adds the action inside the If block. You can move an action into or out of an If block by dragging it or by clicking the up and down arrows at the right end of the action.

Any actions that are inside the If block's box are executed only if the condition is true. If the condition is false, Access skips over the If block and continues executing the macro with the action following the If block.

**Book VI
Chapter 1**

**Making Macros Do
the Work**

If-then-else macros

If you want an if-then-else condition — you want to run one set of actions if the condition is `True` and another set if the condition is `False` — you can add an `Else` or `ElseIf` section to your `If` block. An `Else` section gives you a place to add actions to your macro that will be executed only if the `If` condition is false. An `ElseIf` section enables you to enter a second condition for Access to check.

To add an `Else` or `ElseIf` section to your `If` block, click the Add Else or Add ElseIf link in the lower-right corner of the `If` block's box.

For example, the macro shown in Figure 1-12 prints a receipt if the order has been paid, and it prints an invoice if it has not been paid. The OpenReport actions have been collapsed (shrunk) so that their arguments appear on the same line as the action, to save screen space (and paper).

Figure 1-12:
An if-then-else macro does one set of actions if a condition is True, and another set if the condition is False.

Chapter 2: Making Macros Smarter

In This Chapter

✔ Validating and setting fields in your tables using data macros

✔ Making your forms smarter with macros

✔ Changing form control properties with a macro

✔ Creating your own main menu form

✔ Using temporary variables in macros

The macros we describe in this chapter are fired off automagically by *events* — that is, by things that happen (usually things that the database user does) to tables or forms. Examples of events are a form opening, a record in a table being added, or the value of a field in a table changing. You can tell Access that when one of these events happens, it should run a specific macro. This makes your macros *event-driven*. The events that can trigger data macros, which are attached to tables, are events that happen to records in tables. The events that trigger form macros are events that happen to forms and the objects they contain.

Event-driven macros can be very powerful. You can use them to validate values in your tables, or to set the values of fields based on changes to other fields. You can also use the On Click event of buttons on a form to run any macro you want.

Although macros are simple and powerful, they aren't the full-featured programming language that VBA is. If you create a macro and decide later that you wish you'd written a VBA procedure to do the job, Access can convert the macro to VBA. See Book VIII, Chapter 1 for how to convert a macro to a VBA program. If you want to use navigation forms rather than regular forms, see Book IV, Chapter 3.

This chapter describes some nifty ways to use macros with tables and forms, including how to set up your own main menu form.

Attaching Macros to Tables

When you create a table, you can specify validation rules that control what values can be stored in each field, and defaults that set field values when adding records. However, these validation rules are limited to looking at values in the same record in the same table. Defaults have to be constants. Wouldn't it be cool if you could define smarter validations and defaults that could look at values in any record in any table and use if-then-else logic? Now, you can by defining *data macros* that are attached to your table.

For example, the `Orders` table in an order-entry database might contain information about each order placed at an online store, including how much sales tax the customer owes. If the customer's address is in the same state as your store, the sales tax rate is your state's tax rate; otherwise it's zero. Also, if the customer is tax exempt, then the sales tax for the order is zero. You could make `Sales Tax Rate Applied` a calculated field, but you might need to override it. Instead, you can make a data macro set the field whenever the customer's state and tax exempt status change.

Running data macros

You don't actually run a data macro. Instead, the data macro runs whenever the triggering event happens — someone adds or deletes a record or edits a field. Access automatically runs the data macro, whether the data was changed in Datasheet view, in a form, or by another macro or VBA module. That's why data macros can't include actions that require user input; the macro may be triggered by another program, rather than by a human being.

Creating a data macro

You create data macros as part of a table. Here's how:

1. **Open the table in Design view by right-clicking the table name in the Navigation pane and choosing Design View from the menu that appears.**

   The Access window looks something like Figure 2-1, and the Design tab on the Ribbon shows tools for designing tables.

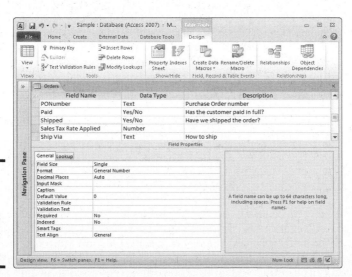

Figure 2-1:
A table in Design view, ready for data macros.

Create Data
Macros ▾

2. Click the Create Data Macros button in the Field Record & Table Events group on the Design tab of the Ribbon.

You see a list of the events that can trigger a data macro, as listed in Table 2-1. When a user, a macro, or a VBA module performs one of these actions on this field, the macro will run.

Table 2-1	Data Macro Events
Event	*Description*
After Insert	After a new record has been added to this table
After Update	After any field in a record in this table has been updated
After Delete	After a record in this table has been deleted
Before Delete	When a record in this table is about to be deleted
Before Change	When a record in this table is about to be updated

3. Choose an event from the list of triggering events.

The most common choices are After Insert and After Update, for checking information that has been entered. Access creates a macro that is attached to the table, named *table name* : *event* (for example, Orders : After Update).

4. Add actions to the macro, based on what you want Access to do when the triggering event has happened.

When you click the Add New Action box or look at the Action Catalog, the available actions are not the same as those available when making regular actions. The actions you can use are centered around editing a record in the table.

For example, Figure 2-2 shows a data macro that sets the Sales Tax Rate Applied field.

• The EditRecord action tells Access to make and save changes to the current record. (Ignore its Alias property; we never use it.)

• The SetField action sets the value of a field (specified with the Name argument) in that record to the value in the Value argument.

5. Close the macro tab to return to your table in Design view.

6. Close the table in Design view, or switch to Datasheet view.

When you save changes to the table design, Access saves changes to the data macros for the table, too.

Now when you edit records in the table, Access runs the data macro after each update. If it makes a change, a red box appears briefly around the field that it is changing.

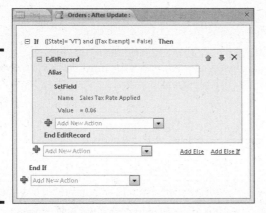

Figure 2-2:
This data macro sets the sales tax based on the state and tax exempt status.

To edit a data macro for a table, open the table in Design view, click the Create Data Macros button in the Field Record & Table Events group on the Design tab of the Ribbon, and choose the same event you chose before — that is, follow the same steps you used to create the macro. Access displays the macro that is saved for that event. We think that the button should be called Create or Edit Data Macros, but a name that long would never fit on the Ribbon!

There's just one data macro for each triggering event for the table, not a separate macro for each field. If you want to update two different fields in a record, your macro can have two `SetField` actions. While a data macro is open in Design view, you can't view any other Access objects until you close the macro — we're not sure why. This limitation is inconvenient, and we hope that Microsoft considers this a bug and fixes it.

Data macros don't show up on the Navigation pane; they aren't considered separate objects. They are stored as part of the table to which they are attached.

Cool data macro tricks

Here are a few interesting functions and properties that you can use in data macros:

✦ **Did the value of this field even change?** When you write a data macro triggered by an `AfterUpdate` or `BeforeChange` event — by an edit to the record — how can you tell whether the value of a specific field changed? Maybe the record was edited, but who knows which fields actually changed? You can know, by using the `Updated("fieldname")` function. For example, this condition is true only if the `ProductCount` field in the Orders table changed, and it's less than 6:

```
If Updated("ProductCount") And ProductCount < 6
```

✦ **What did the value used to be?** If the value of a field changed, you may want to know what the previous value was. For example, if the ProductCount went up, you might want to do something about recalculating the shipping charge. You can use the Old.[*fieldname*] property for a value that the field had before the edit. (Note that there are no quotation marks around the fieldname.)

Running Macros in Forms

Most macros are used with forms — to make form controls smarter or to power command buttons. Every control in a form has events connected to it — things that happen when the user clicks the control, changes its value, or opens or closes the form itself.

You can run these two kinds of macros from a form:

✦ **Regular old standalone macros,** like the ones described in Chapter 1 of this minibook. You can make a macro for the form, and in the macro, you can create a submacro for each event for which you want a macro to run.

✦ **Embedded macros,** which Access creates when a wizard makes a command button on a form. These macros are attached to the form in the same way that data macros are attached to tables. You can get to them when you have the form open in Design view.

The rest of this section describes how to run both types of macros from your forms.

Running a macro when a form event happens

To tell Access to run a macro when an event happens, you enter the macro name in the event property for the control (or for the whole form). Follow these steps:

1. **Create and save the macro you want to run.**

You can store the macro by itself, or as a submacro in a macro for the form. (We usually create one macro for each form and make a submacro for each event for which we want something to happen.) Save the macro before continuing. (But you can keep the macro open in Design view if you plan to make further changes to your macro.)

2. **Open the form in Design view.**

Refer to Book IV, Chapter 2 for how to edit a form in Design view.

Property
Sheet

3. **Display the Property sheet by clicking the Property Sheet button in the Tools group on the Design tab on the Ribbon. Click the Event tab.**

See Book IV, Chapter 1 for information about the Property sheet. The Event tab displays all the events for the selected object.

4. **If you're attaching a macro to a control (such as a command button), click that control. To attach the macro to the form itself, click the box where the rulers intersect in the upper-left corner of the form.**

Now the Property sheet shows the available events for the control or for the form itself.

5. **Click in the event property you want to use.**

For example, if you're attaching a macro to a command button, click in the `On Click` property to run the macro when the user clicks the command button. If you want the macro to run whenever you insert a record using the form, click in the `Before Insert` property.

6. **Click the downward-pointing arrow at the right end of the property and choose the name of the macro.**

Access lists all the macros and submacros, in alphabetical order. For example, if the `Order Form` macro contains a macro named `AddRecord`, choose `Order Form.AddRecord`.

Most controls have a number of different events to which you can assign a macro, including when your cursor enters and exits the control, when you click or double-click it, or when its value changes. Figure 2-3 shows the Event tab of the Property sheet for a command button control, with a macro name in the `On Click` event property.

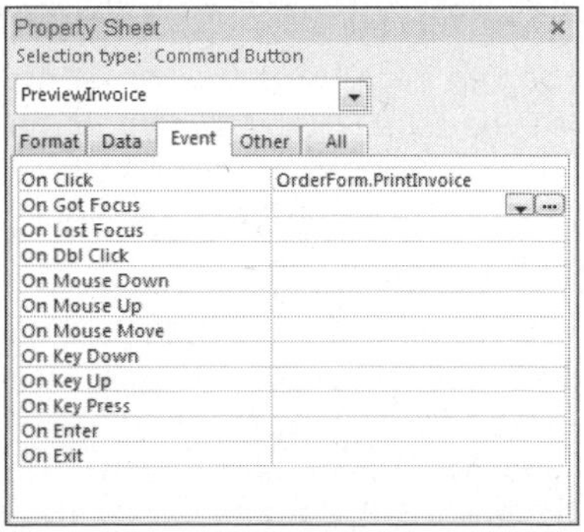

Figure 2-3:
The Event properties of a command button control on a form.

Property Sheet	✕
Selection type: Command Button	
PreviewInvoice	▾

Format	Data	Event	Other	All

On Click	OrderForm.PrintInvoice
On Got Focus	▾ ⋯
On Lost Focus	
On Dbl Click	
On Mouse Down	
On Mouse Up	
On Mouse Move	
On Key Down	
On Key Up	
On Key Press	
On Enter	
On Exit	

Table 2-2 shows the most commonly-used events that can happen to controls in a form.

Table 2-2	Some Form Control Events
Event	*Description*
`Before Update`	When the control or record is about to be updated
`After Update`	Immediately after the control or record is updated
`On Not in List`	When a user tries to enter a value in combo and list boxes that's not in the list of values
`On Enter`	When focus (cursor) moves to the control
`On Exit`	When focus (cursor) leaves the control
`On Click`	When you click the control
`On Dbl Click`	When you double-click the control

Book VI Chapter 2

Making Macros Smarter

For example, you can make a macro for an order form that automatically moves you to the last record in the table. (You rarely want to edit the first, oldest order in the table, but you may well want to edit the newest order.) The macro runs when you open the form. The macro, which we named `GoToLastRecord` and stored in our `Order Form` macro, looks like Figure 2-4. It uses the `GoToRecord` action, with the `Record` argument set to `Last`.

Figure 2-4:
A single-action macro moves the cursor to the last record in the record source of the form.

To make the macro run each time you open the form, set the form's `OnOpen` event property to the name of the macro, `Order Form.GoToLastRecord`.

Keyboard shortcuts for command buttons

Some people would rather use the keyboard than the mouse. You can give your command buttons keyboard shortcuts, in the form of the Alt key combined with a letter or number. To assign a shortcut to a command button, include an ampersand (&) in the Name property of the control. The keyboard shortcut is the Alt key combined with the letter or digit that follows the ampersand. For example, if you name a command button &Print, then its keyboard shortcut is Alt+P.

Creating command buttons on forms

Book IV, Chapter 3 describes how to make command buttons on a form. The Command Button Wizard can write macros for many tasks that you may want a button to do, such as going to the first or last record, applying a filter, or finding a record. The wizard writes a macro that is attached to the form — an *embedded macro*.

To look at or edit an embedded macro, open the form in Design view, display the Events tab on the Properties sheet, and click the control to which the macro is attached. The On Click event of the control says Embedded, and you can click the macro Builder (...) button to open the macro in Design view. While you are editing an embedded macro, you can't view any other objects in the database until you close the macro. Embedded macros don't show up in the Navigation pane; they aren't considered separate objects. They are stored as part of the form to which they are attached.

Referring to form controls in macros

When you write a macro that runs from a form — whether it's an embedded macro or a standalone macro that runs from an event on the form — the macro has to refer frequently to the current value of a control on the form. In the arguments you use to specify macro actions, you can just type the name of the control that displays either the field or the field name. For example, to set the shipping charge to three dollars per item, you can use the SetValue action with these arguments:

```
Name: [Shipping & Handling]
Value: ([Total Qty] * 2) + 3.75
```

However, if you're referring to a control on a form other than the form from which the macro was called, you need to specify which form the control is on, such as

```
[Forms]![formname]![controlname]
```

Replace *formname* with the name of your form and *controlname* with the name of the control on the form.

For example, the OpenReport action displays or prints a report. You can use its Where argument to restrict the records that appear in the report. If you want the report to include only records with the same OrderID value as the order displayed on the Orders form, you type this value in the Where Condition argument of the OpenReport action:

```
[OrderID] = [Forms]![Orders]![OrderID]
```

The first OrderID field is the one in the record source of the report. The second one is the OrderID field on the form. The next section shows how to make a button on your form that prints a report with only records that match the record displayed on the form, using this condition.

In the Where Condition argument of many actions (an argument you use to filter records), you must always use this longer version of the name of the control you want to refer to.

**Book VI
Chapter 2**

**Making Macros
Smarter**

Printing matching records from a form

Now you know everything to create a very useful command button, a button that prints a report for the record displayed in the form. For example, an order form may have a button to print a mailing label, a button to print a packing slip, and a button to print an invoice (if not paid) or receipt (if paid) — all filtered to include only the order that is currently displayed in the form. Store these as submacros in a macro for the form (for example, the Order Form macro).

The PrintInvoiceOrReceipt submacro, shown in Figure 2-5, saves any changes made to the current record on the form and then prints the invoice for the current record. For each macro, you create a button that calls the macro via the button's On Click property. Figure 2-6 shows a form in Design view, with the Property sheet for the Print Invoice/Receipt command button.

Figure 2-5:
A macro
that prints
a report
containing
only records
for the order
currently
displayed on
the form.

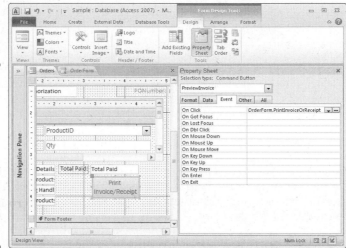

Figure 2-6:
You set the `On Click` property for your button to the submacro you want the button to run.

Changing the Way Your Form Looks Dynamically

A *really* smart form changes in response to the information you type into it. Making smart forms isn't hard: You need only know how to make a macro display, hide, enable, or disable controls on the form in response to what you enter.

Setting the properties of form controls

Macros have no problem changing the *values* of controls — a macro can copy a value from one control to another, for example, or store a calculation in a control, using the `SetValue` action. But that's not all. Macros can also change the properties of controls, in essence changing how controls look or act on-screen. The following properties, for example, are all eminently changeable once a macro gets its hands on them:

✦ `Fore Color`: We're guessing `Fore Color` is short for "Foreground Color." In any event, `Fore Color` refers to the text color property of a label. Changing this property makes the text appear in a different color. Why is this neat? A macro can change the color of a label to, say, bright red based on whether an order is paid for, which makes tracking down deadbeats much easier for you. `Back Color` works the same way for the background color.

✦ `Visible`: If the `Visible` property is set to `No`, the control is hidden. You can have a macro make controls invisible based on the values of other controls. For example, if an order is paid by check, the credit card controls aren't needed and can be hidden.

✦ Enabled: If the Enabled property is set to No, the cursor won't move to it, and you can't change the control's value. You can make a macro that sets the value of some controls and then disables them so that the value can't be changed.

Hiding unneeded controls on a form

For example, on an order form, if the payment method isn't by purchase order, what's the point of displaying a place to type in a purchase order number? How cool would the form be if it could hide the PONumber control if the Payment Method control didn't contain the value Purchase Order? Follow these steps to make a submacro that changes the properties of a form control:

1. **Open your macro in Design view. (Right-click the macro in the Navigation pane and select Design View.)**

2. **Make a submacro named something like ShowHidePONumber.**

    Double-click Submacro in the Action Catalog, or drag a Submacro from the Action Catalog to your macro. It doesn't matter what order the submacros are in a macro; each submacro runs only when called or triggered.

3. **Add an If action to your macro.**

    You can choose If from the Add an Action drop-down list in the submacro box, or drag an If from the Action Catalog into your submacro.

4. **In the If box, type the condition under which you want to change the property of the control.**

    In Figure 2-7, the condition is [Payment Method] = "Purchase Order". The submacro displays the PONumber control if this is true, and hides it otherwise.

    In Figure 2-7, the macro hides a text box control if a control is blank (null) and displays the text box if the control isn't blank. You'd probably want to display or hide the text box's label, too, but we are keeping the macro short.

Figure 2-7: Don't display the PONumber control if the customer isn't paying by purchase order.

5. **Add a `SetValue` action in the `If` block.**

   The `SetValue` action works for setting properties, too.

6. **In the `Item` argument to the `SetValue` action, type the name of the control whose property you want to set, followed by a dot and the name of the property.**

   If the control name includes spaces, enclose it in square brackets. (If there are no spaces, the square brackets can't hurt.) Access adds brackets around the property name for you. In Figure 2-7, the `Item` argument is `[PONumber].Visible` — the `Visible` property of the `PONumber` text box.

7. **In the Expression argument box, type the value to which you want to set the property.**

   To hide the `PONumber` text box, set its `Visible` property to `Yes` or `True`.

8. **Add an `Else` action by clicking the Add Else link in the `If` block.**

9. **Add a `SetValue` action to the `Else` action.**

10. **Set the `Item` argument to the same property as in Step 6.**

    You are still setting the properties of the same control, the `PONumber` text box.

11. **Set the Expression to `No` or `False`.**

12. **Save the macro by pressing Ctrl+S.**

13. **Open the form in Design view.**

14. **Set the `After Update` event property for the `Payment Method` control to the name of the submacro you just created.**

    You might want to set the control's `On Exit` event, too, so that the submacro runs whenever the user's cursor leaves the control.

 When you set the Item argument of the `SetValue` action to the property you want to change, you can click the Build button to the right of the Item box to use Expression Builder.

Show All
Actions
By default, Access displays only the actions that are allowed in databases that have not been trusted. Click the Show All Actions button in the Show/Hide group on the Design tab on the Ribbon to see the complete list of actions in the Action drop-down list.

Setting Up Your Own Main Menu Form

You can make your own main menu form by creating an *unbound form* (a form with no record source) with command buttons that run macros. (See Figure 2-8.) For some commands, you can use the Command Button Wizard to create an embedded macro instead of having to write the macro yourself. Here's the sequence:

1. **Create the main menu form.**

2. **Create a macro to contain submacros run by buttons on the main menu form.**

3. **Create a macro named AutoExec that contains an OpenForm action to open your main menu form so that Access displays the form automatically when you open the database.**

4. **Create each command button that you want on the main menu form.**

5. **For command buttons that do something that the Command Button Wizard doesn't offer, write a submacro for the command button to run, and set the button's On Click event property to run the submacro.**

Figure 2-8:
A completed custom main menu. Each button runs a macro.

Creating a form that appears when the database opens

To create an unbound form (a form with no record source) that appears when you open the database, follow these steps:

1. **Create a new form by clicking the Form Design button in the Forms group on the Create tab of the Ribbon.**

Access opens a form in Design view.

2. **Save the blank form by clicking the Save button on the Quick Access toolbar or by pressing Ctrl+S. In the Save As dialog box, type a name for the form and click OK.**

Call the form something like Main Menu. Leave the form open — you make buttons for it later.

Now you are ready to make the AutoExec macro that opens the form automagically.

3. **Create a new macro.**

A blank macro appears.

4. **Add an OpenForm action to the macro.**

5. **Set the Form Name argument to the name of the form you just created (Main Menu).**

   You click in the Form Name argument, click the down-arrow button, and choose the form from the list that appears.

6. **Close the macro, click the Yes button to save it, and name it AutoExec.**

   You have to name your macro AutoExec if you want the macro to run automatically each time you open the database.

7. **Create another macro by clicking the Macro button in the Macros & Code group on the Create tab of the Ribbon.**

   Your main menu form needs a macro to contain the submacros your buttons will run. It's possible that you can make all your buttons using the Command Buttons Wizard, which stores its submacros as embedded macros. But if you want to make your own submacros for your buttons, you can store them here.

8. **Click the Save button or press Ctrl+S to save the new macro; type a name for the macro, and click OK.**

   You don't *have* to name the macro with the same name as the main menu form — but you'll find yourself less confused if you do! If you took our advice in Step 2, name the macro Main Menu or Main Menu Form.

9. **Click the tab for the Main Menu form so that you can start adding buttons.**

   Now you are ready to return to your main menu form (the one you created back in Step 1 — remember?) and add command buttons.

The form is ready and appears when you open the database — all it needs is buttons!

Creating command buttons for your main menu form

For each button you want on the main menu form, create a command button and (if necessary) a macro for it to run. When you create a command button, the Command Button Wizard writes embedded macros to open forms, print reports, and run queries. The most useful Command Button Wizard choices for buttons on a main menu form are

✦ **Open Form** (in the Form Operations category): Opens any other form.

✦ **Preview Report** (in the Report Operations category): Opens a report in Print Preview.

✦ **Print Report** (in the Report Operations category): Prints a report without previewing it.

✦ **Run Query** (in the Miscellaneous category): Runs an action query or opens a select query in Datasheet view.

✦ **Run Macro** (in the Miscellaneous category): Runs a macro. The macro needs to exist before you create the command button.

If you want to do something else, you need to create a submacro in your macro and then tell the command button to run it. The next two sections describe both ways to make a command button — letting the Command Button Wizard write an embedded macro for your button, or writing your own macro for your button.

Letting the wizard make your command button

If the Command Button Wizard knows how to write the embedded macro for your button, use the wizard. Book IV, Chapter 3 describes how to tell the Command Button Wizard what you want the button to do.

Open your main menu form in Design view and follow these steps:

1. **Click the Button button in the Controls group on the Design tab of the Ribbon and then click the form where you want the button to appear.**

   Access starts the Command Button Wizard. (See Book IV, Chapter 3 for the details.)

2. **Look in the categories and actions that the wizard offers for the action that you want the button to do. Choose the category and the action and click Next.**

   Depending on which action you choose, the wizard asks for specific information about what you want to do. For example, if you choose Open Form for the action, the wizard asks which form you want to open — and whether you want it to display all or specific records.

3. **Answer the wizard's questions about what form you want to display, what report you want to preview or print, or what query you want to open or run. Click Next.**

4. **When the wizard asks what the button should look like, click Text or Picture and specify the text or icon to appear on the button. Click Next.**

5. **Type a short name for the command button. Choose a name that has something to do with what the button does, and then click Finish.**

   The wizard creates the command button and sets the button's On Click property to execute the embedded macro it just wrote. This property causes Access to run the embedded macro when someone clicks the command button.

6. **Move or resize the command button as you like and create a label to go next to it.**

   If the button displays text, it may not need a label.

The Command Button Wizard sets the On Click property of each command button to an embedded macro that it writes. In the Property sheet, you see Embedded macro in the property; click in the property and then click the Macro Builder (...) button to see the submacro in Design view.

If you want to change the button to run a different macro, you can click in the On Click property on the Event tab of the Property sheet, click the down-arrow button for the property, and choose your macro from the list that appears.

If you're not sure whether the Command Button Wizard can write an embedded macro for the task you want the button to perform, run the wizard according to the preceding steps to find out. In Step 2, browse through the various programs that the wizard knows how to write. If you don't see the program you need, cancel the wizard and try the steps in the next section of this chapter.

Making command buttons that run your macros

There's a chance that you ran the Command Button Wizard but couldn't find the option you need — the wizard just doesn't do everything. In that case, you can create a button and then write a macro for the button to run.

If you followed the steps in the section, "Creating a form that appears when the database opens," earlier in this chapter, you already created a macro for the macros run by command buttons on your main menu form. Follow these steps for each command button that runs a macro:

1. **Open the macro in Design view by right-clicking the macro name in the Navigation pane and selecting Design View.**

   If you already created macros for this form, this macro already contains submacros. No problem! Just add another submacro.

2. **Create a submacro by double-clicking Submacro in the Action Catalog. Then add actions and enter arguments for each action.**

   Chapter 1 of this minibook describes how to choose the actions and arguments for a macro.

3. **Save the macro by pressing Ctrl+S or clicking the Save button on the Quick Access toolbar.**

   You can't assign the macro name to the command button's On Click property if the macro isn't saved.

4. **Switch to the form in Design View by clicking the form's tab.**

   If your main menu form isn't open in Design view, open it now. (In the Navigation pane, right-click the form name and select Design View.)

5. **Click the Button button in the Controls group on the Design tab of the Ribbon and then click the form where you want the button to appear.**

   Access starts the Command Button Wizard. The wizard creates a command button and starts asking questions.

6. **Click Cancel to dismiss the wizard.**

7. **Move or resize the command button as you like, and create a label to go next to it.**

8. **Set the button's properties to display the text or picture you want.**

   Book IV, Chapter 3 describes how to configure a command button.

9. **Set the button's On Click event property to run the macro you created in Steps 2 and 3.**

Save the macro and the form, and try out your new button!

Using Temporary Variables in Macros

Now that Microsoft has decided that macros are here to stay, they have decided to beef up their features. One new feature is *temporary variables* — variables that are like fields that belong to no table. You can use a temporary variable to store a value that you will need later in the macro's execution. You can make as many temporary variables as you like well, up to 255, but that's a lot! — and they stick around even after your macro stops running. You can set a temporary variable in one macro and read its value in another macro, or when the same macro runs again later.

Each temporary variable has a name that you choose. To create a temporary variable, or change the name of an existing one, use the SetTempVar action in your macro. It has two arguments:

✦ **Name:** A name that you create, like RecordID

✦ **Expression:** The value to assign to (or store in) this temporary variable, which can be any expression

To refer to the temporary variable later so that you can use the value it contains, type an expression like this:

[Tempvars]![*varname*]

(Replace *varname* with the name of the temporary variable.)

If the temporary variable doesn't exist, Access doesn't complain. Instead, you get the value Null as the value of the non-existent temporary variable. To delete a temporary variable, you can use the RemoveTempVar action.

Book VI Chapter 2

Making Macros Smarter

Nobody's perfect: Dealing with errors

Originally, when a macro ran into a problem (like a reference to a record or control that didn't exist, or an expression that divides a number by zero), it just died with a message displayed for the user to see. Error-handling, which was new in Access 2007, allows the macro to detect an error and do something about it.

If you want macros to try to handle errors that might arise, you can use the On Error action to tell Access what to do if it runs into an error. You set its Go To argument to one of these options:

✔ Next: Just ignore the error and go on to the next action in the macro.

✔ Macro Name: Run a macro. Set the Macro Name argument to the macro you want it to run.

✔ Fail: Give up and display an error message.

If you choose Next or Macro Name, your macro can find out what the error was by looking at [Macro Error].[Number] to see the error number or [Macro Error].[Description] to see a description of the error. You can use an If action to determine what to do depending on the type of error.

Book VII

Database Administration

The 5th Wave   By Rich Tennant

"Your database is beyond repair, but before I tell you our backup recommendation, let me ask you a question. How many index cards do you think will fit on the walls of your computer room?"

Contents at a Glance

Chapter 1: Database Housekeeping

In This Chapter

✔ Taking out the garbage (compacting your database)

✔ Backing up part or all of the database

✔ Analyzing how the objects in your database work together

✔ Loading Access add-ins

An Access database can get big and complicated, with dozens or even hundreds of different objects — tables, queries, forms, reports, macros, and other stuff you find out about in other parts of the book. You need to keep your database neat and tidy, or it becomes just plain confusing to use, and the file size balloons. This chapter describes how to compact, repair, back up, analyze, and configure your database.

Compacting and Repairing Your Database

When you make changes to your database, Access stores new information in the database file and marks the old information for deletion. However, the old information isn't actually removed from your database file right away. In fact, most database files have a tendency to get larger and larger because Access (like most other programs) isn't very good at taking out the garbage. To shrink your database, you have to compact the database file.

The process of compacting a database also repairs errors that crop up in the file. Occasional Access bugs, Windows bugs, or cosmic rays from the planet Jupiter can cause objects in the database to become corrupted — or broken, if you prefer a more straightforward term. Compacting the database repairs these corrupted objects.

To compact and repair your database when the database is open, follow these steps:

1. **Close all tables, queries, forms, reports, and other database objects, including the Visual Basic Editor.**

   Access can't compact the database if objects are open.

2. **Click the File tab on the Ribbon to see Backstage View, click Info (if it isn't selected already), and then click Compact & Repair Database.**

Access compacts the database. When the status indicator at the bottom of the Access window hits 100 percent and the mouse pointer no longer looks like an hourglass, the compacting is complete. If you don't see any error messages, the compacting worked perfectly and needs no repairs.

If your computer is on a network and you suspect other people may be using your database, make sure that no one else has your database open before compacting it.

Making Backups

Backing up your database is vital. If you're not sure about this, think about the amount of effort the database required. Think about your boss's fury if the database vanished from your hard disk. Think about the killing boredom of typing all that information again. Okay, you get the idea — backups are a good thing.

Ideally, you should back up your entire hard drive — at least the files that you create or edit. (Backing up program files is usually pointless: You should have all the CDs or downloaded executable installation files to reinstall your programs, if need be.) A good backup system creates backup copies of all your files — perhaps all the files in your Documents or My Documents folder — on a regular basis onto tapes, writable CDs, writable DVDs, or another hard disk (your organization's file server, for example). Follow these steps to back up your database:

1. **With your database open, click File on the Ribbon and click Save & Publish.**

2. **Double-click Back Up Database.**

It's under the Advanced heading. You see the Save As dialog box. Access has conveniently added today's date, in the format YYYY-MM-DD, to the end of the filename.

3. **Navigate to the folder where you want to store the backup, and click Save.**

If you use Access at work, consult your system administrator. If you store your Access databases on a network drive, they may back up automatically for you on a regular basis.

You may also want to back up only part of your database — maybe only a few tables contain data that changes frequently. You can export objects to another Access database for backup. The first order of business is to create a blank database to which you can export objects; then, when they have some place to go, you can export them.

Follow these steps to create a new, blank database:

1. **Click the File tab and then click Close Database to close the database you're working with (if any).**

Don't close the Access window, stay in Backstage View — you still need to use Access for this task.

2. **Click New and then click the Blank Database button, if it isn't selected already. On the right side of the Access window, browse to the folder where you want to make this new database and give the database a name. (How about Backup followed by the name of your main database?)**

Click the folder icon to the right of the File Name box to browse to a folder.

3. **Click the Create button.**

Access displays a new, blank database and opens a new, blank table to encourage you to start.

4. **Close your new backup database.**

If you are exporting a table, you see the Export dialog box shown in Figure 1-1. Otherwise, you see a dialog box with no Export Tables section.

Follow these steps each time you want to back up an object in your Access database:

1. **Open the database that contains the object that you want to export.**

2. **In the Navigation pane, select the object that you want to export.**

3. **Click the Access button in the Export group on the External Data tab of the Ribbon.**

You see the Export – Access Database dialog box.

4. **Click the Browse button to select the backup database you created earlier, click the Save button, and then click OK.**

You see the Export dialog box shown in Figure 1-1.

5. **Choose whether to export the structure only or the data, too, if you're exporting a table.**

Select the Definition and Data option if you want all the records in the table, or the Definition Only option if you want a blank table with no records. For backup purposes, go with Definition and Data.

Figure 1-1:
You can
export a
single table,
form, or
other object
from one
Access
database to
another.

6. Click OK.

Access creates a duplicate object in the backup database with the same information stored in the current database. Then it asks whether you want to save these export states so that you can back up in the same manner later.

7. If you plan to back up this object regularly, click the Save Export Steps check box. Either way, click Close.

If you choose to save your steps, one more dialog box, shown in Figure 1-2, asks for a name and description for the saved task.

8. Enter a name (or accept the suggested name) and then click Save Export.

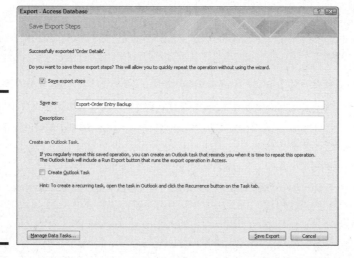

Figure 1-2:
Save the
steps that
you used
to create
a backup
copy of a
database
object.

To export the same object to the same database later, click the Saved Exports button in the Export group on the External Data tab of the Ribbon and choose from among your saved export tasks.

Converting Databases

Access 2010 uses the same file format as Access 2007 for storing its databases, but previous versions of Access use a different format. Book I, Chapter 4 describes how to choose between previous file formats. See Book I, Chapter 2 for what happens when you open older Access databases in Access 2010.

You can tell what version a database is by opening it in Access and looking at the title bar. The title bar may display (Access 2000 file format) or (Access 2002-2003 file format) if it's an old format, and nothing or (Access 2007) if it's the new format.

To convert a database from an older file format to the Access 2010/2007 format, follow these steps:

1. **Open the database and close any open objects.**

2. **Click the File tab on the Ribbon, click Save & Publish, click Save Database As, and then click Access Database.**

   You see the Save As dialog box (the one used in all Microsoft Office programs).

3. **Browse to the folder where you want to store the new version of your database and enter a name for the database.**

   Access creates a new database containing all the objects in the old database, but stored in the new format with the extension .accdb. Additionally, a message warns you that this new database can't be opened using Access 2003 or earlier versions.

4. **Click OK.**

Analyzing and Documenting Your Database

Access includes a number of commands that help you analyze your database, especially how the objects in your database connect. The following sections detail some of them.

Viewing relationships in the Relationships window

Relationships

Keeping the relationships straight between tables can be tricky. For help, click the Relationships button in the Relationships group on the Database Tools tab of the Ribbon to display the Relationships window (shown in Figure 1-3), which shows you how your tables connect. For example, in an order-entry database, your Customers table has a one-to-many relationship with your Orders table because one customer may place zero, one, or many orders. (See Book II, Chapter 6 for how to use this window, including how to move items around.)

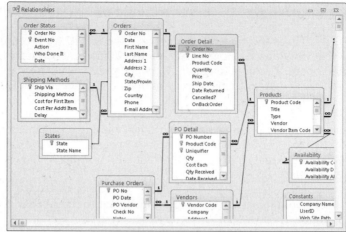

Figure 1-3:
The
Relationships
window
can get
complicated
if your
database
has a lot of
tables.

Viewing object dependencies

Access can show you a list of the tables, queries, forms, and reports that depend on an object. Say you have a query in your database that you never use, but you're not sure you can delete it because it may very well be the record source for a form or report. Access can ease your worried mind on this subject. To display a list of object dependencies, click an object in the Navigation Pane and click the Object Dependencies button from the Relationships group on the Database Tools tab of the Ribbon. You may see a message saying that the Track Name AutoCorrect Info option must be enabled and a warning that various steps may take a few minutes; click OK for each. The Object Dependencies pane appears on the right side of the Access window, as shown in Figure 1-4.

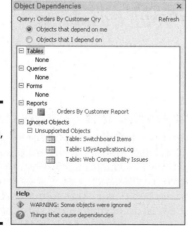

Figure 1-4:
What tables,
queries,
forms, and
reports
depend on
this query?

At the top of the Object Dependencies pane is the name of the object that you're analyzing. In Figure 1-4, the object in question is the Orders By Customer Qry query. (It has to be a table, query, form, or report; Access can't show the dependencies of macros or VBA modules.) Two options follow the object name:

✦ **Objects That Depend On Me:** Choosing this option lists the tables, queries, forms, and reports that use this object as a data source. The objects that depend on a table include the queries based on the table and the forms and reports that use the table as a record source. The objects that depend on a form include forms of which this is a subform.

✦ **Objects That I Depend On:** Choosing this option lists the tables, queries, forms, and reports that directly provide input for this object. The objects that a report depends on include the query or table that makes up its record source and any reports used as subreports on this report.

After the Object Dependencies pane displays information about one object, you can't simply switch to another object. To see the dependencies for another object, click the object in the Navigation pane and then click the Refresh link in the Object Dependencies pane. When you finish looking at object dependencies, click the X button in the upper-right corner of the pane.

Analyzing database performance

The Performance Analyzer examines and improves the speed and efficiency of your database and suggests changes, such as shrinking unnecessarily large fields and adding indexes. Creating indexes for fields in your tables speeds up sorting and searching. (See Book II, Chapter 1 for how to create an index for a field in a table.)

To improve your database's performance, follow these steps:

1. **Open the database and close any open objects.**

The Performance Analyzer can't analyze an open object.

2. **With the database open, choose the Analyze Performance button in the Analyze group on the Database Tools tab of the Ribbon.**

You see the Performance Analyzer dialog box, shown in Figure 1-5.

3. **Select the objects you want to analyze.**

Click the object types you want (from the Tables, Queries, Forms, Reports, Macros, or Modules tabs) and then click the check boxes next to the specific objects to include in the analysis. To select all the objects of an object type, click the tab for the type and click the Select All button. On the Current Database tab, click the Relationships check box to ask Access to look at the relationships among your tables. If you want Access to analyze all the object types, click the All Object Types tab and then the Select All button.

Analyze
Performance

Figure 1-5:
The
Performance
Analyzer
improves
your
database's
performance
—in this
case, the
relationships
among
tables.

4. **Click OK to begin the analysis.**

   This may take a few minutes. When the analysis is complete, a new
   Performance Analyzer dialog box appears, as shown in Figure 1-6. Each
   result on the list is classified as a Recommendation (a change that
   Access recommends and can make for you), a Suggestion (a change that
   Access can make for you that may have some drawbacks), or an Idea (a
   change that Access can't make that you can make yourself). When you
   click a result, more information about the result appears in the lower
   part of the Performance Analyzer dialog box.

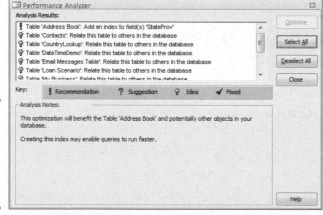

Figure 1-6:
The
Performance
Analyzer
lists its
results.

5. **For each recommendation or suggestion that you want Access to fix,
   select the result and then click the Optimize button.**

   Access tries to make any recommended or suggested change and displays a message about its success.

6. **Make a note of the ideas that you may want to try.**

   Write down any of the ideas that you want to look into because you can't print the ideas, and you can't give any commands until you close the Access windows.

7. **Click the Close button to close the Performance Analyzer dialog box.**

The Performance Analyzer does a good job of spotting fields that should be indexed to speed up searches and sorts.

Documenting your database

You can create reports that describe the design and properties of the objects in your database. With the database open and all closed, choose the Database Documenter button in the Analyze group on the Database Tools tab of the Ribbon to open the Documenter dialog box.

The Documenter dialog box works (and looks) just like the Performance Analyzer dialog box shown in Figure 1-5 — you click tabs and select check boxes to specify which objects in your database you want to document. When you click OK, Access creates a report showing details about the properties of the object. If you select a table, the report looks similar to Figure 1-7 and includes information about the table and each field (column) in the table. The report about a form or report includes the properties of all the controls in the form or report design.

TIP

Choose just one object to document at a time — the report can be many pages long!

**Book VII
Chapter 1**

**Database
Housekeeping**

Figure 1-7:
The Documenter's report includes the gory details about a form.

C:\Users\Margy\Documents\Sample.accdb   Sunday, December 20, 2009
Form: Address Book   Page: 1

Properties

AllowAdditions:	True	AllowDatasheetView:	False
AllowDeletions:	True	AllowDesignChanges:	True
AllowEditing:	True	AllowEdits:	True
AllowFilters:	True	AllowFormView:	True
AllowLayoutView:	True	AllowPivotChartView:	False
AllowPivotTableView:	False	AllowUpdating:	None
AlternateBackShade:	90	AlternateBackThemeColorIn	3
AlternateBackTint:	100	AutoCenter:	False
AutoResize:	True	BackShade:	100
BackThemeColorIndex:	-1	BackTint:	100
BorderShade:	100	BorderStyle:	Edited Record
BorderThemeColorIndex:	3	BorderTint:	100
CloseButton:	True	Container:	Forms
ControlBox:	True	Count:	51
CurrentView:	0	Cycle:	Transparent
DataEntry:	False	DatasheetAlternateBackColor	13092021
DatasheetBackColor:	16777215	DatasheetBackShade:	100
DatasheetBackThemeColorIn	-1	DatasheetBackTint:	100

Loading and Managing Add-Ins

As with all of the programs in Microsoft Office, Access allows you to extend the functionality of Access with add-ins. An *add-in* is a custom component, usually created by professional programmers. If you work in a large corporation that has an Information Technology (IT) department, programmers may create an add-in to make Access easier to use with your company's data.

To use an add-in, you must first copy it to your computer's hard drive. To do that, you need the name and location of the add-in. If your company's IT department created the add-in, they can tell you the name and location of that add-in. After you copy the add-in to your hard drive, using the add-in is simple. Just follow these steps:

1. **Click the Add-Ins button in the Add-Ins group on the Database Tools tab of the Ribbon. From the menu that appears, choose Add-In Manager.**

   The Add-in Manager dialog box appears, listing the add-ins you've installed already.

2. **To install an add-in, click the Add New button.**

   An Open dialog box appears.

3. **Navigate to the folder in which the add-in is stored and then click the Open button.**

4. **Repeat Steps 2 and 3 to add as many add-ins as you wish. Then click the Close button in the Add-in Manager dialog box.**

To remove an add-in, open the Add-in Manager dialog box, select the name of the add-in you want to remove, and click the Uninstall button.

Chapter 2: Sharing the Fun: Managing Multiuser Access

In This Chapter

✔ **Sharing an Access database over a LAN**

✔ **Splitting your database into a front end (for each user) and a back end (where the data lives)**

✔ **Editing data when someone else may be editing the same record**

*Y*our database probably contains such terrific information that lots of people in your organization want to use it. If the database stores customer names and addresses, for example, your colleagues may want to use this information. And, wouldn't it be great if only one person had to enter an address correction in a shared address book instead of everyone maintaining a separate one?

Well, Access has been a multiuser database right from the beginning. Many people can get at the information in your database. Here's how:

✦ **Everyone can use Access to open the database.** If your computer is on a LAN (local area network), you can store your Access database on a shared network drive, and other people can run Access and open your database. However, this option works for only a small number of users.

✦ **People can see the database information via Web-based forms.** You can allow anyone on your LAN (anyone with access to the database file, that is) to see or edit database information by using a Web browser. Book IX, Chapter 3 describes how to use Access with SharePoint to create Web-based forms.

✦ **You can store your data in a big, industrial-strength database server application.** If your database gets really large, or you want a lot of people (more than, say, 15 or 20 people) to be able to see and maintain it simultaneously, Access may not be able to handle the load. Not a big problem. Move the tables to a database server program, such as Oracle or SQL Server, and continue to use your Access queries, forms, or reports to work with it. You just link your Access database to the tables in the database server. Because this is an increasingly common situation, Access 2010 comes with an option to migrate the data to an SQL Server database, which we describe in Book IX, Chapter 2.

This chapter describes the first method — setting up a database in order for more than one person to open it at the same time, using computers that connect to a LAN.

Putting Your Database Where They Can See It

For other people on a LAN to be able to open your Access database, you need to store it in a shared folder — a *share,* for short. The shared folder can be on your computer or on a file server — a computer whose primary job is storing files for use over the LAN. If you work in an organization, check with your LAN administrator to find out the best place to store your database.

If you decide to store the database on your own computer, you need to share the folder with other people. Choose Start⇨Computer or Start⇨ My Computer to run Windows Explorer and find or create the folder where you plan to store the database. Here's how to share a folder on your LAN, depending on which version of Windows you use:

✦ **Windows XP:** Put the database in a folder in the Shared Documents folder. Or, to configure any folder as shared, right-click the folder in Windows Explorer and choose Sharing and Security. On the Sharing tab of the Properties dialog box that appears, click the Share This Folder option and give the folder a name, which appears on other users' computers. Click the Permissions button to set whether other people can only read files in the folder, or edit them. Click OK twice.

✦ **Windows Vista:** Put the database in a folder in the Public folder.

✦ **Windows 7:** In Windows Explorer, click the folder name. Click Share With on the menu and then choose Homegroup (Read), Homegroup (Read/Write), or Specific People.

You can tell that a folder is shared because its icon includes a little hand.

If you store a shared database on your computer, everyone else depends on the stability and speed of your computer. If you restart Windows after installing the latest update to your favorite game of Solitaire, everyone else loses the edits they make to the database. If you decide to run a big, hairy application that slows your computer to a crawl, the other users of your database crawl, too. If your database is important, consider storing it on a network server, or at least on a little-used or lightly used PC.

Read *Windows 7 For Dummies, Windows Vista For Dummies,* or *Windows XP For Dummies* (by Andy Rathbone) for more information on sharing files on a LAN.

Splitting Your Database into a Front End and a Back End

If you create a multiuser database, consider splitting your database into two pieces: the data (the tables and the relationships among them) and everything else. The database with the data is the *back end* and the database with everything else — the queries, forms, reports, macros, and VBA procedures — is the *front end.* You and other database users open the front-end database, which contains links to the tables in the back-end database.

Why split?

Splitting your database has some advantages. Two scenarios that have nothing to do with multiuser databases are

✦ You don't need to back up the front end nearly as often as the back end because the front end rarely changes. By splitting your database into two files, you can back up just the back end, where the constantly updated data lives. (You do back up your data every day, right? See Chapter 1 of this minibook to find out how.)

✦ You improve the front-end database and replace everyone's old front-end database with your new one without messing up each person's data, which is stored safely in the back end. For example, you may create a database that tracks church members, committees, and donations, and then sell the database to zillions of congregations. By splitting the database, you can provide updates to the front end later (with improved forms, reports, and programming) without disturbing each congregation's data in the back-end database.

Splitting your database is even more important if you create a multiuser database in which everyone opens the same forms and edits the same data, possibly at the same time. Here's why:

✦ **Each person has his or her own front-end database with user-specific forms and reports.** All the front ends can connect to the shared back-end database. Each user is free to make new queries, forms, and reports in the front-end database without affecting any other user.

✦ **You can protect the front-end database by saving it as an ACCDE file.** (See Chapter 3 of this minibook for instructions.) People can't change the VBA code, macros, forms, or reports in an ACCDE file.

✦ **Performance is better.** Your database will run faster if the front-end objects — queries, forms, and reports — are stored on the local computer instead of transmitted across the LAN.

✦ **Security is better.** In an organizational setting, if you store the back-end database on a file server, it can be backed up with the rest of the files on the server. Also, server security is usually better than security on a local PC.

✦ **If the database grows into a huge project, you can move the data from the back-end Access database to a larger database system, such as MySQL or SQL Server, without changing the Access front end.** Your Access front end can link to large corporate databases as well as to an Access back-end database.

Of course, a few disadvantages exist:

✦ **You need to keep track of both files.** You can't get far with only one of the two databases. If you need to move your database to another computer, be sure to move both files. Back up both files regularly, too.

✦ **If you want to change the design of the tables in your database, remember to make your changes in the back-end database.** Make sure that the links still work from the front end.

What if some people have older versions of Access?

Be aware of which Access version you use for your database files. Access 2010 and 2007 use a different file format from previous versions of Access. If anyone uses older versions of Access, you have two options: Upgrade this person to Access 2007 or later, or make your database readable by earlier versions. You can choose to create your database in Access 2000 format or Access 2002/2003 format or Access 2007/2010 format. If people are using versions of Access earlier than Access 2000, make them upgrade — too much has changed since Access 95 and Access 97!

If you have to support older Access users, your back-end database must be stored in the appropriate format. In Access 2010, choose the appropriate file format when you're creating your database: Click the File tab on the Ribbon, click New, click Blank Database, browse to the folder where you want to store the database, and set the Save as Type option in the File New Database dialog box to the appropriate version of Access. Put this older-format database in the shared folder that everyone links to. Fortunately, because of the differences in the filename extensions, these older versions can have the same name and reside in the same location as your Access 2010 versions.

You also need to create a front end in the same version of Access as the back end that you just created. The best idea is usually to maintain as many front ends as you have database users: one version in Access 2010, one in Access 2003 (for your version 2002 and 2003 users), and one in Access 2000 (for your version 2000 users). Tell your users to copy the appropriate version to their computers for their use.

Let's split!

Access comes with a Database Splitter Wizard that splits a database into front and back ends and creates the links between the two databases.

To split your database into front-end and back-end databases, follow these steps:

1. **Make a backup copy of your database.**

   You never know what could go wrong, and you certainly don't want your entire database trashed. (See Chapter 1 of this minibook for info on backing up your database.)

2. **Open the database.**

   Close all tables and anything that may refer to a table because the wizard can't run if any are open.

Access
Database

3. **Click Access Database in the Move Data group on the Database Tools tab of the Ribbon.**

   The Database Splitter Wizard appears, as shown in Figure 2-1, explaining its plans.

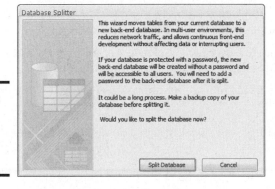

Figure 2-1:
The
Database
Splitter
Wizard.

Database Splitter

This wizard moves tables from your current database to a new back-end database. In multi-user environments, this reduces network traffic, and allows continuous front-end development without affecting data or interrupting users.

If your database is protected with a password, the new back-end database will be created without a password and will be accessible to all users. You will need to add a password to the back-end database after it is split.

It could be a long process. Make a backup copy of your database before splitting it.

Would you like to split the database now?

Split Database   Cancel

4. **Click the Split Database button.**

   You see the Create Back-End Database dialog box, which looks just like a Save As dialog box.

5. **Type a name for the back-end database and click the Split button.**

   The wizard suggests the name of your original database, followed by *-be* (for back end). You may want to use the original name plus the word *Data*.

   Access creates a new, empty database with the name you specify. It exports every table from your original database to this new database, including the relationships among the tables, and then creates links from the original database to the tables in the new back-end database. The original database becomes the front-end database.

The wizard displays a message when it finishes, indicating whether the split was successful.

6. **Click OK.**

If you open the back-end database directly in Access, you find only tables — no queries, forms, reports, macros, or VBA modules. If you open the original database (which is now the front end), the tables are replaced by links to the tables in the back end.

Splitting by hand

Some people just don't trust wizards. If you'd rather split your database manually rather than use the wizard, follow these steps:

1. **Create a blank database in your shared folder and name it** `filename_be.accdb`, **or** `filename_data.accdb`, **where** `filename` **is the original database name (or whatever name you want to use for the database).**

   This database is the back end. Make sure to store it in a shared folder if other users need to access it. Refer to Book I, Chapter 3 for more information on how to create a new database. If Access creates a new blank table after creating the new database, close the table without saving it.

Access

2. **With this new database open, click the Access button in the Input & Link group on the External Data tab of the Ribbon.**

   The Get External Data dialog box, shown in Figure 2-2, appears.

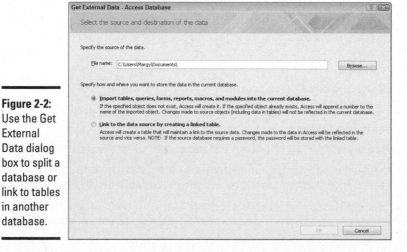

Figure 2-2: Use the Get External Data dialog box to split a database or link to tables in another database.

3. **Choose the name of the database you want to split (either type the path or browse for it).**

4. **Click the Import Tables, Queries, Forms, Reports, Macros, and Modules into the Current Database option and then click OK.**

   The Import Objects dialog box appears, looking similar to Figure 2-3.

Book VII Chapter 2

Sharing the Fun: Managing Multiuser Access

Figure 2-3: Which objects do you want to import?

5. **Select the Tables tab, click Select All, and click OK. When Access asks whether to save your import steps, don't click the Save Import Steps check box; just click Close.**

   There's no point saving these steps because you'll never need to perform them again in this database.

   Access imports all the tables from your original database and the table names appear in the Navigation pane. The back-end database is ready to roll!

6. **Close the back-end database by clicking the File tab and choosing Close Database.**

7. **In Windows Explorer (My Computer), make a copy of the database you want to split. Name the copy with the name you used in Step 1 but end it with _fe instead of _be.**

   This copy is the front end. You're making a copy so you leave your original database untouched, just in case something goes wrong.

8. **Open the new front-end database.**

9. **In the Navigation pane, delete all the tables, one by one, by selecting each one, pressing the Delete key, and clicking the Yes button to confirm the deletion.**

    If Access reports a relationship between the table you're deleting and other tables, click the Yes button to delete it.

10. **Click the Access button in the Import & Link group on the External Data tab of the Ribbon.**

    You see the Get External Data dialog box again, shown in Figure 2-2.

11. **Select your back-end database in the File Name box, click the Link to the Data Source by Creating a Linked Table option, and then click OK.**

    The Link Tables dialog box appears, with a list of the tables in the back-end database.

12. **Click the Select All button and then OK to make links to all the tables in the back-end database.**

    Your table names reappear in the Navigation pane, but with an arrow next to the icon for each one to indicate that the table links from another database. Access even imports the relationships between the tables!

Handing out front ends

Each person who uses your shared database needs a copy of the front-end database on his or her computer. (You can open a front-end database from a shared folder, but it loads and runs much more slowly.) You can copy the front end to each person's computer, or copy the front end to a shared folder and tell everyone to copy the file.

Before you pass out the front-end database, consider saving it as an ACCDE file, so people can't accidentally mess up the forms, reports, or VBA code. (See Chapter 3 of this minibook for more on saving a database file as an ACCDE file.) If you do, save a copy of the ACCDB file, too, so you have a way to make updates.

The Navigation Pane lists every object in an Access database, but having to click and scroll around the list to find the forms and reports you use most can be annoying. Wouldn't it be nice to have a list of just the objects you usually use? Better yet, if several people use the database, each person might like a list of favorite objects in daily use. You can create a group on the Navigation pane for each user; see Book I, Chapter 2 for instructions.

Relinking your tables

The links between the front-end and back-end databases work only as long as the files are in the same positions relative to each other. If you create the back-end database in the same folder as the original database, the two databases need to be in the same folder to work. If you need to move one of the files, you have to re-link the tables. (For example, you decide to move the back-end database to a network drive where you can share it with other users on a LAN and give copies of the front-end to people in your office.) To re-link tables, follow these steps:

1. **Put the front and back end databases in their new locations.**

    The two databases need to be in their new positions to ensure that everything works.

2. **Open the front-end database and view the list of tables in the Navigation pane.**

    Now you're ready to re-link the tables.

Linked Table
Manager

3. **Right-click any table name and choose the Linked Table Manager option from the shortcut menu that appears, or choose the Linked Table Manager button in the Import & Link group on the Database Tools tab of the Ribbon.**

    The Linked Table Manager opens, showing a list of your linked tables along with the name of the database that each links to. (Not all linked tables have to link to the same database!)

4. **Click the Select All button and then click OK.**

    The Select New Location Of dialog box appears.

5. **Navigate to the folder in which you put the back-end database and click its icon.**

6. **Click the Open button in the dialog box where you selected the name of the database you want to work with and then click the Close button in the Linked Table Manager dialog box.**

    Now Access knows the correct locations of your linked tables.

See Book II, Chapter 4 for more on how to create a link in one database to a table in another database.

Editing with Multiple Users

To set up Access for more than one person to open your database, you don't have to do a thing other than store the database file in a shared folder. Access has multiuser features built in! Just open the database one time on your computer and again from a second computer. Poof! You're both using the database!

Everything works fine if multiple people use front-end and back-end databases, too. One back-end database lives in a shared folder, and multiple people have copies of the front-end database running on their computers.

When several people open the front end at the same time, they all link to tables in the back end. No problem!

Multiuser access works great as long as everyone looks at the data without making any changes. Two people can look at the same table — even the same record — at the same time. People can open forms and print reports. Peachy.

Fixing exclusive access

Okay, you may have to do one thing. If the second person who tries to open your database gets an error message saying that the database is already in use, it means that the database is in exclusive mode and can be opened by only one person at a time. (How very exclusive!) If this happens, the person who has the database open must follow these steps:

1. Click the File tab on the Ribbon and click Options.

2. Click Client Settings in the pane on the left, scroll down to the Advanced section, set the Default Open Mode to Shared (as shown in Figure 2-4), and then click OK.

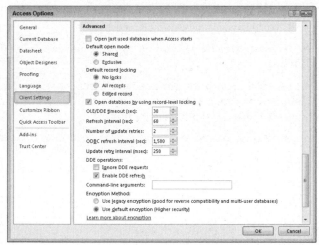

Figure 2-4: Use the Access Options dialog box to choose Shared or Exclusive mode and to configure record-locking.

3. Close the database and reopen it.

Access now opens the database in Shared mode.

Managing record-locking

Okay, everyone can look at the information in the database. But what happens when two people want to edit a table at the same time? Worse, two people want to edit the same record at the same time? The Access record-locking feature handles this situation.

To turn on the record-locking feature, click the File tab on the Ribbon, click Options, click Client Settings, scroll down to the Advanced section, and look at the Default Record Locking section (refer to Figure 2-4). You have three options: No Locks, All Records, and Edited Record. The following sections detail how these options work.

No Locks (no record-locking)

Multiuser editing works as follows without record-locking (when you uncheck the No Locks check box in the Options dialog box):

1. Person A opens a table or query (or a form based on a table or query) and begins editing a record.

2. Person B opens the same table or query, or a form or other query based on the same table that Person A is editing. Person B starts making changes to the exact same record that Person A is editing.

3. When Person A or Person B tries to save the record, Access displays the Write Conflict dialog box shown in Figure 2-5.

**Book VII
Chapter 2**

Sharing the Fun: Managing Multiuser Access

Figure 2-5: Two people are trying to change this record at the same time.

If one person clicks the Save Record button, his or her changes write over whatever changes the other person made to the record. Not good. If the person clicks the Drop Changes button, he or she loses the changes in process. Also not good. Clicking the Copy to Clipboard button allows a person to compare the two people's changes and either choose between them or combine them. (This process is usually a pain — you have to check with the other person, compare changes, and decide which to keep.)

The No Locks option is usually a bad choice because people can end up losing changes to records. Why not let Access prevent this from happening? Sometimes the computer really does know best.

Records versus pages

Sometimes, Access locks more than just the record being edited. Access (and most other programs) stores information in chunks called *disk pages* or *pages.* Access retrieves information from your hard drive a page at a time, and Access can lock an entire page worth of information much more easily than locking a single record, which is usually smaller than a page. (How many records fit in a page depends on how big each record is. If your table has large records with lots of fields, a record may even be larger than a single page of storage.)

Rather than locking individual records, this system is called *page-level locking* rather than real record-level locking. Page-locking is faster and easier for Access than real record-locking, but in some applications, page-locking just isn't good enough. If you have several people entering and editing orders in an order-entry database at the same time, they may end up constantly locking each other out of records — very annoying.

You can control whether Access does true record-level locking or just page-level locking. In the Advanced section of the Client Settings page of the Access Options dialog box (refer to Figure 2-4), check the Open Databases by Using Record-Level Locking check box to use record-level locking.

The solution is for Access to lock the information that someone is editing. While the user is editing the information, no one else can make any changes. When the first person saves the changes, the next person can start editing. Each takes a turn; simple enough.

All Records (lock the whole table)

If you choose the All Records option, when someone starts editing a record, Access locks the entire table that contains the record. When someone else tries to edit any record in the table, Access just beeps and refuses to allow changes. This option means that two people can't change different records at the same time. Some databases require this option — for example, if each record contains information based on the records before it. However, for most databases, each record stands on its own; you can allow simultaneous editing of separate records.

Edited Record (lock one record)

Our favorite record-locking setting is to lock only the record you're editing. Leave the rest of them available for other people to edit.

If you try to edit a record that someone else is editing, Access beeps and doesn't allow you to make changes. The international "don't even think about it" symbol (a red circle with a diagonal line through it) appears in the record selector when a record is locked. Within a few seconds after the other person saves the changes, Access displays the changes on-screen, too. Then you can make your changes.

Programming your locks

If you use forms to edit your tables (and most people do), you can control how each form locks records when someone uses the form to edit a record. Open the form in Design view by right-clicking the form in the Navigation pane and choosing Design View from the menu that appears. Display the Properties sheet for the form by clicking the Property Sheet button in the Tools group on the Design tab of the Ribbon. Click the Data tab on the Property sheet and look at the Record Locks property of the form. You can set it to No Locks, All Records, or Edited Record.

You can also write VBA code to control the way that tables and records are locked. See Book VIII, Chapter 5 for how to write VBA code that edits records.

If you want different people to have permission to see or change different information, you need to find out about the Access security features, which we describe in Chapter 3 of this minibook.

What's happening behind the scenes?

Whenever anyone opens an Access database, Access creates a *Locking Information File* that contains information about who's doing what with the information in the database. Even if only one person opens the database, Access makes the file in the same folder and with the same filename as the database, but with the extension `.laccdb` (people usually refer to this file as the *LDB file*). When you close the database, Access deletes the file. If more than one person has the database open, Access doesn't delete the file until the last person closes the database.

Chapter 3: Securing Your Access Database

After you create a database, you may want to control who can open the database and change the data. If you're creating a database in which many people link to a shared back-end database, you should design security from the beginning; otherwise, your data is sure to deteriorate as different people use the database in different ways. Consistency may be the hobgoblin of little minds, but it's vital for clean data. You owe the users of your database protection from them accidentally doing something dumb.

Be sure to use validation in your tables and forms, too. Read all about it in Book II, Chapter 5.

Access has several mechanisms for adding security to your database:

✦ Startup options that you use to display your own forms, or run other code, when the database opens. See the "Controlling What Happens When You Open the Database" section, later in this chapter.

✦ Password-protecting your database. See the "Password-Protecting and Encrypting Your Database" section, later in this chapter.

✦ Converting your database to an ACCDE file to prevent anyone from editing forms, reports, and VBA modules. The upcoming "Locking Up Your Database as an ACCDE File" section describes this process.

Granting database access to specific users

Access 2003 and earlier versions had a system of user-level security in which you could create users and groups of users and grant them specific permissions. When each user opened the database, he or she typed a username and password, so Access always knew who was using the database and allowed or disallowed commands accordingly. This system still works with old-format (.mdb) database files.

However, the system was confusing, hard to set up, and not very hard to break in to, so Microsoft abandoned it in Access 2007. Access 2010 can still open an MDB file that has user-level security, if you have the necessary permissions and password, but you can't set up or change this type of security for use with ACCDB files.

If you want different security settings for different users, you should use a more secure back-end database, such as SQL Server or MySQL, to store your tables and give each user an account on that database with appropriate permissions. When you link to each table from Access, you enter the user's username and password, which prevents them from viewing or editing tables for which they don't have permission. Book IX, Chapter 2 describes how to use Access to link to SQL Server.

For a detailed, if slightly out-of-date, write-up about Access user-level security, see the following Web page:

```
http://office.microsoft.com/
     en-us/assistance/
     HA011381161033.aspx
```

Don't Forget Basic Windows Security

Your first line of defense for your Access database — no matter what Access security options you choose — is securing the computer where you store the database. Be sure you set a Windows password. If the database lives in a shared folder on a local area network, check with your LAN administrator to make sure that only the right people have access to the shared folder.

Part of security is making sure no one walks off with your database — such as copying it and taking it off-site — or deletes it! That's why Windows-level and LAN-level security are important.

For information about networking and Windows security, see *Networking For Dummies,* by Doug Lowe, or *Windows 7 For Dummies, Windows Vista For Dummies,* or *Windows XP For Dummies,* all by Andy Rathbone.

Controlling What Happens When You Open the Database

If you don't want users entering data (except in the forms you create); modifying your tables, queries, forms, and other database objects; and generally screwing up your lovely Access system, you can prevent them from using (or even seeing) the Design view and Layout view in Access. You can set the startup options to control what the database user can see and do.

Click the File tab on the Ribbon, click Options to display the Access Options dialog box, and click Current Database (see Figure 3-1). The settings in the dialog box apply to the current database. If you change them, many don't take effect until you exit and reopen the database. Table 3-1 lists some settings that control what users can see and do when they open your application.

Table 3-1	Access Settings for the Current Database
Setting	*What It Does*
Application Options	
Application Title	Sets the title of the application in the title bar.
Application Icon	Associates a unique icon with the application. Overrides the default "Access" icon.
Display Form	Designates the form that opens automatically when the database opens.
Display Status Bar	Specifies whether the status bar shows at the bottom of the Access window.
Document Window Options	*Overlapping Windows:* Specifies that you want the default action of windows opening one at a time and overlapping each other, as used in older versions of Access.
	Tabbed Documents: Specifies that you want new windows to open as one document with tabs rather than individual windows. (We use this style for the figures in this book.)
	Display Document Tabs: If you choose Tabbed Documents, this determines whether the tabs appear. (We recommend that you keep this checked.)
Use Access Special Keys	Sets the database to allow the use of Show Navigation Pane, Show Immediate Window, Show VB Window, and Pause Execution key combinations.

(continued)

Table 3-1 *(continued)*

Setting	What It Does
Application Options	
Compact on Close	Sets the database to compact automatically each time a database closes rather than only when you compact it manually.
Enable Layout View	Allows users to view (and usually alter) forms and reports in Layout view.
Enable Design Changes for Tables in Datasheet View	Allows users to make design changes to tables in the database when they view them in Datasheet view.
Check for Truncated Number Fields	Makes sure that you aren't losing significant digits in numbers. For example, if users are entering numbers that are 10 digits and your field is defined as only 8 digits, you would lose information unless you check for truncated number fields.
Picture Property Storage Format	*Preserve Source Image Format (smaller file size):* Allows you to store TIFF or JPG or GIF images as in their original format rather than converting them to bitmap images.
	Convert All Picture Data to Bitmaps (compatible with Access 2003 and earlier): Converts all images to bitmaps (the default in older versions of the database).
Navigation	
Display Navigation Pane	Allows all users to see the Navigation pane. Clicking the Navigation Options button opens a dialog box with additional options for how grouping objects.
Ribbon and Toolbar Options	
Ribbon Name	Specifies a custom Ribbon for the application. You can create your own Ribbon; even define your own buttons.
Shortcut Menu Bar	Specifies a custom Shortcut Menu Bar (the menu of keyboard shortcuts you see when you press Alt).
Allow Full Menus	Allows users to see the full menu options for all menus.
Allow Default Shortcut Menus	Allows users to use the default shortcut menus and any new custom ones.

Setting	What It Does
Name AutoCorrect Options	
Track Name AutoCorrect Info	Tells Access to track name changes to your objects.
Perform AutoCorrect	If name-change tracking is on, when you rename an object, Access automatically changes the object name wherever it is referred to. (For example, if you change a field name in a table, Access updates the field name in all queries and forms that refer to the table.)
Log Name AutoCorrect Changes	Logs any object name changes made by the Perform AutoCorrect feature.

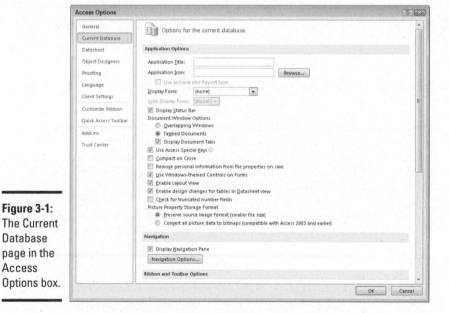

Figure 3-1:
The Current Database page in the Access Options box.

What's been going on in this database?

Access keeps a log of errors that occur in your database. Click the File tab on the Ribbon, click Info, and click the View Application Log Table button to see a table of suspicious or erroneous events. Then close the table as usual.

Consider changing these settings:

✦ Do you want people to be able to use Layout view to change your forms and reports? If not, uncheck the Enable Layout View check box.

✦ Do you want a form to open automatically when the database opens? Set the Display Form setting to the form of your choice.

✦ Do you want a macro to run automatically when the database opens? After you customize a database using the Access Options dialog box, when you (or anyone) open this database, Access performs the startup actions you specify. Then Access runs the `AutoExec` macro, if any, which performs additional actions. (See Book VI, Chapter 2 for how to create an `AutoExec` macro.)

✦ Do you want to create any keyboard shortcuts? You can define them using an `AutoKeys` macro, which we describe in Book VI, Chapter 1.

Sometimes you need to bypass the settings in the Current Database section of the Access Options dialog box. No problem! Hold down the Shift key while the database opens.

Password-Protecting and Encrypting Your Database

Halt — who goes there? You can tell Access not to allow anyone to open your database until he or she enters the right password. This system is all-or-nothing, which is a problem. After you allow someone to open the database, he or she can do anything to the database unless you take additional security measures. When you add a password to your database, Access takes the additional precaution of encrypting the database, too.

The database may work a little more slowly, however, because Access has to encrypt and decrypt the information every time it reads or writes the database file.

Encrypting your database with a password

Follow these steps to encrypt your database with a password:

1. **Make a backup copy of the database and store it somewhere safe.**

This backup copy doesn't have a password. If you lose the password to the database, at least you have this backup. You may want to burn it to a CD and store the CD in something heavy that's locked.

2. **Close the database, and make sure no one else has the database open.**

You need sole access to the database to assign a password. In fact, you need exclusive access, in which everyone is locked out temporarily.

You're in Backstage View, with no database open, right?

3. **Click Open and select the name of the database in the Open dialog box.**

4. **Click the little arrow to the right of the Open button (instead of the Open button) and choose Open Exclusive from the menu that appears.**

    Access opens the database with exclusive access.

Encrypt with Password

5. **Click File on the Ribbon, click Info, and click the Encrypt with Password button.**

    You see the Set Database Password dialog box, shown in Figure 3-2.

Figure 3-2: Setting a password for a database.

6. **Type the database password once in each box and click OK.**

    If you don't type the password the same way in both boxes, Access complains, and you have to type them again. Encryption may take a few minutes. You may see a message if your database uses any features that are incompatible with encryption.

    Capitalization counts in passwords. A password can be up to 20 characters and include letters, numbers, and some punctuation.

Opening a password-protected database

After you set a password, whenever you (or anyone else) try to open the database, you see the Password Required dialog box.

If you forget your database password, you're hosed. No command, service, or secret incantation can get your password back.

What happens if another database (one with no password) links to your password-protected database? Answer: When you create a link to a password-protected database, Access asks you for the password. If you don't know it, you can't create the link. However, after you create the link, Access saves the password so you can see the linked table without entering a password. Therefore, you have an unguarded backdoor into your password-protected database (to the linked tables in your database, at least). Keep this in mind when you split databases into a front-end and a back-end. Password-protecting the back-end database does no good if the front-end databases that link to it aren't protected, too.

Book VII Chapter 3

Securing Your Access Database

Decrypting a database

Decrypt
Database

You can change your mind about encrypting a database. Click the File tab on the Ribbon, click Info, and click the Decrypt Database button.

Locking Up Your Database as an ACCDE File

If you make an Access database for other people — especially people who may be a teeny bit clueless about Access — you may want to lock your database to prevent other users from making changes that may break it. One option is to turn your database from an ACCDB file to an ACCDE file.

What's an ACCDE file, we hear you asking. An *ACCDE file* is the same as a regular Access ACCDB database file, with the following changes:

✦ All VBA procedures are *compiled* — converted from human-readable code (more or less readable, anyway) to a format that only the computer understands. This change prevents a database user from reading or changing your VBA code. (See Book VIII for how to write VBA procedures.)

✦ No one can create forms or reports or modify the existing ones (you can't even open them in Design or Layout view). You can't import any forms or reports, either.

Be sure to keep a copy of your original ACCDB file! If you need to make changes to your VBA code, forms, or reports (or create new ones), you need to use the ACCDB file, not the ACCDE file. ACCDE files are most commonly used for the front-end database when you split an application into two databases (front end and back end), as we describe in Chapter 2 of this minibook.

Creating an ACCDE file

Saving your ACCDB file as an ACCDE file is easy. Follow these steps:

1. **Make sure your database is in Access 2007/2010 file format by opening the database.**

   Look at the title bar of the Access window. If the title bar says anything but (Access 2007 file format), you need to convert it to the latest file format. (See Chapter 1 of this minibook.)

2. **Click the File tab on the Ribbon, click Share, click Save Database As, and click Make ACCDE.**

   Access closes the database to do the conversion. Then you see the Save As dialog box.

3. **Specify the folder and filename for the file and click the Save button.**

   Access creates the new ACCDE file while leaving the original ACCDB file untouched. Then the new ACCDE file opens.

If Access runs in to a problem while making the ACCDE file, a message appears with a Show Help button. Click the button to find out what's wrong.

Making updates later

Eventually, you're going to want to make a new report or fix an annoying typo in a form. You have to go back to your ACCDB file to make these kinds of changes because you can't make changes in an ACCDE file.

If the ACCDE file is a front-end file, with no data stored in it, you can just make your changes to the original ACCDB file and resave it as an ACCDE file. Because all your data lives in the back-end database, you're all set. (If you're wondering what we're talking about, see Chapter 2 of this minibook.)

However, if your ACCDE file contains tables full of valuable information, you can't just abandon it. If you use the ACCDE file for data entry and editing, that file contains your up-to-date tables. The original ACCDB file has editable forms, reports, and VBA code, but doesn't have the latest version of the data stored in your tables.

Not a problem. Follow these steps:

1. **Rename your ACCDE file as a backup file.**

   For example, add today's date to the end of the filename (right before the .accde part). You're about to create a new ACCDE file, but you don't want to lose the data in this file.

2. **Open the original ACCDB file and make any changes to the forms, reports, and VBA code that you want.**

   If you plan to make drastic changes, make a backup copy of the ACCDB file first.

3. **Save this database as an ACCDE file with the name that your ACCDE file originally had. Click the File tab on the Ribbon, click Share, click Save Database As, and click Make ACCDE.**

   Now you have an updated ACCDE file with new, improved forms, reports, and VBA procedures with old data. You also have an updated ACCDB file with your new, improved forms, reports, and VBA code with out-of-date tables.

4. **Delete all the tables from this new ACCDE file.**

   Deleting tables sounds dangerous, but remember you have all these tables stored safely in your old ACCDE file.

5. **Import the tables from the old ACCDE file to the new one.**

   Click Access on the Import & Link group on the External Data tab of the Ribbon and choose the name you gave your old ACCDE file in Step 1.

You see the Import Objects dialog box with tabs for Tables, Queries, Forms, Reports, and other objects.

6. **Click the Select All button with the Tables tab selected and then click OK.**

Access imports your tables from the original ACCDE to the new ACCDE file, replacing the older data in the tables.

7. **Import any queries or macros in the old ACCDE database that you created or changed.**

Repeat Steps 5 and 6, but use the Queries and Macros tabs on the Import Objects dialog box to import whatever changed.

If you're going to do this often, consider splitting your table into a front end and a back end, as described in Chapter 2 of this minibook. With a split database, you don't have to re-import your updated tables; you can just leave them in the unchanged back-end database.

Using the Trust Center

Access 2010 moved many of its security settings to one dialog box — the Trust Center. One new feature is that Access wants to know whether you *trust* the database because you trust the folder where it's stored, you trust the publisher who created and signed the database, or you just trust this specific database. If you trust a database, then you can use the macros and VBA modules in the database. Book VI, Chapter 1 describes the settings that determine how to tell Access that you trust a database.

The Trust Center has a few other settings that affect the security of the database and your computer. To see the Trust Center dialog box, click the File tab on the Ribbon, click Options to see the Access Options dialog box, click Trust Center in the left pane, and then click the Trust Center Settings button. Figure 3-3 shows one page of the Trust Center dialog box. Here are some settings to consider:

✦ **Add-Ins:** Add-in programs could be malicious, so you might want to select the Require Application Add-Ins to be Signed by Trusted Publisher check box on the Add-Ins page of the Trust Center.

✦ **ActiveX Settings:** ActiveX controls are tiny programs that can be included in Web pages and various Office applications. They can carry viruses, so you should be aware when an ActiveX control is installed on your computer. The default setting on the ActiveX page of the Trust Center is a prudent one: Prompt Me before Enabling All Controls with Minimal Restrictions.

✦ **Macro Settings:** Macros (described in Book VI) are programs that you can write to automate objects in your Access database. We like to leave the Macro Settings option set to the default, Disable All Macros with Notification.

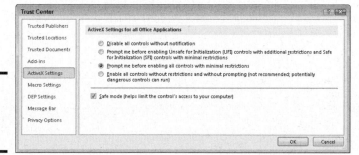

Figure 3-3:
The Trust Center dialog box.

Book VII
Chapter 3

Securing Your
Access Database

Book VIII

Programming in VBA

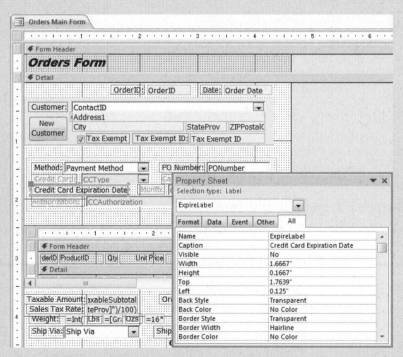

Controls on a form in Design view

Contents at a Glance

Chapter 1: What the Heck Is VBA?

In This Chapter

✔ **Understanding Visual Basic for Applications (VBA)**

✔ **Using the Visual Basic Editor**

✔ **Discovering code as you go**

*V*isual Basic for Applications — often abbreviated *VBA* — is a programming language that you can use to extend the functionality of Microsoft Access and other products in the Microsoft Office suite of programs. A *programming language* is a means of writing instructions for the computer to *execute* (perform). Programmers often refer to the written instructions as *code* because the instructions aren't in plain English. Rather, they're in a code that the computer can interpret and execute.

You can create sophisticated Access databases without using VBA at all. In most cases, the other objects offered by Access — tables, queries, forms, reports, and macros — offer more than enough flexibility and power to create just about any database imaginable. But once in a while, you come across a situation where you want to do something that none of those other objects can do. That's where VBA comes in. If you can find no other way to accomplish some goal in Access, writing VBA code is usually the solution.

Finding VBA Code

So what the heck is VBA code, anyway? To the untrained eye, VBA code looks like gibberish — perhaps some secret code written by aliens from another planet. But to Access, the code represents very specific instructions on how to perform some task.

Within any given database, Access stores code in two places:

✦ **Class modules (code-behind forms):** Every form and report you create automatically contains a *class module* (also called a *code-behind form*), as illustrated in Figure 1-1. The class module for a given form or report is empty unless you place controls that require VBA code on that form or report.

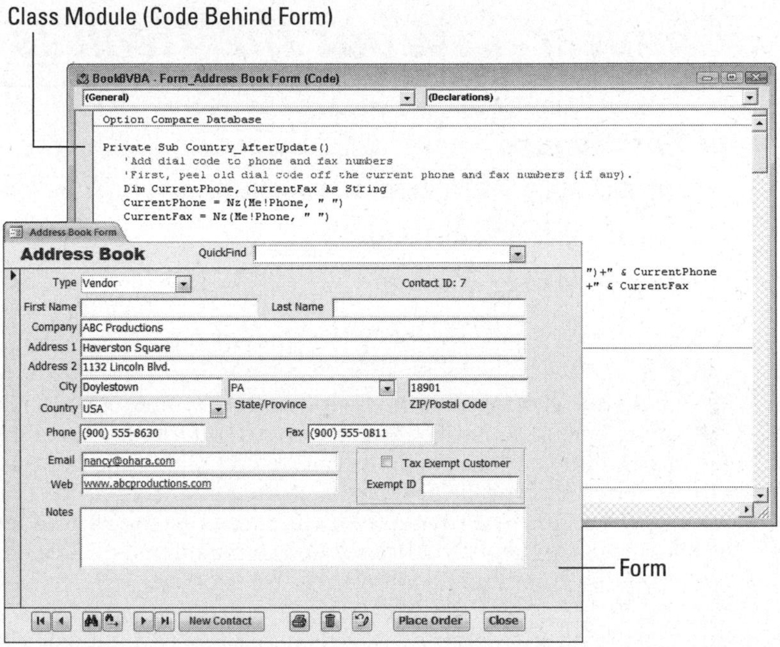

Class Module (Code Behind Form)

BookIVBA - Form_Address Book Form (Code)

(General) · (Declarations)

```
Option Compare Database

Private Sub Country_AfterUpdate()
    'Add dial code to phone and fax numbers
    'First, peel old dial code off the current phone and fax numbers (if any).
    Dim CurrentPhone, CurrentFax As String
    CurrentPhone = Nz(Me!Phone, " ")
    CurrentFax = Nz(Me!Phone, " ")
```

")+" & CurrentPhone
+" & CurrentFax

Address Book Form

Address Book   QuickFind [

| Type | Vendor | | Contact ID: 7 |

First Name [   ] Last Name [

Company [ABC Productions]

Address 1 [Haverston Square]

Address 2 [1132 Lincoln Blvd.]

City [Doylestown] [PA] [18901]

Country [USA] State/Province ZIP/Postal Code

Phone [(900) 555-8630] Fax [(900) 555-0811]

Email [nancy@ohara.com] [ ] Tax Exempt Customer

Web [www.abcproductions.com] Exempt ID [

Notes [

———— Form

[◄◄] [◄] [▲▲] [►] [►►] [New Contact] [🖨] [🗑] [↻] [Place Order] [Close]

Figure 1-1:
Every form
and report
has a class
module
behind it.

✦ **Standard modules:** Code can also be stored in *standard modules*. Code in standard modules is accessible to all objects in your database, not just a single form or report.

Opening a class module

If you want to view or change the code for a form or report's class module, first open, in Design view, the form or report to which the module is attached. Then click the (Form Design Tools) Design tab, and then click the View Code button in the Tools group, shown near the mouse pointer in Figure 1-2.

Figure 1-2:
The View
Code button.

Add Existing Property Tab
Fields   Sheet Order
Tools

View Code

You can also get to a class module from the Event tab of the Property sheet in the Design View window. The Property sheet allows you to zoom right in on the VBA code that's associated with a given control. For example, some controls contain code created by wizards. When you click such a control and then click the Events tab in the Property sheet, the property value chose

[Event Procedure]. When you click [Event Procedure], you see a button with three dots, like the one near the mouse pointer in Figure 1-3. That's the Build button. Click it to see the code that executes in response to the selected event.

Figure 1-3:
Look for the code that executes in response to the event.

To write custom code for a control, select the control in Design view, open the Property sheet, click the Event tab, click the event to which you want to attach some custom code, click the Build button, and then choose Code Builder.

After you open a module, you're taken to an entirely separate program window called the *Visual Basic Editor* (VBE), where you see the module in all its glory.

Creating or opening a standard module

Standard modules contain VBA code that isn't associated with a specific form or report. The code in a standard module is available to all tables, queries, forms, reports, macros, and other modules in your database. You won't see Module as an option when you're viewing All Access Objects in the Navigation pane until you create at least one standard module. You have to go looking for options to create and work with modules.

To create a new module, click the Create tab. Then click the Module command in the Macros & Code group (see Figure 1-4). The Visual Basic Editor opens.

To show a list of modules in the Navigation pane, click the drop-down button in the top of the Navigation pane and choose Modules, as in Figure 1-5. If you already created and saved a standard module, you can open it by double-clicking its name. If the current database contains no standard Modules, you won't even see Modules as a category.

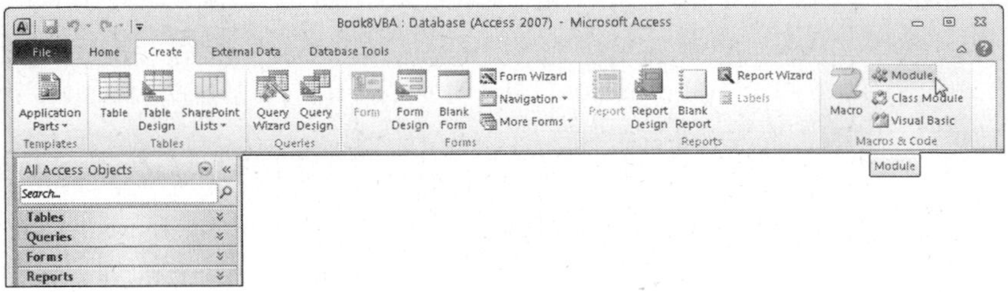

Figure 1-4:
Create
a new
module.

Figure 1-5:
Open a
pane to see
standard
modules.

Regardless of whether you create or open a module, you end up in the Visual Basic Editor. The editor is a completely separate program with its own Windows taskbar button. The editor retains the old-style Windows look and feel with menus instead of the Ribbon. We cover that in more detail in a moment. For now, keep in mind that you can close the Visual Basic Editor and return to Access at any time. Just click the Close (X) button in the editor window upper-right corner.

Enabling VBA Code

Like any programming language, people can use VBA to create code that does good things or code that does bad things. Whenever you open a database that contains code, Access displays a warning in the Security bar. The warning doesn't mean that there's "bad code" in the database; it just means that there *is* code in the database. Access has no way of determining whether the code is beneficial or malicious. That's a judgment call only a human can make.

If you trust the source of that code, you have to click the Enable Content button to make the code executable. Otherwise, the code is disabled, as are many features of the Visual Basic Editor.

How code is organized

All modules organize their code into a Declaration section at the top, followed by individual procedures, as shown in Figure 1-6. The Declaration section contains options, written in code format, that apply to all procedures in the module. Each procedure is also a chunk of VBA code that, when executed, performs a specific set of steps.

Sub procedure

Declarations

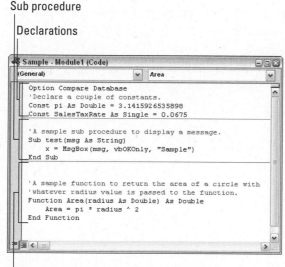

```
Sample - Module1 (Code)
(General)                               Area

    Option Compare Database
    'Declare a couple of constants.
    Const pi As Double = 3.1415926535898
    Const SalesTaxRate As Single = 0.0675

    'A sample sub procedure to display a message.
    Sub test(msg As String)
        x = MsgBox(msg, vbOKOnly, "Sample")
    End Sub


    'A sample function to return the area of a circle with
    'whatever radius value is passed to the function.
    Function Area(radius As Double) As Double
        Area = pi * radius ^ 2
    End Function
```

Figure 1-6:
Modules consist of declarations and procedures.

Function procedure

Procedures in a module fall into two major categories: sub procedures and function procedures. Both types of procedures use VBA code to perform some task. The next sections outline some subtle differences in how and where they're used.

Sub procedures

A *sub procedure* is one or more lines of code that make Access perform a particular task. Every sub procedure starts with the word `Sub`, `Private Sub`, or `Public Sub` and ends with `End Sub`, using one of the following general structures:

```
Sub name()
    ...code...
End Sub

Private Sub name()
    ...code...
End Sub
```

**Book VIII
Chapter 1**

What the Heck Is VBA?

```
Public Sub name()
    ...code...
End Sub
```

name is the name of the procedure, and ...*code*... is any amount of VBA code.

Text that appears to be written in plain English within a module represents *programmer comments* — notes for other programmers. The computer ignores the comments. Every comment starts with an apostrophe (').

Function procedures

A *function procedure* is enclosed in Function...End Function statements, as the following code shows:

```
Function name()
    <...code...>
End Function

Public Function name()
    <...code...>
End Function

Private Function name()
    <...code...>
End Function
```

Unlike a sub procedure, which simply performs some task, a function procedure performs a task and returns a value. In fact, an Access function procedure is no different from any of the built-in functions you use in Access expressions. And you can use a custom function procedure wherever you can use a built-in procedure.

A Public procedure is available to all modules in Access. A Private procedure is only available to other procedures in the same module.

Using the Visual Basic Editor

Regardless of how you open a module, you end up in the Visual Basic Editor. The Visual Basic Editor is where you write, edit, and test your VBA code. The Visual Basic Editor is entirely separate from the Access program window. If you click outside the Visual Basic Editor window, the window may disappear because whatever window you clicked comes to the front.

The Visual Basic Editor retains the view that it had in previous versions of Access. There is no Ribbon or Navigation pane. In fact, the Visual Basic Editor is similar to Microsoft *Visual Studio,* the Integrated Development Environment (IDE) used for all kinds of programming with Microsoft products.

Like all program windows, the Visual Basic Editor has its own Windows taskbar button, as shown in the top half of Figure 1-7. If the taskbar is particularly crowded with buttons, the editor and Access may share a taskbar button, as in the bottom half of Figure 1-7. If you suddenly lose the VBA Editor window, click its taskbar button to bring the window back to the top of the stack of program windows on your desktop.

Figure 1-7:
Taskbar
buttons for
Access and
the Visual
Basic Editor.

In most versions of Windows, you can right-click the Windows taskbar and choose the Tile Windows Vertically option from the shortcut menu to make all open program windows visible on-screen without overlap.

The Visual Basic Editor provides many tools designed to help you write code. Most of the tools are optional and can be toggled via the View menu in the Visual Basic Editor menu. The windows are shown in Figure 1-8. We provide more information on each of the optional windows when they become relevant to the type of code we're demonstrating. For now, knowing how to make them appear and disappear is sufficient.

Talkin' the talk

Programmers have their own slang terms to describe what they do. For example, the term *code,* which refers to the actual instructions written in a programming language, is always singular, like the terms *hardware* and *software.* You don't add *hardwares* and *softwares* to your computer system. You add hardware and software. Likewise, you never write, or cut and paste *codes.* You write, or cut and paste, code.

The term GUI (*goo-*ey) refers to *graphical user interface.* Anything you can accomplish by using a mouse (that is, without writing code) is considered part of the GUI. You create tables, queries, forms, reports, and macros with the GUI. You only need to write code in modules.

A database may be referred to as an *app,* short for *application.* If a programmer says, "I created most of the app with the GUI; I hardly wrote any code at all," he means he spent most of his time creating tables, queries, forms, reports, and macros — using the mouse — and relatively little time typing code in VBA.

Project Explorer   Locals window

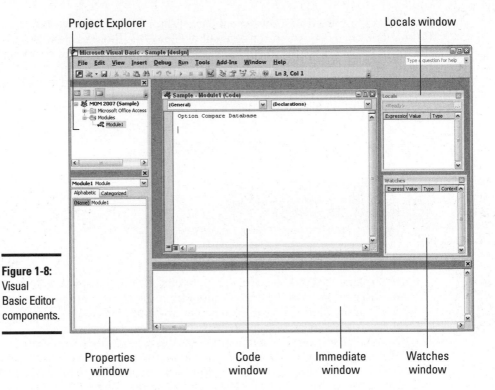

Figure 1-8:
Visual
Basic Editor
components.

Properties   Code   Immediate   Watches
window   window   window   window

You can move and size most of the windows in the Visual Basic Editor by using standard methods. For instance, you can move most windows by dragging their title bars. You size windows by dragging any corner or edge. Most of the time, you won't need to have all those optional windows open to write code. Feel free to close any optional window open in your editor by clicking its Close (X) button. To open a window, choose View from the menu, and click the name of the window you want to open.

If you have multiple monitors connected to your computer, you can put the Access window on one monitor and the Visual Basic Editor window on the other.

Using the Code window

The Code window is where you type your VBA code. Similar to a word processor or text editor, the Code window supports all the standard Windows text-editing techniques. You can type text and use the Backspace and Delete keys on your keyboard to delete text. You can use the Tab key to indent text. You can select text by dragging the mouse pointer through it. You can copy and paste text to, and from, the Code window. In short, the Code window is a text editor.

The Code window acts like the document window in most other programs. Click its Maximize button, shown near the mouse pointer at the top of Figure 1-9, to enlarge it. To restore it to its previous size, click the Restore Window button, shown at the bottom of that same figure.

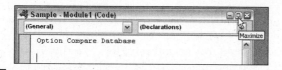

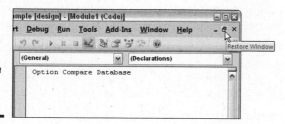

Figure 1-9:
Code Windows Maximize and Restore Window buttons.

Tools in the Code window are pointed out in Figure 1-10 and summarized in the following list:

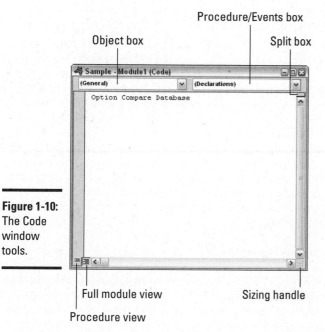

Figure 1-10:
The Code window tools.

✦ **Object box:** When you're viewing a class module, this box shows the name of the object associated with the current code and allows you to choose a different object. In a standard module, only the word `General` appears because a standard module isn't associated with any specific form or report.

✦ **Procedure/Events box:** When you're viewing a class module, this box lists events supported by the object whose name appears in the Object box. When viewing a standard module, the Procedure/Events box lists the names of all procedures in that module. To jump to a procedure or event, just choose its name from the drop-down list.

✦ **Split bar:** This divvies up the screen for you. Drag the Split bar down to separate the Code window into two independently scrollable panes. Drag the Split bar back to the top of the scroll bar to unsplit the window.

✦ **Procedure view:** When clicked, the window displays only one procedure (or the declarations section) at a time. This is useful when scrolling through a long procedure and you don't want to scroll past the end.

✦ **Full Module view:** When clicked, the window lets you scroll through all of the declarations and procedures in the module. This is useful when browsing through a module.

✦ **Sizing handle:** Drag it to size the window. (You can drag any corner or edge as well.)

Using the Immediate window

The *Immediate window,* or *debug window,* in the Visual Basic Editor allows you to run code at any time, right on the spot. Use the Immediate window for testing and debugging (removing errors from) code. If the Immediate window isn't open in the Visual Basic Editor, you can bring it out of hiding at any time by choosing View⇨Immediate Window from the editor's menu.

When the Immediate window is open, you can anchor it to the bottom of the Visual Basic Editor just by dragging its title bar to the bottom of the window. Optionally, you can make the Immediate window free-floating by dragging its title bar up and away from the bottom of the Visual Basic Editor program window. You can also dock and undock the Immediate window by right-clicking within the Immediate window and choosing the Dockable option from the shortcut menu that appears.

The Immediate window allows you to test expressions, run VBA procedures you create, and more. To test an expression, you can use the `debug.print` command, or the abbreviated `?` version, followed by a blank space and the expression. Which command you use doesn't matter, although obviously, typing the question mark is easier. You may think of the `?` character in the Immediate window as standing for *"What is . . . ?"* Typing `? 1+1` into the Immediate window and pressing Enter is like asking, "What is one plus one?"

The Immediate window returns the answer to your question, 2, as shown in Figure 1-11.

Figure 1-11:
The free-
floating
Immediate
window
solves 1 + 1
calculation.

If you see a message about macro content being blocked, switch over to the Access program window and click the Enable Content button on the Security bar.

If you want to re-execute a line that you already typed into the Immediate window, you don't need to type that same line again. Instead, just move the cursor to the end of the line that you want to re-execute and press Enter. To erase text from the Immediate window, drag the mouse pointer through whatever text you want to erase. Then press the Delete (Del) key; or, right-click the selected text and choose the Cut option from the shortcut menu.

You see many examples of using the Immediate window in the forthcoming chapters of this book. For the purposes of this chapter, knowing the Immediate window exists and basically how it works is enough.

Do bear in mind that the Immediate window is just for testing and debugging. The Code window is where you type (or paste in) VBA code.

Using the Object Browser

VBA code can manipulate Access objects programmatically. Remember, everything in Access is an object — tables, forms, reports, and even a single control on a form or report are objects. Every Access object you see on-screen in Access is managed either interactively or programmatically. When you work with objects in the Access program window, using your mouse and keyboard, you use Access interactively. You do something with your mouse and keyboard, and the object responds accordingly.

When you write code, you write instructions that tell Access to manipulate an object *programmatically,* without user intervention. You write instructions to automate some task that you may otherwise do interactively with mouse and keyboard. To manipulate an object programmatically, you write code that refers to the object by name.

All the objects that make up Access and the current database are organized into an *object model,* which comprises one or more object libraries. An *object library* is an actual file on your hard drive that provides the names of objects that VBA refers to and manipulates.

Each object consists of *classes,* where each class is a single programmable object. Each class has *members,* and some members are *properties.* Properties are characteristics of the class, such as its name, or the number of items it contains. Other members are *methods,* which expose things you can do to the class programmatically.

The object model is huge and contains many libraries and classes. There's no way to memorize everything in the object model. It's just too darn big. The Visual Basic Editor provides an Object Browser that acts as a central resource for finding things as well as getting help with things in the model. It's especially useful for deciphering other peoples' code, like the examples you'll see in this book.

To view the objects that VBA can access, follow these steps to open the Object Browser:

1. **Make sure that you're in the Visual Basic Editor.**

2. **Click the Object Browser button in the toolbar, choose View⇨Object Browser from the menu, or press F2.**

The Object Browser opens. Figure 1-12 shows the Object Browser and points out some of the major features of its window. The following list describes each component:

✦ **Project/Library list:** This allows you to choose a single library or project to work with, or <All Libraries>.

✦ **Search tools:** Use these tools to help you find information in the libraries.

✦ **Classes list:** This shows the names of all classes in the currently selected library or project name (or all libraries).

✦ **Members list:** When you click a name in the Classes list, this pane shows the members (properties, methods, events, functions, objects) that belong to that class.

✦ **Details pane:** When you click a member name in the Members list, the Details pane shows the syntax for using the name as well as the name of the library to which the member belongs. You can copy text from the Details pane to the Code window.

✦ **Split bar:** Drag the Split bar left or right to adjust the size of the panes. (Drag any edge or corner of the Object Browser window to size the window as a whole.)

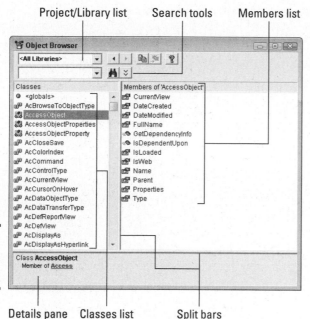

Project/Library list   Search tools   Members list

Figure 1-12:
The Object
Browser.

Details pane   Classes list   Split bars

Searching the Object Library

For a beginning programmer, the sheer quantity of items in the Object
Browser is daunting. However, learning about the pre-written code you pick
up elsewhere is useful. Suppose you find and use a procedure that has a
DoCmd object in it. You're wondering what this DoCmd thingy is.

You can search the Object Library for information about any object, including DoCmd, by following these steps:

1. **In the Object Browser, type the word you're searching for in the
Search box.**

In this example, type **DoCmd**, as shown in Figure 1-13.

2. **Click the Search button.**

The search results appear in the Search Results pane.

3. **Click the word you searched for.**

4. **Click the Help (question mark) button on the Object Browser toolbar.**

Search button   Show/Hide search results

Search box   Help   Search results

Figure 1-13:
Object
Browser
search
tools.

Figure 1-14 shows the Help window for the DoCmd object. For the absolute beginner, even the information in the Help text may be a bit advanced. However, as you gain experience and dig a little deeper into VBA, you'll find the Object Browser and Help windows useful for constructing references to objects, properties, and methods from within your code.

Referring to objects and collections

Objects in the object model all have a syntax that works like this: You start with the largest, most encompassing object, and work your way down to the most specific object, property, or method. Sort of like a path to a filename, as in C:\My Documents\MyFile.doc, where you start with the largest container (disk drive C:), down to the next container (the folder named My Documents), and then to the specific file (MyFile.doc).

For example, the Application object refers to the entire Access program. It includes a CurrentProject object. If you were to look up the CurrentProject object in the Object Browser and view its Help window, you see that CurrentProject houses several collections, including one named AllForms. The AllForms collection contains the name of every form in the current database.

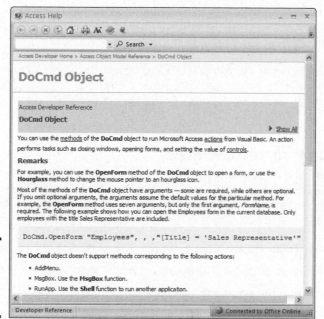

Figure 1-14:
Help for the
DoCmd
object.

The `AllForms` collection, in turn, supports a `Count` property. That property returns the number of forms in the collection. Say that you have a database open and that database contains some forms. If you go to the Immediate window and type

```
? Application.CurrentProject.AllForms.Count
```

and then press Enter, the Immediate window displays a number matching the total number of forms in the database.

At the risk of confusing matters, typing the following line in the Immediate window returns the same result:

```
? CurrentProject.AllForms.Count
```

The shortened version works because the `Application` option is the default parent object used if you don't specify a parent object before `CurrentProject`. (The `Application` object is the parent of `CurrentProject` because `CurrentProject` is a member of the `Application` object library.)

The bottom line is that when you see a bunch of words separated by dots in code (such as `CurrentProject.AllForms.Count`), be aware that those words refer to some object. In a sense, the words are a path to the object — going from the largest object down to a single, specific object, property, method, or event. You can use the Object Browser as a means of looking up the meanings of the words to gain an understanding of how the pre-written code works.

As you gain experience, you can use the Object Browser to look up information about objects, collections, properties, methods, events, and constants within your code. For now, consider the Object Browser as a tool for discovering VBA as you go.

Choosing object libraries

Most likely, the object libraries that appear automatically in the Object Browser's Project/Library drop-down list are all you need. However, should a given project require you to add some other object library, follow these steps to add it:

1. **Choose Tools⇨References from the Visual Basic Editor main menu.**

The References dialog box opens.

2. **Choose any library name from the list.**

In the unlikely event that you need a library that isn't in the list — but you know you stored it on your hard drive — click the Browse button, navigate to the folder that contains the object library you need, click its name, and then click the Open button.

3. **Click OK when the object libraries you need have check marks.**

The Project/Library list in the Object Browser now includes all the libraries you selected in the References dialog box.

Closing the Visual Basic Editor

When you're done working in the Visual Basic Editor, you can close it by using whichever of the following techniques is most convenient for you:

✦ Choose File⇨Close and return to Microsoft Access from the Visual Basic Editor main menu.

✦ Click the Close button in the upper-right corner of the Visual Basic Editor program window.

✦ Right-click the Visual Basic Editor button on the taskbar, and then choose the Close option from the shortcut menu.

✦ Press Alt+Q.

Access continues to run even after you close the Visual Basic Editor window.

Discovering Code as You Go

Most beginning programmers start by working with code they pick up else-where, such as code generated by code wizards, or code copied from a Web site. You can also create VBA code, without writing it, by converting any macro to VBA code.

Converting macros to VBA code

Any macro that you create in Access can be converted to VBA code. Converting macros to code is easier than writing code from scratch. For example, say you need to write some code because a macro can't do the job. But, say that a macro can do 90 percent of the job. If you create the macro and convert it to VBA code, 90 percent of your code is already written. You just have to add the other 10 percent (which is especially helpful if you can't type worth beans).

See Book VI, Chapter 1 for how macros work and how to create them.

As an example, suppose you click the Create tab, and then click Macro in the Macros & Code group, as in Figure 1-15, to create a new macro.

Figure 1-15:
Create a
new macro.

Then you create your macro. The macro can be as large or as small as you want. Figure 1-16 shows a small simple example of a macro that shows a message on-screen. After you create your macro, close and save it. For this example, say we saved the macro in Figure 1-16 with the name `TinyMacro`.

Figure 1-16:
Sample
`TinyMacro`
macro.

When you convert a macro to VBA code, you actually convert all the macros in the macro group to code. Follow these steps for the basic procedure of converting macros to VBA:

1. **Open the Macro in Design view.**

2. **Click the (Macro Tools) Design tab, and then click the Convert Macros to Visual Basic button in the Tools group, as shown in Figure 1-17.**

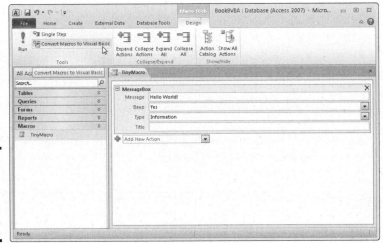

Figure 1-17: Convert Macros to Visual Basic button.

A dialog box appears, asking whether you want to include error-handling code or comments in the code. If you want to keep the code relatively simple, you can clear the first option and select only the second option.

3. **Click the Convert button and then click OK when your conversion is complete.**

To see the name of the converted macro, expand the Modules category, as shown in Figure 1-18. The name of the module is `Converted Macro -` followed by the name of the macro you converted.

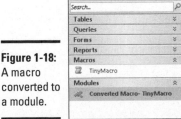

Figure 1-18: A macro converted to a module.

To see the converted macro as VBA code, double-click its name. Like all VBA code, the code from the converted macro opens in the Visual Basic Editor Code window, as shown in Figure 1-19.

```
Book8VBA - Converted Macro- TinyMacro (Code)

(General)                              TinyMacro

Option Compare Database
Option Explicit

'------------------------------------------------------------
' TinyMacro
'
'------------------------------------------------------------
Function TinyMacro()
On Error GoTo TinyMacro_Err

    Beep
    MsgBox "Hello World!", vbInformation, ""


TinyMacro_Exit:
    Exit Function

TinyMacro_Err:
    MsgBox Error$
    Resume TinyMacro_Exit

End Function
```

Figure 1-19:
Converted macro in the Code window.

Copying and pasting code

Many VBA programmers post examples of code they've written on Web pages. When you come across some sample code you want to incorporate into your own database, retyping it all into the Visual Basic Editor isn't necessary. Instead, just use standard Windows copy-and-paste techniques to copy the code from the Web page into the Visual Basic Editor.

Say you come across some code in a Web page that you want to use in your own database. Here's the sequence:

1. **In the Web page, drag the mouse pointer through the code you want to copy to select that code. Then press Ctrl+C to copy that selected code to the Windows Clipboard.**

2. **Back in Access, create a new module or open an existing module in which you want to place the code.**

3. **In the Code window, click where you want to put the copied code. Then paste the code to the cursor position by pressing Ctrl+V.**

Bear in mind, however, that just pasting code into the Code window doesn't make the code do anything. Most code examples are based on a sample database. Just dropping the example into your database may not be enough to get it to work.

**Book VIII
Chapter 1**

What the Heck Is VBA?

When you copy and paste from a Web page, you might get some HTML tags, weird characters, weird spacing, and so forth. If that happens, you can copy the code from the page and paste it into a simple text editor like Notepad first. That should get rid of any unusual tags and characters. Then copy and paste the text from the Notepad document into the Visual Basic Editor's Code window.

But even if you do find an example that's generic enough to work in any database, the code won't actually do anything until some event in your database triggers it into action. We look at the many ways you can trigger code into action in the next chapter.

Chapter 2: Writing Code

In This Chapter

✔ Understanding VBA syntax

✔ Writing your own custom VBA procedures

✔ Running and testing your custom procedures

Writing VBA code is different from writing in English or some other human language. When you write in English, you're presumably writing to another human being who speaks the same language. If your English isn't so great (bad spelling, poor grammar), your recipient can probably still figure out what your message means. Humans have flexible brains that can figure things out based on context.

Not so for computers. Computers don't have brains and can't figure out anything based on context. When you write code, the computer does exactly what the code tells it to do. If the computer can't read and process a statement, the procedure stops running, and an error message appears on-screen.

Before you start writing your own custom code, you need to know about syntax and also the resources available for finding the syntax for the tasks you want to program. And you need to know at least some basic techniques for testing your code to see whether it's going to work — before you try putting it to use.

How VBA Works

VBA code is organized into procedures. Each procedure contains any number of lines of code called *statements*. Each statement instructs VBA to perform some action. The procedure sits in its module, doing nothing, until some event calls the procedure.

When a procedure is called, each statement *executes* (runs) one at a time. VBA fully executes the first statement, then fully executes the second statement, and so forth, until the `End Sub` or `End Function` statement, which marks the end of the procedure. At that point, the code stops executing. Figure 2-1 summarizes how procedures work.

```
Function IsOpen(strFormName As String) As Boolean

    'Declare an Access Object named myObject.
    Dim myObject As AccessObject
    'Set myObject to passed form name.
    Set myObject = CurrentProject.AllForms(strFormName)

    'If myObject is open (loaded)...
    If myObject.IsLoaded Then
        '...and is not in Design View (acCurViewDesign)...
        If myObject.CurrentView <> acCurViewDesign Then
            '...then return True.
            IsOpen = True
        End If
    End If
'If IsOpen isn't assigned a value in this procedure,
'IsOpen() automatically returns False.
End Function
```

Figure 2-1:
Code execution from top to bottom.

The top-to-bottom flow of execution can be altered using loops and decision-making code, as we describe in Chapter 3 of this minibook.

VBA Syntax

Each statement within a procedure must follow strict rules of syntax. You can't just write text that looks like VBA code. All languages, including English and VBA, have rules of syntax. Rules of *syntax* define the order in which words must be placed so a statement makes sense. For example, the following sentence — which is English, by the way, and not VBA — doesn't make sense because grammar rules are broken (similar to the way they're mangled in some of those e-mails we get):

    moon the yapped sullen dog at irritating the.

If we rearrange the letters and words of that sentence so they follow the correct rules of syntax for the English language, the sentence makes sense:

    The irritating dog yapped at the sullen moon.

The rules of VBA syntax are more rigid than the rules of human language. Even the slightest misspelling or missing punctuation mark causes a statement to fail.

Most statements start with a *keyword,* which is a word that has a specific meaning in VBA. As soon as you type a complete keyword you typically see a brief Quick Info *syntax chart* for the keyword. Figure 2-2 shows an example. If you don't see the syntax chart, you can right-click the keywords and choose Quick Info.

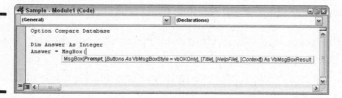

Figure 2-2:
A Quick
Info syntax
chart.

The Quick Info syntax chart doesn't give you any details. Instead, it just guides you through typing the entire statement according to the syntax rules. For detailed information on each item in the syntax chart, you have to look in Help. Here are several ways to get to the help for a keyword:

✦ Type the keyword in the Type a Question for Help box (upper-right corner of the VBA editor) and then press Enter.

✦ Select the keyword in the Code window and press Help (F1).

✦ Search the Object Browser for the keyword and use its Help, as described in the previous chapter.

When you get to the help page, you see a description of what the keyword performs. You also see a syntax chart similar to the one in Quick Info, but you get a lot more information, too. You see the meaning of each part, acceptable values of each part, one or more examples, and perhaps links to related help pages. Figure 2-3 shows a small portion of the Help screen for the MsgBox keyword. Use the scroll bar at the right side of the window to scroll through it all.

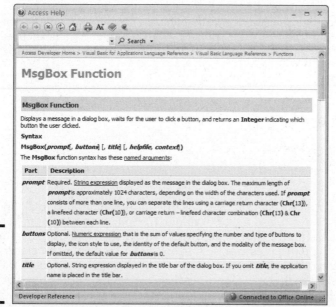

Figure 2-3:
Help for the
MsgBox
keyword.

The most important things to know about the syntax charts are quick to list:

✦ In the Quick Info syntax chart, boldface indicates the part you're about to type.

✦ Items in square brackets are optional and can be omitted from the statement you're typing.

✦ Never type the square brackets into your statement.

✦ If you skip over an optional part, you must still type the comma.

Arguing with VBA

Each part that follows the keyword is generally referred to as an *argument*. Most arguments are actually expressions, similar to expressions used in calculated controls. A string expression can be a literal string enclosed in quotation marks (such as `"Smith"` or `"Jones"`), or the name of a field — or, for that matter, the name of a variable (as described in the next chapter of this book) that contains a string, such as `[LastName]` (which refers to a field in a table).

A numeric expression can be anything that results in a valid number. For example, 10 is a valid numeric expression, as is 2*5 (two times five), as is the name of a field or variable that contains a number.

Given all this information, take a look at some `MsgBox` statements that follow the rules of syntax and are considered valid:

```
MsgBox("Slow, children at play")
```

The preceding statement is valid because the one-and-only required named argument — the `Prompt` argument — is included. When executed, the `MsgBox()` statement displays that prompt as shown in Figure 2-4.

Figure 2-4:
Result of
`MsgBox`
statement.

As you scroll through the Help for the `MsgBox` function, you'll find that there are many ways to use it. For example, the following statement is perfectly valid syntax for the `MsgBox` keyword, where `vbYesNo` is the setting that tells the box to display Yes and No buttons — and replaces the placeholder text buttons in the `MsgBox` syntax chart — and `"Question"` is literal text that appears in the title bar of the message box (and replaces the placeholder text title in the same chart).

```
x = MsgBox ("Are we having fun yet?", vbYesNo, "Question")
```

That variation displays the message shown in Figure 2-5 and stores the user's answer to the question in a variable named x. (We talk about variables in the next chapter.)

Figure 2-5:
Result of
`MsgBox`
function
with three
arguments.

You can combine two or more options for the `Buttons` argument by using a plus sign. For example, the preceding `MsgBox` statement uses the vbYesNo and vbQuestion constants to specify that the box show a question mark icon as well as the Yes/No buttons:

```
x = MsgBox ("Are we having fun yet?", vbYesNo + vbQuestion,
    "Question")
```

When executed, the preceding statement shows the box in Figure 2-6. Unlike the previous example, this new box shows a question mark icon because of the + vbQuestion added to the second argument.

Figure 2-6:
`MsgBox`
with a
question
mark icon.

Although you have some flexibility in how you express values for arguments, you have almost no flexibility in terms of the order in which you place the arguments within a statement. For example, if you want to use just the first and third arguments in a syntax chart, such as the Prompt and Title arguments of the MsgBox function, you still need to include a comma for the second argument to make clear that the last argument is the title, as in the following example:

```
x = MsgBox("Howdy", , "I am the Title")
```

The first comma after the `"Howdy"` prompt shows the start of the second argument. No argument shows between the two commas because you're not using that argument. The second comma then shows that the next argument is actually the third one, `Title` (hence the text, `"I am the Title"` appears in the title bar of the message box). Because there is no value for the `Buttons` argument, the box shows only the default OK button.

Module level versus procedure level

As you work with the VBA Help windows and syntax charts, you often come across the terms *module level* and *procedure level*. These terms refer to the location of code within the module. Simply stated, anything that's defined near the top of the module above the first `Function` or `Sub` procedure is a module-level declaration. Anything defined within a procedure is said to be defined at the procedure level, as illustrated in Figure 2-7.

Module level

```
Option Compare Database
Const pi As Double = 3.1415926535898
Const SalesTaxRate As Single = 0.0675

Sub Test()
        Dim x As Integer
        x = MsgBox("Are we having fun yet?", vbYesNo)
End Sub

Function Area(radius As Double) As Double
        Area = pi * radius
End Function
```

Procedure level

Figure 2-7: Module level and procedure level.

All procedures that you add to a module should be placed below the declarations section of the module. When you see one or more `Option` statements at the top of a module, make sure that any procedures you add to the module start below all the `Option` statements at the top of the module.

Declaring Module Options

When you create a new standard module, it has just one declaration at the top. Typically it reads `Option Compare Database`, which doesn't even seem to make any sense. And frankly, changing or deleting that is extremely unlikely. However, the declaration actually has meaning.

The word `Option` tells the VBA to set an option. The specific option to set is the `Compare` option. The `Compare` option tells VBA what rules to use when comparing values. The word `Database` means to use the same rules that the rest of the database uses when comparing values. Using the same rules is always a good idea because otherwise things could get very confusing. However, the other two possible settings are the `Binary` and `Text` options:

- ✦ `Option Compare Binary`: When comparing strings, uppercase letters are considered to be smaller than lowercase letters. (With `Option Compare Database`, uppercase and lowercase letters are considered equal.)

- ✦ `Option Compare Text`: The sort order of your system's *locale* (the country and spoken language of your location) is used to compare strings. This option may be useful when creating a database that's used in non–English-speaking countries.

Writing Your Own VBA Procedures

All the code that you write will be contained within procedures. A *procedure* is a single chunk of code that performs a series of actions when called. A sub procedure always begins with a `Sub` statement or a `Private Sub` statement, and ends with an `End Sub` statement. A function procedure begins with a `Function` statement and ends with an `End Function` statement. You can add new procedures to class modules or standard modules. How you do so depends on where you want to place the procedure.

Creating a new standard procedure

A procedure in a standard module is available to all Access objects and isn't tied to any particular control or event. To create a new procedure in a standard module

1. **Create a new standard module as described in Book VIII, Chapter 1.**

   or

   Open an existing module by double-clicking its name in the Navigation pane.

2. **Choose Insert⇨Procedure from the Visual Basic Editor menu.**

   The Add Procedure dialog box opens, as shown in Figure 2-8.

Figure 2-8:
Add
Procedure
dialog box.

3. **Type a name for the procedure in the Name field.**

   The name can be anything you choose but must start with a letter and cannot contain any blank spaces.

4. **Under Type, choose Sub to create a sub procedure or Function to create a function procedure.**

   The Property option in the Type list has to do with creating custom objects, which isn't relevant to the topic at hand.

5. **Choose either the Public procedure type (to make the procedure available to all Access objects) or the Private procedure type (to make the procedure visible only to the current module) from the Scope section.**

   If you're not sure whether to choose the Public procedure or the Private procedure, choose Public.

   Private procedures are generally used only in class modules, not standard modules.

6. **Select the All Local Variables as Statics check box if you want to ensure that variables in the procedure retain their values between calls.**

   If you're not sure what to do with the All Local Variables as Statics option, your best bet is to leave it unselected.

7. **Click OK in the Add Procedure dialog box.**

   You see a new, empty procedure in the Code window.

If you chose the `Function` procedure type, the procedure looks something like this:

```
Public Function name()

End Function
```

If you chose the `Sub` procedure type, the code looks something like this:

```
Public Sub name()

End Sub
```

where *name* is the name you typed into the Add Procedure dialog box.

Creating a procedure through the Add Procedure dialog box is not really necessary. You can just type the `Function` statement or `Sub` statement into the Code window, and VBA automatically adds a corresponding `End Function` or `End Sub` statement.

The statements that the Add Procedure dialog box adds to the module use only the bare minimum of optional arguments supported by the `Function` and `Sub` statements. Depending on what the procedure does, you may need to define some additional arguments, as discussed in the section, "Passing arguments to procedures," later in this chapter.

Creating a new event procedure

Recall that an event procedure is already tied to some event, such as clicking a button on a form. If you want to create a new event procedure for a control on a report or form, follow these steps:

1. **In Design view, open the form or report that contains the control for which you want to create a new procedure.**

In the Navigation pane, right-click the object's name and choose Design View from the shortcut menu that opens.

2. **Select the control for which you want to create a procedure.**

3. **Click the Event tab in the Property sheet.**

If the Property sheet isn't open, right-click the selected control, choose the Properties option from the shortcut menu to see its properties, and then click the Event tab.

4. **Click in the event that should trigger the procedure into action and then click the Build (...) button that appears.**

For example, if the selected control is a button and you want a user to click that button to trigger the procedure into action, click in the `On Click` event and then click its Build button.

The Choose Builder dialog box opens.

5. **Click the Code Builder button and then click OK.**

The class module for the form or report opens in the Visual Basic Editor, with the cursor resting in a new procedure.

The name of the new procedure is a combination of the control's name and the event that triggers the procedure into action. The name is one that appears at the top of the All tab in the Property sheet. For example, if you right-click a button named `MyButton` and then build the procedure from the `On Click` event on the Event tab of the Property sheet, the procedure looks like this:

```
Private Sub MyButton_Click()

End Sub
```

Passing arguments to procedures

When you create your own expressions in Access, you often use built-in functions that are capable of accepting arguments. For example, there's a built-in UCase() function that takes any string of text as an argument. The argument is text or a number that you hand over to the function to operate on. The function does its thing on the argument and then returns the results.

To pass an argument to a built-in function, you place it in the parentheses after the function name. If you're passing a literal string, that string must be enclosed in quotation marks. For example, say you type the following into the Immediate window in the Visual Basic Editor:

```
? UCase("howdy world")
```

In this example, UCase() is the function and "howdy world" is the argument, the value being passed to the function. The UCase() function returns that same chunk of text with all the letters converted to uppercase, HOWDY WORLD.

When you create your own procedures, you can define what arguments, if any, the procedure is capable of accepting. If you create a function procedure, you can also define what the procedure returns. (A sub procedure doesn't return a value.)

If you were to look at the syntax chart for the Sub statement and take away some of the optional stuff from that chart, you see the syntax for the Sub statement looks something like this:

```
Sub name [(arglist)]

End Sub
```

What's with the simplified syntax?

Many optional arguments available in VBA statements represent very advanced concepts that are difficult to describe out of context. This book often shows a simplified version of the syntax for a given statement, focusing just on those arguments you either need to use or are likely to want to use. When you compare the simplified syntax shown in this book with the actual syntax shown in the Visual Basic Editor Help windows, the two may not be the same. Don't be alarmed. It's not a mistake.

Using the simplified syntax in this book allows you to discover VBA programming in a manner that focuses on the most basic — and most important — stuff first. You can work your way to the more advanced — and mostly optional — stuff as needed. The simplified syntax may well be all you ever need to use when writing your own code.

The simplified syntax for the `Function` statement (with some of the optional stuff removed) looks similar, as the following:

```
Function name [(arglist)] As type

End Function
```

In both cases, the `arglist` is optional, as indicated by the square brackets. But even the optional `arglist` has a syntax, the simplified version of which is

```
name [As type]
```

where *name* is a name you make up. You can list multiple arguments by separating their names with commas.

The *type* component specifies the data type of the data. Like Access tables, VBA supports multiple data types. These data types are similar (but not identical) to data types defined for fields in the structure of a table. For example, the `String` data type in VBA is similar to the `Text` data type in an Access table, in that both contain text.

Table 2-1 lists the VBA data types that work best with Access. The Storage Size column shows how many bytes each data type assumes. The Declaration Character column shows an optional character used at the end of a name to specify a data type. For example, the name `PersonName$` defines `PersonName` as containing a string. But in the real world, you really need not concern yourself too much with those columns. The first two columns in the table provide the information you really need to know.

Table 2-1	VBA Data Types		
Data Type	*Acceptable Values*	*Storage Size*	*Declaration Character*
Boolean	True (–1) or False (0)	2 bytes	
Byte	0 to 255	1 byte	
Currency	–922,337,203,685,477.5808 to 922,337,203,685,477.5807	8 bytes	@
Date	January 1, 100 to December 31, 9999	8 bytes	
Double	–1.79769313486231E308 to –4.94065645841247E-324 for negative values; 4.94065645841247E-324 to 1.79769313486232E308 for positive values	8 bytes	#

(continued)

Table 2-1 *(continued)*

Data Type	Acceptable Values	Storage Size	Declaration Character
Integer	–32,768 to 32,767	2 bytes	%
Long	–2,147,483,648 to 2,147,483,647	4 bytes	&
Object	Name of any object	4 bytes	
Single	–3.402823E38 to –1.401298E-45 for negative values; 1.401298E-45 to 3.402823E38 for positive values	4 bytes	!
String (fixed length)	Any text from 1 to 65,400 characters in length	10 + string length	$

You define the names and data types of arguments within the parentheses that follow the name of the procedure. Separate the name from the data type using the word As. For example, the following Sub statement defines a sub procedure named SampleSub(). That sub procedure accepts two arguments: a single-precision number named Amount and a string named Payee:

```
Sub SampleSub(Amount As Single, Payee As String)
...code...
End Sub
```

Unlike a sub procedure, a function procedure can return a value. You define the data type of the returned value after the parentheses and the word As. The returned data doesn't need a name, just a data type. For example, the following Function statement defines a function procedure named IsOpen(). That function accepts one argument — a string. The name FormName refers to that passed string within the function. The function returns either a True or False value (the Boolean data type).

```
Function IsOpen(FormName As String) As Boolean
     ...code...
End Function
```

Don't bother to type either of the preceding procedures because they don't actually do anything. They just demonstrate the syntax of the Sub and Function statements. Figure 2-9 further points out the purpose of the various components of the sample Function statement.

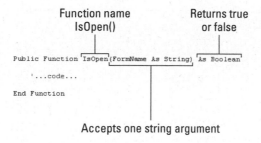

Function name
IsOpen()

Returns true
or false

Figure 2-9:
Components
of a sample
function
procedure.

```
Public Function IsOpen(FormName As String) As Boolean
      '...code...
End Function
```

Accepts one string argument

Returning a value from a function

Any function can return a value. To define the value that a function returns, you use the following syntax within the body of the function:

```
functionName = value
```

where *functionName* is the name of the function and *value* is the value that the function returns. The following function is an example:

```
Function WithTax(AnyNumber As Currency) As Currency
    WithTax = AnyNumber * 1.065
End Function
```

Multiplying a number by 1.065 is equivalent to adding 6.5 percent sales tax to that number. Do this little trick with any sales tax rate. For example, to add 7.75 percent sales tax, you would multiply by 1.0775.

The `WithTax()` function is a complete VBA procedure that actually works. If you type it into a standard module, you can use it anywhere in your database just as you would a built-in function. You could even test it out in the Immediate window. For example, after you type the `WithTax` function into the Code window, you can type the following into the Immediate window and press Enter:

```
? WithTax(10)
```

The Immediate window displays `10.65` because 10 times 1.065 equals 10.65. Figure 2-10 shows the function and the Immediate window.

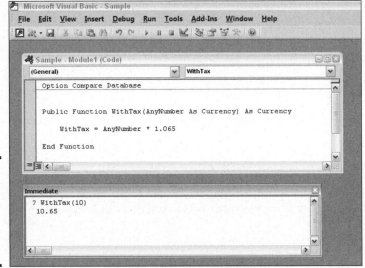

Figure 2-10:
Sample function tested in the Immediate window.

Typing and Editing in the Code Window

For a procedure to actually do anything, it has to contain some valid VBA code. As you type statements in the Code window, the VBA Editor offers a little help along the way. Figure 2-11 shows an example. As you type your line of code and get to a place where only certain words are allowed, a drop-down menu appears to let you know what those words are. This autocomplete feature is *IntelliSense,* which assists you in writing code.

Figure 2-11:
Drop-down menu of acceptable words.

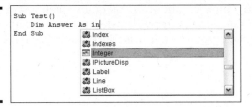

As you continue to type, the drop-down menu moves down to the first item that matches what you typed so far. Rather than type the whole word, you can type until the selected item in the drop-down menu matches what you intend to type; then press Enter. The word in the menu replaces what you typed so far. This saves you some typing and also ensures that the word you typed is spelled correctly.

Shortcut keys used in the Code window

While typing in the Code window, you can use the various shortcut keys listed in Table 2-2 to navigate, make changes, and so forth. Most of the shortcut keys are identical to those found in other text-editing programs and word processors.

Table 2-2	Code Window Shortcut Keys
Action	*Shortcut Key*
Move cursor right one character	→
Select character to right	Shift+→
Move cursor right one word	Ctrl+→
Select to end of word	Ctrl+ Shift+→
Move cursor left one character	←
Select character to left of cursor	Shift+←
Move cursor left one word	Ctrl+←
Move cursor to start of line	Home
Select text to start of line	Shift+Home
Move cursor to end of line	End
Select text to end of line	Shift+End
Move cursor up a line	↑
Move cursor down a line	↓
Move cursor to next procedure	Ctrl+↓
Move cursor to previous procedure	Ctrl+↑
Scroll up one screen	PgUp
Scroll down one screen	PgDn
Go to top of module	Ctrl+Home
Select all text to top of module	Ctrl+ Shift+Home
Go to bottom of module	Ctrl+End
Select all text to bottom of module	Ctrl+ Shift+End
Cut selection	Ctrl+X
Copy selection	Ctrl+C
Paste	Ctrl+V
Cut current line to Clipboard	Ctrl+Y
Delete to end of word	Ctrl+Delete
Delete character or selected text	Delete (Del)

(continued)

Table 2-2 *(continued)*

Action	Shortcut Key
Delete character to left of cursor	Backspace
Delete to beginning of word	Ctrl+Backspace
Undo	Ctrl+Z
Indent line	Tab
Outdent line	Shift+Tab
Find	Ctrl+F
Replace	Ctrl+H
Find Next	F3
Find Previous	Shift+F3
View Object Browser	F2
View Immediate window	Ctrl+G
View Code window	F7
View shortcut menu	Shift+F10 (or right-click)
Get help with currently selected word	F1
Run a Sub/UserForm	F5
Stop code execution	Ctrl+Break

Typing comments

When typing VBA code, you can mix in programmer comments (usually called *comments* for short). A *comment* is plain-English text for human consumption only. VBA ignores all comments and processes only the code. As such, comments are entirely optional. The purpose of a comment is simply to "jot down notes" within the code, either as a future reminder to yourself or to other programmers working on the same project.

The first character of a comment must be an apostrophe ('). In the Code window, comments appear as green text. Each comment is on its own line or follows a line of VBA code. Never put VBA code to the right of a comment on the same line because VBA assumes all text after the apostrophe (on the same line) is just a comment and ignores everything to the right of the apostrophe.

Breaking lines of code

Unlike a word processor, where long lines of text are word-wrapped (broken between words as necessary), text in the Visual Basic Editor never wraps. You (and Access) really need to be able to see each line independently. If the Visual Basic Editor were to word-wrap, you wouldn't really know exactly where one line ends and the next one begins.

Sometimes you may end up typing a statement that extends beyond the right border of the window. For example, the line that begins with `AnyText =` in Figure 2-12 is actually much longer than it appears. Most of the line is invisible, cut off at the right margin. The statement works as is. Still, you may want to see the entire statement when writing, testing, or modifying your code.

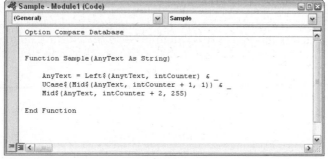

Figure 2-12: Line starting with `AnyText=` is cut off in window.

If you want to break a single long statement into two or more lines, you must insert a *continuation character* (an underscore _) at the end of the line, just before you press Enter to break the line. Essentially, the continuation character tells Access, "The line break that follows isn't the end of this statement. Rather, I want to break up this lengthy line." Figure 2-13 shows the lengthy line broken into three shorter lines using the continuation character.

Figure 2-13: Line starting with `AnyText=` broken into three lines.

Book VIII Chapter 2

Writing Code

Although you can break a statement into two or more lines using the continuation character, you cannot break a literal string in the same manner. A *literal string* is text enclosed in quotation marks, as in the following example:

```
SomeChunk = "A literal string is text in quotation marks"
```

If you try to break a literal string into two lines by using a continuation character, as the following example does, you get an error message:

```
SomeChunk = "A literal string is _
text in quotation marks"
```

To break a literal string, you need to terminate the top line with a quotation mark ("), followed by an ampersand (&), and then the continuation character (_). On the next line, enclose the entire second half of the literal text in quotation marks, as the following example shows:

```
SomeChunk = "A literal string is " & _
"text in quotation marks"
```

Because breaking up lines is entirely optional, you may never have to concern yourself with these nitpicky details of breaking lines within literal text. However, when you cut and paste code written by others, you may find that the programmer has broken up lengthy lines to make them more readable. Just be aware that an underscore (_) at the end of a line means, "The line below is a continuation of this line, not a new and separate statement."

Dealing with compile errors

Each statement in VBA code must be syntactically correct, complete, and must be either on its own line or correctly broken across several lines by using a continuation character. If you press Enter to end the line before you type a complete, syntactically correct statement, an error message appears on-screen.

For example, Figure 2-14 shows what you see if you type **MsgBox("Hello World"** and press Enter. The `MsgBox()` statement requires a closing parenthesis, which is missing in this example — so the editor displays an error message. In the Code window, the faulty line is shown in red.

Figure 2-14: Sample compile error.

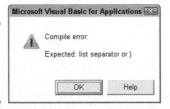

The compile error means that the line you typed cannot be translated to instructions that Access can perform. Access can compile and execute only syntactically correct and complete statements. The part that says `Expected: list separator or )` tells you that Access expected to find either a comma (to separate the first argument from the second) or a closing parenthesis.

The box displaying the error message contains two buttons:

✦ **OK:** Closes the error message box so you can type in the correction

✦ **Help:** Provides some general information about the type of error discovered and provides some suggestions for fixing the problem

Regardless of which button you click, you need to correct the statement before it can work correctly. After you type the correct statement and press Enter, the error message no longer appears, and the line no longer displays in red.

Testing and Running Your Code

A completed procedure is generally called from some object, such as a button on a form. But as you write code, you may want to make sure that it will work before you start attaching a procedure to objects in your database. You can use the Immediate window to run the procedure right on the spot. The syntax varies depending on whether you're testing a sub procedure or function as well as whether the procedure accepts arguments.

Testing sub procedures

To test a sub procedure that accepts no parameters, you simply type the name of the sub procedure into the Immediate window, and then press Enter. The following procedure accepts no parameters and displays a message box when called:

```
Sub ShowThanks()
   MsgBox ("Thank you")
End Sub
```

To test the preceding procedure, simply type its name without the parentheses into the Immediate window, as the following:

```
ShowThanks
```

The procedure switches to the Access window and shows a message. Then close the message box and switch back to the Visual Basic Editor to continue writing code.

If a sub procedure accepts arguments, you follow the procedure name by a blank space and the value to pass to the sub procedure. For example, the following sub procedure accepts one argument:

```
Sub WarnUser (msg as String)
   x = MsgBox(msg, vbCritical, "Warning")
End Sub
```

Access assumes that the passed parameter is a string. To test the procedure, you need to pass some text to it. Type the following into the Immediate window to test this procedure:

```
WarnUser "Don't move!"
```

When you press Enter, the procedure executes, displaying a message box in the Access window. Close the message box and return to the Visual Basic Editor.

If a procedure accepts more than one argument, separate the arguments by a comma. The following procedure accepts two string arguments:

```
Sub TakeTwo(msg as String, tBar As String)
    x = msgbox(msg, vbOKOnly, tBar)
End Sub
```

To test the procedure, you need to pass two parameters to it from the Immediate window, as in this example:

```
TakeTwo "Hello World", "Sample"
```

The result is a message box with `"Hello World"` on-screen, a single OK button, and `"Sample"` in the title bar. The result is the same if you execute this statement directly:

```
    x = msgbox("Hello World", vbOKOnly, "Sample")
```

Running sub procedures from Access

The real goal of a sub procedure, of course, is to run when appropriate from within Access. Sub procedures in a class module are usually tied to a control on the corresponding form or report. To actually run a procedure, open the corresponding form or report and trigger the event that causes the code to run. For example, if the code is attached to the `On Click` event of a button on a form, you need to open the form in Form view and click the button that runs the code.

Calling a procedure from another procedure

Any VBA procedure can call another procedure, using exactly the same syntax used to test the procedure in the Immediate window. If the sub procedure accepts no arguments, just call the procedure by name. If the sub procedure does contain arguments, include the passed values in the command.

You can use the `Call` keyword in front of the procedure name as a reminder that you're calling some other procedure, but the `Call` keyword is optional.

Figure 2-15 shows two sub procedures: one named `SampleSub()`, and the other named `SecondSub()`. The `SampleSub()` procedure includes a `Call` statement that calls upon `SecondSub()` to do its job. What happens when you execute `SampleSub()` is the following:

Figure 2-15:
One sub
procedure
calls
another.

```
Sub SampleSub()
    Statement1A
    Statement2A
    Call SecondSub("Howdy World")
    Statement3A
    Statement4A
End Sub

Sub SecondSub(AnyText As String)
    Statement1B
    Statement2B
End Sub
```

1. *Statement1A* and *Statement2A* in `SampleSub()` are each executed.

2. The `Call SecondSub ("Howdy World")` statement is executed, causing *Statement1B* and *Statement2B* in `SecondSub()` to be executed.

3. The `End Sub` statement at the end of `SecondSub()` returns control to the next line in the calling procedure — *Statement3A*.

4. Both *Statement3A* and *Statement4A* in `SampleSub()` are executed next.

5. The `End Sub` statement at the end of the `SampleSub()` procedure is executed, and no more VBA code is executed.

Running sub procedures from macros

You can also call VBA sub procedures from macros although technically, a macro only calls a function procedure, not a sub procedure. You have two choices if you still like to have a macro call a sub procedure:

✦ Convert the sub procedure to a function procedure.

✦ Write a function procedure that calls the sub procedure, and then call the function procedure from the macro.

Converting a sub procedure to a function procedure is a simple matter of changing the `Sub` keyword at the top of the procedure to `Function`, and the `End Sub` statement at the bottom of the procedure to `End Function`.

If you want to leave the procedure as is and call it from a function, place the call to the sub procedure within a function procedure. When executed, the following `DoMySub()` function procedure calls the `MySub()` sub procedure.

```
'The sub procedure below is named MySub()
Sub MySub()
    MsgBox ("MySub Ran")
End Sub

'Function procedure below calls MySub sub procedure.
Function DoMySub()
    Call MySub
End Function
```

To run `MySub` from a macro, you choose `RunCode` as the macro action. Then type the name of the function procedure — in this example, `DoMySub()` — as the action argument for the `RunCode` action, as shown in Figure 2-16.

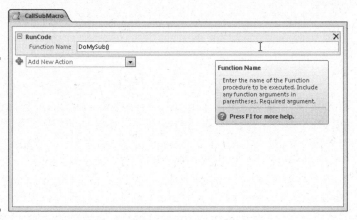

Figure 2-16: Run a function procedure (which runs the sub procedure) from a macro.

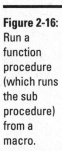

For a reminder on defining macro actions, see Book VI, Chapter 1.

Testing function procedures

Unlike sub procedures, which return no value, a function procedure always returns a value. To test a function from the Immediate window, use the ? ("What is . . . ?") symbol, followed by the function name — and, if necessary, use the values that pass to the function.

For example, the following custom function accepts no arguments. When called, the day of the week is returned:

```
Function Today() As String
    Today = WeekDayName(Weekday(Date))
End Function
```

To test the function, type the following into the Immediate window and press Enter:

```
? Today()
```

The Immediate window then displays the value returned by the function. If you ran the test on a Monday, the function would return

```
Monday
```

The following function procedure accepts a single number as an argument (and returns a number):

```
Function Area(radius As Double) As Double
    Area = 3.141592654 * (radius ^ 2)
End Function
```

To test the function, call it with the ? symbol and pass some number to it, as in this example:

```
? Area(10)
```

The Immediate window then displays the value returned by the function, as the following shows:

```
314.1592654
```

If the function accepts multiple arguments, you just separate the arguments with commas, like when using the Access built-in functions.

Using function procedures in Access

When you create a function procedure in VBA, you can use that function any place within the database where you use a built-in function. Wherever you use an expression in Access, that expression can contain built-in functions, custom function procedures, or both. Here are some examples:

✦ In an expression used in the `Control Source` property of a calculated control on a form or a report

✦ In an expression that defines a calculated field in a select query

✦ In an expression in the Update To row of an update query

✦ In an expression used in a macro

✦ As a custom action called from a macro, such as the example shown in Figure 2-16

In Access, function procedures are generally easier to use than sub procedures. Calling a function procedure from within any expression is easy. Most pre-written, custom VBA code examples you may find on the Web is organized into function procedures rather than sub procedures.

Chapter 3: Writing Smarter Code

In This Chapter

✓ Using variables and constants to store temporary data

✓ Having your code make decisions

✓ Executing the same code repeatedly

✓ Managing data with custom VBA functions

*L*ike with all programming languages, VBA offers certain concepts and statements designed to allow you to write the code necessary to make a computer do — well, *anything*. Those concepts and statements are the subject of this chapter.

We must point out, though, that the underlying VBA concepts described in this chapter aren't unique to VBA. Virtually all programming languages are built around these same concepts. If you ever have aspirations of learning to program in any language — Java, JavaScript, C++, C#, VBScript, or whatever — the concepts that you discover in this chapter apply equally to most programming languages.

Creating Variables and Constants

Within a procedure, you define and use *variables*. A variable is a name — a placeholder — for any data that may change. You make up your own variable names. Choose names that indicate what information the variable contains, so you don't have to wonder later. Variable names must begin with a letter, cannot contain spaces or punctuation, and cannot be the same as any built-in keyword.

Unlike data stored in a table, data stored in a variable isn't permanent. Data stored in a variable is fleeting and exists only for as long as VBA needs the information contained within the variable.

Make me a variable

You can create variables in a couple of ways in VBA code. The quick-and-dirty way is to simply make up a variable name and assign a value by following the name with an equal sign (=) and the value to be stored in the variable. The following VBA statements define three variables named x, y, and ExtPrice. The variable x stores the number 10, the variable y stores the number 9.99, and the variable ExtPrice stores the result of multiplying the contents of x by the contents of y (or 99.9 by the time all three lines are executed):

```
x = 10
y = 9.99
ExtPrice = x * y
```

These statements are all examples of *implicit variable declarations.*

Explicit variable declaration, as the name implies, requires that you assign a data type to each variable before you assign the variable a value. Explicit variable declaration is a little more work, but your code runs more smoothly and efficiently because Access doesn't have to figure out the best data type to use when it encounters the data lurking in the variable.

Two steps go into using a variable explicitly. First you *define* (or *declare*) the variable, which gives the variable a data type. After the variable exists, you assign a value using the same syntax as for implicit declarations: *variableName = value*.

The command for defining a variable explicitly is Dim, short for *dimension.* But thinking of Dim as standing for "Define In Memory" may be easier because variables exist only in the computer's random access memory (RAM). The simplified syntax for the Dim statement looks like this:

```
Dim varname [As type] [,...]
```

where *varname* is a name of your own choosing. The *type* refers to one of the acceptable VBA data types or object types. The data types you assign to variables in a Dim statement are the same as those used in defining arguments in a Function or Sub statement.

The comma and ellipsis in the syntax chart mean that you can define multiple variables, separated by commas, within a single statement. For example, the following statement declares one variable, named ReportName, as a string (textual data):

```
Dim ReportName as String
```

The following sample Dim statement declares two variables: a string named ReportName and a long integer named Qty. The lines after the Dim statement then assign a value to each variable using the standard variableName = value syntax:

```
Dim ReportName as String, Qty as Long
ReportName = "Sales Summary Report"
Qty = 50
```

Scope and lifetime of variables

All variables and constants have a scope and a lifetime. The *scope* of a variable defines to which procedures the variable is visible. You determine the scope of a variable when you declare the variable. Variables declared at the beginning of a module (before the first procedure in the module) can be either *private* (visible only to procedures within the same module) or *public* (visible to all procedures in all modules). These variables have *module-level scope.*

If you use the `Public` keyword (rather than `Dim`) to declare a variable at the module level, the variable is visible to all procedures in all modules. On the other hand, if you use a `Dim` or `Private` statement to define a variable at the module level, the variable is private to the module. All procedures defined within the same module can see the variable, but the variable is invisible to procedures defined in other modules.

When you define a variable within a procedure, that variable has *procedure-level scope,* meaning that the variable is *private* (visible only) to the procedure in which it is defined. Only the procedure in which the variable is defined can see, and use, the variable.

Figure 3-1 shows a module with several variables declared using `Dim`, `Private`, and `Public` keywords. Comments in the code describe the scope of the variables declared within the module as follows:

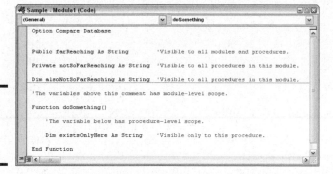

Figure 3-1:
Scopes
of sample
variables.

✦ `Public farReaching As String`: The variable named `farReaching` is visible to all procedures in all modules because it's declared by using the `Public` keyword.

✦ `Private notSoFarReaching As String` and `Dim alsoNotSoFar Reaching As String`: These variables are visible to all procedures in the same module but are not visible to procedures defined in other modules. `Dim` and `Private` have the same meaning in this context.

✦ `Dim existsOnlyHere As String`: Because this variable is declared within a procedure, the variable is visible only to that procedure.

The *lifetime* of a variable defines how long a variable retains a value. When you open a database, variables defined at the module level of standard modules are created and can be assigned a new value at any time. The lifetime of such variables is lengthy — these variables exist and can contain values for the entire session — from when you open the database to the time you close it.

Variables declared with a `Dim` keyword at the procedure level have a much shorter lifetime. The variable retains its value only for as long as the procedure runs. A second call to the same procedure re-creates the variables and assigns new values to them.

Although it's rare to do so, you may want to make one or more variables retain their values between calls to the procedure in some instances. For example, you may have a variable that keeps track of how many times the procedure is called. In that case, you can use the `Static` keyword, rather than `Dim`, to declare the variable or variables. The following statement defines a static variable named `howMany`, which stores an integer (whole number).

```
Static howMany as Integer
```

You can make all variables declared within a procedure static by preceding the `Sub` or `Function` keyword with `Static`. All variables defined within the following procedure are static because the `Static` keyword in front of the word `Function` makes all that procedure's variables static:

```
Static Function myFunction()
    'Both variables below are static
    Dim var1 As String
    Dim var2 As Byte
End Function
```

If you find this terribly confusing, you rarely need to be so picky about the scope and lifetimes of variables. In fact, if you never use the `Public`, `Private`, or `Static` keywords in any code you write, chances are that the code will still work perfectly — the default scope and lifetime assigned to a variable through the `Dim` statement is usually exactly what you need. Exceptions are few and far between, and are not likely to show up until you start developing huge and complex databases.

Defining constants

A *constant* is similar to a variable: It has a name, a data type, and a value. However, unlike a variable (whose contents can change at any time), a constant's value never changes. Constants are often used to assign a short name to some value that must be used repeatedly throughout the code, but never changed.

To declare a constant, you use the `Const` keyword. The simplified syntax for the `Const` keyword is

```
Const name [As type]=value [, name [As type]=value]...
```

You define the name, data type (`type`), and value of the constant on a single line. The rules for coming up with a name are the same as those for a variable: It must start with a letter, cannot contain blank spaces or punctuation, and cannot be the same as a VBA keyword.

As an example of creating a constant, the following statement defines a constant named `pi` as a double-precision number containing the value `3.141592654`:

```
Const pi As Double = 3.141592654
```

You can declare multiple constants in a single `Const` statement by separating them with a comma. For example, the following statement declares two constants, a number named `x` of the Byte data type with a value of `10`, and a string named `myName` containing the text `"Billy"`:

```
Const x As Byte = 10, myName As String = "Billy"
```

Constants tend to be private to the module in which they're defined. If you want to ensure that a constant is available to all objects and all modules within the database, precede `Const` with the `Public` keyword, as the following shows:

```
Public Const pi As Double = 3.141592654
```

Organizing variables into arrays

An *array* is a collection of variables organized into a list or table. Each item's name is the same, but each has one or more *subscripts* that uniquely identify each item in the array based on its position in the array. The subscript is one or more numbers, enclosed in parentheses, that follow the name. If `Colors` is the name of an array, `Colors(1)` (pronounced *colors sub 1*), is the first item in the list, `Colors(2)` is the second item in the list, and so forth.

In a sense, an array is like a database table, in that the data can be organized into rows and columns. And you can use VBA to manipulate data stored in tables. The only time you really want to use an array is when you work with a small amount of data that either never changes or changes only while the code is running. The data in an array is defined in code, not in a table, so getting to the data stored in the array is not easy.

The syntax for declaring an array is almost identical to that of creating a variable. However, you need to define the number of *dimensions* in the array and the number of *elements* in each dimension of the array. An array can have up to 60 dimensions and virtually any number of elements within each dimension. The basic syntax for declaring an array using the `Dim` statement is

```
Dim varname[([subscripts])] [As type] [,varname[([subscripts])]] [As type]] . .
```

In this statement

- ✦ *varname* is the name assigned each element in the array.
- ✦ *subscripts* is the number of elements in each dimension, with each dimension separated by a comma. It can contain the optional keyword `To` to specify the starting and ending subscripts.
- ✦ *type* is any valid VBA data type.

All arrays are zero-based unless you specify otherwise, which means that the first item in the array has a subscript of zero, rather than one. The number of elements specified is actually one less than the total number of elements that the array contains.

For example, the following `Dim` statement declares a one-dimensional array named `Colors` that contains four string elements (numbered 0, 1, 2, and 3):

```
Dim Colors(3) as String
```

The following lines of code show how you can then assign a value to each element in the array. Because the first item always has a subscript of 0 (zero), you actually place four, rather than three, items into the array:

```
Colors(0) = "black"
Colors(1) = "red"
Colors(2) = "blue"
Colors(3) = "green"
```

Having the first element in an array start with a 0 can be counterintuitive for us humans, who tend to think of the first item in a list as being number 1. You can force the first element to be 1 by specifying a range (rather than a number) of elements in the `Dim` statement. The following `Dim` statement declares an array of three elements, with subscripts ranging from 1 to 3. The lines after the `Dim` statement assign a value to each of those elements:

```
Dim Colors(1 To 3) as String
Colors(1) = "red"
Colors(2) = "blue"
Colors(3) = "green"
```

Another alternative, if you want all your arrays to start at 1 rather than 0, is to simply put the following statement up in the `Declarations` section of the module, before the first procedure in the module:

```
Option Base 1
```

After you add the `Option Base 1` statement to the top of a module, all arrays within that module start at 1 rather than 0. Thus the `Dim Colors(3)` statement creates an array of three elements, numbered 1, 2, 3, as you expect. There is no `Colors(0)` when the optional base for arrays is set to 1 via the `Option Base 1` module declaration.

Multidimensional arrays

A *multidimensional array* offers more than one subscript per name. The simplest example is a two-dimensional array, which you can envision as a table. The first subscript in a two-dimensional array represents the element's row position in the array. The second subscript represents the element's column position in the array. For example, in the following array, `State(3,2)` refers to "row 3, column 2" in the `States` array, which contains `"AZ"`.

```
State(1,1) = "Alabama"        State(1,2) = "AL"

State(2,1) = "Alaska"         State(2,2) = "AK"

State(3,1) = "Arizona"        State(3,2) = "AZ"

State(50,1) = "Wyoming"       State(50,2) = "WY"
```

The `Dim` statement that creates a two-dimensional array named `States`, with 50 row elements and 2 column elements, is shown with the following statement. If you use the `Option Base 1` statement in the `Declarations` section, the starting number for each array is 1:

```
Dim States (50,2) as String
```

The code to *populate* the array (that is, to assign a value to each variable) looks like this:

```
State(1,1) = "Alabama"
State(1,2) = "AL"
State(2,1) = "Alaska"
State(2,2) = "AK"
State(3,1) = "Arizona"
State(3,2) = "AZ"
...
State(50,1) = "Wyoming"
State(50,2) = "WY"
```

Although all programming languages support multidimensional arrays, you won't use them in Access very often. Instead, you can use a table to store lists and tables of data, and then use Access code to extract data, as needed, from that table.

Naming conventions for variables

Some programmers use *naming conventions* to identify the data type of a variable as part of the variable's or constant's name. The naming conventions are entirely optional — you don't have to use them. But a lot of VBA programmers follow them, so you're likely to see them in any code you happen to come across.

The idea behind a naming convention is simple. When you define a new variable, make the first three letters of the name (referred to as the tag) stand for the type of variable or object. The following line creates an `Integer` variable named `intMyVar`, where `int` is short for *integer*.

```
Dim intMyVar As Integer
```

The tag added to the front of the name doesn't affect how the variable is stored or how you can use it. The tag serves only as a reminder that `MyVar` is an `Integer`. Table 3-1 summarizes the tags you'll most likely encounter when reading other people's code. In the Sample Declaration column of the table, the italicized word *Name* means that you can put in any variable name of your own choosing.

Table 3-1   Naming Conventions Used among VBA Programmers

Tag	Stands For	Sample Declaration
byt	`Byte` data type	`Dim byt`*Name* `As Byte`
cur	`Currency` data type	`Dim cur`*Name* `As Currency`
dtm	`Date/Time` data type	`Dim dtm`*Name* `As Date`
dbl	`Double` data type	`Dim dbl`*Name* `As Double`
int	`Integer` data type	`Dim int`*Name* `As Integer`
lng	`Long integer` data type	`Dim lng`*Name* `As Long`
sng	`Single` data type	`Dim sng`*Name* `As Single`
bln	`Boolean` data type	`Dim bln`*Name* `As Boolean`
str	`String` data type	`Dim str`*Name* `As String`
var	`Variant` data type	`Dim var`*Name* `As Variant`

Making Decisions in VBA Code

Decision-making is a big part of programming because most programs need to be smart enough to figure out what to do depending on circumstances. Often, you want your code to do one thing "if such-and-such is true," and do something else "if such-and-such is false." You use conditional expressions to determine whether something is true or false. A *conditional expression* is one that generally follows the syntax

```
Value ComparisonOperator Value
```

where *Value* is some chunk of information and the *ComparisonOperator* is one of those listed in Table 3-2.

Table 3-2	Comparison Operators
Operator	*Meaning*
=	Equal to
<	Less than
<=	Less than or equal to
>	Greater than
>=	Greater than or equal to
<>	Not equal to

For example, the expression

```
[Last Name] = "Smith"
```

compares the contents of the Last Name field with the string "Smith". If the [Last Name] field does, indeed, contain the name Smith, the expression is (or *returns*) True. If the [Last Name] field contains anything other than Smith, the expression returns False.

Another example is the following statement:

```
[Qty] >= 10
```

The content of the Qty field is compared with the number 10. If the number stored in the Qty field is 10 or greater, the expression returns True. If the number stored in the Qty field is less than 10, the expression returns False.

You can combine multiple conditional expressions into one using the logical operators summarized in Table 3-3.

**Book VIII
Chapter 3**

Writing Smarter Code

Table 3-3	Logical Operators
Operator	*Meaning*
and	Both are true.
or	One or both are true.
not	Is not true.
xor	Exclusive, or: One — but not both — is true.

The following conditional expression requires that the [Last Name] field contain "Smith" and the [First Name] field contain "Janet" in order for the entire expression to be True:

```
[Last Name] = "Smith" and [First Name] = "Janet"
```

An example of an expression that returns True if the State field contains either NJ or NY is the following:

```
[State] = "NJ" or [State] = "NY"
```

Using If...End If statements

You can have VBA code make decisions as the code is running in several ways. One method is to use the If...End If block of code. The syntax for If...End If looks like this:

```
If condition Then
    [statements]...
[Else
    [statements]...
End If
```

where *condition* is an expression that results in True or False, and *statements* refers to any number of valid VBA statements. If the condition proves True, the statements between Then and Else execute, and all other statements are ignored. If the condition proves False, only the statements after the Else statement execute, as illustrated in Figure 3-2.

As an example, imagine that a State variable contains some text. The following If...End If block checks whether the State variable contains NY. If the State variable does contain NY, the TaxRate variable receives a value of 0.075 (7.5%). If the State variable does not contain NY, the TaxRate variable receives a value of 0.

```
If State="NY" Then
    TaxRate=0.075
Else
    TaxRate=0
End If
```

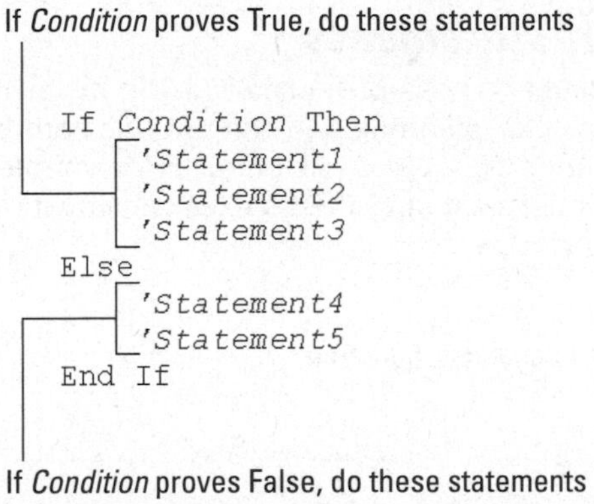

If *Condition* proves True, do these statements

```
If Condition Then
      'Statement1
      'Statement2
      'Statement3
Else
      'Statement4
      'Statement5
End If
```

Figure 3-2:
Basic idea
behind
If...
End If.

If *Condition* proves False, do these statements

You have a little bit of flexibility when using If...End If. If only one line of code executes for a True result and only one line executes for a False result, you can put the whole statement on a single line and omit the End If statement, as the following shows:

```
If State="NY" Then TaxRate=0.075 Else TaxRate=0
```

Because you can use any built-in function in VBA, and Access supports the use of the iif() *(immediate if)* function, you can also write the preceding statement as an expression:

```
TaxRate = iif([State]="NY",0.075,0)
```

In the block format, you can also write code that tests for more than just two possible conditions, using the optional ElseIf statement. Suppose the Reply variable stores a string of text. If Reply contains the word "Yes", your code does one thing. If Reply contains "No", your code does something else. If Reply contains neither "Yes" nor "No", you want your code to do something else instead. You could set up an If...End If block to test for and respond to all three conditions, as the following:

```
If Reply = "Yes" Then
    statements for "Yes" reply
ElseIf Reply="No" Then
    statements for "No" reply
Else
    statements for any other reply
End If
```

TIP

When the code has to make a decision from many possibilities, you may find using a Select Case...End Select block is easier, described in the section, "Using a Select Case block," later in this chapter.

**Book VIII
Chapter 3**

Writing Smarter Code

Nesting If...End If statements

What if you have more than two possible scenarios? No problem — you can nest If...End If blocks, meaning you can put one complete If... End If block inside another If...End If block. For example, in the code shown in Figure 3-3, the innermost statements execute only if Condition1 and Condition2 result in True.

Executed only if Condition1 and Condition2 both true

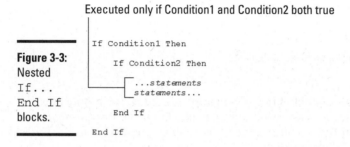

Figure 3-3:
Nested
If...
End If
blocks.

```
If Condition1 Then

    If Condition2 Then

        ...statements
        statements...

    End If

End If
```

You can see why the nested If...End If statements work if you look at what happens when either test proves False. For example:

✦ If *condition1* proves False, all code down to the last End If statement is skipped over. The inner If...End If block isn't seen or executed.

✦ If *condition1* proves True but *condition2* proves False, all the statements in the nested block are ignored. The innermost statements still don't execute.

✦ If both *condition1* and *condition2* prove True, no code is skipped over, and the innermost statements execute normally.

You can nest If...Else...End If blocks as deeply as you want. However, you have to make sure each one has its own End If statement.

Using a Select Case block

But what if you have more than two or three cases to check for? For example, what if you need to perform different statements depending on which of ten product types a person ordered? You could nest a lot of If...End If blocks, but it would be confusing. Luckily, Access provides a better way.

A Select Case block of code performs a particular set of instructions, depending on some value. Typically, the value is stored in a variable or field in a table, and is a number that represents some previous selection. The basic syntax of a Select Case block of code looks like this:

```
Select Case value
    [Case possibleValue  [To possibleValue]
        [statements]]
    [Case possibleValue [To possibleValue]
        [statements]]...
    [Case Else
        [statements]]
End Select
```

where *value* is some value (like a number), and *possibleValue* is any value that could match the value. You can have any number of `Case` *possibleValue* statements between the `Select Case` and `End Select` statements. Optionally, you can include a `Case Else` statement, which specifies statements that execute only if none of the preceding `Case` *possibleValue* statements prove `True`.

Each `Case` statement can have any number of statements beneath it. When the code executes, only those statements after the `Case` statement that match the *value* at the top of the block execute. Figure 3-4 shows the idea.

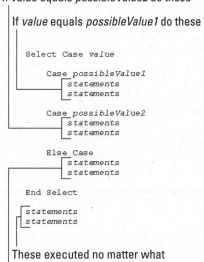

If *value* equals *possibleValue2* do these

If *value* equals *possibleValue1* do these

```
Select Case value
    Case possibleValue1
        statements
        statements
    Case possibleValue2
        statements
        statements
    Else Case
        statements
        statements
    End Select

    statements
    statements
```

These executed no matter what

If *value* equals no *possibleValue* above do these

Figure 3-4:
A `Select Case...` `End Select` block.

As an example, suppose you create a custom option group named `WhereTo` and a command button named `OKButton` on a form like the one in Figure 3-5. When the user chooses an option and clicks OK, you want to have the appropriate form open.

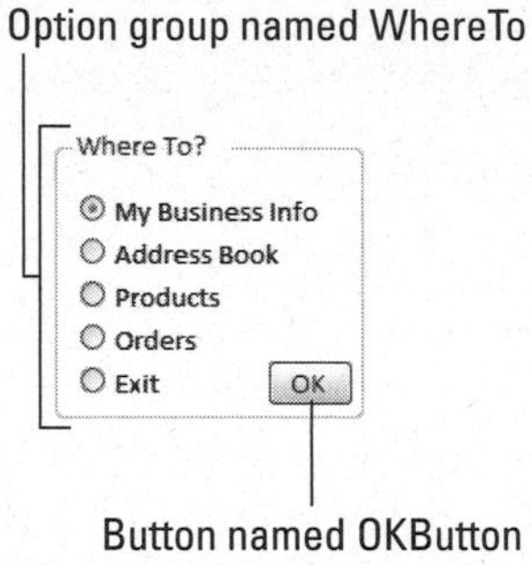

Option group named WhereTo

Figure 3-5:
Option
group and
button on a
form.

Button named OKButton

In the class module for that form, a sub procedure named OKButton_
Click() executes whenever someone clicks OK. The sub procedure, as
shown in Figure 3-6, opens a form, exits Access, or does nothing, depending
on what's selected in the WhereTo option group.

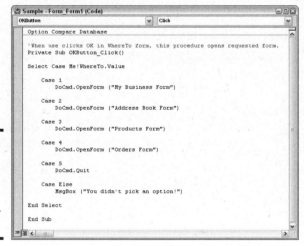

Figure 3-6:
Sub
procedure
to handle
OKButton_
click().

The OKButton_Click() procedure does its job this way: When called, the
following statement executes first:

```
Select Case Me!WhereTo.Value
```

This statement uses the Me!WhereTo.Value expression to refer to the
value of the WhereTo option group on the form. The word Me! is used
mainly in class modules to refer to the form or report to which the class
module is attached. Me!WhereTo.Value is a number between 1 and 5 when
the code executes. If no option is selected, Me!WhereTo.Value equals
Null. In that case, the code after the Case Else statement executes.

If you omit the `Case Else` statement from the sample code, no code within the `Select Case...End Case` block executes when `Me!WhereTo.Value` contains something other than a number from 1 to 5. Execution still continues normally, however, at the first line after the `End Case` statement.

The optional `To` keyword of the `Case` statement can be used to specify a range of values to compare against. In the following code, statements after `Case 1 To 9` execute only if `SomeNumber` contains a value from 1 to 9. Statements after `Case 10 To 99` execute only if `SomeNumber` contains a value from 100 to 999, and so forth.

```
Select Case SomeNumber
   Case 1 to 9
      Statements for when SomeNumber is between 1 and 9
   Case 10 to 99
      Statements for when SomeNumber is between 10 and 99
   Case 100 to 999
      Statements for when SomeNumber is between 100 and 999
End Select
```

Executing the Same Code Repeatedly

Occasionally, a situation occurs where you want to execute one or more VBA statements multiple times. Say you write some VBA statements that need to operate on each record in a table, and there are 1,000 records in the table. You have two choices: Write each set of statements 1,000 times, or create a loop that repeats the one set of statements 1,000 times. Needless to say, typing the statements once rather than 1,000 times saves you a lot of time. A loop is your best bet.

Using Do...Loop to create a loop

The `Do...Loop` block is one method of setting up a loop in code to execute statements repeatedly. Two syntaxes for using `Do...Loop` exist. The first syntax evaluates the condition of the loop, as the following shows:

```
Do [{While | Until} condition]
   [statements]
   [Exit Do]
   [statements]
Loop
```

The second syntax provides the option of defining the condition at the bottom of the loop, using this syntax:

```
Do
   [statements]
   [Exit Do]
   [statements]
Loop [{While | Until} condition]
```

As an example of the first syntax, the code in the following `Do Until` loop executes once for each record in a recordset named `rst`. (A recordset, as discussed in Chapter 5 of this minibook, is the VBA equivalent of a table in Access.)

```
'Example assumes recordset named rst already exists.
rst.MoveFirst
Do Until rst.EOF()
   Debug.Print rst.Fields("Product Name")
   rst.MoveNext
Loop
```

How the loop works is as follows: The `rst.MoveFirst` statement moves the cursor to the first record in the table. At that point, `EOF()` (which stands for End Of File) is `False` because `EOF()` means "past the last record in the table." Because the cursor is at the first record, `EOF()` is `False`.

Within the loop, the `rst.MoveNext` statement moves the cursor to the next record in the table. But `EOF()` remains `False` until `rst.MoveNext` executes a sufficient number of times to have visited every record in the table. After visiting the last record, `rst.MoveNext` moves the cursor to the end of the file — past the last record. When the cursor is past the last record, `EOF()` becomes `True`, and the loop doesn't repeat anymore. Instead, Access resumes executing your code normally at the first statement after the `Loop` statement.

Using the alternative syntax, where you define the condition at the bottom, rather than at the top of the loop, you can construct that same sort of loop as follows:

```
'Example assumes recordset named rst already exists.
rst.MoveFirst
Do
   Debug.Print rst.Fields("Product Name")
   rst.MoveNext
Loop Until rst.EOF()
```

You'll notice one subtle difference between setting the loop condition at the top of the loop rather than at the bottom of the loop. Access checks the condition *before* the loop executes for the first time (and each time thereafter). When you set the condition at the top of the loop, none of the statements in the loop may execute. Forgetting about recordsets and tables for the moment, consider the following more generic example:

```
Counter = 101
Do While Counter < 100
   Counter = Counter +1
Loop
'Statements below the loop.
```

Because `Counter` already has a value of `101` when the `Do While Counter <
100` statement executes, the looping condition is `False` right off the bat.
Thus, everything between the `Do While` and `Loop` statements is skipped
over completely, and code execution resumes at the statements after the
loop.

In the following code, we move the looping condition, `While Counter <
100`, to the bottom of the loop:

```
Counter = 101
Do
    Counter = Counter +1
Loop While Counter < 100
'Statements below the loop.
```

In the preceding loop, `Counter` receives a value of `101`. The `Do` statement
doesn't specify a condition for starting the loop, so the `Counter =
Counter + 1` statement within the loop executes. The `Loop While
Counter < 100` condition then proves `False` (because `Counter = 102`
by then), so code execution continues at the statements after the `Loop`
statement at the bottom of the loop.

In short, when you define the condition for the loop at the top of the loop,
the code within the loop may not execute at all. But if you define the condition at the bottom of the loop, the code within the loop executes at least
once.

Using While...Wend to create a loop

The `While...Wend` loop is similar to `Do...Loop`, but it uses the simpler
(and less flexible) syntax shown in the following code:

```
While condition
    [statements]
Wend
```

where *condition* is an expression that results in a `True` or `False` value,
and *statements* are any number of VBA statements, all of which execute
with each pass through the loop.

The condition is evaluated at the top of the loop. If the condition proves
`True`, all lines within the loop execute (down to the `Wend` statement) and
then the condition at the top of the loop is evaluated again. If the condition
proves `False`, all statements within the loop are ignored, and processing
continues at the first line after the `Wend` statement.

Using For...Next to create a loop

When you want to create a loop that keeps track of how many times the loop repeats, you can use the `For...Next` block of statements. The syntax for a `For...Next` loop is as follows:

```
For counter = start To end [Step step]
    [statements]
    [Exit For]
    [statements]
Next [counter]
```

where

+ *counter* is any name you want to give to the variable that keeps track of passes through the loop.

+ *start* is a number that indicates where the loop should start counting.

+ *end* is a number that indicates when the loop should end.

+ *step* is optional and indicates how much to increment or decrement *counter* with each pass through the loop. If omitted, *counter* increments by 1 with each pass through the loop.

+ *statements* are any number of VBA statements that execute with each pass through the loop.

Figure 3-7 shows a simple example of a `For...Next` loop within a sub procedure. This loop starts at 1 and increments the `Counter` variable by 1 with each pass through the loop. The loop continues until `Counter` reaches a value of 10, at which point the loop is done and processing continues at the first line after the `Next` statement. Within the loop, the `Debug.Print` statement simply prints the current value of the `Counter` variable to the Immediate window.

Figure 3-7:
A simple
`For...`
`Next` loop
in a sub
procedure.

The results of testing the procedure in the Immediate window are shown in Figure 3-7. As you can see, the Counter value displays once with each pass through the loop. Then processing continues at the lines that use Debug. Print to display the words "All Done".

Note that if you change the loop so that it counts from 2 to 10 and adds 2 (rather than 1) to Counter with each pass through the loop, the code looks like the following:

```
For counter = 2 to 10 Step 2
    Debug.Print counter
Next
```

Running the preceding loop displays the following in the Immediate window:

```
2
4
6
8
10
All Done
```

Looping through an array

You can use the Counter variable for a For...Next loop as the subscript for elements in an array. You can use the LBound() (lower boundary) and UBound() (upper boundary) functions to automatically return the lowest and highest subscripts in the array. You can use those values as the *start* and *end* values in the For... statement. The following code creates an array of four elements and assigns a value — a color name — to each element in the array. The For...Next loop that follows the array prints the contents of each array element by using the Counter value as the subscript for each pass through the loop:

```
Sub LoopArrayDemo()
    'Declare and variable and an array.
    Dim counter As Integer
    Dim Colors(3) As String

    'Fill the array.
    Colors(0) = "Black"
    Colors(1) = "Red"
    Colors(2) = "Green"
    Colors(3) = "Blue"

    'Create a loop that shows array contents.
    For counter = LBound(Colors) To UBound(Colors)
        Debug.Print Colors(counter)
    Next

End Sub
```

**Book VIII
Chapter 3**

Writing Smarter Code

In the `For` statement, `LBound(Colors)` and `UBound(Colors)` automatically fill in the lowest and highest subscript numbers. On the first pass through the loop, the `Debug.Print` statement prints the contents of `Colors(0)`. On the second pass through the loop, `Debug.Print` displays the contents of `Colors(1)`, and so forth, until all array elements print.

Analyzing each character in a string

You can also use a `For...Next` loop to look at each character in a string. First, be aware that these two built-in Access functions help with the loop:

✦ `Len(`*string*`)`: Returns the length of a string in number of characters

✦ `Mid(`*string*`,`*start*`,`*length*`)`: Returns a portion of *string* starting at character *start* that's *length* characters long

As an example, if *string* is `"Hello World"`, `Len(`*string*`)` returns 11 because there are 11 characters in `"Hello World"` (counting the blank space that separates the two words). The expression `Mid(string,7,3)` returns a substring of *string* that starts at the seventh character and is three characters in length. In this case, that would be `Wor` (because W is the seventh character, and the returned substring is three characters in length).

Text-handling functions are described in more detail in Book III, Chapter 3.

To create a loop that looks at each character in a string, one at a time, start the loop at `1` and end it at `Len(string)`. Within the loop, use `Mid(string,counter,1)` to isolate the single character at the position indicated by `Counter`. A simple loop that just prints each character from the string names `strFull` in the Immediate window looks like this:

```
Sub LookAtEachCharacter()
    'Declare a couple of string variables.
    Dim strFull As String, thisChar As String

    'Give strFull a value.
    strFull = "Hello World"

    'Now isolate and display each character from strFull.
    For Counter = 1 to Len(StrFull)
        thisChar = Mid(strFull,Counter,1)
        Debug.Print thisChar
    Next

End Sub
```

The `For Each...Next` loop is a slight variation on the `For...Next` loop, and is discussed in Chapter 4 of this minibook.

Using Custom Functions

Access has many built-in functions that you can use in expressions. One of the beauties of VBA is that you can create your own custom functions. They're commonly referred to as *user-defined functions* or *UDFs*. After you create such a function in a standard module, you can use it throughout your database as you would a built-in function.

To illustrate, we show you a function that converts numbers like 123.45 to words like One Hundred Twenty Three and 45/100. It's handy for printing checks. This function also requires using a little bit of everything that VBA has to offer — variables, arrays, loops, and decision-making. So it works as an example of how programmers combine all aspects of programming languages to come up with solutions to problems. Comments throughout the function explain what's going on, but it's not important to understand everything about how it works. Rather, it's just an example of what a large custom function might look like.

To create a custom function that's accessible to all objects in a database, you have to put the function in a standard module. Listing 3-1 shows the NumWord() custom function used to convert numbers to words as it would appear in a module under the words Option Compare Database in the module:

Listing 3-1:   NumWord() **custom function**

```
'Declare variables for NumWord to use
Dim English As String, strNum As String
Dim Chunk As String, Pennies As String
Dim Hundreds As Integer, Tens As Integer
Dim Ones As Integer, LoopCount As Integer
Dim StartVal As Integer, TensDone As Boolean
Dim EngNum(90) As String

'NumWord converts a number to its words,
'Useful for printing checks.
Function NumWord(AmountPassed As Currency) As String

    'Just bail out if no valid check amount passed.
    If AmountPassed <= 0 Then
        NumWord = "Void"
        Exit Function
    End If

    'Set up the array of words for numbers.
    EngNum(0) = ""
    EngNum(1) = "One"
    EngNum(2) = "Two"
    EngNum(3) = "Three"
    EngNum(4) = "Four"
    EngNum(5) = "Five"
    EngNum(6) = "Six"
    EngNum(7) = "Seven"
```

(continued)

Listing 3-1 *(continued)*

```
EngNum(8) = "Eight"
EngNum(9) = "Nine"
EngNum(10) = "Ten"
EngNum(11) = "Eleven"
EngNum(12) = „Twelve"
EngNum(13) = „Thirteen"
EngNum(14) = „Fourteen"
EngNum(15) = „Fifteen"
EngNum(16) = „Sixteen"
EngNum(17) = „Seventeen"
EngNum(18) = „Eighteen"
EngNum(19) = „Nineteen"
EngNum(20) = „Twenty"
EngNum(30) = „Thirty"
EngNum(40) = „Forty"
EngNum(50) = „Fifty"
EngNum(60) = „Sixty"
EngNum(70) = „Seventy"
EngNum(80) = „Eighty"
EngNum(90) = „Ninety"

,** Copy amount passed to a string with leading zeroes.
strNum = Format(AmountPassed, „000000000.00")

'** Put last two digits in Pennies variable for later use.
Pennies = Mid(strNum, 11, 2)

'Set starting values for some local variables.
English = ""
LoopCount = 1
StartVal = 1

'** Now do each 3-digit section of number.
Do While LoopCount <= 3
   Chunk = Mid(strNum, StartVal, 3)      '3-digit chunk
   Hundreds = Val(Mid(Chunk, 1, 1))      'Hundreds portion
   Tens = Val(Mid(Chunk, 2, 2))          'Tens portion
   Ones = Val(Mid(Chunk, 3, 1))          'Ones portion

   '** Do the hundreds portion of 3-digit number
   If Val(Chunk) > 99 Then
      English = English & EngNum(Hundreds) & " Hundred "
   End If

   '** Do the tens & ones portion of 3-digit number
   TensDone = False
   '** Is it less than 10?
   If Tens < 10 Then
      English = English & " " & EngNum(Ones)
      TensDone = True
   End If

   '** Is it a teen?
   If (Tens >= 11 And Tens <= 19) Then
      English = English & EngNum(Tens)
      TensDone = True
   End If
   '** Is it evenly divisible by 10?
   If (Tens / 10) = Int(Tens / 10) Then
      English = English & EngNum(Tens)
```

```
               TensDone = True
           End If
           '** Or is it none of the above?
           If Not TensDone Then
               English = English & EngNum((Int(Tens / 10)) * 10)
               English = English & " " & EngNum(Ones)
           End If

           '** Add the word "Million" if necessary
           If AmountPassed > 999999.99 And LoopCount = 1 Then
               English = English + " Million "
           End If

           '** Add the word "Thousand" if necessary
           If AmountPassed > 999.99 And LoopCount = 2 Then
               English = English + " Thousand "
           End If

           '** Do pass through next three digits
           LoopCount = LoopCount + 1
           StartVal = StartVal + 3
       Loop

       '** Done: Return English with Pennies/100 tacked on
       NumWord = Trim(English) & " and " & Pennies & "/100"
   End Function
```

You can test any custom function you create right at the Immediate window. For example, to test the NumWord() function, you'd use a question mark followed by a space and then NumWord with some number you want to convert to words. For example, suppose you type the following and press Enter:

```
? NumWord(123456.78)
```

NumWord() does its thing and spits back the result:

```
One Hundred Twenty Three Thousand Four Hundred Fifty Six and 78/100
```

Of course, in real life, you'd most likely use NumWord() in a database that has the ability to print checks. For example, suppose that in the same database as the NumWord() function, you have a table like the one in Figure 3-8 that contains information for writing checks.

Book VIII
Chapter 3

Writing Smarter Code

Figure 3-8:
Table of data for printing checks.

CheckID	PayTo	CheckNumb	CheckAmt	DatePrinted
1	Tori Pines	1001	$1,331.47	4/1/2010
2	Marilou Midcalf	1002	$123,456.78	4/1/2010
3	Wilma Wannabe	1003	$76,543.00	4/6/2010
4	Frankly Unctuous	1004	$644.45	4/7/2010
5	Margaret Angstrom	1005	$19.37	5/1/2010
6	Margie McDonald	1006	$782.35	5/2/2010
7	Hortense Higglebott	1007	$6.23	5/9/2010

Next, you'd need to create a report format that can print on pre-printed checks. Most of the controls on that report come straight from the table, except that you need one calculated control to print the check amount in words. That calculated control uses the expression =NumWord(CheckAmount). In other words, it uses the NumWord() function in the same way you use a built-in Access function. Figure 3-9 shows what that report design looks like.

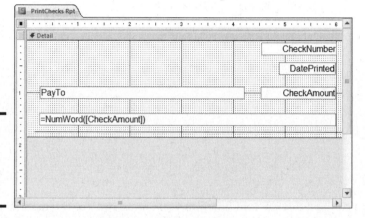

Figure 3-9:
Report
format for
printing
checks.

Of course, the tricky thing is getting all the boxes on the report format to line up correctly with areas on the pre-printed checks, but that's something you do in the report design. VBA is out of the loop on that part of the deal. The NumWord() function just saves you from having to hand-write the check amounts in words on all of the printed checks.

Chapter 4: Controlling Forms with VBA

In This Chapter

✔ Displaying — and responding to — custom messages

✔ Opening a form with the DoCmd object

✔ Changing form controls with VBA

✔ Using objects and collections in code

*W*hen you create a database for other people to use, making things as automatic as possible is to your advantage. The more automated your overall database, the less likely that *users* — the people who actually use the database — will make mistakes (even if the user is you!). This chapter explores some techniques for using Visual Basic for Applications (VBA) to display custom messages to users, to automatically open and close forms, to change form controls, and more.

Displaying Custom Messages

In your day-to-day work with your computer, programs occasionally pop little messages on-screen to ask you questions, such as, "Are you sure you want to delete . . .?" You can then click the Yes or OK button to delete, or click the No or Cancel button to change your mind. You can add similar custom messages to your database.

Displaying a message box

As we discuss in Chapter 2 of this minibook, VBA can also display custom messages. By using a variable and the MsgBox() function, you can display a question and then have VBA perform some task based on the user's answer to that question. The syntax for creating such an interactive message box is

```
Dim myVar as Byte
myVar = MsgBox(prompt[, buttons] [, title])
```

where the Dim statement defines a variable as the Byte data type, a number in the range of 0 to 255. *myVar* is any variable name of your choosing, *prompt* is the text of the message, and *title* is the text to appear in the title bar of the message. The *buttons* argument is a constant, or sum of constants, that specify the buttons and icons to show in the box, as summarized in Table 4-1.

Table 4-1   Constants Used for the MsgBox Buttons Argument

Constant	Description
vbOKOnly	Display OK button only
vbOKCancel	Display OK and Cancel buttons
vbAbortRetryIgnore	Display Abort, Retry, and Ignore buttons
vbYesNoCancel	Display Yes, No, and Cancel buttons
vbYesNo	Display Yes and No buttons
vbRetryCancel	Display Retry and Cancel buttons
vbCritical	Display Critical icon
vbQuestion	Display Question icon
vbExclamation	Display Warning icon
vbInformation	Display Information icon

For example, the following statement shows a message box that contains a Question icon and Yes and No buttons. Figure 4-1 shows the message box that the code displays when executed.

```
Dim myVar as Byte
myVar = MsgBox("Are you sure?",vbYesNo+vbQuestion)
```

Figure 4-1:
Sample
MsgBox
message.

When someone clicks a button in the message box, the variable (myVar in this example) receives a value. That value tells you which button the person clicked, as summarized in Table 4-2.

Table 4-2	Values That MsgBox Passes to the Variable	
Button Clicked	*Variable Receives*	*Numeric Value*
OK	vbOK	1
Cancel	vbCancel	2
Abort	vbAbort	3
Retry	vbRetry	4
Ignore	vbIgnore	5
Yes	vbYes	6
No	vbNo	7

Responding to what the user clicks

By using decision-making code, you can then have your VBA procedure do something when someone clicks a button on your message box, based on the contents of the myVar variable. For example, the sample message box displays a Yes button and a No button. If the user clicks the Yes button, myVar contains vbYes (or 6). If the user clicks the No button, myVar contains vbNo (or 7). The skeletal structure of the code that decides what to do — based on the button clicked (where Do these statements can be any number of VBA statements) — is shown in Listing 4-1:

Listing 4-1: Message box response code in which a constant refers to myVar

```
'Show a message box with Yes and No buttons.
Dim myVar as Byte
myVar = MsgBox("Are you sure?",vbYesNo+vbQuestion)
'Decide what to do next based on button clicked in box.
If myVar = vbYes Then
    'Do these statements if Yes
Else
    'Do these statements if No
End If
```

You can use either the constant or the numeric value to refer to the contents of the myVar variable. The following code in Listing 4-2 works exactly the same as the code in Listing 4-1:

**Book VIII
Chapter 4**

**Controlling Forms
with VBA**

Listing 4-2: Message box response code in which a numeric value refers to myVar

```
'Show a message box with Yes and No buttons.
Dim myVar as Byte
myVar = MsgBox("Are you sure?",vbYesNo+vbQuestion)
'Decide what to do next based on button clicked in box.
If myVar = 6 Then
    'Do these statements if Yes
Else
    'Do these statements if No
End If
```

If you need three buttons, you can use a `Select Case` statement to choose what to do. For example, the following code displays a message box with Yes, No, and Cancel buttons. The `Select Case` block of code shown in Listing 4-3 decides what to do based on the button that was clicked. (Again, `Do these statements` represents any number of VBA statements.)

Listing 4-3: Message box response code for three buttons

```
'Show a message box with Yes, No, and Cancel buttons.
Dim myVar as Byte
myVar = MsgBox("Overwrite?",vbYesNoCancel+vbQuestion)
'Decide what to do next based on button clicked in box.
Select Case myVar
    Case vbYes
        'Do these statements if Yes clicked
    Case vbNo
        'Do these statements if No clicked
    Case vbCancel
        'Do these statements if Cancel clicked
End Select
```

Message boxes are handy for presenting short little messages or asking the user questions. Often, though, you want your code to open an entire form.

Opening Forms with DoCmd

Although you can access countless objects in VBA, the `DoCmd` object (pronounced *do command*) is one of the easiest and handiest for manipulating Access objects. The `DoCmd` object gives you access to all the commands — including options on all menus, Ribbon groups, and shortcut menus — found in the Access program window. The basic syntax of a `DoCmd` statement is as follows:

```
DoCmd.methodName(arglist)
```

where *methodName* is any method that's supported by the DoCmd object, and *arglist* represents required and optional arguments that a given method accepts.

Like with any VBA keyword, as soon as you type DoCmd into the Code window, a menu of acceptable words that you can type next appears, as shown in Figure 4-2. Use the scroll bar at the right side of the list to see all your options.

Figure 4-2:
Sample
drop-down
menu that
appears as
you type in
VBA.

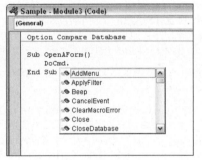

Of course, you can also use the VBA Help system to find more information on the DoCmd object and its methods. For instance, type **DoCmd** in the Type a Question for Help field in the VBA editor. Then click the DoCmd Object option to get help with that object.

Umpteen ways to open a form

Although many methods are available to choose from in the DoCmd object, the OpenForm method provides a good example. The syntax of the OpenForm method is

```
DoCmd.OpenForm FormName, [View], [FilterName],
    [WhereCondition], [DataMode], [WindowMode], [OpenArgs]
```

where

✦ *FormName* represents the name of the form that you want to open.

✦ *View* represents the view in which you want to open the form using the built-in constants:

- acNormal: Form view. This view is used if you omit the View argument in the statement.

- acDesign: Design view.

- acLayout: Layout view.

- `acFormDS`: Datasheet view.

- `acFormPivotChart`: PivotChart view.

- `acFormPivotTable`: PivotTable view.

- `acPreview`: Print Preview.

✦ *FilterName* specifies the name of a query within the current database, which limits records displayed by the form. If omitted, no query filter is applied.

✦ *WhereCondition* represents an expression, enclosed in quotation marks, that specifies records to include. If omitted, all records are available. For example, entering a *WhereCondition* such as `"[State] = 'CA'"` displays only records that have CA in the State field.

✦ *DataMode* specifies the data entry mode in which the form opens, using one of the following constants:

  - `acFormatPropertySettings` opens the form in its default view as specified in the form's `AllowEdits`, `AllowDeletions`, `AllowAdditions`, and `DataEntry` properties. If you don't specify a `DataMode` argument in the statement, this setting is used by default.

  - `acFormAdd`: Opens the form with the ability to add new records enabled and the cursor in a new, empty record.

  - `acFormEdit`: Opens the form with the ability to edit records contained within the table.

  - `acFormReadOnly`: Opens the form in read-only mode so that the user can only view — not change — the data.

✦ *WindowMode* specifies the appearance of the form window upon opening, using any of the following options:

  - `acWindowNormal`: Opens the form in its normal view. If you omit this argument, `acWindowNormal` is the setting that's applied automatically.

  - `acDialog`: Opens the form by using a fixed-size, dialog-box-style border.

  - `acHidden`: Opens the form so that the code can have access to the form's controls and data but doesn't make the form visible on-screen.

  - `acIcon`: Opens the form minimized to an icon in the Access program window.

✦ *OpenArgs* can be used to pass data to the form's class module, where other code can use it.

Macros and the DoCmd object

Access macros (see Book VI) use the DoCmd object to carry out most of their actions. Often, you can use macros to write a series of DoCmd statements without the complexities of manually typing each statement. Create a macro to do whatever you want your code to do. Then convert the macro to VBA code, as we discuss in Chapter 1 of this minibook. When you open the converted macro in VBA Editor, you see that most, if not all, of its actions are converted to DoCmd statements. You can then cut and paste those statements into some other procedure that you're writing. Or, just add any necessary code to the converted macro.

When you type a DoCmd.OpenForm statement into the Code window, the Quick Info syntax chart keeps you posted on which argument you're currently typing (by showing that argument in boldface). When you get to an argument that requires a constant, the Code window displays a drop-down list of acceptable constants. You can just double-click, rather than type, the constant that you want to use.

Look at some examples of using the OpenForm method of the DoCmd object. The following line opens a form named Products Form:

```
DoCmd.OpenForm "Products Form"
```

Because no optional arguments are specified, no filter is applied, and all other optional settings take on their default values. Opening the form by double-clicking its name in the Navigation pane accomplishes the same thing.

The following statement opens a form named Products Form, displaying only those records where the Selling Price field contains a number greater than 100:

```
DoCmd.OpenForm "Products Form", , , "[Selling Price] > 100"
```

The following statement opens a form named Sales Tax Calcs with the Window Mode property set to the dialog box style:

```
DoCmd.OpenForm "Sales Tax Calcs", , , , , acDialog
```

As you can see, the DoCmd object offers a lot of flexibility in specifying how you want to open a form. The same is true of many other methods of the DoCmd object. These few examples don't even come close to showing all the variations. The important thing is knowing that the DoCmd object exists and that you can perform many Access actions on objects within your database.

Book VIII
Chapter 4

Controlling Forms
with VBA

Closing a form with DoCmd

Just like you can open a form with `DoCmd`, you can also close it. The syntax to close an object using `DoCmd` is

```
DoCmd.Close(ObjectType, ObjectName, Save)
```

Each argument in the syntax represents the following:

✦ `ObjectType`: The type of object that you want to close expressed using one of the available constants, such as `acForm`, `acReport`, `acTable`, `acQuery`

✦ `ObjectName`: A string expression that identifies an object currently open

✦ `Save`: One of the following constants:

  • `acSaveNo`: Closes the object without saving any changes

  • `acSavePrompt`: (Default) Displays the standard `Do you want to save...` message so the user can choose whether to save

  • `acSaveYes`: Saves all changes to the form and then closes it

If you want to close a form, from code, and save the user's changes without prompting, use the following syntax:

```
DoCmd.Close acForm, formName, acSaveYes
```

where `formName` is the name of the form that you want to close. If you want a line of code to close a form named `Products Form`, the syntax is

```
DoCmd.Close acForm, "Products Form", acSaveYes
```

Changing Form Controls with VBA

When a form is open, you can use VBA code to change the contents and even the appearance of the form — from the big picture down to the individual controls on the form. Suppose you have a form that includes a control for choosing a payment method. When the user chooses a payment method, you want to enable or disable other controls on the form based on the selected payment method. Or, you might want to auto-fill some other controls on the form. You might even want to make some controls visible or invisible, depending on which payment method the user selected.

Figure 4-3 shows a few examples. When the user selects `Cash`, the `Paid` field is marked `True`, and all other fields are disabled. When the user selects `Credit Card`, the fields for entering credit card information are enabled. When the user selects `Purchase Order`, the P.O. Number control is enabled, and the Paid check box is emptied.

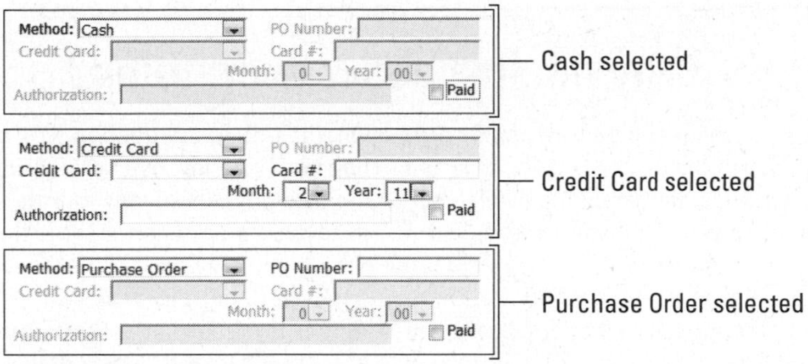

Figure 4-3:
Enabling/
disabling
controls
with VBA.

Cash selected

Credit Card selected

Purchase Order selected

Within VBA, use the following syntax to change a control's property:

```
ControlName.PropertyName = Value
```

where `ControlName` is the complete name of a control on an open form, `PropertyName` is the name of the property that you want to change, and `Value` is the new value for the property. A dot separates the control name from the property name. The complete name means that the name has to contain both the name of the form and the name of the control. However, in a class module, you can use the keyword `Me` to stand for the form name. The keyword `Me` means "the form to which this class module is attached."

Some cool control properties

To make a control invisible, use the following syntax:

```
Me.ControlName.Visible = False
```

To make the control visible, use the syntax

```
Me.ControlName.Visible = True
```

To disable a control so that it's dimmed and doesn't respond to mouse clicks or the keyboard, set the control's `Enabled` property to a `False` value:

```
Me.ControlName.Enabled = False
```

To set the control back to its normal `Enabled` status, use this syntax:

```
Me.ControlName.Enabled = True
```

Book VIII
Chapter 4

Controlling Forms
with VBA

Why not just show everything?

In case you're wondering why we don't show all the methods of the DoCmd object, or all the objects, properties, and methods available in all the object libraries, the truth of the matter is this: It's too many words. No, we're not too lazy to type that many words. Rather, there aren't enough pages in this entire book to fit that many words.

The sheer quantity of information makes remembering every detail of every VBA statement and object nearly impossible, so it

wouldn't do much good to print that information here anyway. Even professional programmers spend a lot of time looking up the syntax of keywords and objects in the Help system (or the Object Browser). The sooner you become fluent in using the VBA Editor's Help or the Object Browser (or both), the better off you are. See Chapters 1 and 2 of this minibook for more information on the Object Browser and VBA Help.

To change the value (contents) of a control, set the control's Value property equal to the value you want to put in that control. Here's the syntax:

```
Me.ControlName.Value = desiredValue
```

The *desiredValue* part has to be an appropriate data type for the control. For example, suppose that a control named Paid is on the form that's bound to a Yes/No field in the underlying table. The following statement makes that control True, thereby putting a check mark in its check box:

```
Me.Paid.Value = True
```

To clear that check mark, use

```
Me.Paid.Value = False
```

To insert new text into a text box, use the standard syntax but enclose the new text in quotation marks. For example, if the current form has a Text Box control named Product Name that's bound to a Text field, the following statement puts the text in quotation marks into that control:

```
Me.ProductName.Value = "9-Passenger Lear Jet"
```

To increase or decrease a value in a numeric field, set the Value property of its control to an expression that does the appropriate math. Suppose that a form contains a UnitPrice control that's a Currency field. The following statement increases that control's current value by 10 percent:

```
Me.UnitPrice.Value = 1.10 * Me.UnitPrice.Value
```

Controlling properties example

Take a look now at how you might use the preceding techniques to control what happens to controls in the payment method example shown near the start of this chapter. Figure 4-4 shows those controls on a form, in Design view, so that you can see the actual control names. The `Label` control named `ExpireLabel` doesn't show a name, so we pointed that one out. We also selected that control — and are showing its Property sheet — so you can see its `Name` property and some of the other properties it offers. The Property sheet for a control is how you find out exactly what properties the control offers.

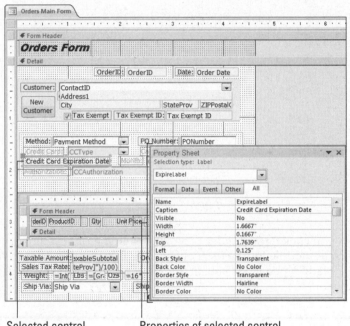

Figure 4-4: Properties of a control in Design view form.

Selected control (ExpireLabel)

Properties of selected control

The Payment Method control in the example is named `Payment Method`. It's a combo box that allows the user to choose one of four possible payment methods: Cash, Check, Credit Card, or Money Order. As soon as the user makes a selection from that combo box, we want some VBA code to change some other controls. In particular, we want it to disable controls that aren't relevant to the selected payment method. We can also have it mark the `Paid` field as `False` when Purchase Order is selected. And just as an example, we'll have it hide the `ExpireLabel` control when the user selects anything except Credit Card.

So the first question is, when should this custom VBA code be executed? The `After Update` event is the best event for this situation because that event occurs after a new value is selected, and any validation criteria for the field have already been met. So in this case, you click the `Payment Method` control (in Design view) to select it. If the Property sheet isn't already open, right-click that control and choose Properties. Click the Event tab in the Property sheet. Click the `After Update` event, click its Build button, and then choose the Code Builder from the dialog box that appears, as illustrated in Figure 4-5.

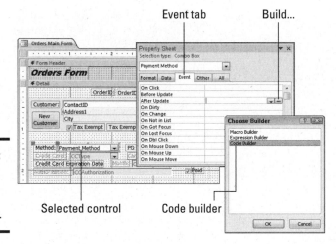

Figure 4-5: Manually creating an event procedure.

After you click Code Builder and then OK in the Choose Builder dialog box, the class module for the form opens. The first and last lines of the procedure are already typed in for you. In this example, the lines look like this in the module:

```
Private Sub Payment_Method_AfterUpdate()

End Sub
```

When writing the procedure, be sure to put all the lines between the `Private Sub` and `End Sub` statements. We typed in the necessary code in Listing 4-4. Just to make things even fancier, we threw in a few `DoCmd.GoToControl` statements to position the cursor to the next control that the user would likely type in next. For example, the statement `DoCmd.GoToControl "CCType"` means "move the blinking cursor into the control named `CCType`."

Listing 4-4:   An event procedure

```
Private Sub Payment_Method_AfterUpdate()
   'First, disable controls and hide the label,
   'to create a simple starting point.
   Me.CheckNo.Enabled = False
   Me.PONumber.Enabled = False
   Me.CCType.Enabled = False
   Me.CCNumber.Enabled = False
   Me.CCExpireMonth.Enabled = False
   Me.CCExpireYear.Enabled = False
   Me.CCAuthorization.Enabled = False
   Me.ExpireLabel.Visible = False

   'Now selectively show and enable controls,
   'and fill the Paid field, based on the
   'contents of the Payment Method control
   Select Case Me.[Payment Method].Value

       'If selection is Cash...
       Case "Cash"
          Me.Paid.Value = True

       'If selection is Check...
       Case "Check"
          Me.CheckNo.Enabled = True
          Me.Paid.Value = True
          'Move cursor to CheckNo control
          DoCmd.GoToControl "CheckNo"

       'If selection is Credit Card...
       Case "Credit Card"
          Me.CCType.Enabled = True
          Me.CCNumber.Enabled = True
          Me.CCExpireMonth.Enabled = True
          Me.CCExpireYear.Enabled = True
          Me.CCAuthorization.Enabled = True
          Me.ExpireLabel.Visible = True
          Me.Paid.Value = True
          'Move cursor to CCType control
          DoCmd.GoToControl "CCType"

       'If selection is Purchase Order...
       Case "Purchase Order"
          Me.PONumber.Enabled = True
          Me.Paid.Value = False
          'Move cursor to PONumber control
          DoCmd.GoToControl "PONumber"

   End Select
End Sub
```

Looks can be deceiving

When you create a lookup field, what you see in that field may not match what Access has actually stored in the field. For example, you may have a `ContactID` field that shows a customer name in the format `Jones, Hank`. However, Access actually stores that person's `ContactID` as a number (perhaps `39` or whatever).

VBA sees what Access sees — the `ContactID` number in the preceding example, not the name. Any code that you write needs to take that into consideration. To create an `If` statement that makes a decision based on the contents of the `ContactID` field, use something like this:

```
If Me.ContactID.Value = 39
```

If you use the following statement instead, the code either generates an error message or perhaps doesn't give the result that you think it should:

```
If Me.ContactID.Value =
    "Jones. Hank"
```

You can add a `Debug.Print` statement to your code and run it from the Immediate window to see what type of data is stored in a control. For example:

```
Debug.Print Me.ContactID,Value
```

displays the contents of the `ContactID` control. If that's a number, you know that the `ContactID` field in every record contains a number.

The code and comments should be fairly easy to read. For starters, the sub procedure name, `Payment_Method_AfterUpdate()`, tells you that this code executes after a user makes a selection from the `Payment Method` control, and Access accepts that change.

The first lines under the `Sub` statement disable most controls and hide the expiration label, just so that we know the status of each control before the `Select Case` statement executes.

The `Select Case Me.[Payment Method].Value` statement uses the value (contents) of the `Payment Method` control to make a decision about which controls to enable and make visible. When the `Cash` option is selected, only this code is executed, filling the Paid check box with a check mark:

```
Case "Cash"
    Me.Paid.Value = True
```

When the `Check` option is selected, the following lines execute to enable the `CheckNo` control, place a check mark in the Paid check box, and move the cursor to the `CheckNo` control:

```
Case "Check"
    Me.CheckNo.Enabled = True
    Me.Paid.Value = True
    'Move cursor to CheckNo control
    DoCmd.GoToControl "CheckNo"
```

And so it goes, each `Case` statement modifying certain controls and positioning the cursor based on the current value of the `Payment Method` control.

After typing in the code, close the Code window and Visual Basic Editor to return to your form. There you can save the form, open it in Form view, and try out your code.

If you have difficulty with your own code, you may find some of the debugging techniques described in Chapter 6 of this minibook useful for diagnosing and fixing problems.

Understanding Objects and Collections

Working with controls on a form or report from within a class module is greatly simplified by the `Me` keyword, which refers to the form or report to which the class module is attached. Things become more complicated when you write code in standard modules, where the keyword `Me` doesn't refer to anything because a standard module isn't attached to any particular form or report. The moment you step outside a class module, you have to think more in terms of the object models.

As you (hopefully) know, just about everything you work with in Access is an object — tables, queries, and forms are all objects. Some objects are very much alike; tables are alike in that they all contain data. Forms are alike in that they all present data from tables in a certain format. A group of like objects forms a *collection*. For example, all the tables within your database represent that database's tables collection.

In some cases, a single object may be a collection as well. A single form is one object in the collection of forms, but a single form is also a collection in its own right — a collection of controls. Each control on a form is also an object in its own right, but even a single control is a collection. A control has lots of properties, as you can see on any control's Property sheet in Design view. Figure 4-6 shows how a collection is a bunch of objects that have something in common, and how any given object can also be a collection.

Properties, methods, and events

All objects have some combination of properties, methods, and events. Objects in the real world as well as objects in Access have properties, methods, and events. You can describe a car in terms of its properties (make, model, size, color, and so forth), methods (you drive a car), and events (you press the brake pedal, which causes a series of actions that slow the car down). Getting back to Access, we define those terms as follows:

✦ **Property:** A *property* of an object (or collection) is some characteristic of that object, such as size, color, font, and so forth.

✦ **Method:** A *method* is something that you can do to the object. Every form has an `Open` method and a `Close` method because you can open and close forms. (The `DoCmd` object that we mention earlier in this chapter provides access to the methods provided by most Access objects.)

✦ **Event:** An *event* is something that happens to an object. When you click a button on a form, you trigger its `On Click` event (or `Click` event).

Virtually everything in Access is an object that has properties, methods, and events. If you open a form in Design view, you can click any control to see its properties in the Property sheet. If the Property sheet isn't open, press Alt+Enter or right-click a control and choose Properties.

Many objects support methods. For example, if you right-click a form name in the Navigation pane, you see a shortcut menu like the one in Figure 4-7. Most of the items you see on the shortcut menu are methods — things you can do to the object.

Of course, when you're working in VBA, the visual interactive tools that Access offers — tools such as shortcut menus and Property sheets — aren't visible. In VBA, you write code to access collections, objects, properties, methods, and events.

Collection of Forms   Collection of Controls   Collection of Properties

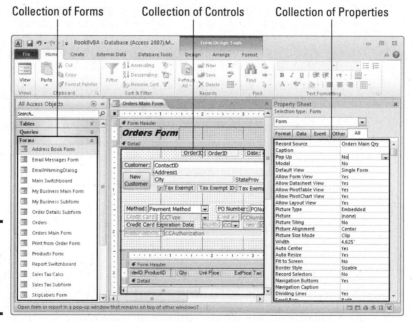

Figure 4-6:
Collections are everywhere in Access.

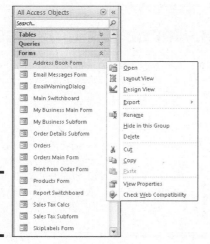

Figure 4-7:
Form
methods.

Referring to objects and collections

Manipulating an object through VBA code starts with a two-step process:

1. Declare an object variable (by using `Dim`) as the appropriate object or collection type.

2. Set the object variable (by using the `Set` keyword) to a specific object or collection within your database.

The syntax of the statements for performing those two steps looks like this:

```
Dim anyName As objectType
Set anyName = specificObject
```

where *anyName* is a variable name of your choosing, the *objectType* is one of the keywords shown in the first column of Table 4-3, and *specific Object* represents a specific named object.

Table 4-3	Common Types for Object Variables
Object Type	*Use to Declare*
`AccessObject`	Any type of Access object in `AllForms`, `AllReports`, and other collections
`Form`	A form
`Report`	A report
`Control`	A control on a form or report
`Property`	A property of an object
`RecordSet`	A group of records (see Chapter 5 of this minibook)

Naming conventions for object variables

In this chapter, we use the letters `my` at the start of variable names, just to provide some consistency. Some programmers, however, follow certain naming conventions, replacing the letters `my` with a tag that represents the object type that the variable refers to. If an object variable refers to an `AccessObject`, programmers may use `obj` as the first letters of an object variable name, as in `Dim objForm as AccessObject`. Some may use `ctl` as the first letters of an object variable that refers to a control, as in `Dim ctlProductID as Control`.

Naming conventions are especially useful in large projects where many different programmers work with code. They help identify the object type each variable refers to. However, naming conventions are also entirely optional. Don't feel that you must use them in your own code.

At the highest level of the object model, you can use the `AllForms`, `AllReports`, and other collections contained within the `CurrentProject` object to refer to any form or report — even forms and reports that aren't open. Each object in those collections has a general type called `AccessObject`.

For a detailed explanation of the `CurrentProject` object and the collections that it supports, look up the `CurrentProject` object in the VBA Editor Help and look at the `CurrentProject Object` link.

If you want to create a reference to a form named `Products Form`, in code, and give that form a short variable name, like `myForm`, declare `myForm` as an `AccessObject`. Then set that variable's value to the form by using the syntax `Set myForm = CurrentProject.AllForms("FormName")`, as the following shows:

```
Dim myForm As AccessObject
Set myForm = CurrentProject.AllForms("Products Form")
```

After the code runs, the variable named `myForm` refers to the form named `Products Form`.

An example: Seeing whether a form is open

You can create a custom VBA function that uses a collection and an object variable. You can prevent your code and macros from opening multiple copies of a form. The name of this custom function is `isOpen()` and is shown in Figure 4-8.

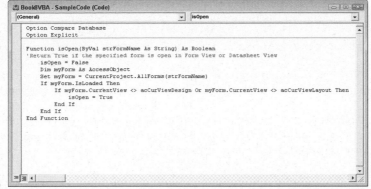

Figure 4-8:
The
`isOpen()`
function
determines
whether
a form is
open.

The `isOpen()` function is stored in a standard module, rather than a class module, so you can access it freely from anywhere in your database.

You use the `isOpen()` custom function, just like you would a built-in function, by passing a form name to the function, as the following shows:

```
isOpen("Products Form")
```

When called, the `isOpen()` function returns `True` if the specified form is open or `False` if the specified form is closed. The first statement of the `isOpen()` function is the following:

```
Function isOpen(FormName As String) As Boolean
```

which defines the name of the function as `isOpen`, accepting a single string value that is referred to as `FormName` within the procedure. This custom function returns either `True` or `False` (a Boolean value).

The `ByVal` keyword, used in front of an argument name in a `Sub` or `Function` statement, passes the value directly instead of as a reference to the object. `ByVal`, although optional, can speed the processing.

The next line sets the initial value to be returned by the function to `False`. Later code in the procedure turns that to `True` if the form is open in Form or Datasheet view:

```
isOpen = False
```

The next line in the code declares an object variable named `myForm` and sets its type to `AccessObject`:

```
Dim myForm As AccessObject
```

**Book VIII
Chapter 4**

**Controlling Forms
with VBA**

The next line then makes the `myForm` object variable refer to the specific form, based on the name that passes to the function:

```
Set myForm = CurrentProject.AllForms(strFormName)
```

If you call the function by using `isOpen("Products Form")`, the variable name `myForm` refers to the Products Form after the line is executed.

The next statement uses the built-in `IsLoaded` property to determine whether the form is open. If the form is open, `isLoaded` returns `True`. If the form is closed, `isLoaded` returns `False`:

```
If myForm.IsLoaded Then
```

If (and only if) the form is indeed open, the next statement uses the `CurrentView` property to see whether the form is currently open in Design view or Layout view. (`CurrentView` is a property of all form objects; `acCurViewDesign` is a constant that means "currently open in Design view"; `acCurViewLayout` is a constant that means "currently open in Layout view"):

```
If myForm.CurrentView <> acCurViewDesign And _ myForm.
    CurrentView <> acCurViewLayout Then
```

If (and only if) the form is open — but not open in Design view or Layout view — the following statement sets `isOpen` to `True`. If the form isn't open or is open in Design view or Layout view, the next line doesn't execute, so `isOpen` retains its original value of `False`:

```
isOpen = True
```

The rest of the procedure just contains an `End If` statement for each `If` block, and the `End Function` statement to mark the end of the procedure.

To see some practical uses of the custom `isOpen()` function, imagine that you already added that custom function to a standard module in your database. Now you want to use the function to see whether a form is open before you execute code to open that form. In particular, you want the code to see whether `Products Form` is open — and, if it isn't, to go ahead and open the form. Use the following code to open a form:

```
'Open Products Form, but only if it isn't open already.
If Not isOpen("Products Form") Then
    DoCmd.OpenForm "Products Form"
End If
```

Suppose you want a procedure to close the form, but you want to make sure the form is indeed open before using `DoCmd.Close` to close the form. In that case, use these statements:

```
'Close Products Form if it is currently open.
If isOpen("Products Form") Then
    DoCmd.Close acForm, "Products Form", acSaveNo
End If
```

In a macro, you can use `isOpen()` to ensure that the macro doesn't try to open a form that's already open. You can also use `isOpen()` to make sure that a form is open before you close it, as shown in Figure 4-9.

Figure 4-9:
Using
`IsOpen`
function
in macro
Condition.

Looping through collections

Access provides a slight variation on the `For...Next` loop, known as the `For Each...Next` loop, that's designed to specifically repeat once for each item within a collection. With each pass through the loop, the object variable used in the `For Each...Next` loop refers to the next object in the collection. The syntax of the `For Each...Next` loop is

```
For Each element In collection
    [statements]
[Exit For]
    [statements]
Next [element]
```

where *element* is an object variable of the appropriate type for the collection, *collection* is the name of a collection, and *statements* are any number of statements to be executed within the loop.

Whether you ever need a `For Each...Next` loop in your own code depends on how fancy things get. However, if you use other peoples' code, you may come across an occasional `For Each...Next` loop, so you need to have an idea of what that loop does.

For example, recall that the `AllForms` collection in the `CurrentProject` object contains all the forms in the current database. Each form in the collection is a type of `AccessObject`.

The `Forms` collection contains only the forms that are open. The `AllForms` collection includes both closed and open forms.

In Listing 4-5, we use the `Dim` statement to declare an object variable named `myForm` as an `AccessObject`. Then we use a `For Each...Next` loop to loop through the `AllForms` collection and print the `Name` property of every form in the database:

Listing 4-5:   Looping through the AllForms collection

```
Dim myForm as AccessObject
For Each myForm In CurrentProject.AllForms
    'Code to be performed on every form.
    Debug.Print myForm.Name
Next
```

Running the code in Listing 4-5 prints the name of each form in the current database to the Immediate window.

Recall, too, that a form is a collection in its own right — a collection of controls. To set up a loop that looks at each control on a form, you first need to make sure that the form is open. Then, define an object variable as the `Control` element type. The collection name used in the `For Each...Next` loop needs to be a specific open form.

The following code snippet opens a form named `Products Form`. The `Dim` statement creates an object variable, named `myCtl`, as the generic `Control` type of object. The `For Each...Next` loop specifies all the controls on the current form as the collection. With each pass through the loop in Listing 4-6, the `Debug.Print` statement prints the name of the current control:

Listing 4-6:   Looping through the controls

```
DoCmd.OpenForm "Products Form"
Dim myCtl as Control
For Each myCtl In Forms![Products Form]
    'Code to be performed on every control goes below.
    Debug.Print myCtl.Name
Next
```

A control, as you may recall, is also a collection: A collection of properties defines the control's name, contents, appearance, type, and behavior. If you want to set up a loop that accesses each property that a control supports, first ensure that the form is open. With that accomplished, define an object variable of the `Property` type and use the specific control's name as the collection name in the `For Each...Next` loop, as Listing 4-7 shows:

Listing 4-7: Looping through the properties

```
DoCmd.OpenForm "Products Form"
Dim myProp as Property
For Each myProp In Forms![Products Form].[Product Name]
    'Code to be performed on every control goes below.
    Debug.Print myProp.Name & " = " & myProp.Value
Next
```

The first line opens a form named `Products Form`. The next line defines an object variable named `myProp` as the `Property` type. Then the `For Each...Next` loop displays the name and value of every property for the `Product Name` field.

Using With...End With

If you need to change a whole bunch of properties associated with an object, you can save a little typing by using a `With...End With` block. The syntax for the block is

```
With objectName
    .property = value
End With
```

where `objectName` is the name of an open object, or the object variable name that points to the object; `.property` is a valid property for that object; and `value` is the value you want to assign to that object. Assuming that `myCtl` refers to a control on an open form, as in Listing 4-8, you can use a `With myCtl...End With` block to change several properties of that control:

Listing 4-8: Using a With myCtl...End With block to change a control's properties

```
Dim myCtl As Control
Set myCtl = myForm.[Selling Price]
With myCtl
    .Visible = True
    .SpecialEffect = Flat
    .FontBold = True
    .Value = 1.1 * myCtl
End With
```

The `With...End With` block changes the `Visible` property of the `Selling Price` control to `True`, sets its `Special Effect` property to `Flat`, sets its font to bold, and increases the value stored in that field by 10 percent.

As in the case of the `For Each...Next` loop, the `With...End With` statement is optional and not something you must use in any code you write. Our main purpose is to take the mystery out of it in case you should ever come across `With...End With` in someone else's code.

Chapter 5: Using SQL and Recordsets

In This Chapter

✔ **Creating quick and easy recordsets**

✔ **Using SQL to create recordsets**

✔ **Running action queries from VBA code**

*W*orking with data in tables and queries through Visual Basic for Applications (VBA) is — in a word — weird. You don't exactly work with a table or query directly in VBA. Instead, you work with a recordset. As the name implies, a *recordset* is a set of records. A recordset can be all the records in a given table, all the records in the results of a query involving two or more tables, or a subset of particular records from any table or query. In other words, a recordset can contain any records from any tables you want.

Recordsets and Object Models

Because Access offers two different object models for the purpose of working with recordsets, you may find recordsets confusing. One is DAO (Data Access Objects); the other is ADO (ActiveX Data Objects). The DAO model is the older of the two. DAO works only with Access tables. ADO, the newer of the two, works either with Access tables or external data sources, such as Oracle and Microsoft SQL Server.

At first glance, you may think, "Well, I'll never use external data sources, so I'll stick with the DAO object model." Picking an object model, though, isn't that easy. The newer ADO model is currently favored by Microsoft, meaning that ADO will continue to grow and get better while DAO remains in maintenance mode, which generally spells doom for a technology. If a technology is in maintenance mode today, that pretty much guarantees that it won't exist in the not-too-distant future.

Given the bias of Microsoft, we stick with ADO in this book. To make sure the stuff that we do in this chapter works on your computer, make sure the ADO object model is loaded in your copy of Access. To do so, open the Visual Basic Editor, choose Tools⇨References from the VBA Editor menu, and select the Microsoft ActiveX Data Objects 6.0 Library option. (See Figure 5-1.) If you don't see that one in your References dialog box, you'll have to scroll down to find it.

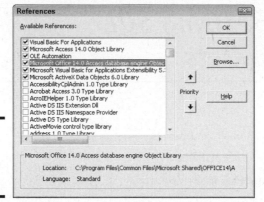

References

A̲vailable References:

☑ Visual Basic For Applications
☑ Microsoft Access 14.0 Object Library
☑ OLE Automation
☑ Microsoft Office 14.0 Access database engine Object
☑ Microsoft Visual Basic for Applications Extensibility 5.
☑ Microsoft ActiveX Data Objects 6.0 Library
☐ AccessibilityCplAdmin 1.0 Type Library
☐ Acrobat Access 3.0 Type Library
☐ AcroIEHelper 1.0 Type Library
☐ Active DS IIS Extension Dll
☐ Active DS IIS Namespace Provider
☐ Active DS Type Library
☐ ActiveMovie control type library
☐ address 1.0 Type Library

OK
Cancel
Browse...
Priority
Help

Microsoft Office 14.0 Access database engine Object Library
    Location: C:\Program Files\Common Files\Microsoft Shared\OFFICE14\A
    Language: Standard

Figure 5-1:
The
References
dialog box.

Because ADO is evolving quickly, you'll likely find several versions of the ActiveX Data Objects library in your References dialog box. Select only the most recent one — the one with the highest version number. Then click OK.

Quick and easy recordsets

If your goal is to create a recordset that contains all the fields and records from a single table in your database, the job is fairly straightforward. Just type the following code, exactly as shown, into a procedure — but replace *tableName* with the name of the table that you want to open:

If you don't yet know how to type code into a procedure, see Chapter 2 of this minibook.

```
Dim myConnection as ADODB.Connection
Set myConnection = CurrentProject.Connection
Dim myRecordset as New ADODB.Recordset
myRecordSet.ActiveConnection = myConnection
myRecordset.Open "tableName", , adOpenStatic, adLockOptimistic
```

After all the lines execute, the myRecordSet object variable refers to all the fields and records in whatever table you specified as tableName in the last line of code.

ADO recordset properties and methods

Most ADO recordsets support the following methods, which allow you to manipulate the data in the recordset with VBA code:

✦ .AddNew: Adds a new, blank record to the recordset

✦ .MoveFirst: Moves the cursor to the first record in the recordset

✦ .MoveNext: Moves the cursor to the next record in the recordset

✦ .MovePrevious: Moves the cursor to the previous record in the recordset

✦ .MoveLast: Moves the cursor to the last record in the recordset

✦ .Move *numrecords, start*: Specifies the number of records to move through and the starting point

✦ .Open: Opens a new recordset

✦ .Close: Closes a recordset

✦ .Update: Saves any changes made to the current row of a recordset

✦ .UpdateBatch: Saves all changes made to the current recordset

Some properties you can use to determine the number of records in a recordset, as well as the current position of the cursor within the recordset, are the following:

✦ .RecordCount: Returns the total number of records in the recordset

✦ .AbsolutePosition: Returns a number indicating which row the cursor is in (1 is the first record, 2 is the second record, and so forth.)

✦ .BOF: Beginning Of File; returns True when the cursor is above the first record in the recordset

✦ .EOF: End Of File; returns True when the cursor is past the last record in the recordset

Looping through a recordset

When a recordset is open, you can use a loop to step through each record within the recordset. As an example, Figure 5-2 shows some code that creates a recordset named myRecordSet. The While...Wend loop steps through each record in the recordset — one record at a time — and prints the record's position and the contents of the first couple of fields in each record.

Figure 5-2:
Sample sub procedure loops through records in a recordset.

The code in Figure 5-2 isn't exactly simple. The sections that follow, however, shed some light on some of its meaning.

Flip to Chapter 3 of this minibook to review `While...Wend` loops.

Defining a recordset's cursor type

When you open a table in Datasheet or Form view, you see the blinking cursor and move it around freely using your mouse or keyboard. With recordsets, you can choose from different types of cursors. The *cursor* is a pointer to the current record in the recordset. These types of cursors have nothing to do with how the cursor looks because in a recordset, you can't see the cursor (or the data)! Rather, the cursor type in a recordset defines how the cursor behaves within the recordset. You can define a recordset's cursor type two separate ways: One is to change the recordset's `CursorType` property by using the following syntax:

```
recordsetName.CursorType = constant
```

where `recordsetName` is the name of the recordset, and `constant` is one of the constants listed in the first column of Table 5-1. You must define the recordset's cursor type before opening a recordset.

You can also specify the cursor type when opening the recordset by using this syntax:

```
myRecordset.Open "tableName/SQL", , CursorType
```

where `tableName/SQL` is the name of the table in the current database or a valid SQL statement (which we discuss in a moment), and `CursorType` is one of the constants listed in Table 5-1.

Many cursor type options are relevant only to multiuser databases. When working with a single-user database, the `adOpenStatic` setting is the easiest to work with.

Table 5-1	Recordset Cursor Types	
Constant	*Name*	*Description*
`adOpenDynamic`	Dynamic Cursor	Allows unrestricted cursor movement. You can modify data in the recordset. Changes made by other users in a multiuser setting reflect in the recordset.
`adOpenStatic`	Static Cursor	Recordset is a nonchanging version of the table. Changes made by other users have no effect on the recordset.

Constant	Name	Description
adOpen ForwardOnly	Forward-Only Cursor	Same as Static Cursor, but the cursor moves only forward through the table. This setting is the default if you don't specify a cursor type.
adOpenKeyset	Keyset Cursor	Like a Dynamic Cursor, but records added by other users aren't added to the recordset. Records deleted by other users are inaccessible to your recordset.

The .RecordCount and .AbsolutePosition properties only return correct values when you're using a static cursor type, which is another reason why we use adOpenStatic as the cursor type in our examples. When using a dynamic cursor, .RecordCount and .AbsolutePosition always return -1. because the number and position of the records in the recordset may change.

Field names in recordsets

In a recordset, each *record* is a collection of fields. You can refer to fields by their position in the record. myRecordSet.Fields(0) refers to the first field in the record, myRecordset.Fields(1) refers to the second field, and so forth. You can also refer to fields by their names. The syntax is

```
myRecordSet.Fields("fieldname")
```

where *fieldname* is the name of the field as defined in the table. You must type the fieldname exactly as it appears in the table's Design view (including spaces).

SQL and Recordsets

You don't have to base a recordset on a single table. You can base it on a query if you like. However, you can't use the query's name in the myRecordset.Open statement because only table names are allowed there. If you want to base a recordset on a query, you need to use the query's SQL statement to create the query.

SQL (*see*-quel), stands for *Structured Query Language*. You can't get very far in database management without hearing some reference to SQL, because SQL is "the" standard language for extracting information from data stored in Access tables, Microsoft SQL Server, Oracle, and a whole bunch of other database products.

As a language, SQL can get fairly complex. The syntax of a basic SQL statement looks something like this:

```
SELECT fields1 FROM table(s) [WHERE criterion] [ORDER BY
     fields2]
```

where *fields1* represents a list of fields from the table (or * for all fields), *table(s)* represents the name of the table (or tables) where the data are stored, *criterion* represents an expression that filters records (for example, State="CA"), and *fields2* represents fields to use for sorting the records. The WHERE and ORDER BY portions are optional.

Writing SQL statements is fairly easy after a bit of practice; don't worry, you rarely need to write them by hand. Every time that you create a query by using Design view, you actually write a SQL statement. The fields that you choose for the query become the fields included in the recordset, although only those fields that have a check mark in the Show box are actually included. The FROM table that you select records from is plainly visible at the top of the grid. The Sort row defines the ORDER BY clause. The Criteria row specifies the WHERE clause, as illustrated in Figure 5-3.

Select (fields)   From (tables)

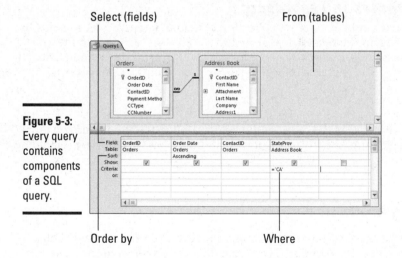

Figure 5-3:
Every query
contains
components
of a SQL
query.

Order by   Where

To see the SQL statement for any query you create, right-click the title bar or document tab of your query (in Design view) and choose the SQL View option from the shortcut menu. Or, click the Ribbon's (Query Tools) Design tab and choose View⇨SQL View in the Results group. You see the SQL statement the query uses to get the data specified, as shown in Figure 5-4. The SQL statement may already be selected (highlighted); copy it to the Clipboard, if you wish, by pressing Ctrl+C.

Figure 5-4:
Sample SQL
statement
produced by
a query.

```
Query1
SELECT Orders.OrderID, Orders.[Order Date], Orders.ContactID, [Address Book].StateProv
FROM [Address Book] INNER JOIN Orders ON [Address Book].ContactID = Orders.ContactID
WHERE ((([Address Book].StateProv)='CA'))
ORDER BY Orders.[Order Date];
```

If the SQL statement isn't already selected, drag the mouse pointer through
the entire SQL statement to select it, and then press Ctrl+C. After you copy
the SQL statement to the Clipboard, you can paste it into a `myRecordSet.`
`Open` statement in VBA code where indicated by the SQL statement here:

```
myRecordset.Open "SQL statement here", , cursorType
```

Unfortunately, just pasting the SQL statement isn't quite enough to get the
job done. You have to change some things in the VBA code, namely:

✦ You must remove the semicolon (`;`) from the end of the SQL statement.

✦ If the pasted SQL statement breaks across multiple lines, gather the lines
together into one long line. (Or break up the line by using the continuation character, as we discuss in a moment.)

✦ If the SQL statement contains any double quotation marks (`"`), replace
them with single quotation marks (`'`).

Take a look at Figure 5-4 (earlier in this chapter) for an example of a big
SQL statement. The first step is to select the SQL statement by dragging the
mouse pointer through it until you highlight all the text. Then press Ctrl+C
or right-click the highlighted text and choose Copy from the shortcut menu
to put a copy of the SQL statement on the Clipboard.

Within your procedure in the Code window, type out the `recordset.Open`
statement, followed by two sets of double quotation marks. Place the cursor
between the two quotation marks, as in the following example (where the |
character represents the cursor):

```
myRecordSet.Open "|"
```

Press Ctrl+V to paste the SQL statement between the quotation marks.

The cursor lands at the end of the SQL statement, just to the right of the
semicolon at the end of the statement. Press Backspace to delete the
semicolon.

If the SQL statement breaks into multiple lines, you need to unbreak it. Move
the cursor to the end of the first line. If a quotation mark is at the end of the

**Book VIII
Chapter 5**

**Using SQL and
Recordsets**

first line, delete it. Then press Delete (Del) key to delete the line break and bring the next line up to the current line. Leave a blank space between any whole words. Repeat this process until the entire SQL statement is one big, long line in the Code window.

Finally, look through the SQL statement for any double quotation marks. Don't disturb the quotation marks surrounding the whole SQL statement. Just change any double quotation marks within the statement, as in the following example:

```
WHERE (((Address Book].State="CA" ORDER BY
```

to single quotation marks as the following shows:

```
WHERE (((Address Book].State='CA' ORDER BY
```

When everything is clean, the Code window accepts the statement without showing any red lines (lines with code that VBA doesn't recognize) or `Compile Error` messages.

Breaking up long SQL statements

In the previous section, we said that for a copied SQL statement to work in your code, you have to treat it as one extremely long line. An alternative to the one-extremely-long-line approach is to store the SQL statement as a string variable. Then use that variable name in your `myRecordset.Open` statement. Within the code, build the lengthy SQL statement by joining short chunks of text together.

The first step is to declare a string variable, perhaps named `mySQL`, to store the SQL statement, as the following variable shows:

```
Dim mySQL As String
```

Assign the SQL statement to the string. Use the following rules to assign the SQL statement:

✦ Each chunk is fully enclosed in quotation marks.

✦ If a blank space is after a word, leave that blank space in the line.

✦ Follow each line with an ampersand (`&`) character (the join strings operator), a blank space, and the continuation character (`_`).

✦ Use the variable name in the `recordset.Open` statement.

You still have to convert any embedded double quotation marks to single quotation marks, and then remove the ending semicolon.

The following example shows an original SQL statement. (Just imagine that the code stretches out as one long line, which the margins of this book prevent us from showing.)

```
SELECT Orders.*, [Address Book].* FROM [Address Book] INNER JOIN Orders ON
    [Address Book].ContactID = Orders.ContactID WHERE ((([Address Book].
    State)="NY")) ORDER BY Orders.[Order Date];
```

The following statements show some VBA code to store that SQL statement in a mySQL string variable. The myRecordSet.Open statement creates the recordset from the SQL statement:

```
'Form a SQL statement from "chunks".
Dim mySQL As String
mySQL = "SELECT Orders.*, [Address Book].* FROM [Address Book] " & _
    "INNER JOIN Orders ON [Address Book].ContactID = Orders.ContactID " & _
    "WHERE ((([Address Book].State)='NY')) " & _
    "ORDER BY Orders.[Order Date]"
'Fill the recordset with data defined by the SQL statement.
myRecordSet.Open mySQL, , adOpenStatic, adLockOptimistic
```

Notice a few essential characteristics of this code:

✦ Each chunk of the SQL string is enclosed in double quotation marks.

✦ The blank space after a word is included at the end of the line.

✦ The ampersand and continuation character, separated by single blank spaces, end each line.

✦ The myRecordSet.Open statement then uses the mySQL variable name in place of the lengthy SQL statement.

Figure 5-5 shows how this all looks in the Code window.

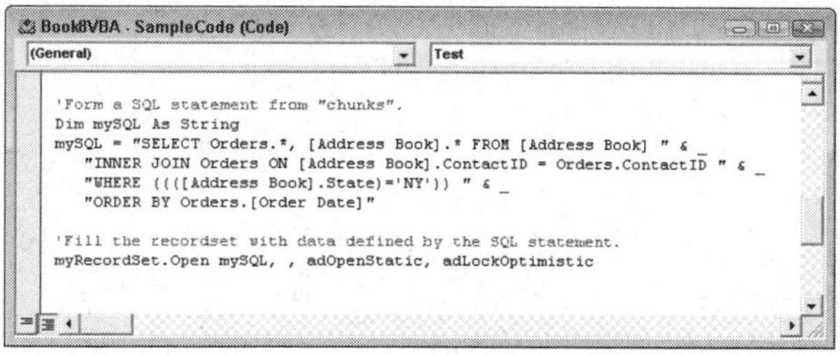

Figure 5-5:
A SQL
statement
stored in a
String
variable
named
mySQL.

Running Action Queries from VBA

Everything we discussed about SQL so far in this chapter is about *select queries* — queries that select data from tables to display but don't in any way alter the data from the tables. *Action queries* actually change the contents of tables.

Book III, Chapter 3 introduces the update and append form of action queries.

To execute an action query from VBA, you don't need to define a recordset or use a `RecordSet.Open` statement. Instead, use the `RunSQL` method of the `DoCmd` object as follows:

`DoCmd.RunSQL SQLstatement`

Follow the same rules for composing the SQL statement for an action query as you do a select query, as described in the "SQL and Recordsets" section earlier in this chapter. Figure 5-6 shows a sample action query to update records in Design view and SQL view.

Design View   SQL View

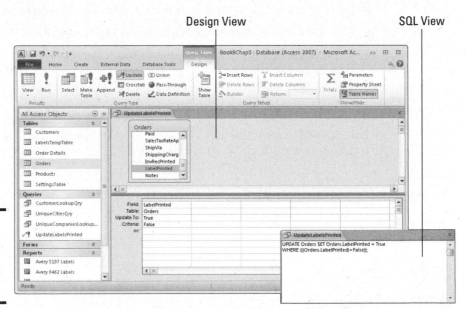

Figure 5-6:
An update query in Design and SQL views.

In the VBA Code window, store the SQL statement in a string variable and follow the `DoCmd.RunSQL` statement with that variable name — as in the following example, where `mySQL` is the name of the variable that stores the SQL statement:

```
Sub RunUpdateQry()
    'Declare a string variable named mySQL
    Dim mySQL As String
    'Store an action SQL statement in the mySQL variable.
    mySQL = "UPDATE Employees SET Employees.[Country/Region] = 'USA' " & _
            "WHERE (((Employees.[State/Province])='WA'))"
    'Run the action query.
    DoCmd.RunSQL mySQL
End Sub
```

Normally, when you run an action query — whether from Access or from VBA — Access displays a warning before the query actually runs, stating that you're about to change records in a table — which gives you a chance to change your mind. In many cases, though, you won't want that warning to appear. For example, if you know the query does what it purports to do and you're writing code for other people to use, presenting them with a warning message that they may not know how to respond to is pointless.

To prevent that warning from appearing when your code executes, and in order for the query to run without asking for permission, use the SetWarnings method of the DoCmd object to disable the warnings. In Figure 5-7, the code includes a DoCmd.SetWarnings False to turn off permission-asking just before executing a RunSQL statement. The code then turns the normal warning messages back on (DoCmd.SetWarnings True) after the query runs.

Figure 5-7:
Code used
to execute
action query
without
warning
messages.

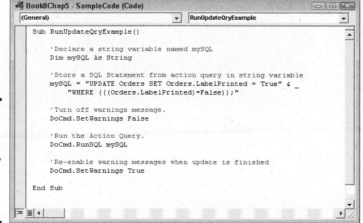

When you run an update, append, make a table, or delete a query from within a VBA procedure, use the query's SQL statement as the argument to a RunSQL statement in your code.

Cleaning up connections

Before your procedure ends, you may want to close both the recordset and the active connection to the local tables to prevent those objects from remaining open after your code moves on to other tasks. To close a record-set, follow the recordset's name with a `.Close` method, as in the following example:

```
myRecordSet.Close
```

To terminate the connection to the local tables in the database and remove the recordset and connection objects from the computer's memory, set each one to the keyword `Nothing`, as shown here:

```
Set myRecordSet = Nothing
Set myConnection = Nothing
```

So that's what SQL and recordsets are all about in VBA. Will there ever come a time where you *need* to write all this complex code to perform some task? It depends on how complex your database projects are. But one thing is for sure: If you ever inherit a database that someone else wrote and come across a bunch of code with SQL statements and recordsets, the information in this chapter will at least help you better understand what's going on with that code.

Chapter 6: Debugging Your Code

In This Chapter

- ✓ Identifying types of errors (bugs)
- ✓ Figuring out how to solve compiler errors
- ✓ Trapping and fixing runtime errors
- ✓ Digging out logical errors

*I*nstant gratification is rare in the world of programming. Nobody writes perfect code every time. Usually it takes some trial and error: You write a little code, test it, find and fix any *bugs* (errors), write a little more, test a little more, and so on until the code is fully *debugged* (free of errors) and runs smoothly every time. With the help of some debugging tools built in to Visual Basic for Applications (VBA) and the Visual Basic Editor, you can usually track down, and fix, any problems that are causing your code to fail.

Considering Types of Program Errors

Many things can go wrong while writing code, especially for a beginner. The ability to identify what type of error you're dealing with is helpful. The three types of errors that all programmers have to contend with are

- ✦ **Compiler errors:** These indicate a problem with the code that prevents the procedure from running at all. Messages alerting you to compiler errors often appear right in the Code window — such as when you type a faulty VBA statement and press Enter before you catch the goof.

- ✦ **Runtime errors:** The code compiles okay but fails to run properly in practice, often because of a problem in the environment. For example, if a procedure assumes that a certain form is already open in Form view, but the form is not, the code *crashes* — stops running — before the procedure completes its task.

- ✦ **Logical errors:** The code compiles and runs without displaying any error messages, but the code doesn't do what it's supposed to do.

Fortunately, the Visual Basic Editor contains tools that help you track down, catch, and fix all these different errors. We start with compiler errors because you have to fix them before the code can do anything at all.

Fixing Compiler Errors

When you write code, the stuff that you're writing is referred to as *source code*. Before your code executes, VBA compiles your source code to an even stranger language that the computer executes very rapidly. You never actually see that compiled code — humans only work with source code. If a problem in the source code prevents compilation, though, you definitely see the error message.

Most compiler errors happen immediately. For example, if you type just **DoCmd.** and press Enter, you get a compiler error. The DoCmd. statement alone on a line isn't enough for VBA to compile the line. You need to follow DoCmd. with some method that's specific to the DoCmd object.

Not all compiler errors are caught the moment that you press Enter. Furthermore, code may be in your database (or project) that's never been compiled. When you call the code, it compiles on the spot and then executes. That extra step slows performance. To compile all the code in a database (or project) — both to check for errors and to improve performance — follow these steps:

1. **If you're currently in the Microsoft Access window, go to the VBA Editor.**

   When you're in the Microsoft Access window, you can press Alt+F11 to quickly switch to the Visual Basic Editor.

2. **Choose Debug⇨Compile *name* (where *name* is the name of the current database or project) from the Visual Basic Editor menu.**

   Doing so compiles all the code in all standard and class modules. If any errors lurk anywhere, you see a Compile Error message box. The message provides a brief, general description of the problem, as in the example shown in Figure 6-1.

Figure 6-1:
A sample
Compile
Error
message.

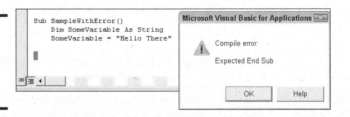

```
Sub SampleWithError()
    Dim SomeVariable As String
    SomeVariable = "Hello There"
```

Microsoft Visual Basic for Applications

⚠ Compile error:

Expected End Sub

OK   Help

The location of the error is highlighted in gray. The Compile Error message box in Figure 6-1 shows that the compiler was expecting an End Sub statement at the gray highlight. You can click the Help button for more information about the error — although in this example, the fix is pretty easy. Every sub procedure needs an End Sub statement, and one of the procedures in this module has no `End Sub` statement. Click OK to close the error message box. Then type in the missing `End Sub` statement at the gray highlight.

When you can choose Debug➪Compile name without seeing any error messages, you know that all your code is compiled and free of compiler errors. The Compile command on the Debug menu is also *disabled* (dimmed) because no uncompiled code is left to compile. Any remaining errors are runtime or logical errors.

Trapping Runtime Errors

Some VBA errors may be caused by events in the environment rather than in the code. Here are a couple of examples:

✦ Your code performs some operation on data in an open form. If the form isn't open when the code executes, code execution stops, a runtime error occurs, and an error message pops up on-screen.

✦ Another example may be when an expression performs division using data from a table, and the divisor ends up being 0 (zero). Because dividing a number by 0 doesn't make sense, code execution stops, a runtime error occurs, and an error message appears.

If people who know nothing about Access use the database that you create, the error messages that pop up on-screen won't likely help those users much. What you want to do is anticipate what kinds of errors may occur, *trap* them (that is, tell Access to let you know when they happen), and fix them when they occur. To do this, you add an *error handler* to your code, which is a chunk of code within the procedure that intercepts the error and fixes the problem without stopping code execution or displaying an error message.

To create an error handler, the first order of business is to add an `On Error` statement to your code — preferably just after the `Sub` or `Function` statement that marks the beginning of the procedure. Use one of the following three different ways to create an `On Error` statement:

✦ `On Error Goto label`: When an error occurs as a statement runs, code execution jumps to the section of code identified by label within the same procedure.

✦ `On Error Resume Next`: If an error occurs as a statement runs, that statement is ignored, and processing just continues with the next line of code in the procedure.

✦ `On Error GoTo 0`: This disables any previous `On Error Goto` or `On Error Resume Next` statements, so VBA handles future runtime errors rather than your own code.

You can use the `Resume` statement in any error-handling code to tell VBA exactly where to resume code execution after the runtime error occurs. The syntax for the `Resume` statement can take any of the following forms:

✦ `Resume`: Causes VBA to re-execute the statement that caused the error. You only want to use this statement if the error-handling code fixed the problem that caused the error in the first place. Otherwise, executing the same statement again just causes the same error again.

✦ `Resume Next`: Causes execution to resume at the first statement after the statement that caused the error. The statement that caused the error does not execute at all.

✦ `Resume label`: Causes execution to resume at the label specified.

In addition to the `On Error` statements, VBA includes a helpful object known as an `ErrObject`, which stores the error message that pops up on-screen when an error occurs. Each of those built-in error messages has its own number and text. The `ErrObject` stores that number and text, so you can write code to identify the error and work around it. The `ErrObject` has several properties. The two main ones — essential to understand first — are

✦ `Err.Number`: Returns either the number (integer) of the error that occurred or `0` for no error.

✦ `Err.Description`: Returns the textual description of the error that occurred as a string.

The `ErrObject` also supports a couple of methods, whose jobs can be summed up like this:

✦ `Err.Raise(errNo)`: Causes the error specified by `errNo` to occur. Generally used for testing error-handling code. (No practical reason exists to intentionally cause an error in actual working code.)

✦ `Err.Clear()`: Clears all current properties of the `ErrObject`. (`Err.Number` returns to zero, `Err.Description` returns to a null string, and so forth.)

Code created by Control Wizards and macro conversions may already have error-handling code written into it. Fortunately, you can easily enter such code into any procedure that you write. As a rule, you want the `On Error Goto label:` statement to execute early in the procedure. That way, no matter where an error occurs in the procedure, execution passes to the error handler.

The label text can be any text at all, provided that it starts with a letter and contains no blank spaces. Using the word `Err` and an underscore, followed by the procedure name and a colon, is customary. (The colon is mandatory.)

Place the error-handling code at the bottom of the procedure, just before the End function or End Sub statement. You need to place an Exit Sub statement, as well, before the error handler. That prevents code execution from reaching the error-handler code when no runtime error occurs.

Because you can't always anticipate every conceivable runtime error, having the error handler display the error number and error description is best — that way, at least, you know what caused the error. The following example shows an error message, where *[main body of code]* stands for all the code that makes up the actual procedure.

```
Sub myProcedure()
On Error GoTo Err_myProcedure
    [main body of code]
Exit_MyProcedure:
    Exit Sub 'Returns control to whomever called procedure.
'Error handler starts below.
Err_MyProcedure:
    Msg = Err.Description & " - " & Err.Number
    MsgBox Msg
    Resume Exit_MyProcedure
End Sub
```

The following list details what happens when a runtime error occurs while code in *[main body of code]* executes:

✦ On Error GoTo Err_myProcedure: Because this statement told VBA to transfer execution to the Err_myProcedure label, execution does not stop cold. Instead, execution continues at the first line after the Err_myProcedure label.

✦ Msg = Err.Description & " - " & Err.Number: Creates a string of text that contains the description of the error and the error number.

✦ MsgBox Msg: Displays the error message text and number in a message box with an OK button. Code execution stops until the user clicks the OK button in the message box.

✦ Resume Exit_MyProcedure: Causes execution to resume at the first line after the Exit_MyProcedure label.

✦ Exit Sub: Causes the procedure to exit without any further error messages.

Error-handling code, by itself, doesn't fix the error or allow the procedure to continue its job. However, if an error does occur, you see the message (text) and the number that identifies that message. So then you can add code to your custom error handler to fix the problem and resume code execution normally.

Suppose that the main body of the code is just trying to move the cursor into a control named `Company` on the current form, using the statement `DoCmd.GoToControl "Company"`. If you run the procedure when the form that contains the `Company` field isn't open, a runtime error occurs. The error handler displays the message box, shown in Figure 6-2. Code execution stops because nothing in the error handler takes care of the problem.

Figure 6-2:
A sample
message
displayed
by an error
handler.

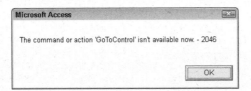

The error description and number (`2046`) display in the error message. In this particular example, the `GoToControl` action isn't available because the form that the code expects to be open isn't open. The solution is to come up with a means of making sure that the appropriate form is open before the code executes.

Fixing the runtime error

One way to handle the problem is to use an `If...End If` block (or `Select Case...End Select` block) to provide a solution to error 2046. Because error 2046 is telling us that a form the code expects to be open is in fact closed, the solution is to open the appropriate form, as in the following example:

```
[code above handler]
Err_MyProcedure:
    'Trap and fix error 2046.
    If Err.Number = 2046 Then
       DoCmd.OpenForm ("Address Book Form")
       Resume    'Try again now that form is open.
    End If
    'Errors other than 2046 still just show info and exit.
    Msg = Err.Description & " - " & Err.Number
    MsgBox Msg
    Resume Exit_MyProcedure
End Sub
```

Preventing the runtime error

A cleaner, more elegant solution to the problem, though, is to rewrite the procedure so that the runtime error can't possibly occur. In the following example, the procedure starts by checking to see whether the required form is already open. If it's not, the procedure opens the form before the `DoCmd.GoToControl` statement executes:

```
Sub myProcedure1()
    On Error GoTo Err_myProcedure

    'Make sure Address Book form is open.
    If Not isOpen("Address Book Form") Then
        DoCmd.OpenForm "Address Book Form", acNormal
    End If

    'Now move the cursor to the Company field.
    DoCmd.GoToControl "Company"
Exit_myProcedure:
    Exit Sub
Err_myProcedure:
    Msg = Err.Description & "-" & Err.Number
    MsgBox (Msg)
End Sub
```

The `isOpen()` function used in the preceding example isn't built into Access. (See Chapter 4 of this minibook for a description of the `isOpen()` function.)

Dealing with Logical Errors

After your code is free of compile and runtime errors, Access executes every statement perfectly. But that doesn't necessarily mean that the code does exactly what you intended. If you were thinking one thing but wrote code that does something else, an error in the logic of the code occurs — a logical error.

Logical errors can be tough to pinpoint because when you run a procedure, everything happens so fast. You'll find slowing things down and watching what happens while the procedure runs helpful. Several tools in Access can help with that.

Watching things happen

You can use the `Debug.Print` statement anywhere in your code to print the value of a variable, a constant, or anything else. Because all output from the `Debug.Print` statement goes to the Immediate window, those statements don't disrupt the normal execution of your procedure.

Imagine writing a procedure that's supposed to make some changes to all the records in a table with the help of a loop embedded in your code. When you run the procedure, though, the expected result doesn't happen. You can put a `Debug.Print` statement inside the loop to display the current value of some counting variable within the loop, as in this example:

```
Function Whatever()
    [code]
    For intCounter = LBound(myArray) To UBound(myArray)
        'Show value of inCounter with each pass through loop
        Debug.Print "intCounter = " & intCounter
    [Code]
    Next
    [maybe more code]
End Function
```

If you run the procedure with the Immediate window open, the Immediate window displays something like this:

```
intCounter = 0
intCounter = 1
intCounter = 2
etc..
```

If some problem with the loop's conditional expression exists (the logic that makes the loop repeat *x* number of times), you may just see something like the following:

```
intCounter = 0
```

The preceding output tells you the loop repeats only once, with a value of zero. You need to go back into the code, figure out why the loop isn't repeating as many times as you expect, fix that problem, and then try again.

After you solve the problem, remove the Debug.Print statements from the code because they serve no purpose after the debugging phase is done. Optionally, you can comment out the Debug.Print statement by adding an apostrophe to the beginning of its line, thereby making it appear as a comment to VBA. After you comment out a statement, it is no longer executed in the code. To reactivate the Debug.Print statement in the future, uncomment it by removing the leading apostrophe.

Slowing down procedures

Another way to check for logical errors in code is to slow things way down to see exactly what's happening, step by step, while the procedure runs. To do this, you set a breakpoint at the line of code, right where you want to start slowing things down.

If you want the entire procedure to run slowly, you can set the breakpoint in the first line of the procedure (the Sub or Function statement). To set a breakpoint, right-click the line where you want to set the breakpoint and then choose Toggle⇨Breakpoint from the shortcut menu, as in Figure 6-3. The line where you set the breakpoint is highlighted in red — and has a large red dot to the left.

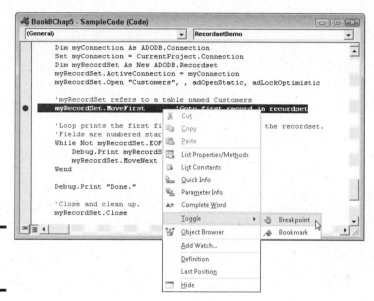

Figure 6-3:
Setting a breakpoint.

You can also open the Locals window to watch the values of variables change as the code is running in break mode. (After you set a breakpoint, the code runs in break mode, or one line at a time.) To open the Locals window, choose View⇨Locals Window from the VBA Editor main menu. Like other windows in the Visual Basic Editor, you can dock the Locals window to the Visual Basic Editor program window or drag it away from the window border to make it free-floating.

After you set a breakpoint, just run the code normally. Before executing a line of code, VBA highlights the line in yellow that's about to execute and shows an arrow to the left of that line. You have three choices at that point:

✦ To execute the one line (only), press F8 or choose Debug⇨Step Into.

✦ To skip the currently selected line without executing it, press Shift+F8 or choose Debug⇨Step Over.

✦ To bail out of break mode, press Ctrl+Shift+F8 or choose Debug⇨Step Out.

Some types of runtime errors cause VBA to go into break mode automatically. You see the yellow highlight line when that happens.

While your code executes, the highlight moves from line to line. Each time that an executed statement changes the value of a variable, the Locals window updates to reflect that change, as in Figure 6-4.

**Book VIII
Chapter 6**

Debugging Your Code

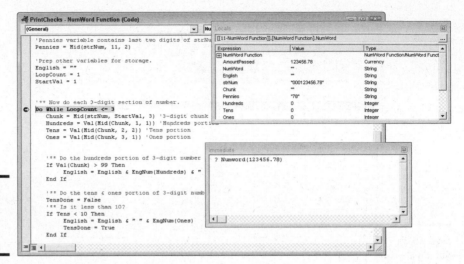

Figure 6-4:
Stepping
through
code.

Cleaning up

When you finish debugging or just want to start over with a clean slate, do one of the following:

✦ To clear the Locals window, right-click any text within the window and then choose the Reset option from the shortcut menu that appears.

✦ To clear all breakpoints from your code, choose Debug⇨Clear All Breakpoints.

Of course, you can also close the Locals window by clicking the Close button in the window's upper-right corner.

Book IX

Going Beyond Access

The 5th Wave   By Rich Tennant

"Our automated response policy to a large company-wide data crash is to notify management, back up existing data and sell 90% of my shares in the company."

Contents at a Glance

Chapter 1: Automation with Other Office Programs

In This Chapter

✔ **Understanding Automation**

✔ **Adding a contact to Microsoft Outlook**

✔ **Merging data with a Word document**

✔ **Exporting data to Excel**

*I*n Book VIII, we show you VBA (Visual Basic for Applications) and give you an understanding of some of the wonderful ways you can take control of your Access database. You can use VBA to open and close forms, print reports, loop through tables and change data, and modify form properties.

Well, VBA isn't there just for Access; you can also use VBA to control other Microsoft Office applications including Outlook, Excel, Word, and PowerPoint. With VBA, the possibilities are virtually endless when you consider what some advanced users do in these Office applications on a daily basis. This chapter explains Automation and gives several examples of how Access can interact with these other Office programs.

What Is Automation?

Automation came about during the industrial revolution to replace tasks performed by humans with faster, more efficient methods. Instead of phone operators manually plugging and unplugging wires to make a connection, large systems handle this automatically. Rather than having people assemble cars on the assembly line, industrial robots now handle the bulk of the duties. Us humans just get in the way.

In the world of VBA, *Automation* (with a capital A) refers to the ability of a program to expose itself to VBA so that VBA can control it behind the scenes, with little or no human interaction. Humans just slow down the process anyway. Other programming languages such as C++ and C# use Automation as well, but since VBA is the language of Access, we focus on using VBA.

Automation with other Microsoft Office programs works only when you have these programs installed on your computer. If you don't have Word, Excel, or Outlook installed, you won't be able to control them from Access.

Using Object Libraries

To use VBA to control another program, you need to have access to that program's object library. Each program has its own set of properties and methods, which allows VBA to control it. Just as each object (forms, text boxes, buttons) has its own properties and methods, each application — including Access — has a set of properties and methods, which is referred to as the *object library*.

In order to access another program's object library, you first have to tell VBA where to find it. To add an object library to your VBA project, choose Tools⇨References from the Visual Basic Editor menu, and add the desired object libraries, as shown in Figure 1-1.

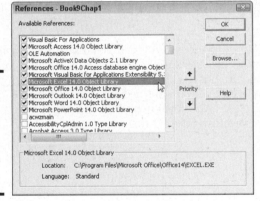

Figure 1-1:
Choose
the object
libraries
from the
References
window.

For this example, we added the Microsoft Excel 14.0 Object Library, Microsoft Office 14.0 Object Library, Microsoft Outlook 14.0 Object Library, Microsoft Words 14.0 Object Library, and Microsoft PowerPoint 14.0 Object Library.

 If you have multiple versions of a program installed on your computer (for instance, Excel 2003 and Excel 2010), you'll see different versions of the Excel Object Library in the References window. If you're sure you'll be working in the latest version only, choose the version with the highest number. Applications in Office 2010 are version 14.0, whereas applications in Office 2007 are version 12.0. I guess the superstitious programmers at Microsoft skipped version 13.0.

Exploring an object library

After adding a reference to a program's object model, you can explore that program's objects, properties, and methods through the Object Browser. In the Visual Basic Editor, choose View➪Object Browser from the Visual Basic Editor menu or press F2. When you open the Object Browser, it shows the objects for everything VBA has access to. To limit the list to a specific library, choose the library's name from the Project/Library drop-down list in the top-left corner of the Object Browser window. In Figure 1-2, we selected Excel to show only the classes and members related to Microsoft Excel.

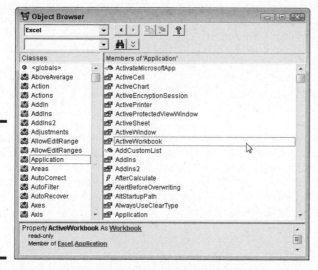

Figure 1-2:
Use the
Object
Browser
to view a
program's
object
model.

Each application exposes a lot of objects to VBA — way too many for you (or any sane person) to remember. We don't have enough room in this book to define every property and every method for each Office application. We'd probably need a book just for each application, which wouldn't make too many trees very happy, would it? Instead, you have to be able to get the information you need when you need it.

To find out more about a selected object, property, or method in the Object Browser, click the Help icon — the yellow question mark — in the Object Browser window.

The Application object

Each application exposes (makes available) its own set of objects to VBA, but one object that each application has in common is the `Application` object. The `Application` object exposes that program's objects, properties, and methods to VBA. When a program is open, its objects are available to VBA. For example, if VBA opens a Word document, everything in that Word document is also exposed. VBA can do anything in the Word document that a human can do from the Word Ribbon.

In order to take control of an application, you first have to create an instance of the application in VBA. An *instance* is basically the same as opening the program from the Windows Start menu. For example, when you start Microsoft PowerPoint on your computer, you're creating an instance of PowerPoint on your computer.

To create an instance of an application in VBA, you have to declare a variable that references that object. The variable name can be any name you like, but you should attempt to give it a meaningful name. The syntax for declaring an object variable is

```
Dim objectVariable as New program.Application
```

For more information on declaring and using variables, see Book VIII, Chapter 3.

The *objectVariable* in the above example is the name of the variable. The *program* is a reference to one of the Office applications (such as Word, Excel, Outlook). The Application part refers to the program's Application object of that program. The New keyword ensures that VBA creates a new instance of the program. Here are some examples of declaring new instances of the Office programs:

```
Dim XL as New Excel.Application
Dim Wrd as New Word.Application
Dim Olk as New Outlook.Application
Dim PPT as New PowerPoint.Application
```

After you declare the object variable for the desired program, you can now control that program. In order to take control of the program, you must open the program from VBA. The syntax for opening a program in VBA is

```
Set objectVariable as CreateObject("program.Application")
```

where the *objectVariable* is the same name you specified in the Dim statement and *program* is the name of the application. When using the Dim statements described above, the corresponding Set statements for opening the applications are:

```
Set XL as CreateObject("Excel.Application")
Set Wrd as CreateObject("Word.Application")
Set Olk as CreateObject("Outlook.Application")
Set PPT as CreateObject("PowerPoint.Application")
```

In order to control another program using VBA, you must first add the program's object library to VBA using the References window.

In the next few sections, you'll see how Access can share information with Outlook, Word, and Excel — oh my!

Adding a Contact to Outlook

Suppose you're working on an Access program and your users suggest that it would be a good idea to include in your program the capability to add a contact from your Access database to the Microsoft Outlook contacts. You could be mean and tell them to just type it in themselves, or you can impress them by adding a button to a form that adds the current contact to their Outlook contacts.

Consider the form shown in Figure 1-3. This form is a basic customer contact form that you might find in one of your applications, with one exception — the addition of an Add to Outlook Contacts button.

Figure 1-3: Changing an Access form to add a contact to Outlook.

Now just adding the button doesn't accomplish much; you have to add code to the button's `Click` event procedure. In the form's Design view, double-click the button to show the Property sheet, click the Event tab, click the ellipsis button on the right of the `On Click` event property, and then click Code Builder to open the Visual Basic Editor to the button's `Click` event procedure. The code looks something like this:

```
Private Sub cmdOutlook_Click()

    'Open Instance of Microsoft Outlook
    Dim Olk As Outlook.Application
    Set Olk = CreateObject("Outlook.Application")

    'Create Object for an Outlook Contact
    Dim OlkContact As Outlook.ContactItem
    Set OlkContact = Olk.CreateItem(olContactItem)
```

```
'Set Contact Properties and Save
With OlkContact
  .FirstName = Me.FirstName
  .LastName = Me.LastName
   Me.Email.SetFocus
  .Email1Address = Me.Email.Text
  .CompanyName = Me.Company
  .BusinessAddressStreet = Me.Address1
  .BusinessAddressCity = Me.City
  .BusinessAddressState = Me.StateProv
  .BusinessAddressPostalCode = Me.ZIPCode
  .BusinessTelephoneNumber = Me.Phone
  .BusinessFaxNumber = Me.Fax
  .Save
End With

'Let User know contact was added
MsgBox "Contact Added to Outlook."

'Clean up object variables
Set OlkContact = Nothing
Set Olk = Nothing

End Sub
```

This might look like a lot of code, but it's just a series of small steps. In laymen's terms, this procedure creates and sets a variable for the Outlook Application, creates and sets a variable for an Outlook contact, sets the properties of the Outlook contact object to values from the form, saves the Outlook contact, displays a message box, and cleans up the object variables. Let's take a detailed look into this example.

The first two statements under the first comment declare an object variable named `Olk` and set it to an open instance of Microsoft Outlook.

```
'Open Instance of Microsoft Outlook
Dim Olk As Outlook.Application
Set Olk = CreateObject("Outlook.Application")
```

The `Application` object for Outlook lets you create items within Outlook, just as if you open Outlook and navigate through the program. The second comment and the next two lines are as follows:

```
'Create Object for an Outlook Contact
Dim OlkContact As Outlook.ContactItem
Set OlkContact = Olk.CreateItem(olContactItem)
```

These lines declare an object variable named `OlkContact` and create that contact using the `CreateItem` method of the Outlook Application object. This is the VBA way of clicking Contacts and clicking the Click Here to Add a New Contact line at the top of the Outlook window.

Now let's look at the next block of code:

```
'Set Contact Properties and Save
With OlkContact
  .FirstName = Me.FirstName
  .LastName = Me.LastName
   Me.Email.SetFocus
  .EmailAddress = Me.Email.Text
  .CompanyName = Me.Company
  .BusinessAddressStreet = Me.Address1
  .BusinessAddressCity = Me.City
  .BusinessAddressState = Me.StateProv
  .BusinessAddressPostalCode = Me.ZIPCode
  .BusinessTelephoneNumber = Me.Phone
  .BusinessFaxNumber = Me.Fax
  .Save
End With
```

The `With...End With` block of code sets the properties of the Outlook `ContactItem`. The `ContactItem` object has many properties that you can see via the Object Browser. This example uses only a few of these properties and sets them to the values from the form. Everything that uses the `Me` keyword reads a value from the form shown in Figure 1-3.

The last few statements tell the user that the contact was added and resets the object variables.

The one tricky part of the above code lies in how Access stores an e-mail address. Access doesn't just store the e-mail address as text. Instead, it stores additional information along with the e-mail address. So when reading the e-mail address from the form, we want only the text component of the e-mail address field on the form. In order for VBA to read this property on the form, we must first use the `SetFocus` method of the Email text box to make sure that the control has the focus — the cursor is in that field.

The `Save` method of the `ContactItem` object saves the contact in Outlook. The remaining code displays a message letting you know that the contact was added to Outlook, and it then cleans up the variables before the `Click` event procedure ends. Figure 1-4 shows the contact in Outlook.

Outlook's Object Library exposes many more objects and methods than described here. You can do anything from VBA that you can do from the Outlook program. You can compose and send e-mail messages, create and schedule calendar items, and build tasks and to-do lists. To find out more about these objects, properties, and methods, use the Object Browser and select Outlook from the Project/Library drop-down list in the top-left corner of the Object Browser window.

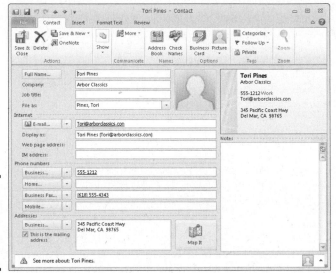

Figure 1-4:
The contact
added to
Outlook
from VBA.

Merging Data with a Word Document

Microsoft Word is probably the most widely used word-processing program in the world, if not the universe. If you have Microsoft Office installed, then you have Word installed as well. Many people in any given work environment know how to use and edit Word documents, but they might not know how to create and modify an Access report. Using Automation, you can give some users the ability to edit the body of a form letter in Word, and then allow them to print that letter from Access.

Creating a Word template

In order to put data from Access into a Word document, you have to tell Access where in the Word document to put the data. One method is to create bookmarks in the Word document that Access can later replace with data from the database. A *bookmark* in Word is just a placeholder. If you do this in a Word template file (`.dotx` file), you can easily create new documents based on this template.

First, use Word to create a template file and format the document however you want. You can add a company logo, other letterhead information, and type the body of the letter. So far, this should be pretty easy.

When you get the document ready, you'll need to add bookmarks where you want the data from Access to go. Bookmarks in Word are usually hidden, so you need to display them so you can see what you're doing. In Microsoft Word, choose File⇨Options. Click the Advanced option on the left side of the Word Options window, scroll down to the Show Document Content section, select the Show Bookmarks option, and click OK.

You can insert bookmarks into your Word template as follows:

1. **Move the cursor to where you want the bookmark to appear in the Word document.**

2. **Type a short, meaningful name for the bookmark.**

   The name cannot contain spaces or punctuation, and it must start with a letter.

3. **Select the text by double-clicking the name you just typed and copy it to the Clipboard. (Press Ctrl+C.)**

4. **On the Word Ribbon, click the Insert tab, and then click Bookmark in the Links group.**

   The Bookmark dialog box appears, as shown in Figure 1-5.

5. **Paste (Ctrl+V) the typed name into the Bookmark Name field.**

6. **Click the Add button to create the bookmark.**

   Square brackets appear around the text to indicate the bookmark.

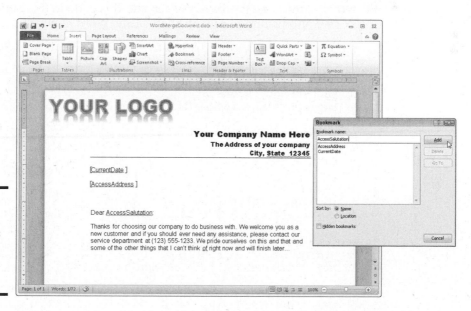

Figure 1-5:
Adding bookmarks to a Word template (DOTX).

For this example, we created three bookmarks: `CurrentDate`, `AccessAddress`, and `AccessSalutation`. We then saved the `.dotx` file in the same folder as our database.

Writing the merge code

Now that the Word template is ready to go, we can create another button on the Customer form that sends data from the form into Word, as shown in Figure 1-6.

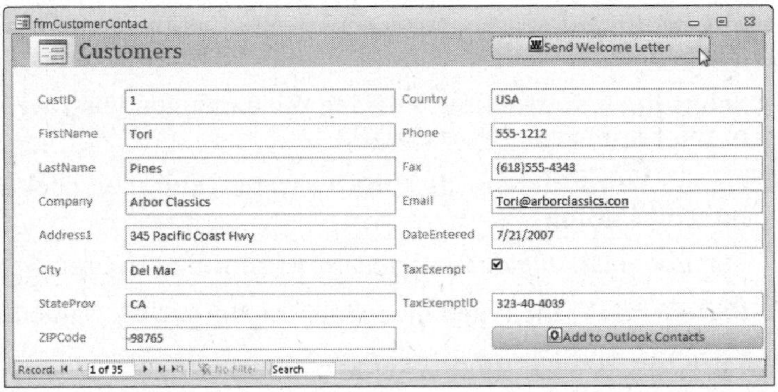

Figure 1-6: Adding another button to send data to Word.

When the button is on the form, you can add this code to this button's `Click` event procedure to send the data to the Word document:

```
Private Sub cmdWord_Click()

    'Declare Variables
    Dim sAccessAddress As String
    Dim sAccessSalutation As String

    'Build sAccessAddress
    sAccessAddress = FirstName & " " & LastName & _
        vbCrLf & Company & vbCrLf & Address1 & _
        vbCrLf & City & ", " & StateProv & "   " & ZIPCode

    'Build sAccessSalutation
    sAccessSalutation = FirstName & " " & LastName

    'Declare and set Word object variables
    Dim Wrd As New Word.Application
    Set Wrd = CreateObject("Word.Application")

    'Specify Path to Template
    Dim sMergeDoc As String
    sMergeDoc = Application.CurrentProject.Path & _
        "\WordMergeDocument.dotx"
```

```
'Open Word using template and make Word visible
Wrd.Documents.Add sMergeDoc
Wrd.Visible = True

'Replace Bookmarks with Values
With Wrd.ActiveDocument.Bookmarks
  .Item("CurrentDate").Range.Text = Date
  .Item("AccessAddress").Range.Text = sAccessAddress
  .Item("AccessSalutation").Range.Text = sAccessSalutation
End With

'Open in PrintPreview mode, let user print
Wrd.ActiveDocument.PrintPreview

'Clean Up code
Set Wrd = Nothing

End Sub
```

Again, there's a lot of code here, but it breaks down into a number of different sections. We declare the variables we're going to use, set the address and salutation variables, open Word using the template we created, replace the bookmarks with values from Access, and show the Print Preview view for the document. Let's take a closer look at some key components of this code.

After declaring the string values, we set the sAccessAddress variable to a concatenated string of values from the form. We use the line continuation character (an underscore) as well as the vbCrlf keyword, which starts a new line in the string variable:

```
'Build sAccessAddress
sAccessAddress = FirstName & " " & LastName & _
  vbCrLf & Company & vbCrLf & Address1 & _
  vbCrLf & City & ", " & StateProv & "  " & ZIPCode
```

We also build the sAccessSalutation variable by combining just the first and last name fields on the form with a space in between:

```
'Build sAccessSalutation
sAccessSalutation = FirstName & " " & LastName
```

Next, we use the syntax described earlier in this chapter to open an instance of Microsoft Word. Here's the code:

```
'Declare and set Word object variables
Dim Wrd As New Word.Application
Set Wrd = CreateObject("Word.Application")
```

In order to control Word 2010 using VBA, you must first add the Microsoft Office Word 14.0 Object Library to VBA using the References window.

After opening an instance of Word, we set the location of the Word template created earlier. We use the `Path` property of `Application.CurrentProject` in order to get the location, and then concatenate it with the filename. In this case, we named the Word template file `WordMergeDocument.dotx`, as follows:

```
'Specify Path to Template
Dim sMergeDoc As String
sMergeDoc = Application.CurrentProject.Path & _
    "\WordMergeDocument.dotx"
```

Next, we use the `Add` method of the `Application.Documents` object to create a new document based on the template file. After creating a new Word document, we set the `Visible` property of the `Wrd` object to true, letting the user see Word. When you open Word from VBA, it's invisible to the user unless you specify otherwise, as we've done here:

```
'Open Word using template and make Word visible
Wrd.Documents.Add sMergeDoc
Wrd.Visible = True
```

After viewing the document, we use the `Bookmarks` collection within the `ActiveDocument` to add the values from Access. We replace the `CurrentDate` bookmark with the system date using the `Date()` function. Then we replace the `AccessAddress` and `AccessSalutation` bookmarks with the variables set earlier in the code, as follows:

```
'Replace Bookmarks with Values
With Wrd.ActiveDocument.Bookmarks
    .Item("CurrentDate").Range.Text = Date
    .Item("AccessAddress").Range.Text = sAccessAddress
    .Item("AccessSalutation").Range.Text = sAccessSalutation
End With
```

Finally, we switch to Print Preview view and clean up the code in Word. Figure 1-7 shows the document with the bookmarks replaced with data from Access.

Just like with the Outlook Object Library, the Word Object Library contains many more properties and methods that allow you to control Word as if you were clicking on the various Ribbon commands and typing in the Word window. For more assistance on all of these commands, use the Object Browser available by choosing View⇨Object Browser from the Visual Basic Editor menu or pressing F2.

Figure 1-7:
The final
merged
document in
Word.

Exporting Data to Excel

Many Office users familiar with Excel just don't understand the power and flexibility of Access. And many higher executives are used to viewing and printing tables of data from an Excel spreadsheet. So even though you're convinced that everyone in your organization (and perhaps, the world) should use Access instead of Excel, you'll still come across quite a few people who'd rather see the data in Excel than open an Access database.

Sure, you can export data to Excel (or a number of other formats) from the Export group on the External Data tab, but that requires one of those pesky humans to know what to do. As a compromise, you can automate the process by writing VBA code to export the data, plus do a number of other formatting tasks as well.

Let's pretend once again that we're going to create a spreadsheet of everyone's phone number in the Customer table. We also want to add a meaningful title with the date the phone numbers were exported. You can create a button anywhere in your application to do this, so we'll just show you the code:

```
'Declare and set the Connection object
Dim cnn As ADODB.Connection
Set cnn = CurrentProject.Connection
```

```
'Declare and set the Recordset object
Dim rs As New ADODB.Recordset
rs.ActiveConnection = cnn

'Declare and set the SQL Statement to Export
Dim sSQL As String
sSQL = "SELECT FirstName, LastName, Phone FROM Customers"

'Open the Recordset
rs.Open sSQL

'Set up Excel Variables
Dim Xl As New Excel.Application
Dim Xlbook As Excel.Workbook
Dim Xlsheet As Excel.Worksheet

Set Xl = CreateObject("Excel.Application")
Set Xlbook = Xl.Workbooks.Add
Set Xlsheet = Xlbook.Worksheets(1)

'Set Values in Worksheet
Xlsheet.Name = "Phone List"
With Xlsheet.Range("A1")
   .Value = "Phone List " & Date
   .Font.Size = 14
   .Font.Bold = True
   .Font.Color = vbBlue
End With

'Copy Recordset to Worksheet Cell A3
Xlsheet.Range("A3").CopyFromRecordset rs

'Make Excel window visible
Xl.Visible = True

'Clean Up Variables
rs.Close
Set cnn = Nothing
Set rs = Nothing
Set Xlsheet = Nothing
Set Xlbook = Nothing
Set Xl = Nothing
```

As you can see, the code is starting to grow. It's not out of control, but it's common to have procedures that grow to pages in length. But don't be afraid; as long as you break it down into small chunks, it's not so hard to understand.

The first chunk of code sets up the Recordset object with a simple SQL Select statement that gets the first name, last name, and phone number from the Customers table, as follows:

```
'Declare and set the Connection object
Dim cnn As ADODB.Connection
Set cnn = CurrentProject.Connection

'Declare and set the Recordset object
Dim rs As New ADODB.Recordset
rs.ActiveConnection = cnn

'Declare and set the SQL Statement to Export
Dim sSQL As String
sSQL = "SELECT FirstName, LastName, Phone FROM Customers"

'Open the Recordset
rs.Open sSQL
```

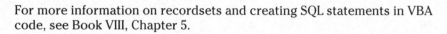

For more information on recordsets and creating SQL statements in VBA
code, see Book VIII, Chapter 5.

The next chunk of VBA code initializes the Excel objects so that you can
manipulate them. There are three objects to declare when working with
Excel: `Application`, `Workbook`, and `Worksheet`. By default, when you
open Excel from the Start menu, it opens to a new workbook, and each workbook contains at least one worksheet. Here's the code:

```
'Set up Excel Variables
Dim Xl As New Excel.Application
Dim Xlbook As Excel.Workbook
Dim Xlsheet As Excel.Worksheet

Set Xl = CreateObject("Excel.Application")
```

After opening the Excel `Application` object, we use the `Add` method of the
`Workbooks` collection to create a new workbook, stored in the `Xlbook` variable:

```
Set Xlbook = Xl.Workbooks.Add
```

After adding a new `Workbook` to the Excel `Application`, we set the
`Xlsheet` variable to the first `Worksheet` of the `Workbook` object using the
`Worksheets` collection:

```
Set Xlsheet = Xlbook.Worksheets(1)
```

Now that the worksheet is initialized and set, it's time to start playing
around. First, we set the `Name` of the worksheet to something other than
Sheet1. Then we change cell A1 to a meaningful heading that includes the
date, and format the cell to a larger, bolder, more colorful font:

```
'Set Values in Worksheet
Xlsheet.Name = "Phone List"
With Xlsheet.Range("A1")
  .Value = "Phone List " & Date
  .Font.Size = 14
```

```
    .Font.Bold = True
    .Font.Color = vbBlue
End With
```

Now it's time to take the data from the `Recordset` object and put it into the spreadsheet. There's no looping through the recordset here; just use the `CopyFromRecordset` method to copy the contents of a recordset into a particular range of cell. Here, we copy the data from our recordset, starting with cell `A3`, as follows:

```
'Copy Recordset to Worksheet Cell A3
Xlsheet.Range("A3").CopyFromRecordset rs
```

Finally, we make the Excel application visible so we can see our data in Excel (shown in Figure 1-8) and clean up our variables.

You can add so much more code to this routine to fully customize the look of the spreadsheet. You can change the column widths, change the cells' background colors, and sort the data. Just remember, if can perform a task with the mouse and keyboard in the Excel window, you can find a way to do it using VBA.

Automating Access with other Office programs can seem overwhelming at first, but once you know where to find help and examples, you'll be well on your way to beefing up your Access applications and relying less and less on those humans to perform these tasks.

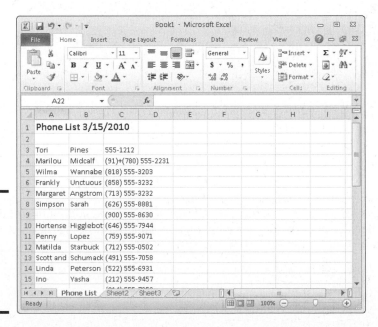

Figure 1-8:
The Excel worksheet with customer phone numbers.

Chapter 2: Using Access as a Front-End to SQL Server

In This Chapter

✓ **Understanding SQL Server**

✓ **Using ODBC to connect to SQL Server**

✓ **Creating an Access Data Project**

Access is more than just a relational database; it's a robust development environment where you can create queries to view and manipulate subsets of data, build forms to view your data in an easy-to-read format, and generate reports to print your data on paper. You can even create macros and VBA code to perform common tasks and routines automatically. But the data itself resides in the Access tables.

When you're building your beautiful application, you aren't limited to working exclusively in Access. You can use Access as a front-end to a number of different data sources. In Book II, Chapter 4, we show you how to import and link to data from a number of data sources such as Excel and Outlook. In this chapter, we demonstrate how to connect to and use data from other relational databases, such as Microsoft SQL Server.

What Is SQL Server?

SQL Server is a relational database management system (RDBMS) produced by Microsoft — just like Access. SQL Server is built primarily as a database engine, and it has much higher hardware requirements to achieve a faster performance than a database designed for the desktop, such as Access. SQL Server is a product from Microsoft that you must purchase — usually at a high cost — in order to achieve the maximum benefits. For large companies with lots and lots of data, it's a no-brainer. For individuals and smaller companies, the cost involved will probably break the bank.

Downloading SQL Server Express Edition

If you have access to a full-blown version of Microsoft SQL Server or if there's one in your company (or basement) already, then consider yourself lucky. But if you're trying to get familiar with SQL Server and haven't hit the lottery lately, you can download a scaled-down version for free. It slices and it dices just like the full version of SQL Server, but it has a database size limitation. As of this printing, you can download it at the URL listed below. However, since Microsoft likes to change their URLs more often than gas stations change their prices, you can just do an Internet search for *SQL Server Express download*.

`www.microsoft.com/Sqlserver/`
`2005/en/us/express.aspx`

SQL Server is a *client/server* database, which means there are usually two computers involved — sometimes three, four, or a hundred. The network computer with SQL Server installed and running is (you guessed it) the server; the computers with Access (or another program that's retrieving data) are the clients. The client/server architecture allows the client computers to focus on displaying the data to the end user, and the server computer to retrieve, insert, update, and delete data. Client/server databases like SQL Server are optimized for dealing with data and perform tasks on large sets of data much quicker than Access.

The Internet is a perfect example of client/server computing. It's nothing more than a bunch of servers networked together and a bunch of client computers using their Web browsers to retrieve and update information on these servers. In fact, many of these server computers use SQL Server to store data.

Plenty of client/server databases besides SQL Server are on the market, and Access can link to and import data to a number of them, including Oracle, Sybase, and MySQL — just to name a few. If your organization is using any of these databases and you need to connect to them, you'll have to talk to the system administrator and refer to the documentation for these databases in order to gain access to these servers.

Using ODBC

ODBC — Open Database Connectivity, for short — is a standard method to communicate with a database management system. ODBC was created to allow programs to communicate with different databases regardless of the manufacturer or how the database engine is constructed. Think of ODBC as a translator that speaks many different languages; Access has to know one language, and ODBC talks to the other databases.

Access uses ODBC to connect to a variety of data sources, including dBase, Excel, Paradox, Visual FoxPro, Oracle, and of course, SQL Server. Once Access connects to any of these data sources, it can communicate with them in the same way, all because of ODBC.

Connecting to SQL Server with ODBC

We could spend all day typing about client/server computing and the intricacies of how the ODBC architecture allows programmers to add additional drivers for databases not currently supported. But honestly, you don't need to know any of that in order to connect to a SQL Server database using ODBC. Sure, it helps to know a little bit about these topics, but you don't have to be an expert on the subject.

To connect to a SQL Server database, click the Ribbon's External Data tab, and then click the ODBC Database command in the Import & Link group, as shown in Figure 2-1.

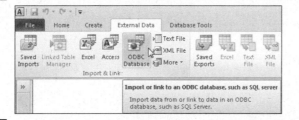

Figure 2-1: Linking to an ODBC database from the Access Ribbon.

After the Get External Data — ODBC Database window opens, you're presented with two choices: Import or Link to the data. Because you're using Access as a front-end to manipulate data in SQL Server, select the option to link to the data source, as shown in Figure 2-2. If you import the data, you'll get a snapshot of the data at the time you performed the import, and any changes you make won't be reflected on the SQL Server.

For further assistance on when to import data and when to link to data in another data source, see Book II, Chapter 4.

Next, you're presented with the Select Data Source dialog box shown in Figure 2-3. This dialog box lets you choose an existing ODBC data source or create a new one. After you create the connection to a particular database, it appears in the list. If this is your first time connecting to a data source, you'll have to create a new data source.

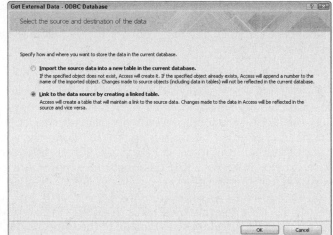

Figure 2-2:
Select
the Link
To option
when using
Access as a
front-end.

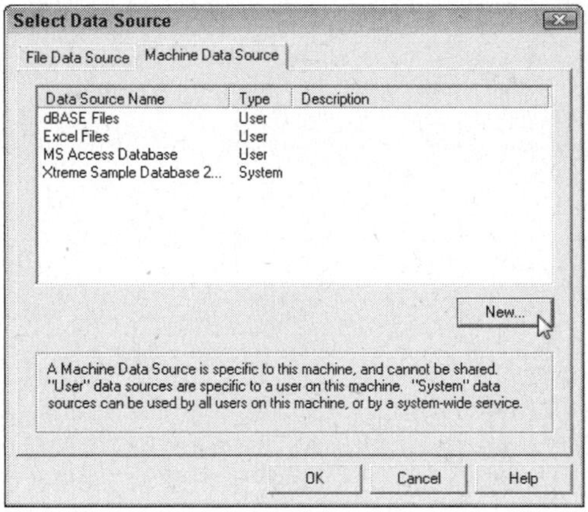

Figure 2-3:
Create or
select a
data source.

You can create a file data source, which is a file that can be shared with
other computers, and may reside somewhere on your company's network;
or you can create a machine data source, which is specific to the computer
you're working on. If you're using only the data source on your computer,
then machine data source is the better option. Follow these steps to create
your data source:

1. **Click the Machine Data Source tab, and then click the New button
   under the list of data sources to open the Create New Data Source
   dialog box.**

   From this dialog box, you can choose to create a User Data Source,
   which can be used only by the current user, or a System Data Source,
   which can be used by anyone using the machine. If many users log in to

this computer, then a System Data Source is the better option so that you won't have to create one for each user.

In order to create a System Data Source, you must be logged on to the computer with administrative rights. If you don't have administrative rights, you won't be allowed to create a System Data Source.

2. **Select an option — User or System Data Source — and click Next to display the list of ODBC drivers, as shown in Figure 2-4.**

   The list contains all the available ODBC drivers installed on your computer. Some may even appear to be in other languages, such as Spanish or German.

Figure 2-4:
Select the correct ODBC driver.

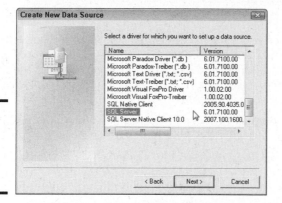

If you're connecting to a database and don't see a specific driver in the list, you might have to download and install it, if it even exists. Search the Internet for your database with the words *ODBC driver* after the database name (such as *Oracle ODBC driver*, *MySQL ODBC driver*, and so forth).

3. **Scroll down and click the SQL Server driver, and then click Next to display the confirmation page for creating a new data source.**

4. **Click Finish to start another wizard to configure the data source for SQL Server, as shown in Figure 2-5.**

   The Name is whatever name you want to give the data source, and it's how Access refers to the ODBC connection. It helps to keep the name short and memorable, in case you need to create it on another computer. The Description lets you type something more descriptive than a name, so that later on, you know what the data source connects to. You might give it a description of, for example, "Contact Database on SERVER1."

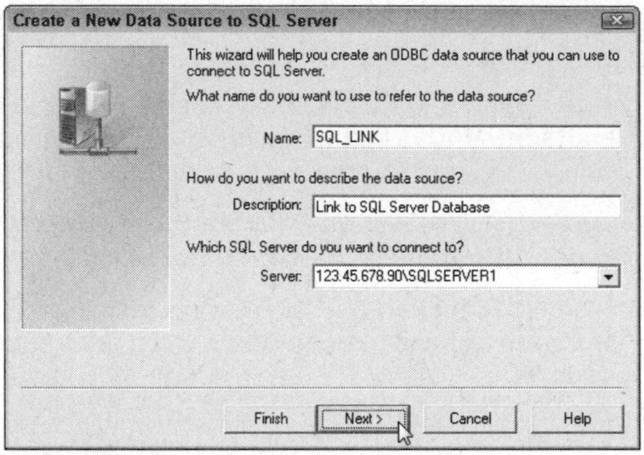

Create a New Data Source to SQL Server

This wizard will help you create an ODBC data source that you can use to connect to SQL Server.

What name do you want to use to refer to the data source?

Name: SQL_LINK

How do you want to describe the data source?

Description: Link to SQL Server Database

Which SQL Server do you want to connect to?

Server: 123.45.678.90\SQLSERVER1

Finish   Next >   Cancel   Help

Figure 2-5:
Enter the user-friendly name and the SQL Server name.

The SQL Server you want to connect to field is where you enter the server name or IP address followed by the name of the server. If you don't know the address and name of the server, contact the database administrator for help. If there are registered servers on your network, then you can simply select one from the drop-down menu.

5. **Click Next to display the screen to configure how you log in to the server, shown in Figure 2-6. You have two choices:**

    • *With Windows NT authentication using the network login ID:* Use this option if the username and password for the server match the username and password you use to log in to your computer.

    • *With SQL Server authentication using a login ID and password entered by the user:* Use this option if you have a separate username and password for the SQL Server. If you select this option, you enter the Login ID and Password at the bottom of the window.

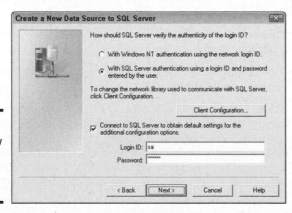

Create a New Data Source to SQL Server

How should SQL Server verify the authenticity of the login ID?

○ With Windows NT authentication using the network login ID.

◉ With SQL Server authentication using a login ID and password entered by the user.

To change the network library used to communicate with SQL Server, click Client Configuration.

Client Configuration...

☑ Connect to SQL Server to obtain default settings for the additional configuration options.

Login ID: sa

Password: ******

< Back   Next >   Cancel   Help

Figure 2-6:
Choose how to log in to the SQL Server.

6. **Click Next to display a slew of additional options for connecting to the server, as shown in Figure 2-7.**

7. **The only option you need to be concerned with is Change Default Database. Select this option, and then select the desired database from the drop-down menu.**

If you'd like to find out more about the other options available, click the Help button.

If you click Next and it won't let you continue because your server name is wrong or the login fails, make sure you have everything typed correctly and check with your system administrator to make sure you have the rights to log in.

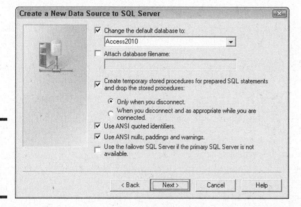

Figure 2-7:
Selecting
the default
database.

8. **After selecting the default database, click Next to display another screen of options. Usually, the default settings on this page of the wizard are OK. However, if you'd like to know more about these options, click the Help button. If you just want to connect to the database, click Finish.**

You'll see the ODBC Microsoft SQL Server Setup confirmation dialog box with a bunch of settings that you typed in over the past few minutes.

9. **At the bottom of the dialog box, click the Test Data Source button to make sure all the settings, login IDs, and passwords are entered correctly.**

If you click this button and see "TESTS COMPLETED SUCCESSFULLY!," then you did a good job. If not, you'll have to go back and tweak your settings.

10. **When you have a successful connection, click OK in the ODBC Microsoft SQL Server Setup dialog box.**

You're taken back to the Select Data Source dialog box shown in Figure 2-3; only this time, the data source you created appears.

11. Click the data source and click OK.

Just when you thought no more windows would appear, you're prompted to log in to the SQL Server again.

12. Enter the Login ID and the Password and click OK.

The Link Tables dialog box appears, as shown in Figure 2-8, which is where you select which tables to link to.

13. Select the tables you want to import from the list.

You'll also see a bunch of system tables listed that you don't normally see. You can ignore these.

Figure 2-8: Selecting tables and views to link to.

You can use the Select All button to select all the tables, but if you have a lot of tables to select and don't want all the system tables, forget about using the Shift key to select a range. Instead, you can click the first table you want to select, then alternate pressing the down arrow and space-bar until you reach the last table you want to link to.

In addition to seeing the tables from SQL Server, you also see the views. A *view* in SQL Server is the same as a select query in Access; it just returns data. When you link to a view in SQL Server, it appears as a table in Access. Opening a SQL Server view in Design view shows you only the list of fields, not the criteria or source tables.

14. In the Link Tables dialog box, there's a Save password check box. Select this option if you want Access to remember the password when connecting.

If you leave this deselected, users of the database will have to know the password to log on to the SQL Server. Consider the security and sensitivity of the data when choosing this option.

15. **Click OK.**

Access begins linking to the tables in SQL Server. You might be prompted to select a unique identifier for some of the tables being linked to — particularly if it's a SQL Server view. Just click the unique identifier for each table, and you're on your way.

After Access is done linking to the tables, they appear in the Navigation pane, as shown in Figure 2-9. Instead of the table icon you're used to seeing, each table has an icon with an arrow, indicating it's a linked table.

Figure 2-9:
SQL Server
tables and
views in the
Navigation
pane.

When you attach a table from an ODBC data source, Access prefixes dbo_ at the beginning of the table's name. This prefix indicates the owner of the table in SQL Server. If you don't want to see the SQL tables with the dbo_ prefix, simply right-click the table, choose Rename from the pop-up menu, and give the linked table a new name.

If you don't see the arrows in the icons next to the table names, you probably chose to import the tables instead of linking to them. No problem, just delete the tables and click the ODBC Database command on the External Data tab and start over, unless, of course, you meant to import them.

Using linked tables in Access

Now that you have these tables from SQL Server appearing inside Access, what do you do with them? Well, you use them just as you use any other local table in Access. You can build queries, forms, reports, macros, and modules that reference these tables just like you did throughout the previous eight minibooks.

The main difference is that you cannot alter the structure of a linked table. So if you need to add a field or change a field size, you have to log in to the SQL Server to perform that operation.

You can mix and match tables in your Access database. For example, create a few local tables to place data that doesn't need to be on the server. Connect to a number of different databases and gain access to the data from one ACCDB file. The possibilities are endless once you know where all of this data resides.

Maintaining linked tables

Different things happen that cause the links to an ODBC database to break. The Server might change locations, someone may change the structure of the SQL Server table or database, or you may move the ACCDB file to another machine. Whatever the reason, if the link is broken, you'll know it, as the tables won't display any data, or you get an error when opening a linked table.

To fix this, click the Ribbon's External Data tab and click the Linked Table Manager command in the Import & Link group. Select all of the linked tables, click the Always prompt for new location check box in the bottom-left corner of the window, and then click OK. This displays the Select Data Source dialog box shown in Figure 2-3. Then either select the existing Data Source or create a new Data Source to correct the problem.

For more information on using the Linked Table Manager, see Book II, Chapter 4.

Using ODBC, you can use data from any number of data sources, including SQL Server. From just one simple command on the Ribbon, your world opens up to a number of options. Whether you're in a small company with one server, or a large organization with multiple servers around the world, you can use Access to connect to these databases and build eye-catching front-end applications to view and manipulate this data.

Using pass-through queries

Pass-through queries let you send commands directly to an ODBC database server. By using a pass-through query, you work directly with the server tables instead of having the Microsoft Jet Database Engine process the data. Sometimes, the Jet Database Engine can't process the information or criteria you're entering in the query window. A pass-through query lets you interact directly with the SQL Server (or any other ODBC-linked database).

To create a pass-through query, click the Ribbon's Create tab, and then click the Query Design command in the Macros & Code group. When the Show Table dialog box appears, click Close without selecting any tables. On the Ribbon's (Query Tools) Design tab, click the Pass-Through command in the Query Type group, shown in Figure 2-10.

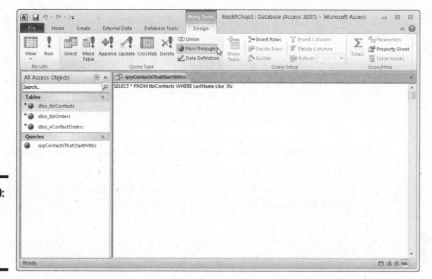

Figure 2-10:
Creating
a pass-
through
query.

Access gets rid of the fancy query builder interface and shows you a blank
area where you can type any SQL statement you want. You must know the
native syntax of SQL Server (or the ODBC database you're working with) in
order to have a successful result.

For instance, the following SQL Select statement shows all of the records from
the SQL table tblContacts, where the LastName field starts with the letter J:

```
SELECT * FROM tblContacts WHERE LastName Like 'J%'
```

Notice that this query uses the name of the table from SQL Server, not the
name assigned in the Access Navigation pane. Because SQL Server processes
this query, it doesn't care what you called it in Access. Also, instead of using
an asterisk (*) for a wild-card character, this query uses a percent sign (%).
Again, since the query gets passed through directly to SQL Server, you must
use the syntax that SQL Server recognizes.

If you typed the same SQL statement in a non–pass-through query, the
Access equivalent would be

```
SELECT * FROM dbo_tblContacts WHERE LastName Like 'J*'
```

In the preceding Access example, you must use the table name as it appears in
the Navigation pane — with the dbo_ prefix. This query would not work as a
pass-through query, since dbo_tblContacts doesn't exist on the server.

When using pass-through queries, always type the SQL statement using the
syntax the ODBC data source recognizes. Also, use the table names as they
appear on the server.

Creating an Access Data Project

An *Access Data Project* — ADP — is an Access data file that provides access to a SQL Server database. Using an *ADP*, you can create a client/server application using Access forms, reports, macros, and modules, while using SQL Server tables, views, stored procedures, and functions.

To create an ADP, follow these steps:

1. **Start Access and choose New on the left side of the opening screen.**

2. **Select Blank Database in the middle part of the screen, and then click the folder to the left of the File Name text box to display the File New Database dialog box, shown in Figure 2-11.**

Figure 2-11:
Creating an Access Data Project (ADP).

3. **Give the file a meaningful name, and then select Microsoft Access Projects (*.adp) from the Save as Type drop-down list.**

4. **Click OK in the File New Database dialog box, and then click the Create button in the lower-right corner of the Access startup screen.**

For more information on creating an opening database, see Book I, Chapter 2.

After clicking the Create button, Access displays a message box asking if you want to connect to an existing SQL Server database. Click Yes if you want to use a SQL Server database already in place. Click No to create a new SQL Server database. Click Cancel if you don't want to do either. (Why did you click it in the first place?)

5. **For our purposes — and, we think, for most people out there — we want to connect to an existing database, so click Yes to connect to an existing SQL Server database.**

    Access displays the Data Link Properties dialog box, shown in Figure 2-12.

Figure 2-12:
Entering
SQL Server
database
information.

To connect to a SQL Server database, you have to have rights — permissions — to do so. If you don't have access to the SQL Server or the database on the server, you won't be able to connect to the server.

6. **If you do have rights, enter the server name, choose the type of authentication, enter a username and password — and whether to save the password — and choose the database on the server. After entering this information, click Test Connection to make sure you entered everything without a dreaded typo.**

    For more information on SQL Server settings and types of authentication, see the section, "Connecting to SQL Server with ODBC," earlier in this chapter.

7. **Click OK.**

    If you chose to save the password, Access lets you know that the password won't be encrypted before it's saved.

8. **If this is OK, click Save Password. If this is not OK, choose Cancel to select other options or Help to read more about it.**

After creating the ADP — and waiting for Access to connect to the server and get all the information about the database — the Navigation pane shows all of the tables, views, stored procedures, and functions from the SQL Server. Unlike an ODBC-linked database (discussed earlier in this chapter), you don't have to tell Access which tables and views you want. An ADP is linked to every table and view on the SQL Server.

One advantage of using an ADP over ODBC-linked tables is that if someone changes the structure of the tables on the SQL Server, you don't have to tell Access to refresh the tables. Access retrieves all the tables and views every time you open an `.adp` file.

Designing ADP tables and views

Because an ADP is a direct link to the SQL Server database, you can actually create and modify these objects on the SQL Server. For example, when you open a table in Design view, as shown in Figure 2-13, you'll notice that it looks slightly different from a local Access table's Design view.

If you're familiar with SQL Server, you'll notice that the data types for the fields are shown as SQL Server data types. SQL Server uses different types, such as `int` instead of `Number` and `nvarchar` instead of `Text`. It also displays different properties for each field, like the `Precision` and `Identity` properties for a number field. You're modifying a SQL Server table, so you see what you'd see if you were doing it from within SQL Server.

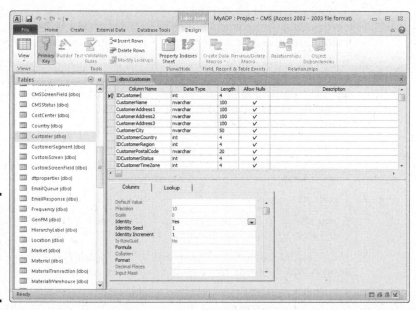

Figure 2-13:
A SQL Server table in Access's Design view.

Unlike an ODBC-linked database, you cannot have a hybrid of local tables and linked tables; every table in an ADP is in the SQL Server database. If you're used to using tables to temporarily store data when analyzing data or running reports, you'll have to create these on the SQL Server instead of in the local Access file.

Any SQL Server views, stored procedures, and functions appear in the Access Navigation pane under Queries. You can, of course, run any of these objects from the Navigation pane and even open them in Design view and make modifications. You'll notice that the designers for these objects closely mimic the designers in SQL Server Management Studio — SQL Server's tool to modify databases and database objects. Figure 2-14 shows a SQL Server view in Design view.

Keep in mind that when you modify the design of any of the tables, views, stored procedures, and functions, you're changing them on the SQL Server, and your changes could affect hundreds or thousands of users. Be careful when working with any SQL Server database, and make sure you understand the ramifications of making changes.

Creating other objects in an ADP

Now that you have these tables and views from SQL Server appearing inside Access, what do you do with them? Just like with an ODBC-linked database, you can create local forms, reports, macros and modules that will reside in the local .adp file — not on the SQL Server.

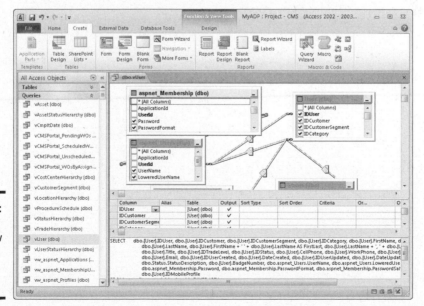

Figure 2-14:
A SQL
Server view
in Access's
Design
view.

The .adp file format is an Access 2002-2003 file format, so when working with forms, reports, macros, and modules, you're limited to features available at that time. Many things have changed since 2002-2003, so listing them here would be quite difficult. If you're trying to implement a feature that you can't figure out in an ADP, use the Access Help feature and the Internet for assistance.

When you're working with data from SQL Server — or another data source — the data is coming from somewhere other than Access. Once you establish the connection to the server and the database, you can build the rest of your Access objects — forms, reports, macros and modules — to create a robust front-end to a SQL Server database. You can even create an Access Data Project to change the design of SQL Server tables, views, stored procedures, and functions.

Chapter 3: Using Access with SharePoint

In This Chapter

✔ **Understanding SharePoint**

✔ **Using a SharePoint list as a data source**

✔ **Building a Web database**

*U*nless you've been living under a rock for the past 20 years, you're probably aware of the Internet — the all-encompassing network of information at your fingertips. The popularity of the Internet has soared more than anyone can imagine. Twenty years ago, did you ever think that parents and grandparents would ever need a reason to have a computer in their houses? This is mainly due to the convenience of e-mail and social networking sites like Facebook and MySpace — and let's not leave out shopping!

But what does the Internet mean to Microsoft Office Access? Until recently, it hasn't meant too much to the Access user. With SharePoint, Microsoft built — and continues to enhance — a wonderful collaborative tool to share information with users around the world. And Access takes advantage of this information in some pretty interesting, yet limited, ways. In this chapter, we explore using this information from Access as well as creating a rich user interface for use on a SharePoint site.

What Is SharePoint?

According to Microsoft, *SharePoint* — the short name for Microsoft Office SharePoint Server — is "an integrated suite of server capabilities that can help improve organizational effectiveness by providing comprehensive content management and enterprise search, accelerating shared business processes, and facilitating information-sharing across boundaries for better business insight. Additionally, this collaboration and content management server provides IT professionals and developers with the platform and tools they need for server administration, application extensibility, and interoperability."

Huh? Basically, SharePoint's another product from Microsoft that some IT person must set up and administer so that its users can access information stored on that server. Using SharePoint, you can set up lists of contacts and other information, create calendars, share documents, and have discussions on a message-board–style interface. SharePoint is Microsoft's vision for sharing information, and Access is fully capable of utilizing SharePoint to share and manage this information.

In order to use SharePoint, you must have access to a SharePoint server. If you work for a medium- to large-size organization, chances are good that it might have one or more SharePoint servers used for collaboration. If not — and if you can't afford the cost of installing and maintaining your own SharePoint server — you can rent one from a number of SharePoint hosting sites. Just open your favorite Internet browser and search for *SharePoint hosting.* Then get out your credit card and start sharing.

Using a SharePoint List as a Data Source

A *SharePoint list* is a table where SharePoint stores its data. Just like an Access table, a list contains columns or fields that define the items and rows that house the information. From the Access interface, you can create new lists on a SharePoint server — or you can link to an existing list.

Creating a new SharePoint list

If you want to create a SharePoint list on the server, one that the SharePoint administrators and developers didn't already create, you can do so from within Access. To create a new SharePoint list, follow these steps:

1. **Click the Ribbon's Create tab, and then click the SharePoint Lists command in the Table group.**

Access displays a menu of choices, as shown in Figure 3-1.

Figure 3-1:
Using
SharePoint
lists from
the Create
tab.

SharePoint provides five types of lists you can create.

- *Contacts:* Creates a contacts list when you want to manage information about people that your team works with, such as customers or partners.

- *Tasks:* Creates a tasks list when you want to track a group of work items that you or your team needs to complete.

- *Issues:* Creates an issues list when you want to manage issues or problems. You can assign, prioritize, and follow the progress of issues from start to finish.

- *Events:* Creates an events list when you want a calendar-based view of upcoming meetings, deadlines, and other important events.

- *Custom:* Creates a custom list when you want to specify your own columns.

Each option walks you through the steps of creating a new SharePoint list. If you choose Contacts, the Create New List dialog box for a Contacts list appears, as shown in Figure 3-2.

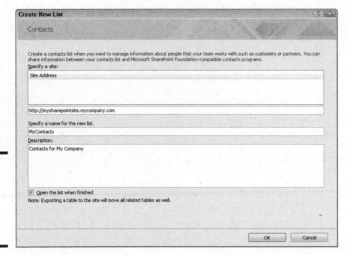

Figure 3-2:
Creating
a new
Contacts
list.

2. **Specify the location of the SharePoint server in the Specify a Site text box.**

   This typically looks like any other URL for an Internet site. You'll need to get this information from your SharePoint administrator or from your SharePoint hosting site. After you specify a site in Access, it appears in the list of Site Addresses when you create and manage these lists.

3. **Specify a name for the list in the Specify a Name for the New List text box.**

If you're creating a catalog of products for your company, you can give the list a name, such as Catalog.

4. **Enter a description for the new list.**

   Don't be too wordy, but type something that will be meaningful to others using this new list.

5. **After you enter in all the information for the new list, click OK.**

   Access shows a login screen for the SharePoint server you specified in the Create New List dialog box.

6. **Enter the username and password for this SharePoint site, and then click OK.**

   If you selected the Open the List when Finished option, the new list appears in the Access window — as well as a linked table in the Navigation pane — as shown in Figure 3-3.

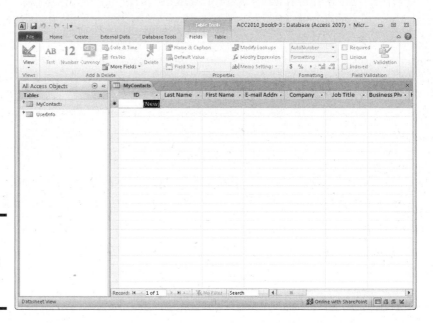

Figure 3-3:
The new SharePoint list in Access.

After you create the SharePoint list from Access, you can add and modify data just as you would with any other local or linked table. The changes you make will be accessible to anyone else with access to the SharePoint site.

To make changes to the design of the SharePoint list, right-click the table name in the Navigation pane and choose More options➪Modify Columns and Settings from the pop-up menu. The Customize page on the SharePoint site loads in a new browser window in which you use the SharePoint tools to modify the list's structure.

Linking to an existing SharePoint list

If your SharePoint site already has lists — usually created by a SharePoint administrator or developer — that you want to get information from and make changes to, then you want to link to those SharePoint lists. To link to an existing SharePoint list, follow these steps:

1. Click the Ribbon's Create tab, click the SharePoint Lists command in the Tables group, as shown in Figure 3-1, and then choose the Existing SharePoint List option.

2. When the Get External Data – SharePoint Site Wizard loads, enter or choose a SharePoint site at the top of the first screen.

As with linking to other external data sources, you're prompted to either import the data to you database or link the data source in a linked table. If you import the data, you'll get a snapshot of the list at the time you performed the import, and any changes you make won't be reflected on the SharePoint server. If you choose to link to the data source, you'll see the data that other users enter and modify — and they'll see your changes, too.

For further assistance on when to import data and when to link to data in another data source, see Book II, Chapter 4.

3. After choosing to link or import, click Next to display the list of SharePoint lists to link to or import, as shown in Figure 3-4.

4. Simply click the check box to the left of each list that you want to link to, and then click OK in the bottom-right portion of the screen.

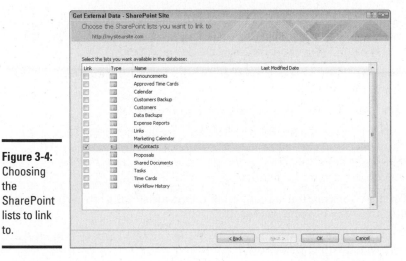

Figure 3-4:
Choosing the SharePoint lists to link to.

The SharePoint lists you choose to link to appear in the Access Navigation pane as linked tables, just like they appear in Figure 3-3. If you chose to import the lists, the data will be stored in local Access tables and will appear with the standard Access table icon — without an arrow — next to the table name.

You may notice that when you create a new list or link to an existing list, some other tables appear in the Access Navigation pane. If these lists are linked in SharePoint, they also need to be a part of the Access database that's manipulating them. So if you see tables that you didn't create or select, don't be alarmed. Access is smart enough to know you need them and just brings these lists along for the ride.

Moving an existing database to SharePoint

If you've already taken the time to build an Access database with tables, queries, forms, and reports that all work together and are automated with modules and macros, you don't have to reinvent the wheel on SharePoint. Access provides a tool that moves your existing tables to SharePoint and links them to the Access database.

To move your database to a SharePoint site, follow these steps:

1. **Click the Ribbon's Database Tools tab and click the SharePoint command in the Move Data group.**

   This starts the Export Tables to SharePoint Wizard.

2. **Enter the SharePoint site where you'll place these tables as SharePoint lists.**

   If you've used your SharePoint site before, it appears in the list of available sites. If you're moving these tables to a site that's not in the list, type the site information in the provided text box.

3. **Click Next, and you're prompted for the login information for the SharePoint site.**

4. **Enter your username and password, and click OK.**

   Access creates the SharePoint lists, moves the data from Access to these lists, and then links these lists to the Access database. If everything goes smoothly, you're shown a message that the tables have been successfully shared, as shown in Figure 3-5.

5. **On the confirmation screen, click the Show Details check box to show the summary of what Access did.**

   You'll see that it created new lists on the specified SharePoint site and made a backup copy of the original database.

6. **Click Finish, and your database opens, displaying the linked tables in addition to your other database objects.**

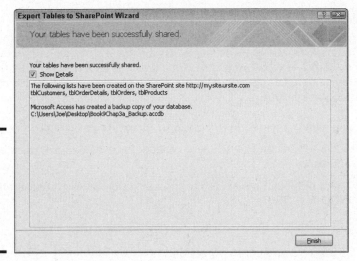

Figure 3-5:
Success
in moving
Access
tables into
SharePoint
lists.

If something goes wrong and Access can't move the tables to the SharePoint site, or other issues occur during the process, the wizard creates a table called Move to SharePoint Site Issues that lists the issues that prevented the tables from being moved. Just open this table in Datasheet view to review and correct these issues as they're found.

By linking tables to a SharePoint site, you can create front-ends to an existing SharePoint site or give users access to data from your database in SharePoint. And these users don't even have to have Microsoft Office Access installed to edit the data in a SharePoint list; they just need access to the list on the SharePoint site.

Building a Web Database

If you've worked through all the chapters in this minibook, you can see how to create a rich, data-driven Windows application that you or your company can use to track all kinds of information. You can build a database that can track your music collection at home one day, and the next day work on a database to track sensitive corporate data — so that you can continue to finance that music collection that's large enough to require a database.

And, like many Access developers before you, you're probably thinking, "Wow, it would be great if I could put this database online so I can access it from anywhere." With the release of Microsoft Office Access 2010 and SharePoint 2010, you can. However, this comes at a cost — there are some limitations on the formatting and structure of the database. The first big limitation is this: You must deploy this application using SharePoint. We discuss other limitations throughout the rest of this chapter.

What is a Web database?

An Access database consists of a number of objects — tables, queries, forms, reports, and macros. In Access 2010, each of these objects can be a Web object or client object. A *client object* is an Access object that runs on the client machine using Access. Some characteristics of client objects include the following:

✦ Any object created in Access 2007 or earlier is a client object.

✦ Access 2010 can create client objects for use in an Access client database.

✦ Client objects have access to the full set of Access functionality — including VBA.

✦ Client objects can reference Web objects.

A *Web object* is an Access object that is both client and server compatible publishable to a SharePoint server. In order to make this functionality possible, a Web object has some different characteristics than the client objects, such as:

✦ Web objects can be created only in Access 2010 — and, we assume, every version after that.

✦ Web objects have a limited subset of the functionality, compared to the corresponding client objects.

✦ Web objects — with the exception of Web tables — can be referenced only by other Web objects and cannot reference client objects.

✦ Web objects are visible in the browser when the database is published to the SharePoint server.

✦ Web objects are limited to expressions supported by the server, and they do not support VBA.

Queries, forms, reports, and macros can either be Web objects or client objects. These objects cannot be converted from a client object to a Web object or from a Web object to a client object. However, you can save a Web object as a new client object.

Tables can also be client objects or Web objects; however, any given database can contain one or the other not both. In Access 2010, a database that contains Web tables is called a *Web database,* and it can contain a mix of Web and client objects. A database containing client tables is called a *client database* — a traditional Access database — and cannot contain any Web objects. Both types of databases are stored in the ACCDB format.

Creating a Web database

Because of the restriction of a database to contain only client tables or Web tables, you must first create a Web database. To create a blank Web database, follow these steps:

1. **Start Access 2010.**

The Access home screen appears, as shown in Figure 3-6.

2. **On the left side of the home screen, click New.**

The list of available templates appears in the center of the home screen.

3. **Under Available Templates, click Blank Web Database.**

4. **In the File Name text box on the lower-right portion of the screen, enter a name for your Web database.**

5. **Click the Create button.**

Access creates the new Web database and displays Table1 in the Access window, as shown in Figure 3-7.

Figure 3-6: Creating a new blank Web database.

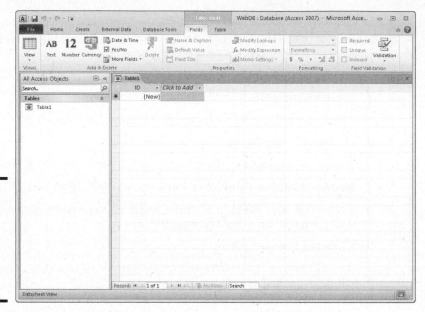

Figure 3-7:
Starting
from
scratch
in a new
blank Web
database.

For more information on creating and opening databases, see Book I, Chapter 2.

Designing Web Databases

As discussed in the previous section, Web objects do not fully represent all the functionality of client objects. Because of these limitations, Microsoft restricted the design functionality for Web objects in a Web database. When working with Web objects, you'll see changes such as these:

✦ Web tables do not support Design view. To compensate, you can modify the table and field properties from the Ribbon, which is shown in Figure 3-7.

✦ Web queries can't be opened in SQL view, and the query designer restricts you to settings that are valid on the Web.

✦ Web forms and reports cannot be opened in Design view, and there are some formatting restrictions that don't allow you to place controls wherever you want. The layout designers have expanded tools for changing the layout and a Property sheet that shows only the properties available on the Web.

✦ The Macro designer is filtered to expose the macros that will function correctly on the server.

Because a Web database's primary purpose is to show information on the Web via SharePoint, the Ribbon's Create tab shown in Figure 3-8 — changes for a Web database. The icons for the commands to create forms, reports, queries, and macros have a small globe in them indicating that you're creating a Web object.

Figure 3-8:
The Create tab for a Web database.

You can still create client forms, reports, queries, macros, and modules in a Web database, but these objects will work only when the database is opened in Access. When you publish the database to the SharePoint server, these objects will not appear there. Use these commands on the Ribbon's Create tab to create client objects:

✦ In the Queries group, click the drop-down for Client Queries and choose either Query Wizard or Query Design.

✦ In the Forms group, click the drop-down for Client Forms and choose a type of form from the list.

✦ In the Reports group, click the drop-down for Client Reports and choose a type of report from the list.

✦ In the Macros & Code group, click the drop-down for Client Objects and choose the appropriate option to create a query, macro, or module.

You might consider using client objects in your database primarily for users who need to perform tasks on the data that the Web object forbids them to do. For instance, you can create a form that runs some VBA code against the data to perform some calculations that a macro just doesn't allow. In order to run these client objects, users must have a copy of the ACCDB file and have Access installed on their computers.

Creating a Web table

If you're used to building a table through the Table designer, you can rid yourself of that habit real quick when building a Web table. In a Web table, you add and remove fields to and from the table and modify field properties in the table's Datasheet view. Remember, there is no Design view for a Web table.

For more information on designing tables in Datasheet view, using the various field types and properties, and editing data, see Book II.

Utilizing the commands on the Ribbon's (Table Tools) Fields tab (shown in Figure 3-7), we created a simple table with three fields: FirstName, LastName, and Birthday. We saved the table as tblBirthdays and populated it with some data, as shown in Figure 3-9.

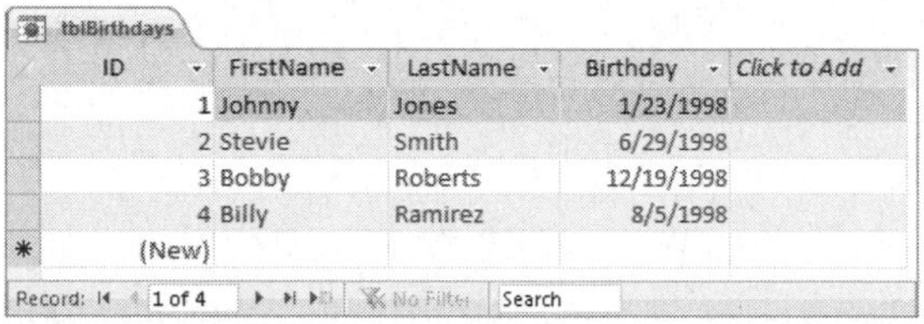

Figure 3-9: A simple Web table with three fields.

▾ tblBirthdays				
ID ▾	FirstName ▾	LastName ▾	Birthday ▾	Click to Add ▾
1	Johnny	Jones	1/23/1998	
2	Stevie	Smith	6/29/1998	
3	Bobby	Roberts	12/19/1998	
4	Billy	Ramirez	8/5/1998	
*	(New)			

Record: I◀ ◀ 1 of 4 ▶ ▶I ▶⁕ ☒ No Filter Search

Other than the table's icon with a globe, it's difficult to see any difference between this Web table and a client table when looking at it in Datasheet view. Data is as data does, in both types of tables. Using the commands provided on the table-specific tabs on the Ribbon, you can create many tables with many fields to house all the data you want to put out there on the Web.

Creating Web forms and reports

One reason people love to create applications in Access is the form/report designer, which lets you create a form or report however you want. You can place controls anywhere on the form or report, and it displays your data exactly how you want. If you want to indent a field underneath another field, you simply drag the field to its new location. If you want to create a form that looks like a baseball diamond and use it to pick players who will start in those positions, you're limited only by your artistic skills.

With Web forms and reports, you can be Vincent van Gogh and still have trouble getting a form to look exactly how you want. But for straightforward, data-driven applications, you can get the results you want with a little bit of practice.

Creating Web forms

When creating a form based on a table, you're limited by the form's layout as to where you can place controls — text boxes, labels, check boxes, and so forth. When creating a multiple items form, this isn't an issue, as the table's data displays in the row and column format.

For more information on designing forms in Layout view, see Book IV, Chapter 1.

To create a multiple items form, click a table name in the Navigation pane, select the Ribbon's Create tab, and then click the Multiple Items command in the Forms group. (See Figure 3-8.) Because you're using a Web database, the icon for this command contains a globe. Figure 3-10 shows a multiple items form based on tblBirthdays, which was created in the previous section.

Figure 3-10:
A Web form
showing
multiple
items.

Not all controls supported by client forms are available when you're building a Web form. When you're adding controls to a Web form, the following controls which you can use on client forms — aren't available:

✦ Navigation

✦ Option Group and Option Buttons

✦ Insert Page Break

✦ Chart

✦ Toggle Button

✦ Line and Rectangle

✦ Bound and Unbound Object Frame

✦ Subform/Subreport

✦ Image

If you're used to performing a certain task or setting a certain property of a client form, keep in mind that it might not be available in a Web form.

Set the `Caption` property for all your forms so that the Web pages in SharePoint have a user-friendly title. To view the properties in Layout view, click the Ribbon's (Form Layout Tools) Design tab, and then click the Property Sheet command in the Tools group.

Creating Web reports

Just like client reports, Web reports are used for getting data out of your application — and usually onto a piece of paper that goes on somebody's desk. And just like Web forms, Web reports lack a Design view, so you're stuck using Layout view. Luckily, the skills needed to work in a report's Layout view are similar to those for a form, so you don't have to retrain yourself twice.

Not all controls supported by client reports are available when building Web reports. The list of controls that you can't use is longer than the list of available controls. When adding controls to a Web report, you *can* use the following:

✦ Text Box
✦ Label
✦ Hyperlink
✦ Checkbox

You can also use the Ribbon commands to insert images and logos into your report.

For more information on creating and designing reports, see Book V.

Creating a navigation form

To tie everything together, we recommend creating some type of form that displays when you run your application. Access introduces the navigation form in Access 2010, which provides a sleek interface for navigating through your forms and reports.

To build one: After building your Web tables, forms, reports, queries, and macros, click the Ribbon's Create tab, and then click the Navigation command in the Forms group. Select the type of Navigation you'd like from the list of available formats, and then start dragging forms and reports from the Navigation pane onto the form. Figure 3-11 shows a navigation form, with a form and a report added to the navigation portion — the left side of the form.

In the Navigation pane in Figure 3-11, all the icons next to the table, form, and report names contain a globe, indicating they're Web objects.

Now that you have a navigation form, it's time to set that form as your startup form. Click File⇨Options to display the Access Options dialog box. Select the Current Database option on the left side of the screen, and then set the Display Form under Application Options to the form you want to open when you first open the database.

For more information on creating a navigation form and setting the startup form, see Book IV, Chapter 3.

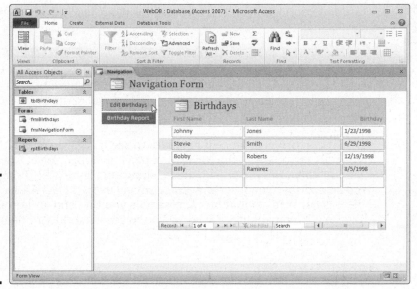

Figure 3-11:
Creating a
Navigation
form
for your
application.

Creating Web macros

In addition to creating tables, queries, forms, and reports in your Web database, you can also automate tasks in your application through macros. The list of macros available in a Web database is smaller than the list available in a client database. (See Table 3-1.)

Table 3-1	**Macros Available in a Web Database**	
Macro Action		
Comment	MessageBox	RunMenuCommand
Group	OnError	SaveRecord
If	OpenForm	SetFilter
Submacro	OpenReport	SetLocalVar
BrowseTo	RefreshRecord	SetOrderBy
ClearMacroError	RemoveAllTempVars	SetProperty
CloseWindow	RemoveTempVar	SetTempVar
DeleteRecord	Requery	StopAllMacros
GoToControl	RunDataMacro	StopMacro
GoToRecord	RunMacro	UndoRecord

For more information on creating and designing macros, see Book VI.

Converting client databases to Web databases

If you already have a database and want to put that data out there on the Web using SharePoint, the good news is, you don't have to start over. The bad news is, it will probably take some additional effort to sort through any Web-compatible issues.

To check an object in a client database to see if it's Web-compatible, right-click the object in the Navigation pane, and then select Check Web Compatibility from the pop-up menu, shown in Figure 3-12. If the object is Web-compatible, you'll get a message saying everything's A-Okay. If the object is not Web-compatible, Access tells you that and creates a table called Web Compatibility Issues for you to see what the problems are.

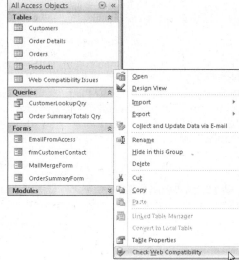

Figure 3-12: Checking a client object for Web compatibility.

Some examples of Web compatibility issues are

✦ The Column data type is incompatible with the Web.

✦ Tables with lookups must have a primary key, and the `DataType` property of the primary key must be `Long`.

✦ The Column data type for a value list must be Text to be compatible with the Web.

+ Lookup row sources must be complete SQL statements that specify one table and fields from that table to be compatible with the Web.

+ The Column data type is incompatible with the Web.

+ Access was unable to convert the query for use on the Web because it relies on a different query that is not Web compatible.

If your client database contains lots of objects and you don't have the time to check each one individually, you can check the compatibility of all the objects at once. Click File⇨Save & Publish, select Publish to Access Services, and then click Run Compatibility Checker in the Check Web Compatibility section on the right side of the screen, as shown in Figure 3-13.

After the compatibility checker runs — which could take some time on large databases — the screen will indicate if the database is compatible or incompatible with the Web. You can click the Web Compatibility Issues button or open the Web Compatibility Issue table from the Navigation pane.

After you repair any issues found with your client database, you can publish it to the SharePoint server, which is covered in the next section.

Creating a Web database is nearly identical to creating a client database. Just start with your baseline of Web tables and build your forms, reports, queries, and macros to be Web compatible — and you'll be ready to publish your database to a SharePoint server.

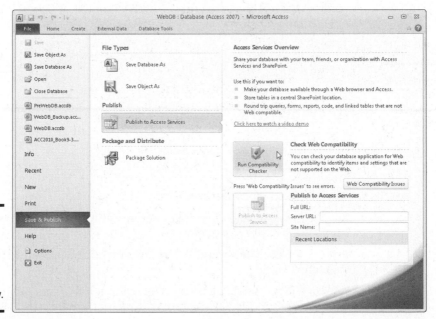

Figure 3-13:
Checking
a client
database
for Web
compatibility.

Publishing a Web Database

After you've built your Web database with Web tables, forms, reports, queries, and macros — and set your startup form — you'll want to publish that application to a SharePoint server so that others can use that application on the Web — without installing Access on their computers.

To publish an Access database to a SharePoint server, you must have SharePoint Server 2010 with Access Services installed. Make sure this is available on the server before attempting to publish your database.

To publish your database to a SharePoint server, follow these steps.

1. **In the database that you want to publish to SharePoint, click File⇨Save & Publish, and then select Publish to Access Services.**

2. **If you haven't already done so, click the Run Compatibility Checker button.**

   If your database isn't Web compatible, fix any issues before you continue. For more information on dealing with compatibility issues, see the previous section.

3. **In the Publish to Access Services section in the bottom-right portion of the screen, enter in the Server URL and Site Name, as shown in Figure 3-14.**

   The Server URL is the location of your server, and the Site Name is the name of the site that will appear on the SharePoint server when you navigate to that site.

Figure 3-14: Entering the server URL and site name.

4. **Click Publish to Access Services.**

   If you entered a valid SharePoint server URL, Access displays the Windows Security dialog box.

5. **Enter your user name and password for the SharePoint server and then click OK.**

   Access checks the database for Web compatibility and — if everything is compatible — displays a status dialog box like the one in shown in

Figure 3-15 and begins synchronizing the database with the SharePoint server.

Figure 3-15:
Synchroniz-
ing your
Access Web
Database
with
SharePoint.

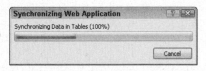

6. **Watch and wait.**

When Access is done synchronizing, it displays the Publish Succeeded message with the URL of your Web site, as shown in Figure 3-16.

Figure 3-16:
Publishing
success and
your Web
site URL.

Publishing a database to a SharePoint 2010 server requires you to create a Web-compatible database and — using a valid account on the server — synchronizing the Access Web objects with the server. Don't forget to write down and save the URL, so you can find your Web site later.

Viewing the results in a browser

So you've successfully published your Access Web database to a SharePoint Server and you're probably wondering, "Now what?" Well, once your database is published, you can view the database using a Web browser, such as Internet Explorer.

To view your application in a Web browser, you can either click the link in the Publish Succeeded dialog box (refer to Figure 3-16) or type the URL into the Address bar of your Web browser. Windows requires you to log in to the SharePoint site in order to view your page.

When the page loads in your Web browser, it displays the form you specified in the Display Web Form option from the Access Options screen. Normally, you create a navigation form, like the one shown in Figure 3-17, to navigate through your application.

Go ahead, click the Navigation control and your forms and reports load right in the Web browser. If you don't believe us when we say you can view this page without Access 2010 installed, go to a different computer and type the URL for your site and edit the data on the Access-less computer.

Although you can view your Access Web database through a Web browser, don't get too carried away with designing Web sites for the general public. You will have to create accounts on the SharePoint server in order to let someone use your application on the Web. Please see your SharePoint Server administrator for assistance in setting up your application for others to use.

When publishing fails

If you build your Web database correctly, make sure everything in your database is Web compatible, and log in with a valid account to a SharePoint 2010 server with Access Services installed, the publishing will most likely go smoothly. However — as most of us have experienced — things don't always go as planned.

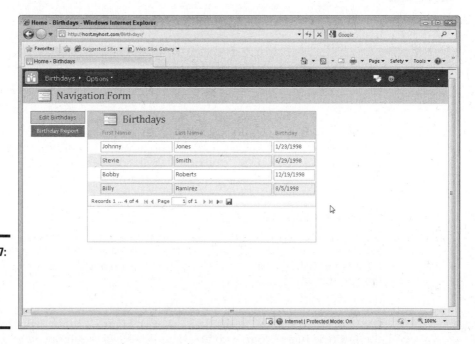

Figure 3-17:
A Web Database finally on the Web.

Here are a few scenarios that might cause publishing a Web database to a SharePoint server to fail:

✦ **You don't have a valid account on the SharePoint server.** Check with your SharePoint administrator for valid account information.

✦ **The SharePoint server you're trying to synchronize with is not a SharePoint 2010 Server with Access Services installed.** This will not work with older versions of SharePoint.

✦ **The database is not Web compatible.** Access checks for Web compatibility before attempting to synchronize with the server. For more information on Web compatibility, see the section "Converting client databases to Web databases" earlier in this chapter.

✦ **The synchronization has object conflicts.** If another user makes changes to the server database, and you attempt to change those same objects, you'll get a message explaining how Access handled these conflicts.

Whatever the cause of the failure, simply follow the prompts on the screens to remedy the situation. The displayed messages are actually quite helpful.

Synchronizing changes

We're pretty sure that you didn't create the Web database exactly how you wanted on the first try — we'd even bet money on it. After viewing your Web database in a browser, you might notice that things didn't look how you expected. A text box might be too big, or you might have to scroll to see a button or image.

To correct these issues, just use the designers in the same way you modify client objects. After correcting these issues in the Access Web database, you must synchronize with the SharePoint server. Synchronizing with the server also updates your copy of the Web database with any changes that another user might have made.

To update the SharePoint server with changes to the Web database, follow these steps:

1. **In the database that you want to update on SharePoint, click File➪Info, and then click Sync All, as shown in Figure 3-18.**

Access begins the synchronization process and displays status dialog box like the one in shown in Figure 3-15. Access reopens the database in Access when the synchronization completes.

2. **After the synchronization completes, refresh your browser window to see the changes on the Web.**

Depending on where you are in the application in the Browser, you might have to navigate to the URL of the application shown in Figure 3-16. If the application doesn't show the changes made, try closing and re-opening your Web browser.

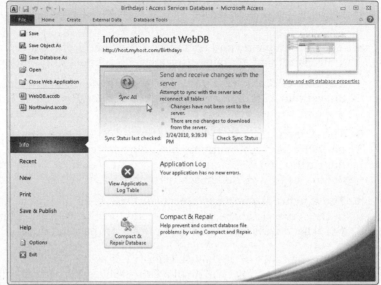

Figure 3-18:
Synchroniz-
ing database
changes
with
SharePoint.

If there aren't any changes made to the Web database or the SharePoint server, clicking the Sync All button displays a message that the application is already in sync with the server.

Appendix: Installing Microsoft Access

*I*f Microsoft Access is already on your computer, you don't need to read this appendix, unless you want to change something related to your current installation. If Microsoft Access 2010 isn't on your computer, you need to install it before you can use it. Microsoft Office Access 2010 isn't a program that comes free with Windows. You have to purchase it separately.

If you've just bought Access new, don't even think about throwing away the packaging until after the installation is complete. And never throw away the Product Key. You never know when you might need it to re-install the program again at some time in the future.

To install Access 2010, you need a Microsoft Office Professional 2010 or Microsoft Office Access 2010 disc, and the 25-character Product Key that came with it. You find the Product Key included with the packaging that came with your product. To get started with the installation, follow these steps:

1. **If you're currently using any programs, close them and save your work.**

   You don't need to close programs whose icons show in the Notification area, just the application programs on the desktop.

2. **Insert your Microsoft Office Professional or Microsoft Access disc into your computer's CD or DVD drive.**

   Wait a minute for the installation program to start. If no program starts automatically, choose Start⇨Computer, right-click the icon for your CD or DVD drive, choose the Open AutoPlay option from the shortcut menu, and click the option to Install or Run the program from your media.

3. **You may see some security warnings asking for permission to proceed. These are standard warnings that appear whenever you install any program. It's okay to proceed with the installation.**

4. **After a brief delay, the installation program prompts you to enter your Product Key. (See Figure A-1.)**

   You don't need to type the hyphens in the key. You can use lowercase letters.

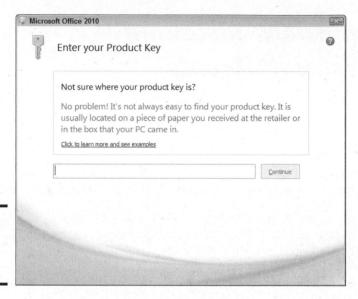

Microsoft Office 2010

Enter your Product Key

Not sure where your product key is?

No problem! It's not always easy to find your product key. It is usually located on a piece of paper you received at the retailer or in the box that your PC came in.

Click to learn more and see examples

Continue

Figure A-1:
Enter the
Product
Key.

5. **When you've correctly typed the key, the installation program verifies it, and the Continue button becomes available. Click Continue.**

6. **Select the Attempt to Automatically Activate My Product Online check box if your computer is connected to the Internet. If your computer isn't online, then leave this deselected.**

   Microsoft requires activation to prevent people from installing Access on multiple computers.

7. **The End-User License Agreement (EULA) appears next, containing the usual legalese about licensing. Read the agreement (yeah, sure), which says you won't sell or give away copies of the program — and then select the I Accept the Terms of the Agreement check box and click Continue.**

8. **The next page you see depends on whether you have a previous version of Office software installed on your computer.**

   If you have a previous version of Access (or other Office programs) installed, the next page asks whether you want to upgrade or customize. Before you choose an option, keep these points in mind:

   - *Upgrade:* Your current versions of Access and any other programs you're installing will be replaced by the new 2010 versions, which means you can't use the old versions anymore.

   - *Customize:* You can opt to keep your old versions and still have the new 2010 versions, too. Not a bad idea because it may take some time to get used to the new interface in 2010.

If you're installing the software on a computer without a previous edition of Access (or other Office programs), the next page gives you two choices:

- *Install Now:* The program installs with Microsoft's default settings.

- *Customize:* You can choose which programs and features of the software you want to install. We tell you more about this in Step 11.

9. **If you choose Upgrade, click the Upgrade button. Follow any remaining on-screen instructions to completion. You can ignore the steps that follow.**

If you want to use Access's new ability to use e-mail as a means of populating a table, you must upgrade to Outlook 2010. You cannot keep previous versions of Outlook on your system. However, you will not lose your existing e-mail messages, contacts, or other Outlook information. All of that will appear automatically in Outlook 2010.

10. **If you click the Customize button while upgrading, your first decision is whether to remove all previous versions, keep all previous versions, or just replace certain ones.**

If you want to keep your previous version of Access, be sure to choose Keep All Previous Versions. Alternatively, you can choose the option to remove only certain programs, but be sure to deselect the check box for Access.

11. **After choosing to upgrade or keep certain versions (or after clicking Customize on a new install), the Installation Options appear. To install all of Microsoft Access 2010, click the Installation Options tab, and choose Run from My Computer, as shown in Figure A-2.**

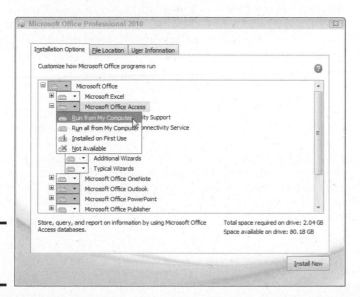

Figure A-2:
Installation
options.

If you're installing a full Microsoft Office suite, you can make similar selections for other programs.

Selections you make here will not override selections you previously made concerning upgrading versus keeping old versions.

Each time you choose Run from My Computer to install a component, the Total Space Required on Drive indicator (in the lower-right corner of the Installation Options window) shows how much hard-drive space the program will use, as compared to available disk space (shown in the Space Available on Drive indicator).

12. Optionally, you can click the File Location tab and choose a different location for the installed programs.

It isn't necessary to change the File Location to keep previous versions of programs. Use that tab only if you have some other good and compelling reason to store the installed programs on another drive or a folder other than the Program Files folder.

13. (Optional) Click the User Information tab and enter information about yourself.

User information is used by some programs to identify you as author or reviser of documents.

14. Click Install Now on the bottom-right corner of the window and follow the on-screen instructions.

15. Wait.

The rest of the process is largely automatic. If you see any additional on-screen instructions, follow them. But the installation should proceed on its own from this point forward. When it's done, you'll see a Continue Online option. It's a good idea to do that because those services may prove to be a valuable resource for future information. But if you miss that opportunity, no big deal. You can register for online services at any time.

If you see an option to Delete Installation Files, it's best to leave that alone. The installation files make it easier to install any components you may have skipped on the first pass. If you choose that option, you can still install those components; you'll just need to insert the original disc to do so.

Be sure to store your original disc and Product Key in a safe place where you can easily find them in the future. You just never know when a bad disk crash or nasty virus will force you to reinstall Access (or Office) from scratch!

Activating Access

If you didn't choose to attempt to activate during installation, Microsoft now requires *product activation,* which is a process designed to prevent people from installing their products on multiple computers. The first time you start Access (or some other Office application program), you're prompted to activate the product. Just go ahead and follow the instructions on-screen to activate.

When Microsoft came out with product activation, many people were alarmed that Microsoft would spy on them, correlating their Access usage with their personal information, and other appalling privacy invasions. As it turns out, product activation doesn't do any of those things. Product activation is unconnected with *product registration,* which is when you give Microsoft your name and address. Activation just connects your Office Product Key with your specific computer so that no one else can install your Office license on his or her computer. Go ahead and activate Office with no worries!

Repair, Reinstall, or Uninstall Access

If something bad happens to your hard drive and you can't start Access on your computer, you may have to reinstall or repair it. Or, if you opted to omit some optional components, you may later change your mind and want to install some component you previously declined.

First, close the program you want to change or repair. Then go to your list of installed programs in one of these ways:

✦ In Windows XP, choose Start⇨Control Panel⇨Add or Remove Programs.

✦ In Windows Vista and Windows 7, choose Start⇨Control Panel⇨Programs⇨Programs and Features.

Click the Microsoft Office Access 2010 or Microsoft Office Professional 2010 option that contains your Access installation. Then click the Change button. You're taken to a set of options where you can do these things:

✦ **Add or Remove Features:** This shows you a window similar to the one in Figure A-2, where you can choose which features of Access (and other Office programs) you want installed or removed from your computer.

✦ **Repair:** This option attempts to repair a damaged installation of Access or Office. What might damage an installation, you may ask? All of those nasty viruses, Trojan horses, and Internet worms can cause various things to go wrong with your computer.

✦ **Remove:** This option removes Access or Office from your computer.

✦ **Enter a Product Key:** This option lets you enter a new Product Key if yours expires or becomes invalid. It may expire if you're using a trial edition of Office that lets you use it for a short period of time.

If a repair operation doesn't work, you may have to remove Access (or Office) completely and reinstall from scratch. You'll need to search through your desk and dig out your CD and Product Key for this.

Index

Business/Accounting & Bookkeeping
Bookkeeping For Dummies
978-0-7645-9848-7

eBay Business
All-in-One For Dummies,
2nd Edition
978-0-470-38536-4

Job Interviews
For Dummies,
3rd Edition
978-0-470-17748-8

Resumes For Dummies,
5th Edition
978-0-470-08037-5

Stock Investing
For Dummies,
3rd Edition
978-0-470-40114-9

Successful Time
Management
For Dummies
978-0-470-29034-7

Computer Hardware
BlackBerry For Dummies,
3rd Edition
978-0-470-45762-7

Computers For Seniors
For Dummies
978-0-470-24055-7

iPhone For Dummies,
2nd Edition
978-0-470-42342-4

Laptops For Dummies,
3rd Edition
978-0-470-27759-1

Macs For Dummies,
10th Edition
978-0-470-27817-8

Cooking & Entertaining
Cooking Basics
For Dummies,
3rd Edition
978-0-7645-7206-7

Wine For Dummies,
4th Edition
978-0-470-04579-4

Diet & Nutrition
Dieting For Dummies,
2nd Edition
978-0-7645-4149-0

Nutrition For Dummies,
4th Edition
978-0-471-79868-2

Weight Training
For Dummies,
3rd Edition
978-0-471-76845-6

Digital Photography
Digital Photography
For Dummies,
6th Edition
978-0-470-25074-7

Photoshop Elements 7
For Dummies
978-0-470-39700-8

Gardening
Gardening Basics
For Dummies
978-0-470-03749-2

Organic Gardening
For Dummies,
2nd Edition
978-0-470-43067-5

Green/Sustainable
Green Building
& Remodeling
For Dummies
978-0-470-17559-0

Green Cleaning
For Dummies
978-0-470-39106-8

Green IT For Dummies
978-0-470-38688-0

Health
Diabetes For Dummies,
3rd Edition
978-0-470-27086-8

Food Allergies
For Dummies
978-0-470-09584-3

Living Gluten-Free
For Dummies
978-0-471-77383-2

Hobbies/General
Chess For Dummies,
2nd Edition
978-0-7645-8404-6

Drawing For Dummies
978-0-7645-5476-6

Knitting For Dummies,
2nd Edition
978-0-470-28747-7

Organizing For Dummies
978-0-7645-5300-4

SuDoku For Dummies
978-0-470-01892-7

Home Improvement
Energy Efficient Homes
For Dummies
978-0-470-37602-7

Home Theater
For Dummies,
3rd Edition
978-0-470-41189-6

Living the Country Lifestyle
All-in-One For Dummies
978-0-470-43061-3

Solar Power Your Home
For Dummies
978-0-470-17569-9

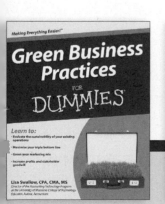

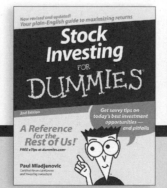

Available wherever books are sold. For more information or to order direct: U.S. customers visit www.dummies.com or call 1-877-762-2974.
U.K. customers visit www.wileyeurope.com or call (0) 1243 843291. Canadian customers visit www.wiley.ca or call 1-800-567-4797.

Internet

Blogging For Dummies,
2nd Edition
978-0-470-23017-6

eBay For Dummies,
6th Edition
978-0-470-49741-8

Facebook For Dummies
978-0-470-26273-3

Google Blogger
For Dummies
978-0-470-40742-4

Web Marketing
For Dummies,
2nd Edition
978-0-470-37181-7

WordPress For Dummies,
2nd Edition
978-0-470-40296-2

Language & Foreign Language

French For Dummies
978-0-7645-5193-2

Italian Phrases
For Dummies
978-0-7645-7203-6

Spanish For Dummies
978-0-7645-5194-9

Spanish For Dummies,
Audio Set
978-0-470-09585-0

Macintosh

Mac OS X Snow Leopard
For Dummies
978-0-470-43543-4

Math & Science

Algebra I For Dummies,
2nd Edition
978-0-470-55964-2

Biology For Dummies
978-0-7645-5326-4

Calculus For Dummies
978-0-7645-2498-1

Chemistry For Dummies
978-0-7645-5430-8

Microsoft Office

Excel 2007 For Dummies
978-0-470-03737-9

Office 2007 All-in-One
Desk Reference
For Dummies
978-0-471-78279-7

Music

Guitar For Dummies,
2nd Edition
978-0-7645-9904-0

iPod & iTunes
For Dummies,
6th Edition
978-0-470-39062-7

Piano Exercises
For Dummies
978-0-470-38765-8

Parenting & Education

Parenting For Dummies,
2nd Edition
978-0-7645-5418-6

Type 1 Diabetes
For Dummies
978-0-470-17811-9

Pets

Cats For Dummies,
2nd Edition
978-0-7645-5275-5

Dog Training For Dummies,
2nd Edition
978-0-7645-8418-3

Puppies For Dummies,
2nd Edition
978-0-470-03717-1

Religion & Inspiration

The Bible For Dummies
978-0-7645-5296-0

Catholicism For Dummies
978-0-7645-5391-2

Women in the Bible
For Dummies
978-0-7645-8475-6

Self-Help & Relationship

Anger Management
For Dummies
978-0-470-03715-7

Overcoming Anxiety
For Dummies
978-0-7645-5447-6

Sports

Baseball For Dummies,
3rd Edition
978-0-7645-7537-2

Basketball For Dummies,
2nd Edition
978-0-7645-5248-9

Golf For Dummies,
3rd Edition
978-0-471-76871-5

Web Development

Web Design All-in-One
For Dummies
978-0-470-41796-6

Windows Vista

Windows Vista
For Dummies
978-0-471-75421-3

Available wherever books are sold. For more information or to order direct: U.S. customers visit www.dummies.com or call 1-877-762-2974.
U.K. customers visit www.wileyeurope.com or call (0) 1243 843291. Canadian customers visit www.wiley.ca or call 1-800-567-4797.

DUMMIES.COM®

How-to?
How Easy.

Go to www.Dummies.com

From hooking up a modem to cooking up a casserole, knitting a scarf to navigating an iPod, you can trust Dummies.com to show you how to get things done the easy way.

Visit us at Dummies.com

Dummies products make life easier!

DVDs • Music • Games • DIY • Consumer Electronics • Software • Crafts • Hobbies • Cookware • and more!

For more information, go to **Dummies.com®** and search the store by category.

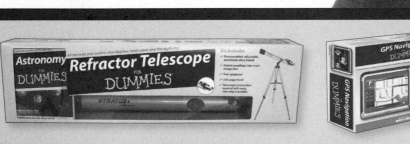

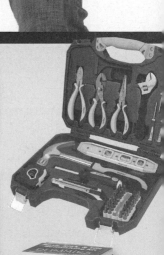

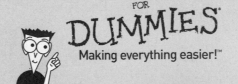

FOR **DUMMIES**
Making everything easier!™